Isobel Shaw was born in Ireland. Since graduating from Cambridge University, she has travelled and worked in many different countries and continents. Her lasting love has been for Pakistan where she lived for four years, and which she has explored more completely than any other Westerner, visiting it several times every year since she left. She has written two other guides to Pakistan, and is currently preparing a forthcoming trekking guide to Pakistan.

Pakistan

HANDBOOK

Isobel Shaw

Liberty Books

This edition first published in 1989 by
the Guidebook Company Limited, Hong Kong
The Penthouse, 20 Hollywood Road, Hong Kong

ISBN: 962-217-065-1

Editors: Peter Fredenburg, Stephanie Holmes, Ralph Kiggell
Additional text contribution: Kent Obee
Map Editor: Patrick R Booz
Picture Editor: Carolyn Watts
Cover photograph: Patrick R Booz
Photography: Peter Fredenburg (facing page 160); John King (facing page 193);
James Montgomery (facing pages 384, 385); Photobank (facing pages 96, 128,
129, 161—both, 256—both, 289—both, 417); Joseph Rupp (facing page 97);
Isobel Shaw (facing pages 192—all, 257—both, 288—all, 416—both)

Design: Unity Design Studio
Map artwork: Bai Yiliang
Colour Separation: Sakai Lithocolour

Printed in Hong Kong

Contents

Contents

Contents

Contents

Contents

Contents

Appendices 457

Index 469

Contents

List of Maps

Contents

Legend for Maps

■ **ISLAMABAD**	national capital	⛪	church
● **Peshawar**	provincial capital	⌂	stupa
● **Abbottabad**	district capital	∴	cultural site
• Passu	town, village	△	mountain
▬▬▬	major highway	7706	altitude in metres
══	road	〜〜	glacier
═══	jeep road	⤙	river
··········	footpath	⊢·⊣	national boundary
▬·▬	railway	—··—	provincial boundary
▣	mosque	—···—	district boundary

All maps © copyright The Guidebook Company Ltd. except where indicated otherwise. The author, Isobel Shaw, provided source material for all maps except where indicated otherwise. The publisher wishes to thank her.

Preface

Parts of this book are a rewrite of *A Traveller's Guide to Pakistan*, written by Hilary Adamson and myself in 1981 and published by the Asian Study Group in Islamabad. Some of the descriptions of the northern Punjab are based on *Between Indus and Jhelum*, by Malcolm Hardy, also published by the Asian Study Group (1976). Hilary Adamson has given me continual support and help throughout the writing of this book, accepting with good humour whatever I sent her to edit and criticize, and generally cheering me along.

It is impossible to list all the people who have helped in the production of this book. The government support I received from Aslam Khattak, minister of the interior, Makhdoom Sajjad Hussain Qureshi, governor of the Punjab, and Jam Ghulam Quadir Khan, chief minister of Baluchistan, made my travel throughout the country comfortable and easy. My patron, Begum Mumtaz Rashdi, smoothed my path with essential introductions and enthusiastic support. And the help of other friends, especially Minoo Marker, Aban Marker Kabraji, S M Shahid, Shirin Walji, Nasir Abbas Mirza, Tonny Rosiny, Paddy Booz, Asghar Ahmad, Javed Jabbar and Hakim Feerasta, made the whole project considerably easier.

I owe a debt to many commissioners, deputy commissioners and assistant commissioners who took time from their busy schedules to find me the necessary accommodation and guides. Shams Jafrani, AC Sehwan; Nazar Hussein Mahar, DC Dadu; S A Zulqarnain, commissioner Bahawalpur; Sher Mohammad Iqbal, DC Bahawalpur; Choriasat Ali Khan, protocol officer Bahawalpur; Mansoor Ahmed Bajwa, AC Ahmedpur East; Sheikh Labib-ur-Rehman, DC Dera Ismail Khan; Ahmed Salim Hussain, DC Leah; Raja Irshad-ul-Haq Kayani, DC Mianwali; Buxial Khan Gudaro, DC Sukkur; Tariq Mahmood, DC Multan; Aman Shah, home secretary Baluchistan; Anwar Salim, DC Quetta; Akbar Ahmed, commissioner Sibi; Ejaz Chaudry, AC Jacobabad; the commissioner and ADC, Swat; Prince Aurangzeb of Swat; Sajid, SP Dassu; Sami Khilji, DC Gilgit; Rajah Ali Ahmed Jan of Gilgit; and finally the mir and rani of Hunza.

I do not know how I can repay the patient guides who spent long hours escorting me round, often at the most frenetic pace: Mohammad Ashraf, Dadu, who spent three days guiding me round western Sind; Izaz Ahmed, Quetta, who escorted me round Baluchistan; Pir Ghulam Shah Gilani, Naing, who took me to his village; Nazir Ahmad Quereshi and Amanullah Chachar, Sukkur; Talib Hussain and Farrukh Ahmad Khan, Multan; Syed Khursheed Abbas Shah Gardezi, who showed me round his ancestral tomb and home in Multan; M A Shah, administrator of the Lal Suhanra National Park; Ashraf Jalal, chief librarian, Bahawalpur; Rana Md Afzal and Saeed Khan, Mianwali; Masud Mukhtar and C M Zahid, Khushab; Qadar Ali Khan, Tharparkar; Iqbal Rahman, Mingora; Muneeruddin of the Tourism Division; Siddique, the curator of Harappa; and Rafique Mughal, director of archaeology, Lahore.

Special credit must be given to those who have contributed to this book, read parts of the manuscript and given advice: Prince Salahuddin Abbasi, Bahawalpur, Jonathan Addleton, Ameneh Azam Ali, Ashraf Aman, Zee Arif, Claus Bally, Jon Beeny, Henri Behar, Saeeda Chaudhry, Carolyn Eastham, John Elliott, Holly Edwards, Seemin Asif Ezdi, Sue Farrington, Wolfram Fischer, Hasan-Uddin Khan, Ron Pont, Andre Roch, Ahsan Tayyab, Peter Treloar, Deborah Turrell, Pir Abdul Haque Sirhindi and Hans van Hoeflaken.

Most of all I would like to thank the friends who provided a home away from home and encouraged me throughout: Sue and Malcolm Bannister, Eryll and Paul Fabian, Margaret and Terry Benson, Margaret and Tom Green, Shona Falconer, Suzanne and Rocky Staples, Rosi and Dyno Keatinge, Musarrat and Shoaib Sultan Khan, Tariq and Maliha Husain.

And I am very grateful to my dedicated editors, Yolanda King and Sally Alderson, who went through the text checking punctuation and grammar.

But it is to my husband, Robert, and my children, Dominique, Katherine and Benedict, that I owe everything. Without their unfailing support and tolerance through all the months of work and long absences from home this book could not have been completed.

Finally I would like to ask the reader to remember that conditions change rapidly in Pakistan, especially the state of the roads and the availability and prices of transport and hotels. Telephone numbers and village names change and archaeological sites disappear, so it is likely that before you ever see this book, some details will be already out of date. In order to keep reprints of *The Pakistan Handbook* as accurate as possible, I will be most grateful to anyone who sends me corrections and suggestions on how to improve this guide.

Isobel Shaw
Geneva, February 1989

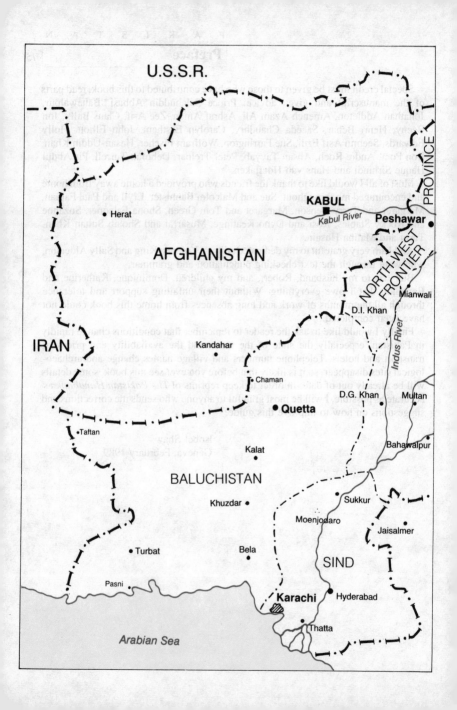

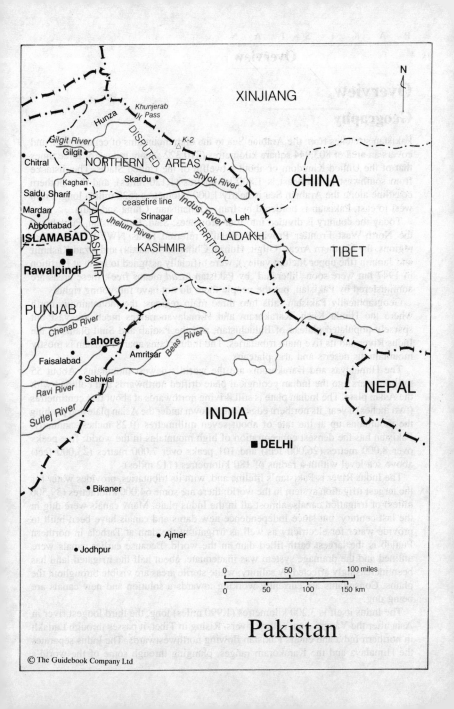

N

XINJIANG

Khunjerab
Pass

Hunza

DISPUTED

K-2 △

Gilgit River

Gilgit

NORTHERN AREAS

CHINA

Chitral

Skardu

Shyok River

Kaghan

Indus River

AZAD KASHMIR

Saidu Sharif

ceasefire line

Mardan

Jhelum River

Srinagar

Leh

Abbottabad

LADAKH

ISLAMABAD

KASHMIR

TERRITORY

TIBET

Rawalpindi

PUNJAB

Chenab River

Lahore

Beas River

Faisalabad

Amritsar

NEPAL

Sahiwal

Ravi River

Sutlej River

INDIA

DELHI

• Bikaner

0   50   100 miles

0   50   100   150 km

• Ajmer

• Jodhpur

Pakistan

© The Guidebook Company Ltd

Overview

Geography

Pakistan stretches from the Arabian Sea to the high mountains of central Asia, and covers an area of 803,944 square kilometres (310,322 square miles), or three times that of the United Kingdom or about a twelfth of the United States. The distance from southwest to northeast is 1,800 kilometres (1,120 miles), and the southern coastline along the Arabian Sea is nearly 1,000 kilometres (620 miles) long. From west to east, Pakistan is bordered by Iran, Afghanistan, China and India.

Today the country is divided into four provinces: Sind, Baluchistan, Punjab and the North-West Frontier Province (usually referred to as NWFP). Two other regions, the Northern Areas (Gilgit, Hunza, Chilas and Skardu) and Azad Kashmir and Jammu (the upper Jhelum valley), were officially assigned to India at Partition in 1947 but were soon 'liberated' by Pakistan (*azad* means free); these areas are administered by Pakistan, but the people there do not have full voting rights.

Geographically Pakistan falls into three main regions: the mountainous north where the Hindu Kush, Karakoram and Himalayan ranges meet; the vast but sparsely populated plateau of Baluchistan; and the Punjab and Sind plains of the Indus River and its five main tributaries. The Indus plains apart, Pakistan is mostly mountainous deserts and arid plateaux.

The Himalayas and Karakorams are the world's newest mountains. About 55 million years ago the Indian geological plate drifted northwards and collided with the Asian plate. The Indian plate is still driving northwards at about five centimetres (two inches) a year, its northern edge nosing down under the Asian plate and pushing the mountains up at the rate of about seven millimetres (0.28 inches) annually. Pakistan has the densest concentration of high mountains in the world: five peaks over 8,000 metres (26,000 feet) and 101 peaks over 7,000 metres (23,000 feet) above sea level within a radius of 180 kilometres (112 miles).

The Indus River is Pakistan's lifeline and, with its tributaries, provides water for the largest irrigation system in the world; there are some 64,000 kilometres (39,500 miles) of irrigation canals, almost all in the Indus plain. Many canals were dug in the last century, but since Independence new dams and canals have been built to provide water for electricity as well as irrigation; the dam at Tarbela in northern Punjab is the largest earth-filled dam in the world. Because earlier canals were unlined and the drainage system was inadequate, about half the irrigated land has been increasingly affected by salinity; white sterile areas are visible throughout the plains. Consultants are currently working towards a solution and new canals are being dug.

The Indus itself is 3,200 kilometres (1,990 miles) long, the third longest river in Asia after the Yangzi and Yellow rivers. Rising in Tibet, it passes through Ladakh in northern India and enters Pakistan flowing northwestwards. The Indus separates the Himalaya and the Karakoram ranges, plunging through some of the world's deepest gorges as it twists between the mountains until it finally finds an exit south to the plains of the Punjab and Sind. The river then meanders across the plains, as wide as 30 kilometres (20 miles) in places, flowing in channels separated by large islands. It floods every summer, when the melting of the mountain snows coincides with the monsoon in the Punjab. In recent years this flooding has been controlled, but previously the river used to change course frequently. The river deposits millions of tons of silt annually before it finally oozes out into the Arabian Sea through a giant delta 150 kilometres (95 miles) long and 250 kilometres (155 miles) wide, stretching east from Karachi to the border of India.

Climate

Pakistan is dry. A quarter of the country has less than 120 millimetres (4.7 inches) and over three-quarters less than 250 millimetres (9.7 inches) of rain annually. Only on seven percent of the land, mostly in the narrow belt of the Punjab from Lahore to Islamabad, and on the mountain slopes north of Islamabad, does the rainfall exceed 500 millimetres (19.5 inches) a year; this is the only area reached by the monsoons which blow across the northern Punjab from India, causing heavy summer storms from July to September. They usually reach Islamabad about a week after arriving in Delhi. Occasional winter rain from the west also falls in the northern Punjab and North-West Frontier Province. The north, west and south are deserts dependent on irrigation for agriculture.

June and July are the hottest months, with mid-day temperatures in the 40°s C (over 104°F) in most places. In upper Sind and neighbouring Baluchistan, the temperature occasionally goes into the 50°s C (over 122°F). It is naturally cooler at higher altitude, especially in the mountain valleys of Swat and Kaghan and around Murree, where there is rain, but it can be very hot in summer along the dry northern valleys of the Indus and Gilgit rivers, where the heat radiates off the bare mountains. Above 2,500 metres (8,200 feet) it is usually pleasant during the day and cool at night.

December, January and February are the coldest months. At this time it is pleasantly cool in Sind, the southern Punjab and the lower areas of Baluchistan, with daytime temperatures ranging between 10° and 25°C (50° and 77°F). In Islamabad the winter climate is crisp during the day and cold at night, and above 1,500 metres (5,000 feet) it is cold during the day and very cold at night.

Population

The estimated population figure for 1988 was 105 million. (The 1981 census figure of 83.79 million represented a five-fold increase since the turn of the century but did not include some three million Afghan refugees or the two to three million Pakistanis who work abroad.)

A quarter of the population lives in the large cities, the chief of which are Karachi

(8 million), Lahore (3 million), Faisalabad (1.25 million), Rawalpindi-Islamabad (1 million), Hyderabad (1 million), Multan, Gujranwala and Peshawar (.75 million), Sialkot, Sargodha and Quetta (.5 million). About three-quarters of all Pakistanis live in the Indus Valley, while some of the desert areas are almost empty.

Although Urdu is the lingua franca of Pakistan, it is actually the mother tongue of only a small proportion of the population; it is, however, claimed as the 'language of speech' by a greater number, and most Pakistanis possess a rudimentary knowledge of Urdu. The word *urdu* itself means army or camp; the language evolved from an amalgam of local languages and the Persian spoken by invading armies from the north. Many educated Pakistanis speak English as well as Urdu.

In fact, the Pakistanis are an ethnically diverse people and speak a variety of languages. The major ones are Punjabi in the Punjab; Sindhi in Sind; Baluchi, Pushtu and Brahui in Baluchistan; Pushtu, Kashmiri, Khowar, Kohistani and Kafiri in the North-West Frontier Province; and Balti, Shina, Burushaski and Wakhi in the Northern Areas. This picture is complicated further by the multiplicity of tribal dialects that have evolved in isolated valleys.

Although Muslims account for the overwhelming majority of the population, there are a small number of Hindus (about 1.2 percent), mostly nomads living in the south, and even smaller Christian and Zoroastrian communities.

Economy

Pakistan's economy is heavily dependent upon agriculture, which accounts for 32 percent of the gross national product and employs nearly three-quarters of the country's population. Wheat is the main food crop, followed by rice, millet, maize, barley and pulses. Cotton is by far the most important cash crop and accounts for five percent of world production. High-quality Basmati rice, grown mainly in Lahore Division, is also a major export. Other crops include sugar-cane, oil-seeds (mustard, rape, sesame, linseed and castor), tobacco, fruit, vegetables, chillies and fodder crops.

Textile manufacture is Pakistan's most important industry, followed by light engineering (electrical goods, metalworking, precision equipment), food processing (vegetable oils, sugar, soft drinks), cement, pharmaceuticals, leather and rubber. The abundant supplies of natural gas (particularly in Baluchistan) mean that Pakistan has a substantial fertilizer industry, and the Soviet Union has helped to build an iron and steel works near Karachi.

Hydroelectric power is the largest source of energy in the country. There is also oil in the Potwar Plateau, and there have been some new finds in southern Sind.

Nearly half of Pakistan's foreign exchange earnings come from remittances sent home by the country's estimated two to three million expatriates, who work mainly in the Middle East. This money makes a considerable difference to the lives of the poorer families in Pakistan, many of whom have at least one member working in the Gulf.

The tourism industry remains almost totally undeveloped, although its great potential is recognized.

Religion

There are few countries where religion plays such an important role in the life of its people as it does in Pakistan. Islam is the binding force of the nation. The muezzin's call to prayer from the minarets of the mosques; the men bowed in prayer in the fields, shops and airports; the *qibbla* (direction of Mecca) marked in every hotel room; the veiled women in the streets—all are constant reminders of the devotion and religious fervour of the Pakistanis.

Islam

The founder of Islam was the Prophet Muhammad, who was born in Mecca (Saudi Arabia) on 29 August 570 and died at Medina on 18 June 632. Muhammad forged a new monotheistic religion which incorporated ideas from both Judaism and Christianity and was acceptable to the war-weary Middle Eastern population. Not only was Muhammad a great religious leader, he was also a great statesman: no Arab has ever succeeded in holding his countrymen together as he did. The Islamic Empire expanded rapidly and within 100 years stretched from Pakistan to Spain.

The word Islam means 'submission to the will of God and peace among His creation'. Muslims believe that the teaching of Islam was first given to man at the time of creation and that prophets have been sent from time to time to convey or renew the divine instruction. Some of these prophets—such as Abraham, Moses and Jesus—have been divinely inspired, and those who follow these prophets are called *ahl-e-kitab*, 'people of revealed books'. Islam recognizes the great Hebrew prophets, as well as Jesus Christ, but it does not believe in the divine nature of Christ, only in his prophethood. Muslims further believe that, despite the teaching of the prophets, man consistently erred so that the teaching became obscured and overladen with false interpretation. Muhammad was sent to restore purity and bring to the entire world the true teachings of God. There will be no other prophet until the Messiah comes.

Muslims have five fundamental religious duties; these are called the Pillars of Islam. They must recite the creed 'There is no God but God and Muhammad is his Prophet' (*La illaha illa 'llah Muhammad Rasulu 'llah*), and must also pray five times a day, fast during the month of Ramazan, give alms (*zakat*) for distribution among the poor and save for a pilgrimage to Mecca.

The Koran, the holy book of Islam, containing God's message as revealed to Muhammad, is a distillation of written and oral records compiled during Muhammad's lifetime and after his death which lays down the Islamic philosophy and code of behaviour. The word of the Koran is infallible: it is the supreme authority to which Muslims look for guidance.

Islam suffered a major split almost from the beginning, as Muhammad died without a clearly appointed successor. There followed a power struggle which saw most of the early leaders dying violently. Two main sects of Islam emerged: the Sunnis, who followed a line of elected leaders called caliphs (the word *khalifa* means representative or deputy); and the Shias (or Shi'ites), who followed a line of hereditary leaders called *imams*, who were directly descended from Muhammad through his daughter Fatima and his son-in-law and cousin Ali. The third most important sect, and very active in Pakistan today, are the Ismailis, a branch of the Shias who follow their living imam, the Aga Khan.

Today the majority of the Muslims in Pakistan are orthodox Sunnis; most of the rest are Shias, and a smaller number are Ismailis. There are a few Ahmadis or Ahmediyas, followers of the newest Islamic sect (founded in 1908), who are also known as the Qadianis, after Qadian in the Punjab where the sect started.

Islam arrived in Pakistan 80 years after Muhammad's death. An Arab army conquered Sind in AD 711, and soon afterwards holy men travelled to the subcontinent and converted the local population to Islam. In the 11th century, Islam became the dominant religious force in Pakistan under the Afghan Mahmud of Ghazni.

Today Pakistan is combining the needs of a modernizing society with the beliefs of Islam. The government has introduced interest-free banking and a systematic collection of zakat, the welfare tax prescribed by Islam.

Sufism

Sufism is the name given to Islamic mysticism, and Sufis are Muslim holy men who develop their spiritual lives through prayer, self-denial and meditation. The word *sufi* is derived from *safa*, meaning purity.

The first Sufis were ninth-century ascetics who wandered around the Islamic world, through Persia, Afghanistan and the subcontinent, preaching love, peace and brotherhood, and teaching Islam by pious example. Many of them were scholars, poets and musicians, who attracted large followings to their gentle form of Islam. Some of Pakistan's finest religious music and literature was written by Sufi saints who portrayed a life of perfection embodying the noblest moral teachings of Islam.

The places where Sufi saints settled and died have become important centres of pilgrimage, attracting hundreds of thousands of devoted followers who admire the saints' holiness and hope that they will intercede for them with God in the granting of some favour, such as health, fertility, peace or success. The Sufi saints have given hope to the poor and sick for over 1,000 years.

The most famous Sufi saints in Pakistan, each with hundreds of thousands of devotees, are Lal Shahbaz Qalandar, whose shrine is in Sehwan Sharif; Data Ganj Bakhsh of Lahore; Baba Farid Shakar Gunj of Pakpatan; Shah Latif of Bhit Shah near Hala; Pir Baba of Buner; Bari Imam of Nurpur, near Islamabad; and Shah Shams Tabrez of Multan. There are hundreds of other shrines all over the country, each with its followers who visit the shrine to pray and make offerings.

Visitors are always welcome at Sufi shrines, providing they remove their shoes, cover their heads and show respect. The shrines are centres of religious, cultural and social interest where rich and poor alike come to pray. The best time to go is on Thursday evening, when the shrines are crowded and there is often devotional singing and dancing. Some Sufi followers use music, dancing and incense to reach a trancelike state in which they feel very close to God.

Each shrine has a festival, or *urs*, once a year at the anniversary of the saint's death. The shrine becomes a fairground with musicians and folk singers playing ancient musical instruments and singing mystical songs. Dervishes and mendicants dance themselves into a state of devotional frenzy, and there are also trade fairs and sports competitions. At the best-known festivals there are displays of Pakistan's traditional martial arts, such as wrestling, swordsmanship, riding, tent-pegging and dagger fighting.

Sikhism

Guru Nanak, the founder of the Sikh religion, was born near Lahore in 1469 and died in 1538. Central to his teaching, which embraced certain aspects of both Hinduism and Islam, was the concept of one God as Truth. Unlike the Hindus, the Sikhs did not adhere to a caste system. The Sikhs developed into a strong military brotherhood, reaching the height of their power under Ranjit Singh at the beginning of the 19th century. By this time they controlled the Punjab; Lahore was their political capital, Amritsar (now in India) their religious centre. At Partition the Sikhs migrated to India, where they are now agitating for a separate Sikh state. The Sikh shrines in Pakistan are maintained by the government and are visited by Sikh pilgrims during their annual festivals.

Hinduism

Pakistan played an important role in the historical development of Buddhism and Hinduism, the latter taking its very name from the Indus River, along the banks of which it evolved some time after the Aryan invasion in 1700 BC. About four million Hindus left Pakistan at Partition in 1947, and fewer than 1.5 million remain in the country today.

Buddhism

Buddhism arrived in the Indus Valley from the Ganges Valley in the third century BC, about 230 years after the death of Buddha. During the great age of Gandhara (second to fifth centuries AD), northern Pakistan was the centre of Buddhism, and it was from here that the religion spread to China and Tibet.

The Buddha, Siddhartha Gautama, was born in Nepal in 624 BC. The son of a rich prince, he became increasingly troubled by the suffering in the world and at the age of 29 decided to renounce all worldly pleasures. He left his wife and young son, and surrendered himself to the search for inner peace. Though unsuccessful at first, he finally attained enlightenment as he sat meditating under the Bodi tree. Buddha spent the rest of his life teaching the way of righteousness and truth, and died aged 80 in Gorakpur, India.

Buddhists do not believe in a supreme god. They look to Buddha to guide them to perfection, and finally to nirvana, a sinless, calm state of mind beyond human existence. The path to perfection embraces the principles of charity, compassion, truthfulness, chastity and self-restraint. Essentially, Buddhists try to follow the middle path between worldliness and asceticism, believing that suffering can be avoided only after suppressing the sensual passions.

After his death, Buddha was cremated and his ashes buried under various stupas (burial mounds) across northern India—some of the stupas in Pakistan supposedly once housed the Buddha's ashes. Though Buddha never visited Pakistan, the Jataka legends relate that he went there in previous incarnations. Shrines were built at the locations described in the legends—there are several such shrines in the Peshawar area. Though there are no Buddhists in Pakistan today, the country's museums are full of Buddhist art from the first to seventh centuries, mostly statues of Buddha and scenes from his various lives, carved in stone or modelled in plaster.

History

Prehistory

Ten million years ago the common ancestors of men and apes roamed in the open woodland south of Islamabad. About two million years ago our own genus, *Homo*, evolved here and began making stone tools and eating meat. The species *Homo sapiens* lived here as far back as 50,000 years ago, as the stone tools scattered along the banks of the Soan River attest. Approximately 9,000 years ago man learned to tame animals and plant crops; early peasant farming villages dating from 6000 BC have been excavated in Baluchistan, the North-West Frontier Province and in the Punjab.

The Ancient Empires

The farming communities were the forerunners of the great Indus Valley Civilization, which developed between 3000 and 1500 BC, or at roughly the same time as the Mesopotamian and Egyptian empires. The Indus Valley Civilization was a well-organized urban society that united the Indus Valley under a strong central government and developed a system of pictograms which has not been deciphered to this day. The two major excavated sites of this civilization are at Moenjodaro in Sind and Harappa in the Punjab.

In about 1700 BC, Aryans swept down from central Asia. Though culturally less advanced than the Indus Valley Civilization, they were the forerunners of the

Hindus and authors of the *Rigveda*, the oldest religious text in the world, which describes battles against people living in cities.

In the sixth century BC, Pakistan became the easternmost province of the Achaemenid Empire of Persia, which was then at its height under Darius the Great. Gandhara, which covered most of northern Pakistan, was a semi-independent kingdom with capitals at both Pushkalavati (now Charsadda) and Taxila. In the fourth century BC, Taxila was the site of one of the greatest universities in the ancient world.

Alexander the Great conquered the Gandharan region between 327 and 325 BC. He visited Taxila and crossed the Salt Range before reaching the Beas River, then sailed down the Indus to the sea and marched west across the Makran Desert in Baluchistan. His empire, however, was short-lived.

In 321 BC, Chandragupta founded the Mauryan Empire, controlling Gandhara from his capital at Patna on the Ganges. His grandson, Ashoka, promoted Buddhism and built Buddhist shrines all over the empire.

From the third century BC to the sixth century AD little is known about the history of Sind and Baluchistan, which were on the far western edge of Indian, and on the eastern edge of Persian, influence. The Kingdom of Gandhara, however, has a fully documented history. Wave after wave of invaders from Persia, Afghanistan and central Asia entered through the passes in the northwestern corner of what is now Pakistan and flowed down across the Punjab towards Delhi.

The Bactrian Greeks arrived in Gandhara in 185 BC, about 50 years after the death of Ashoka. The descendants of Alexander the Great's armies from Bactria (now Balkh, in northern Afghanistan) built new Greek cities at Taxila and Pushkalavati.

In 75 BC the Scythians (Sakas), Iranian nomads from central Asia, invaded the Gandharan region, followed in about AD 20 by the powerful Parthians from east of the Caspian Sea. The Parthians had grown rich as middlemen on the Silk Route between China and the Roman Empire, and had defeated the Romans in 53 BC, terrifying their enemies with their silken banners.

The Kushans from central Asia overthrew the Parthians and established themselves at the centre of the lucrative silk trade, the Roman demand for the gossamer fabric having by this time become virtually insatiable.

By the second century AD the empire under the Kushans extended from eastern Iran to the Chinese frontier and south to the Ganges River. The imperial winter capital was at Peshawar; the summer capital was north of Kabul. Under the most famous Kushan king, Kanishka (*c.* AD 128–51), Buddhism flourished and thousands of monasteries and stupas were built. The Gandharan school of art combined the traditions of east and west to produce art forms so dynamic that they survived for five centuries.

When the Kushans declined, their Gandharan Empire was absorbed by the Sassanian Empire of Persia in the north and the Gupta Empire in the south. In the fourth century a new dynasty of Kidar (Little) Kushans came to power and established their capital at Peshawar.

In about 455 the White Huns (Hephthalites) invaded Gandhara from the northwest. They worshipped Shiva and the sun god Surya, and under their sway Buddhism began to go into decline, although it continued in Tantric form, which incorporated elaborate rituals and theurgy, and did not finally die out until the 16th century in Swat. The White Huns were converted to Hinduism and were possibly absorbed into the Rajput warrior caste.

The Sassanians and the Turks overthrew the Huns, but by the late sixth and seventh centuries the Turki Shahis, the Hindu rulers of Kapisa in Afghanistan, controlled the area west of the Indus, including Gandhara. The raja of Kashmir ruled east of the Indus and the northern Punjab, and there were numerous smaller kingdoms, all Hindu, throughout the country. Brahmanical Hinduism, a sect which performed elaborate ceremonies and animal sacrifice and had a dominant priestly class, overtook Buddhism.

In 870 Hindu Shahis from central Asia overthrew the Turki Shahis and established their capital at Hund on the Indus. They ruled the area from Jalalabad in Afghanistan to Multan, including Kashmir, until 1008.

The Coming of Islam

Islam arrived in Pakistan from two directions, south and north. In 711 an Arab expedition under Muhammad bin Qasim arrived by sea to suppress piracy on Arab shipping and established control of the Indus Valley as far north as Multan. Although most of the local rulers were left in power, they were forced to pay taxes to the caliph of Baghdad.

In the 11th century, the Turkish rulers of Afghanistan began the Islamic conquest of India from the northwest. Mahmud of Ghazni (979–1030) led a series of raids against the Rajput kingdoms and the wealthy Hindu temples. Gandhara, the Punjab, Sind and Baluchistan all became part of the Ghaznavid Empire, which had its capital at Ghazni, in Afghanistan. The Ghaznavids developed Lahore as a centre of Islamic culture in the Punjab; mass conversions to Islam began at this time.

The Ghaznavid Kingdom was destroyed by the Ghorids, the Turkish Muslim rulers of Ghor in Afghanistan. Muhammad of Ghor swept down the Indus into India, defeating the Rajput confederacy in 1192 and capturing Delhi in 1193. This marked the beginning of the sultanate period, which lasted for over 300 years and saw five dynasties of Muslim sultans succeeding one another in Delhi. The Mongol Genghis Khan harried the Delhi sultans during the 13th century but never succeeded in overthrowing them. The sultans' defensive border, which stretched from Lahore to Multan, was penetrated by the great Turkish conqueror Tamerlane between 1398 and 1399, when he succeeded in sacking Delhi.

The Moghul Period

Early in the 16th century, Babur, the first Moghul emperor and a descendant of Tamerlane and Genghis Khan, raided the Punjab from Afghanistan and in 1526 defeated the last of the Delhi sultans, the Lodis, at the battle of Panipat.

Babur was succeeded by Humayun in 1530. Humayun was more of an intellectual than a statesman, and was ousted by the Pathan Sher Shah Suri, who ruled the empire until his death in 1545. Humayun returned from exile in Persia and regained the throne in 1554 but died two years later after falling down his library stairs. He was succeeded by his son Akbar.

Akbar was the greatest of the Moghul emperors. He improved the centralized administrative system established by Sher Shah Suri and was a great patron of Moghul art and literature. By the time of his death in 1605, his empire stretched from central India to Kashmir, and included Sind and Rajasthan.

Moghul art and architecture reached its height under Akbar's son Jahangir, and later under his grandson Shah Jahan. Together they left a legacy of magnificent mosques, palaces, forts and gardens embellished with luxurious but delicate decorations.

Aurangzeb, who ruled from 1658 to 1707, was a pious man and an efficient administrator, but within a few decades of his death the empire disintegrated into several independent regions, and Muslim power declined.

In 1739, Nadir Shah of Persia invaded the subcontinent and sacked Delhi, taking the territories west of the Indus. After his death, Ahmad Shah Durrani founded the Kingdom of Afghanistan and acquired the Punjab and Kashmir.

In the early 19th century, the Sikhs, a militant religious group derived from Hinduism in the early 16th century, began to rise to power in the Punjab, and by the 1830s they had pushed the Afghans back across the Indus to the Khyber Pass. Ranjit Singh, their greatest leader, consolidated Sikh power in the Punjab and ruled from his capital at Lahore from 1799 to 1839.

The British Period

The British were in the subcontinent for over three centuries. Arriving as merchants with the British East India Company at the beginning of the 17th century, they sought concessions first from local rulers and later from the Moghul emperors. They traded in cotton, wool, opium, indigo, sugar, jute, diamonds—anything, in fact, which would make them a profit—and with force, bribery, usury and intrigue they made their trade routes secure.

By the mid-18th century, the British were becoming increasingly involved in Indian politics and, after the battle of Plassey in 1757, began a systematic conquest of the subcontinent. As Moghul power weakened and the Sikhs rose to power in the Punjab and the north, the British rapidly extended their influence over the rest of the country. By 1843 Sind, the corridor to Afghanistan, was in their hands. British and Sikh territories met at the Sutlej River in eastern Punjab, and it was here that in 1845 the British defeated the Sikhs in the First Anglo-Sikh War; they subsequently set up a British political resident at Lahore. In 1849 the British defeated the Sikhs in the Second Sikh War and annexed the Punjab and the North-West Frontier area.

After the First War of Independence in 1857 (also known as the Indian or Sepoy Mutiny), the British government took direct control of India. This marked the beginning of the British Raj (British rule), and in the name of Queen Victoria the British continued to expand their empire. Hunza on the Chinese border was the last area to fall into British hands, in 1891; only Afghanistan continued to elude their grasp.

In 1893 the British established the Durand Line, which separated British India from Afghanistan and cut straight through the Pathan tribal lands. There are now about ten million Pathans on the Pakistan side of the border and five million on the Afghan side. The British allowed the tribal areas to govern themselves under the supervision of a British political agent, a system which by and large has been adopted by the Pakistani government.

The British have, in fact, had a strong influence on modern Pakistan. They not only introduced their administrative and legal systems, they also mapped the entire country, demarcated borders and built an impressive network of roads, railways and canals. The British brought with them their culture, language, art and architecture, some of which is still in evidence in Pakistan today. Their cantonment areas (see page 222) with wide, tree-lined avenues and imposing public buildings are a curious mixture of Victorian Gothic and classic Moghul.

The Emergence of Pakistan

After the unsuccessful First War of Independence in 1857, the British determined to suppress and weaken the Muslims, whom they held mainly responsible for the uprising. Sir Syed Ahmed Khan (1817–98) made one of the first attempts to restore Muslim status by founding the Aligarh Movement, which later became the Muslim League. The latter was initially part of the Hindu-dominated Indian National Congress, founded in 1885 to promote political freedom for all communities in the subcontinent, but the Muslims broke away because they felt their interests were being neglected.

In 1930, the great Muslim poet and philosopher Dr Muhammad Iqbal proposed the creation of a separate Muslim state for those areas of the subcontinent with a Muslim majority. His proposal was adopted by Muhammad Ali Jinnah, a British-trained lawyer and Pakistan's first head of state. Once the British realized that they would have to relinquish their hold upon the subcontinent, they tried without success to keep the country intact by suggesting that there should be autonomous Muslim states under a united central government; their plans were rejected by both the Muslim League and the Indian National Congress. It was finally agreed that the subcontinent should be partitioned at Independence in 1947.

The division of the subcontinent proved difficult, particularly as it had to be accomplished in less than four months. It was decided that Pakistan would comprise the eastern and western wings of the country, where there were Muslim majorities, while India would retain the predominantly Hindu central parts. The main area of contention was the fertile Punjab, where Hindu, Muslim and Sikh populations were inextricably mixed. The result was that at Independence an estimated six million Muslim refugees, mainly from the Punjab, streamed across the border into Pakistan, and about 4.5 million Sikhs and Hindus crossed into India. This migration was accompanied by terrible violence and bloodshed: about 500,000 people lost their lives.

There were other problems. One concerned Kashmir, whose maharaja opted to join India upon Independence (under pressure from Nehru) although the Kashmiris are predominantly Muslims. This led to the division of Kashmir in 1948. Today both Pakistan and India still claim Kashmir, and the territory has been a central issue behind most of the disputes between the two countries since Independence.

Yet another problem of Partition was the division of water for irrigation, as all Pakistan's great rivers pass first through India. A solution was not found until 1959, when a treaty was drawn up under the auspices of the World Bank (see page 110).

Another issue concerned the status of the hundreds of princely states. Those absorbed into Pakistan were Khairpur in Sind; Bahawalpur in Punjab; Kalat and Las Bela in Baluchistan; Dir, Swat and Chitral in NWFP; and Gilgit, Hunza, Punial, Gupis and Yasin in the north.

Pakistan After Independence

The greatest difficulty facing the new Pakistan was that it consisted of two parts separated by nearly 2,000 kilometres (1,200 miles) of hostile India, with populations that had nothing in common except religion. The western half was dominant in political and economic terms despite having a smaller population. It took nearly ten years to draft a new constitution. Almost immediately General Ayub Khan took over the government; in 1969 he was succeeded by General Yahya Khan. During this time the eastern wing of the country became increasingly unhappy with its status, and in 1970, following a disastrous cyclone in the area, things came to a head. In December of that year elections were held which resulted in wins for the Pakistan People's Party in the western half and for the Awami League in the eastern half. The dispute over which party had the right to form a government led first to strikes and then to outright revolt in East Pakistan. The Indians declared war on Pakistan and supported the creation of an independent Bangladesh.

Zulfikar Ali Bhutto remained as prime minister of Pakistan and ruled until 1977, pursuing a policy popular with the urban masses and rural poor, especially in Sind. He nationalized basic industries, banks and insurance, began to democratize the civil service and started reforming the health and education systems. When Britain recognized Bangladesh, Bhutto pulled Pakistan out of the British Commonwealth and strengthened ties with China in an attempt to balance the threat from India.

Bhutto's downfall came after the general elections in 1977, which opposition parties alleged were rigged in the Punjab.

General Zia-ul-Haq took over the administration of Pakistan, and Bhutto was charged with the murder of the father of a political opponent; he was tried, found guilty and was hanged on 4 April 1979. Under martial law there was steady economic growth favouring the private sector, and some effort was made to Islamize the political, legal and economic structures. In 1985, 'non-party' elections were held and a civilian government was installed. Martial law was lifted in 1986, though President Zia remained in power.

Zia was killed in a plane crash in August 1988, free party elections were held in November, and the Pakistan People's Party was returned to power with Benazir Bhutto as prime minister.

Facts for the Traveller

The Pakistan Tourism Development Corporation (PTDC) is the main source of information inside Pakistan; their head office is at House 2, Street 61, F 7/4, Islamabad. For PTDC hotel bookings contact PTDC Motel Head Office, Room 30, Flashman's Hotel, The Mall, Rawalpindi, tel. 581480–4. The PTDC also has offices in the Metropole Hotel in Karachi, Faletti's Hotel in Lahore, Dean's Hotel in Peshawar, the Muslim Hotel in Quetta, PTDC Motel in Ziarat, Club Annex in Abbottabad, PTDC hotels in Balakot and Naran in the Kaghan Valley, Swat Serena Hotel in Swat, PTDC Motel in Chitral, Chinar Inn in Gilgit, K-2 Motel in Skardu, and at the archaeological sites of Moenjodaro, Taxila and Thatta. They arrange trips, accommodation and transport and publish a series of booklets on areas of tourist interest.

Outside Pakistan, Pakistan International Airlines (PIA) offices and the Pakistani embassies and consulates supply information.

Visas

A valid passport is required for all visitors. All nationalities need visas for Pakistan, except nationals of Hong Kong, Ireland, Malaysia, Singapore, Tanzania, Tonga, Trinidad and Tobago, and Uganda. Nationals from the following countries can stay in Pakistan without a visa from between one and three months: Fiji, Japan, Republic of Korea, Maldives, Mauritius, Nepal, Philippines, Romania and Western Samoa. Israelis and South Africans are not admitted to Pakistan. A maximum of three months' stay is allowed on a tourist visa. Short extensions can be obtained from regional Passport Offices in Islamabad, Karachi, Lahore, Peshawar and Quetta (see relevant chapters for details). The length of the extension is up to the officer in charge. Contact your local Pakistan consulate or PIA office for the latest information as these rules are subject to change.

Exit Formalities

Antiques may not be exported from Pakistan. Jewellery and precious stones worth less than Rs10,000, and carpets worth less than Rs25,000 are allowed out, but you must produce foreign exchange certificates up to the value you claim for the articles. Unaccompanied baggage needs an export permit.

All travellers must pay an airport tax of Rs350 for international flights and Rs10 for domestic flights.

Health Regulations

Visitors need cholera and yellow fever vaccination certificates if coming from an infected area. Malaria exists all year round in the whole of Pakistan below 2,000 metres (6,500 feet), so malarial prophylactics are essential. Anti-malaria pills should be taken for one week before arriving and for six weeks after departure; ask your doctor which prophylactic is recommended for the type of malaria prevalent in Pakistan.

Tourists are advised to have up-to-date vaccinations against typhoid, tetanus and polio. Cholera vaccine is only 50 percent effective and may have quite severe side effects, so it is not always recommended. Some doctors suggest you have an injection of gamma globulin a few days before departure; this gives 80 percent protection for five months against hepatitis, which is widespread in Pakistan.

Customs Regulations

Alcohol is not admitted to Pakistan; bags are almost always searched and the alcohol impounded if found. Non-Muslims can buy liquor in Pakistan if they have a liquor licence, obtainable in some large hotels authorized to sell alcohol to hotel residents, and from government liquor shops in the main cities if they have a permit from the Excise and Taxation Department of that area.

Officially, 200 cigarettes, a half pint of perfume and only one camera, tape recorder and typewriter are allowed in. Officials are less strict about these restrictions for tourists, though visiting Pakistanis and Indians are thoroughly searched.

Money

Rupees and paise are the currency of Pakistan: 100 paise = 1 rupee. Approximate rates (1989) are US$1=Rs19, British £1=Rs33, Dm1=Rs11. There is no restriction on the amount of foreign currency or travellers cheques brought into Pakistan. Only Rs100 in cash may be taken in or out of Pakistan, and only Rs500 can be changed back from rupees to foreign currency. Save your encashment slips as you may need them when leaving. It is an offence to sell foreign currency in Pakistan except to authorized dealers.

US dollars—both currency and travellers cheques—are the most useful. (English pounds and Deutsche Marks are also accepted, but avoid other currencies.) American Express has offices at Karachi, Lahore, Islamabad and Rawalpindi, but the Islamabad and Rawalpindi branches have a bad reputation. Travellers cheques can be changed in major cities. Only foreign banks, the National Bank of Pakistan and Habib Bank are permitted to deal in foreign exchange; the rates differ depending on the town and bank. Large hotels will change travellers cheques for guests, but they usually give a lower rate than banks; they also accept credit cards.

If you need to have money sent to you in Pakistan, ask for a bank draft to be sent registered airmail to a specific address. This is quicker than having it sent bank to bank.

Getting to Pakistan

By Air

More than 20 international airlines fly to Pakistan from over 40 countries. Most international flights arrive in Karachi or Islamabad–Rawalpindi but a few go to Lahore or Peshawar. You can change travellers cheques and foreign money at these airports. There are taxis and public buses from the airports to the city centres. You should bargain with the taxi driver and agree on the fare before setting off. From Karachi airport to the downtown hotels it should cost about Rs80 by taxi, Rs10 by airport coach and Rs2 by bus. From Islamabad–Rawalpindi airport to Islamabad it is about Rs70 by taxi, Rs5 by wagon and Rs3 by bus. A taxi to Rawalpindi costs about Rs50, a bus about Rs2.

Overland

From China: The Khunjerab Pass border crossing is open from 1 May to 31 October for tours, and from 1 May to 30 November for individual travellers (see pages 427–8 for details).

From India: The border at Wagah, near Lahore, is open only a few days each month due to unrest in the Indian Punjab. India and Pakistan have agreed to open the railway line from Jodhpur in Rajasthan to Hyderabad in Sind, but this is not yet running (see pages 81–2).

From Iran: The border is open only at Taftan, from where it is a 15- to 24-hour bus ride to Quetta in Baluchistan (see page 126).

From Afghanistan: Afghanistan is closed to foreigners because of the troubles. There are two entry points to Pakistan from Afghanistan—from Kabul via Torkham and the Khyber Pass, and from Kandahar via Chaman and the Khojak Pass—but both are closed except to local traffic and authorized refugees (see pages 145 and 293).

By Sea

No boats for the general public sail to or from Pakistan. However, a few pilgrim boats ply between Karachi and the Gulf States.

When to Go

The climate in Pakistan is so varied (see page 19) that no matter what time of year you go, somewhere will be pleasant at that time. Winter (November to February) is the best time to visit southern Pakistan (Sind and southern Punjab). The rest of the country is at its most beautiful in spring (March to May depending on the altitude) and autumn (mid-September to mid-November) when the spring flowers and autumn colours are at their best. For trekking and mountaineering, June to September are the recommended months. Avoid Ramazan (see page 39).

Travelling Inside Pakistan

By Air

PIA operates flights to Bahawalpur, Bannu, Chitral, Dera Ismail Khan, Faisalabad, Gilgit, Gwadar, Hyderabad, Islamabad–Rawalpindi, Jacobabad, Jiwani, Karachi, Khuzdar, Kohat, Lahore, Mianwali, Moenjodaro, Multan, Nawabshah, Panjgur, Pasni, Peshawar, Saidu Sharif, Sargodha, Sindhri, Skardu, Sui, Sukkur, Turbat, Zhob.

Flights to Gilgit, Skardu and Chitral are cheaper when tickets are bought in Pakistan and are extremely good value, at about twice the bus fare. Gilgit and Chitral flights operate only when visibility is good, so they can be delayed for some days.

Discounts: Pakistani students, or foreigners under 26 at local universities or colleges, are eligible for a 30 percent discount on internal flights. Apply to the public relations officer at the PIA offices in Karachi, Lahore, Rawalpindi, Peshawar, Multan or Quetta. Journalists and groups are also eligible for discounts.

By Train

This is the best way of travelling if you are not in a hurry. The main lines run from Karachi via Multan, Lahore and Rawalpindi to Peshawar, and from Karachi via Sukkur and Quetta to the Iranian border, and there is an extensive network of branch lines. Trains are frequent, but they are very slow, unpunctual and crowded. There are two classes of train, express and ordinary, and three classes of compartment, air-conditioned, first and second. Air-conditioned and first class have sleeper compartments, and there are special ladies' compartments recommended for women travelling alone. Air-conditioned sleeper class on an express train is almost as expensive as flying, but second class on an ordinary train is extremely cheap. You usually need to book several days in advance, especially if you want a sleeper. Most passengers bring their own bedding, but this can sometimes be hired at major stations. Buying a ticket can be time-consuming and frustrating, so an agency or hotel employee willing to take this on is a great asset. If all else fails, you can pay a station porter (distinguishable by his red turban and armband) to buy you a ticket and find you a seat.

Parties can hire luxurious **tourist cars** complete with dining and sitting rooms, which can be attached to certain trains and detached at any railway station for as many hours as the occupants wish. These can be hired from the Divisional Superintendent's Office, Pakistan Railways, Karachi. The cost is reasonable when divided among a fairly large party.

Discounts: Foreign tourists can get a 25 percent discount, and foreign students a 50 percent discount, on most rail fares. First apply to the Tourist Information Centre at the PTDC at Karachi, Lahore, Rawalpindi, Islamabad, Peshawar or Quetta. Next go to the Divisional Superintendent with your passport and student card at Karachi, Lahore, Rawalpindi, Peshawar, Quetta, Sukkur or Multan railway stations for the necessary concession order before you buy your ticket. You are allowed to break your journey only once. Indians and visiting Pakistanis are not given discounts.

By Bus

Buses are the cheapest but most uncomfortable and dangerous way of travelling in Pakistan. Buses go everywhere from everywhere. Seats cannot be reserved in advance. Bus stations are usually near the railway stations in larger towns, and near the bazaars in smaller places. On longer journeys the buses make scheduled stops for food, but it is wise to take food (especially fruit) and drink with you.

Minibuses are faster, more comfortable and only slightly more expensive; seats can be booked in advance. There are also several private luxury bus services between Rawalpindi and Lahore.

By Jeep-taxi

Jeep-taxis are used for public transport in the northern valleys where the roads are too narrow for buses. The drivers are excellent, but the jeeps are neither cheap nor comfortable, and they do not run to a timetable. As many passengers as possible perch on top of the cargo (usually sacks of grain or fertilizer) and crouch on the front and back bumper. In the remoter valleys, jeeps are quite rare.

The Northern Area Transport Company (NATCO) runs buses and jeeps up the Karakoram Highway and into some of the side valleys off the main road. They offer a discount to a limited number of Pakistani and foreign students on each vehicle.

Jeeps with drivers can easily be hired in the mountains. The government-approved rate in the Punjab, on the Karakoram Highway and in Gilgit District is Rs6 per mile plus Rs75 overnight charge; in Chitral Rs8 per mile plus Rs30 overnight charge; and in Skardu Rs10 per mile plus Rs200 halt charge—but you are unlikely to get them for as little as this, so bargain hard.

By Car

The main roads in Pakistan are surfaced and generally in reasonable condition. Drivers are not conscientious about traffic rules, so those unused to driving in Asia may find it harrowing and dangerous. The main Karachi–Lahore–Rawalpindi–Peshawar highway is always very crowded with particularly reckless drivers. The minor roads are often impassable for ordinary cars; four-wheel drive vehicles with high clearance are recommended. In the mountains it is essential to have a small four-wheel drive vehicle, as the roads have been built for small jeeps and the bridges are very narrow.

Signposts are few and far between and often written in Urdu. Finding your way around the larger cities can be difficult, especially as the names of many streets have changed since Independence and the locals use both names interchangeably. Distances are measured in kilometres in the Punjab, but since Pakistan has fairly recently transferred to the decimal system, not all signposts in the rest of the country have been changed, so, particularly in Baluchistan, you never know if you still have eight kilometres or eight miles to go. Driving at night is especially hazardous, as trucks, bicycles and bullock carts rarely have lights; it is also dangerous to drive in some parts of Sind at night because of bandits.

Cars with drivers can be hired at the airport and big hotels. Hotel cars are usually air-conditioned and expensive, but are often worth the price as the drivers can speak some English. Check with the hotel rental agency that the driver knows where you want to go before you set off. You can hire a small local taxi (black with a yellow roof) in the street for about Rs300 for the day, which is often the most satisfactory solution if you have several places to visit. Taxi drivers usually know only the main locations in town and will expect you to direct them to offices or private houses.

Self-drive cars are not usually available and are not recommended unless you speak some Urdu and know your way around; a valid driving licence is required.

Inner-city Transport

In big cities buses run along set routes but not to a schedule. Datsun wagons and Suzuki vans run everywhere possible in Pakistan; in the cities the fare is usually Rs2. There are few designated stops—simply wave down a passing wagon or Suzuki and ask the driver if he is going in your general direction. In some towns there are also motorized rickshaws charging about half the local taxi fare. Lastly, bicycle rickshaws in the lower Punjab, and horse-drawn *tongas* in Lahore, provide alternative methods of transportation in these areas.

Maps

Maps are difficult to find in Pakistan—good maps do not exist. The best overall map is Bartholomew's road map of the entire subcontinent; the best general road map of Pakistan is the 1:2,000,000 1976 road map. The most useful maps are the 1:1,000,000 (ten kilometres to one centimetre) contour maps issued by the Survey of Pakistan. Occasionally you can buy some of these in bookshops or hotel lobbies, but usually the only place to get them is at the Survey of Pakistan office on Murree Road in Faizabad between Islamabad and Rawalpindi. (The office is 200 metres, or 220 yards, from the Airport Road-Murree Road intersection, on the right going towards Rawalpindi.) They may also be available in the Survey of Pakistan office in Karachi near the Metropole Hotel. The drawback is that they are reprints of old maps and are sometimes very blurred. The road grading is usually 50 years out of date, and new roads and lakes—and even the present cease-fire line with India—are not shown. The Pakistan Tourism Development Corporation publishes pamphlets with sketch maps which contain much useful information.

For **trekking maps** see page 432.

The maps in this guide mark everything mentioned in the text. These are more-or-less to scale and fairly accurate, but road conditions can change rapidly.

Accommodation

Hotels in Pakistan should be seen in perspective and not judged by western standards. Throughout this guidebook hotels in every major town or place of tourist interest are listed by price and quality.

There are good **international class hotels** in Karachi, Islamabad, Rawalpindi, Lahore, Peshawar, Quetta and Faisalabad, but outside these major cities there is a shortage of good accommodation. However, the situation is improving rapidly: the Serena chain has hotels at Quetta, Faisalabad, Swat and Gilgit, and the Shangrila chain is expanding into the northern areas at Chilas, Skardu, Muree, Gilgit, Sost, Raikot and Fairy Meadows. These hotels are all comfortable but relatively expensive (between US$20 and US$80 a night) as they cater for businessmen and wealthy travellers. The best hotels are usually fully booked all the time, so advance booking is essential.

The **Pakistan Tourist Development Corporation** runs motels and guest houses at the most popular tourist resorts and places of interest. These are at Besham and Gilgit (on the Karakoram Highway), Miandam and Kalam (in Swat), Balakot and Naran (in the Kaghan Valley), Chitral town, Skardu, Taxila, Moenjodaro and Keenjhar Lake. They charge US$18–40 a night, but the staff is usually extremely helpful.

Every town has a wide range of **locally run hotels** which vary greatly in price and standard (anything from US$1 to US$40 a night). Many of them are cheap by western standards but adequate. Some are exceptionally good value, but it is usually worth checking the room and sanitary facilities before signing in.

It is the custom in Pakistan to provide only a bottom sheet and a well-used blanket in local hotels. It is advisable to carry your own sheet and pillow case (or a sleeping-bag liner), towel and soap. In winter, or in the mountains, you will need a sleeping bag.

In local hotels you should order any food you want for the next 24 hours as soon as you arrive. However, it is often more satisfactory to go out and find a food stall or local restaurant than to eat in the hotel.

At the bottom end of the scale are the **musafar khanas**, local inns where a *charpoy*, or rope bed, is provided (without bedding) in a communal dormitory or outside. These local inns and the really cheap hotels will not usually accept foreigners except in very remote areas where there is no other accommodation. Prices range from US$.50 to US$1.50 a night.

There are **youth hostels** at Lahore and Taxila and **YMCA hostels** at the major cities of Karachi, Lahore, Peshawar and Abbottabad; at Bhurban and Khanpur (in the Murree Hills); at Balakot, Sharan, Naran and Bat Kundi (in the Kaghan Valley); and at Ketas (in the Salt Range). There are YWCA Hostels at Karachi and Lahore. Nightly charges vary between US$1.50 and US$2.50.

Railway Retiring Rooms are a remnant from British days. They are rooms with beds at certain railway stations which are available to passengers holding air-conditioned or first-class tickets. These are good value at between Rs20 and Rs40 and are available at Karachi (City and Cantonment), Lahore (City and Cantonment), Multan Cantonment, Rawalpindi Cantonment, Peshawar Cantonment, Sargodha, Taxila, Bahawalpur and Quetta.

There are hundreds of **government rest houses** all over the country belonging to the various government departments—Forestry, Highway, Irrigation, Public Works, etc. They are often in the most beautiful and inaccessible places, and can usually be booked providing no government official is using them. Charges are moderate and fixed—usually US$1.50–8.00 a night. The problem is to identify and contact the appropriate authority to make a reservation. The best rest houses are listed in this guide and in the PTDC brochures, but there are many more. You need a letter from the appropriate government agency to show to the watchman at the rest house. It is best to collect this personally at the government office. It is not possible to book much in advance as rest houses are primarily for the use of government officials on duty, and other visitors can only use them if they are not needed for official use, which cannot always be foreseen. The whole process requires considerable patience and is far from foolproof. Standards in rest houses are variable. It is usually necessary to take bedding, food, crockery, cutlery and basic cooking utensils. The best can be very beautiful and comfortable indeed, but these are obviously the most sought after.

Camping

Islamabad has the only official camp site in Pakistan, but it is often possible to camp in the garden of small hotels, rest houses or youth hostels and to use their facilities; Rs10 per tent is the usual charge. You are not allowed to camp by the roadside, in tribal areas or in some parts of the northern valleys. Camping in the open can be difficult, as the locals are very curious and in some areas hostile.

Showers

Major railway stations usually have free shower rooms. In most towns and villages barber shops also provide *hammams*, cubicles with buckets of water (hot in winter).

Food and Drink

The best Pakistani food is delicious, lightly curried and varied. Most restaurants serve chicken, mutton and beef with lentils (*daal*), vegetables (*subzi*), yoghurt (*dahi*), and *chapatis* or *naan* (two varieties of unleavened bread, usually made with wheat flour). Lahore is famous for its Moghul cuisine, Karachi for its seafood and Peshawar for its kebabs, naan and green tea. Pakistani curries are usually not as hot as Indian ones, and many dishes have no chillies at all, though they are well seasoned with other spices.

Visitors should be sensible about what they eat; it is easy to avoid an upset stomach by taking a few simple precautions. Seasoned travellers in Asia will have developed some immunities, but new arrivals should avoid eating anything that has not been freshly cooked, especially salads, sliced tomatoes, even raw onion slices. Fruit is particularly good in Pakistan, but it is wise to peel all fruit with a clean knife before eating it; pocket folding knives are available in most bazaars. Cut fruit, mixed fruit juices and ice cream sold in bazaars spell danger. Boil it, bake it, peel it or forget it, is a good motto to remember.

It is perfectly safe to eat at roadside stalls, but make sure that the food comes out of a boiling pot on to a clean dry plate. Chapatis and daal make for a good, high-protein, cheap meal and are available everywhere. As a general rule, follow the crowds: the most popular stalls have the best, and the freshest, food.

Buffet meals in first-class hotels can be a problem, as food kept warm for long periods may be contaminated.

In most areas restaurants serve only chicken and fish on Tuesdays and Wednesdays. This is an attempt to cut down on meat consumption.

Avoid drinking water that has not been boiled or purified; this can sometimes be embarrassing as very few Pakistanis boil water at home. International-class hotels claim that their water is drinkable, but it is wise not to risk it unless you know you have built up some immunities. Smaller hotels sometimes have a sign saying 'Water personally passed by the manager'! Don't believe it (in either sense). Avoid ice everywhere, even in major hotels, as it is not made with boiled water. A small plastic bottle in which to carry purified water is useful when travelling.

Tea is usually a safe drink, and as it is the custom in Pakistan to boil milk before serving, it is also safe to take milk in tea. Be sure the tea is poured into a clean, uncracked, dry cup. Bottled soft drinks are safe and are available in all major towns and many smaller ones.

During Ramazan, the fasting month, no food or drink is sold during the day except in a few Chinese restaurants and in the dining rooms of large hotels. (Poolside service is usually suspended.) Travel is difficult during this month; tourists should be careful not to eat, drink or smoke in public. See page 465 for relevant dates.

Health Facilities

Pakistan has a good supply of doctors, many English-speaking, in the major towns. Chemists stock a wide range of medicines which can often be obtained without prescription. There are hospitals in many towns; the best is the Aga Khan Hospital in Karachi.

Clothes

Loose cotton clothes are recommended for hot weather. In winter and in the mountains you will need sweaters and an anorak. Many Pakistanis wear a large woollen shawl day and night—you might think of following their example.

Women should dress modestly in loose trousers and a long, loose shirt. Legs and shoulders should be covered at all times, so dresses should not be worn. The lightweight scarf (*dupatta*) worn by Pakistani women is useful for draping round your shoulders and head in remoter areas or when visiting mosques and shrines. The women's national dress of Pakistan, the *shalwar-kameez* (loose shirt and baggy trousers), is very comfortable and can be bought cheaply ready-made in Karachi, Lahore and Islamabad; elsewhere it can be quickly and inexpensively made by a dressmaker. See what is in fashion in these three cities and choose something similar. Pakistani ladies are very fashion-conscious and fashions change frequently.

Men should wear shorts only for playing sports, and tracksuits to and from the sports ground.

Visiting Mosques and Shrines

Tourists are welcome in mosques and shrines providing they remove their shoes, show respect and are suitably dressed. Women should cover their heads, shoulders and legs. A pair of socks, or the bootees provided by some airlines, are very useful, especially in summer, as the stones can get extremely hot. In some shrines women are not allowed into the inner sanctum, but may look in through a side window. Many mosques close their doors to tourists half an hour before prayers.

Hints for Women

Pakistani women never travel alone: many never even leave their houses unless accompanied by a family member, friend or servant. Foreign women tourists are advised not to travel alone in Pakistan, not because there is any danger, but because it offends a good Muslim male to see a woman being so immodest as to travel unaccompanied. Older Muslim men may look at a lone woman with disgust; teenage boys usually think it very funny and may gang up and tease—like adolescents anywhere, they can be extremely offensive and cruel. Some Pakistani men are sexually frustrated and believe in the myth that western women, especially if alone, are available. They often bring the subject round to sex and ask the most personal of questions. To talk about politics or sport is an excellent distraction, and I always carry photos of my husband and children and produce them at every opportunity. I have travelled alone on assignments over most of Pakistan and have never felt in danger. Once Pakistani men realize that you are serious and working they quickly understand and are extremely helpful and courteous, often going out of their way to escort you around and see that no disrespect is shown to you. A well brought-up Pakistani male will consider it his 'duty' to look after you. Most have spent many boring hours escorting their sisters to school and around the bazaar, so they accept it as natural. They are genuinely worried and uncomfortable if you go out on your own. Pakistanis are very friendly and extremely helpful and obliging. Do not misinterpret their good intentions, but do make it clear what yours are, and be especially sensitive not to offend, provoke or excite with what they see as western lack of modesty.

It pleases Pakistanis to see you wearing their national dress, and they are delighted if you make the effort to learn a few words of Urdu.

Items to Carry

Here is a checklist of useful items to carry with you in Pakistan: sunglasses; some sort of head-covering to keep off the sun and dust and for women to wear in mosques and shrines; lavatory paper; water-purifying tablets and pills for upset stomachs; insect repellent; suntan lotion; a zippered bag to protect your camera and other possessions from dust; a plastic water bottle and a pocket knife. If you are using the cheaper hotels take a plug for washbasins, soap, towel, insect powder and a sheet or sleeping bag. If you are using rest houses you might also need some food and drink to supplement the local diet, and a torch or candle and matches.

Women should be sure to take all the moisturizing cream and tampons they need with them, as these are difficult to find in Pakistan.

The most popular presents for Pakistani friends are imported cosmetics, creams, perfumes, fabrics, cheese and chocolate.

What to Buy

Rugs and carpets, leather goods, embroidered and appliquéd bedspreads and table linen, pottery, copper and brassware, onyx ornaments, woodwork and gold and silver jewellery—all can be found in government-sponsored handicraft shops, where the prices are controlled, or in the bazaars, where it is necessary to bargain to get a good price.

Business Hours

All shops and offices in Pakistan are closed on Fridays. Government office hours are 8.30 am–2 pm in summer and 9 am–2.30 pm in winter. Normal business hours are 7.30 am–2.30 pm in summer, and 9 am–4 pm in winter.

Pakistan is five hours ahead of GMT. It gets dark at about 5 pm in winter and 7.30 pm in summer.

Electricity

220–40 volts, with fluctuations in voltage. In the north the electrical supply is very erratic. Paraffin lamps or candles are usually supplied in hotels. Electric hairdryers and razors are usable only in large cities.

National Holidays

23 March — Pakistan Day
1 May — Labour Day
14 August — Independence Day
6 September — Defence of Pakistan Day
11 September — Anniversary of the death of M A Jinnah, the Quaid-e-Azam
9 November — Allama Iqbal Day
25 December — Birthday of the Quaid-e-Azam

The dates of religious holidays vary each year. See page 465 for details.

Newspapers and Periodicals

There are two English-language daily newspapers in Karachi, *Dawn* and *Morning News*, and four in Lahore and Islamabad, *The Pakistan Times*, *The Muslim*, *The Nation* and *The Observer*. Foreign newspapers and periodicals are available at large bookstalls and the big hotels, as are English-language books.

The Great Outdoors

Bird-watching: Over 740 species of birds have been identified in Pakistan. The Indus is one of the major migration paths of the world, so the lakes and reservoirs of Punjab and Sind are alive with migrant birds during the winter months. The coastline and the deserts are also good places to see unusual birds. Pakistan also has seven national parks, 72 wildlife sanctuaries and 76 game reserves.

Fishing: There is excellent deep-sea fishing off Karachi and equally good fresh-water fishing in the northern valleys. Fishing permits usually cost Rs10 per day and are available from local fishing authorities.

Sports: Pakistanis are sports mad and excel at cricket, hockey, badminton and squash. They are also famous for their polo playing, and in the Northern Areas play a local variety of the game which is faster and visually more exciting than the staider international game. In many areas you can hire horses. There are golf courses in Rawalpindi, Islamabad, Murree, Quetta, Abbottabad and Swat.

Trekking: The Himalayas, Karakorams and Hindu Kush offer excellent trekking. See Trekking Guide, pages 431–50, for details.

Mountaineering: Pakistan has five peaks over 8,000 metres (26,250 feet) and 101 over 7,000 metres (23,000 feet), some of which are still unclimbed. In 1985, some 54 expeditions attempted 62 peaks. Applications for permission to climb K-2 must be made two years in advance; applications for other peaks one year in advance. For rules, regulations and application forms write to the Tourism Division, College Road, F-7/4, Islamabad, Pakistan, or to any Pakistani Embassy or Office abroad.

Desert safaris: Camel safaris in the Cholistan Desert are very popular and best arranged by Lal Suhanra National Park or a good travel agent.

Rafting and kayaking: This is allowed on the Indus, Hunza, Gilgit, Swat and Kunhar rivers, but the sport is in its infancy in Pakistan, and the rivers have not yet been graded for difficulty. Apply to a good travel agency for details.

Hunting: Officially boar-hunting is the only hunting now allowed in Pakistan.

Photography and Film

Pakistan and its people are superbly photogenic. Very few travellers have the time to wait for the perfect light, but beware the noon-day sun, which tends to flatten the subject and dull the colours. For best results, take photos before 10 am and after 3 or 4 pm (depending on the season). Underexposing midday shots by half a stop or even more can help, as will the use of a daylight or haze filter, but the results may be slightly disappointing and washed out.

Film for colour prints is widely available in Pakistan, but it is often old and overheated. Film for colour slides and black-and-white prints is available only in Karachi, Lahore and Islamabad, where it is expensive. Enthusiasts are advised to bring all the film they need with them and to store it in as cool a place as possible.

You are not allowed to photograph military installations, airports or bridges. Pakistani men generally like to be asked permission before being photographed, then they usually assume manly poses and stare straight into the camera; a very discreet telephoto lens may be useful for spontaneous shots. Men should not attempt to photograph women, though female photographers usually have no problem at all, especially if there are no men around to disapprove, and if a little time is first spent making friends and asking permission.

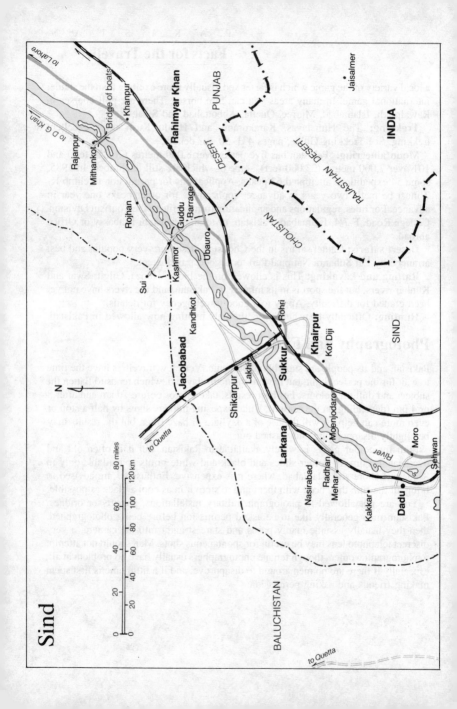

Sind

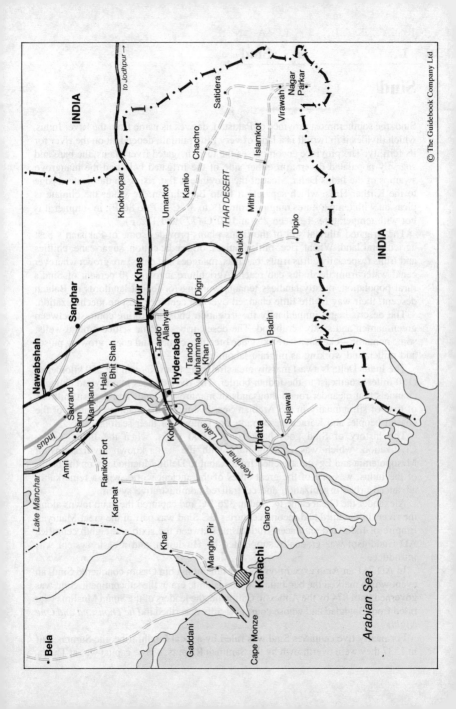

© The Guidebook Company Ltd

Sind

Sind, the southernmost province of Pakistan, derives its name from the River Indus, which divides it in two. It is a land of very little rainfall, dependent on the river for its fertility. The province encompasses the lush, irrigated river plains, the bare and sparsely populated deserts on either side of the irrigated belt, and the mangrove swamps of the Indus Delta. Most of the province is flat, rising on the western edge to the Kirthar Hills, which separate it from Baluchistan. In winter the climate is pleasant with temperatures ranging from 10° to 30°C (50° to 86°F); in summer it is hot with temperatures between 25° and 50°C (77° and 122°F).

The irrigated alluvial soil of the Indus plains provides some of Pakistan's best agricultural land. Wheat, rice, millet, pulses, oil-seeds, cotton, sugar-cane, chillies and fruits (especially citrus fruits, bananas, mangoes and dates) are grown wherever canal water from the Indus can reach. Agriculture involves 70 percent of Sind's rural population, mostly landless tenants working for feudal landlords of Baluch descent, their way of life little changed over the centuries despite mechanization.

The deserts begin immediately the irrigation ends: a striking contrast between green garden and sandy scrubland. The desert tribes—some settled around wells, some nomadic—eke out a bare existence breeding camels and goats, growing pulses and millet, and working as migrant labourers.

The Indus Delta is a vast marshy area stretching from Karachi for 250 kilometres (150 miles) southeast to the Indian border. The river divides into myriad sluggish channels that meander round thousands of mangrove islands and deposit millions of tons of silt annually in the Arabian Sea. Fishing is the main occupation of the coastal people, and Karachi restaurants are famous for their seafood.

The history of Sind goes back some 5,000 years, when the Indus Valley Civilization, which was contemporary with the better-known civilizations of Mesopotamia and Egypt, stretched from Kabul to Delhi. Moenjodaro, on the banks of the Indus, was one of the great cities of the ancient world, with a remarkably advanced urban organization and centralized administrative system.

Alexander the Great came to Sind in 326 BC and captured the main towns along the river. In the third and second centuries BC Sind was part of the great Mauryan Empire of India and embraced Buddhism. Between the sixth and eighth centuries AD Buddhism was gradually supplanted by Hinduism, and a caste system was introduced.

In AD 711 an Arab expedition under Muhammad bin Qasim conquered Sind, an event which marked the beginnings of the Islamic era in the subcontinent. Sind was governed until 874 by the Abbassid Caliphate, the leaders of the Sunni Muslims who ruled from Baghdad and whose court is vividly described in *The Thousand and One Nights*.

For nearly five centuries Sind was ruled by a local Sindhi tribe, the Sumras, but in 1337 they were overthrown by the Sammah Rajputs, whose capital was at Thatta.

In 1524 Sind was taken by Shah Beg Arghun from Kandahar in Afghanistan; he in turn was ousted in 1545 by the Tarkhans, who ruled first independently then as governors under the Moghul emperors. As Moghul power waned, the Kalhoras from Upper Sind took control in 1736, ruling the region from Khudabad. The Kalhoras were overthrown by the Talpurs from Baluchistan in 1789 and moved their capital to Hyderabad. In 1843 the British defeated the Talpurs at the battle of Miani and ruled the territory until Independence in 1947. It was under the British that Karachi grew from a small fishing village to a large industrial city.

Industry, both rural cottage industries and large-scale factories, is now developing quickly in Sind. For some 4,000 years cotton and textiles have been Sind's major industry (cloth in ancient Greek was *sindonion*, and in Latin *sindon*), and textiles and carpets are still the province's most important industries. More recently sugar, oil, flour and rice mills have been joined by factories producing steel, fertilizers, cement, electrical goods, pharmaceuticals and rubber.

Sind is famous for its handicrafts, particularly its textiles, pottery and lacquered woodwork. Patchwork quilts, block-printed cloth and striped woven cloth are available in bazaars all over the province. Hala is the centre for Pakistan's woodworking industry, and blue glazed tiles from Sind decorate most shrines and mosques in the country.

Religion is intensely important to all Sindhis. Along the roadside and beside most houses, they mark out prayer areas about two metres (yards) square and surrounded by stones, with the *mehrab* (prayer niche) oriented towards Mecca. Anyone can stop here, remove their shoes and pray. (Tourists should be on the look-out for these areas and be careful not to step into them with their shoes on.) Much of Sind's cultural life revolves around the shrines of the Sufi saints (see pages 22–3), where music and singing are a major part of the traditional devotional ceremonies.

The Sindhis are the most colourfully and exotically dressed of Pakistan's people. Shocking pink is a favourite colour for men's turbans in central Sind. The men also wear little embroidered caps speckled with tiny mirrors, brightly coloured long shirts and *lunghis* (pieces of cloth wrapped round the lower half of the body instead of trousers). Many wear traditional embroidered slippers with long, pointed, upturned toes. The desert women dress in long red skirts and bright tie-dyed shawls.

The Sindhi language is both spoken and written, the Sindhi script being based on the Arabic alphabet, with additional letters. A number of other languages are also spoken in the province: Thari in the Thar Desert, Kutchi in the Rann of Kutch, Lari in lower Sind, and Saraiki in upper Sind, to name a few. Karachi, the capital, is not representative of the rest of the province, as most of the inhabitants are Urdu-speaking *Mohajirs* (immigrants) from India and their descendants, who came at Partition in 1947.

The best time to visit Sind is the winter months, from mid-November to mid-March, when the daytime temperature fluctuates between 15° and 25°C (60° and 80°F); in summer it hovers around 35° to 45°C (95° to 115°F). In the monsoon season—June, July and August—it is very humid, though there is little rain.

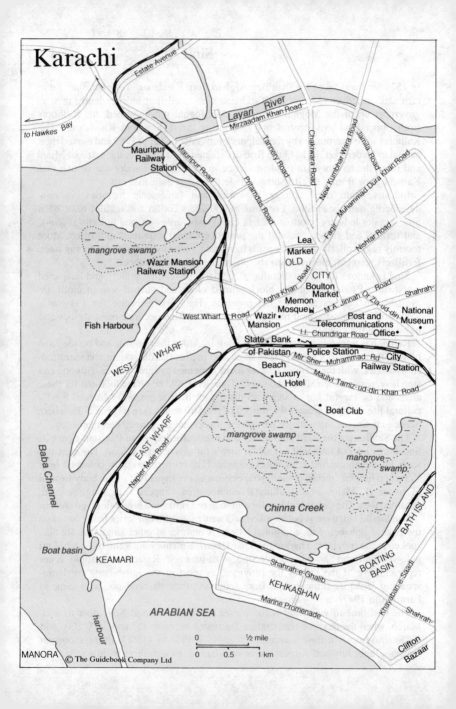

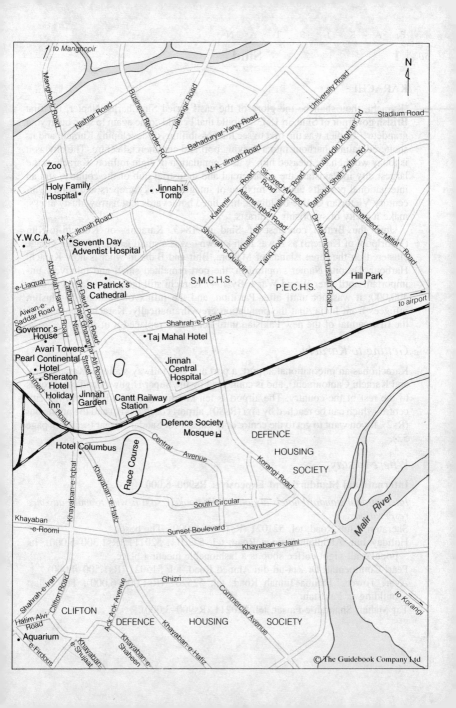

KARACHI

'Karachi, thou shalt be the glory of the east!' cried Sir Charles Napier, the first British governor of Sind, in 1843. 'Would that I could come again to see you in your grandeur!' Napier was the first to see the possibilities of developing Karachi and its sheltered natural harbour into a thriving port and commercial centre. The city as it is today would have pleased him; with a population of eight million, Karachi is the largest city in Pakistan, the commercial and industrial hub of the country, and an international port. Its unusual mixture of imaginative skyscrapers and solid 19th-century Victorian Gothic buildings, tree-lined boulevards and narrow dusty alleys, make it a city of surprising contrasts.

Until the British conquest of Sind in 1843, Karachi—or Kolachi-jo-Kun (Whirlpool of Kolachi) as it was then known—was a small isolated fishing village clustered on the three islands of Manora, Bhit and Baba in what is now Karachi Harbour. Despite Napier's optimism, the port remained small and relatively unimportant until after World War I. By 1947 Karachi still had a population of only 400,000; it was not until after Partition, and the influx of millions of Muslim refugees from India, that the population grew dramatically. Karachi then became the first capital of the new Pakistan until Islamabad replaced it in 1963.

Getting to Karachi

Karachi has an international airport, a port and two railway stations (Karachi City and Karachi Cantonment), and is connected by the Super Highway and other roads to the rest of the country. The airport is ten kilometres (six miles) from the city centre, which can be reached by taxi (Rs80), airport coach (Rs10) and the public bus (Rs2). If you want to get to the centre of town, ask for Saddar Bazaar (see map, page 52).

Where to stay

International Standard and Expensive: Rs900–6,000

International standard hotels are often fully booked, so it is wise to make advance reservations.

Sheraton, Club Road, tel. 521021 (Rs1,400–6,000). The best.

Holiday Inn, Abdullah Haroon Road, tel. 522011, 520111 (Rs1,300–5,000). Its popular all-night coffee shop is a fashionable meeting place.

Pearl Continental, Dr Zia-ud-din Ahmed Road, tel. 515021 (Rs1,500–4,000).

Avari Towers, Fatima Jinnah Road, tel. 525261 (Rs1,000–6,000). The tallest building in Pakistan.

Taj Mahal, Shahrah-e-Faisal, tel. 520211 (Rs900–3,000).

Moderate: Rs200–800

Midway House, Star Gate Road, near airport, tel. 480371 (Rs550–1,000). The usual in-transit hotel.

Beach Luxury, Maulvi Tamiz-ud-din Khan Road, tel. 551031 (Rs500–1,750). Excellent seafood restaurant in garden.

Metropole, Club Road, tel. 512051 (Rs500–1,200). The oldest hotel in town.

Mehran, Shahrah-e-Faisal, tel. 515061 (Rs350–850).

Airport, Star Gate Road, near airport, tel. 480141–5 (Rs320–450).

The best value moderate and cheap hotels are in Saddar Bazaar along and between Daud Pota Road and Raja Ghazanfar Ali Road. It is easy to walk from one to the other until you find one to your liking. Try:

Sarawan, Raja Ghazanfar Ali Road, tel. 525121–5 (s/d Rs235/305). All facilities, excellent value.

Jabees, Abdullah Haroon Road, tel. 512011 (s/d Rs300/450).

Gulf, Daud Pota Road, tel. 515831–5, 525146–9 (s/d Rs165/236).

Reliance, Daud Pota Road, tel. 510036, 521921 (s/d Rs116–171/171–278).

Sarah, Parr Street, tel. 527160–2 (s/d Rs145–205/210–270).

United, Daud Pota Road, tel. 515010–4 (s/d Rs118/172–247). Helpful.

Chiltan, National City, Ocean, Al-Mashriq, and many more in Saddar Bazaar.

Inexpensive: Rs25–100

These recommended cheapies supply a room with bath—hot water in winter, but no AC in summer. I only list a few—there are many others worth trying in Saddar Bazaar, and also around Cantonment Station, in Boulton Market and along Shedi Village Road in Lee Market.

Al-Salatin, Daud Pota Road, Saddar, tel. 516362, 527368 (s/d Rs60/100).

Ambassador, Daud Pota Road, Saddar, tel. 514820, 514200 (s/d Rs60–75).

Shalimar, Daud Pota Road, Saddar, tel. 529491, 527671 (s/d Rs50–65).

Chandni, Daud Pota Road, Saddar, tel. 511487, 529467 (s/d Rs45/50).

De Paris, Mir Karamali Talpur Road, Saddar, tel. 524411–3 (s/d Rs60/75).

International, Sheikh Chand Street, Saddar, tel. 511471 (s/d Rs70/95).

Al-Farooq, Summerset Street, Saddar, tel. 511031–2 (s/d Rs55–100).

Royal, I I Chundrigar Road, near Habib Plaza, tel. 211089 (s/d Rs20/35).

Sunshine, Cantonment Station, tel. 512316 (s/d Rs20/35).

Hostels

Amin House Youth Hostel, 2 Maulvi Tamiz-ud-din Khan Road (Rs15–25).

YMCA, Strachen Road, opposite Governor's House, tel. 516927, 613022 (s/d Rs25–40).

YWCA, M A Jinnah Road, tel. 71662. Recommended for women travelling alone.

Salvation Army, Frere Road, behind Empress Market, tel. 74262 (Rs30). Dorm only.

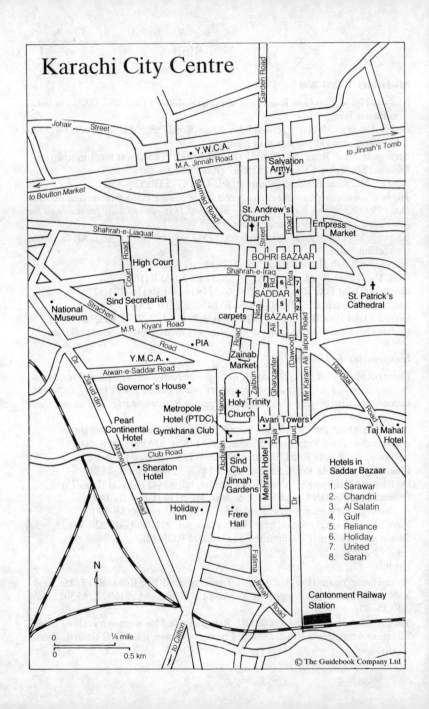

Karachi City Centre

Johair Street

Garden Road

Y.W.C.A.

M.A. Jinnah Road

Salvation Army

to Jinnah's Tomb

Sarmad Road

to Boulton Market

St. Andrew's Church

Empress Market

Shahrah-e-Liaquat

Road

Court Road

High Court

BOHRI BAZAAR

Shahrah-e-Iraq

Strachen Road

Sind Secretariat

National Museum

M.R. Kiyani Road

Road

SADDAR

BAZAAR

carpets

St. Patrick's Cathedral

Pota Rd

Nisa Road

Ali Road

Ghanzanfer

8 6 7
5 4
3
2
1

PIA

Zainab Market

Dr Zia-ud-din

Y.M.C.A.

Aiwan-e-Saddar Road

(Dawood)

Mir Karam Ali Talpur Road

Hospital Road

Governor's House

Zaibun

Holy Trinity Church

Road

Pearl Continental Hotel

Metropole Hotel (PTDC)

Gymkhana Club

Avari Towers

Raja

Daud

Dr

Taj Mahal Hotel

Ahmed Road

Club Road

Abdullah

Haroon

Sheraton Hotel

Sind Club

Jinnah Gardens

Mehran Hotel

Hotels in Saddar Bazaar

Holiday Inn

Frere Hall

1. Sarawar
2. Chandni
3. Al Salatin
4. Gulf
5. Reliance
6. Holiday
7. United
8. Sarah

N

Fatima Road

Jinnah Road

Cantonment Railway Station

0   ¼ mile

0   0.5 km

to Clifton

© The Guidebook Company Ltd

Where to eat

Karachi now has hundreds of good restaurants, especially in Clifton shopping centre and along Airport Road.

Beach Luxury Hotel, Casbah Restaurant, tel. 551031. Excellent grilled seafood; good ambience (outdoors).

Sheraton Hotel, tel. 521021, has four good restaurants: French, Italian, Chinese and Pakistani.

Pearl Continental Hotel, Chandni Lounge on ninth floor, tel. 515021. International food, seafood, and Thai restaurant

Avari Towers, Teppanyaki Restaurant on rooftop, tel. 525261. Japanese cuisine, magnificent view. Also buffet restaurant on rooftop.

Ponderosa, Stadium Road, opposite A K Hospital. Good South Indian food.

Red Carpet, Seabreeze Centre, Boat Basin, Clifton. Barbecue and curries.

Seagull, Seabreeze Centre, Boat Basin, Clifton, tel. 531244.

Kebabish, Seabreeze Centre, Boat Basin. Afghan barbecue.

Mr Burger, Seabreeze Centre, Boat Basin, tel. 535957, and off Tariq Road, tel. 439682. Beefburgers and snacks.

Silver Spoon, off Tariq Road. Barbecue and snacks.

Shezan Kohsar, Hill Park, tel. 428628. Good Pakistani food.

The Village, Merewether Road, tel. 512880. Barbecue.

Bundu Khan, M A Jinnah (Bundar) Road. Chicken tikka and parathas.

Star of Pakistan, Boulton Market, tel. 225219.

The best cheapies are in Lee Market near the bus station. Also good value (Rs8–20) are the stalls in Burns Road, Napier Road and Hill Park—and the Chinese stalls near Merewether Tower.

Boutiques

Iridescence, 10 A-7 Amir Khusro Road, off Karsaz Road, opposite the American school. Latest Pakistani fashions and modern Western dress; block-printing on the premises.

Haveli, 10 C-1 Gizri Lane, DHS 1V. Saris, traditional shalwar-kameez and Western clothes.

Chaman, 43 B-4 Block 1V, PECHS, and F-31 Block 1V, Kehkashan, Clifton. Hand-printed fabrics and traditional Pakistani ready-to-wear.

Cleos, Hilltop Shopping Centre, 4 D-2 Gizri Boulevard, DHS 1V. Modern shalwar-kameez and some Western clothing.

Fusun, 9 A-1 Khayaban-e-Shujaat, DHS V. Western export clothing; by appointment only.

Koel, 36-1 Khayaban-e-Hafiz, DHS V. Hand-block printed and embroidered traditional Pakistani clothing, cushion covers, table linen, wall hangings, silver jewellery; block printing and hand-embroidery on the premises.

Sehr, opposite back entrance of Metropole Hotel. Export clothing and shalwar-kameez.

Nicky Malik, C178-2 PECHS Main Tariq Road, above International Furnishers. Smart Western clothes.

Aliya Iqbal, 16-1-2 3rd Zamzama Street, Clifton. Western couture clothes.

Furs are a good buy in Karachi; try the shops in the Sheraton Arcade, Club Road, which has an excellent collection of antique jewellery, brass and copper ware, and precious and semiprecious stones.

Useful Addresses

Tourist Information Centre, PTDC, Metropole Hotel, Club Road, tel. 510234, and International Arrivals Lounge, Karachi Airport, tel. 482441.

PTDC, Karachi, tel. 516397. For booking PTDC hotels in Sind.

Sind Wildlife Management Board, Strachen Road, tel. 523176.

Archaeological Office, Karachi, tel. 431821.

Passport Office, Saddar Bazaar, tel. 510360.

Sights

Karachi's three main attractions are its bazaars, architecture, and coastline.

The Bazaars

If you only have a few hours in Karachi, the most exciting way to spend them is at the bazaars in the old city in the area north of M A Jinnah (Bundar) Road, behind Boulton Market. Hindu women in bright full skirts over baggy trousers and Baluchi men sporting huge coloured turbans jostle with donkey and camel carts in the narrow streets. Deeper into the market the alleyways, too narrow for carts, are crammed with tiny, box-sized shops; each lane specializes in a different commodity. Ask the taxi driver to drop you in the **Sarafa (Silver) Bazaar**. Opposite a shop called Bombay Jewellery Mart a narrow lane leads into the heart of the bazaar, where exquisite old silver tribal jewellery is sold by weight. Wali Muhammad Chandiwala at Baguari Street, Kundan Chowk, is one of the more reliable stalls.

The Sarafa Bazaar runs into the **Bartan Gali**, where all sizes of pots and pans—copper, aluminium and steel—are stacked up the walls and sold by weight. A tinsmith sits on the ground in front of his stall coating the copper pots with tin: copper is poisonous and must be coated before it can be used for cooking.

Next comes the **wholesale cloth bazaar**, the most colourful of all: gold and red, turquoise and blue, the lengths of cloth festoon the alleys. This is the best place to buy traditional Sindhi fabrics: *sussi*, a striped, hand-woven cloth; *ajrak*, block-printed cloth with geometric designs; and *bandini*, a tie-dyed cloth.

This market opens out into a wider area, the **Khajoor (Date) Bazaar**. Tarpaulin awnings flap in the wind over piles of dates, and hawkers wander up and down offering anything from embroidered Sindhi hats to coloured pyjama cords and strips of walnut bark for cleaning your teeth.

From the Khajoor Bazaar a short rickshaw ride of about one kilometre (half a mile) will take you to the **Botal Gali**, or the bottle market, proof that nothing is ever thrown away in Pakistan, and well known to serious bottle collectors for the occasional rare and beautiful bargain.

Saddar Bazaar, the central shopping area in Karachi, is spread around and between the two main thoroughfares, Abdullah Haroon (Victoria) Road and Zaibun Nisa (Elphinstone) Street, and stretches for about one kilometre (half a mile) from south to north. Victorian brick architecture rubs shoulders with modern concrete, not always harmoniously, in the noisy, lively alleyways. A great variety of shops follow each other in a succession of specialist bazaars.

Going north up Abdullah Haroon Road you come first to **Zainab Market** on the right. Inside are dozens of little shops selling new copper and brass, onyx, inlaid woodwork, lacquerwork, hand-printed cloth and appliquéd bedspreads (*rillis*). One or two shops sell some excellent old embroidered Sindhi cloth, traditional wedding dresses with mirror embroidery work, and old tribal silver jewellery. Two recommended shops are Marvi Handicrafts and Village Handicrafts. Zainab Market also sells very good, extremely cheap cotton shirts, ready-made shalwar-kameez, general export rejects and T-shirts saying, 'I caught crabs in Karachi.'

A little further up Abdullah Haroon Road are the **carpet shops** selling both new Pakistani carpets and old tribal rugs from Baluchistan, Afghanistan and Iran.

Bohri Bazaar, down the side lanes to the north of the carpet shops, is another cloth bazaar. Traditional women in purdah and modern Karachi ladies all flock here to choose material from the huge selection on display.

Empress Market, further north, was opened in 1889. It is a huge Victorian Gothic building with a clock tower 50 metres high. Inside are hundreds of stalls selling fruit, vegetables, meat, fish and groceries. Housewives hire coolies to carry their shopping bags and to bargain for them (for a small commission). A stall behind the market sells hookahs of all shapes and sizes.

Architecture

The **Tomb of Muhammad Ali Jinnah**, the Quaid-e-Azam, or Father of the Nation, is Karachi's most impressive monument. Jinnah led the movement for a separate Muslim state and at Partition in 1947 became governor-general of Pakistan. He died from tuberculosis one year later. The tomb stands on a hill at the east end of M A Jinnah Road, from where there is a good view down over the city. High-pointed arches with copper grills lighten the solid effect of the square base and heavy marble dome. The crystal chandelier inside is a gift from the People's Republic of China, the blue-tiled ceiling from Japan, the silver railing from Iran. A colourful changing-of-the-guard ceremony takes place every two hours.

The **National Museum of Pakistan**, off Dr Zia-ud-din Ahmed Road, houses a good, well-displayed collection of Indus Civilization artefacts dating back 4,500 years, some impressive, 1,500-year-old Gandharan Buddhist stone sculpture, tenth-century Hindu sculpture from Bangladesh, and various Muslim art objects including miniatures, carpets, and brass and copper bowls and plates. There is also an interesting ethnological gallery, an illustrated manuscripts and coins room, and a special exhibition hall.

Defence Society Mosque, Karachi's largest and best-known modern mosque, has a huge flat dome supported on a low redbrick wall. The excellent acoustics enable the *maulana*'s voice to be heard clearly by each of the 20,000 worshippers.

Those interested in colonial history and church architecture might enjoy a visit to **Holy Trinity Cathedral**, north of the Metropole Hotel on Abdullah Haroon Road, which was built as the garrison church in the mid-19th century. Of main interest here are the many brass and marble memorials around the inside walls recalling the history of British life in Sind.

There are a number of other 19th-century churches in Karachi, including **St Andrew's Church** and **St Patrick's Cathedral**. There are, however, no graveyards nearby, as all Christians are buried in the Christian cemetery on Drigh Road.

The enthusiast of British social history and architecture will enjoy visiting the **Sind Club** on Abdullah Haroon Road. The club was founded in the mid-19th century exclusively for British civil servants and did not accept Indian or Pakistani members until the early 1950s. The casual visitor can wander in to look at the spacious halls, wide verandahs and beautifully tended gardens; the billiards room and reading room are particularly evocative. Only members and their guests may eat at the club, where a dark suit and tie are obligatory in the evenings.

Frere Hall, set in the spacious Jinnah Gardens, opposite the Holiday Inn, is a charming Victorian Gothic hotchpotch. Built as a social and cultural centre in 1865, it is now a public library. The ceiling has recently been painted by Sadequain, an eminent Pakistani artist.

The **Sind High Court**, on Court Road, is a 19th-century red sandstone building with cupolas, balconies and pillars. Opposite it is the late 19th-century limestone **Sind Assembly Building**, typically colonial in style with wide verandahs and high ceilings.

A drive west on I I Chundrigar Road takes you past the vast **Cotton Exchange Building**, followed by the new **Habib Bank Plaza**, an elegant round building and the second tallest in Karachi. Further along on the left is the 19th-century Greek-porticoed **State Bank of Pakistan**, and beside it the new **State Bank Building**.

The Coast

The sea is the most romantic of Karachi's attractions, especially if you sail out into the harbour at sunset to catch and eat crabs in the moonlight, or anchor at Oyster Rocks for a picnic under the stars. You can also stroll along the beaches to watch the giant sea turtles lay their eggs in the sand. By day you can swim and bodysurf on Karachi's many beaches and see the newly hatched turtles attempt their hazardous first journey across the beach to the sea.

The Harbour

You can happily spend a whole day in **Keamari Harbour**, riding the public launches or hiring a private sailing boat or motor launch. It is a 15-minute ride by minibus or taxi to Keamari from central Karachi. If you take your own car, you can park it safely in the guarded parking lot. At the end of the wharf dozens of eager boatmen clamour for your attention. It costs about Rs50 an hour to hire a private boat, but public launches ply the harbour all day long; they leave whenever they are full. For only Rs1 you can cross to Manora Point or to the islands of Bhit or Baba. Either crossing takes only about ten minutes from Keamari. You are not allowed to take photographs in the harbour area. Swimming in this area is not advisable.

Manora Point, once the island home of the original fishing community of Karachi, is now connected to the mainland by Sandspit and can be reached by car in less than an hour from central Karachi. But it is easier and more fun to go by boat. Once there you can travel by public Suzuki or walk. The beach here is clean enough for swimming, and you can take a leisurely walk along the sand or ride a camel. Manora also has a large naval base, a lighthouse, two British churches and a ruined Hindu temple.

The islands of **Bhit** and **Baba** in the shelter of the harbour are still inhabited by the descendants of Karachi's original fishermen. They are members of the dark-skinned Mohana tribe and related to the fishermen on Manchar Lake (see pages 93–4) and are very friendly.

If you have only one evening in Karachi, perhaps the best way to spend it is **crabbing** from a local sailing boat in the harbour. You should arrive at Keamari about one hour before sunset to hire your boat. Haggle hard. An outing of three or four hours should cost about Rs300 including the cooking of your crabs. Before you leave, check that your boatman has on board crabs (in case you don't catch any), potatoes, onions and seasonings. To avoid disappointment it is best, though not essential, to arrange all this in advance. Captain Abdullah is a recommended boatman; others are cheaper but may not be such good cooks. You should provide your own drinks. Ten is a comfortable number for one boat, 15 a crowd.

The boat moves out into the harbour, and a boy shins up the mast to unfurl the sail. The captain drops anchor and provides you with fishing lines and raw fish for bait. While you are fishing the crew fry up potatoes and onions and boil water (the crabs are either boiled or fried with spices). As the sun sets, long lines of cormorants fly westward in V-formation to their roosts. You can also see flamingos flying along the coast in the evening.

At full moon, a romantic sail further up the sheltered harbour takes you to **Sandspit**, a nine-kilometre (six-mile) -long sandbank that protects the harbour from the open sea. You can wade ashore on the sheltered side and walk 100 metres (yards) over the spit to the open sea. From July to November giant sea turtles lumber up out of the sea to lay their eggs in the sand. To find them, walk along the edge of the sea and look for their tracks, which resemble caterpillar tractor tracks about 1.5 metres (five feet) wide. If you follow these up the beach, you should find a turtle digging in. At this stage she is easily frightened, but once she starts laying, the sound of voices and even a weak light will not disturb her. In season you can find turtles laying on any of the sandy beaches from the mouth of Keamari Harbour to Cape Monze. The Sind Wildlife Management Board (tel. 523176) will arrange guided tours of the turtle project at Sandspit and Hawkes Bay.

The **fish harbour** is at the end of West Wharf Road. Hundreds of fishing boats with coloured sails or outboard motors bring their catch here daily. The wharf is always bustling with men unloading fish or loading ice, and children sluicing down boats and sitting in circles peeling shrimps. At the top of the creek, boat builders working with bow drills, hand adzes and saws make new fishing boats from shisham wood. No metal is used in the boats; the hulls are pegged to the ribs with wooden dowels.

The Beaches

Clifton Beach is the easiest beach to get to. It is only ten minutes from the city centre by taxi or by bus number 20 from Shahrah-e-Iraq Road. You can paddle, but the water is not clean enough for swimming. Clifton is five kilometres (three miles) south of central Karachi along Abdullah Haroon (Victoria) Road. Clifton Road passes two modern monuments, the first of which is locally known as the Three Swords and represents the Pakistani national motto: Unity, Faith and Discipline. The second, known as One Sword, commemorates the 1965 war with India.

Originally a tiny coastal village, Clifton was developed by the British in the 19th century as a health resort for the military. Its tree-lined streets are graced by old colonial houses set in spacious, shady gardens.

Clifton Viewpoint, a hill about 20 metres (65 feet) high, overlooks the whole of Karachi, with Mohatta Palace in the foreground. The palace, a red sandstone Moghul Gothic building with dome and cupolas, was built early this century. Jinnah's sister Fatima lived here until she died in 1978; it is now empty. Out to sea the smooth Oyster Rocks wallow in the foreground, with Manora Lighthouse beyond, and to the west (right) the tops of cranes poke up from Keamari Harbour. Halfway down the hill towards the sea is the well-stocked aquarium and amusement park with rollercoaster, ferris wheel, bumper cars and merry-go-round.

A paved road leads several miles along Clifton Beach. On Thursday evenings and Fridays the residents of Karachi flock here to enjoy camel and horse rides, eat at the food kiosks, stroll round the souvenir stalls, and paddle. You can easily get away from the crowds and walk a long way down the beach. The huge hall near the beach was built as a casino but has never been used.

The **Shrine of Abdullah Shah Ghazi** dominates the top of the hill near Clifton Viewpoint. Its tall square chamber and green dome are typical of Sufi shrines all over Pakistan. Abdullah Shah Ghazi, a ninth-century saint and direct descendant of the Prophet Muhammad, has one of the largest followings in Pakistan. As he is also the patron saint of Karachi, 1,000 believers a day (and 10,000 at weekends) visit his shrine in the hope that their prayers will be answered. Abdullah Shah Ghazi is particularly famous for helping women who have marital problems or cannot conceive.

Foreigners are welcome to enter the shrine, providing they remove their shoes and are suitably dressed with heads, legs and arms covered. An atmosphere of reverence pervades the shrine. The crowd shuffles slowly forward to caress the silver railing around the saint's tomb, the depth of feeling and hope reflected in their faces. Every Thursday evening Sind's most famous devotional singers gather for the *qawwali* ceremony, the singing of plaintive mystical songs to the accompaniment of stringed instruments and drums. Many devotees spend the night at the shrine wrapped in their shawls. Free food is given daily to the poor by the shrine attendants. There are always beggars around shrines—they provide the faithful with the opportunity to gain blessing by giving alms. There is a devotional connection between the shrine of Abdullah Shah Ghazi and the Pathan Kafi in Sehwan Sharif (see page 93).

From Sandspit a continuous line of beaches stretches west for hundreds of kilometres along the coast of Sind and Baluchistan to Iran. Only those beaches near Karachi and open to foreigners are listed here.

Hawkes Bay, 25 kilometres (15 miles) from the centre of Karachi, has beach huts for rent, complete with cooking facilities, bathrooms and changing spaces. Long stretches of fairly clean sand sweep round the curve of the bay, and camel rides and other seaside amusements are available. The swimming is particularly good in March and April. From May until October the sea is dangerously rough, and you should not swim; in winter the sea is colder, though still very pleasant.

Further west, about 45 minutes from the centre of Karachi, is **Baleji Beach**. At this point the road lies a few hundred metres (yards) inland; the track (on the left) down to Baleji village and the beach is just past the small fishing village of Abdur Rahman. Baleji Beach itself is a succession of secluded bays with rocky sections between each. There are a few private huts, but otherwise no shade or greenery of any kind. The rock pools are interesting and the waves dramatic and good for body surfing, but beware the undertow.

Beyond Baleji Beach is Karachi Nuclear Power Plant (KANUPP). The road makes a detour round this for about three kilometres (two miles) then returns to the coast at **Paradise Point**, where the waves crash through a hole in a pointed rock like the eye of a needle. From here the road follows the top of a low cliff—you need to stop occasionally and peer over the edge to choose your own private cove. From December to March this is the place to go snorkelling. **Cape Monze**, about 25 kilometres (15 miles) beyond the nuclear power plant, has a lighthouse and some attractive isolated coves.

Gaddani Beach, about 50 kilometres (30 miles) west of Karachi across the Hub River in Baluchistan, is famous as the biggest ship-breaking yard in the world. Ships of up to 20,000 tons are beached by driving them at full speed onto the sand at high tide, then dismantled with a minimum of mechanization. Beyond Gaddani lie about 50 kilometres (30 miles) of smooth sand and long lazy waves, perfect for swimming and sunbathing. Foreign visitors in private cars may be stopped unless they have a permit (obtainable from the government of Baluchistan in Quetta) and turned back at the check-post at the Hub River Bridge. You are less likely to get stopped on the public bus which leaves Lee Market (to the north of old Karachi).

The Mangrove Swamps

The **mouths of the Indus** empty into the Arabian Sea southeast of Karachi through channels that wander round thousands of mangrove-covered islands. Here fishermen from nearby villages, or from temporary camps on the more remote islands, work in every creek, using all means imaginable to land their catch. Lonely men in small canoes fish with lines; others wade in the shallows throwing wide circular nets weighted at the rim. Some set elaborate fish traps. Whole families work together stretching nets on poles across lagoons and chasing fish into them.

To get there hire a local sailboat for the day or a weekend at Korangi or Keamari and head southeast along the coast.

From your boat you will see an amazing variety of wildlife. Green mudskippers with goggly eyes chase each other and mate on the mudflats. Fiddler crabs wave to each other before being gobbled up by terns and Braminy kites. Reef herons sit along the water's edge and, perched on the mangrove roots, kingfishers wait to dive. Waders of every sort stalk about in the mud. Dolphins, seasnakes and shoals of tiny fish leap and swim fearlessly near the boat.

Outings from Karachi

Karachi is surrounded by dozens of places of interest, many easily reached on a day's outing. You can explore Sindhi history at a number of archaeological excavations and hundreds of 14th- to 19th-century tombs, or immerse yourself in Sind's rich spiritual life at its many shrines and mosques. Naturalists can visit some of Sind's 32 wildlife sanctuaries and 13 game parks.

Bird-watchers are in their element. The Indus River lies on one of the northern hemisphere's major flight paths for migrating birds. Waterbirds and birds of prey fly south from their summer breeding grounds to winter in Sind from October to April. You can easily make daytrips to go bird-watching at Haleji Lake, Hadiero Lake, Keenjhar Lake, Gharo Creek, the lake above the Hub River dam, the mouth of the Hub River, the mangrove swamps south of Karachi or the riverine forest along the Indus near Thatta.

The most popular outing is the daytrip to Thatta (see pages 72–3).

Mangho Pir, Hub Dam and Khar Wildlife Preserve

The road north from Karachi runs out through the poorer section of town for 18 kilometres (11 miles), past some steep ridges, to the village of Mangho Pir. The **Shrine of Pir Mangho** stands on a low hill to the left of the road beside two hot sulphur springs guarded by crocodiles. An amusing legend relates that when the saint Pir Mangho came from Arabia in the 13th century, he inadvertently brought crocodiles with him in the form of head lice. Soon after his arrival two oases sprang up from the desert, with hot springs gushing out from a clump of date palms; the crocodiles jumped in and have lived there ever since.

The crocodiles are of a snub-nosed variety, different from the long-snouted gavial of the Indus, and are thought to be particularly dangerous. Zoologists claim—rather more plausibly—that they were stranded here when the Hub River changed its course.

On Fridays the shrine is thronged with pilgrims seeking blessings and cures, particularly for rheumatism, skin diseases and leprosy. Pilgrims used to enter the pool with the crocodiles, but they are now spared this ordeal as a separate bathing place has been built nearby. The supplicants offer goats to the crocodiles; only if the meat is eaten will the pilgrim's prayers be answered. The five crocodiles, stuffed to bursting, lie with lumps of meat hanging from their jaws. It is not inconceivable that there is some connection with crocodile worship in ancient Egypt, with which the Indus people traded 5,000 years ago.

Pilgrims climb the hill to the shrine to pray at the saint's tomb. Bearded holy men in green wander aimlessly through the crowd. A fortune teller sits on the ground with his trained parakeets, who take one-rupee notes from the passers-by before picking out their fortune cards from a pile. Food and drink sellers do a roaring trade. Everyone is very friendly, and foreigners are welcome to enter the shrine. To the right of the entrance are three heavily carved old Baluchi tombs similar to those at Chaukundi (see page 66).

From Mangho Pir a paved road runs northwest for 33 kilometres (20 miles) to the **Hub Dam**. Mango and papaya orchards give way to rolling scrubland with a low line of hills on either side. The escarpment on the west overlooking the Hub Valley is the home of several groups of **Baluchi tribespeople**. Small temporary settlements of wattle houses surrounded by thorn hedges cluster along the top of the ridge. Men may not approach, but foreign women are welcome to wander into the settlement and meet the Baluchi women.

The Hub Dam is almost five kilometres (three miles) long and holds back a shallow lake trapped between low barren hills; one narrow canal carries water from the lake to Karachi. A grove of trees cooled by the breeze off the water at the Baluchistan end makes a pleasant picnic spot.

A sandy track, for four-wheel drive vehicles only, skirts to the right along the bottom of the dam and continues for about 20 kilometres (12 miles) along the east (Sind) side of the lake through the Kirthar National Park to **Khar Wildlife**

Preserve. If you have more time, you can stay at the small Sind Wildlife Guest House, bookable through the Sind Wildlife Management Board, Strachen Road, Karachi, tel. 523176.

The track twists through low hills close to the lake, past several Baluchi villages with herds of camel, goats and sheep. In winter Hub Lake is alive with birds, and you can expect to see 100 species in a day. The many crocodiles in the lake make it inadvisable to swim. There are also plenty of monitor lizards in the rocks around Khar. The wildlife complex is a breeding centre for blackbuck; you can see peacocks and urial sheep as well. There is a shady picnic spot nearby.

Kirthar National Park

A four-hour drive north from Karachi, for four-wheel drive vehicles only, takes you deep into the heart of the Kirthar National Park, over 3,000 square kilometres (1,160 square miles) of game reserve in the Kirthar Hills. October to February are the coolest months, although the flowers bloom during the monsoon in August. Five furnished rest houses with cooking facilities and running water, located on the edge of a wide valley in the centre of the park at **Karchat**, are bookable through the Sind Wildlife Management Board, Strachen Road, Karachi, tel. 523176. It is also safe and enjoyable to camp, and tents can be hired from the SWMB. Some food is available if ordered well in advance, but it is advisable to take everything you need to eat and drink and all your bedding with you.

To get there take the Super Highway out of Karachi and turn off at kilometre stone 80 beside the National Tile and Ceramic Factory (almost opposite the enormous Dadabhoy Cement Factory). After 15 kilometres (nine miles) you reach Zero Point at the Sui Gas Pumping Station (locals will direct you to this); follow the gas pipeline to the Esar Checkpost at the entrance to the park. It is 72 kilometres (45 miles) from the Super Highway to the Karchat Centre.

Green after the monsoon and golden in autumn, the rolling valleys and contorted, rugged lines of the hills form a natural haven for the urial sheep and ibex goats that bound up the vertical cliffs. Chinkara gazelle graze in the eroded gullies; jungle and desert cats stalk through the rocks. There is even the occasional leopard or desert wolf in the park, though you will see them only if you are very lucky. Pangolins, porcupines and monitor lizards are more in evidence.

From the Karchat Centre you can climb at dawn up the 1,000-metre (3,300-foot) -high **Karchat** (or **Rano**) **Hill**, take a jeep ride to the 18th-century Chaukundi-style carved tombs at **Taung** (see page 66), or take a trip to the prehistoric archaeological remains at **Koh-Tarash**. The enormous **Ranikot Fort** (see pages 88–9) is also within the park, a two-hour jeep drive from the Karchat Centre. From Ranikot it is about a four-hour drive back to Karachi via the Indus Highway and the Super Highway.

Khadeji Falls

Trickling down an escarpment a couple of kilometres (a mile or so) to the north of the Super Highway is Khadeji Falls, a pleasant winter picnic place. Take the Super Highway out of Karachi. From the toll gate the road runs flat across an arid plain for 25 kilometres (15 miles) before twisting up a sharp escarpment. A blue tiled mosque on the left at the top stands beside a local restaurant. Immediately beside the mosque turn left and follow the dirt road to a hut with a parking lot, where you must leave your car and walk on down a steep track into the gorge. Check at the restaurant that this road is open.

KARACHI TO HYDERABAD

Via the Super Highway

The railway, the Super Highway and the National Highway connect Karachi to Hyderabad, about 150 kilometres (90 miles) as the crow flies, away to the northeast on the River Indus.

The Super Highway is fast and dangerous; you can cover the 164 kilometres (102 miles) to Hyderabad in about two and a half nerve-wracking hours. The highway has two lanes and gravel shoulders. Cars overtake, undertake and double-overtake, and sometimes four lanes of traffic race abreast in one direction. The toll for cars is Rs8—save your receipt as it will be collected at the other end. The Super Highway is the starting point for trips to Kirthar National Park (see page 62) and Khadeji Falls (see above).

The road passes straight across the semi-desert, which is mainly scrub with the odd sparse crops of pulses and mustard. Occasional low limestone ridges run down from the Kirthar Hills on the left. Halfway between the two towns is a tax-free zone, where huge factories line the road on either side.

The Super Highway ends just past the second toll gate, where it joins the Indus Highway to Sehwan Sharif and Larkana. To enter Hyderabad turn left on the Indus Highway and right five kilometres (three miles) later at an unmarked junction, passing the **University of Sind** and the **Institute of Sindology** on the left. The latter is worth visiting for its good collection of old books, coins and other articles relating to Sind. The road crosses the Indus on the **Ghulam Muhammad Barrage** (sometimes called the **Kotri Barrage**), built in 1955 and the last of six great barrages controlling the flow of the Indus between Tarbela Dam and the sea. There is a popular fish restaurant with a shady garden beside the barrage and a good view of the river.

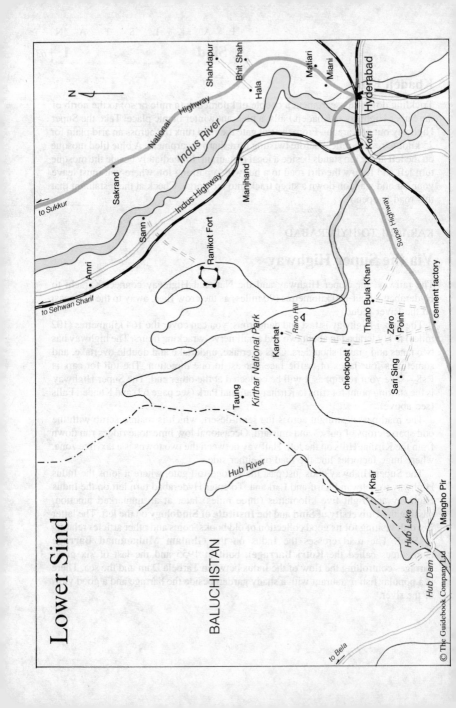

© The Guidebook Company Ltd

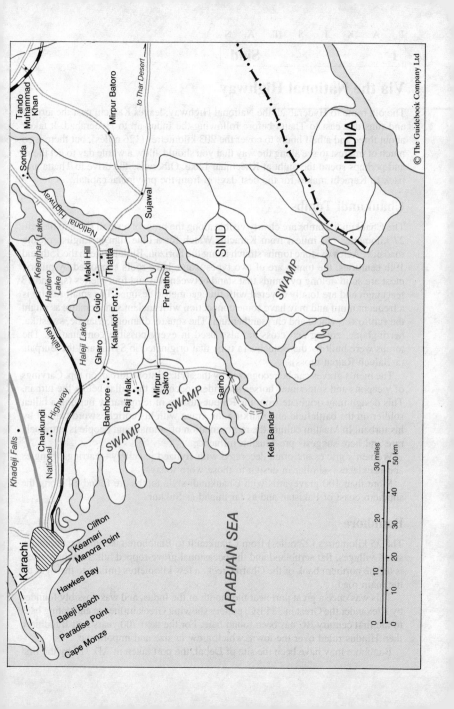

© The Guidebook Company Ltd

Via the National Highway

The old route to Hyderabad, the National Highway, leaves Karachi past the airport and runs due east to Thatta before following the Indus up to Hyderabad. It takes about three and a half hours to cover the 203 kilometres (126 miles), but there is so much of interest to see along the way that you should allow a whole day to get there, and perhaps spend the night at Kheenjhar Lake. Otherwise the drive to Thatta and back to Karachi makes for the best daytrip from the provincial capital.

Chaukundi Tombs

The Chaukundi Tombs are clearly visible along the brow of a small ridge to the left, 27 kilometres (17 miles) from Karachi. Watch for a blue sign in English on the roadside. Acres of stone tombs stretch along the horizon. Built between the 15th and 19th centuries, the tombs are of two types: some have roofs supported by pillars; most are solid oblong pyramids that stand between two and four metres (six and 13 feet) high and are totally covered with fine geometric designs. The small rosette is a frequent motif and may have some connection with ancient sun worship, as might the sunflower, wheel and chrysanthemum. The square, diamond, triangle, swastika, herringbone, zigzag and cross are also used in every possible combination. The tombs were built by the Baluchis (a tribe that originated in Syria) and the Burpats (a Baluch-Rajput cross).

The men's graves can be recognized by the stylized stone turban on top. Carvings of weapons and sometimes horses and riders decorate the pillar below the turban. This design may originate from the Rajput custom of temporarily burying a fallen soldier on the battlefield and marking the grave with his upright sword capped by his turban. In Muslim culture the representation of animals and people is extremely rare and here suggests pre-Muslim influence.

Women's graves are often decorated with stylized jewellery—earrings, bangles and necklaces—similar in design to those worn today.

More than 100 graveyards with Chaukundi-style tombs are found all along the southern coast of Pakistan and as far inland as Sukkur.

Banbhore

The 35 kilometres (22 miles) from Chaukundi to Banbhore take you past nomads, small villages, flat scrubland and the occasional grave-topped hill. Banbhore itself is on the northern bank of the Gharo Creek, a few kilometres (miles) to the right off the main road.

This was once a great port near the mouth of the Indus, and was possibly founded by Alexander the Great in 325 BC; pottery showing Greek influence and dating back to the first century BC has been found here. For the next 700 years first Buddhists, then Hindus ruled over the town, which grew in size and importance.

Banbhore may have been the site of Debal, the port taken in AD 711 by the first

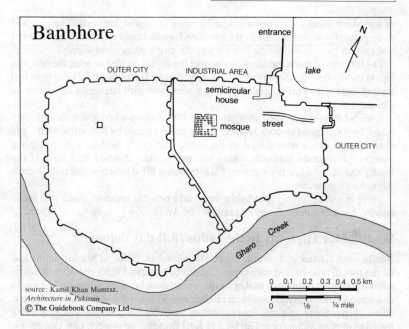

of the Arab invaders, Muhammad bin Qasim. Sent to the subcontinent by the caliph of Baghdad, the 17-year-old Muhammad bin Qasim arrived with a force of 15,000 infantry, plus horse and camel cavalry. According to an eighth-century text, the *Chach Nama*, he was armed with rockets, firearms and five catapults, the biggest of which, the 'wee bride', took 500 men to operate and had been used by the Prophet Muhammad himself. The catapult destroyed the Hindu temple in Debal and the garrison surrendered. Every man over 18 was beheaded.

The mosque at Banbhore is of particular interest, as it dates from AD 727 and is the earliest to be found in the subcontinent. Its floor and foundations can still be seen today. The mosque was about 40 metres (yards) square and consisted of an open courtyard surrounded by covered cloisters on three sides and a prayer chamber on the fourth. The roof of the prayer chamber was supported on 33 pillars arranged in three rows.

Though no longer visible owing to extensive excavation of the site, a palace and some administrative buildings once stood to the north of the mosque. The wealthier houses were made of stone and plastered with lime, and were built round a central courtyard; wooden beams were used in the roofs. Evidently the port was comfortable and prosperous.

The most impressive remains at Banbhore are the eighth-century **city walls** built of limestone blocks with semicircular bastions at regular intervals. The city had three gates: the main gate lay to the south and opened onto the creek; the northern and eastern gates led to a lake, which was the city's main water supply.

The little museum on the site helps to give the visitor an idea of what the port was like in its heyday. The display of pottery and coins indicates that Banbhore once had trading links with Muslim countries to the west, and with territories as far east as China.

It seems that the port died abruptly in the 13th century when it was sacked, then razed, by the Afghan invader Jalaluddin; skeletons pierced by iron arrowheads, and charcoal and ashes were found in the ruins. The city's decline was inevitable, however, as over the centuries silting and earthquakes changed the course of the Indus, and the sea has been driven back by some 80 kilometres (50 miles) since Alexander's time.

There is a shady picnic spot by the small lake near the museum, and a rest house nearby, bookable through the Department of Archaeology, Karachi, tel. 431821.

South of the Highway to the Indus (full-day detour)

Just beyond **Gharo** is a turning right, signposted in Urdu, to Mirpur Sakro and Garho (not to be confused with Gharo). Halfway between Gharo and Mirpur Sakro, a dirt track to the right leads to **Raj Malk**, where there are three white-domed tombs and some Chaukundi-style tombs, including one with a stone warrior on horseback. From Mirpur Sakro you can either continue south for a day's bird-watching along the edge of the swamps near **Garho** and **Keti Bundar**, or you can turn east for Pir Patho and make a round trip via Thatta.

At **Pir Patho** is the 17th-century Muhammad bin Qasim Mosque, set in a spacious courtyard; the brick tower beside the mosque is of an earlier date and was possibly used as a watch tower as well as a minaret. Nearby stands a second, newer mosque.

From Pir Patho two roads lead north to Thatta and one south to **Puricha** and **Gafar Mori**, a shady spot on the canal popular with fishermen. The Irrigation Department bungalow there is bookable at Thatta.

Haleji Lake

Haleji Lake, one of Karachi's reservoirs, is a nature reserve just north of the National Highway. In the winter months birds migrate from the north and settle here in their thousands. On a good day, from October to February, you can see as many as 100 species here, including flamingos, pelicans, kingfishers and up to 20 different species of birds of prey.

The turning to Haleji is on the road to Thatta 87 kilometres (54 miles) from Karachi and five kilometres (three miles) before the village of Gujo; it is signposted in English. You pay at the barrier to enter the sanctuary. The road runs all round the lake on an embankment from which you have an excellent view of the birds. The Sind Wildlife Information Centre provides ornithological details, and there is a

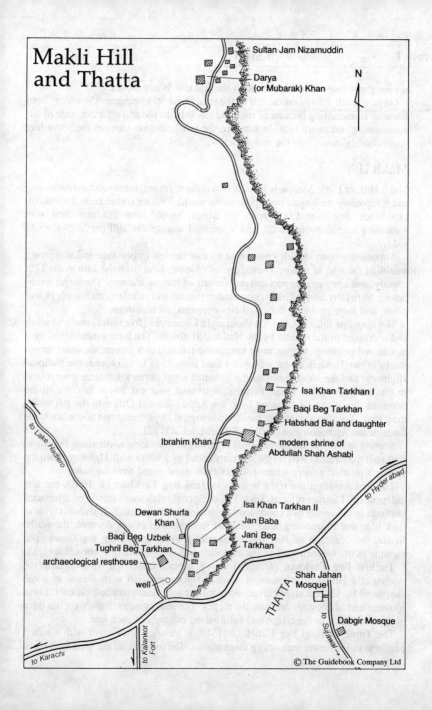

Makli Hill
and Thatta

N

Sultan Jam Nizamuddin

Darya
(or Mubarak) Khan

to Lake Hadero

Isa Khan Tarkhan I

Baqi Beg Tarkhan

Habshad Bai and daughter

Ibrahim Khan

modern shrine of
Abdullah Shah Ashabi

to Hyderabad

Isa Khan Tarkhan II

Dewan Shurfa
Khan

Jan Baba

Baqi Beg Uzbek

Jani Beg
Tarkhan

Tughril Beg Tarkhan

archaeological resthouse

THATTA

to Hyderabad

well

Shah Jahan
Mosque

to Sujawal

Dabgir Mosque

to Kalankot
Fort

to Karachi

simple guest house bookable through the Karachi Water Board.

Gujo, a small village on the left of the road about 90 kilometres (56 miles) from Karachi, is interesting because of the wind catchers (an old and effective form of air-conditioning) on every roof. In summer, the wind catchers channel the prevailing southwesterly down into the rooms below.

Makli Hill

Makli Hill, or Little Mecca, is the site of a million graves, tombs and mausoleums, and is reputedly the largest necropolis in the world. Visiting it is an eerie, impressive experience. For over 1,000 years the Sindhi people have felt that there was something sacred about Makli, and a spiritual atmosphere still pervades the site today.

Atmosphere apart, Makli gives some idea of the self-importance and staggering wealth of the elite of nearby Thatta, capital of lower Sind from the 14th to the 17th century, and a prosperous port and great centre of Islamic learning. The larger tombs belong to royalty and military commanders, saints and scholars, philosophers and poets, and were probably built to their occupants' own designs.

The long low hill stretches for about eight kilometres (five miles) north to south and is crossed in the middle by the National Highway. The tombs themselves vary in size and grandeur, but the most interesting fall into two groups: the more recent tombs of the Tarkhan kings, who ruled Sind from 1545 to 1614, near the National Highway; and the older tombs of the Sammah kings, three kilometres (two miles) to the north along the ridge. Permission to take your car inside to drive to the Sammah tombs can be obtained from the Archaeological Office to the left of the main gate. You can also stay at the Archaeological Department rest house bookable through the Archaeological Office, Karachi, tel. 431821.

Starting at the gate on the National Highway and working north along the ridge, first visit the unusual **well** on the left surrounded by a white wall. Halfway down the well is a pillared gallery where soldiers once stood guard over the water.

The first tomb on the right belongs to **Jani Beg Tarkhan** (d. 1601), the last independent Tarkhan ruler of Sind. The octagonal brick tomb stands on a terraced platform in the centre of a courtyard surrounded by a brick wall. Alternate layers of dark blue and turquoise glazed tiles and red unglazed bricks decorate the walls. Inside, the cenotaph of Jani Beg is inscribed with verses from the Koran. The mosque in the western wall of the enclosure has an exquisitely decorated mehrab.

Tughril Beg Tarkhan (d. 1679) was a general under the Moghul emperor Aurangzeb. His tomb consists of a small square pavilion with a conical dome supported by 12 delicately carved stone pillars with honeycombed capitals. Lotus blossom and sunflowers decorate the niches. The wall mosque to the west has three elegant mehrabs in the centre and solid raised minarets at each end.

The **Tomb of Baqi Beg Uzbek** (d. 1640) is an open brick court with a raised platform in the centre supporting three graves. The mosque on the west wall has a domed chamber with a zigzag-patterned brick ceiling.

The **Tomb of Isa Khan Tarkhan II** (d. 1644), the finest on Makli Hill, is a magnificent two-storey stone building in the centre of a square courtyard surrounded by a high stone wall. Isa Khan II, who died aged 90, was governor of Gujerat in India under the Moghul emperor Shah Jahan, and also governor of Thatta for one year. The tomb has a high dome surrounded by a two-tiered verandah. The upper verandah, roofed with small domes, is reached by stairs on the east and is decorated inside and out with delicate tracery like that at Akbar's palace at Fatipur-Sikri, near Agra in India. Floral and geometric designs, surrounding a lattice window, decorate the mehrab of the wall mosque in the west wall of the enclosure.

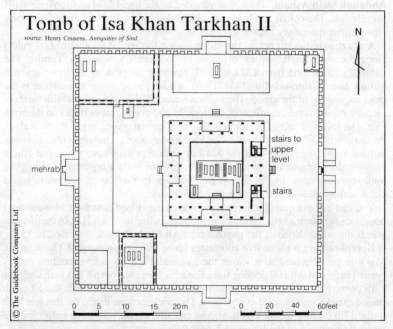

Tomb of Isa Khan Tarkhan II

source: Henry Cousens. *Antiquities of Sind*

© The Guidebook Company Ltd

Jan Baba's Tomb, built in 1608, is in a stone enclosure entered through an elegant portico of later date. In a row, under a pillared pavilion, lie the graves of seven family members. The walls are covered in carved tracery that looks like fine brown lace. Two ladies' tombs in the northeast corner are hidden by a wall. There is an excellent view of Thatta from the eastern doorway. Jan Baba was the son of Isa Khan I and the father of Isa Khan II.

The best-preserved tomb is that of **Dewan Shurfa Khan**, a revenue collector who died in 1638. The tomb leaves you in no doubt as to how some of the revenue was used. A square brick building with heavy round towers at the corners stands in the centre of a walled court. When the traveller Richard Burton saw it in 1876, he found the tiled dome 'gaudy, with more the appearance of a pleasure house than a mansion of the dead'. Inside it is richly decorated so that, according to Burton, 'Your eye rejects the profuseness of square and circle, spiral and curve, diamond and scroll work, flowers, border pattern and quotation from the Koran.' Perhaps time has softened the effect, for a hundred years later the blue, red and white zigzags of the ceiling and the ornately decorated cenotaph delight the eye.

Thousands of graves of all sizes and designs cover the ridge. The paved road twists and turns between them for one kilometre (half a mile) to the **Shrine of Abdullah Shah Ashabi**, which is surrounded by the usual food and souvenir stalls for pilgrims. The colour and lively activity of the saint's devotees make a welcome change after the empty tombs.

A dirt road to the left before the shrine leads a further 2.3 kilometres (1.4 miles) along the ridge to the group of 14th- to 16th-century **Sammah Tombs**. The Sammahs ruled Sind from 1337 to 1524, reaching the peak of their power under **Sultan Jam Nizam-ud-din** (1461–1509), whose square stone mausoleum is the most impressive of the group. The walls are decorated inside and out with bands of medallions, diamonds, sunflowers, calligraphy and even a row of ducks on the north side. The loveliest part of the tomb is the richly carved projection of the mehrab on the outside of the west wall with its arched balcony above, showing Gujerati Hindu influence and suggesting that the Muslim architects may have employed Hindu stonesmiths. Because the architects were unable to build a big enough dome, the tomb remains open to the sky. Stairs lead up to the top of the walls and a commanding view of the surrounding countryside.

You can enjoy a quiet picnic in the shade of the ruined **Sammah Mosque** next door, looking north across the ravine to the next section of Makli Hill. In the distance stands the white shrine of the popular saint **Ali Shah Shirazi**, who died in 1572.

Kalankot Fort is about five kilometres (three miles) southwest of Thatta on the Makli ridge. The road to it leaves the National Highway a few hundred metres (yards) before Makli Hill coming from Karachi. There has been a fort here since the 12th century, though most of the surrounding brick walls date from the Sammah period. Bricks are scattered everywhere. The brick mosque inside the fort was built in the 17th century by the Tarkhans; you can still see the sandstone pulpit and the water tank cut out of the living rock near the mosque.

Hadiero Lake, a permanent natural salt lake surrounded by low hills is 6.6 kilometres (4.1 miles) along the paved road which leads left (north) from the gate of the Makli Hill tombs. You cross three canals in quick succession. The turning to the lake is an unmarked dirt track, passable in an ordinary car, 500 metres (yards) past the last canal, on the right, just before a row of tea shops. You cannot see the lake from the road. Like other lakes in Sind, Hadiero is the winter quarters for thousands of birds, especially ducks, gulls, terns and pelicans. It is the perfect place for a picnic and a quiet day's bird-watching. Baluchi nomads camp in temporary settlements around the water's edge. Female tourists are welcome to enter the camps, where the women are friendly, and, if there are no men around, are quite happy to be photographed. Men should not try to enter the camps unless invited by a man.

Thatta

Thatta, about 100 kilometres (60 miles) from Karachi, is well worth a visit for the **Shah Jahan Mosque** and its bazaar. The mosque is a reminder of Thatta's past as a thriving port and the capital of lower Sind before the Indus abandoned it for new channels to the east.

Some experts believe that Thatta was the site of the ancient city of Pattala, where Alexander the Great rested his weary troops before his near-fatal march across the Makran Desert in Baluchistan, and where his admiral Nearchus readied the fleet for the voyage along the Arabian Sea coast. Alexander built a wall around Pattala's citadel and a dockyard known as the Wooden City (timber being the only material to hand) at the head of the Indus estuary.

Thatta's known history goes back at least 600 years. From the 14th to the 16th century it was the seat of the Sammahs, the independent Muslim rulers of lower Sind, who had rebelled against Delhi. In the mid-16th century the Portuguese, who controlled the lucrative spice trade to Indonesia, burned and ransacked the town, and in 1592 it became a part of the Moghul Empire. For the next 150 years it was a prosperous port famous for its handloom cotton-weaving and its wood-carving. In the 18th century Thatta declined; not only had the Indus shifted its course, but Britain had begun exporting cotton lunghis to India which were better and cheaper than the once-famous Thatta product. By 1851 the population had fallen from its height of 300,000 to 7,000. Today only a dozen or so of the old carved wooden houses remain near the bazaar.

The **Shah Jahan** or **Jami Mosque** was built by the Moghul emperor Shah Jahan in 1647 in gratitude to the people of Thatta for harbouring him when, as a young man, he incurred his father's displeasure. It is easy to find: just past the bazaar take the paved road right, signposted in Urdu, to Sujawal, and you will find the mosque on the right a few hundred metres (yards) further on.

The Jami Mosque comes as something of a surprise to those used to the white marble and pink sandstone of the Moghul monuments in Lahore and other cities of northern India. Built of red brick, the mosque is decorated with blue and green glazed tiles and unlike its contemporaries elsewhere is long and narrow, with arcades on all sides of its central court. The effect of the red brick arches in the arcades, highlighted with bands of white paint, is extremely striking. The arcades are covered with no fewer than 93 domes, which enable prayers said in front of the mehrab to be heard in any part of the mosque. The ceilings of the domes over the entrance, and the dome over the mehrab, are completely covered in blue, turquoise and white glazed tiles decorated with suns and stars. The mosque has now been extensively renovated with a modern entrance and a garden laid out in front.

Before leaving Thatta take a walk through the **Shahi Bazaar**, 500 metres (yards) down the lane beside Shah Jahan's mosque. This is a good place to buy sussi (striped hand-loom) and ajrak (hand-block printed) cloth, which is cheaper here than in Karachi. There are wind catchers on the roofs of the houses and a few remaining carved wooden balconies. Just before the bazaar on the right is **Khizri Mosque**, built in 1613, a small brick building set in a tiny courtyard behind a high wall, with the usual blue and white glazed tiles. Wind catchers on the roof of the mosque funnel cool air down to the faithful.

Dabgir Mosque, built in 1588, is one kilometre (half a mile) south of Shah Jahan's mosque on the road to Sujawal. This mosque originally stood in the heart of old Thatta and was paid for by Khusro Khan Charkas, a finance officer who was caught with his hand in the till, but escaped punishment owing to the sudden suspicious death of the governor. He atoned by building the mosque.

The **Yahya Khan Bridge**, the last bridge across the Indus before it reaches the sea, is only eight kilometres (five miles) past the Dagbir Mosque on the road to Sujawal. The bridge is about one kilometre (half a mile) long, but for two or three kilometres on either side the road runs along a high embankment across the flood plain, which is filled with surprisingly dense riverine forest, and is another good place for bird-watching.

The single-lane road continues through **Sujawal** for about 100 kilometres (60 miles) to **Tando Muhammad Khan**, commonly called T M Khan and famous for its hand-printed ajrak cloth. There is a good road through plantations of sugar-cane and bananas for the remaining 40 kilometres (25 miles) to Hyderabad, but this is not the best route from Thatta to Hyderabad unless you particularly wish to go to T M Khan.

Keenjhar Lake

The National Highway to Hyderabad follows the west bank of the Indus across rich farmland irrigated by water from Keenjhar Lake. The access road to the lake is 22 kilometres (14 miles) from Thatta and ten kilometres (six miles) after you first see the water.

Keenjhar Lake, formerly Kalri Lake, is another of Karachi's sources of water. About 32 kilometres (20 miles) long and ten kilometres (six miles) wide, it has also been developed as a resort and offers sail-boats for hire, fishing facilities and excellent bird-watching. It is crowded on Fridays, but quiet during the rest of the week. The new PTDC motel here, bookable through PTDC Karachi, tel. 516252 and 510301 (s/d Rs275–550), is a much more agreeable place to spend the night than Hyderabad.

On the banks of the lake is the tomb of Noori, a fishergirl from the Mohana tribe who married King Jam Tamachi of the Sammah dynasty. This romantic rags-to-riches story is very popular in Sind. Jam Tamachi is buried at Makli Hill.

Sonda Graveyard, on the right of the National Highway, and 14 kilometres (nine miles) beyond the entrance to Keenjhar Lake, has the best of all the Chaukundi-style decorated stone tombs (see page 66). Almost every one has a carving of a horse and rider or jewellery. On the embankment behind the graveyard is an Engineering Department bungalow which overlooks the white sands of the Indus on one side and Keenjhar Lake in the distance on the other.

The road is very quiet from Sonda for the 60 kilometres (37 miles) to Kotri. This stretch is mostly flat and bleak, with strange table-topped hills rising to the left and the Kirthar Hills in the distance. You enter **Kotri** through ten kilometres (six miles) of industrial suburbs. Turn left in the town to find the Kotri Bridge which crosses the Indus River to Hyderabad. The railway runs across the centre of the bridge with a single lane for cars on either side. You have to take your turn between camel and ox carts, so it can be slow getting across.

HYDERABAD

Hyderabad, Pakistan's fifth-largest city after Karachi, Lahore, Faisalabad and Islamabad-Rawalpindi, is a bustling industrial metropolis on the Indus River. Tumbling in all directions from its central hill, the city is a maze of narrow streets without any signposts or street signs, so it takes patience (and a local guide) to unravel its mysteries. Hyderabad's chief attractions are its bazaars, forts and tombs.

The city was known as Neroon when Muhammad bin Qasim took it during his invasion of Sind in 711, and it may also have been the site of one of Alexander's cities on the Indus. The present city was laid out by one of the Kalhora rulers in 1786 to replace the former capital of Khudabad when it was abandoned by the Indus. It was the capital of Sind from 1789 to 1843 under the Talpur *mirs* (kings).

At the end of the 18th century Sind owed only very nominal allegiance to Afghanistan, and was coveted by both the British East India Company and the Sikhs (who controlled the Punjab)—not least because the Indus flowed through the territory. When the First Afghan War broke out in 1838, Sind provided the only feasible corridor for British forces en route to Kabul. Sir Charles Napier wrote in his private journal: 'We have no right to seize Sind, yet we shall do so, and a very advantageous, useful, humane piece of rascality it will be.'

The British annexed Sind, and the mirs took to arms, attacking the residency in Hyderabad. Napier came to the rescue with a small force of 2,800 men and 12 guns; the mirs had assembled a force of 20,000. Nonetheless, at the final battle for Sind at Miani (see page 106) in February 1843, the British emerged as victors. Napier subsequently telegraphed to London: 'Peccavi' (or 'I have sinned').

Getting to Hyderabad

Hyderabad can be reached from Karachi in two and a half hours via the Super Highway (164 kilometres or 102 miles) and in three and a half hours nonstop via the

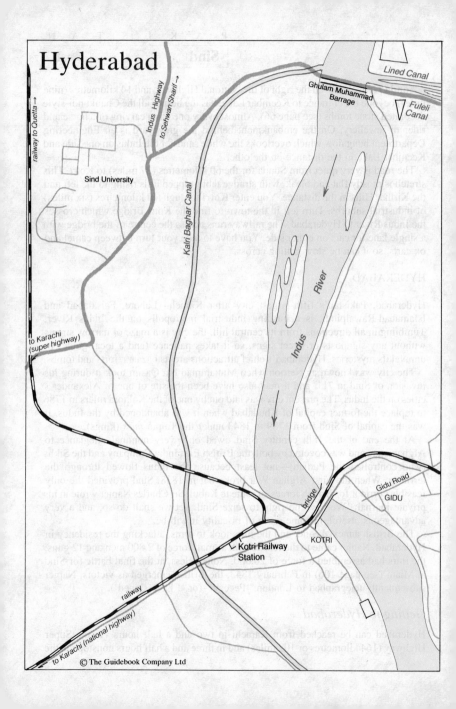

Hyderabad

railway to Quetta →

Indus Highway

to Sehwan Sharif →

Ghulam Muhammad Barrage

Lined Canal

Fuleli Canal

Sind University

Kalri Baghar Canal

Indus River

to Karachi (super highway)

bridge

Gidu Road

GIDU

KOTRI

Kotri Railway Station

railway

to Karachi (national highway)

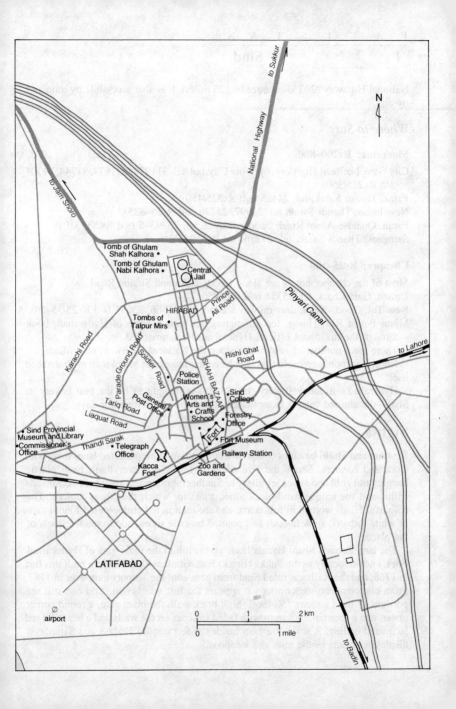

National Highway (203 kilometres or 126 miles). It is also accessible by train and by air.

Where to Stay

Moderate: Rs200–800

City Gate, National Highway, opposite City Jail, tel. 31197–8, 31677, 31744, 31707 (s/d Rs225/350).
Fataz, Thandi Sarak, tel. 24425 (s/d Rs325/450).
New Indus, Thandi Sarak, tel. 23997, 25276 (s/d Rs25–325).
Faran, Quaid-e-Azam Road, Saddar Bazaar, tel. 23993–5 (s/d Rs200/310).
Saingees, Thandi Sarak, tel. 27276 (s/d Rs150/270).

Cheaper: Rs25–100

Most of the cheaper hotels are along Goods Naka and Station Road.
United, Gari Khata, tel. 25354 (s/d Rs30/50).
New Taj, Goods Naka, near railway station, tel. 25566, 23691 (s/d Rs25/35–50).
Miani Forest Rest House, ten kilometres (six miles) north of Hyderabad; book through the divisional officer, Hyderabad. Recommended.
There are a number of new hotels along the National Highway, near Miani.
Note: It is more agreeable to stay at Keenjhar Lake or at Miani than in Hyderabad itself.
Hyderabad's Bombay Bakery (tel. 23479) is thought to be the best bakery in Sind—the almond cake is exceptionally good and keeps fresh for days.

Sights

Resham and **Shahi bazaars** comprise a labyrinth of interconnected lanes hung with cloth and banners. Shops the size of horse-boxes sell everything from plastic bangles and gold and silver jewellery to Sindhi embroideries, appliquéd bedspreads (rillis) and the unique hand-block ajrak prints for which the city is famous. The colourful Hindi women in full skirts, and the men in red embroidered Sindhi caps or white turbans, ajrak *lunghis* and pointed brocade shoes, add to the liveliness of the place.

The lane through Shahi Bazaar leads up the hill to the main gate of **Hyderabad Fort**, known locally as the Pukka (Brick) Fort. Ghulam Shah Kalhora built this fort in 1768, and the Kalhoras ruled Sind from here until the Talpurs took over in 1787. From contemporary descriptions it appears the fort was lavish. You can still see portions of the 15-metre (50-foot) -high brick wall, the main gate, a round corner tower, and a room in the harem with faded frescoes on the walls and a beautiful red lacquered ceiling. A small museum inside the fort (closed Fridays and Saturdays) displays portraits of the mirs and weapons.

To the west of the Pukka Fort is the **Kucca (Mud) Fort,** built by Ghulam Shah Kalhora in 1772 to defend the main fort from the west. It rains little in Hyderabad, as the 200-year-old unbaked mud brick walls bear out. The only entrance to the fort is up some steep steps and through the **Shrine of Maki Shah Baba** just inside the walls.

Maki Shah Baba is said to have arrived from Mecca in 1260, although his mausoleum was not built until 1671. Sindhis, ever devoted to their saints, flock to Maki Shah Baba seeking blessings and cures, particularly for mental disorders resulting from possession by evil spirits. Men are allowed to enter the central tomb and touch the saint's grave, which is covered with rich cloths; women may only look in through the stone lattice windows on either side. Devotees tie threads to the lattice; as the threads rot, their prayers are answered. A tiny decorated mosque, its low ceiling covered with frescoes, is set into the western wall of the compound. Behind the tomb is a courtyard and a very ancient khakar tree, also festooned with votive threads. In the corner there is a room where sick women can lie waiting for their cure, cared for by the shrine attendants. The rest of the fort is now a shady graveyard.

The huge decorated **Tombs of the Kalhora and Talpur Mirs** testify to the wealth of Hyderabad in the 18th and 19th centuries. There are 21 tombs in all, and the oldest and most majestic is that of **Ghulam Shah Kalhora** (d. 1772). The tomb stands to the north of the central jail in a peaceful, shaded compound enclosed within a high mud wall. The gate is locked, but a watchman and his family live inside. Shout *chowkidar* through a crack in the large carved doors and someone will open up. The square tomb, with cupolas at each corner, rests on a sandstone platform. The walls are covered with decorative panels with enough blue and white tiles still in place to give a good idea of the original beauty and variety of the floral design. Though the tomb is square outside, the chamber is octagonal inside, and was once totally covered in elaborate frescoes with bands of Persian script. On one panel is written, 'The emperor of the world, Ghulam Shah; before him the firmament kissed the earth.' A broad band of coloured tiles runs round the walls.

About 500 metres (yards) to the south is the **Tomb of Ghulam Nabi Kalhora** (d. 1776), Ghulam Shah's brother, who usurped the throne after murdering his nephew. The large octagonal tomb with four cupolas and a dome is situated to the northwest of the central jail behind Government College. What remains of the blue and white tiles that once covered the outside, and the frescoes that covered the inside, is beautiful. You can climb the outside stairs on the northwest corner for a good view over Hyderabad.

The **tombs of the Talpur mirs** are in two adjacent walled compounds off Jail Road, less than a kilometre (half a mile) south of the central jail. They are less interesting architecturally, but are worth a visit for their blue tilework and geometric and floral frescoes.

The **Sind Provincial Museum** is one of the most pleasant museums in Pakistan. It has three galleries: one for very young schoolchildren; a second with an

Tombs of the Talpur Mirs

N

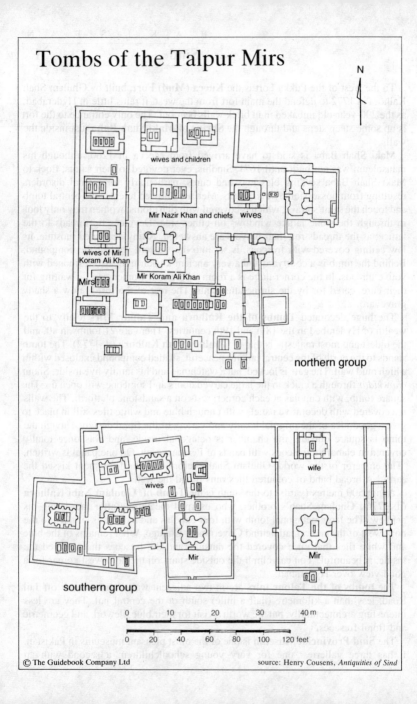

wives and children

Mir Nazir Khan and chiefs   wives

wives of Mir
Koram Ali Khan

Mir Koram Ali Khan

Mirs

northern group

wife

wives

Mir

Mir

southern group

| 0 | 10 | 20 | 30 | 40 m |

| 0 | 20 | 40 | 60 | 80 | 100 | 120 feet |

© The Guidebook Company Ltd

source: Henry Cousens, *Antiquities of Sind*

archaeological display covering prehistoric Sind to the British period; and a third with a display of Sindhi embroidery, wood-carving, household utensils and models of village life.

EAST OF HYDERABAD

One hundred kilometres (60 miles) of well-irrigated land divides the Indus from the Thar Desert. Fed by two of the great canals that leave the Indus at Sukkur, this newly fertile belt is one of the fruit gardens of Pakistan. Shady avenues of shisham, acacia and neem trees line the roads. Rows of eucalyptus windbreakers divide the banana gardens from dark green mango orchards interplanted with wheat, lucerne, vegetables and cotton. There are sugar-cane plantations in all stages of development, from newly planted reedy spikes to densely packed mature canes; three crops can be cut off one sugar-cane root before replanting is necessary. Patches of over-irrigated salty wastes highlight one of the problems of irrigation; today the rising watertable is lowered by pumping water into huge drainage ditches that flow out to sea.

The road and railway run east together from Hyderabad to Mirpur Khas, passing through **Tando Jam** (*tando* meaning place), a shady, peaceful academic town.

Kisano Mori, six kilometres (four miles) beyond Tando Jam, is a popular spot, particularly for the young. Men can swim in the canal, and you can have lunch at one of the many local restaurants.

Mirpur Khas

About one and a half hours by road and two hours by train from Hyderabad, Mirpur Khas is the district headquarters of Tharparkar. Known today as the 'City of Mangoes', its name actually means 'Town of the Mirs'. It was important in the fourth century AD for its Buddhist monastery and stupa, the sad remains of which lie two kilometres (a mile) to the north of the town on the road to Khar. Many Buddhist treasures were uncovered here, but now that it has been robbed even of its brick facing, a long bare mound is all that remains.

Mirpur Khas is the jumping-off point for trips into the Thar Desert. Information and guest house bookings are available through the deputy commissioner here.

Where to Stay

Hotel Abaseen, M A Jinnah, tel. Mirpur Khas 2153 (s/d Rs15/20).
The Irrigation Department Rest House and the Building Department Rest House are both bookable through the deputy commissioner.

The railway to the border with India is a metre-gauge track with a daily service to **Khokhrapar** just before the border. This border remained closed in 1988, but India and Pakistan have agreed to open it, with Indian trains travelling to Khokhrapar in

Pakistan and Pakistani trains stopping at Munabao in India. The line continues to Barmer and Jodhpur.

There are two paved roads from Mirpur Khas to the edge of the Thar Desert, one to Umarkot, the other to Naukot. For those without four-wheel drive vehicles, and who do not plan to enter the desert proper, the two-hour drive to the historic town of Umarkot is recommended. The road runs east through increasingly barren land that was once more fertile: a few hundred years ago the main channel of the Indus flowed here. The remains of the ancient west embankment which was built to contain the Indus River floods runs southwards just after the level crossing about 20 kilometres (12 miles) from Mirpur Khas, and a branch of the Nara Canal now follows the old river bed. The new Left Bank Outflow Drain, a huge drainage channel about ten kilometres (six miles) east of Mirpur Khas, should reduce the salinity problem in the area.

Umarkot

Some 160 kilometres (100 miles) and three hours' nonstop driving time from Hyderabad, Umarkot has a strong feel of Hindu Rajasthan about it. It lies at the end of the paved road and is fringed on the east by ridges of sand which roll without interruption for 200 kilometres (125 miles) across the border with India and deep into Rajasthan.

Umarkot was founded in the 11th century by King Umar, the first king of the Sumrah Dynasty. A legend tells of his love for a beautiful and virtuous desert girl called Marvi, whom he kidnapped one evening at the local well. But Marvi remained faithful to her village husband and, despite Umar's entreaties and gifts, refused to marry him. Her modesty and virtue are still celebrated in Sind today.

Umarkot gave refuge in 1542 to the Moghul emperor Humayun, who was overthrown in Delhi by the Afghan Sher Shah Suri and fled to Sind, where he married a 15-year-old Sindhi girl, Hamida. Later Humayun, his pregnant bride and a small retinue started out for Jodhpur across the Thar Desert, but fearing attack by Sher Shah Suri's troops turned back. It was the hottest time of year, and the wells along the route had been filled with sand by his enemies. At one point he was forced to ride a camel so that his wife could ride his horse. The party was unexpectedly welcomed at Umarkot, where Hamida gave birth to Akbar, later to become the greatest Moghul emperor. A small engraved stone half a kilometre (a quarter mile) to the north of the town marks the supposed site, but you need a guide to help you find it. It is surrounded by orchards and agricultural land and makes a peaceful picnic spot.

Umarkot Fort, built in 1746, is nearly 250 metres (yards) square and has 12-metre (40-foot) -high walls of unbaked brick. Round towers of baked brick stand at each corner and on either side of the main gate. Inside there is a small museum with Moghul arms, coins, miniatures, history books and an interesting map of Humayun's travels. The fort also contains the government offices and a fully equipped, colonial circuit house, built in 1877 and bookable through the deputy commissioner at Mirpur Khas.

In the centre of the fort a watch tower oversees the surrounding countryside. On top was the place of public execution. A bronze cannon with dragon handles protrudes through a hole in the parapet. The small town of Umarkot, with its wind catchers and three Hindu temples, nestles below the fort, and beyond to the east rise the sandy hills of the desert and pillared Muslim tombs on the horizon. To the northeast are a white Hindu temple dedicated to Shiva and, to its left, a high-domed Muslim tomb.

The ruined **Fort of Momal-ji-Mari** is about five kilometres (three miles) out of Umarkot on the Karna road. According to Sindhi legend, it was here that Princess Momal burned herself to death after being deserted by her lover Rano.

Umarkot Bazaar is a happy hunting-ground for village textiles, Sindhi hats, embroidered leather shoes, felted horse saddles, camel trappings, carved wooden boxes and old silver jewellery. Hindu blacksmiths squat along the edge of the road. One turns a piece of iron in the fire and holds it on the anvil while his wife wields the sledgehammer, her bangles rattling in time with her blows. Blacksmiths belong to a caste who traditionally worship the snake, Nag Devta. In fact, hundreds of people die each year in the desert from snake bites; the Jogis, Hindu desert dwellers and also worshippers of the snake, suck the poison from bites. As medical facilities are minimal or non-existent in the area, this is often the only cure.

Both petrol and diesel are available in Umarkot.

The Thar Desert

The border of Pakistan and India runs through desert for 500 kilometres (300 miles) from the Rann of Kutch to Bahawalpur in the Punjab. The Thar, Rajasthan and Cholistan deserts form a continuous belt of dry, sparsely populated land.

The Thar Desert, however, is not an inhospitable, empty wasteland, but is often called, with good reason, the 'Friendly Desert'. It is accessible, not too hot, and colourful and makes a perfect four-day trip from Karachi.

More than half a million people, 70 percent of whom are Hindu, live in the desert, spread out over 13,000 square kilometres (5,000 square miles). The women wear long, full, red or orange skirts and cover their heads with embroidered or tie-dyed shawls. Married women encase their arms in bone or plastic bangles from wrist to shoulders (widows wear bangles above the elbows only; single girls wear them only round the wrist). The people live in round mud-walled huts thatched with grass and surrounded with thick thorn hedges. These are clustered round the more reliable wells or along the tops of ridges. There is always plenty of activity in the villages: women come with pots on their heads or with donkeys to fetch water; herds of camels and cattle drink from the pond. The wells are generally very deep and animals are needed to haul the water up—a 50-metre (150-foot) -deep well requires the strength of a camel, while the shallower wells can be worked by two or four donkeys harnessed together. Wandering Sindhi musicians sometimes sit by the wells or at shrines and give impromptu concerts.

The villagers eke out a living from the desert by growing sparse crops of millet, sorghum, pulses, mustard, rape, sesame and red chillies. In a good year approximately 120 millimetres (4.7 inches) of rain falls in four or five showers from mid-July to mid-September. For a few weeks starting in mid-August, the sand becomes a green carpet, flowers and shrubs bloom, fields are quickly cultivated and the atmosphere is clear.

The towns marked on the map are market centres with brick or mud houses, narrow lanes and bazaars that are always worth exploring for tribal embroidery and silver jewellery. Foreigners are a rarity and cause great excitement, especially those with blue eyes and blond hair. Women wearing trousers and shirts are presumed to be men.

When to Go

The desert is at its best—green from the rains and cooled by the desert breeze—in August and September. From December to February it is cool during the day and cold at night.

Where to Stay

Mithi, Islamkot, Nagar Parkar, Chachro and Kantio all have rest houses bookable through the deputy commissioner at Mirpur Khas. The rest houses in Islamkot, Chachro and Kantio are basic and have no running water, so take everything you need with you. The local 'hotels' available in most towns are really nothing more than rows of charpoys in the street. It is safe to camp.

Suggested Desert Tours

Four days: Naukot—Mithi—Nagar Parkar—Chachro—Umarkot
Three days: Naukot—Mithi—Islamkot—Chachro—Umarkot
Three days: Naukot—Mithi—Nagar Parkar and back
(Naukot is a five-hour nonstop drive from Karachi.)

The best way into the Thar Desert is via **Naukot**, which can be reached from Mirpur Khas by paved road with frequent (but unscheduled) bus services or by three daily trains. Naukot is the headquarters for the desert bus service. Converted army trucks, some of them Studebakers that saw service in the Sahara Desert in World War II and are now painted with lurid scenes of mountains, aeroplanes and war heroes, ply all over the desert. Known locally as GMC trucks or *kekra* (crabs), they consist of three rows of seats inside and can comfortably take ten; there is also plenty of space in the back on top of the cargo. It costs Rs35 to travel the 175 kilometres (109 miles) to Nagar Parkar. The trucks can be hired for private parties from Ahmed

Transport Company, tel. Naukot 15; there is also a Toyota land cruiser for hire. One recommended driver-mechanic is Mr Arshad Ali. Jeeps are also available from Sona Mal and from Ahmed Ali Petrol Pump. If you bargain hard, you should get a vehicle for Rs1,000 per day, including fuel and driver (tips are extra). The GMC trucks use a lot of diesel, so expect to pay a little more for them; in the mid-'80s they cost Rs5,000 for three days.

The desert roads are deeply rutted sandy tracks for experienced desert drivers only. If you are driving yourself, plan your trip carefully, take two four-wheel drive vehicles and a guide-mechanic, and be prepared for all emergencies. A shovel, axe (for cutting desert shrubs to put under your wheels when you are stuck on steep sand dunes), gardening gloves (for protecting your hands when you are gathering shrubs) and a compass are vital. Do not follow the Pakistan Survey map of Sind, as the roads marked on it bear little relation to reality. Follow the advice of your guide and let him plan your route for you. Ask the truck drivers about the condition of the tracks and the time it takes between various towns. Lower the air pressure in your tyres when driving on sand, and take plenty of extra fuel.

Naukot Fort, a few kilometres along the road to Mithi, was built by Mir Ali Murad Talpur in 1814. It soars majestically out of the desert, its immense thick walls dominating the landscape. You can walk round the top of the wall to look out over the desert, which at this point is covered with thick scrub. Some of the soldiers' quarters are still intact and give some idea of what life there was once like. The huge elephant doors have been taken down and the main entrance bricked up in an attempt to make the fort suitable for modern defence: India invaded the Thar Desert in 1971 during the Indo-Pakistan War.

A paved road connects Naukot to Mithi, but it is wise to check its condition in Naukot before setting out in an ordinary car.

Mithi, with a population of 20,000, is the biggest town in the desert and a famous centre for Thari handicrafts, appliquéd bedspreads, embroidered shirts, shawls, babies' hats, wall hangings, horse and camel trappings, silver jewellery and old carved wooden chairs and boxes. However, the goods are for sale in private houses and are quite difficult to find.

Hindus and Muslims live peacefully side by side in the desert, and in Mithi even enjoy each other's festivals. There are a number of Hindu temples in town, and these are at their best when there is a festival. The **Temple of Nag Devta**, the snake, has its festival in June. The Muslim **Shrine of Sayed Ali Shah**, an 11th-century Arab settler, celebrates its urs (death anniversary) on the 27th day of Ramazan.

Beyond Mithi the real feeling of the desert begins. Sandy tracks weave between hills covered with low flowering shrubs. Vultures, buzzards, eagles, kites and many species of smaller bird are easily spotted. House crows and brown-necked ravens scavenge in the villages. Some of the remoter Hindu villages keep tame peacocks. The peacock is considered sacred by the Hindus, although it has been hunted almost to extinction where not protected.

Mammals are more difficult to spot. Indian and red foxes, jackals, gerbils, mongoose and squirrels are fairly common, but you are unlikely to see a pangolin, porcupine, desert hare, wolf or hyena. Desert-cat, jungle-cat and lynx pelts are for sale in Rawalpindi and Karachi bazaars, so presumably they are to be found somewhere in the desert.

Islamkot, about two hours from Mithi, is another predominantly Hindu town with two mosques and five Hindu temples. Almost every house has a wind catcher on the roof. From here a little-used track cuts north across country to Chachro. This track is not a bus route and is particularly difficult to negotiate, so it is essential to take a guide. It is an interesting route, however, as the villages are remote and untouched. **Arnaro**, about one hour north of Islamkot, is a Hindu village with protected peacocks.

On the main track to Nagar Parkar, about 45 kilometres (28 miles) from Islamkot, is the **Jain Temple of Gori**, said to date from 1376. The pillared porch with its carved ceiling leads into a multi-domed chamber, divided into little cubicles; crumbling stone statues decorate the walls. The Jains are followers of Mahavira, a contemporary of Buddha, and though no Jains live in Pakistan today and the temple is abandoned there is still a festival here on 20–25 March in honour of the Jain god Parasnath.

The village of **Bahalwar**, famous as the home of Marvi (see page 82), is about eight kilometres (five miles) from Gori. The well from which she was kidnapped is still there. Happily, Umar returned Marvi undefiled to Bahalwar and was content to call her 'Sister' from then on.

Virawah, 22 kilometres (14 miles) from Gori, is the last town before the sand dunes end and the pinkish hills of Nagar Parkar rise up like an island between the desert and the swamps. The brick ruins of the old city of Pari-Nagar are on the west side of Virawah and overlook the completely flat plain below. When a channel of the Rann of Kutch was actually navigable, more than 1,000 years ago, Pari-Nagar was a seaport. The town declined in the sixth century AD when the port silted up, and today a small stone temple is all that remains.

Beyond Virawah the sand becomes firmer and, because of a greater availability of well water, the desert ends. At Virawar there is an Indus Rangers checkpost, where tourists without permits are likely to be turned back. The Indian border area is sensitive for security reasons and because of the existence of a lucrative smuggling racket.

Nagar Parkar, only 13 kilometres (eight miles) from the Indian border, lies at the base of the volcanic Karunjhar Hills, which loom up unexpectedly on the horizon. Nagar Parkar has two recommended rest houses, both bookable through the mukhtiarkar in Nagar Parkar. The town is small, with a long narrow bazaar of stone stalls and shops opening into a small square with an ornate Hindu temple. This is a centre of some religious significance, and clustered at the edge of the green cultivated plain that lies at the foot of the hills are Muslim, Hindu and Jain places of worship.

Bhodisar, a few kilometres (miles) away, was once the site of a prosperous town established in about 515 BC. Two plain **Hindu temples** here possibly date from the sixth century. A ninth-century Jain temple, prominently built on a mound, features intricate tiny figures and other carvings. The buildings are all in poor condition and show signs of recent vandalism. Nearby two ancient *suttee* stones, decorated with turbaned knights carrying swords, mark the spot where the faithful Hindu widows were burned with their husbands. They stand on the bank of an artificial lake, or tank, which is as large as a football field and is said to be 600 years old. Local tribal women in bright clothes and carrying brass water pots on their heads come to get water.

A short walk from the lake is the **Bhodisar Mosque**, built of marble in 1436 by a Gujerati king to mark the spot where his mother was attacked by bandits. Ironically an inscription on the mosque reads: 'If this mosque is not kept in good repair by whoever is in power, God will consider him to be a sinner.'

At **Anchlasar**, three kilometres (two miles) away in the hills, there is a sacred Hindu water tank where women bathe as a cure for infertility. In nearby **Sardharo** Hindus throw the ashes of their dead into the water. A walk up to **Tyrwhitt Thullo**, the smooth flat platform on top of the highest hill (356 metres or 1,168 feet above sea level) takes a couple of hours and gives views across the salt flats to the Rann of Kutch. This is where Colonel Tyrwhitt, political superintendent from 1860 to 1873, sat in judgment at the local assizes. The flat rocks on top, apparently smoothed by the sea centuries ago, make a superb place for a picnic.

To make a round trip in the desert you can take a different route out through Chachro to Umarkot. This track is less used, so you might run into problems with the security forces. Ask for advice and hire a guide before setting out. It is about 100 kilometres (60 miles) to Chachro and a further 80 kilometres (50 miles) to Umarkot.

Chachro has never really recovered from its year-long occupation by the Indian army in 1971. A tablet in the Chachro guest house claims the town was 'retaken from the occupation by the enemy in January 1973'. Some 4,000 Hindus and tribals are said to have fled to India during the occupation; today the gradual depopulation of the Thar area continues, as Hindus filter across the border into Rajasthan and Muslims leave to find work in Karachi. Chachro is another smuggling centre; Indian whisky, betel nut and cardamom are brought into Pakistan, and edible oil and more valuable items are taken back.

The Chachro District rest house is well sited on the edge of town, with a verandah looking out to the desert, but it is sparsely furnished and does not always have running water. The watchman and restaurant owner nearby are both extremely helpful. Local musicians will entertain travellers after supper with Sindhi and Urdu music. Chachro is a collecting point for Thari handicrafts, and it is worth asking around to find out if there are any dealers in town with embroideries or woodwork for sale.

There are bus services from Chachro to most places in the desert. Allow an hour to travel from Chachro to **Kantio** and two hours to cover the last 45 kilometres (28 miles) from Kantio to Umarkot, as this area is particularly dry and the track runs across deep, soft sand through a forest of euphorbia cactus. It is very slow going.

HYDERABAD TO SUKKUR

There are two routes from Hyderabad to Sukkur, one up either side of the Indus. The National Highway up the east bank is fast and busy and takes about six hours (see pages 106–10). The Indus Highway up the west bank is much quieter and takes considerably longer, but is recommended for those travelling at a more leisurely pace and with time to stop in Sehwan Sharif and Moenjodaro.

Hyderabad to Sukkur via the Indus Highway (west bank)

Leave Hyderabad across the Ghulam Muhammad (Kotri) Barrage and turn north up the Indus Highway for Sehwan Sharif, 135 kilometres (84 miles), or about two hours away without stops.

The road is subject to flooding from the Indus, and several new stretches of raised road have been built further west. Whenever there is a choice of roads take the one to the west (the furthest from the Indus). There are no diversion signs; the road just forks, and the fork nearest the Indus peters out.

The long low line of the barren Kirthar Hills keeps you company on the left; the

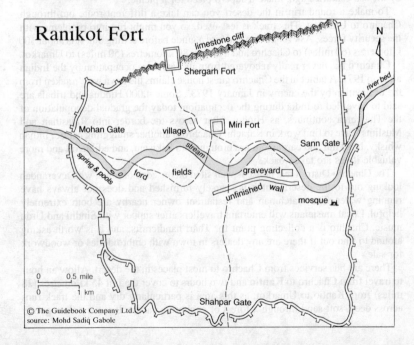

Ranikot Fort

© The Guidebook Company Ltd.
source: Mohd Sadiq Gabole

right is marked by the green line of irrigated land that borders the Indus. Baluchi and Sindhi villages dot the landscape; brightly dressed Hindu women carry water pots on their heads, and Baluchi tribesmen tend their herds of cattle, sheep, goats and camels.

Ranikot Fort

The turning for Ranikot Fort is at the **Sann** crossroads, 76 kilometres (47 miles) from the Hyderabad turning and about three hours from Karachi. There are no buildings at the crossroads, which is marked in Urdu only. Sann is one kilometre (half a mile) to the east, and its railway station is located to the west of the main road. Ranikot Fort is about 30 kilometres (19 miles) from Sann Railway Station on a jeepable track. As it is sometimes used as a hideout by brigands, it is vital to enquire in Sann if it is safe to go there.

The size of Ranikot Fort defies all reason. It stands in the middle of nowhere, defending nothing; there is no trace of an old city inside. It does not overlook any important trade route or mark the boundary of any known historical kingdom. The walls, 29 kilometres (18 miles) round, would in any case have been indefensible. In short, it appears to be the monstrous folly of a ruler of large imagination but little sense. There is no mention of the fort in any history of Sind until 1812, when, according to their records, the Talpur mirs spent Rs1.2 million repairing it.

Visible from five kilometres (three miles) away, Ranikot's massive undulating walls twist and dip over the hills. Built of dressed sandstone and reinforced with round bastions, they stand ten metres (30 feet) high on three sides of the fort; the northern side is protected by a natural limestone cliff.

You enter the fort by the Sann Gate after crossing the dry bed of the Rani River, and climb up through a tiny pass to a fertile oasis about two kilometres (a mile) away. The track continues for another three kilometres (two miles) to Miri Fort, a fortified residence for the Talpur mirs in the heart of Ranikot. You can explore the ruins of the court, harem, guest rooms and soldiers' quarters. It is also possible for you to stay at the guest house or camp under the protection of the Gabols who live in the village nestled below Miri. The headman Sadiq Gabol acts as a guide to the fort.

From Miri you look up to **Shergarh Fort** (Abode of the Lions), Ranikot's fortified citadel. The steep climb up to Shergarh gives a commanding view down over the whole fort and its four gates—Sann, Shahpar, Amri and Mohan. On a clear day you can even see the Indus, 36 kilometres (22 miles) away to the east.

The river enters the fort from the west at Mohan Gate, which is guarded by a small fortification on the east bank, and then tumbles in a series of turquoise pools to irrigate the fields of the Gabols.

Shahpar Gate to the south takes its name from a limestone rock with the rough shape of a foot imprinted on it. The Sacred Footprint supposedly belongs to Hazrat Ali, son-in-law of the Prophet Muhammad, and is venerated by the locals. This is the most spectacular portion of the fort. From the middle of a narrow, boulder-strewn gorge you can see the great wall rise and dip out of sight along the crests of the distant hills. Allow at least three hours to see the fort.

Amri, 20 kilometres (12 miles) north of Sann on the Indus Highway, has been occupied for over 5,000 years. Broken pottery shards dating from 3000 BC to the present day and 4,000-year-old Indus Civilization bricks lie scattered all over the high mounds beside the road. These mounds are the result of thousands of years of building new mud houses on top of old. The Amri people predated the Indus Civilization but disappeared in about 2500 BC, when the latter rose to power. A walk across the ancient mounds on the right, which are marked by a blue sign in English, gives you a chance to stretch your legs, but there is very little to see. After Amri the road moves closer to the almost impenetrable wall of the Kirthar Hills.

Lakhi Shah Saddar Sulphur Springs, at the foot of the hills 2.5 kilometres (1.5 miles) off the main road, was a popular Hindu shrine before Partition. The turning to it comes immediately after the Lakhi level crossing (marked in English). Take the dirt road to the left back across the railway; the first few hundred metres (yards) have been washed away, but you soon get onto a good paved road. It is a 500-metre (yard) walk up the steps to the shrine and the two sulphur springs.

The springs bubble out at the base of an immense wall of rock, with a sponge-like texture and swirling lines, that rears straight up behind the shrine. The nearby cave where Shah Saddar meditated is now a Muslim shrine.

A strong stench of sulphur leads you to the two hot springs. At present only 20 pilgrims a day come to bathe in the hot turquoise water as a cure for skin diseases and rheumatism; the thick green scum from the pool's surface is taken home and used as an ointment.

Lakhi village is almost deserted, but the ruined guest house and large Hindu houses give some indication of the revenue once derived from the hot springs. The small white tomb of Shah Saddar is on the left between the road and the railway.

The road and railway now hug the higher ground at the foot of the hills above the flood plain of the unpredictable Indus, which meanders, deceptively calmly in winter, on the right.

Now comes your chance to get cool: an 'air-conditioned' cave, marked by flags on the left of the road just before Pagho Toro Station. This is a popular truck stop. Currents of cold air from the heart of the hills keep the cave shivering cold, even in summer.

The hills come to an abrupt end, and Sehwan Sharif lies scattered before you. The town is famous for the Shrine of Lal Shahbaz Qalander, renowned for his great learning and virtue and for his ability to perform miracles. The town is a permanent carnival with a holiday air.

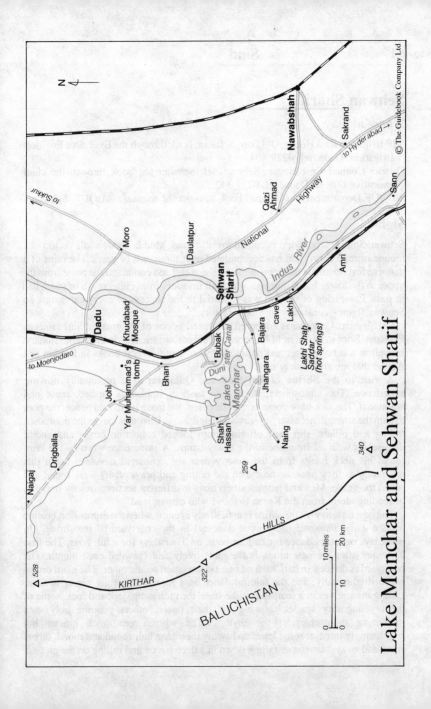

© The Guidebook Company Ltd

N

to Sukkur

to Hyderabad

Nawabshah

Sakrand

Qazi Ahmad

Daulatpur

National Highway

Moro

Indus River

Sann

Amri

Sehwan Sharif

Dadu

Khudabad Mosque

cave

Lakhi

Bubak

Bajara

Lakhi Shah Saddar (hot springs)

to Moenjodaro

Bhan

Jhangara

Lake Manchar

Duni

Minster Canal

Yar Muhammad's tomb

Johi

Shah Hassan

Naing

Drigbala

△ 340

△ 259

Naigaj

△ 528

KIRTHAR

HILLS

△ 322

BALUCHISTAN

0   10   20 km

0   10   10 miles

Lake Manchar and Sehwan Sharif

Sehwan Sharif

Where to Stay

VIP Irrigation Rest House, Old Fort, Sehwan; book through the Executive Engineer Irrigation, Dadu, tel. 0229 404.

District Council Rest House, Sehwan, tel. Sehwan 68; book through the chief executive officer, Dadu, tel. 0229 342.

AUQUF Department Rest House, book through the manager AUQUF, Sehwan.

Sights

Sehwan Sharif is the oldest occupied town in Sind. Mud houses huddle on top of a mound of mud debris that has accumulated over thousands of years. The ruins of a massive fort dominate the town at the northern end and command the route from the upper to the lower Indus, through which all invaders from either north or south had to pass. Possession of the fort was essential to the success of every campaign, so Sehwan figures constantly in Sind's history.

Lal Shahbaz Qalandar is honoured and loved as one of the greatest Sufi saints in Pakistan. Born in Persia in 1177, he was a celibate, mystic wanderer and missionary, as well as a scholar, poet and philologist who wrote several books in Persian and Arabic that are still widely read today.

A visit to the **Shrine of Lal Shahbaz Qalandar** is a profoundly moving experience. The atmosphere, thick with hashish smoke, is hushed, tense and emotional. The sick have come here to be cured, the troubled to find peace, the poor to gain the strength necessary to survive their misery. Devotees caress the doorposts, railing and pillars, slip their offerings into locked collection boxes and anoint themselves with oil from one of the many lamps. A stone once worn by the saint round his neck hangs from the canopy over the cenotaph; devotees touch this reverently as they pass. Some clutch the railing and pray, others walk round and round the grave. Men and women sit on mats in different sections quietly praying, or reading aloud from the Koran to those who cannot read.

The best time to visit the shrine is at 6.30 any evening when the drums start beating for the daily *dhammal* (devotional dancing) in the courtyard of the shrine. On weekdays devotees dance for half an hour, on Thursdays for a full hour. The first Thursday after the new moon is the most lively and crowded each month. The courtyard is divided in half, men on one side, women on the other. The giant drums boom rhythmically, and the faithful dance as a means of getting closer to God. Losing themselves in a semi-trancelike state, the men jump, jerk and rock, some of them young city spades showing off their paces, others genuine holy men immersing themselves in the rhythm. The women are much quieter but frighteningly intense: some kneel and swing their long hair round and round, others stand and sway, sometimes falling down in a deep trance and rolling on the ground.

The timekeeper bangs his gong to signal the passing quarter hours, which he measures by floating a bowl with a hole in it in a pot of water; the bowl takes 15 minutes to sink.

There is no climax. The drumming gets faster and faster and then just stops, and everyone goes home or settles down for the night, rolled up in their quilts in the shrine.

An added interest to the shrine is Alam Channa, at 2.52 metres (8 feet 4 inches), one of the tallest men in the world. Alam, who was born in 1957, works for Pakistan television, but spends most evenings helping in the shrine.

The annual urs (death festival) of Lal Shahbaz Qalandar is held on the 18th, 19th and 20th days of Shaban, according to the Muslim calendar. At this time Sehwan is thronged with devotees from all over Pakistan.

The shrine complex is rather confusing. To reach the courtyard where the dancing takes place you can enter through the new entrance built by Bhutto on the south; the huge gold-covered doors were a gift from the Shah of Iran. From here you pass through the new pilgrims' hall, which connects directly with the shrine beyond. Alternatively, the old gateway on the east leads straight into the shrine courtyard, where pilgrims can spend the night under the covered arcades. The great drums are stored in the first alcove on the left.

The shrine was originally built in 1356, but was enlarged by subsequent rulers. It is so hemmed in by the bazaar that it is difficult to see its design. The eastern entrance from the main courtyard is covered in blue and white tiles and has minarets at each corner.

The pilgrim industry works hard to extract rupees from the faithful. Colourful bazaars selling food and souvenirs surround the shrine, and everyone does the rounds to see the sights. There is something of a carnival about it all. Outside the town, tombs crown the small hillocks and many sites are associated with the saint: you pay to crawl under a fallen khabar tree under which Lal Shahbaz prayed and which reputedly cures any ailments you might have; or to drink from the spring from which the saint drank; or to enter the pavilion where he meditated.

Each day about 1,500 pilgrims are fed free at the Pathan Kafi, a pilgrim hostel near the shrine financed mainly by donations from the Pathan truck drivers. The Pathans have the monopoly on the transport business in Pakistan and form a powerful brotherhood that travels continuously to every corner of the country.

Outings from Sehwan Sharif

Manchar Lake, reputedly the largest natural lake in the subcontinent, is a half hour's drive from Sehwan. A large natural depression fed by streams from the Kirthar Hills and water from the Indus, the lake is a wildlife preserve that gives sanctuary to an extraordinary number of birds. It is also the home of the Mohanas, an aboriginal tribe of fishermen (sometimes called the Mirbahars or Sealords), who live in colonies along the canals and in houseboats out on the lake.

The lake is best visited during the cool months from November to February. The recommended route to the lake is via Bubak and the Dunister Canal, a 20-kilometre (12-mile) drive in an ordinary car.

Turn right at the T-junction just before **Bubak** and continue for four kilometres (2.5 miles) to the end of the paved road. This takes you to the top of the canal embankment. A Mohana settlement is strung along the bank of the Dunister Canal on the other side. Park here and ask Haji Abdul Karim to arrange for a boat to punt you down the canal to the lake, an hour away. A boat for the day costs Rs200 to Rs300 (tips are extra). Ten will fit comfortably in a middle-sized boat, but larger and smaller craft are also available. Take your picnic and drinks and all you need for a full day on the water, plus some extra fruit and biscuits to share with the boatman's family. Alternatively you can walk the three kilometres (two miles) along the canal bank to the lake.

Like the boats on the lakes in Kashmir, the Mohana boats are shaded by reed awnings and padded with embroidered cushions. The square mud houses of the canal-dwelling Mohanas stretch along the bank, their boats of all sizes moored in front. Women do their washing, cooking and embroidery by the water's edge. Children run along the bank flying dragonflies on strings. Blindfolded camels and oxen plod round in circles turning the wheels of the lift-irrigation systems which bring water up from the canal to the fields.

At the end of the canal you punt out into the shallow, reedy lake, where you can see as many as 12 boat villages clustered round the edges and across the horizon. The high-prowed, flat-bottomed houseboats give their inhabitants little privacy: apart from one small room in front, the rest of the canopied deck is open-sided. There are other boats of various sizes, including little fishing canoes. Some fishermen stretch a semicircle of nets on poles, into which they chase the fish by banging pots and pans and beating the water with their punt poles; others use long submerged baited lines. Many boats have trained fishing cormorants tied up on deck. The Mohanas also net waterfowl by wading in up to their necks and placing blinded egrets on their heads as decoys.

You can make two other trips from Sehwan: south of Manchar Lake to Naing or north to Naigaj.

Naing is a small oasis watered by a hot sulphur spring at the foot of the Kirthar Hills, 45 kilometres (28 miles) from Sehwan. The paved road to the village leaves the Indus Highway just south of Sehwan, immediately after crossing the Manchar Lake outflow canal. It passes through Bajara to the ancient raised village of **Jhangara** with its high-domed Kalhora tomb on the right. A long, flat-topped escarpment on the right hides Manchar Lake as you cross the sandy landscape dotted with tamarisk and khabar trees. Suddenly, round a corner, the green fields of Naing appear. Just outside Naing the remains of an ancient fort crown a low hill, and nearby the hot sulphur spring bubbles gently up in a clear pool shaded by acacia trees. According to legend, if the pure in heart stand beside the pool and call '*Ya Ali*', the spring answers with a vigorous bubbling. It did not disturb its gentle rhythm for us.

Naigaj, meaning Hill Torrent of the Gaj River, is a picturesque picnic spot on the banks of the Gaj River where it leaves the Kirthar Hills and wanders off across the plain. The jeep track to Naigaj leaves the Indus Highway north of Sehwan, and passes through **Johi**, a busy colourful bazaar. The area west of Johi is controlled by armed bandits, so you must stop at the Johi police station to arrange for an armed escort. From Johi the track runs northwest for 40 kilometres (25 miles) across the dusty flood plain that was once the main channel of the Indus. Halfway to Naigaj, near the village of **Drighballa**, a cluster of tall 17th- and 18th-century Muslim mausoleums rises unexpectedly up out of the semi-desert, on what was once the bank of the Indus. Ten large tombs stand in a huge graveyard, against a backdrop of the Kirthar Hills, the largest being that of **Mir Allahyar Khan**, which is stucco-painted inside and out. Two remarkable scenes are painted in Moghul style: one depicts a battle with soldiers on elephants and horses; the other the love story of Sassi and Punho—Sassi, separated from her lover on their wedding night, runs weeping through a jungle filled with tigers and crocodiles, while Punho is led reluctantly away on horseback. Some of the other tombs have well-preserved paintings of figures and gently flowing floral sprays. There are three or four more groups of tombs similar to these along the foot of the hills, one west of Kakkar and another west of Nazirabad.

At Naigaj an Irrigation Department Inspection bungalow stands at the foot of the hills surveying the flood plains of the Indus below.

A jeep track south from Johi leads past Shah Hasan village, at the western end of Manchar Lake, to Jhangara.

Sehwan Sharif to Moenjodaro

It takes three hours to reach Moenjodaro from Sehwan. The trip is perfectly safe in daylight, but you are advised not to travel after dark.

This area is the rice bowl of Pakistan. The rich green paddies are a haven for migrating birds in winter; even from a fast car you should be able to spot about 50 species. Of special interest along this stretch are the big mud and dung storage bins for grain lined up in the courtyards of the village houses. They are built up ten centimetres (four inches) each day and allowed to dry overnight; this storage system has not changed for centuries.

Khudabad, halfway between Bhan and Dadu, is so small you can speed through it without noticing. Astonishingly the town once lay on the banks of the Indus; it was the capital of Sind in the 18th century and is reputed to have been bigger than Delhi at the time. However, the city was built of mud and today only two monuments remain: the mosque and the tomb of Yar Muhammad, the first Kalhora ruler.

The **Khudabad Jami Mosque** is right beside the road. A large square building, with a high-walled courtyard in front that holds 1,600 for prayers, it is renowned for the two beautiful panels of glazed tiles on either side of the entrance to the prayer chamber. Each panel is decorated with a fluid and realistic white floral design on a dark blue background—quite unlike anything else in Sind. The leaves twist and curl gracefully from a central stem; the flower heads and buds, no two alike, seem to move naturally. A staircase leads to the roof for a view of the mud mounds that were once a city and the traces of the outer walls that once defended it.

The glazed tile façade of the **Tomb of Yar Muhammad Kalhora** features a magnificent circular floral design in blue and white tiles above the central door. Though quite a number of tiles have fallen down, you can still appreciate the beauty and intricacy of the pattern; again no two tiles are alike. The tomb is one kilometre (half a mile) to the west of the mosque down a paved road marked 'Garhi Rashdi Fruit Farm' in English. The watchman lives nearby and will open the gate into the tomb, which is still venerated by pilgrims. On request he will show you the knobbly staff with which Yar Muhammad ruled his kingdom and which lies beside the cenotaph wrapped in sacred cloths. The view from the roof across agricultural land to the Kirthar Hills in the west, and across the mounds of Khudabad to the mosque in the east, is worth the climb.

Dadu, the capital of Dadu Division, is bypassed by the Indus Highway and is not worth a visit—there is nothing of interest to see there and nowhere to stay.

Beyond Dadu a new road east leads to the new **Moro Bridge** across the Indus and the National Highway, the quickest route to Sukkur (two and a half hours) if you do not wish to visit Moenjodaro. It takes three hours on the Indus Highway. Moenjodaro is about half an hour's drive to the east of the Indus Highway, and two hours from Moro Bridge. To get there, you can either turn right at Mehar and go through Radhan or continue further up the main road and turn east at Nazirpur.

Mehar is famous for *mawar*, a sweet made of milk boiled down to a thick curd and mixed with dried fruit and nuts. It is delicious and makes a perfect gift. The first turning to Moenjodaro is just at the north end of Mehar bazaar. The sign, in Urdu and Sindhi only, reads 'Radhan Station'. It is 45 kilometres (28 miles) from here to Moenjodaro.

The level crossing at Radhan is a few hundred metres (yards) south of the station with no obvious road leading to it. The road from Radhan to Moenjodaro through the rice fields is very quiet and it is wiser not to stop along this stretch. Turn right at a T-junction 22 kilometres (14 miles) from Radhan and you will soon see the ruins of Moenjodaro on your right. Turn right at the next T-junction to find the gate.

Moenjodaro

Moenjodaro (Mound of the Dead) is the ruins of a 4,000-year-old Indus Civilization city. It is one of the most important archaeological sites in the subcontinent, and a must for anyone interested in ancient history. Enthusiasts should allow a whole day there to tour the ruins and see the excellent museum; even nonspecialists will enjoy at least a couple of hours.

Getting to Moenjodaro

There are daily return flights from Karachi to the airport near the site. A guide meets the plane every day and takes tourists to the ruins. Bring along your own food and drink, as both are usually unobtainable for day visitors. Moenjodaro Railway Station is eight kilometres (five miles) from the archaeological site—good news for the horse-drawn tonga wallahs who charge Rs25 for the hour's drive.

Where to Stay

Archaeological Department Rest House, tel. Moenjodaro 3. The PTDC in Karachi or Islamabad will make the booking for you. Order your meals for your whole stay as soon as you arrive. The rest house is quite comfortable and right beside the ruins. There is nowhere recommended for the general tourist to stay in Larkana, the nearest town, though there are three cheapies (s/d Rs20/30) near Larkana station.

Moenjodaro Museum

An hour in Moenjodaro's museum will give you a firm grounding in the cultural and economic basis of the Indus Civilization, and a good idea of what the ancient city of Moenjodaro looked like.

At its height the Indus Civilization comprised at least 400 cities or towns extending along the Indus and its tributaries, covering most of present-day Pakistan and stretching north to Kabul and as far east as Delhi. The waterways connected the empire, and flat-bottomed barges, almost identical to those still used today, plied the rivers between the cities. Few of the cities have been excavated; what little we know of the civilization has been pieced together from the finds at Moenjodaro and Harappa (see pages 172–4).

According to excavators John Marshall and Mortimer Wheeler, the land was probably irrigated, but Pakistan was slightly wetter and more wooded in those days, and the land along the Indus more fertile. The farming techniques must have been sufficiently advanced to produce a large surplus; wheat, barley, sesame and vegetables were grown, and cotton was already a major trade item in 2000 BC, as it still is today. Draught and food animals were domesticated; even dogs and cats were tamed. There is one particularly evocative brick in the museum with a set of dog and cat prints—presumably the dog chased the cat over the brick when it was still unbaked.

Trade between the three contemporary civilizations of the Indus, Egypt and Mesopotamia was well organized. Indus merchants drove caravans of camels and horses transporting cotton across the hills to Mesopotamia (later, in Mesopotamia, cotton was called *sindu*, and in Greece today cloth is still called *sindonian*). Whatever was traded in return was perishable, for no traces remain, but on their way back through Baluchistan, the merchants picked up bitumen, alabaster and steatite stone for making seals. Silver, lead, tin, turquoise and lapis came from Persia and

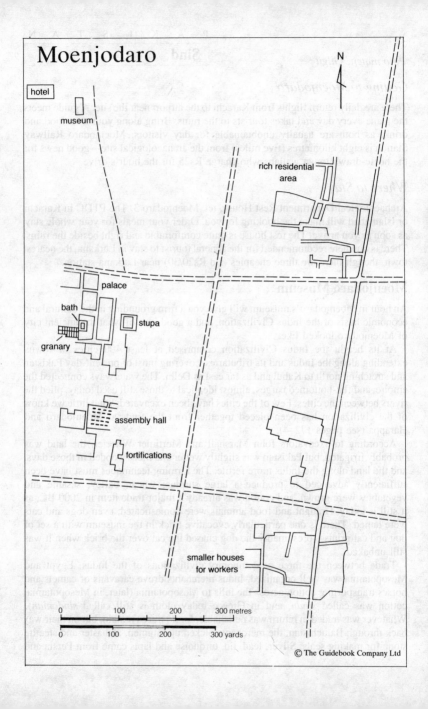

Moenjodaro

N

hotel

museum

rich residential area

palace

bath

stupa

granary

assembly hall

fortifications

smaller houses for workers

0   100   200   300 metres

0   100   200   300 yards

© The Guidebook Company Ltd

Afghanistan; red iron oxide for colouring was imported from the islands of the Persian Gulf; and from India came copper and semi-precious stones for beads.

The Indus people had a strong central administrative system. All the cities were built on the same highly organized plan with a raised citadel in the west and the streets laid out in neat blocks below, the wide main avenues intersecting at right angles. Indus city plans were not unlike that of modern Islamabad, different sectors being reserved for different functions. There was an administrative area, a wealthy residential area, an area for workers' houses and separate areas for the different trades and artisans.

Two large murals in the museum show a reconstruction of Moenjodaro, with its high outer walls narrowing at the top, a walkway for soldiers, and square watch towers. Down by the river, boats unload cotton and grain into the same two-wheeled ox carts still used today for transportation to the granary. Nearby, priests mill around the great bath and the palace, and in the distance stretch the two-storeyed, flat-roofed houses of the prosperous city.

Among the most interesting exhibits in the museum are the traders' seals, the pottery figurines of a priest-king and mother goddesses, and the bronze dancing girl. The exquisite seals are two to four centimetres (0.8 to 1.6 inches) square and made of steatite, a soft, easily carved stone. On each seal, an animal, or composite mythical animal, is delicately and realistically engraved. The carvings range from naturalistic representations of roaring tigers and rough-skinned rhinoceros, to pictures of deities and fighting demons. Across the top of most seals are inscriptions in the as yet undeciphered Indus Civilization script, presumably the merchants' names. Unfortunately, philologists cannot decipher a language from a list of personal names. Other short inscriptions have been found on some pots, but no lengthier writings or bilingual tablets have survived.

The famous little statue of the haughty priest-king (the original is on display in the National Museum in Karachi) indicates there was a ruling religious class. In fact, the central government was so strong that it was able to regulate the entire empire. The brick size was standardized throughout the empire, as were the shopkeepers' little cube weights (on display in the museum).

The pottery mother goddesses found in Moenjodaro suggest that the people here, as elsewhere in the ancient world, were devoted to this fertility deity.

The bronze dancing girl, pert and provocative, indicates either a tradition of temple girls or a normal sense of fun. (The original is in Delhi, but not on display.) There are also numerous terracotta figurines, some plainly phallic, which may symbolize fertility—or merely show an earthy sense of humour.

The little statues and the selection of jewellery indicate that the Indus women wore short skirts and dressed their hair in high complicated coiffures. Hairpins, earrings and strings of beads of carnelian, agate, faience, ivory, cowrie shells and gold seem to have been popular. The priests wore robes thrown over one shoulder (like Buddhist monks today) and their hair either short or gathered into a bun behind and held in place by a headband.

Moenjodaro: State Buildings

N

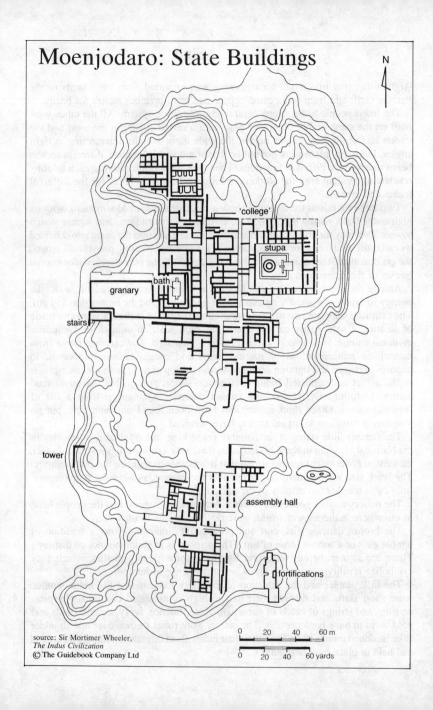

'college'

stupa

bath

granary

stairs

tower

assembly hall

fortifications

source: Sir Mortimer Wheeler,
The Indus Civilization
© The Guidebook Company Ltd

0   20   40   60 m

0   20   40   60 yards

The pottery on display reflects efficient mass production rather than great elegance, but what is interesting is that the potters in the village nearby are still making identical ware.

In about 1500 BC Moenjodaro was abandoned, although the civilization lingered on until about 1000 BC. This was probably due to a combination of factors. There were environmental changes: many trees were cut to fire bricks, the land was overgrazed and the monsoon may have moved slightly further north; the soil was gradually impoverished and became increasingly saline; and there was general cultural decline. Towards the end more fortifications were hastily built, presumably to defend the city against the warlike Aryan nomads who began invading the subcontinent from central Asia in about 1700 BC. The *Rigveda* (see page 25) relates that the Aryans overthrew people with flat noses who spoke a strange language and lived in walled cities. Among the more striking finds at Moenjodaro were skeletons in contorted positions, as though lying where they had been slain. However, the theory that the city ended suddenly after the deliberate slaughter of its inhabitants is probably an overdramatic interpretation.

Excavations

Moenjodaro was about five kilometres (three miles) in circumference, and 4,000 years ago stood on the banks of the Indus; a 1,500-metre (one-mile) -long embankment controlled the floods. Today the river has moved five kilometres (three miles) further east, and a modern embankment controls its flow. Only parts of the city have been excavated.

If you stand at the museum and look south, the first thing you will notice are the remains of the Buddhist stupa on the highest point and dominating the other ruins. Built 2,000 years later than the Indus Civilization city, it stands on top of the ruins of the ancient acropolis, or fortified citadel, which once crowned the 15-metre (50-foot) -high artificial hill.

Moenjodaro's administrative and religious buildings—the public bath, state granary, palace and assembly hall—are just to the west of the Buddhist stupa.

The great bath, probably used for ritual bathing, is more than two metres (six feet) deep and was sealed with a bitumen lining; today it has been completely restored with new brick and gives you a fairly good idea of what it was once like. Broad steps lead down to the water at either end. A cloister surrounds the bath, and on three sides are a series of small rooms (possibly private baths for the priests), in one of which is a well. A neatly arched and brick-lined drain leads out of the bath.

The state granary stands beside the bath. This was, in effect, the state bank, where the wheat, barley and sesame collected as taxes were stored. Today you can see three rows of nine high brick platforms separated by ventilation channels. According to Wheeler, wooden storage bins stood on top of these foundations. On the north side was a loading bay for ox-drawn carts, but this has deteriorated to such an extent that it is difficult to make out.

The palace or priests' college, a cloistered court surrounded by rooms, is situated to the north of the bath. The assembly hall is about 100 metres (yards) away to the south. You can still see the foundations of a large, square, pillared room and a portion of the city fortifications. There is no temple building; if there ever was a great temple, today it probably lies under the Buddhist stupa.

The city lies to the east of the citadel area and is laid out in a neat chessboard pattern. Wide main streets divide the city into 12 regular blocks; narrower side streets lead off these to give access to the individual houses. The city once covered about a square kilometre (25 acres), but only a small portion has been excavated so far.

The rich residential area (see map) is the most exciting part of Moenjodaro. Here you can stroll down the narrow side streets between high, forbidding, blank walls. It is dark and claustrophobic. Periodically a set of steps leads up to a front door, but there are no windows on the outside. Inside the doors you find yourself in the shell of a house. About ten rooms of different sizes lead off a central courtyard, and originally most of the houses had two storeys. A stair led up to the second storey, which probably had a wooden balcony round the courtyard giving access to the upper rooms; you can still see holes in the walls that once held wooden beams supporting the second floor. The only windows were small and high up, protected by a wooden or stone grille, and overlooking the courtyard.

In the streets you can see the remains of the famous drainage system of the Indus people. This was both elaborate and efficient: carefully graded brick-lined drains flowed down the centre of the streets to the river; the drains were covered, but at intervals there were inspection holes so that they could be unblocked when necessary. Tributary drains flowed from each house, first into a cesspit where solid matter was deposited; when the pit was half full the water drained off into the main sewer. The richer houses had bathrooms with carefully lined brick floors; some even had separate lavatories, and most had their own brick-lined well. Many houses had rubbish chutes running out through the wall to rectangular brick rubbish bins outside, which were emptied by the city's dustmen. The streets even had periodic sentry boxes to shelter the city police from the sun and rain.

The wells now stand up like tall factory chimneys: over the centuries new houses built on top of old ones raised the ground level, and as the excavators worked through the different levels of occupation, the brick-lined wells were completely exposed. The later brickwork near the top of the wells is rougher and of poorer quality than that lower down.

On the east side of the rich residential area is a wide main street leading south. From artefacts found here, Wheeler deduced that this was the old bazaar area. As in modern Pakistan, jewellers, fabric sellers, coppersmiths and potters all had their own areas.

The smaller working-class houses are about 300 metres (yards) south along the main street. In the northwest corner of this area, you can see the foundations of a block of 16 little cottages in two rows of eight with a narrow lane on one side and

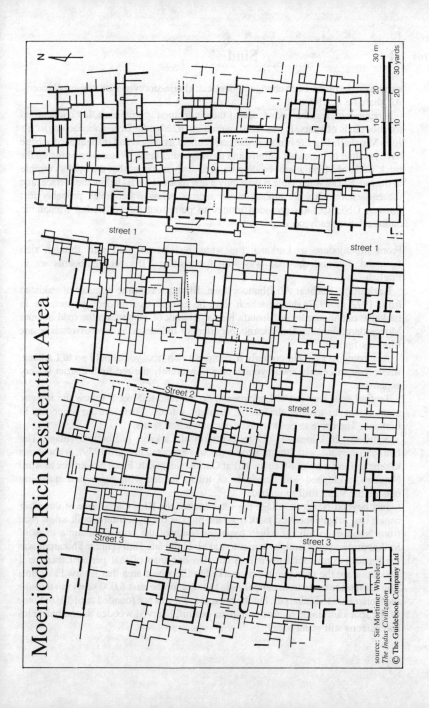

Moenjodaro: Rich Residential Area

street 1

street 1

Street 2

street 2

Street 3

street 3

source: Sir Mortimer Wheeler,
The Indus Civilization
© The Guidebook Company Ltd

N

0   10   20   30 m

0   10   20   30 yards

a street on the other. Each cottage is identical: single-storeyed with two small rooms. All shared a nearby well.

Moenjodaro, and the knowledge of the civilization it represents, lay undisturbed for thousands of years. It was rediscovered in 1922 by the British archaeologist Sir John Marshall. The site is now in danger; years of irrigation and inadequate drainage have resulted in increased salinity and a rising water table. Water is creeping up the brick walls of Moenjodaro, eroding them to such an extent that the bricks crumble to the touch. The water table is now only a few metres (yards) below the surface, and the earliest remains are already many metres below water level, probably lost forever. UNESCO has provided money to pump out the water, but irreparable damage has already occurred.

From Moenjodaro to Larkana, the wide, well-paved road runs through rich farmland. Because the road was built for visiting VIPs, the signboards are in English.

Larkana is Zulfikar Ali Bhutto's town. Bhutto was prime minister of Pakistan from 1972 to 1977, during which time he erected two modern monuments in Larkana: one in honour of Mustafa Kemal Ataturk of Turkey, on the road in from Moenjodaro; the other for Sukarno, president of Indonesia, at the crossroads beside Bhutto's house.

According to a Sindhi proverb, if you are a rich man you should go to Larkana, where you can easily spend your money; apparently the red-light district is very expensive.

To find your way out of Larkana and on the road to Sukkur follow the railway north down an avenue shaded by eucalyptus trees. There are no signposts in Larkana. The drive to Sukkur takes one and a half hours.

Naudero, 20 kilometres (12 miles) north of Larkana, is Bhutto's village. The family graveyard, with Bhutto's tomb (he was executed in April 1979), is about one kilometre (half a mile) off to the left at Gari Khudabaksh. From November to April Naudero is clogged with hundreds of trucks loaded with sugar-cane queueing outside the sugar mill to unload.

Just beyond Naudero village the road crosses the **Rice Canal**, one of three big canals that irrigate the west bank from the Sukkur Barrage. Bhutto built a new road from Naudero to Sukkur which bypasses south of the once-flourishing town of **Shikarpur** and cuts straight across to Lakhi. In the late 18th century Shikarpur was the greatest commercial town in Sind. (On one map of that period Lahore and Shikarpur are the only two towns marked in the whole area that is now Pakistan.) The main trade route from central Asia to India for the past 6,000 years ran through the Bolan Pass to Shikarpur, but the present town was not founded until 1616. Some of the spacious Hindu houses with their beautiful carved wooden doors, balconies and screens still stand today.

Jacobabad

Jacobabad, 44 kilometres (27 miles) north of Shikarpur on the road to Baluchistan, is a 40-minute drive across irrigated farmland, and worth a visit because of its association with John Jacob, who was largely responsible for creating the town as it is today. Jacobabad has an airport served by one weekly flight from Karachi and is connected by rail with the rest of the country.

The highest temperature recorded in Jacobabad is 54°C (129°F), which makes it the hottest place in the entire subcontinent. Even in January the average temperature is 14°C (58°F).

John Jacob was one of those extraordinary men produced by mid-Victorian society. When he arrived in upper Sind in 1847, the whole country around Khangher (as Jacobabad was then known) was in a state of anarchy: in theory the tribespeople owed allegiance to the khan of Kalat, but in practice they followed their own inclinations. Jacob established his headquarters at Khanger and, dedicated administrator that he was, set about enforcing law and order. In order to lessen the tribespeople's economic dependence on plundering, he concentrated on irrigating and settling the land and found work for the tribesmen digging wells, planting trees and building houses. He also built a network of roads and canals, which he aligned by the simple method of lighting a fire on the horizon and aiming the road or canal straight at it. With two regiments of irregular horse (the Sind horse) Jacob so chastised the tribesmen that they no longer dared to raid, quickly bringing peace and relative prosperity to the area.

Jacob then turned his attention to education and health. In the midst of all this activity, and despite the harsh living conditions (for Jacob and his officers scorned such luxuries as fans, thermantidotes and ice), he found the time to be a considerable craftsman and adviser to local tradesmen. He was an engineer, architect, designer, inventor; he made guns far in advance of the time, and an ingenious clock which tells the time, day, month and phase of the moon, and is still in perfect working order in the deputy commissioner's house.

Jacob's architecture is more exuberant than tasteful. His residency, now the much-altered deputy commissioner's house, has a ten-storey dovecote in the shape of a pagoda with holes for almost 400 pigeons. He designed and built the police station, which can perhaps best be described as a cross between a fort and a mosque, with round towers and domes that would not be out of place at a fun fair. Other British landmarks in the town include the district jail, courthouse, clocktower and station. The tomb of Jacob's favourite horse stands incongruously in the yard of the Red Crescent Hospital; the inscription reads, 'Here lies Messenger, the favourite charger of General John Jacob C.B.'

Jacob achieved all this in seven years. He died, aged 36, of heatstroke while working in the fields and is buried in the Jacobabad cemetery. His tomb, a veiled urn standing on a pedestal, has become a shrine. The people of Jacobabad hang fresh garlands on his tomb and place votive lamps before it. It has been suggested several times that the name of Jacobabad be changed back to Khanger, but so far the townspeople have voted to keep the English name.

Hyderabad to Sukkur
via the National Highway (east bank)

The National Highway runs from Hyderabad to Sukkur up the east bank of the Indus. Bypassing Hyderabad to the west, the highway is joined by traffic from the Ghulam Mohammad Barrage and the Super Highway from Karachi. The Tomb of Ghulam Shah Kalhorais on the right just after the junction with the road from the barrage.

North from Hyderabad the National Highway carries almost all the traffic from the port of Karachi to the rest of the country, so it is extremely busy and fast, but is usually in good repair. Though you never actually see the river, the road runs parallel to the Indus all the way through fertile irrigated land. The drive is shaded by avenues of acacia trees, and surrounded by orchards of mangoes, guavas and citrus fruits and fields of wheat, lucerne, cotton, sugar-cane and fennel. Ox carts, camel caravans, laden bicycles and pedestrians all vie for space; cold drink and fruit stalls and local restaurants line the way. There are no tourist restaurants, but it is perfectly safe to eat at one of the truck stops.

Miani is clearly marked to the left, with a sign to the comfortable Miani Forest Rest House, about ten kilometres (six miles) from Hyderabad. The memorial to the fallen of Napier's force in the battle of Miani (see page 75) is in the forest some five kilometres (three miles) from the rest house. Ask for directions, as it is difficult to find.

Matiari, an old town on the right, about 30 kilometres (19 miles) from Hyderabad, looks more interesting from a distance than it proves on closer inspection. The two high, square, 18th-century tombs of Pir Hashim Shah and Pir Rukan Shah are clearly visible from the road. The multi-domed mosque beside the road, with its heavy, freestanding minaret, was built in 1807; it is now abandoned and in very bad repair.

To the left you can see the embankment that controls the course of the Indus; there are good picnic places behind it.

Bhit Shah

Bhit Shah, the shrine of Shah Abdul Latif, one of the most beloved of Pakistan's mystic Sufi poet-musicians, is only four kilometres (2.5 miles) to the right off the main road. The turning is marked by a mass of signs in Urdu, five kilometres (three miles) before Hala and about 50 kilometres (30 miles) from Hyderabad, down a broad divided highway with lights.

Shah Abdul Latif (1689–1752) is the author of the *Risalo*, the best-known collection of romantic poetry in the Sindhi language. According to the journalist Ameneh Azam Ali:

His heroes and heroines have become symbols of Sind's oppression and sorrow through the ages . . . . [They tell] the story of Sind itself. The agony of foreign occupation and feudal strongholds, loot and plunder and rampaging armies and the struggle to survive against the odds, are all there in these folk myths. Sufi mysticism is the soul of this poetry, the solace and hope which give the people of Sind the courage to face another day.

'Songs of Love and Hope', *The Herald*, January 1984

At his urs (death festival) on the 14th, 15th and 16th of the Islamic month of Safar, Bhit Shah becomes the capital of Sind. A huge fair with amusements, wrestling matches, transvestites dancing, a circus, theatre, and food and souvenir stalls surrounds the shrine. Wildly dressed fakirs mingle with the crowds. Inside the shrine the atmosphere is reverently hushed. There is devotional singing, and, as Shah Latif was Sind's greatest musician, the classical and folk music performed here is by Sind's best-known groups. The main event each evening of the urs is an official concert organized by the Bhit Shah Cultural Committee, at which the annual Latif Award is presented to the best performers. For details and dates contact the Bhit Shah Cultural Committee, Bhit Shah.

The best time to visit Bhit Shah (or any shrine) is on a Thursday evening, when the devotional singing continues for most of the night. There are enough pilgrims present to make it interesting, but it is not overcrowded as at the time of the urs. Many devotees spend all night in the shrine rolled up in their blankets and rillis.

If you arrive on a weekday morning, drive up through the empty fairground past the souvenir stalls to the main gate of the shrine. There are always a few pilgrims wandering about or camping under the arcades of the courtyard. As part of their daily devotions, pilgrims and shrine attendants sweep the compound with palm fronds.

The **Mausoleum of Shah Latif** and the mosque stand side by side. The 18th-century mausoleum, built by Ghulam Shah Kalhora on the sand dune where Shah Latif lived and meditated during the last years of his life, is a square, high-domed building covered in blue and white tiles and frescoes. Inside, the tombs of Shah Latif and his cousin are surrounded by a carved wooden screen; devotees walk around this touching the pillars and praying, or sit and read aloud from the Koran. A box of holy clay beside the graves is reputed to cure all aches and pains when eaten or rubbed on the skin. The beautifully proportioned mosque next door is also covered in blue and white tiles and has carved marble pillars.

Hala

Hala, 56 kilometres (35 miles) from Hyderabad, is Sind's most famous handicraft centre. A blue tiled archway on the left of the National Highway marks the entrance to New Hala, which was relocated three kilometres (two miles) away from the banks of the Indus after disastrous floods destroyed the old city. Today potters' clay from the Indus is transported to the new town, and Hala's potters still produce the best blue and white ceramics in Pakistan. The new main street is lined with handicraft shops and runs for one kilometre (half a mile) from the tiled archway on the National Highway to the tiled archway entrance to the Makhdoom Nooh Mausoleum. Leading off to the left of the mausoleum is a crowded covered bazaar filled with shops selling sussi and ajrak handloomed and printed cloth, Sindhi embroidery, Hala blue and white pottery vases, birds and tiles, lacquerwork chairs, beds and cots and wood-carvings.

The **Mausoleum of Makhdoom Nooh** was built in 1790 when the old mausoleum on the banks of the Indus was flooded. Some of Hala's best blue and white tilework in floral and geometric designs covers the façade of the shrine.

Makhdoom Nooh, born in 1505 near Hala, is renowned for having moved the great Shah Jahan Mosque at Thatta by the force of prayer. Apparently the mosque was not correctly aligned, and in despair the builders went to Makhdoom Nooh. Telling them not to worry, he spent the night in prayer, and in the morning the mosque was facing directly towards Mecca.

In the street behind the mausoleum is the workshop of Gul Muhammad Samro, a tilemaker who welcomes visitors and will describe all the stages of making, glazing and firing tiles. In the next street you can watch the handblock printing of ajrak at the works of Maghomal Khatri; the freshly printed cloth is then laid out in the sun and covered with camel dung to fix the colours.

Brahmanabad-Mansura, once the capital of lower Sind, is east of Hala, 13 kilometres (eight miles) south of Shahdapur. Founded in the fifth century BC, and mentioned by all the major historians of Sind, the town was abandoned in the 14th century when the Indus changed course. The site has been extensively excavated, but despite its former importance there is little for the general tourist to see.

Moro, 110 kilometres (68 miles) from Hala, is the turning point for the new bridge across the Indus to Dadu. You can detour here to Moenjodaro, about two hours and 130 kilometres (80 miles) away (see page 96).

Kot Diji

Kot Diji, 226 kilometres (140 miles) from Hala, is the next place of interest on the National Highway. It is a magnificent early 19th-century Talpur fort perched on the ridge of a steep, narrow hill just beside the road on the right. The Talpurs ruled Sind from 1789 to 1843 and built a number of huge brick forts at strategic points. Kot Diji was undertaken by Mir Suhrab Khan (1803–30) and is the best preserved and most interesting of them all.

The entrance to the fort is located in the village on the other side of the hill and is barred by enormous spiked elephant gates set between massive round bastions. The gates are protected by a projecting wall with battlements erected so they could not be charged. A steep road between high walls leads up to the narrow top of the ridge. Extensive soldiers' quarters, a royal residence, a pavilion with fluted arches

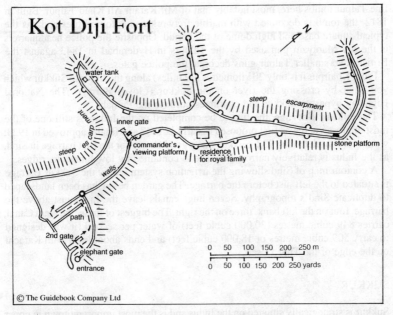

Kot Diji Fort

water tank

main

inner gate

commander's
viewing platform

steep escarpment

steep escarpment

residence
for royal family

stone platform

walls

path

2nd gate

elephant gate

entrance

0   50   100   150   200   250 m
0   50   100   150   200   250 yards

© The Guidebook Company Ltd

under which the commander sat, and a parade ground fill the space at the top of the
hill, which is surrounded by a crenellated wall.

The prehistoric site at Kot Diji at the foot of the hill is no less exciting for the
archaeologist. The people who lived here were the forerunners of the Indus
Civilization. The lowest levels of the site are under water and cannot be excavated,
but from their discoveries here archaeologists have found that the Indus Civilization
borrowed or developed some of the basic cultural elements of the Kot Dijians in
about 2800 BC.

The site consists of two parts: the citadel area on high ground where the elite lived,
and an outer area for the artisans and workers. The people built houses of mud brick
on stone foundations and made pottery which differed in style and technique from
that of the later Indus people, who nonetheless seem to have adapted Kot Dijian
designs—horizontal and wavy lines, loops and simple triangular patterns. There are
hundreds of shards on the site.

It is not clear yet where the people of Kot Diji came from or how they disappeared.

Khairpur

Khairpur, 23 kilometres (14 miles) beyond Kot Diji, was the capital of a small
independent state ruled until 1947 by a member of the Talpur family. There are some

fine Talpur tombs here, most notably that of Mir Karam Ali Khan Talpur. Built in
1812, the tomb is decorated with marble fretwork and coloured tiles and has the
typical square base and high dome of the period. Opposite the police headquarters
is the old Marayam gun used by the Talpurs in Hyderabad in 1843 against the
British; two smaller Talpur guns decorate the police gates.

From Khairpur it is only 20 kilometres (12 miles) along the Indus to Sukkur which
you enter by crossing the river on the Sukkur (Lloyd) Barrage. The National
Highway bypasses Sukkur and continues north to the Punjab.

The **Sukkur Barrage**, the first to be completed on the Indus, is still one of the
most impressive. It was first proposed as early as 1847 and finally approved in 1923;
work was completed in 1932. Sukkur was a good choice for the first barrage in Sind,
as the Indus is relatively narrow here and is contained by low limestone ridges.

A contour map of Sind showing the irrigation system fed by the Sukkur Barrage
is situated to the left just before the barrage. The garden below has been landscaped
to duplicate Sind's topography. Seven huge canals leave the Indus just above the
barrage, four on the left bank, three on the right. The biggest of these, the Nara Canal,
carries 849 cubic metres (30,000 cubic feet) of water per second (it was designed
to carry 509 cubic metres or 18,000 cubic feet) and ends about level with Karachi
on the edge of the Thar Desert.

SUKKUR

Sukkur is strategically situated on the Indus and is the most important town in upper
Sind. It is connected by air, rail and road to the rest of the country.

For over 2,000 years the capital of upper Sind has stood on low limestone hills
near Sukkur. The capital was originally located at Aror (or Alor), nine kilometres
(six miles) to the east of Sukkur (see page 117), but in AD 962 an earthquake
diverted the Indus to its present channel, and by the 13th century the twin towns of
Sukkur and Rohri, which face each other across the river, had become busy ports
with the impregnable fort on the island of Bukkur between them. Traders, scholars,
saints and adventurers thronged here. Sukkur reached its height in the 17th century,
at which time it took 15 days to reach the sea by boat.

Before the Partition of the subcontinent in 1947 more than 13 million hectares (33
million acres) of the Indus plains were irrigated by 50,000 kilometres (15,500
miles) of irrigation canals. The division of the Punjab led to a lengthy dispute
between Pakistan and India over the control and use of the canal waters; the rivers
of the Pakistani Punjab—the Jhelum, Chenab, Ravi and Sutlej—flowed through
Indian territory before joining the Indus. The threat to Pakistan's agriculture was
great, as India could at any time (and did, once) cut off water to the Pakistani Punjab.
The dispute was eventually resolved in 1960 under the auspices of the World Bank,
and Pakistan set out to develop her own water resources to replace the waters being
lost to India. Pakistan built a series of huge diversionary channels which fed water

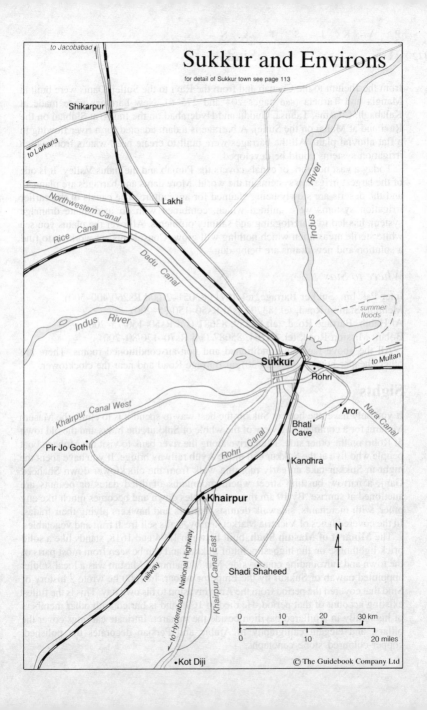

Sukkur and Environs

for detail of Sukkur town see page 113

to Jacobabad

Shikarpur

to Larkana

Northwestern Canal

Lakhi

Rice Canal

Dadu Canal

Indus River

Indus River

summer floods

Sukkur

Rohri

to Multan

Khairpur Canal West

Aror

Nara Canal

Bhati Cave

Pir Jo Goth

Rohri Canal

Kandhra

Khairpur

railway

Khairpur Canal East

to Hyderabad National Highway

N

Shadi Shaheed

0   10   20   30 km

0   10   20 miles

Kot Diji

© The Guidebook Company Ltd

from the Jhelum to the Chenab and from the Ravi to the Sutlej. Dams were built at Mangla and Tarbela (see pages 204 and 275–6). New barrages were made at Kalabagh, Chasma, Taunsa, Guddu and Hyderabad on the Indus, at Sidhnai on the Ravi and at Mallsi on the Sutlej. A barrage is a dam adapted for a river flowing in a flat alluvial plain. All the barrages were built to create head-waters from which irrigation systems could be developed.

Today a vast network of canals covers the Punjab and the Indus Valley. It is one of the largest irrigation systems in the world. More dams and barrages are planned, and the deserts are slowly being claimed for agriculture. The canals of the earlier irrigation systems were unlined which, combined with an inadequate drainage system, has led to waterlogging and salinity problems. All over the plains you see white sterile areas upon which nothing will grow. Consultants are working to find a solution and new drains are being dug.

Where to Stay

Inter Pak Inn, Sukkur Barrage, tel. (071) 83051–2 (s/d Rs260/400–500).
Mehran, Station Road, tel. 83792 (s/d Rs50–150/75–200).
Al Habib, Barrage Road, tel. 84359, 83681 (s/d Rs50–150/75–200).
Bolan, Mission Road, tel. 84264, 85087 (s/d Rs70–170/80–200).

All the above have air-conditioned and non-air-conditioned rooms. There are other cheaper hotels (s/d Rs20/30) on Barrage Road and near the clocktower.

Sights

If you only have one hour in Sukkur the best way to spend it is to climb the Masum Minaret for a commanding view of the whole of Sukkur, the Indus and the old town of Rohri on the other side. Then drive along the river bank to visit the Mohana boat people who live at the Sukkur end of the Ayub railway bridge. If you have spent the night in Sukkur take an early morning walk from the clocktower down Shaheed Ganj, a narrow bustling street where mountains of dried dates or peanuts are auctioned at sunrise. By 10 am this street settles down and becomes much like any other, with merchants, sidewalk dentists, barbers and hawkers plying their trades. In the covered lanes of Victoria Market nearby, stalls sell fresh fruit and vegetables.

The **Minaret of Masum Shah**, built between 1594 and 1618, stands like a solid brick lighthouse on the highest point of Sukkur and can be seen from most parts of the town and surrounding countryside. Mir Muhammad Masum was a local soldier appointed nawab of Sukkur by the Emperor Akbar. In 1600 he wrote a history of Sind that covered the period from the Arab invasion to his own day. This is the fullest existing account of that period. He died in 1605 and is buried with other members of his family in a pillared pavilion beside the minaret. Intricate carvings cover the pillars, and elegant calligraphy in Arabic and Persian decorates the polished, copper-coloured stone cenotaphs.

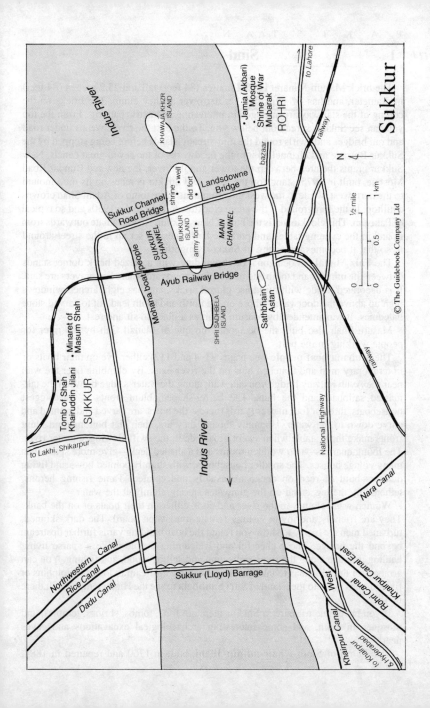

Sukkur

to Lahore

Indus River

KHAWAJA KHIZR
ISLAND

Jamia (Akbari)
Mosque
Shrine of War
Mubarak

ROHRI

railway

bazaar

shrine • well
• old fort

Landsdowne
Bridge

Sukkur Channel,
Road Bridge

SUKKUR
CHANNEL

BUKKUR
ISLAND
• army fort

MAIN
CHANNEL

N

0   0.5   1 km

0   ½   1 mile

© The Guidebook Company Ltd

Mohana boat people

Ayub Railway Bridge

SHRI SADHBELA ISLAND

Sathbhain
Astan

railway

Minaret of
Masum Shah

Tomb of Shah
Khairuddin Jilani

SUKKUR

to Lakhi, Shikarpur

Indus River

National Highway

Nara Canal

Northwestern Canal
Rice Canal
Dadu Canal

Sukkur (Lloyd) Barrage

Rohri Canal
Khairpur Canal East
West
Khairpur Canal

to khairpur
& Hyderabad

to khairpur

The brick Masum Minaret is 25.2 metres (84 feet) tall and 25.2 metres (84 feet) in diameter, and has 84 steps that get narrower as they climb. The bricks on the ceiling of the stairway are arranged in interesting geometric patterns. From the top you can see Sukkur spread out below you. To the east the river sweeps under road and rail bridges and swirls round the mid-stream islands before being stopped by the Sukkur Barrage and channelled into the headworks of the seven great canals. New Sukkur crams the area between the tower and the river; the new red Bundar Road Mosque, built in 1975, stands on the bank. Old Sukkur perches on its mud mound to the northwest, while to the west the prominent white tomb of Adam Shah crowns a hilltop. In the foreground is the green clocktower, built in the 1930s and so typical of Pakistan. This clocktower is the hub of New Sukkur. Roads radiate outwards from it, and in the evening tables and portable barbecues are set up in the street around it, so that it becomes the centre of Sukkur's nightlife.

The **Faiz Mahal**, an octagonal brick building with a glazed brick dome, stands between the minaret and tomb and overlooks a courtyard where Eid prayers are said. It is decorated inside with turquoise glazed bricks, and has eight arched windows high up above the doorways—those on the north and south lead out to carved stone balconies. It was intended by Masum Shah as a place to sit and rest.

Masum Shah also built the octagonal mosque of Manzil Gah by the river for people working in the port.

The **Mohana boat people** (see pages 93–4 and 112) either live on their boats or in temporary mud and thatched huts on the river bank. By climbing over the wall near the Ayub railway bridge you can walk along the water's edge between the tall-masted sailboats and the huts. The barrel-shaped, blunt fronts of the biggest houseboats, three or four metres (yards) across the bows, are carved and painted and curve down to the water. Ungainly though they are, their flat bottoms and blunt fronts make them stable when swept broadside in the swift-flowing summer river. The living quarters—two wooden rooms and a shaded deck—give more space than many village houses. The smaller houseboats, with slightly pointed bows and living quarters built of reed on deck, are usually undecorated. Tame fishing herons, tethered by the leg, stand on the gunwales staring glumly at the water.

Women wash clothes in the river and cook either on their boats or on the bank. They are friendly and invite visiting female tourists on board. The dark-skinned, turbaned men are happy to show you round the boat-building yards further upstream beyond the bridge. These cheerful and welcoming people make a sparse living hauling produce along the river, collecting and selling wood, and fishing. You can arrange for the Mohanas to take you on a boat trip upstream to look for dolphins or five minutes away to the island of **Shri Sadhbela** to see the Hindu temple built there in 1823.

If you have time to spare in Sukkur there are forts, tombs, shrines, temples, and mosques in town, and some interesting archaeological excavations and caves nearby.

The **Tomb of Shah Khair-ud-din Jilani**, built in 1760 and repaired in 1884, looks rather uninteresting when you first step through a doorway in a high wall and enter the tomb courtyard from behind. But the east face on the other side is totally glazed in green, yellow, brown and blue tiles. Silver doors surrounded by coloured stones lead into the burial chamber, where men turn to the right and women duck behind a curtain to the left. A high marble screen with intricate marble fretwork round the top and bottom surrounds the cenotaph. Shah Khair-ud-din is popular with women suffering from 'incurable women's problems'; he is the last resort when all else has failed. He came from Baghdad, founded a spiritual dynasty in Sukkur and is supposed to have died in 1609 at the unlikely age of 116.

Bukkur Island, 300 metres by 800 metres (yards), is the largest of the three islands in the river and can be reached by the Sukkur Channel Road Bridge. The Landsdowne Bridge, built in 1889, takes the road across the main channel of the Indus from Bukkur to Rohri; the Ayub Bridge, built in 1962, now carries the railway across the river just downstream from the road bridges.

On the northern end of Bukkur Island are a ruined fort, a Muslim shrine and a stepwell. The main fort lies at the south end of the island and is occupied by the army; it is out of bounds for tourists. There have been forts on the island since about the 12th century, and Bukkur itself appears frequently in the history of Sind. Its strategic position on the Indus has meant that like Sehwan (see page 92) its capture was essential to every campaign in upper Sind. It was never taken by force, but changed hands many times by treachery, cajolery or treaty.

The old brick fort at the northern end of Bukkur is 100 metres (yards) to the left, just before the Landsdowne Bridge, and can be reached by car. The south gate with its crumbling red brickwork stands guard over the river. Right on the water's edge is the Bloody Tower, where people were executed and thrown into the water. From here you look across to the old holy city of Rohri perched on top of a limestone cliff on the east bank. The white-domed Jamia (or Akbari) Mosque, built by Fateh Khan in 1584, is right by the river in Rohri. Above it rises the green dome of the War Mubarak shrine.

Upstream the small island of **Khawaja Khizr** breaks the force of the river. The old mosque and the Hindu temple of Zinda Pir on this island were both completely destroyed in the flooding of 1976.

Mohana boats lumber through the quieter Sukkur Channel. Beyond, on the flood plains of the Indus north of Sukkur, are winter vegetable gardens; in summer, when the monsoon rains combine with the melting snows, the area is completely inundated.

The **Shrine of Shah Sadr-ud-din**, chief justice of Bukkur in the early 16th century, lies to the west of Bukkur Fort. Nearby is the fort's original well with steps leading down to water level.

As you leave Bukkur Island on the Landsdowne Bridge you can look downriver, under the high sweep of the iron railway bridge, to the Sathbhain Astan (Seven Sisters' Astana) on the east bank and the Sukkur Barrage in the distance.

Sathbhain Astan itself crowns a flat-topped hill. Carved tombs and pavilions dating from the 17th to the 19th century stand on a walled terrace, from which there is a superb view of the chief fort on Bukkur Island, the Hindu temple on Sadhbela Island downstream from Bukkur and the Mohana boats beyond.

To enter Sathbhain Astan you go up a flight of stairs that passes through a blue tiled chamber where you remove your shoes. The walled graveyard with blue tiled minarets at the corners contains heavily carved sandstone tombs reminiscent of Chaukundi (see page 66), but covered in Persian and Arabic script as well as floral and geometric designs. A little blue tiled pavilion (*chaubutro*) provides a cool, shaded spot for sitting and meditation. Beneath the terrace is a series of rooms where, legend has it, seven sisters hid from a cruel nawab who demanded that all beautiful girls be sent to him.

Rohri

The seven-storey houses of Rohri, with carved wooden balconies, doors and windows, face the river at the end of Landsdowne Bridge. To the right the limestone cliffs form a natural defence, with the fort-like houses perched on top. In winter the wide beach below the bridge is the temporary home of herders and their cattle, Mohanas and their boats, and migrant workers.

A visit to the **Shrine of War Mubarak** (Hair of the Prophet) is a moving experience. The shrine is difficult to find, 500 metres (yards) down a maze of twisting side streets where the carved wooden balconies almost touch each other overhead. A blue and green tiled archway with flags marks the turning from the main bazaar; several hundred metres (yards) down this alley are the old carved wooden doors surrounded by glazed tiles that lead into the shrine.

The shrine, built in 1545, is square. Frescoes decorate the inside of the dome. When enough people have assembled, an expectant silence falls. The *makhdoom* (hereditary keeper of the relic) appears from an inner sanctum carrying a bundle wrapped in green cloth in his outstretched hands. He kneels in a glass cubicle in the centre and reverently unwraps cloth after cloth while intoning verses from the Koran. At last he reveals a golden casket studded with rubies. He covers his hand with a white cloth, opens the casket, removes a gold cover and lifts out a gold tube with a padded end. The crowd sighs and murmurs, and presses forward to see a single reddish bristle protruding half a centimetre from the padding. The faithful believe this to be from the beard of the Prophet Muhammad (d. AD 632).

The **Jamia (Akbari) Mosque** is just downhill from the War Mubarak on the edge of the river. It was built in 1584 by Fateh Khan, an officer under Emperor Akbar. Cooled by the river breeze, it is a quiet place to offer prayers on the hottest of summer days. It has frequently been damaged by floods and subsequently repaired, so only a few of the original tiles still cling to the walls. A climb up to the roof with its five brick domes gives another superb view of the river and the Mohana sailboats.

Outings from Sukkur

Aror (or Alor), eight kilometres (five miles) east of Rohri, is the site of the ancient capital, once on the banks of the Indus, that predates Sukkur. The road to it is clearly marked off the National Highway about one kilometre (half a mile) north of Rohri, and follows the old disused channel of the Nara Canal past brick kilns and a cotton ginning mill. After six kilometres (four miles) or so take the right fork across the New Nara Canal and continue one kilometre (half a mile) to Aror. Pottery-strewn mounds and the ruins of the brick **Muhammad bin Qasim Mosque**, not earlier than the 16th century, are all that remain. The present village of Aror, on top of one of the mounds behind the ruined mosque, is worth a visit to see what antiquities the villagers have found in the ruins.

Some authorities believe Aror was the capital of the Kingdom of Musicanus, which Alexander the Great was told 'was the most prosperous in all India'. Alexander's army made a prolonged halt here, fortifying and garrisoning the citadel before moving on down the Indus in 325 BC.

Aror is also thought to be the capital visited in AD 630 by the Chinese Buddhist pilgrim Xuan Zang, who described Sind as stretching from Kashmir to the sea under a Sudra (Buddhist) monarch. Thereafter the Hindus ruled the area until Muhammad bin Qasim defeated the ruler and took the city in 711. The capital then moved to Mansura near Hala, and Aror declined. The final blow came in the tenth century when the Indus changed its course. An attractive but unlikely legend attributes the change to a merchant sailing up the Indus at that time:

The local prince had imposed harsh trading terms upon him, and was also demanding one of his beautiful slave-girls. The merchant asked for three days to consider the matter and during this time found enough men to dig a new channel westwards away from Aror, using the excavated earth to dam and redirect the river. On the morning of the fourth day the people of Aror found they had no river, just mud and muddy water.

Jean Fairley, *The Lion River* (1975)

An earthquake in AD 962 is a more plausible explanation for the river's dramatic move.

The **Tomb of the Unknown Lady**, or **Pir Bacha**, is a brick ruin, possibly dating from the 12th century, one kilometre (half a mile) past Aror on the right. The surfaced road ends here, but you can continue for another 1.5 kilometres (one mile) in an ordinary car. Bear right when the road forks, to the deserted village of Bhatti, with its **Hindu shrine of Kalka** (or Kali Devi, the goddess of death) in a limestone cave. Once an important Hindu shrine, it is still cared for by an attendant and comes to life each August at its festival.

You enter the semicircular cave at the west end. The shrine attendant will tell you the story of each bump and crevice. A passageway to the right is the route taken by

Kalka when she went to visit the Hindu shrine at Hinglaj in Baluchistan near Las Bela. The limestone roof is little more than a metre (three feet) high, but occasional holes allow you to straighten briefly. These are the places Kalka's servants stood to attend her. The altar is on the left, the exit at the east end. In the courtyard outside are the pilgrim centre and shops.

There are no houses left in Bhatti, which was deserted when its water supply dried up, but the large mosque indicates it was once a flourishing town. The Nara Canal follows an earlier channel of the Indus through the limestone hills. All around this area are old tombs and shrines, the most spectacular being **Bhago Takar**, an enormous layered rock cleft in four parts as if by a gigantic sword; it has a square domed shrine on top. A tiny house huddles in a crevice halfway up. One legend says that King Dahir was killed by Muhammad bin Qasim here and that his blood (a streak of red) still stains the rock.

An afternoon's drive **south from Rohri** through Kandhra, Shadi Shaheed, Khairpur, Pir jo Goth and back to Sukkur loops through the rich agricultural land of the east bank. Date gardens, harvested in June and July and intersown with wheat and cotton, alternate with banana and citrus orchards, and fields of sugar-cane and oil-seeds. Tribes of migrant workers camp along the irrigation channels. The Marwari (traditionally woollen weavers), the Marecha (leather workers, tanners and shoemakers) and the Oad (earth movers and wall builders) now all take whatever work they can find. Kandhra and Khairpur are both populated by the descendants of the Talpur mirs. Shadi Shaheed is a small village with an enormous graveyard surrounding the **Shrine of Shadi Khan**, a Baluchi saint who died in 1817; pilgrims flock here for relief of headaches and influenza.

If you have more time it is only about 20 kilometres (12 miles) from Khairpur to Kot Diji down the National Highway (see page 108).

From Sukkur to Multan there is a choice of three routes:
—Up the National Highway via Bahawalpur (see page 158).
—On the National Highway for 290 kilometres (180 miles) then fork left across the Panchnad via Alipur and Muzaffargarh.
—Up the west bank of the Indus from Shikarpur to Dera Ghazi Khan. This route is recommended for bird-watchers only, as the first part of the road is not particularly good and there is little of general interest to see along the way. Kashmor, 110 kilometres (68 miles) from Shikarpur, on the border of Sind and Punjab provinces, is famous for its wooden lacquerwork and for the Guddu Barrage, the second largest in Pakistan, which irrigates 11 million hectares (27 million acres). From here it is about 85 kilometres (53 miles) to Mithankot, where there is a wonderful boat bridge (see page 150) and two 19th-century shrines. The next town, Rajanpur, has a rather dilapidated fort some 700 years old. From there the road improves, but it is still another 114 kilometres (70 miles) or almost two hours to Dera Ghazi Khan (see page 151)

Stone Age Tools

If you are interested in the Stone Age you might like to wander on the flat-topped hill beside the cement factory near Rohri, which is littered with thousands of ancient tools. Blade cores, blades and waste flakes are piled up round cleared patches of ground, where craftsmen must have sat crossed-legged to work thousands of years ago.

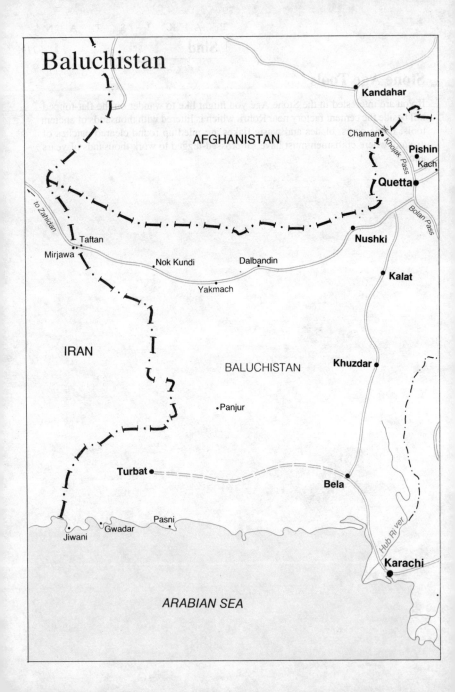

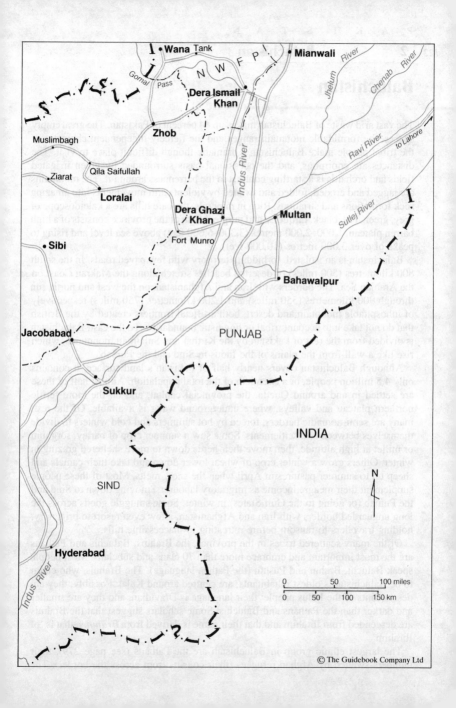

Wana • Tank

N W F P

Gomal Pass

Dera Ismail Khan

• Mianwali

Jhelum River

Chenab River

Muslimbagh

Zhob

to Lahore

Ravi River

Ziarat

Qila Saifullah

Indus River

Loralai

Dera Ghazi Khan

Multan

Sutlej River

• Sibi

Fort Munro

Bahawalpur

Jacobabad

PUNJAB

Sukkur

INDIA

SIND

Hyderabad

Indus River

0   50   100 miles

0   50   100   150 km

N

© The Guidebook Company Ltd

Baluchistan

The vast arid waste of Baluchistan makes up 44 percent of Pakistan. The great empty spaces, the formidable mountain ranges and the fiercely independent character of the tribal people make Baluchistan a dramatic though difficult place to visit. The distances are enormous, and the occasional oasis surrounded by green irrigated fields and orchards is a startling contrast to the barrenness around it. The mountains are jagged and eroded, folded and twisted by violent earth movements into amazing rock formations and striations. Rich in minerals, the bare hills are a kaleidoscope of grey, green, red, black, turquoise and purple. Much of the province consists of a high barren plateau, 1,000–2,000 metres (3,300–6,600 feet) above sea level and rising to peaks of over 3,000 metres (10,000 feet).

Baluchistan is an isolated, forbidding territory with few paved roads. In the south 800 kilometres (500 miles) of deserted beaches stretch along the Makran Coast on the Arabian Sea. The borders with Iran and Afghanistan, on the west and north, run through 900 kilometres (550 miles) and 1,200 kilometres (750 miles) respectively of inhospitable mountain and desert, both artificial frontiers created by the British that do not take into account tribal or linguistic boundaries. To the east, Baluchistan is divided from the rest of Pakistan by the Kirthar and Sulaiman mountains, which rise like a wall from the plains of the Indus in Sind and the Punjab.

Although Baluchistan covers nearly half of Pakistan's land surface, it contains only 4.5 million people, or a twentieth of the total population. Almost half of these are settled in and around Quetta, the provincial capital, and on the more fertile northern plateau and valleys, where underground water is available. Of the rest, many are semi-nomadic herders, forced by hot summers and cold winters to divide themselves between two settlements. Some sow a summer crop of barley, sorghum or millet at high altitude, then move their herds down to more sheltered grazing in winter. Others grow a winter crop of wheat lower down and take their camels and sheep up to summer pastures in April when the snow melts. Most of these people supplement their meagre income as migratory labourers, moving down to Sind and the Punjab (or going to the Gulf States) in winter. Some smuggle goods across the long unguarded borders with Iran and Afghanistan; a few even resort to brigandry, holding travellers to ransom before retreating to inaccessible hills.

Of the many scattered tribes in the province, the Brahuis, Baluchis and Pathans are the most important and embrace more than 70 clans and subclans. Most people speak Baluchi, Brahui and Pushtu (the Pathan language). The Brahuis, who claim to be Baluchistan's oldest inhabitants, are centred around Kalat. Possibly, they are descendants of the Indus people: their language is Dravidian, and they are smaller and darker than the Pathans and Baluchis. Some scholars suggest that the Brahuis are descended from Ibrahim and that their name is derived from *Brahimy*, that is 'of Ibrahim'.

The largest ethnic group in Baluchistan are the Pathans (see page 279), their numbers swelled by Afghan refugees (their cousins from across the border). The

Pakistani Pathans are mostly settled farmers and traders concentrated in the more populated northeast bordering the North-West Frontier Province, but sizeable minorities of them are scattered elsewhere.

Since the arrival of the Afghan refugees, the Baluchis make up only about a quarter of the people of Baluchistan. Surprisingly, there are more Baluchis in the Punjab and Sind than in Baluchistan, and some have settled in Afghanistan and the USSR. The Baluchis claim to be the first converts to Islam after the Arabs. They may have come from Syria and spread through southern Persia before invading Baluchistan. Baluchi is an Indo-Aryan language resembling Farsi (Persian).

Baluchistan has been inhabited for 50,000 years, first by Stone Age hunters and then, before 9000 BC, by settled villagers who collected wild barley and learned how to domesticate goats. According to the French archaeologist Professor Jarrige, by 6000 BC farmers on the Bolan River were cultivating barley and wheat, using flood irrigation and storing their surplus in large mud bins. Sheep, humped cattle and buffalo had also been domesticated by this time. The people here later discovered how to make pottery, and by 4000 BC they were using the potter's wheel and exporting their superior ware to Iran and Afghanistan. Two millennia later they were growing summer crops of rice, millet and sorghum and had tamed horses, donkeys and camels. This early Baluchistan culture, which developed midway between Mesopotamia and the Indus, may well have been the precursor of the great civilizations that evolved in those areas.

Overpopulation and grazing led to a dramatic fall in Baluchistan's productivity. Only in the last 30 years have irrigation and improved farming methods reclaimed parts of the region, giving some idea of what the landscape must have looked like in prehistoric times.

The tribes of Baluchistan have never really been subjugated, though through the centuries they have alternately paid tribute to Persia and India. Proud, uncompromising and inaccessible, they are not easily disciplined by outsiders. In the later 15th century the great warrior (and lover) Mir Chakkar Rind united the main Baluchi tribes with his sword and eloquent words, and also ruled over southern Afghanistan and parts of the Punjab and Sind. For the next three centuries Baluchistan was governed by the Sufavids, Moghuls and Ghilzais. With the support of Nadir Shah of Persia, the khans of Kalat rose to power under the Ghilzais and united the Brahui tribes.

The British first came to Baluchistan during the First Afghan War (1839–42), when their armies marched through the territories of the khan of Kalat on their way to Kandahar. Although the khan was assassinated in 1839, the British returned the occupied lands to his heir after withdrawing from Afghanistan.

After the annexation of the Punjab the British pursued their forward policy of strengthening the borders of British India against possible Russian invasion. In 1876 Sir Robert Sandeman was appointed agent to the governor-general in Baluchistan, by 1887 most of the area was in British hands, and in 1893 the Durand Line between British India and Afghanistan was fixed. But British rule in Baluchistan and the North-West Frontier areas was much less direct than in other parts of British India.

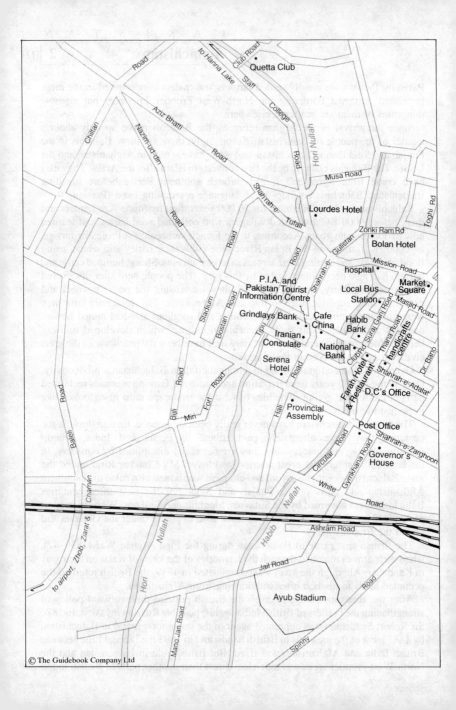

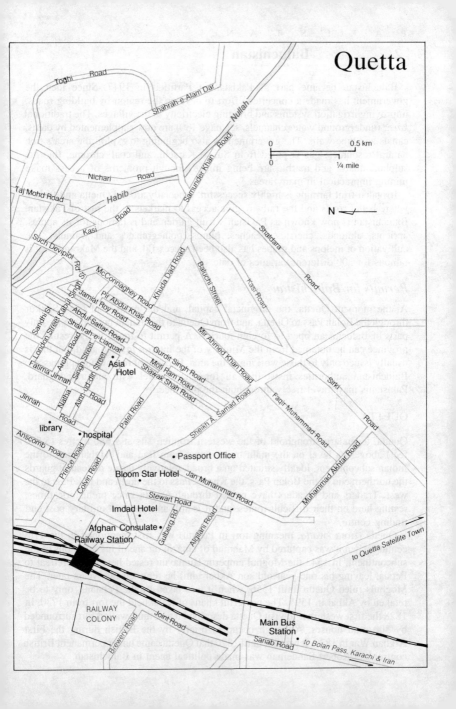

Quetta

Baluchistan became part of Pakistan at Partition in 1947. Since then the government has made a concerted effort to develop the region by building roads, improving irrigation systems and bringing electricity to the villages. The traditional *karez* (underground water channels, see page 130) are now supplemented by dams, canals and tube wells. The government is also beginning to exploit the area's rich natural resources: gas is piped from Sui to Karachi, and coal, chrome, fluorite, sulphur, quartz and marble are being mined, though problems of access make mining impractical in many areas.

Irrigated fruit farming is highly successful, especially around Quetta and Pishin, where better roads and the railway give access to markets in the rest of Pakistan. Baluchistan is now known as Pakistan's fruit garden and is famous for its apples, apricots, almonds, cherries, peaches, plums, pomegranates and walnuts. The cultivation of melons and grapes has also been successful, and the Makran Coast is famous for 300 different varieties of date.

Permits for Baluchistan

At the moment Quetta, the provincial capital, and the main road from Sukkur through the Bolan Pass to Quetta, and from Quetta to the Iranian border, are the only parts of Baluchistan open to foreign tourists. A permit to travel in the rest of the province can be obtained from the Ministry of the Interior in Islamabad, but this is usually issued only to those working in the area. Because of recent kidnappings, the Baluchistan authorities insist that all foreigners travel with an armed guard. Pakistanis may travel freely throughout the province.

QUETTA

Quetta, legendary stronghold of the western frontier, sits at 1,680 metres (5,500 feet) above sea level on the main trade routes from Iran and Afghanistan to the Indian subcontinent. Ideally situated on a broad, relatively fertile plateau, it guards the northern end of the Bolan Pass, the Khojak Pass to the north and Lak Pass to the west. Traders and invaders have passed through Quetta since prehistoric times, resting here on their difficult routes, and it is still an important military post and trading centre.

Quetta (from *kwatta*, meaning fort in Pushtu) was first mentioned in the 11th century when it was captured by Mahmud of Ghazni on one of his invasions of the subcontinent. In 1543 the Moghul emperor Humayun rested here on his retreat to Persia, leaving his one-year-old son Akbar until he returned two years later. The Moghuls ruled Quetta until 1556, when it was taken by the Persians, only to be retaken by Akbar in 1595. The powerful khans of Kalat held the fort from 1730. In 1828 the first westerner to visit Quetta described it as a mud-walled fort surrounded by 300 mud houses. Although occupied briefly by the British during the First Afghan War in 1839, it was not until 1876 that Quetta came under permanent British control and Robert Sandeman was made political agent in Baluchistan.

Since Partition the population of Quetta has increased dramatically. Because of its military base and trading activities, and the introduction of commercial fruit farming, Quetta District can now support half a million people.

Getting to Quetta

Quetta can be reached by daily air and rail services or by road. The four roads from the rest of Pakistan to Quetta are from Karachi via Las Bela and Kalat (about 713 kilometres, 443 miles, or ten to 12 hours—permit required for foreigners); from Sukkur via Jacobabad, Sibi and the Bolan Pass (406 kilometres, 252 miles, or six to eight hours); from Dera Ghazi Khan via Fort Munro and Loralai (529 kilometres, 329 miles, or 13 to 15 hours—jeeps only, permit required); and from Dera Ismail Khan via Zhob and Muslimbagh (about 16 hours—jeeps only, permit required). Quetta is also connected by road with Kandahar in Afghanistan via the Khojak Pass (113 kilometres, 70 miles, or three hours to the border at Chaman—closed to foreigners), and with Zahidan in Iran, a long haul of 724 kilometres (450 miles) across the desert (608 kilometres or 378 miles to the border).

When to Go

The best times to visit Quetta are March through May and September and October, when it is cool at night and not above 30°C (86°F) during the day.

Where to Stay

Moderate: Rs200–800

Serena, Shahrah-e-Zarghun (Lytton Road), tel. 70070–9, Telex 7821 Serena PK (s/d Rs700/800). Swimming pool, tennis and squash courts.

Lourdes, Staff College Road, tel. 70145, 71142–3, 70168–9, 70839 (s/d Rs200/ 300–500). Camping allowed in the garden.

Cheaper: Rs50–300

Gul's Inn, near Jinnah Road, behind Nile Hotel, tel. 70170, 70175, 701178 (s/d Rs250/300).

Marina, Querry Road, tel. 75109 (s/d Rs120/180).

Nile, Jinnah Road, tel. 70736, 77595 (s/d Rs90/135).

Chilton, Jinnah Road, tel. 75635 (s/d Rs85/120).

Imdad, Jinnah Road, tel. 70166, 70167 (s/d Rs50/80).

Al-Muazzam, Jinnah Road, tel. 75884 (s/d Rs45/70).

Al-Shamas, Jinnah Road, tel. 74111 (s/d Rs45/50).

Muslim, Jinnah Road, tel. 74938 (Rs35/55).

Asia, Fateh Muhammad Road, tel. 75181, 73840 (s/d Rs30/45).

Railway Retiring Rooms.

Where to Eat

Serena Hotel, international standard, expensive but worth it.
Cafe China, Staff College Road, tel. 74728. Chinese, moderately priced.

Do not be afraid to eat cheaply on the street. Quetta is famous for its lamb dishes:
try the *sajji* (steamed leg of lamb) at the Lehri Sajji House off Jinnah Road; also
recommended are 'joint' (tender roast lamb) at the Lal Kebab Restaurant on Prince
Road, and 'roast' (another special roast dish) at the Cafe Farah. Other amusing
places to eat are Mir Afzal Karai Kabab Centre and Karam Chat Wala, both on
Circular Road opposite the Caltex petrol pump, and both specialists in *karai tikka*
(braised lamb), which is ordered by weight and cooked in huge pans on the street.
If you are adventurous, try their fried brain and grilled lamb's balls. There are two
Afghan restaurants on Masjid Road, both worth trying, and another on Suraj Road.

Sights

Quetta town was almost completely destroyed in the great earthquake of 1935, when
35,000 people were killed, trapped in their ruined houses in the early hours of 31
May. In the new town, single-storey buildings are set along tree-lined roads that
intersect at clearly labelled roundabouts, and there is a well-maintained administrative centre and thriving university.

The **main bazaar** on Jinnah Road is full of Pathan traders wearing huge turbans,
Baluchi hawkers with red embroidered caps, and full-skirted nomad women
carrying bundles of imported cloth for sale. It is always crowded and colourful. Here
you will also find most of the hotels, restaurants, banks (a notice outside asks you
to enter unarmed), chemists, handicraft and carpet shops, the PTDC Information
Office and the PIA Office.

Baluchi mirror-work embroidery, jackets, fur coats, sandals, Afghan carpets
onyx, semiprecious stones, dried fruit and nuts are the best buys in the bazaar. The
Kandahari Bazaar on Iqbal Road, which crosses Jinnah Road at right angles, and
the **Liaqat Bazaar** on Liaqat Road, are also good hunting grounds for Baluchi
souvenirs. The government offices, Governor's House, new Assembly Hall and
General Post Office are all on Shahrah Zarghun Road (or Lytton Road, or The
Mall—like many towns in Pakistan, Quetta has officially changed the names of its
streets several times; all are still in use).

The **Quetta Staff College**, modelled after Britain's Sandhurst and attended by
such famous men as Auchinleck and Montgomery, has a small museum which is
well worth a visit if you are interested in recent British military history. The
National Museum, just off Jinnah Road, has a good collection of antique arms.
Both museums are usually open to the public 9 am–7 pm except Friday.

While digging the foundations for the Serena Hotel in March 1985, the workers
found an undisturbed **Indus Civilization grave** that dates from 2500–2000 BC. Of
great interest to archaeologists is a cache of gold, copper and stone ornaments found
nearby; the most striking objects are a fishbowl and two gold bulls with long curving

horns. The finds seem to indicate that Quetta was a prosperous settlement before 2000 BC. Though still in Quetta in 1987, the objects were not yet on public display. As they rank among Pakistan's most prized antiques, they merit the trouble of getting special permission from the district commissioner to see them.

A drive out along Brewery Road past the Medical College and Tuberculosis Hospital leads to **Chiltan Hill**. A steep paved road, for jeeps only, winds up to the **Earthquake Recording Office** from where there is a panoramic view down over Quetta. The broad plain behind the town stretches up to the backdrop of Mordar (Dead) Mountain, 3,185 metres (10,449 feet) above sea level. To the far left is Takatu Mountain, 3,455 metres (11,335 feet); mid-left is Zarghun (Green) Mountain, 3,583 metres (11,755 feet), with the road to the picturesque Urak Valley between them. Behind you, completing the rim of mountains around Quetta, is Chiltan (Forty Souls) Mountain, 3,308 metres (10,853 feet). According to local legend, an impoverished couple had 40 sons, and as each was born he was left on the mountain to die. When the parents took their last son to the mountain, the other 39 miraculously appeared, took their youngest sibling and vanished. The children are thought to haunt Chiltan Mountain to this day, luring lone travellers up the slopes and never allowing them to return.

There is a golf course, flying and gliding club, swimming pool, cricket ground and riding stable in Quetta. Ask your local hotel or the PTDC (tel. 72053) for details.

Outings from Quetta

There are checkposts on all the roads leaving Quetta.

From the end of March till the end of April the whole plain around Quetta is tinged with green—even the stony slopes of the hills. Red and yellow tulips, wild hyacinth, iris, wild lavender, aniseed and small red poppies are scattered among the rocks. The orchards, fed from modern tube wells, burst into white, pink and red blossom. The winter wheat makes vivid green patches at the ends of the karez, ancient underground water channels which can be recognized by the line of access holes. surrounded by piles of earth at regular 50-metre (150-foot) intervals. The karez drain water from the side of the valley, where the water table is higher, down to the fields in the centre of the plain.

In May the cherries are harvested, the wheat turns golden and the green vanishes; June sees the apricots ripen and the wheat harvested. Then the long hot summer burns everything that is not irrigated to a crisp brown. October brings the glorious autumn colours and ripe apples. In winter the hills are covered with a blanket of snow and the temperature can drop to −15°C (5°F).

Hanna Lake nestles in the hills ten kilometres (six miles) east of Quetta, a startling turquoise pool within bare brown surroundings. There is a lakeside restaurant with picnic tables shaded by pine trees. You can hire a boat and paddle on the lake and round the island in the middle. To get there take Staff College Road out past the Quetta Club and the School of Infantry, turn after the Staff College and head for Zarghun Mountain. After seven kilometres (4.3 miles) the road forks by a tiny 'hotel' (local restaurant) where you can buy delicious 'roast' (tender lamb) and naan for Rs10 a portion. The righthand fork goes round the back of Mordar Mountain. Take the left fork for Hanna Lake and Urak; the road soon forks again, left to Hanna Lake two kilometres (one mile) away, and right for the eight-kilometre (five-mile) drive up the **Urak Valley**, which is full of orchards; in April cherry, apricot, apple and peach trees form a tunnel of blossom over the road.

Urak, at the top end of the valley, is a village of square, mud houses roofed with roots and mud laid across wooden beams. The village is surrounded on three sides by the Zarghun range of hills. A stream rushes down from Urak Tangi, a narrow gorge in the hills; a short walk will take you up onto the lower slopes where partridge call among the rocks and you can look down on the whole valley. In the little water mill beside the stream two round stones grind wheat into flour.

The two-hour drive round the back of Mordar Mountain leads you 70 kilometres (43 miles) away to the main Quetta-Bolan Pass road. The round trip reveals the complete range of Baluchistan countryside: orchards, reservoir, gorge, hills, coal mines, plains and nomads. To get there, turn right at the local restaurant seven kilometres (four miles) from Quetta on the road to Hanna Lake and Urak. **Spin Karez**, a small reservoir about 15 kilometres (nine miles) from the road fork by the

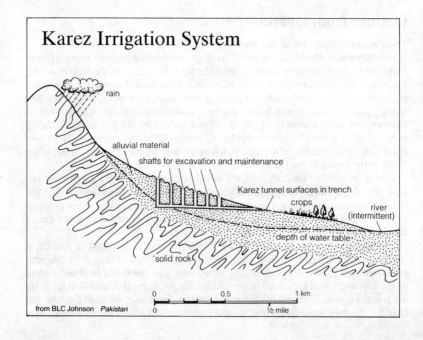

Karez Irrigation System

rain

alluvial material

shafts for excavation and maintenance

Karez tunnel surfaces in trench

crops

river (intermittent)

depth of water table

solid rock

from BLC Johnson *Pakistan*

0   0.5   1 km

0   ½ mile

local restaurant, lies amid the eroded hills. Only shrubs and coarse tufted grasses grow here. For another 35 kilometres (22 miles) the road twists through reddish hills, the white mineheads conspicuous on both flanks. Piles of coal beside the road await collection and transportation by truck to Quetta. The last 20 kilometres (12 miles) take you across the flat plain and past mud-walled settlements where farmers grow wheat, barley, millet, pulses and maize. Camels or oxen pull the ploughs across the light soil, the farmer's wife following behind and scattering seed. Camels also haul water up out of wells that may be up to 40 metres (130 feet) deep. When not in use the wells are covered and locked to prevent animals falling in or others using the water.

In March and April, and later in September and October, caravans of nomads stream across the plains with their herds of camel and sheep, heading up towards Afghanistan in spring and down towards Sind in autumn (see page 140).

You join the main Bolan Pass-Quetta road about five kilometres (three miles) from **Kolpur** gateway to the Bolan Pass, a lively bazaar that has not changed much in centuries. You can make a detour to visit Kolpur before returning to Quetta. Alternatively, you can cut across to the west for about 20 kilometres (12 miles) on the road to Iran along the foot of the Chiltan Hills and over the **Lak Pass** to the customs checkpost. Here the road divides: left to Kalat and Karachi; right to Iran.

The road back to Quetta from Lak Pass goes past the **Hazar Gunji Chiltan National Park**, a fenced area where grass, shrubs and trees grow unmolested, giving some idea of what the whole Quetta plateau would be like if left ungrazed. The Natural History Museum by the gate stood empty in 1987. A good dirt road leads five kilometres (three miles) through the park to two charming, fully equipped rest houses, bookable through the Forestry Department, Quetta. With their back to the Chiltan Hills and a magnificent view down over the plateau and up to the Lak Pass, these rest houses provide a peaceful place to spend a weekend. The park is about 20 kilometres (12 miles) from Quetta and nine kilometres (six miles) from the Quetta-Bolan Pass road.

Ziarat

No trip to Quetta is complete without a visit to the mountain resort of Ziarat, 122 kilometres (76 miles) away to the northeast. At 2,460 metres (8,200 feet), it is pleasantly cool in summer and under snow from December to April. Developed by the British as a summer retreat, Ziarat offers colonial-style accommodation and pleasant walks through the surrounding juniper forest. Ziarat has retained the air of a peaceful British hill station.

Where to Stay

PTDC Motel, tel. Ziarat 15 (Rs230 double). Comfortable but expensive.
Ziarat Hotel, tel. 68 (s/d Rs60/100). Cheap, adequate and quiet.
Grand Hotel, tel. 17 (Rs25 double). Cheap and adequate.

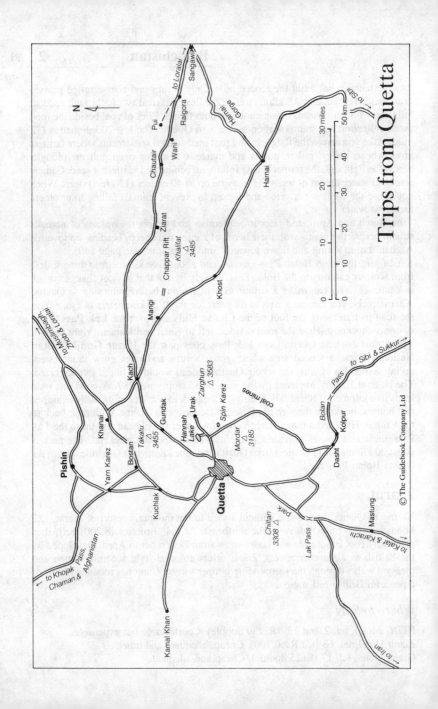

Trips from Quetta

© The Guidebook Company Ltd

Sanubar Hotel, tel. 16 (Rs25 double). Cheap, with dormitories.

All are heavily booked during the summer and closed in winter.

Getting to Ziarat

Three buses and three minibuses ply daily between Quetta and Ziarat. The PTDC rents minibuses and guides, and there are several private taxi companies. Without stops it is a drive of two hours or more. You can go up by public transport and hire a vehicle and guide in Ziarat at either the PTDC, Ziarat or Grand hotels. Ideally, you should allow a minimum of two nights in Ziarat.

There are two roads to Kach, halfway to Ziarat; those with private transport are recommended to go up by one and return by the other.

The main (bus) route to Kach leaves Quetta on the Chaman Road past the Christian cemetery, with its poignantly worded headstones, and the airport. Karez run down from the base of the hills on the right to the fields and villages along the railway.

Kuchlak, 24 kilometres (15 miles) from Quetta, is a busy, colourful bazaar where you can eat excellent 'joint' at roadside stalls. Here the road to Ziarat, Zhob and Loralai branches off to the right at an unmarked and easily missed turning halfway down the main bazaar. Head for the hills and skirt round the northern side of **Takatu Mountain**, past orchards watered by karez and tube wells. Pathan houses, 50 metres (yards) square and built like forts with crenellated walls, corner towers, gun holes and huge corrugated iron gates, guard the orchards. A line of extraordinary eroded red hills rears up in the distance. In warm weather, dust-devil whirlwinds rise from the plain like pillars holding up the sky.

The road forks shortly after **Khanai**, about 25 kilometres (15 miles) from Kuchlak; bear left for Muslimbagh and Zhob; right for Kach and Ziarat. Loralai can be reached by either road. It is faster but longer and less scenic via Muslimbagh, but in winter, when the Ziarat road is blocked by snow, you have to go via Muslimbagh.

As the Ziarat road curves up into the hills there is an immediate change of scenery. The eroded slopes—red and green or black and grey, depending on their mineral composition—are so barren that the pass over to Kach is completely deserted. The road follows the line of the disused railway that once connected Khanai to Sibi but which was washed out by floods in 1942 and never repaired.

The **alternative route from Quetta to Kach**, a dirt road in good condition and usually just passable in an ordinary car, is 20 kilometres (12 miles) shorter than the main road and more scenic. It leaves Quetta on the road to Hanna Lake. Just past the Staff College, Kach Road goes straight north past the Quetta Communication Centre and Army Aviation Base, crosses the Hanna River and winds round between Takatu and Zarghun mountains. Kach Dam has burst and washed out the road below it for a few hundred metres (yards) at the entrance to the hills; in 1987 this was the only bad stretch on the whole road. From the ruined guest house above the dam there is a panoramic view down to Quetta and across the reedy bed of the empty reservoir.

The climb up to the pass on the saddle between Takatu and Zarghun is dotted with twisted juniper trees and nomads tending herds of sheep and goats. The road winds down to **Gundak**, a village in a hollow with a fort and irrigated orchards. From here the hills are extraordinary: some appear to be made of trickled mud; others vary in colour depending on the minerals they contain. Further on, the hills comprise layers of limestone with deep fine striations, and have been thrown up vertically looking for all the world like huge upright slabs of mille-feuille pastry. It is 52 kilometres (32 miles) to Kach by this route.

Kach, with its little fort on a hill, is strategically positioned at a crossroads (where buses now make a rest stop). Before the British leased the Bolan Pass from the khan of Kalat in 1883, the main route, from Sibi to Quetta was via Harnai and Kach. The British built a rail link along this route, and planned a branch line to Ziarat which was never completed. Today the trains run from Sibi as far as **Khost**, about 60 kilometres (37 miles) southeast of Kach. North of Khost there are scenic walks with good hunting along stretches of the unused railway through dramatic cuttings and tunnels. One of the access points is three kilometres (two miles) beyond **Mangi**, about 20 kilometres (12 miles) from Kach on the road to Harnai. Here you can explore the exciting **Chappar Rift**, a narrow limestone gorge nearly 100 metres (300 feet) deep, from where there are superb views of **Mount Khalifat**, at 3,485 metres (11,434 feet) the highest peak in Baluchistan. It is a 33-kilometre (20-mile) walk, jeepable part of the way, from Mangi through the deep gorge of Mir Kasim to Ziarat.

If you drive on down to **Harnai** you can stay in the Community Development rest house, bookable through the assistant commissioner in Harnai. From Harnai a jeep track cuts north through Harnai Gorge to Sanjawi on the Ziarat-Loralai road, the most spectacular of the passes linking the plains with the uplands. This road is not for the fainthearted, as it runs along a ledge blasted out of the side of a sheer cliff 300 metres (1,000 feet) above the river. At one point a sign reads 'Harnai Gorge—danger of blowing off'; apparently at certain times of year the gorge is subjected to furious convectional air currents. The round trip, out through Harnai and back through Ziarat, is supposed to be the most beautiful in all Baluchistan.

Kach to Ziarat

A scenic drive, with inviting jeep tracks up side valleys to left and right, and footpaths leading into narrow gorges on either side, covers the 53 kilometres (33 miles) from Kach to Ziarat.

The road climbs past **Cheena** to **Ziarat Point**, 15 kilometres (nine miles) from Kach, and is guarded on the north by a line of crenellated limestone hills that resembles a fortress wall. Gnarled juniper trees dot the hills on either side of the pass. The road then winds down through **Wam** to the fruit orchards surrounding **Kahan**. On the right the river flows through **Kahan Tangi**, a narrow limestone gorge; to reach it, park as close to the river as you can get and walk downstream. At **Kawas**,

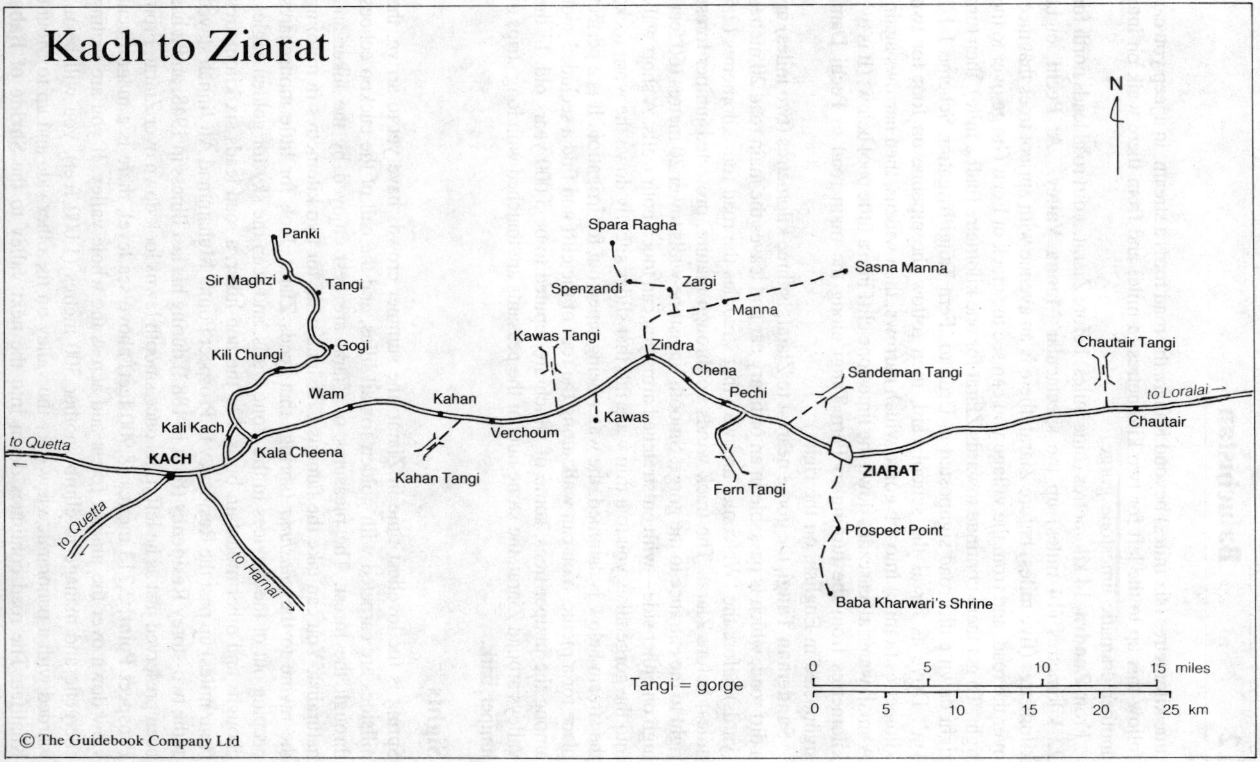

Kach to Ziarat

to Loralai

Chautair Tangi

Chautair

Sasna Manna

ZIARAT

Sandeman Tangi

Prospect Point

Baba Kharwari's Shrine

Manna

Fern Tangi

Zargi

Pechi

Chena

Spara Ragha

Zindra

Spenzandi

Kawas

Kawas Tangi

Verchoum

Kahan

Kahan Tangi

Panki

Tangi

Sir Maghzi

Gogi

Wam

Kili Chungi

Kala Cheena

to Harnai

Kali Kach

KACH

to Quetta

Tangi = gorge

| 0 | 5 | 10 | 15 | 20 | 25 km |
| 0 | 5 | 10 | 15 miles |

© The Guidebook Company Ltd

nine kilometres (six miles) beyond Kahan, the road fords a stream; in a jeep you can follow this up to the left for two kilometres (a mile) and from there walk on into another dramatic limestone gorge.

From **Zandra**, 14 kilometres (nine miles) before Ziarat, a dirt road leads north for 22 kilometres (14 miles) up the spectacular **Manna Valley**. At **Pechi**, eight kilometres (five miles) before Ziarat, there is an avenue with apricot trees that meet over the road, and from the village you can see the crack of **Fern Gorge** over to the right. To get there continue towards Ziarat for one kilometre (half a mile), then turn right down a dirt road signposted in Urdu to 'Fern Tangi Irrigation Scheme 1 1/2 km'. Drive as far as the school yard, then follow the pipeline on foot for two kilometres (a mile) into the gorge which narrows, then widens, then narrows again. A small waterfall cascades down the limestone cliff into a little pool below. (It is two kilometres from the turning to Fern Tangi along the main road to Pechi Dam, signposted in English, on the right.)

Sandeman Tangi, the gorge nearest to Ziarat, is three kilometres (two miles) up a dirt road, which is passable in an ordinary car and leaves the main road 20 metres (yards) before the 'Welcome' archway that straddles the road four kilometres (2.5 miles) before Ziarat. The track winds up through mature, protected juniper forest right to the entrance to the gorge. Smooth limestone walls tower 20 metres (60 feet) high on either side—with outstretched arms you can touch both walls. A short walk into the gorge takes you to a thin waterfall that slides silently down the worn rock; the stream below is dammed, the water being piped out for irrigation. It is a perfect place for a picnic. You can walk along the foot of the cliff and find a secluded spot among the juniper trees, some of which are reputed to be 5,000 years old. In the valleys around Ziarat, the stone huts of the peasants are thatched with long strips of juniper bark.

Sights

Spring is the loveliest time in Ziarat: the summer crowds have yet to arrive, the hillsides are carpeted with golden foxtail lilies, and the call of the cuckoo echoes through the forest. The pleasures of Ziarat are best enjoyed by the hiker and naturalist. You can take the famous Chashma walk for two kilometres (a mile) up the ravine to the *chashma* (spring) that feeds Ziarat, look for little mousehares peeping out of the crevices in the stone walls, and scan the sky for golden eagles, choughs and other mountain birds. For the non-hiker, a road leads six kilometres (four miles) up past the Residency to Prospect Point. Muhammad Ali Jinnah stayed at the two-storey **Residency** (built in 1882) during his last illness in 1948, and it has been preserved just as he left it. Its once smooth lawns look down over Ziarat. From **Prospect Point**, 2,713 metres (8,900 feet) above sea level, there is a magnificent view down over the juniper forest and across the whole valley. If you are feeling energetic and manage to climb another 300 metres (1,000 feet), you will be rewarded with a panoramic view over the valley on the other side and up to Mount Khalifat. The road continues down into the next valley to the **Shrine of Baba**

Kharwari. (*Ziarat* means shrine, and it is after the shrine of this Afghan saint from Kandahar that the town of Ziarat is named.)

Ziarat to Dera Ghazi Khan via Fort Munro

The road from Ziarat continues through more juniper forest and fruit orchards to the picturesque valley of **Chautair**, 23 kilometres (14 miles) away. A road to the left before Chautair leads to **Chautair Tangi**, perhaps the most spectacular gorge of all, and the secret gateway to a hidden valley beyond. The distance between Chautair and Loralai is 70 kilometres (43 miles); the road descends through **Wani** to **Raigora**, and from here a track leads left for 22 kilometres (14 miles) to **Pui**, which is famous for a spring that appears to gush straight out of a rock. A few kilometres (miles) further down the main road to Loralai is the turning south for **Harnai** (see page 134). From **Sanjawi** to Loralai the road is reasonably well paved and runs across barren, rolling hills.

Despite its romantic name, **Loralai** comes as something of a disappointment after the charm of Ziarat and Chautair. It is a dusty, flat cantonment town, famous for its almonds and pomegranates. VIPs can stay in the Circuit House, bookable through the commissioner, Loralai; otherwise there are only local 'hotels'. In former times Loralai suffered much from the attentions of the ferocious Murri people who, together with their neighbours the Bugti, are still considered two of Baluchistan's wildest tribes.

The distance from Loralai to **Fort Munro** on the crest of the Sulaiman Mountains (just over the border in the Punjab) is 200 kilometres (124 miles); the partially surfaced road is known as the Robber Road, and you will be grateful for your armed escort. The landscape is barren and rubble-strewn, the hills dramatically contoured and striated. The road descends to cross a dusty plain, where gusting winds can whip the powdery soil up into a sandstorm and reduce the visibility to almost nothing, before turning south and rising gradually to cross the Sulaimans to the Punjab and Dera Ghazi Khan (see pages 151–2).

Quetta to Dera Ismail Khan via Zhob

The **Zhob Valley**, the northernmost valley in Baluchistan, is populated mostly by Pathans. Though relatively fertile by Baluchistan standards and reasonably accessible, it is seldom visited by foreigners because getting a permit is particularly difficult.

It is an eight-hour trip on one of the five public buses that run daily from Quetta to Zhob, with a stop at Muslimbagh en route. The train runs only once a week and is extremely slow. If you are driving yourself, follow the Ziarat road to Khanai via Kuchlak for the first 50 kilometres (31 miles) from Quetta, then take the left fork, which is signposted in English, for the remaining 68 kilometres (42 miles) to Muslimbagh. The road follows the railway, climbs up out of the Quetta Valley, crossing the continental watershed at **Kan Mehtarzai Pass** on the way, and then

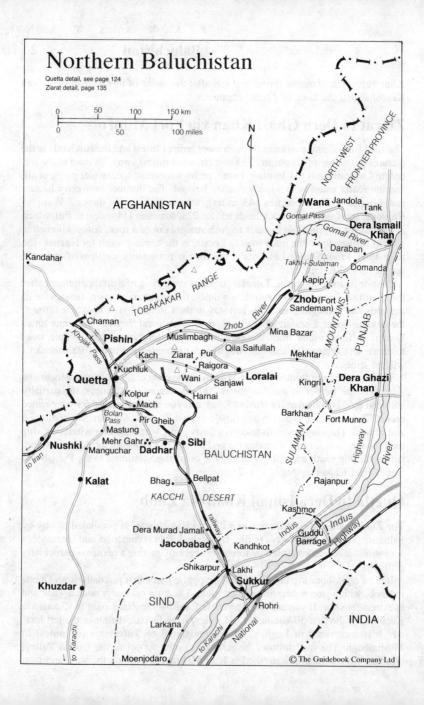

Northern Baluchistan

Quetta detail, see page 124
Ziarat detail, page 135

0   50   100   150 km

0   50   100 miles

N

AFGHANISTAN

NORTH-WEST FRONTIER PROVINCE

Wana   Jandola   Tank

Gomal Pass

Gomal River

Dera Ismail Khan

Daraban

Takht-i-Sulaiman

Domanda

Kandahar

Kapip

TOBAKAKAR   RANGE

Zhob   River

Zhob (Fort Sandeman)

SULAIMAN   MOUNTAINS

PUNJAB

Chaman

Khojak   pass

Zhob

Mina Bazar

Pishin

Muslimbagh   Qila Saifullah

Kach   Ziarat   Pui

Mekhtar

Kuchluk   Raigora

Wani   Sanjawi   Loralai

Dera Ghazi Khan

Quetta

Kolpur

Mach   Harnai

Kingri

Bolan Pass

Pir Gheib

Barkhan   Fort Munro

Mastung

Mehr Gahr   Sibi

SULAIMAN

Nushki   Manguchar   Dadhar

BALUCHISTAN

Highway

River

Kalat

Bhag   Bellpat

Rajanpur

KACCHI   DESERT

railway

Kashmor

Dera Murad Jamali

Indus   Indus

Guddu Barrage

Highway

Jacobabad   Kandhkot

Khuzdar

Shikarpur   Lakhi

Sukkur

to Iran

SIND

Rohri

INDIA

to Karachi

Larkana

National

Moenjodaro

to Karachi

© The Guidebook Company Ltd

follows the River Zhob down again. The rivers in the Quetta Valley drain into the central Asian watershed; the Zhob drains into the Indus via the Gomal River. The highest railway station in Asia is just over the top of the pass at the small village of **Kan Mehtarzai**, 2,222 metres (7,290 feet) above sea level. In May and June the hillsides are covered with lavender and hyacinth. Pathan men stride around with bunches of flowers tucked in their hats, and the women of the nomadic Powindah tribe, who are often seen working in the fields or fetching water, usually wear full-skirted dresses over baggy trousers and large shawls, all in bright red. The brightness of their clothes is to save them from being shot by mistake. The Pathan men are all armed and are always involved in family feuds which do not include the women.

About 12 kilometres (seven miles) before Muslimbagh, the spectacular **Kanchogi Gorge** leads off to the left up into the **Toba Kakar Mountains** with Pathan villages on either side.

Muslimbagh, at 1,774 metres (5,820 feet), has prospered because of its chromite mine. Known before Partition as Hindubagh, it is a well-watered oasis surrounded by fruit orchards and wheat fields and has a comfortable rest house, bookable through the sub-divisional magistrate, Muslimbagh.

It takes about four hours to cover the 212 kilometres (132 miles) from Muslimbagh to Zhob, following the railway and the Zhob River all the way. The turning south to Loralai is at **Qila Saifullah**, famous for its pistachio nuts.

Zhob, at 1,428 metres (4,605 feet), used to be called Fort Sandeman after Sir Robert Sandeman, one-time political agent in Baluchistan; before that it was known as Appozai. Four flights a week connect the local airport to Islamabad, Peshawar, Dera Ismail Khan, Quetta and Multan. There are a few government rest houses where you might be able to spend the night.

The small town of Zhob is divided into cantonment and bazaar areas and is overlooked by two rocky fort-topped hills. The famous Zhob militia live on one, and the political agent lives in **Sandeman's Fort** on the other. The two strongholds are linked by an underground passage, used in times of trouble.

The Zhob Valley has been inhabited since at least 3000 BC. It is ideally situated near the **Gomal Pass**, one of the most important prehistoric trade routes from central Asia to the subcontinent, and preliminary archaeological excavations have revealed several caches of early pottery.

You can make a scenic trip north from Zhob up the Old Valley Road on the east side of the Zhob River to **Brunj Kili** (Brunj Weir), and then back down the west side to **Malazai** on a wonderful switchback road with spectacular views of the mountains. Or you can continue on the Old Valley Road through the **Godray Pass** close to the Afghan border and across the wide Gomal River into South Waziristan, North-West Frontier Province, then through tribal territory to Jandola and Tank, a journey of 247 kilometres (153 miles)(see page 300). The route to Tank via Domanda and Daraban is about 50 kilometres (30 miles) shorter and along a better road.

It is 180 kilometres (112 miles) east from Zhob to **Dera Ismail Khan**. The road winds up through **Kapip**, past steeply terraced vineyards and a new weir. At the top

of the pass across the Sulaiman Mountains there are magnificent views left to
Takht-e-Sulaiman (Soloman's Throne), 3,473 metres (11,290 feet). From the pass
the road descends into the North-West Frontier Province, then via Moghul Kot,
Domanda and Daraban to D I Khan.

Quetta to Sukkur via the Bolan Pass and Sibi

The easiest and most comfortable land route from Quetta to the rest of Pakistan is
via the Bolan Pass, Sibi and Jacobabad to Sukkur. This is the only route for which
you do not need a permit and an armed guard. Buses leave every hour, and there are
several trains daily. It is five hours by bus to Sibi, ten hours to Sukkur. The road is
paved all the way, and in a private car it takes six or eight hours to Sukkur. It takes
about 12 hours by train.

The road south from Quetta to the top of the Bolan Pass follows the railway across
the wide plain, a rocky sea of alluvial gravel that in April is tinged green. The railway
stations of Spezand and Kilidur are lonely platforms in the middle of nowhere.

Kolpur, about 25 kilometres (15 miles) from Quetta, guards the entrance to the
Bolan Pass. An ancient settlement set in a hollow just above the continental
watershed, it is the last place before Sibi to stock up with fruit. In spring and autumn
when the nomads are migrating, you can be held up at Kolpur Bridge by a traffic
jam of laden camels and donkeys as they come up out of the river bed and cross to
the plains of Quetta.

In prehistoric times the **Bolan Pass** was the main route from central Asia to the
subcontinent. It was easier and more hospitable than the Khyber Pass and, as far
back as 50,000 years ago, attracted groups of neolithic nomads who hunted along
the Bolan River. As early as 7000 BC, the settled villagers at the southern end of the
pass were importing lapis and turquoise along this route, and today it is the chief
route to Pakistan from Iran and southern Afghanistan.

The British first passed through here in 1839, on their way to fight the First
Afghan War. In 1883 the British permanently leased the pass from the khan of Kalat
(in return for which the British awarded the khan the privilege of a 21-gun salute,
normally accorded only to the British monarchy), and the following year the whole
of Baluchistan was in their hands. The railway through the pass to Quetta was
completed in 1886; before this the rail link to Quetta was via Harnai.

Officially the pass is 96 kilometres (60 miles) long, but the dramatic narrow gorge
spans only the first 15 kilometres (ten miles). The railway, river and road weave a
plaited path, crossing and recrossing each other; the railway crosses the river nine
times and threads in and out of tunnels. High cliffs enclose the stony river bed, which
is dry most of the year but prone to occasional disastrous flash floods in summer.
An entire British detachment was drowned here in 1841, and the first railway was
washed out in 1889 and had to be completely rebuilt on a new alignment.

Between March and April, and September and October, the nomads lead their
camel caravans in single file along the river bed. Pregnant women, small children,
young lambs and chickens, are piled on the camels on top of tents and water barrels,

and pots and pans are tied on behind. The rest of the women drive donkeys laden with household equipment, small children and chickens along the road. Young men and boys take sheep and goats across the hilltops to graze, somehow managing to keep the herds apart. The families camp in black tents along the way. It takes each family about two weeks to complete the migration.

From the road you can scramble down the side of the gorge and walk along the river bed against the tide of nomads, who are friendly and cheerful, and happy to be photographed. The dogs, however, are very fierce, so take care.

Once out of the gorge, the dry, stony river bed spreads out with an occasional tree and patches of grass along its edge. The Koh-e-Bash Hotel, a local restaurant with charpoys under the trees, is a pleasant place to stop for a cup of tea. A little further down, hot springs bubble up at the side of the valley, and a thin ribbon of water finds its way across the stones. Here the nomads do their laundry and the animals collect to drink. The road winds down to **Mach**, a dusty collection of mud huts clustered round the railway station to the left of the road. Mach was the epicentre of the great earthquake of 1935.

From here on the road and railway take different routes through the hills. The river divides into numerous channels and meanders around the low hills on the valley floor, which is about 20 kilometres (12 miles) wide at this point. Shallow coal mines dot the hillsides to left and right.

At **Pir Gheib** hot water pours out of a natural limestone spout in the cliff face into a chain of turquoise pools surrounded by palm trees. Hidden up a gorge 16 kilometres (10 miles) off the main road, it is the most idyllic and romantic place for a secluded swim. To get there, turn shortly after the kilometre post in Urdu which reads 'Sukkur 316 km'; it is four kilometres (2.5 miles) before the Sibi Scouts post at Bibi Nani Bridge. A rocky cliff overshadows the main road on the east, and the wide, stony flood plain of a tributary stretches for about ten kilometres (six miles) to the foot of the hills on the west. A sign in Urdu to the Holy Shrine of Pir Gheib marks the beginning of the rough track across the flood plain. Four-wheel drive is essential here. Allow about two hours for the detour, including time for a swim. Head for the hills, then turn right up a side valley, past an oasis with date palms and wheat fields, and twist down into the next valley dotted with tamarisk trees and patches of wheat. The track follows the base of a mud cliff. Park by a stream about 15 kilometres (ten miles) from the main road, and follow the track for ten minutes along the top of the cliff, about 30 metres (100 feet) above the stream, to the shrine. Follow the stream up behind the shrine to the highest pool, where the water gushes out of the mountain. The main pool is deep and for confident swimmers only—you can swim up to the spout, then rush down with the fast flowing water. Non-swimmers can paddle in the side pool.

Pir Gheib's shrine is a simple grave with a little bamboo pilgrims' shelter nearby, where the shrine attendants serve tea in return for offerings.

There are various other hot springs and secluded pools in these hills. Most of them are more difficult to get to, but your Baluchi friends can show you the way.

Back on the main road it is four kilometres (2.5 miles) to **Bibi Nani's Bridge** where the khan of Kalat battled against the Panni tribe in the 18th century. Legend has it that Bibi Nani, the guardian of the water source, was killed here.

Gokirat (or Gokurt), an oasis 20 kilometres (12 miles) further downriver, is a small bazaar surrounded by date palms and wheat fields. From here it is 18 kilometres (11 miles) to Pinjera Pul, the bridge that carries the road across to the east bank. You now enter the final stretch of the Bolan Pass through a gorge where the road runs on a ledge along the cliff face and passes through a tunnel. Just past the tunnel, on the other side of the river, there is a rock with a hole in it and below it a lovely natural pool where you can swim. In the flooding in August 1986 the water rose ten metres (30 feet) in this gorge and washed away Bibi Nani and Pinjera bridges.

Once out of the gorge you come to **Bolan Weir**. Here there is a comfortable Irrigation Department guest house set in a shady garden with green lawns, and bookable through the deputy commissioner, Kacchi District, Dadhar. The weir and the headworks for the Dadhar Canal are behind the guest house. You can swim here.

The archaeological site of **Mehrgarh** is on the right, about ten kilometres (six miles) off the main road. Several villages dating from 7000 BC onwards have been discovered on the banks of the Bolan River. The sites themselves are important as they give some indication of the development that led to the Indus Civilization and the nature of trade through the Bolan Pass, but there is little for the general tourist to see. The French archaeologist Professor Jarrige excavates here every winter.

Sibi

The area around **Dadhar** is now completely irrigated. It is less than half an hour from there to Sibi, the divisional headquarters at the edge of the Kacchi Desert. Sibi is accessible by air, rail and road. Named after the Sewa Hindu tribe, it was once the capital of Sewistan, one of the seven kingdoms of Sind. Strategically positioned at the entrance to both the Bolan and Harnai passes, and at the junction of the routes from Sind and the Punjab, it has been an important trading post for thousands of years. The present town was laid out in the 1880s by the British, with wide tree-lined streets and an orderly bazaar, and was called Sandemanabad after Sir Robert Sandeman.

Since the 15th century Sibi has been a meeting place for tribal chiefs, and since the 17th century the annual *durbar* (meeting) has been combined with a *mela* (agricultural fair). Today the annual horse and cattle show is an important national festival that lasts for a full week in mid-February and marks the beginning of spring with tournaments, exhibitions, lively trading and public speeches. Thousands of the best camels, horses and cattle in the country are brought to the show and tended by Pakistan's most colourful tribal people.

Sibi is packed during the show, and lodging is difficult to find. There are no tourist hotels, but there are rest houses bookable through the deputy commissioner, a few local hotels, and the **Sohbat Serai** on Jail Road, a 19th-century inn built by a rich Baluchi chief to accommodate visitors to the durbar. The 42 rooms are set around a shaded courtyard with arched verandahs supported by pillars; above each pillar a blue tiled medallion depicts floral sprays and clock faces (every one of which reads three o'clock). Rooms are bookable through the chairman of the District Committee for about Rs5 each. You can also camp.

The **Jirga Hall**, built in 1903 by the British, is now a museum. Its large central hall has galleries at each end and arched windows under the ceiling. During the *jirga* (tribal assembly), the British authorities, the khan of Kalat and the tribal chiefs would sit up in the galleries looking down on the petitioners in the hall below.

The 15th-century **Chakkar Fort**, built by Mir Chakkar Rind, the Baluchi chief who united Baluchistan, is on the road to Sibi Airport. Crumbling mud walls with round bastions enclose the inner fort, which contains two beehive-shaped stores for food and ammunition. The outer fort for the troops runs along the edge of the railway, and is now a big pond where buffalo wallow.

Sibi is unbearably hot in summer. With Jacobabad (see pages 104–5) it has the highest recorded temperature in the subcontinent—54°C (129°F). The commissioner and district administrators all move up to Ziarat in the hills from June to September.

It is a three-hour drive from Sibi to Jacobabad across the **Kacchi Desert**. Road and railway make two straight lines across the sand, telephone and electricity lines marching alongside. The occasional tuft of grass lines the dry water channels that carry the flashfloods after the sparse summer rains. Lonely platforms mark the desert stations, the stepping-off places for distant villages.

From **Bellpat**, a station halfway across the desert, you can turn west to **Bhag**, one of the khan of Kalat's old winter residences. Bagh is a traditional Kacchi town with an interesting covered bazaar and a fine domed tomb.

Dera Murad Jamali (Temple Dera before Partition) is irrigated by a canal from the Guddu Barrage and signals the end of the desert. Irrigated farmland stretches all the way from here to Jacobabad and on to Sukkur.

Quetta to Karachi via Kalat, Khuzdar and Las Bela

It now takes only ten or 12 hours to reach Karachi on the recently repaired RCD Highway via Kalat, Khuzdar and Las Bela. There is nowhere really acceptable to stay along the way, though there are local 'hotels' in the three main towns. The Communication and Works Department rest house in Kilaro, 40 kilometres (25 miles) north of Las Bela, has no electricity and is very basic.

It takes three hours to cover the 145 kilometres (90 miles) from Quetta to Kalat. You leave Quetta to the south and fork right off the Bolan Pass road along the base of Chiltan Mountain, past the Hazar Gunji Chiltan National Park and over the Lak Pass. At the base of the pass the road to Iran branches off to the right, while the Kalat road continues due south, through **Mastung** and along a dry, sterile valley that follows the line of the Central Brahui Range. The great **Koh-e-Maran** (Mountain of Snakes) towers a threatening 3,277 metres (10,751 feet) on the left, as ominous as its name.

Kalat, the once-splendid capital of the khan of Kalat (head of the Baluchi confederacy), was completely destroyed by the great earthquake in 1935. Today the deserted ruins of the old fortified town sprawl across the Shah Mardan Hills, with Miri, the abandoned castle of the khan, dominating the highest hill. On another crest is the **Shrine of Sheikh Abdul Qadir Jilani**, an 11th-century Shia saint whose descendants are still important chiefs. On the flat land below, the new town of Kalat is a mixture of mud huts and a few modern bungalows. The new palace of the khan of Kalat stands among apple and pomegranate trees surrounded by a high wall on the edge of town. The khans of Kalat were the most powerful central authority in Baluchistan in the 18th and 19th centuries.

The dusty bazaar is crowded with rugged tribesmen in huge turbans who greet each other with tender embraces and enquire with real concern after each other's health and welfare, the health and welfare of each other's families and relations, livestock and lands, the state of the family feud (feuds are common here) and news of travellers. The traditional greeting continues for ten minutes or so, social etiquette demanding that this exchange of news is not cut short. Questions that are considered personal elsewhere are necessary here: a man can be shot for slighting another by not showing enough interest. Understandably, news travels quickly in Baluchistan.

From Kalat the road continues south through several small villages of scattered mud huts and round the southern end of the Harboi Hills for 161 kilometres (100 miles) to **Khuzdar**, a small dusty town where camels are the main form of transport. There are several government rest houses here which you might be able to use if you have to spend the night.

Las Bela, 227 kilometres (141 miles) further south, is the next market town and was once capital of a small independent kingdom. Sir Robert Sandeman is buried here. The main road west from Las Bela to Turbat runs for 30 kilometres (19 miles) through a dramatic landscape of conical black rocks before deteriorating into one of the worst roads in the province (currently being upgraded).

The distance from Las Bela to Karachi is 160 kilometres (100 miles) and takes about two hours on a good road via Uthal, where the Department of Agriculture is experimenting with different types of coconut trees.

Quetta to Iran

The overland route from Quetta to Iran is open, but check with the Iranian Consulate, Hali Road, Quetta, tel. 75054, for up-to-date information. Incoming groups usually camp in the Lourdes Hotel camp ground in Quetta, and they are the best source of information on the latest conditions.

At least ten buses daily leave Quetta for Taftan, 608 kilometres (378 miles) away on the Iranian border, a journey of between 15 and 24 hours. The road is surfaced for the first 500 kilometres (310 miles), or as far as Nok Kundi, where you can spend the night in a local 'hotel'. You leave Quetta to the south and follow the Kalat road over the Lak Pass. At the foot of the pass, about 30 kilometres (20 miles) from Quetta, the road forks and a sign in English informs you it is 2,256 kilometres (1,402 miles) to Tehran and 686 kilometres (426 miles) to Zahidan. The Pakistani customs post stops all incoming and outgoing traffic here.

It is a long haul to Iran, mostly across undulating desert. The first stop is **Nushki**, 115 kilometres (71 miles) away, the next **Dalbandin**, about 180 kilometres (112 miles) further on. Near here are the onyx mines which provide the stone for the green ashtrays, candlesticks and goblets on sale in the Karachi bazaars. It is another 166 kilometres (103 miles) to **Nok Kundi** with a stop for food in **Yarmach**. The road deteriorates and it is slower going for the last 110 kilometres (68 miles) to **Taftan**, where there is another customs and immigration post to negotiate, before you cross the border to Mirjawa and the Iranian authorities. It is still about 100 kilometres (60 miles) to **Zahidan**.

The train to the border is not recommended: it runs only once a week and is extremely slow.

Quetta to Afghanistan via the Khojak Pass

As we go to press, the border at **Chaman** into Afghanistan is closed except to local traffic but, if you can get a permit, it is worth driving the 106 kilometres (66 miles) to the top of the Khojak Pass for a view down into Afghanistan.

At least 25 buses a day make the four-hour journey between Quetta and Chaman, catering for the thousands of Afghan refugees and the brisk local trade. The daily train takes six hours and goes through the Khojak Tunnel.

The road to Chaman runs north past **Kuchlak** and across the plain, where neat, mud-walled villages are surrounded by orchards irrigated by underground karez. It winds through some extraordinary eroded red hills to the **Pishin** junction. You turn right to Pishin, left to Chaman. Pishin District is a comparatively fertile, well-populated area, its underground watertable recharged with water from the Lora River, which drains into central Asia. Bund Khushdil Khan, a reservoir 16 kilometres (10 miles) into Pishin District, is famous for its duck shooting in early winter, providing there is enough water.

The Chaman road continues past two enormous Afghan refugee camps at **Saranan** and **Jungle Piralizai**, each containing more than 10,000 refugees. In the graveyards, black flags fluttering on tall poles mark the graves of the *shahid* (martyrs) who died fighting for Afghanistan. A low pass divides the plain from **Qila Abdullah**, a small bazaar full of overladen trucks and buses plying between Chaman and Quetta. Two checkposts control the route to the pass; all vehicles are stopped and searched for smuggled goods.

At the foot of the Khojak Pass the railway disappears into the 5.2-kilometre (3.2-mile) - long **Khojak Tunnel**, whose entrance is pictured on the five-rupee note. The tunnel, the longest in the subcontinent, was drilled from each end, and apparently when the engineer discovered that it was not meeting in the centre he attempted suicide. By means of a hill and a corner the situation was redeemed and the tunnel completed in 1892.

It is 6.5 kilometres (four miles) from the checkpost to the top of the pass on a winding road through almost barren hills, each crowned by its defensive fort. At the top, **Shelabagh** rest house looks down the 22 kilometres (14 miles) to Chaman and the sandy plains of Afghanistan, which stretch as far as the eye can see. It is about 125 kilometres (78 miles) from Chaman to Kandahar.

The Makran Coast

The Makran Coast is Baluchistan's southern strip and stretches for 754 kilometres (470 miles) along the Arabian Sea. Long sandy beaches, rugged promontories and tidal creeks characterize the coastline. Three ranges of hills, rising to over 1,500 metres (5,000 feet), run parallel to the coast: the Coastal Makran Range, 30 kilometres (20 miles) inland; the Central Makran Range, 130 kilometres (80 miles) inland; and the Siahan Range, 200 kilometres (125 miles) away from the sea. There is very little rain in the Makran region; the few villages and towns along the coast and between the hills are sustained by spring water. The many rivers marked on the map are really eroded gullies scoured by flash floods after the occasional storm.

Many of the Makrani people are dark-skinned and have African features. They are probably descended from slaves brought by Arab merchants to the subcontinent. They subsist on fishing, date farming and camel breeding. Most of the men work part-time in the Gulf states and Oman and send money home to their families.

Alexander the Great marched half his army home along the inhospitable Makran coast in 325 BC, and Muhammad bin Qasim came from Baghdad to Sind through Makran in AD 711. The Makranis stood firm against the Moghuls, but bowed nominally to the British Raj. It is only since 1971 that some effort has been made to develop the region.

Foreigners are rarely given permission to visit the Makran Coast. There is no road along the coast, but daily flights connect the three main coastal towns of **Pasni**, **Gwadar** and **Jiwani** with Karachi, and there are flights to Quetta three times a week. Gwadar and Jiwani, both picturesque towns flanked by cliffs and beaches, belonged to Oman for about 200 years. The khan of Kalat gave them as a present to the sultan in the 18th century, and in 1958 they were sold back to Pakistan.

Turbat, the divisional headquarters for Makran, is a small inland town near the hills, with little to recommend it but its 300 varieties of dates. Turbat is accessible by a rough road from Las Bela, and by daily flights from Karachi and Quetta. **Panjgur**, the main date-growing area further north, can also be reached by air. The track from Khuzdar to Panjgur is very rough.

Punjab

Punjab, meaning Land of Five Rivers, is the richest, most fertile and most heavily populated province of Pakistan. More than 60 million people live here, or about 60 percent of Pakistan's population. Geographically, Punjab is a land of contrasts, encompassing the alluvial plain of the Indus River and its tributaries the rolling sands of the Cholistan Desert, the fairy-tale beauty of the pine-covered foothills of the Himalayas, and the strangely convoluted lunar landscape of the Potwar Plateau and the Salt Range.

Monsoon rains fall in northern Punjab. The belt from Lahore to Rawalpindi– Islamabad, and north into the foothills, is the only area in Pakistan to get more than 500 millimetres (20 inches) of rain a year; the five big rivers—the Indus, Jhelum, Chenab, Ravi and Sutlej—provide adequate water for agriculture in the rest of the province. With the aid of irrigation, the flat, alluvial plain between the rivers is mostly cultivable. The most fertile areas lie between the Jhelum, Chenab, Ravi and Sutlej; the land between the Indus and Jhelum rivers, known as the Thal Desert (not to be confused with the Thar Desert in Sind), is also slowly being reclaimed with water from the Jinnah and Chasma barrages on the Indus.

Most of Pakistan's wheat, rice, barley, maize, pulses, oil-seeds and sugar-cane is grown in Punjab. The area around Multan is the cotton-growing centre of the country. Cotton is Pakistan's most important cash crop and provides fibre for both direct and manufactured exports. Much of Pakistan's industry is located here: textiles, steel, sports goods, electrical appliances, surgical instruments and fertilizers are all made here, mainly around the large cities of Faisalabad, Multan, Sialkot, Gujranwala and the provincial capital, Lahore. Punjab is also rich in natural resources: salt, gypsum, coal and oil.

Prehistoric man lived on the banks of the Soan River 50,000 years ago, and the Indus Civilization flourished at Harappa and other sites from 3000 to 1500 BC. Taxila, near Islamabad, was a centre of culture and learning from about 500 BC to AD 500, and when Alexander the Great visited Taxila in 326 BC it was known throughout the ancient world for its university. Islamic learning and architecture developed at Uch and Multan during the 13th and 14th centuries, and in the 17th century Lahore was one of the greatest Moghul cities of the subcontinent. The founder of the Sikh religion, Guru Nanak, was born in Punjab near Lahore. It was here that the Sikhs rose to power, and in the early 19th century, Maharaja Ranjit Singh ruled his Sikh empire from Lahore. The British took this fertile region from the Sikhs in 1849.

It was at Lahore that the Resolution for the Creation of Pakistan was passed by the All India Muslim League on 23 March 1940. As Hindus, Sikhs and Muslims were inextricably mixed throughout the region, the division of Punjab at Partition resulted in great bitterness and bloodshed.

When Pakistan decided to build a new capital, it was in fertile Punjab that a site

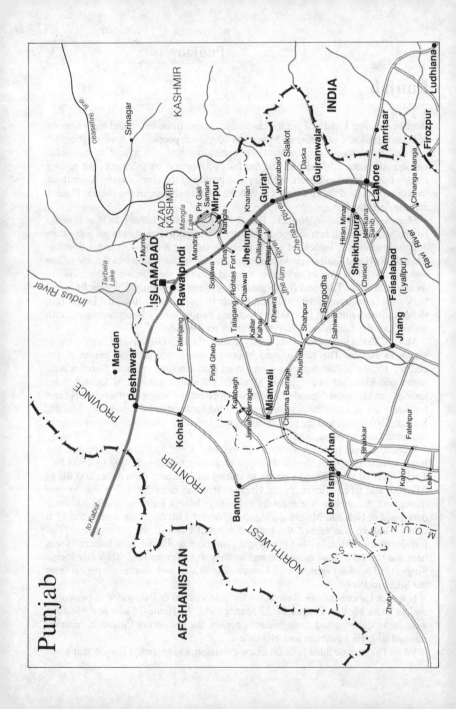

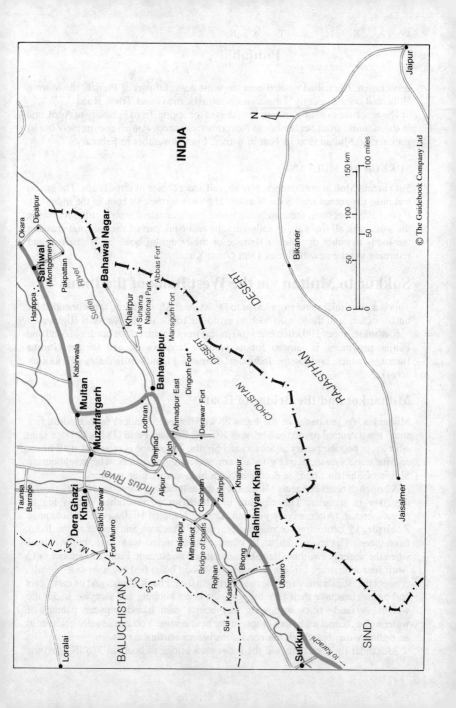

© The Guidebook Company Ltd

was chosen. Islamabad is sited near the most beautiful part of Punjab, the Murree Hills, and on the country's main east-west axis, the Grand Trunk Road.

The best time to visit northern Punjab is in the spring, from February to April, and in the autumn, from September to November. Southern Punjab is extremely hot in summer, so Multan is at its best in winter, from November to February.

SUKKUR TO MULTAN

Sukkur and Multan are connected by air, rail and a choice of three roads. The fastest and most dangerous road is the National Highway up the east bank of the Indus but, if you have more time, there are some interesting alternative routes, either following the west bank all the way, or following the east bank part of the way and crossing the Indus at either the Guddu Barrage or the bridge of boats at Mithankot, and returning via the new bridge at Dera Ghazi Khan.

Sukkur to Multan via the West Bank of the Indus

This is a very quiet route from Lakhi to Dera Ghazi Khan, mainly recommended for bird-watchers and those who wish to avoid the traffic on the National Highway.

Kashmor, about 100 kilometres (60 miles) from Lakhi, on the border of Sind and Punjab provinces, is famous for its wooden lacquerwork and for the **Guddu Barrage**, which bridges the Indus and irrigates 11 million hectares (27 million acres).

Mithankot and the Bridge of Boats

Mithankot, on the banks of the Indus 85 kilometres (53 miles) further north, is a small town centred round the Shrine of Khwaja Ghulam Farid (1815–1901), a saint who wrote popular poetry in Saraiki and Sindhi. The shrine is crowded at all times, and the saint's descendants give a warm welcome to visitors. The neighbouring Shrine of Shidani Sharif is decorated with high-quality blue tilework.

A bridge of boats connects Mithankot to the east bank in winter and a ferry crosses the river in summer. The crossing to **Chachran** on the other side is highly recommended. (Alternatively you can take the National Highway from Sukkur to **Zahirpir**, 15 kilometres, or nine miles, east of Chachran and detour to the Indus from there.) The river is about 18 kilometres (11 miles) wide here, but in winter when the water is low three large islands surface midstream. From 15 October to 15 April four temporary bridges, comprising 90-odd boats tied together side by side, connect the islands and carry the road across to the far bank. Camel and ox carts, cars and pedestrians take their turn to cross, the boats bobbing and swaying under the weight. A sandy track wends its way across each island between patches of watermelon, fennel and other crops, to the next bridge. You can usually get over in an ordinary car, but check the conditions before starting across.

Alexander the Great crossed the Indus on a bridge of boats in 326 BC, and the system was probably used for hundreds of years before that. In summer, when the river is in spate, the boat bridge is dismantled, and an old steamboat dating back to before World War I is brought into service as a ferry; it takes about an hour to cross and is perhaps even more interesting than the boat bridge. You share the deck with both animals and people, and have time to examine all the bits of machinery, all dated and made in England. In winter the steam ferry is moored on one of the islands beside the bridge of boats.

Rajanpur just north of Mithankot has a rather dilapidated fort some 700 years old. From there the road improves for the last 114 kilometres (70 miles), or two hours, to Dera Ghazi Khan.

Dera Ghazi Khan

D G Khan as this District headquarters is commonly called, was originally located on the banks of the Indus, but was destroyed by floods in 1911. The town was relocated 15 kilometres (nine miles) inland, and the new D G Khan bears the unmistakable stamp of a British administrative centre, with its orderly bazaar and spacious bungalows for officials. It is known for its lacquer-, wood- and leatherwork, date-palm baskets, rope-weaving and textiles.

D G Khan has two air-conditioned hotels, the Shalimar (s/d Rs120/180) and the Parkland (d Rs80), plus the cheaper Victory, Al-Habib and Al-Fateh Hotels (s/d Rs20/40), all in the Fareedi Bazaar area. There are also many government rest houses bookable through the deputy commissioner.

From D G Khan you can drive west through Fort Munro to Baluchistan and Quetta, 529 kilometres (329 miles), about 13 hours, away; north along the Indus to the North-West Frontier Province and Dera Ismail Khan, 208 kilometres (129 miles) away; or east to Multan.

The **road west** to Fort Munro and Baluchistan passes the town of **Sakhi Sarwar**, 35 kilometres (22 miles) from D G Khan and named after a popular saint who is buried there in a blue tiled mausoleum. The shrine is at its best on a Thursday evening or during the month of its urs, when devotees dance in the courtyard to the beat of a large drum. During the urs two huge copper pots by the shrine are filled with offerings of food for distribution to the poor.

The road from Sakhi Sarwar to Fort Munro winds dramatically for 50 kilometres (30 miles) to the top of the **Sulaiman Hills**. It cuts along a ledge on the cliff face and climbs up through a narrow gorge in a series of hairpin bends, the rock face towering above on one side and narrow ravines dropping steeply away on the other. Boulders weighing several tons, and washed down by the mountain torrents during the rains, are strewn along the foot of the cliffs. Fantastic contours are carved into the solid rockface above the road.

Fort Munro, the last town in the Punjab, lies among green hills dotted with fruit trees. Built as a summer resort by British colonial officials in the 1920s and '30s, it is now used by tribal leaders from the area around D G Khan as a retreat from the torrid plains. A flat spot above what is left of the old Christian cemetery, where the wind whistles through enormous Himalayan pines, provides a breathtaking vista of the plains of Baluchistan to the west and those of the Punjab to the east.

For the road on to Quetta see page 137.

The **road north** from Dera Ghazi Khan to Dera Ismail Khan (Ghazi and Ismail were brothers in the 16th century; *Dera* means place of), on the west bank of the Indus, is quiet and passable in an ordinary car (except for one river crossing near D I Khan, where there is no bridge). The **Taunsa Barrage**, about 50 kilometres (30 miles) from D G Khan, carries the road and railway bridge across to the east bank. The road north up the east bank through **Leah** to D I Khan is passable all the way in an ordinary car, though it is a little rough between **Karor** and **Bhakkar**. There is a splendid new bridge across the Indus at D I Khan.

From D G Khan to Multan is 94 kilometres (58 miles), a journey which takes about an hour and requires crossing back across the Indus on the new Ghazighat Bridge. Enthusiasts can stop to inspect the *Indus Queen*, the old ferryboat moored below the bridge, with three decks and a special ladies' compartment downstairs (and much grander than the steamboat at Mithan Kot). An old houseboat that once belonged to the nawab of Bahawalpur is moored next door. It is similar in design to the houseboats on the lakes at Srinagar in Kashmir and evokes 19th-century luxury.

Sukkur to Multan via the East Bank of the Indus

The National Highway to Multan runs through 450 kilometres (280 miles) of irrigated farmland. Long avenues of acacia and eucalyptus trees shade the road, and the surrounding orchards of mango, guava, pomegranate and citrus fruits lend an air of lush prosperity. From December to April you can buy freshly picked *kinos*—a delicious cross between an orange and a tangerine—at stalls beside the orchards. Strings of small bazaars along the highway are full of colourfully turbaned men, many of them wearing typically embroidered slippers with turned-up toes. There are plenty of tea shops and local hotels lining the road, but no tourist hotels.

The highway enters the Punjab at a police post about 100 kilometres (60 miles) north of Sukkur, just after **Ubauro**. A road to the west here leads to the Guddu Barrage, where you can cross the Indus to **Kashmor** and Sui in Baluchistan. About 25 kilometres (15 miles) further north on the National Highway is the turning left to **Bhong**, 27 kilometres (17 miles) off the main road, which boasts the most ostentatious mosque in Pakistan, built in traditional style with extravagant use of gold leaf, mirror work and onyx. It is particularly famous for its stylized Arabic calligraphy.

Zahirpir, about 100 kilometres (60 miles) from the Sind-Punjab border, is the turning point for the bridge of boats across the Indus to the west bank. It takes about two hours longer to reach Multan by that route (see above).

About 50 kilometres north of Zahirpir on the National Highway is another choice of alternative routes to Multan. The main road goes via Ahmadpur East and Bahawalpur and is slightly faster but very crowded; the alternative route crosses the **Panjnad** (meaning Five Waters), the confluence of the Chenab and Sutlej rivers where the waters from the Jhelum, Chenab, Ravi, Sutlej and Beas all come together. The place where the road forks is marked in English, but is easy to miss.

Uch (or Uchchh)

Whichever route you choose it is worth making a detour to Uch to see the Muslim tombs of the 13th and 14th centuries. To reach Uch from the Panjnad road turn east (right) across a canal about 20 kilometres (12 miles) after leaving the National Highway, or about 15 kilometres (nine miles) before the bridge across the Panjnad. It is about three kilometres (two miles) from the main road to Uch. To get there from the National Highway turn west just south of Ahmadpur East, where a sign in English reads 'Uch Sharif 20, Panjnad 38'

Uch, near the confluence of the Chenab and Sutlej rivers, has been largely bypassed by the 20th century, and is now just a small country bazaar surrounded by mud houses, but in the 13th and 14th centuries it was the capital of a rich kingdom and, with its sister city Multan, a centre of political, cultural and literary activity. The independent Kingdom of Uch was shortlived, as the river changed course and the town declined, but it still continued to attract the pious and saintly. Today it is always referred to as Uch Sharif (Holy Uch).

Uch was famous long before the advent of Islam. Alexander the Great arrived in 325 BC. Arrian, the second-century AD military historian, records that 'Alexander ordered a city to be built at the confluence of the two rivers, imagining that by the advantage of such a situation, it would become rich and prosperous'. The locals sent Alexander 100 men as hostages and 500 war chariots with the drivers and horses fully caparisoned; apparently Alexander was so touched by this gesture that he returned the hostages.

At the beginning of the eighth century Uch was part of the kingdom of the Brahmin ruler Chach, author of the *Chach Nama* (see page 67), who is believed to have invented and given his name to chess. It then fell in 711 to the Arab Muhammad bin Qasim after a siege of seven days. Five centuries later it reached its height as a great religious centre.

Today Uch is famous for the tombs of its saints, the most exquisite ruins in Pakistan. Of these the most aesthetically pleasing is the blue and white tiled **Tomb of Bibi Jawindi** (d. 1403), a lady famous for her piety. The proportions and colouring of the tomb are lovely, even though 200 or so years ago it was partly destroyed in a flood. Built in 1498, it features two octagonal tiers surmounted by a white dome which are very similar in design to the earlier Rukn-e-Alam Tomb in Multan (see pages 163, 166). Broad bands of brilliant blue tiles laid in pleasing geometric patterns decorate the round buttresses at the corners and surround the arches on each wall. The two ruined tombs of Bahawal Halim and Ustad Ladla stand in the same graveyard.

The **Tomb of Jalaluddin Surkh Bukhari** is right beside the tomb of Bibi Jawindi, but is easily missed as it is a low, square building with a flat roof and a plain brick outside wall. The entrance is on the other side. The tomb consists of an oblong room, built in the 14th century and extensively repaired in the 1800s, with a beautifully painted wooden ceiling held up by 40 carved wooden pillars. Saint Jalaluddin, who came from Bukhara in the 13th century, was a charismatic religious leader and is still greatly revered today. His cenotaph, on a raised platform at one end of the grave-filled room, is surrounded by a carved rail and covered by a wooden canopy, all encased in glass. The square mosque in the same compound has interesting carved brickwork and a wooden ceiling supported by pillars.

Two other tombs in Uch that should not be missed are those of **Shaikh Saifuddin Ghazrooni**, thought to be the oldest Muslim tomb in the subcontinent, and **Makhdoom Jahanian Jahangasht**. You will need a guide to find them as both are square buildings with flat wooden roofs. Saifuddin Ghazrooni came from Baghdad in 980 and was the first Muslim saint to settle in Uch. Jahanian Jahangasht spent his life travelling (his second name means Great Traveller); he was the grandson of Jalaluddin Bukhari.

Ahmadpur East

Ahmadpur East on the National Highway, is the first big town in Bahawalpur District. The main form of transport here is the bicycle rickshaw, and in the bazaar the women all wear handsome white *burkhas* with a blue embroidered grille over the eyes.

The National Highway actually divides Ahmadpur East from the royal suburb of **Dera Nawab Sahib** (Home of the Nawabs) and the **royal palaces** belonging to the nawab of Bahawalpur and his family.

For over 200 years the Nawab Abbasi family ruled the independent princely state of Bahawalpur, which remained independent at Partition in 1947 and was finally absorbed into Pakistan in 1954.

The cluster of 19th-century palaces in Dera Nawab Sahib is enclosed by high walls and is not open to the public. You can catch a glimpse of the largest, **Sadiq Garh Palace**, from the main gate. Built in 1896, its size and imposing design give some idea of the riches once enjoyed by Indian princes. This is Pakistan's only stately home.

Derawar Fort, to the southeast, on the edge of the Cholistan Desert, makes an exciting day's outing from either Ahmadpur East or Bahawalpur. The massive fort towers over the surrounding semi-desert and is visible from miles around. The huge walls, supported by enormous round buttresses, stand 40 metres (130 feet) high and are 1.5 kilometres (a mile) in circumference.

The trip requires careful planning. You need written permission from the nawab's secretary to enter the fort, and it is essential to take a guide. The PTDC in Bahawalpur or the deputy commissioner of Ahmadpur East can arrange this for you. The drive, for four-wheel drive vehicles only, takes from one to two hours from Ahmadpur East, depending on the state of the road and the route your guide has chosen for you. The last 25 kilometres (15 miles) are across desert.

There has been a fort at Derawar for at least 5,000 years, part of a long chain that protected the ancient trade route from central Asia to the Indian subcontinent. The site was captured by the Abassi family from Raja Rawal Singh of Jaisalmer in 1733, at which time the present fort was built. The whole area around Derawar was once well watered by the Ghaggar River (now called the Hakra in Pakistan, and known in ancient Vedic times as the Sarasvati). Along the 500 kilometres (300 miles) of the dry river bed are over 400 archaeological sites, most dating back to the Indus Civilization (see pages 46 and 97–9). In the 18th century 12,000 people lived in the town below the fort walls. Until 1960 Derawar was watered by a canal, but later, under a new international agreement, water from the Sutlej River was diverted to India and Derawar was abandoned. The old canal is being cleaned and new canals dug to reirrigate the area; soon irrigated farmland will once again surround Derawar, and a paved road will connect it to Ahmadpur East.

The fort is more impressive from outside than in. Start your tour with a drive or camel ride (ask your guide to make the necessary arrangements) round the outside of the walls, which are supported by 40 enormous buttresses, ten on each side. Outside the northeast corner are a well and two water tanks where nomads come from miles around to water their camels and fill their goatskin waterbags. The fort entrance is on the east and is now defended by a huge tower with gun emplacements added during the 1965 war with India. At this time many of the buildings inside the fort were removed to make room for a training and parade ground. In the centre of the parade ground stand two cannons and a selection of iron cannon balls and stone sling shots. The remaining buildings, all 19th-century, were vacated by the nawab's family in the 1920s and are now derelict. All that remain are the nawab's quarters, a long corridor with rooms off each side; the ladies' section, behind a locked door and high wall; and some soldiers' barracks. As in most subcontinental forts, the courtyard inside the walls is built on top of a maze of underground cellars and dungeons. At one end of the parade ground, stairs and a trolley on rails lead down to the vaulted cellars, and if you look over the parapet on the south wall you can see the air holes leading to the dungeons.

The most pleasant place in the fort is a painted pavilion on top of the northeast tower and surmounted by a flagpole. This is the best place for a picnic, as it is comfortable, shaded and cool, and looks over the two big water tanks outside and the fort. The walls of the pavilion are covered in frescoes, and the wooden ceiling is painted red, blue, yellow and green.

The white marble mosque in front of the fort was built in 1849 for the nawab's personal holy man, Pir Ghulam Farid, whose name appeared as if by magic (and

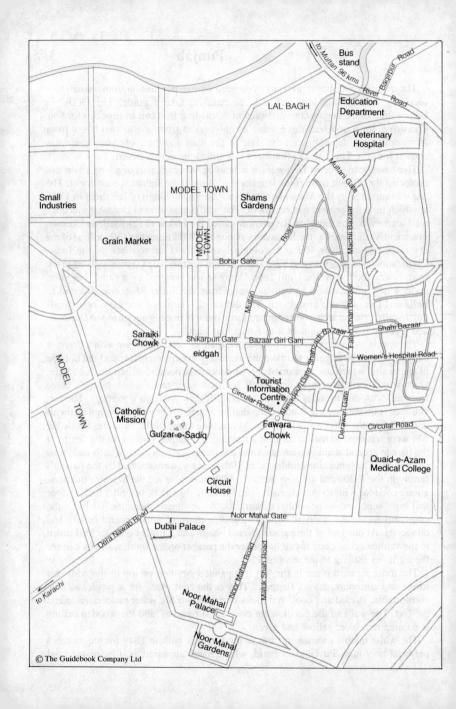

to Multan 96 kms

Bus stand

River Road

Baqirpur Road

LAL BAGH

Education Department

Veterinary Hospital

Small Industries

MODEL TOWN

Shams Gardens

Multani Gate

Grain Market

MODEL TOWN

Machli Bazaar

Bohar Gate

Road

Multan

Fateh Khan Bazaar

Shahi Bazaar

Saraiki Chowk

Shikarpuri Gate

Bazaar Giri Ganj

Shahzadi Bazaar

eidgah

Women's Hospital Road

MODEL TOWN

Ahmadpur Gate

Derawari Gate

Catholic Mission

Tourist Information Centre

Circular Road

Gulzar-e-Sadiq

Circular Road

Fawara Chowk

Quaid-e-Azam Medical College

Circuit House

Noor Mahal Gate

Dera Nawab Road

Noor Mahal Road

Malik Shah Road

to Karachi

Noor Mahal Palace

Noor Mahal Gardens

© The Guidebook Company Ltd

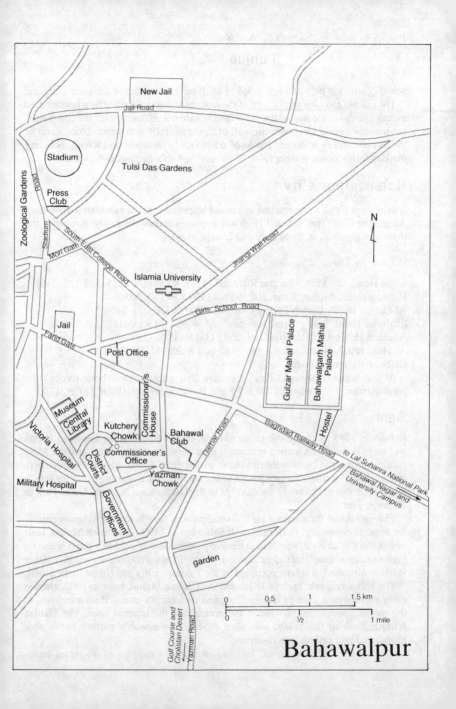

Bahawalpur

possibly with the help of a few drops of acid) on the doorstep of the south entrance.

The marble and blue tiled tombs of the nawabs and their families lie a few hundred metres (yards) to the east of the fort. Tourists are not allowed inside the compound, but there is a good view over the wall of the beautifully decorated oblong tomb of the nawabs and eight domed tombs of other family members and wives, including the elegantly domed marble tomb of the last nawab's English wife.

Bahawalpur City

Bahawalpur City can be reached by air and train and is about one hour's drive from Ahmadpur East. The National Highway bypasses Bahawalpur. The turning to the town is signposted in Urdu only and is easy to miss.

Where to Stay

Erum Hotel, the Mall, Circular Road, tel. 4291, 4730 (s/d Rs85–165/125–210).
Humera Hotel, Multan Road, tel. 5959, 4840 (d Rs150–200).
Al-Hamra Hotel, Berron Fareed Gate, tel. 4291, 4730 (s/d Rs40/70).
Shabrose Hotel, near general bus stand, tel. 4096 (s/d Rs35/45).
Abaseen Hotel, Circular Road, tel. 2591 (s/d Rs35/50).
Al-Hilal Hotel, Circular Road, tel. 2437 (s/d Rs25/45).
Railway Retiring Rooms.

At Lal Suhanra National Park, there are four guest houses; book through the administrator, Lal Suhanra National Park, Bahawalpur, tel. 0621, 3279, 2170.

Sights

Rebuilt in 1748 by the nawab on an old site, Bahawalpur's wide tree-lined streets and large houses with arched verandahs give it an air of calm spaciousness. Most public transport is by bicycle rickshaw, so life here seems graciously unhurried. Bahawalpur is a small but prosperous town, and is an ideal starting-point for safaris into the Cholistan Desert, or for daytrips to the Lal Suhanra National Game Park or Derawar Fort.

The nawabs of Bahawalpur built several palaces here before moving, ostensibly for reasons of privacy, to Dera Nawab Sahib in the 1890s. The **Noor Mahal**, built in 1885 in Italian style, stands in extensive gardens. It was used as a guest house for high-ranking visitors, including Edward VII of Britain who once stayed here. Once lavishly furnished, it is now occupied by the Pakistan army and closed to the public.

The **Bahawalgarh**, built in 1876, and the **Gulzar Mahal**, built in 1902, are two other palaces now used as army offices and the officers' mess. Both are closed to the public, though the mosque in the grounds of the latter is open. The **Daulat Khana**, built in the 1880s, was used by the then-nawab's mother but is now abandoned and falling into disrepair.

The nawabs' elegant capital featured numerous examples of Victorian archi-

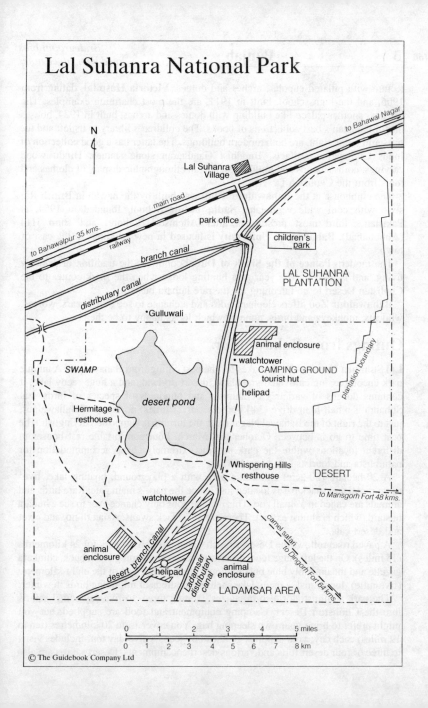

Lal Suhanra National Park

to Bahawal Nagar

N

Lal Suhanra
Village

main road

park office

children's
park

to Bahawalpur 35 kms.

railway

branch canal

distributary canal

•Gulluwali

LAL SUHANRA
PLANTATION

SWAMP

animal enclosure

• watchtower

CAMPING GROUND
tourist hut

○ helipad

desert pond

Hermitage
resthouse

plantation boundary

Whispering Hills
resthouse

DESERT

watchtower

to Mansgorh Fort 48 kms.

camel safari
to Dingorh Fort 64 kms.

animal
enclosure

desert branch canal

○ helipad

Ladamsar
distributary
canal

animal
enclosure

LADAMSAR AREA

| 0 | 1 | 2 | 3 | 4 | 5 miles |
| 0 | 1 | 2 | 3 | 4 | 5 | 6 | 7 | 8 km |

© The Guidebook Company Ltd

tecture with pillared cupolas, arches and domes. **Victoria Hospital**, dating from 1906, and the high school, built in 1911, are the most charming examples. The **library**, another palace-like building with domes and arches, built in 1924, houses one of Pakistan's best collections of books. The children's library to its left and the **museum** to the right, are both modern buildings. The latter has a good collection of Indus Civilization artifacts, Buddhist Gandharan stone statues, Hindu wood carvings, coins, stamps and miniatures, and an ethnographic display of clothes and tools from the Cholistan Desert.

The clubhouse at the **Bahawalpur Club** was built by the nawab in British Raj style with cool wide verandahs. **Sadiq Public School**, founded in 1954, is Pakistan's third most prestigious after Aitchison (Lahore) and Burn Hall (Abbottabad). **Bahawalpur University** is housed in new buildings to the east of town.

The modern **Palace of the Sheik of Dubai** continues the tradition of princely living, and is used once a year as a hunting lodge when the sheik comes to the Cholistan Desert to go falconing for the rare hubara bustard.

Bahawalpur Zoo offers elephant rides and a chance to see lions, bears, wolves, wildcats, monkeys and birds, none of which looks happy to be there.

Outings from Bahawalpur

Lal Suhanra National Park makes for the best outing from Bahawalpur. A unique park encompassing cultivated greenland, desert dryland, and a huge reedy lake, it contains dozens of varieties of animals and hundreds of species of birds. Lal Suhanra is a half-hour drive (34 kilometres or 21 miles) northeast of Bahawalpur, just to the right of the Bahawal Nagar road; the turning is signposted in English. The best time to go is between October and March. Four comfortable rest houses in different locations within the park provide extremely cheap accommodation for naturalists and tourists (see page 158).

A 20-hectare (50-acre) children's park with a playground, boating lake, five-room motel and snack bar is located just inside the park's main gate. Rare birds and animals are caged in a small zoo. This may be your only chance ever to see a hubara bustard, which is almost extinct. There are also black swans, Asian rhino, and civet and desert cats.

A paved road follows the Desert Branch Canal through the park for 24 kilometres (15 miles). On the left, huge fenced enclosures contain leaping black buck, chinkara gazelle and the ungainly blue bull antelope. On the other side of the eight-kilometre (five-mile) -long canal, a reedy lake shelters hundreds of migrating birds in winter.

The park administrator also organizes exciting three- to five-day camel safaris into the **Cholistan Desert**. Camping equipment and food are supplied, but you might prefer to bring your own sleeping bag. You cover 15 to 20 kilometres (ten to 12 miles) each day; your supplies go ahead by jeep. A five-day tour includes visits to three or four desert forts and various desert encampments. Desert safaris are also

organized by Karakoram Tours, Islamabad, tel. 829120, telex 54480 Mirza PK; and by Indus Guides, Lahore, tel. 304190/6, telex 44344 Deens PK.

The desert blooms with the coming of the sparse August and September rains. The nomads spread out with their herds and wander freely across the border into the Rajasthan Desert in India, or the Thar Desert in Sind, building shallow reservoirs in the hollows to catch the rainwater. When these dry up the nomads cluster in temporary villages around the more reliable wells (some up to 30 metres, or 100 feet, deep), eating summer pulses and yoghurt with mutton or goat and, occasionally, camel. The nomads belong to many different tribes, though most of them are descended from settlers who came from Baluchistan at least two centuries ago.

Sixteen desert forts, which protected the ancient trade route, stretch in a long chain for 300 kilometres (200 miles) to Jaisalmer in India. Derawar (see pages 154–5 and 158) is the largest and best preserved.

Shortly after Bahawalpur the National Highway crosses the Sutlej River, and about two kilometres (a mile) further north a high bridge carries the road across the railway. From the top of this bridge you can see the 12th-century **Gardezi Tomb**, one of the oldest Muslim tombs in Pakistan. No one knows who is buried there. A forerunner of the tombs in Multan (see pages 163 and 166), it comprises a square base and high dome. The tomb has lost its outside coating of baked bricks, so that only the core of unbaked mud bricks remains. From here it is about 90 kilometres (56 miles) to Multan.

MULTAN

With four rare things Multan abounds,
Heat, beggars, dust and burial grounds.

Multan is the most important city in the lower Punjab. Strategically placed at the crossroads of the main trade routes through Pakistan, and at what was once the confluence of the Ravi and Chenab rivers (today the Ravi joins the Chenab 40 kilometres, or 25 miles, to the north), Multan has been a rich, well-defended city for more than 2,000 years. Today it is a flourishing industrial city, and can be reached by daily air and rail services from the rest of the country.

Multan was coveted by every invader, and features continuously in the history of Pakistan. Alexander the Great arrived here in 324 BC. His forces were outnumbered ten to one, and Alexander took it upon himself to scale the battlements of the citadel and drop, virtually unaided, into the fortress.

He happened to land on his feet beside a fig-tree . . . . He slashed with his sword and hurled any stones that came to hand: the Indians recoiled as his three attendants leapt down to join him, carrying the sacred shield [of Achilles]. But Indian skills of archery were his undoing; his helpers were wounded, and an arrow, three feet long, struck him through his corslet into his chest. When an Indian ran forward to finish him off, Alexander had strength enough to stab his attacker before he struck home; then he collapsed, spurting blood, beneath the cover of his Trojan shield.

Robin Lane Fox, *Alexander the Great* (1973)

Eventually the walls collapsed and the Macedonians rushed in to massacre the people of Multan 'down to the last of the women and children'.

Multan was later annexed to the Mauryan Empire, became part of the Kushan Kingdom, was sacked by the Huns when they swept across the Punjab, and was later ruled by the Hindus.

The Chinese Buddhist pilgrim Xuan Zang, who visited Multan in AD 641, described the city in detail in his diaries. He found Multan agreeable and prosperous, and wrote at length about a fabulous statue of the sun god, 'cast in gold and ornamented with rare gems'. This statue is mentioned frequently in the history books and was responsible for Multan becoming a prosperous centre of pilgrimage. The statue was broken up by Muslim invaders in the tenth century, then repaired, and was finally destroyed by the Moghul emperor Aurangzeb in the 17th century, 900 years after the first Muslim invasion of Pakistan.

In AD 711, not long before his tragic death, Muhammad bin Qasim became the first Muslim to take Multan, capturing the city for the caliph of Baghdad after a siege lasting over two months. During his earlier invasion of Sind, Muhammad overthrew King Dahir, had him executed, and sent the king's two daughters as a present to the caliph. In order to avenge their father, the women reported that Muhammad bin Qasim had defiled them. The caliph was furious and ordered Muhammad to have himself sewn up in the skin of a freshly killed cow and returned to Baghdad. Muhammad, still only 17 years old, did as he was commanded, and died within three days.

Multan then fell to Mahmud of Ghazni in 1005. The town reached its height as an influential political, religious and cultural centre in the 13th century. Holy men from all over the Muslim world flocked there, and it is their tombs that make Multan so famous today.

Multan fell to Tamerlane the Mongol in 1398. The city later became part of the Moghul Empire in the 16th century and was taken by Nadir Shah of Persia in 1739, by the Afghan Ahmed Shah Durrani in 1752, and by the Sikh Ranjit Singh in 1818.

The 1848 British siege of Multan led to the Second Sikh War and the annexation of the Punjab by the British a year later. The Sikh governor Mulraj had refused to pay his taxes and two young British soldiers, William Anderson and Alexander vans Agnew, were sent to Multan to negotiate a settlement; they were murdered by the Sikhs. Herbert Edwardes, who gained fame as the political agent of Bannu (see pages 299–300), assembled a force and galloped to the rescue in scorching June weather. He defeated Mulraj and drove him into the citadel at Multan. Sikh forces were sent from Lahore to join the rebellion. Mulraj did not surrender until after the citadel's walls were breached in January 1849, nine months after the two Britons were murdered.

Over the last two centuries Multan has developed as the centre for the hides and skin trade in the subcontinent, and since Partition it has become the major cotton-producing region of Pakistan. Spinning and weaving of both cotton and wool and the making of hand-knotted carpets are now important industries. Wherever you look—up on the fort, outside the shrines, in the back alleyways—you will see long skeins of freshly dyed cotton laid out in the sun to dry.

Where to Stay

Moderate

Mangol, LMQ Road, Dera Adda, tel. 30164–5, 74196 (s/d Rs200/350).
Sindbad, Nishtar College Road, tel. 72294–5, 74196 (s/d Rs200/350).
Shezan, Kutchery Road, tel. 30253–6 (s/d Rs170/300).
Silversand, 415 Railway Road, tel. 33061–2, 76800, 76900 (s/d Rs150/200).

Cheaper

Guild, Shershah Road, tel. 40465 (s/d Rs30/50).
Aziz, Shershah Road, tel. 30425 (s/d Rs30/50).
Al-Qamar, Railway Road, tel. 73806, 73845 (s/d Rs30/50).
Plaza, near general bus stand (s/d Rs25/40).
Youth Hostel, opposite Muslim High School.
Railway Retiring Rooms.

Sights

The Fort Mound

Billed as Pakistan's most undiscovered city, Multan is full of unexpected treasures. If your time is limited, the one thing you really ought to see is the elegantly proportioned **Tomb of Rukn-e-Alam**, which dominates the city from the top of the fort mound. It has recently been awarded the Aga Khan Architectural Award for restoration.

The tomb is full of graves; Rukn-e-Alam's grave is covered by a marble canopy which was put up in 1930. Rukn-e-Alam (Pillar of the People) was a pious and learned man, greatly respected in his own day, and head of the mystic Sufi order of Suhrwardia Silsila. His real name was Abdul Fath, but he was also known as Rukn-ud-din (Pillar of the World). When he died in 1334, aged 83, he was buried with his grandfather Baha-ud-din Zakaria (see below). His present tomb was built in 1320 by Emperor Ghiyas-ud-din Tughlaq, who intended it for himself; the emperor's son bequeathed it to the saint instead.

The three-storey, domed building signified a new style of mausoleum archi-

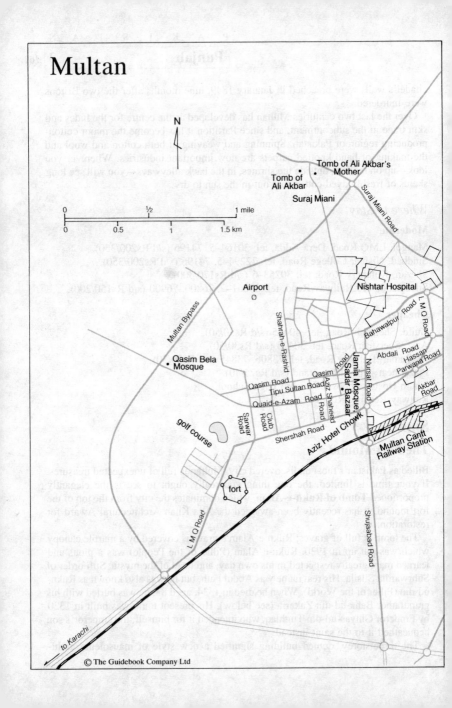

Multan

N

0   ½   1 mile

0   0.5   1   1.5 km

Tomb of Ali Akbar's Mother

Tomb of Ali Akbar

Suraj Miani

Suraj Miani Road

Airport

Nishtar Hospital

Bahawalpur Road

L M Q Road

Multan Bypass

Qasim Bela Mosque

Shahrah-e-Rashid

Abdali Road

Hassan Parwana Road

Jamia Mosque Sadar Bazaar

Nursai Road

Akbar Road

Qasim Road

Qasim Road

Tipu Sultan Road

Quaid-e-Azam Road

Aziz Shaheed Road

golf course

Sarwar Road

Club Road

Shershah Road

Aziz Hotel Chowk

Multan Cantt Railway Station

fort

L M Q Road

Shujaabad Road

to Karachi

© The Guidebook Company Ltd

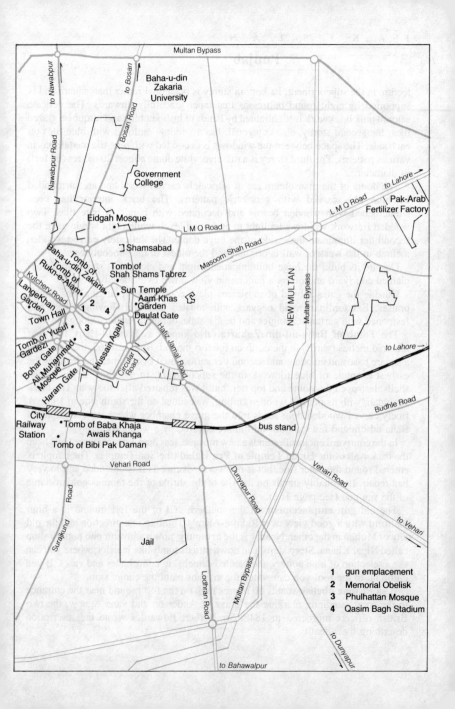

tecture in the subcontinent. Its bottom storey is octagonal rather than square and is supported by eight round buttresses that taper gracefully upwards. The delicate salmon pink brickwork is highlighted by bands of brilliant blue and turquoise glazed tiles; the second storey, also octagonal, has a window outlined with blue tiles on each side. The space between the windows is decorated with blue tile medallions in various patterns. The third storey is a massive white dome almost 20 metres (65 feet) in diameter.

The doors of the mausoleum are of intricately carved wood and are surrounded by blue tiles carved with geometric patterns. The brick interior has been strengthened with wooden beams and decorated with bands of blue tiles. Two wooden fretwork windows let light in at ground level, while eight windows in the second tier illuminate the inside of the huge dome. The delicately carved wooden mehrab in the western wall is original and the oldest in the subcontinent.

Despite its bulk, the huge building seems light and elegant. It stands in a tree-planted courtyard and offers a panoramic view down over the city.

Outside the gates a band of musicians plays continuously, singing the saint's praises. Extraordinary mad beggars with tousled hair and flowing robes, and festooned with garlands, bangles and beads, stake out their territory along the wall.

The **Tomb of Baha-ud-din Zakaria** (also known as Baha-ul-Haq), is a few hundred metres (yards) to the north on the fort mound. Built in 1262, the tomb has a square base and an octagonal second tier surmounted by a dome, and features the earliest example of blue tilework in the subcontinent. In the 1848 siege, British shells destroyed the dome and top tier, but it was repaired after the war. The brick verandah, with its painted wooden ceiling, was added on the south side in 1952. A finely carved wooden door leads into the grave chamber where the cenotaphs of Baha-ud-din and his son Sadr-ud-din are covered by a wooden canopy.

In the courtyard enclosure stands a new mosque, less than a metre (three feet) from the back wall of the Hindu **Temple of Pra Halad** (the Sun Temple). The temple is entered round the other side, but is not worth visiting as it is untended and in very bad repair. It probably stands on the site of the shrine of the famous golden statue of the sun god (see page 162).

The old **gun emplacement** on the southern end of the fort mound is a high platform with a good view over Rukn-e-Alam's Tomb in one direction and the old city of Multan in the other. Nearby is the **armoury**, now a souvenir and pottery shop called Nigar Khana. Steep steps lead down into its tomb-like interior, where you can see a selection of blue pottery and painted camel skin lampshades and vases. If you climb up to the roof you can watch the artisans paint the camel skin.

A **sandstone obelisk** stands 50 metres high on the fort mound near the entrance to the sports stadium, marking the grave of Anderson and vans Agnew, the two British officers murdered in 1848. Sir Herbert Edwardes wrote the inscription describing their death:

... wounded and forsaken
They could offer no resistance,
But hand in hand calmly awaited
The onset of the assailants...

and much more in the same vein.

Old City and Bazaars

Below the fort mound lies the old city, partly surrounded by the old brick wall in which three of the six gates have been restored. Shoppers can explore the bazaars there for Multan's famous textiles: *khes* (cotton and wool bedspreads) and *durries* (jute and cotton woven carpets). To get to the bazaars, walk in from the main square at the bottom of the fort hill. Dominating the square is the 19th-century **Town Hall**, a splendid pink Victorian Gothic building with a clocktower in the centre and cupolas at each corner.

You enter the old town by the **Lohari Gate**. Turn right into a lane selling costume jewellery and plastic utensils. A little further down are the khes and bedsheets in check and flowered patterns. Next come the saris, shalwar-kameez and dupattas, some printed, some hand-embroidered (embroidery being another craft for which Multan is famous). If you have a good sense of direction, the twisting alleys of the bazaar are fascinating. Shops no bigger than cubby-holes line each side of the crowded lanes. Tall narrow houses with carved wooden shutters almost touch across the alleys, and the canvas awnings stretched across between them offer shoppers some shade. For more shopping take a rickshaw to the **Hussain Agahi Bazaar**, also in the old town.

The **Cantonment (Saddar) Bazaar** is easier to get to, though less amusing. Ladies can feel quite comfortable wandering unescorted in this area, with its handicrafts, pottery, brassware, silver jewellery and embroidered cloth. This is also the best place to find durries.

Other Mosques and Tombs

Tomb and mosque enthusiasts can spend their time comparing the early Muslim styles of architecture for which Multan is famous. In the old town are the **Ali Muhammad Mosque,** built in 1758, and the **Phulhattan Mosque**, and nearby, hidden in the back streets off Kotla Tolay Khan Road, is the **Savi Mosque**, built in 1582. This roofless brick mosque features beautiful blue and turquoise glazed-tile panels with white calligraphy. The **Eidgah Mosque**, the most beautiful of all, was built in 1735 and is similar in style to the Badshahi Mosque in Lahore.

The **Gardezi Compound** containing the **Tomb of Syed Yusuf Gardezi** is difficult to find, but worth the effort. It stands near the Bohar Gate to the old city, one kilometre (half a mile) southwest of the fort mound; it is enclosed by a high wall, and entered by a narrow gateway up some steps in an alleyway.

The Gardezis are one of Multan's leading families. Yusuf Gardezi arrived in Multan from Afghanistan in 1080, riding a lion and carrying a snake as his staff. He died here in 1115. The historian Philip Toynbee describes him picturesquely as having as many descendants as there are pigeons on his tomb (of which there are many).

The oblong, flat-roofed 'residential' tomb—so called because it resembles a small windowless house—was rebuilt in 1540 by Salim Shah Suri, the son of Sher Shah Suri (see page 205). It is completely covered outside with blue glazed tiles. The grave of Gardezi's snake lies on the path to the door under the first slab; his lion is buried under the white marble diamond.

Inside, the floral painting on the wooden ceiling makes a pattern of interlocking octagonals. The old frescoes on the walls have been covered with modern oil paint. The cenotaph, which is draped with brocade cloths, has a small wooden lid over where the saint's face should be—Muslims are buried lying on their right side facing Mecca. The lid covers a hole in the sarcophagus: apparently when devout visitors came to the tomb to pray the saint used to speak to them from inside the grave; if the visitors were very holy, he would put his hand out through the hole in greeting.

There are four other buildings in the Gardezi compound. One is a 16th-century mosque with a flat roof supported on eight pillars. The ceiling is painted with black and white geometric rosettes on a red background. Originally built as a hall for dervishes, it is not oriented towards Mecca, but the prayer mats lie diagonally across the floor in the correct position.

The **Tomb of Abdul Jalil**, in the southeastern corner of the compound, has no dome. Had the dome been built it would have been higher than the tomb of Shah Yusuf Gardezi, but as this would have been disrespectful the builders never completed it.

The great **Assembly Hall** in the northeast corner, built in 1878, is used for religious meetings. Here the story of the massacre of Karbala is recited during the month of Muharram: in AD 680, Husein, the grandson of the Prophet Muhammad, was killed with his six-month-old son and all his followers at Karbala (in Iraq), and Shia Muslims mourn this event during Muharram. The small cradles in most Shia tombs are a reminder of the massacred baby. The ceiling in the Assembly Hall is made of wooden beams supported by 16 carved pillars. It was repainted with floral designs in 1944.

A small shrine in the centre of the courtyard contains the 'footprint' of Ali, son-in-law and cousin of the Prophet Muhammad. It is a normal-sized footprint carved in stone. Remove your shoes before climbing the steps up to it.

The ruins on the south side of the compound are the remains of the old Assembly Hall destroyed by British shells in the siege of 1848. Behind stands the Gardezi family house.

The **Tomb of Shah Shams Tabriz**, a Sufi saint born in Afghanistan in 1165, is one kilometre (half a mile) northeast of the fort mound. Shah Shams arrived in Multan from Tabriz in 1201, and apparently died aged 111 in 1276. He is the most popular saint in Multan, and has one of the largest followings in the whole country. His urs is fixed on 1 June, when the tomb is so packed with devotees it is impossible to move. The old tomb was destroyed by fire and rebuilt in 1780 in typical Multan style, with a square bottom tier and a (recently repaired) bright green dome. The carved wooden verandah in front is painted brilliant red, and the grave of the saint inside is covered by a domed wooden screen in brilliant green. The floral frescoes have been whitewashed over, but the wooden ceiling of the verandah is painted in traditional style.

The **Tomb of Ali Akbar** is the second most beautiful tomb in Multan after Rukn-e-Alam's. Ali Akbar was the grandson of Shah Shams Tabriz, and his tomb stands three kilometres (two miles) from the fort mound, or two kilometres (a mile) from the Shezan Hotel, on the road to Suraj Miani. The tomb is 500 metres (yards) to the left of Suraj Miani road down a dirt track. Turn just before a graveyard; there is no sign.

Ali Akbar's Tomb was built in 973 AH (AD 1585), according to an inscription above the door. Similar in shape to the tomb of Rukn-e-Alam, it has an octagonal bottom tier, and Ali Akbar's pedigree is written in white on blue glazed tiles all the way round the top of this. Pleasing blue diamond patterns decorate the brick walls.

Nearby is the **Tomb of Ali Akbar's Mother**. This interesting 16th-century residential tomb is oblong, with a flat roof outside but domed inside. The outside walls are completely covered in glazed tiles in blue, turquoise, brown and white. Only ladies may enter to see the 14 graves, frescoed and tiled walls and domed ceiling.

The **Mosque of Isna Ashrai Jafri** nearby has three domes, each with 16 little niches painted with frescoes round the inside. The verandah features a beautiful ceiling decorated with floral painting on wood.

Before returning to Multan, continue along the Suraj Miani road for four kilometres (2.5 miles) through orchards of mango, pomegranate, lychee, date and falsa trees and past houses with barrel-shaped thatched roofs. This was once swampland between the Ravi and Chenab rivers, and Multan, built on land between the two rivers, was protected on three sides by water. Emperor Shah Jahan decided to drain this land to make it easier to move his troops through the area and diverted the Ravi River to join the Chenab 40 kilometres (25 miles) further north.

The **Tomb of Baba Khaja Awais Khangha** stands about one kilometre (half a mile) south of the Multan City railway station, in the suburb of Basti Daira. The round buttresses at each corner are completely covered in blue, turquoise and white glazed tiles in geometric and floral designs. Blue, brown and white tiles decorate the outside of the mehrab in the west wall. In typical Multan style the second storey is octagonal and surmounted by a dome. The floral paintings on the wooden ceiling in the entrance hall are in good condition, as is the stucco tracery on the walls. Next door there is an elegant little mosque featuring small minarets decorated with blue tiles and with a painted wooden ceiling to the verandah.

The **Tomb of Bibi Pak Daman**, mother of Rukn-e-Alam, is about 500 metres (yards) to the south of Baba Khaja's. This oblong, flat-roofed residential tomb consists of two rooms, and a verandah in front with three wooden fluted arches and two cupolas on the top. The tomb may have been built in the 13th or 14th century.

At the bottom of the hill to the north of the tomb is an enclosed sacred well where women bathe to cure their ills and infertility. The banyan tree beside the well is festooned with coloured votive threads attached by the suppliant women; their prayers are answered as the threads rot.

The **Tomb of Khalid Walid**, about 25 kilometres (15 miles) north of Multan on the way to Kabirwala, is built in the Ghaznavid style and dates from the 12th century. This may be the oldest Muslim tomb in the country and illustrates the Persian influence in the development of tomb architecture in Pakistan. The tomb has massive brick walls with inward-sloping rounded buttresses. The mehrab is marked on the outside of the west wall by a rectangular projection, and on the inside is surrounded by a very fine example of cut-brick calligraphy and other cut-brick decorations. The entrance, on the north side, leads up a flight of steps to an ambulatory passage around the central tomb chamber; at one time this was roofed over, but now only the high-pointed dome over the central tomb chamber remains.

Multan to Islamabad

There is a choice of three routes:

Via Mianwali (nine hours)

The quickest, easiest and most scenic route is west to **Muzaffargarh** and then due north to Mianwali, a five-hour drive on a quiet road in good condition. This road passes through the Thal Desert, much of which is now reclaimed with water channelled from the Indus. Those areas which are still desert offer a startling landscape of thorn trees, camels and high sand hills. From Mianwali to Islamabad it takes about four hours over the extraordinarily dramatic Salt Range via Talagang and Fatehjang (see pages 251–3).

Via Jhang and Khushab (nine hours)

This road through **Jhang** is busier and not in such good condition as the Mianwali Road, but the drive is still much easier than on the National Highway via Lahore. Leave Multan on the National Highway, but after about 35 kilometres (22 miles) fork left at Kabirwala and follow the road north to Jhang, the heart of the Punjab's cotton belt.

At Jhang the direct route is across the Chenab River and north along the Jhelum to **Sahiwal**. (Most confusingly, there are two Sahiwals in the southern Punjab; the other used to be called Montgomery, and is on the National Highway near Harappa.) This road is quiet, but not in very good condition. From Sahiwal continue north to **Shahpur**, then turn left across the Jhelum River on a combined road and rail bridge, built in 1931, to Khushab. It is 30 kilometres (19 miles) from Khushab to the foot of the Salt Range, a spectacular escarpment rising nearly 1,000 metres (3,300 feet) straight up from the plains. The narrow but good road twists up for 15 kilometres (nine miles) to the top of the escarpment. The colours here are extraordinary: the soil is brown, purple, red and grey and dotted with dark green olive bushes and thorn trees. The fastest route from the top to Islamabad is via Talagang, but the more scenic is through Kallar Kahar (see page 245).

Detour to Faisalabad and Chiniot

Alternatively, from Jhang you can detour east to Faisalabad, Pakistan's third-largest city after Karachi and Lahore, and formerly called Lyallpur, after Sir James Lyall, governor of the Punjab. Faisalabad is often referred to as 'little Manchester' because of its textile mills and rapid industrial growth, and is famous for its large Agricultural University. The city was founded in 1890 and offers little of interest to the tourist. Sir James Lyall laid out the town in the shape of the British flag: a rectangle with a cross and two diagonals; a clocktower stands at the crossroads. Each of the eight sections radiating from the centre has its own bazaar.

Faisalabad can be reached by daily air and rail services.

Where to Stay in Faisalabad

Serena, Club Road, tel. 30972–6 (s/d Rs750/1000).
Ripple, 18-A People's Colony, tel. 40973, 41909 (s/d Rs375/500).
Rays, Allama Iqbal Road, tel. 24006, 32605 (s/d Rs200/300).

There are a number of cheaper hotels in the bazaars around the clocktower where you can stay for Rs30/60 a night.

If you want to proceed from Faisalabad to Islamabad the quickest route is via **Sheikhupura** (see page 200) and Gujranwala. A much more interesting route runs north via Chiniot, an attractive little town on the Chenab River. The town's name is a corruption of Chandan, the name of a king's daughter who used to dress as a man and hunt in the area. One day she came to the banks of the Chenab and was so impressed by the beauty of the spot that she ordered a town to be built there. Chiniot today is known for its carved wooden furniture with brass inlay. In the narrow streets of the older parts of town, many of the houses have beautifully carved double gates surrounded by ornate brickwork. The artisans of Chiniot have been renowned for the excellence of their work since the Moghul period. They helped to build the Taj Mahal at Agra in India, the Golden Temple at Amritsar and the Wazir Khan Mosque in Lahore. The mosque in Chiniot with its elegant domes and pillars dates from the 17th century.

From Chiniot you can cross the Chenab River and continue north to **Sargodha**, a large city important for its airforce base, thence via Khushab and the Salt Range to Islamabad. The route from Chiniot to Gujranwala is uninteresting, though in reasonable condition; the stretch from Sargodha to Jhelum is not recommended, as much of it is in poor condition.

Via Lahore (ten hours)

The **National Highway** from Multan to Lahore and Islamabad is fast, busy and dangerous. The 350-kilometre (217-mile) drive to Lahore, through irrigated farmland all the way, takes four to five hours, but you should allow a few hours for a stop at Harappa or Chhanga Manga, or both. It takes ten hours to drive all the way from Multan to Islamabad.

The Multan cotton fields give way to fruit orchards and an extensive forest. The embroidered pointed slippers and brilliantly coloured turbans of the lower Punjab are replaced by sandals, khaki clothes and white turbans.

Harappa

The turning to the Indus Civilization city of Harappa is about 150 kilometres (93 miles) from Multan and is clearly marked in English—'Harappa Museum 6 km' (four miles)—near Harappa railway station.

Harappa was discovered in the mid-19th century by railway engineers building the Lahore–Multan track. David Ross, in *The Land of Five Rivers* (1882), wrote: 'The ruins were extensive enough to provide brick ballast for about 100 miles [160 kilometres] of the railway: in this way several of the large mounds have been entirely cleared away.' What they did not realize was that they were carting off the remains of a 4,000-year-old city, a contemporary of ancient Babylon, Ur and Egypt.

Not until the 1940s was Harappa recognized as an Indus Civilization city of about the same size as Moenjodaro (see pages 96–104). These are the two largest of the Indus Civilization sites excavated so far and have been called the twin capitals. Moenjodaro is more exciting to visit, but at Harappa there is a good **museum**, with Indus Civilization seals, jewellery, stone weights, shell spoons, copper and pottery utensils, and an amusing collection of games (including a type of chess), pottery rattles and whistles, toy carts, and animal and human figurines. There are also displays from other sites along the Indus: Rohri, Kot Diji, Moenjodaro and Amri.

A tour of the site itself takes about an hour. Leave the museum and follow the path past the cemetery. Jars containing human bones were found here, and are thought to be of a later date than the Indus Civilization. Some jars and skeletons are on display in the museum.

The path leads up onto the mound excavated by Sir Mortimer Wheeler in 1946. This is the **citadel area**, with the public buildings and a brick-lined well. If you turn left across the citadel you come to a large trench cut by Wheeler through the

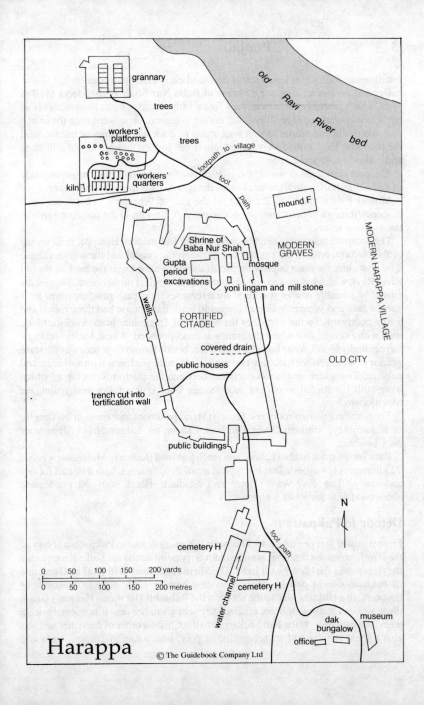

old Ravi River bed

granary

trees

workers' platforms

trees

kiln

workers' quarters

footpath to village

foot path

mound F

MODERN HARAPPA VILLAGE

Shrine of Baba Nur Shah

mosque

Gupta period excavations

yoni lingam and mill stone

MODERN GRAVES

walls

FORTIFIED CITADEL

OLD CITY

covered drain

public houses

trench cut into fortification wall

public buildings

N

cemetery H

cemetery H

water channel

foot path

dak bungalow

office

museum

0   50   100   150   200 yards
0   50   100   150   200 metres

Harappa

© The Guidebook Company Ltd

fortification wall; in its lower levels he found early Harappan pottery.

Beyond the citadel area is the **Shrine of Baba Nur Shah Wali**, a local Muslim saint, which probably dates from the 17th or 18th century, and in front of this is an enclosure containing three stones. According to legend, these were once the saint's ring and pestle and mortar, which were made of gold; when someone tried to steal the treasures, they immediately turned into stone. In fact, they are an old mill stone and a Hindu *yoni* and *lingam*.

The path then leads down off the citadel past the ruins of a brick **mosque**, made of the old Indus Civilization bricks and thought to date from Moghul times.

Mound F (see map), on the right, is the site of Wheeler's deepest trench; it descends through various levels of occupation. A diagram in the museum explains the exposed levels.

The footpath between a neighbouring village and modern Harappa, built on top of the old city, crosses the excavations between the citadel and the workers' area. You now enter the most interesting part of the excavations near the bank of the old River Ravi, which has moved eight kilometres (five miles) further north. Nearest the citadel is a double row of **workers' quarters**, seven in each row, separated by a narrow lane and surrounded by a compound wall. Each house had three rooms and a tiny courtyard. To the north lies the **mill**, with 18 circular brick work-surfaces, each with a central hole where the grain was hand-pounded. Wheat, barley and straw were actually found in one hole. Beyond these, beside the old river bed, was the **state granary**. What you see today are two rows of six brick platforms with a wide central passage. Triangular ventilation ducts ran between the platforms, on top of which were built flat-roofed wood and mud storage bins. (For a fuller description, see Moenjodaro.)

The comfortable two-room rest house at Harappa is bookable through the director of archaeology, Northern Circle, Old Fort, Lahore, tel. Lahore 56747. Bring your own bedding.

Back on the main road to Lahore you reach **Sahiwal** (formerly Montgomery) after 22 kilometres (14 miles). This is a typical small Punjabi town, with a biscuit factory and dairy. The Five-Ways Hotel and Stadium Hotel both offer adequate accommodation for Rs40 a night.

Detour to Pakpattan

From Sahiwal you can take a 48-kilometre (30-mile) detour to **Pakpattan** (Ferry of the Pure), which for centuries was the main ferry point across the Sutlej River; today the river marks the border with India. The **Shrine to Baba Farid Shakar Gunj**, one of Pakistan's most popular saints who died here in 1265, attracts thousands of devotees. In a building next to the shrine is the **Baheshti Darwasa** (Heaven's Gate); those who walk through it are assured they will go to heaven. It is opened once a week, for men only. Baba Farid belonged to the Chishtia order of dervishes and was also a great scholar and an accomplished poet, who wrote in Persian, Urdu and

Punjabi. His urs is held from the 25th day of the lunar month of Zilhij to the 10th of Muharram, when the town is thronged with pilgrims.

From Pakpattan you can continue northeast to **Dipalpur**, another ancient centre of religion and learning, and in the 14th century second only to Multan in size and importance. Turn left here to rejoin the National Highway to Lahore.

Chhanga Manga

The **Chhanga Manga Wildlife Reserve** lies in a huge forest halfway between Sahiwal and Lahore, ten kilometres (six miles) east of the National Highway, and right on the main railway line. The oldest irrigated plantation in the subcontinent, Chhanga Manga was planted by the British in 1890 partly to provide wood fuel for the railway steam engines. Today, train enthusiasts and children can enjoy the five small steam engines which pull narrow-gauge tourist trains through the woods. It costs Rs50 to hire a bogey for 12 passengers. The reserve contains several species of deer in large fenced pens, shady walks, a lake with boating facilities and a restaurant, and is an excellent place to spend the night. Tourist huts with bedding and showers cost Rs20 for 24 hours. It is crowded on Fridays and public holidays but peaceful the rest of the week.

It takes an hour to cover the 70 kilometres (43 miles) from Chhanga Manga to Lahore.

LAHORE

Lahore, the capital of the Punjab, is one of the great Moghul cities of the subcontinent, ranking with Delhi or Agra in its range of superb Muslim architecture. It is Pakistan's cultural and intellectual centre. The faded elegance, busy streets and bazaars, and wide variety of Islamic and British architecture make this a city of atmosphere, surprises and contrasts. As Peshawar looks north to central Asia, so Lahore looks south to the great civilization of the Moghul emperors.

Lahore has been the capital of the Punjab for nearly 1,000 years; from 1021 to 1186 it was governed by Mahmud of Ghazni and the Ghaznavid dynasty, then by Muhammad of Ghor, and finally by the various sultans of Delhi. It reached its full glory under Moghul rule (1524–1752). The third Moghul emperor, Akbar, held his court in Lahore from 1584 to 1598, during which time he built the present Lahore Fort and enclosed the old city within a red brick wall with 12 gates. Jahangir and Shah Jahan added to the fort, built palaces and tombs and laid out gardens. The last of the great Moghuls, Aurangzeb (1658–1707), erected Lahore's most famous monument, the great Badshahi Mosque.

In the 18th and 19th centuries the Sikhs also had their capital at Lahore. It is said that they took enough marble from the city's Moghul monuments to build the Golden Temple at Amritsar twice over.

When the British took over in 1849, they erected the splendid, stolid Victorian

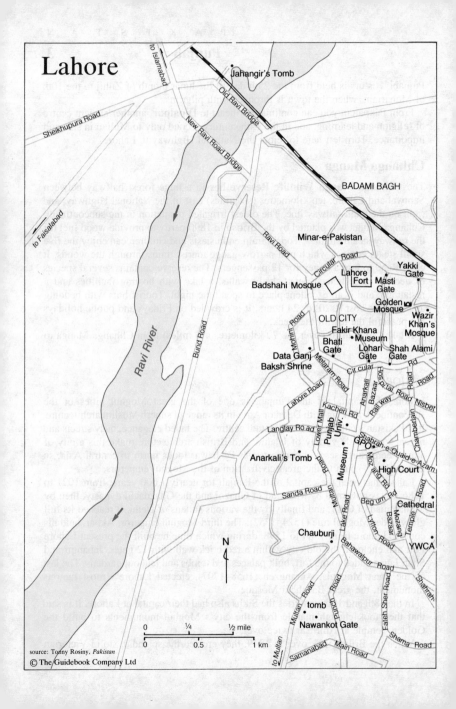

Lahore

to Islamabad

Sheikhupura Road

to Faisalabad

Old Ravi Bridge

New Ravi Road Bridge

Jahangir's Tomb

BADAMI BAGH

Ravi Road

Circular Road

Minar-e-Pakistan

Ravi River

Bund Road

Mohni Road

Badshahi Mosque

Lahore Fort

Masti Gate

Golden Mosque

Yakki Gate

Wazir Khan's Mosque

OLD CITY

Fakir Khana Museum

Bhati Gate

Lohari Gate

Shah Alami Gate

Data Ganj Baksh Shrine

Mclaram Road

Circular Road

Lahore Road

Railway Road

Anarkali Bazaar

Bull Road

Nisbet Road

Kacheri Rd

Langlay Road

Lower Mall Road

Punjab Univ.

Shahrah-e-Quaid-e-Azam

GPO

Chamberlain

Anarkali's Tomb

Museum

Mozang Rd

High Court

Sanda Road

Multan Road

Begum Rd

Mozang Bazaar

Lytton Road

Cathedral

Temple Road

Chauburji

Lake Road

Bahawalpur Road

YWCA

Shahrah

N

tomb

Nawankot Gate

Multan Road

Fateh Sher Road

Shama Road

0   ¼   ½ mile

0   0.5   1 km

Samanabad Main Road

to Multan

source: Tonny Rosiny, *Pakistan*

© The Guidebook Company Ltd

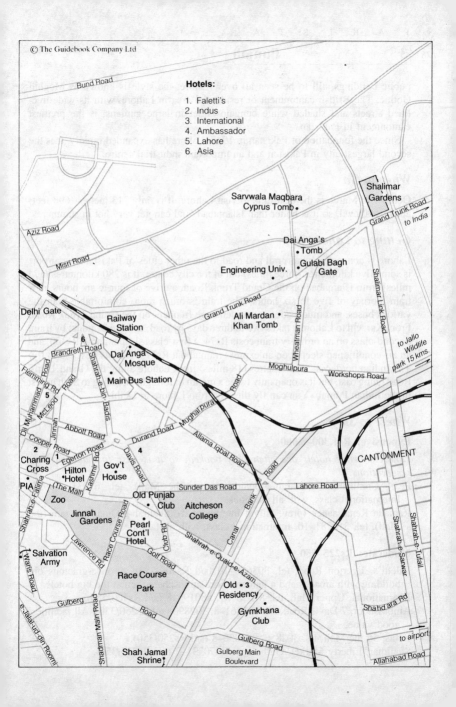

© The Guidebook Company Ltd

Hotels:
1. Faletti's
2. Indus
3. International
4. Ambassador
5. Lahore
6. Asia

public buildings still to be seen all over Lahore; the style is known as Moghul Gothic. The British cantonment or residential area in Lahore, with its wide tree-lined streets and shaded white bungalows set in large gardens, is the prettiest cantonment in Pakistan.

Since the foundation of Pakistan in 1947, Lahore has expanded rapidly. It is the second largest city in Pakistan and an important industrial centre.

When to Go

October to March is the best time to visit Lahore. It is only 213 metres (698 feet) above sea level, so it is hotter than Islamabad, and can get very hot in summer.

Getting to Lahore

Lahore is connected by air, rail and road to the other cities of Pakistan; the airport is some five kilometres (three miles) out of the city centre. It is 280 kilometres (174 miles) from Islamabad on the Grand Trunk Road, a drive of four to six hours, or a train journey of five to six hours. The train is much more comfortable than the various buses, and much safer as accidents are frequent on the Grand Trunk Road. From Karachi to Lahore it takes two to three days by road, or 16 to 21 hours by train. Second-class on an ordinary train costs Rs74, a first-class sleeper about Rs300, and an air-conditioned sleeper on an express train about Rs775. It costs Rs1,530 to fly. The Indian border is 29 kilometres (18 miles) from Lahore along the Grand Trunk Road going east, but it is open only twice a month to foreigners, owing to Sikh unrest in the Indian Punjab. You can fly directly from Lahore to Delhi.

Where to Stay

Expensive: Rs1,300–3,000

Lahore's better hotels are often fully booked, so it is wise to make advance reservations.

Pearl Continental, Shahrah-e-Quaid-e-Azam (the Mall), tel. 67931, 69931. International class, with all facilities.

Ramada Renaissance (prev. Hilton International), Shahrah-e-Quaid-e-Azam (the Mall), tel. 310281–10. International class, with all facilities.

Moderate: Rs225–550

Faletti's, Egerton Road, tel. 303660–10 (s/d Rs400/550). A once-gracious old building with arcades and a garden; more atmosphere than at the big hotels.

International, Upper Mall, tel. 870281–7, 880196–8 (s/d Rs400/550).

Ambassador, 7 Davis Road, tel. 301861–8, 302890 (s/d Rs250/350). All facilities; good value.

Indus, 56 the Mall, tel. 302850, 302856–8 (s/d Rs250/350).

Shalimar, Liberty Market, Gulberg, tel. 870331–3 (s/d Rs225/350).

Cheaper: Rs50–300

Country Club Motel, 105-A the Mall, tel. 311361–2 (s/d Rs200/250).

Orient, 74 McLeod Road, tel. 223906–8 (s/d Rs100–150/200–300).

Lahore, Kashmir Building, McLeod Road, tel. 320257–69, 320250 (s/d Rs70–110/150–200).

Menora, 41 McLeod Road, tel. 224028–9, 224031 (s/d Rs80–190/130–250).

Uganda, 45 McLeod Road, tel. 56077, 310553 (s/d Rs60–140/100–200).

Asia, near railway station, tel. 57429, 57997 (s/d Rs90/130).

Parkway, near railway station, tel. 540547, 320155 (s/d Rs60–190/90–190).

Shabistan, McLeod Road, near railway station, tel. 56744 (s/d Rs50/75).

Inexpensive

The cheap hotels in Lahore, particularly those near the railway station and along McLeod Road, are not safe. Problems range from stolen travellers cheques to planted drugs and blackmail.

Recommended are:

Railway Retiring Rooms, Lahore City Station (s/d Rs20/30).

Youth Hostel, 110-B/3 Firdous Market, Gulberg 111, tel. 83145 (dorm Rs10). Good, but a bit far from the centre; camping allowed.

YMCA Hostel, the Mall, near GPO, tel. 54433 (dorm Rs20). Easy to miss, as it is in part of a large building; usually full.

YWCA Hostel, Fatima Jinnah Road, tel. 304707 (s Rs45, dorm Rs30). Camping allowed in garden.

Salvation Army Hostel, 35 Fatima Jinnah Road (dorm Rs10–30). Camping allowed in garden.

Where to Eat

Restaurant food in Lahore is probably the tastiest in Pakistan. Some of the best-known restaurants are:

Gulberg Kabana, Main Boulevard, Gulberg, tel. 871062, 872255. Pakistani food; quail especially good.

Kababeesh, Main Boulevard, Gulberg, tel. 873218. Pakistani food.

Menage, Main Boulevard, Gulberg.

Rendezvous, Main Boulevard, Gulberg.

Tung Fung, Main Boulevard, Gulberg, tel. 87561. Chinese.

Tai Wah, Main Boulevard, Gulberg. Chinese.

Saloos, WAPDA House, the Mall, tel. 325257.

Lords, the Mall, tel. 312235.

Shezan Oriental, the Mall, tel. 54450; also in Fortress Stadium.

Kabana, Davis Road, tel. 305489.

Kabana, Fortress Stadium, Cantt. tel. 370550.

Tolenton Kabana, the Mall.

Cathay Restaurant, opposite American Express on the Mall. Chinese.

Salt and Pepper, Liberty Market; Fortress Stadium; the Mall (opposite High Court). Most popular of the fast-food places—beefburgers and chips!

Polka Parlour and Carvel, both popular ice-cream parlours on Main Boulevard, Gulberg.

Yummy 36, Liberty Market. Ice-cream parlour.

For cheaper eating it is also worth trying Mozang Bazaar for chicken tikka; the Gamal Mandu area, near the old city, for fried fish; the Anarkali Bazaar for local dishes of every kind; the stalls in Liberty Market; and finally the Abbott Road wayside stalls.

Lahore specialities include a breakfast of *purri*, *halwa* and *lassi*. *Purri* are small, crisp, deep-fried pancakes made of wheat flour; *halwa* is sweet semolina mixed with nuts and raisins, and *lassi* is buttermilk. For lunch try *haleem*, seven types of lentils, rice and meat cooked for hours in a big pot (called a *degh*); or *murgh chola*, chicken and chick peas. The between-meal snacks are endless: *kulfa falooda*, ice cream with rose water and vermicelli on top; *purri bhaji*, chick peas and potatoes with spices; *dhai bara*, yoghurt and lentil-flour fritters; and *kachari*, samoosa balls filled with mince meat or potatoes. Anarkali Bazaar is famous for its fruit *chart*, a fruit salad in juice and spices, and opposite the Gulistan Cinema stop for the 'Kashmiri' tea, pink tea with pistachios, almonds and cream.

Useful Addresses

Tourist Information Centre, PTDC, Faletti's Hotel, Egerton Road, tel. 303660, 303623–4.

Director of Archaeology, Northern Circle, Lahore Fort, Lahore 8, tel. 56747.

Passport Office, Muslim Town, near Canal Bank, tel. 854202.

Sights

The most impressive sights in Lahore are the fort, Badshahi Mosque, Wazir Khan Mosque, the Shalimar Garden and Jahangir's Tomb, all belonging to the Moghul period, and the Lahore Central Museum, built by the British. Only a student of Moghul architecture would want to take the time to explore all the old tombs and gardens, as this would occupy several energetic days. The places of interest are described here in geographical order; many of them can be seen at a glance in passing.

Historic Tour

You pass many of Lahore's most interesting buildings driving from the airport along the Mall to Lahore Fort and Badshahi Mosque. About four kilometres (2.5 miles) along the road into Lahore, you pass the aptly named **Fortress Stadium** on the right, where the famous annual Horse and Cattle Show is held in February or March. This is a national event featuring polo, tent-pegging and dancing camels, among other attractions.

Cross the railway bridge and drive by the modern **New Gymkhana Club**, with its golf course on the left, followed by the British-built **Old Residency** (now the state guest house), set back among the trees in lovely gardens. You can catch a glimpse of its white colonnades through its three gates, just before you cross the canal.

The Mall then becomes wider and is lined with mature trees. Next on the right is **Aitchison College**, Pakistan's most renowned school, which is run on British boarding-school lines. It is in fine Moghul Gothic style (red brick with arches, domes, cupolas and baubles), and surrounded by extensive playing fields. The **Old Punjab Club** is next on the right (opposite the Pearl Continental Hotel), a white colonial building with columns in front. This was the last bastion of colonialism in Pakistan; the government confiscated the building in the early 1950s because the club refused to accept Pakistani members. It is now the Pakistan Administrative Staff College.

The following building on the right, behind its yellow wall, is **Government House**, the residence of the governor of the Punjab. The house was built around the early 16th-century tomb of Qasim Khan, a cousin of Emperor Akbar. Qasim Khan was a great patron of wrestlers and, in fact, until Sikh times the tomb was known as Gumbaz Kushiwala (Wrestlers' Dome); wrestling bouts were staged in the grounds. It was converted into a residence first by the Sikhs and then by the British. The spacious vault is now the dining room, and is beautifully decorated with Moghul fresco paintings of floral and arabesque designs; the small brick sarcophagus lies in a little chamber beneath this room. This sort of conversion was common throughout Pakistan.

The **Old Gymkhana Club**, now the Quaid-e-Azam Library, is located opposite Government House within a lovely garden. The combined Lawrence and Montgomery halls were built in 1862 and 1866 to commemorate the first two British governors of the Punjab. Next door are the spacious **Jinnah Public Gardens** with a small zoo, which is worth a visit if you have children.

On the right is the new **Al-Hambra Art Centre**, followed by the red brick Ramada Renaissance (previously Hilton) Hotel; behind this is the old colonial-style Faletti's Hotel.

The five-road intersection beside the Ramada is popularly known as **Charing Cross**. On the right is the **WAPDA Building**, an impressive modern structure with a roof garden and a glass dome that resembles a flying saucer. In front of the WAPDA building is a modern square marble column which commemorates the Islamic Summit Conference of 1974. Beside the column is the provincial **Assembly Hall**. Also at Charing Cross is the elegant marble pavilion that today houses an open Koran in a glass case and which used to shelter the bronze statue of Queen Victoria now on display in the Central Museum.

If you continue along the Mall, you will see the spire and dome of the modern, red

brick **Catholic Cathedral** off to your left and a modern mosque in front. Further
along on the left is the **High Court**, a red brick Moghul Gothic building replete with
towers and cusped arches; this is followed by what was once the General Post
Office. On your right is the **Anglican Cathedral**, and then the **Punjab University**,
another red brick Moghul Gothic structure with fluted columns, arches and pillared
cupolas.

The **Lahore Central Museum**, on the left, was built by the British in Moghul
Gothic style and opened in 1894. John Lockwood Kipling, Rudyard's father, was
the museum's first curator. It is the best museum in Pakistan, with a superb
collection of Buddhist stone sculpture from the Gandharan period, the best piece
being the statue of the fasting Buddha; a fine Islamic collection of illustrated
manuscripts, miniatures, rugs and carvings; and a good ethnographic display. The
prehistory gallery is also excellent.

The famous **Zam-zama**, the gun which Rudyard Kipling's Kim played on, stands
in the middle of the road in front of the Central Museum, surrounded by water to
discourage anyone from emulating Kim. It has often been said that whoever holds
Zam-zama holds the Punjab. It was cast in 1760 for the Afghan Durranis and used
in the third battle of Panipat a year later, and in the siege of Multan in 1848, where
it was damaged after firing only two rounds.

Next comes the **Town Hall** on the left, a white building with bulbous silver
domes. Turn right (north) for the fort and Badshahi Mosque. Or make a detour to
visit the **Tomb of Anarkali**, which is inside the grounds of the Punjab Secretariat
on the Lower Mall. The tomb is open only from 12 noon to 2 pm Saturday to
Wednesday, and 11 am to 12 noon on Thursday; it is closed Friday. You must ask
at the gate of the Secretariat for a gate pass, and wait for an escort.

Anarkali (Pomegranate Blossom) was a legendary favourite in the harem of
Emperor Akbar. Apparently she had an affair with Akbar's son, Prince Salim. One
day Akbar saw her return Salim's smile, and as punishment she was buried alive.
When Salim became Emperor Jahangir, he built her a magnificent tomb. On the
marble cenotaph, beside the 99 attributes of God, is written:

Ah, if I could again see the face of my beloved,
To the day of judgment I would give thanks to my Creator.

The tomb is a forerunner of the Taj Mahal: it is octagonal, with a huge dome in the
centre surrounded by eight octagonal cupolas supported by columns.

The tomb has had a varied history. It became the residence of Ranjit Singh's son
and successor, Kharak Singh, and was later given to General Ventura, the French
mercenary who fought for the Sikhs, and who lived next door in the present
Secretariat; he used the tomb as his *zenana* (women's house). In 1851 it was
converted into the British civil station's Church of St James; at this time the arches
were blocked up and the Islamic decorations whitewashed over. In 1891 the tomb
became the Punjab Record Room.

The direct road from the museum north to the Badshahi Mosque and Lahore Fort passes **Government College**, a church-like building with a spire and clock behind a red brick wall, and joins the Circular Road which carries traffic all the way around the old city.

This stretch of the Circular Road runs along the west side of the **old city**. The moat is now dry, and most of the defensive wall has been pulled down, but there is still an exciting view on your right of the tall old narrow houses of roughly baked brick crammed together in narrow twisting alleys. Floating above the old city are the white domes and minarets of the Badshahi Mosque. Turn right and follow the road round the north side of the mosque.

The **Minar-e-Pakistan**, in the park on the left of the road, is a modern 'Eiffel Tower', built on the spot where on 23 March 1940 the Muslim League Party of British India passed the resolution for the creation of the independent Muslim country of Pakistan. You can climb to the top for an excellent view of the fort, Badshahi Mosque, the **Tomb of Ranjit Singh** and **Guru Arjan's Memorial** outside the wall of the mosque.

Guru Arjan was the fifth Sikh guru. He compiled the *Adi Granth*, the original Sikh holy book (now in Amritsar in Indian Punjab). Guru Arjan angered Emperor Jahangir by supporting his rebel son Khusrau in the struggle for succession after Akbar's death, and in 1606 Jahangir confiscated all of Guru Arjan's property and condemned him to death. Before his execution Guru Arjan asked permission to bathe in the Ravi River, which flowed where the road now runs beside the Badshahi Mosque and Lahore Fort. He is believed to have stepped into the water and miraculously disappeared. His tomb, built in the early 19th century by the great Sikh leader Ranjit Singh, marks the spot where he disappeared. Its most notable features are the elegant fluted domes covered in gold leaf. The tomb is closed to the general public, but open to Sikhs and Hindus.

Ranjit Singh ruled the Punjab and Kashmir from 1799 to 1839. Known as the One-eyed Lion of the Punjab, this illiterate maharaja controlled his empire with a firm hand. His sons, however, were unable to hold the empire together, and the British annexed the Punjab in 1849.

Ranjit Singh's Tomb, or **Samadhi**, was begun by his son Kharak Singh on the spot where he was cremated, and was completed by Dalip Singh in 1848. The tomb is a splendid example of Sikh architecture, with gilded fluted domes and cupolas and an ornate balustrade round the top. The marble inside was taken from various Moghul monuments in Lahore. Ranjit's ashes are contained in a marble urn in the shape of a lotus, sheltered under a marble pavilion inlaid with pietra dura, in the centre of the tomb. Other tiny urns contain the ashes of his four wives and seven concubines, who threw themselves on his funeral pyre.

Two small monuments to the west of the main mausoleum commemorate Ranjit Singh's son Kharak and grandson Nau Nihal, and their wives.

Badshahi Mosque

The Badshahi Mosque, open 5 am–9 pm, is a superb example of the best of Moghul architecture, with its simple graceful lines and pleasing proportions. It was built by Emperor Aurangzeb in 1674, nearly 30 years after the great Moghul mosques at Delhi and Agra.

The mosque consists of a huge square with a minaret at each corner. To enter, you climb a broad flight of steps and pass through a monumental gateway decorated with floral frescoes. Inside is an enormous open square courtyard paved with red sandstone (and very hot to the bare feet in summer). A square marble fountain stands in the centre, and white-arched arcades surround the courtyard on three sides. On the opposite side to the entrance gate is the prayer chamber, crowned by three elegant marble domes; inside, the ceilings are decorated with carved plasterwork and floral frescoes in subdued colours.

You can climb up the 204 steps to the top of one of the minarets for a bird's-eye view of the mosque, the fort opposite, and the old city of Lahore. The height of each minaret is exactly one third of the length of each side of the courtyard.

In the rooms above the entrance gate (closed to the public) are kept some hair of the Prophet Muhammad and other relics of his daughter Fatima and son-in-law Ali.

Hazuri Bagh

The Hazuri Garden stands between the Badshahi Mosque and Lahore Fort. This square garden was originally built by Aurangzeb as a *serai*, or Moghul hotel. He also reviewed his troops here. The two-storey building by the southern gate was a boarding house for the scholars who studied at the Badshahi Mosque. The garden's north gate is called the **Roshnai Darwaza** (Gate of Light) because it was brightly lit at night. Nobles visiting the palaces inside the fort used this entrance. Ranjit Singh's grandson was killed here—probably not accidentally—by falling masonry while on his way from his father's cremation to his own coronation.

The **Hazuri Bagh Baradari**, the marble pavilion in the centre of the garden, was built by Ranjit Singh in 1818 with marble taken from various Moghul tombs and from the floor of the Hammam, or royal bath, in Lahore Fort. It is one of the few remaining Sikh monuments in Lahore. Elegant carved marble pillars support delicate cusped arches; the central area, where Ranjit Singh held court, has a mirrored ceiling. The pavilion consisted of two storeys until it was damaged by lightning in 1932.

The **Tomb of Allama Muhammad Iqbal** (1873–1938), the great poet-philosopher who conceived the idea of Pakistan as a separate Muslim state, is on the left of the gate to the Badshahi Mosque. Built in 1951, the small red sandstone tomb has marble doorframes and an interior completely faced with decorated white marble. The translucent marble headstone, a gift from Afghanistan, is inscribed with two of the poet's couplets summing up his views against racial discrimination.

Lahore Fort

Lahore Fort is a huge rectangle, 380 by 330 metres (1,250 by 1,080 feet), standing on the northwestern edge of the old walled city of Lahore. It ranks in size and beauty with the Moghul forts at Delhi and Agra.

Akbar began building the fort in the 1560s on the site of an older fort beside the Ravi River (now about one kilometre, or half a mile, away). The next three emperors extended and improved the fort. Some of the buildings today are in their original condition, but others have been damaged or altered by the Sikhs and British. Fountains, lawns and flower arrangements embellish the courtyards and help to give some idea of what it looked like in Moghul times.

You can expect to spend about two hours here, so wear comfortable shoes. It is best to follow the route on the map, as it is easy to get lost in the fort and the signposting is not perfect.

You enter the fort through the **Alamgiri Gate** (1) built by Aurangzeb in 1674 at the same time as the Badshahi Mosque opposite. Inside the gatehouse you can buy souvenirs and softdrinks. From the gate a ramp leads up to the old **Musamman Burj Gate** (2) on the left, and the royal **kitchens** (3) on the right (now occupied by the police and closed to the public). This takes you up to the level of the courtyards, underneath which is a maze of dungeons, storerooms and offices. The central rooms are dark—only those along the walls have windows. This area is also closed to the public.

The **Maktab Khana**, or Clerks' House (4), is a small cloistered court with arcades on all four sides, where clerks sat recording the names of visitors. According to the inscription outside, it was built by Jahangir in 1618; some authorities claim that he built the Maktab Khana as his own private residence. To the north lies a large courtyard with a snackbar under a huge tree. From the corner of this court steps lead up to the tiny **Moti Masjit** (5), the quiet and secluded Pearl Mosque built by Shah Jahan in 1644. Shah Jahan later built a similar mosque in the Agra Red Fort in 1654; Aurangzeb built the most exquisite pearl mosque of all in 1662 in the Delhi Red Fort. All three are faced in white marble, charmingly intimate, and noteworthy for their delicate proportions and purity of line. In Sikh times the mosque was used as a treasury, but in 1904 British Governor-General Lord Curzon ordered its restoration.

The **Diwan-e-Am** (6), or Hall of Public Audience, an open pavilion with 40 pillars, was built by Shah Jahan in 1631. The original building collapsed when it was shelled in 1841 by the Sikhs from the top of a minaret of the Badshahi Mosque. It was rebuilt (badly) by the British in 1849 and used as a hospital. The British covered the spacious lawn in front with barracks and offices, but these have since been removed.

The **marble pavilion**, with its red sandstone balcony, at the back of the Diwan-e-Am is the original built by Akbar. Akbar appeared here daily before the public, who crowded below under a canvas awning. The serpentine sandstone brackets show Hindu influence, as does much of Akbar's architecture. Akbar's two-storey

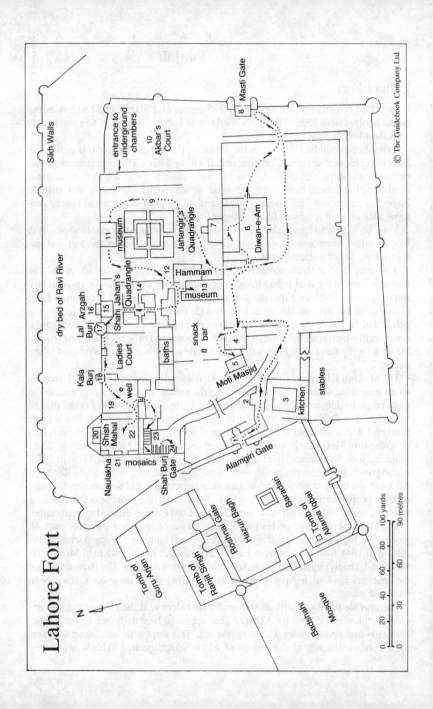

Lahore Fort

© The Guidebook Company Ltd

Sikh Walls

dry bed of Ravi River

entrance to underground chambers

8 Masti Gate

10 Akbar's Court

11 museum

9

7

6 Diwan-e-Am

Jahangir's Quadrangle

12 Hammam

13 museum

14 Shah Jahan's Quadrangle

15 Lal Arzgah Burj

16

17

snack bar

baths

4

5 Moti Masjid

3 kitchen

stables

Ladies Court

Kala Burj

18

well

19

2

20 Shish Mahal

21

22

23

24

Alamgiri Gate

Naulakha

mosaics

Shah Burj Gate

1

Baradari

Tomb of Allama Iqbal

Tomb of Guru Arjan

Tomb of Ranjit Singh

Roshnai Gate

Hazuri Bagh

Badshahi Mosque

N

0 10 20 30 40 60 80 100 yards

0 30 60 90 metres

Hall of Private Audience (7), built in 1566, lies behind the balcony and is reached by stairs on the left. Inside you can still see traces of the original painted and gilded stucco work; the marblework is the oldest in Lahore.

Masti (or **Masjidi**) **Gate** (8) is east of the Diwan-e-Am. Built by Akbar in 1566, this was the fort's original main gate. It is so called because of the Masjid (Mosque) of Maryam Zamani just outside. The gate is defended by heavy octagonal bastions equipped with battlements, loopholes and machicolations for pouring boiling oil on attackers.

Jahangir's Quadrangle (9), north of the Diwan-e-Am, is one of the most attractive parts of the fort. It was begun by Akbar in 1566 and finished by Jahangir in 1617. Three sides of the court are taken up by buildings in typical Akbari style, with richly carved red sandstone columns and elaborate animal brackets. The latter again show Hindu influence. In British times the central fountain in Jahangir's Quadrangle was filled in and converted into a tennis court, but this has now been removed. Behind the buildings on the right is **Akbar's Court** (10), which houses the fort offices and the conservation laboratories in the underground rooms.

The **Khwabhah-e-Jahangir** (11), Jahangir's Room of Dreams, or sleeping quarters, is the main building across the north side of Jahangir's Quadrangle. Its austere character is typical of the period. It is now a museum and contains a huge ivory model of the Taj Mahal, returned from England in 1950; some excellent illustrated manuscripts, including the *Akbar Nama*, the daily chronicle of Akbar's reign; some good Moghul miniatures; and a collection of Moghul coins.

The **Hammam** (12), Jahangir's bathhouse, is situated in the southwest corner of the quadrangle. It was once very luxurious, being paved with marble and decorated with delicate floral wall frescoes—today only traces of these remain. A cascade of water flowed over the carved sandstone in the niche on the southern wall. The bath was remodelled in Sikh times and used as a kitchen by the British.

The new **museum** (13) to the west of the bath contains a fine collection of Moghul and Sikh arms, and paintings of battle scenes and charging horses belonging to the Sikh period. Outside, stairs lead to the second floor, where there are more Sikh paintings.

From the museum you again enter the quadrangle of the Moti Masjid. From here turn north to enter **Shah Jahan's Quadrangle** (14) through the window to Shah Jahan's sleeping quarters. These comprise five connecting rooms built in 1633; the central room has white marble latticework screens, marble doorframes and a marble fountain in the centre. The fresco of Radha and Krishna on the back wall of the central chamber dates from the Sikh period.

The **Diwan-e-Khas** (15), or Hall of Private Audience, on the north side of Shah Jahan's Quadrangle, is a graceful arcaded marble pavilion built by Shah Jahan in about 1645. Delicate marble latticework screens overlook the now dry bed of the Ravi River, and the floor is paved with different coloured marble laid in geometric patterns. A small fountain in the centre was once inlaid with pietra dura work, but only a few pieces remain in place today. The British converted the pavilion into a church. Below the pavilion at the foot of the fort wall is the ruined **Arzgah** (16), where nobles assembled every morning to pay their respects to the emperor. On the outer wall at this point are some particularly fine tile mosaics of blue dragons, the imperial emblem (see next page).

The **Lal Burj** or Red Tower (17), in the northwest corner of Shah Jahan's Quadrangle, is an octagonal summer pavilion built by Jahangir and Shah Jahan between 1617 and 1631. It forms part of the north wall of the fort and is decorated with tile mosaics and filigree work. Most of the floral scrolls inside belong to the Sikh period. The Sikhs also added the third storey. The present sandstone floor was originally marble, and water channels, fountains and a central pool must have made it delightfully cool in summer. On the staircase in the northeast corner you can see the remains of the gilded and painted honeycomb cornice, which give some indication of how lavishly decorated the whole pavilion once was.

You now enter the **Ghusl Khana**, or Ladies' Courtyard, built by Shah Jahan in 1633. The small marble pavilion in the middle of the north side overlooking the river, which was reserved for the emperor when he came to visit his harem, is the only building still standing, though you can also see the foundations of the ladies' apartments and private mosque. On the north side of the courtyard is the **Hammam** (bathhouse), almost in ruins, built in Turkish style with dressing room and warm and hot baths. In the southwestern room the original marble floor is still intact, and you can see the terracotta water pipes built into the wall. The heating system was at the western end beside the original *baitul khana* (lavatory).

The **Kala Burj**, or Black Tower (18), a summer pavilion built as a twin to the Lal Burj, is in the northwest corner of the ladies' court. All its decoration has gone, and the central portion is barred off, but you can still get through it to the **garden court** (19), the ladies' private garden.

The **Court of the Shish Mahal** (Palace of Mirrors) (20) is the best-preserved and most interesting part of the whole fort. The Shish Mahal, private apartments for the empress, was built by Shah Jahan in 1631. It was here that the sovereignty of the Punjab was assumed by the British government in 1849. The inside of the palace is completely covered in mirror mosaics, carved and gilded plasterwork and pietra dura work—the ceiling is original Moghul work. The walls, with shards of blue and white china and floral fresco paintings, are later Sikh work. The front of the main hall of the palace is open. Five cusped arches are supported by delicate fluted double pillars; pietra dura work decorates the base of each pillar and the tops of the arches, and the vine pattern over the two outer arches is particularly fine. The floor is a geometric marble mosaic. Surrounding the main hall is a string of nine connecting rooms overlooking the dry river bed. Through exquisite marble screens the ladies could gaze out without being seen and enjoy the cool river breeze. The easternmost room is covered in floral frescoes. From here there are excellent views along the outer walls of the fort: you can see the windows of the underground rooms and the remains of the brilliantly coloured tile mosaics of animals, people and geometric designs that once decorated the arched niches on the outer face of the wall.

The **Naulakha** (21), on the west side of the court, is a small marble pavilion with a curved roof in the style of a Bengali bamboo hut. It is called the Naulakha because it cost nine lakh (900,000) rupees to build in 1631. Decorating this dainty little pavilion is the finest pietra dura work in Lahore, with little pieces of carefully selected jade, carnelian, lapis, agate, jet and other semi-precious stones set into the marble in delicate floral and geometric designs. In one tiny niche above the double pillars supporting the archway, 102 minute pieces of stone are inlaid to make one floral pattern. Through a lovely marble screen you can see the Badshahi Mosque, Ranjit Singh's Tomb, the gold dome of Guru Arjan's Memorial, and the Minar-e-Pakistan.

On the south side of the court is a **row of rooms** (22). On the back wall of the central room is a water cascade which once filled the water channels and fountains in the courtyard. Behind this wall is the exit.

Follow the broad shallow steps of the **Hathi Paer** (23), or Elephant Path, the private entrance of the royal family, from the **Shah Burj Gate** (24). In the western wall overlooking the path are niches where eunuchs watched and a crier announced the comings and goings of royalty; above this is the upper gallery where servants stood in attendance. A door on the right leads to the underground rooms, but these are closed to the public.

As you leave the Shah Burj Gate, look to your right along the wall at the 350-year-old mosaic pictures set into the outer face of the fort wall. These glazed ceramic tile mosaics are of Persian origin, and during the reign of Shah Jahan were widely used to decorate the brick monuments of the Punjab, where stone is scarce. The mosaics decorating the west and north walls of Lahore Fort are unique in the variety and style of their design, for here the geometric patterns are liberally interspersed with animals and humans, which, like the Moghul miniature paintings, illustrate the court life and pastimes of the Moghuls. There are vigorous scenes of elephant, camel, and bull fights, a polo game and winged Persian fairies (*paris*) in floating robes. On the north wall are blue dragons and court scenes.

Complete your tour of the fort by driving all the way round the outside walls. On the other side of the fort, opposite the Masti Gate, is an old mosque, usually called the **Begum Shahi Mosque**, which was built by Empress Muryam Zamani, mother of Jahangir. There are original frescoes inside.

Old City and Wazir Khan's Mosque

Lahore Fort was built on the northwest corner of the old walled city of Lahore. When Akbar built the fort he also enclosed the old city inside a high brick wall with 12 gates, six of which are still standing.

To get to Wazir Khan's Mosque you can either walk from the Hazuri Bagh, through the maze of narrow lanes in the old city, or else take a tonga, rickshaw or car from the Hazuri Bagh round to the other side of the old city to **Delhi Gate**, a massive brick structure now painted white, and walk from there. Delhi Gate leads

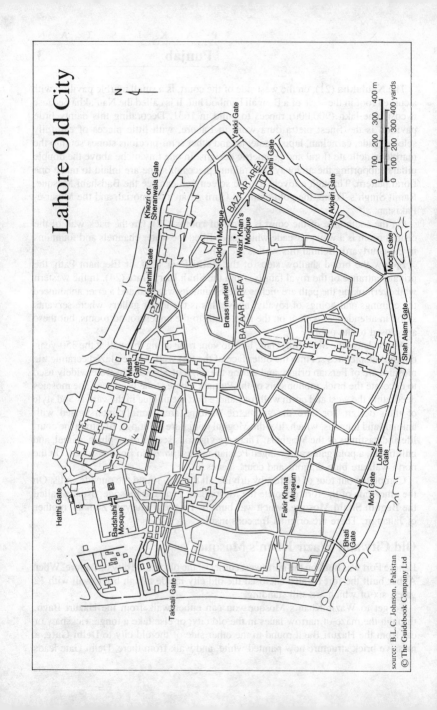

Lahore Old City

Yakki Gate

Delhi Gate

Akbari Gate

Mochi Gate

Shah Alami Gate

BAZAAR AREA

Golden Mosque

Wazir Khan's Mosque

Khezri or Sheranwala Gate

BAZAAR AREA

Brass market

Kashmiri Gate

Masti Gate

Hatti Gate

Badshahi Mosque

Fakir Khana Museum

Lohari Gate

Mori Gate

Bhati Gate

Taksali Gate

N

0   100   200   300   400 m
0   100   200   300   400 yards

source: B.L.C. Johnson, Pakistan
© The Guidebook Company Ltd

into the bazaar area, a narrow lane lined with tiny shops which sell everything from patent medicines to paper money garlands, from nail polish to rat traps. After about 300 metres (yards) you come to Wazir Khan's Mosque on the left.

This unique mosque is decorated with glazed mosaics and is one of the most beautiful in Pakistan. It was built in 1634 by Hakim Ali-ud-din (popularly known as Wazir Khan), from Chiniot (see page 171), governor of the Punjab under Shah Jahan. The mosque is made of brick and faced with brightly coloured glazed tile mosaics of Moghul floral designs on a clear yellow background. The enamelled mosaic work and fresco painting have been carefully restored by the few remaining Islamic craftsmen in Pakistan. The effect is very fine, particularly that of the mosaic calligraphy. Over the entrance is written in Persian:

Remove thy heart from the gardens of the world,
and know that this building is the true abode of man.

In the centre front of the mosque is the Muslim credo, and in panels along the façade are verses from the Koran. The prayer hall has five chambers, each surmounted by a dome. Octagonal minarets stand at each corner of the courtyard. The custodian will unlock one so you can climb up the 69 steps to the muezzin's gallery for excellent views over the old city. The grave in the courtyard belongs to Syed Muhammad Ishaq, or Miran Shah, a saint who died in the 14th century.

From the mosque continue west into the bazaar along a narrow lane lined with more tiny shops and,overhung by precarious wooden balconies. Overhead a maze of electric wires, within easy reach of the balconies, are festooned with wrecked kites. You pass all the exotic sights, sounds and smells of an Asian bazaar. After about 500 metres (yards) you emerge into the square of the **Golden Mosque**, or Sonehri Masjid, with its three gilded domes. This was built in 1753 by Bokhari Khan, a favourite of the powerful widow of Mir Mannu. Bokhari Khan is said to have displeased the lady, whose female attendants then beat him to death with their shoes.

In the courtyard behind the mosque is a large well, with steps leading down to the water. This is said to have been dug by Guru Arjan, the fifth Sikh guru.

Take the narrow alley that runs close along the left (south) wall of the mosque, and continue west along a very narrow lane where all shapes and sizes of pots and pans are sold by weight. This is the **brass bazaar**, where you can still pick up some fine antique brassware. After 200 metres (yards) you come out into a wider street, with a tonga and rickshaw stand straight in front of you. You can hire one very cheaply to take you out of the city via what was once the **Shah Almi Gate**; an abandoned Hindu temple now stands where the Moghul gate used to be.

Further to the west is the **Bhati Gate**. About 500 metres (yards) into the old city from the gate is the **Fakir Khana Museum**, a modest house on the right with a charming collection of family relics: Moghul miniatures, carpets, Gandhara statues, Chinese silks and jade.

The **Mausoleum of Data Ganj Baksh** stands outside Bhati Gate. This is the tomb of Syed Ali Abdul Hasan Bin Usman Hajweri, commonly known as Data Ganj Baksh or 'He Who Gives Generously'. This Sufi saint came from Ghazni in 1039 and lived in Lahore until his death in 1072. He was a great scholar and author of the *Kashful Mahjub*, a basic text in Persian on the fundamentals of Sufism. He is one of the most popular saints in Pakistan and every day hundreds of pilgrims flock to his shrine to pray and ask for blessings and favours. The urs (death festival) of Data Ganj Baksh, on the 18th and 19th days of the month of Saffar, is virtually a national event: thousands of devotees throng to Lahore to visit the shrine. (See pages 22–3 for more information on Sufism and Sufi shrines.)

Jahangir's Tomb

Another cluster of Moghul monuments in Lahore that should not be missed are the tombs of Jahangir, his wife Nur Jahan and her brother Asaf Khan. These are on the Grand Trunk Road to Rawalpindi, on the right just past the toll bridge across the River Ravi, about five kilometres (three miles) from the centre of Lahore. You can get there by buses 6 and 23 in about 20 minutes from Lahore Railway station. Turn right about 700 metres (half a mile) past the toll gate on the bridge. From the main

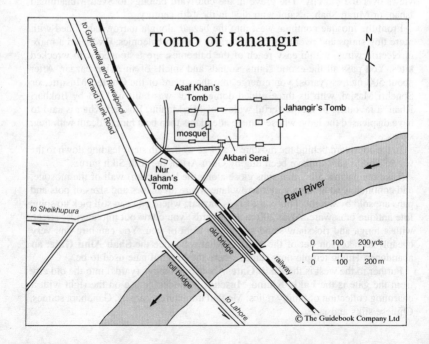

Tomb of Jahangir

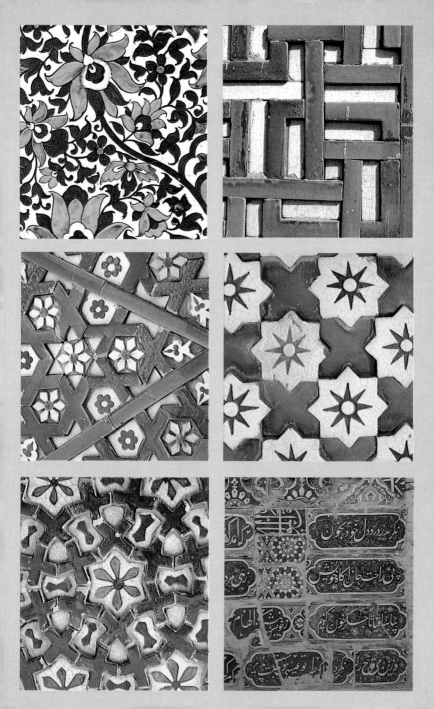

road you can see the dome and minarets of the tombs above the palm trees. If you are on foot follow the path across the railway to the tombs; if you are driving turn left after 600 metres (yards) and cross the railway level crossing. About 700 metres (yards) further on is the massive Moghul gateway leading into the tombs. The entrance fee is Rs2 for all three tombs.

The gateway of plastered red brick is covered in recently restored floral and geometric frescoes. It leads into the **Akbari Serai**, built by Shah Jahan in about 1637 as a travellers' hotel. The spacious garden is filled with huge chinar, plane, shisham (rosewood), peepul and banyan trees and divided into quarters by paths. Around the four sides are 180 small rooms, each with a verandah in front and connected by a wide sandstone terrace with a water channel carrying fast-flowing water round the edge. On the east side a handsome red sandstone gateway inlaid with marble leads into the tomb of Jahangir. Jahangir died in 1627; his tomb was built by his son Shah Jahan, of Taj Mahal fame. It stands in the centre of a large garden filled with mature spreading trees and divided by paths and water channels into 16 square segments.

There is a stall selling cold drinks just inside the gate on the right. This is a good place from which to admire the tomb.

The low square mausoleum has a flat roof, with tall octagonal minarets at the corners, decorated with zigzag designs and crowned with marble cupolas. The red sandstone walls are intricately decorated on the outside with geometric patterns of inlaid white marble. Inside, the floors are highly polished variegated marble, and the walls and ceilings of the surrounding arcade and 30 rooms are covered in geometric and floral fresco paintings. Four passages lead into the centre, where the white marble cenotaph stands on a plinth decorated with delicate floral designs in pietra dura work; the 99 attributes of God are inlaid in black marble. An inscription on the south side of the cenotaph reads:

The Glorious Tomb of His High Majesty, Asylum of Pardon
Nur-ud-din Muhammad, the Emperor Jahangir, 1627.

Marble latticework screens fill the arches on all four sides of the cenotaph.

A staircase in each of the five-storey minarets leads up to the flat roof, which is paved with white marble inlaid with geometric patterns in yellow and black and is surrounded by a balustrade. (Ask for the key at the ticket office.) There was originally another marble cenotaph surrounded by a marble railing in the centre of the roof; the Sikhs took this to Amritsar.

A French officer in Ranjit Singh's army, General Amise, converted Jahangir's Tomb into a residence. After the general's death, Sultan Muhammad, brother of the Afghan ruler Amir Dost Muhammad, resided there.

To the west, on the other side of the Akbari Serai, opposite the gate of Jahangir's tomb, is a red sandstone mosque. To the left of this a passage leads through to the

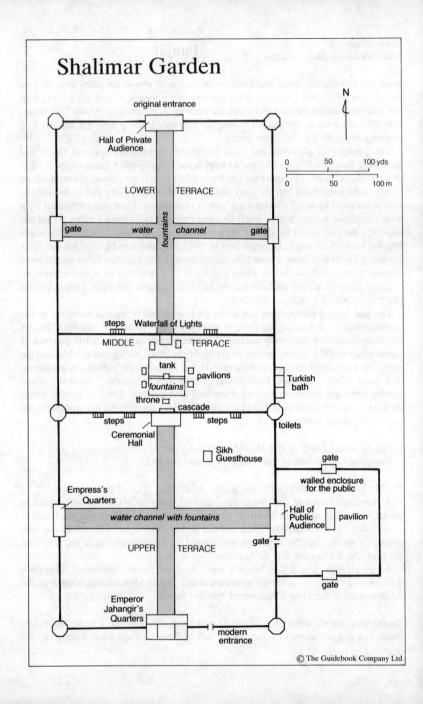

Shalimar Garden

N

original entrance

Hall of Private Audience

LOWER TERRACE

0 50 100 yds

0 50 100 m

gate   water   channel   gate

fountains

Waterfall of Lights

steps   steps

MIDDLE TERRACE

tank

pavilions

fountains

Turkish bath

throne

cascade

steps   Ceremonial   steps   toilets
               Hall

Sikh Guesthouse

gate

walled enclosure for the public

Empress's Quarters

Hall of Public Audience

pavilion

water channel with fountains

gate

UPPER TERRACE

gate

Emperor Jahangir's Quarters

modern entrance

© The Guidebook Company Ltd

Tomb of Asaf Khan, which stands in the centre of another large walled garden. You can see the bulbous dome of the tomb over the top of the mosque.

Asaf Khan was the brother of Jahangir's wife Nur Jahan, and father of Mumtaz Mahal, the lady for whom the Taj Mahal was built. He supported his son-in-law Shah Jahan in his struggle for succession, and on his death in 1641 Shah Jahan built him this huge mausoleum. It is a typical Moghul tomb in the middle of a walled garden with a graceful highpointed dome set on an octagonal base. No doubt it was spectacular when its arches were fully lined with blue, green, yellow and orange glazed tile mosaics, and its dome was covered in shining white marble (no traces of which remain). The marble cenotaph, once inlaid with pietra dura work, still displays the 99 attributes of God inlaid in black. Four fountains once stood at the four cardinal points on the plinth around the tomb. Of the two massive gates to the garden, the one to the north still retains some of its glazed tilework.

Further to the west, on the other side of the railway, is the **Tomb of Nur Jahan**. To get there follow the road west outside the south wall of Asaf Khan's Tomb. Turn left across the railway, and the tomb is immediately on the left.

Nur Jahan (d. 1645) survived her husband, Jahangir, by 18 years, during which time she lived in forced retirement. Her magnificent square tomb is similar in design to Jahangir's. The building was stripped down to its brick core by the Sikhs, and although it has recently been restored with a new sandstone facing inlaid with marble, it is still only a shadow of its former self. The four minarets and the garden wall have fallen, and inside only traces of fresco work remain. The original marble cenotaphs of Nur Jahan and her daughter Lakli Begum have disappeared; the existing ones, and the marble platform, are 20th-century replacements.

To return to the Grand Trunk Road go on past Nur Jahan's Tomb and turn right.

Shalimar Garden

The impressive Shalimar Garden is five kilometres (three miles) from the centre of town on the Grand Trunk Road toward the Indian border. You can get there in about 20 minutes from the railway station on bus 20. If you are going there by car from Jahangir's Tomb you can bypass Lahore on Bund Road from the toll bridge across the Ravi.

The best times to visit the gardens are when the fountains are playing: 10–11 am and 4–5 pm in summer, and 11 am to 12 noon and 3–4 pm in winter.

The garden was built by Shah Jahan in 1642 as a pleasure garden for the royal household; it follows the Moghul concept of the perfect walled garden, with three terraces of straight shaded walks, geometrically arranged ponds, fountains, and marble pavilions, surrounded by flowers and fruit trees. (English and European 17th-century gardens were very similar in their rigid geometrical layout.) The garden is especially lovely in February and March when the flowers are at their best; in summer it can be dry and dusty, though it is still a pleasant place to relax after a sightseeing expedition.

The garden is completely surrounded by a high brick wall with serrated battlements, and decorated on the inside with cusped arched panels of different sizes. Originally it was plastered and painted, and you can still see traces of frescoes on the lowest terrace. The garden was actually used as a palace, the court often staying here for days or weeks at a time.

Originally one entered the garden by two gates in the lowest terrace and progressed upwards against the stream of flowing water to discover new and greater delights at each higher level. Today the entrance is off the Grand Trunk Road through the emperor's private sleeping quarters, straight onto the upper terrace and on down to the least beautiful terrace at the bottom.

The **upper terrace**, once the inner sanctum of the royal family, comprises nine buildings. Ponds with fountains divide the court into four quarters.

The **emperor's sleeping quarters**, in the centre of the south wall, consist of three rooms with a wide verandah in front and five graceful cusped arches supported by pillars. Originally the walls and ceilings were covered in frescoes, of which today only traces remain.

In the centre of the west wall of the upper terrace are the **empress's quarters**, and in the centre of the east wall is the **Hall of Public Audience**. This building juts through the walls to the outside. The emperor used to walk through the building daily to show himself to the public, who gathered in a separate walled garden outside. The arcaded pavilion on the north side is the **Grand Hall** and was used for ceremonial functions. It, too, was once covered with frescoes. An octagonal tower house stands in each corner.

The little house in the northeast quarter of the terrace was built by the Sikhs in the early 19th century and used as a guest house. The English traveller William Moorcroft stayed here in 1820. Cold softdrinks are now sold here, and you can sit on sandstone benches beneath spreading mango trees.

The **middle terrace** is four metres (13 feet) lower than the upper terrace and is reached by two flights of steps in the wall on either side of the Grand Hall. Between the flights of steps a cascade carries water down from the upper ponds to the great square central pond with its 150 fountains. Between the cascade and the pond stands a marble throne surrounded by a marble railing where the emperor sat and listened to his musicians and watched his *nautch* girls dance by moonlight.

Set into the wall in the southeast corner of the terrace is the **Turkish bath house**, with its changing room and cold and hot baths. Originally the inside was completely decorated with pietra dura work.

The way down to the lower terrace is guarded by two pavilions on either side of a waterfall. In the marble wall behind the waterfall are rows of hundreds of little cusped niches which held flowers in golden vases by day and lamps by night. From the lowest terrace and through a double row of five cusped arches, the waterfall looked like a sheet of shimmering light.

The **lower terrace** has two gates decorated with glazed tile mosaics, two corner towers and the **Hall of Private Audience**, which was once decorated throughout with white marble and fresco paintings.

The Shalimar Garden took less than 18 months to build. Water from the Royal Canal was carried up into raised water tanks outside the garden so that there would be enough pressure to feed the hundreds of fountains.

Other Monuments Along the Grand Trunk Road

Located outside the Shalimar Garden in Moghul times was a rich suburb with luxuriant gardens belonging to the nobility. Though some trees immediately beside the royal garden are still standing, the gardens themselves have for the most part disappeared as Lahore spread outwards. To the north lay the **Mahtabi Bagh**, now a fruit orchard, and about two kilometres (a mile) to the west along the main road was the **Gulabi Bagh**, or Rose Garden, of which only the gateway beside the road remains. It is covered in glazed tile mosaics and calligraphy. The garden was built in the mid-17th century by Mirza Sultan Baig, the admiral of Shah Jahan's fleet. He died in 1657 when a gun presented to him by Shah Jahan exploded on a hunting trip.

Behind the Gulabi Bagh gate is the **Tomb of Dai Anga**, Shah Jahan's wetnurse. The square brick tomb, built in 1671, has a squat dome in the centre and cupolas supported by 12 pillars at each of the four corners. Some original glazed tilework still remains around the top. Inside there is a central chamber surrounded by eight rooms, all once decorated with glazed tile mosaics and fresco paintings. The original cenotaphs have been replaced by brick. It was Dai Anga who built the **Dai Anga**

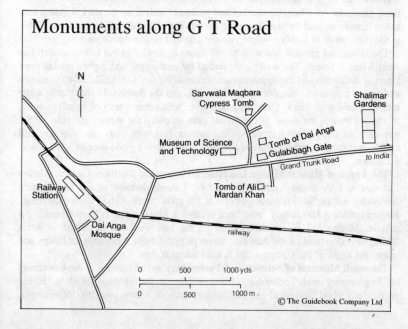

Monuments along G T Road

N

Sarvwala Maqbara
Cypress Tomb

Shalimar Gardens

Museum of Science and Technology

Tomb of Dai Anga

Gulabibagh Gate

Grand Trunk Road

to India

Railway Station

Tomb of Ali Mardan Khan

Dai Anga Mosque

railway

0   500   1000 yds

0   500   1000 m

© The Guidebook Company Ltd

Mosque in 1635 near the railway station (see map). The mosque has been painted over, but it still retains some of the original mosaics and calligraphy. To reach it, turn left off Allama Iqbal Road about one kilometre (half a mile) from the railway station.

North of Dai Anga's Tomb is the **Sarvwala Maqbara** or Cypress Tomb. This tall, square, brick tomb, decorated with cypress trees in glazed tile mosaics, was built in the mid-18th century for Sharfun Nisa Begum, sister of the governor of Lahore. The burial chamber is at the top, about five metres (16 feet) above ground level, and can only be reached by a ladder. The surrounding garden has completely disappeared.

To the south of the Gulabi Bagh, on the other side of the Grand Trunk Road, is the **Tomb of Ali Mardan Khan**. Its dome is visible from the road; the guard at the Gulabi Bagh will direct you. It is located inside a heavily guarded railway yard. You reach it down a walkway between high brick walls.

Ali Mardan Khan (d. 1657) was a Persian nobleman and the 'faithful friend' of Shah Jahan. He was governor of Kandahar in Afghanistan for the Persian ruler Shah Safi, and then in 1637 he changed allegiance, surrendering Kandahar and Quetta to Shah Jahan without a battle and taking refuge in his court. He was made governor of Kashmir, and later of Punjab. A skilled administrator, he was responsible for many public works, including the building of the Royal Canal, which took water from further up the River Ravi to Lahore and fed the Shalimar and other gardens.

The chowkidar (watchman) at Ali Mardan Khan's Tomb is so excited at having a visitor that he will conduct you all over the tomb: down into the crypt to see the three graves of Ali Khan, his mother and younger brother; up the dark winding stair to the terrace around the dome; and on up into the chamber inside the dome. (This is the only tomb in Lahore where you are allowed inside the dome.)

The octagonal mausoleum with its tall dome is similar to but not as graceful as Asaf Khan's Tomb. The walls are pierced by archways, and eight cupolas once stood at the corners of the upper terrace surrounding the dome. Glazed tile mosaics and fresco paintings once decorated the walls, and the dome was covered in white marble inlaid with black. Only the brick core, with some traces of fresco painting in the archways, remains. A colony of bats inhabits the dome, clinging to the remnants of the plaster tracery. Of the surrounding wall only one gateway still stands, but there is enough glazed tilework left to give a good idea of what it was once like.

The **Tomb of Hazrat Madho Lal Hussain** is near the Shalimar Garden. Madho Lal was a 17th-century saint who roamed Lahore dressed in red and singing devotional songs; he is regarded as one of the great poets of the Punjabi language. He befriended a Hindu boy, who later became a Muslim and is buried beside the mystic. Madho Lal is commemorated on the last weekend of March at Mela Chiragham (Festival of the Lamps), when pilgrims light thousands of lamps and spend the night at the shrine; a fair is held the next day.

The small **Museum of Science and Technology** on the campus of the University of Engineering and Technology features largely push-button exhibits. It has particularly good biological and mechanical sections where you can, for example, test your own hearing range. It is on the right of the Grand Trunk Road close to the Gulabi Bagh gate.

Other Moghul Ruins in Lahore

On the other side of Lahore, on the road to Multan, are a group of ruins for the truly dedicated student of Moghul architecture. The **Chauburji** (Four Towers), the gateway to a Moghul garden that no longer exists, stands at the junction of the Multan and Bahawalpur roads. The gate is richly decorated with glazed tile mosaics; its four octagonal towers (one recently rebuilt) were once crowned by cupolas supported on pillars. The inscription on the gate says that the garden was founded in 1646 by 'a lady endowed with elegance, the lady of the age', and was bestowed upon one Mian Bai. The founder was probably Jahan Ara Begum, eldest daughter of Shah Jahan and, after her mother's death, first lady of the land; it is not known who Mian Bai was.

The **Nawankot Gateway** is another gate to a Moghul garden, probably also built by Jahan Ara Begum soon after the Chauburji. It is about two kilometres (a mile) further out on the Multan road on the left. To find it look for an old Moghul tomb on the left, about 200 metres (yards) past the Samanabad Main Road intersection. The square pyramidal dome of this tomb is the only one of its kind in Lahore. The Nawankot Gateway is about 200 metres behind this tomb. You can only approach on foot, as it is surrounded by hovels. A hundred metres (yards) of garden wall and one garden corner tower still remain. The gateway itself is square with four elegant cupolas, each supported by 12 pillars. You can still see some of the green, blue, yellow and orange glazed tile mosaics that once covered the walls, and enough of the fresco decoration inside, to get an idea of how opulent it once was. The garden was 200 metres square (ten acres) when it was built in 1646, with an octagonal tower at each corner.

Shopping

Lahore is famous for its carpet weaving. New handmade carpets are for sale in the shops around Charing Cross, along the Mall and in the hotel lobbies; some original Persian and Afghan carpets are also for sale. Carpet weaving in Lahore started on a large scale after 1947, with the arrival of the Muslim carpet-weavers from established centres in Amritsar and Shahjahanpur, in India. There are now many large carpet factories using best-quality wool, where you can buy carpets and rugs in any design you can imagine, or have one made to your own specifications.

Ask at one of the hotel shops if you want to see inside a carpet studio. It is quite an experience. The looms are in long rows inside a vast shaded courtyard, each loom with its team of boys and a master. The masters sing out the colours and the eldest boys repeat them. Sometimes there are 150 masters and 500 boys at work at the same time, all concentrating furiously. When the carpet is cut down, it is sheared and then washed; up to eight men work rhythmically together scrubbing the carpet with stiff fibre brushes. Sometimes the carpet is treated chemically to tone down the bright colours, although this shortens its life considerably. Pakistani carpets are durable and attractive, and usually good value.

Old brass and copper ware are another good buy from the shops around Charing Cross, and from Faletti's Hotel arcade. At the brass bazaar in the old city (see page 191), the prices are usually cheaper, but the brass is often unpolished or still coated in tin, so it is more difficult to see what you are getting.

In **Mozang Bazaar**, south from Charing Cross, you can find the best cloth and silk. There is a calico-printing shop, selling handblock-printed cloth, bedspreads and tablecloths near the Mozang tonga stand. Other handicrafts can be found in the shops along the Mall near Charing Cross. Especially recommended is the Technical Services Association, 65 the Mall, which sells beautiful shadow-work embroidery at reasonable prices.

Anarkali Bazaar is a treasure-trove selling virtually everything from handicrafts to transistor radios, tin saucepans to refrigerators. It is a maze of lanes and alleys stretching northwards from the Central Museum end of the Mall. Shopping is more fun here than in the shops along the Mall, and prices are cheaper. Bargain hard.

Lahore is famous for its red-light district in the old city near the Badshahi Mosque. The tempo picks up around midnight. Women wearing heavy white makeup play instruments in the doorways to the brothels. Plush red velvet abounds inside; some of the women limit themselves to dancing in the traditional style—others offer more.

Outings from Lahore

Sheikhupura and the Hiran Minar

Emperor Jahangir enjoyed hunting in the area around Sheikhupura, where in 1616 he built himself a hunting pavilion in the centre of an artificial lake and a tower, the Hiran Minar, in memory of his pet deer. Three years later he built a massive brick fort in Sheikhupura, which still stands today.

You can get to Sheikhupura by bus from Lahore. If you are driving yourself, turn left (west) onto Sheikhupura Road, 700 metres (0.4 miles) from the toll gate on the Ravi River Bridge. After two kilometres (a mile) take the right fork onto the dual carriageway, an excellent road that goes straight across flat farmland for 30 kilometres (19 miles) to Sheikhupura.

Jahangir's Fort stands in the centre of Sheikhupura. To find it turn left about 300 metres (yards) past the traffic lights at the intersection with the Gujranwala–Faisalabad road. The fort is 200 metres (yards) down this side street on the right.

In the 19th century the fort was used by Rani Nakayan, one of Ranjit Singh's wives, and most of the buildings inside the fort belong to this period. The most impressive is the rani's private house, which is covered inside with fresco paintings in very good condition. Some of the other buildings have intricately carved wooden doors. The views from the battlements are most impressive.

The fort belongs to Lahore's Department of Archaeology; the chowkidar may refuse to let you in unless you have a note from the director of archaeology, Lahore Fort. The place is definitely worth visiting for its air of 18th-century opulence.

To get to the Hiran Minar continue straight through Sheikhupura on the Sargodha road for four kilometres (2.5 miles) to the end of the dual carriageway. About 100 metres (yards) past the railway level crossing, turn right on a paved road along the canal. There is a yellow signpost, but in Urdu only. Turn left two kilometres (a mile) later at the bridge over the canal; the Hiran Minar is 500 metres (yards) further on.

The deer park is lovely and makes the perfect picnic spot. Its central feature is the large, square, artificial lake. An arched causeway leads out to the three-storey octagonal pavilion in the centre of the lake, where Jahangir sat beneath the arcade to watch the wild animals. Near the beginning of the causeway is the Hiran Minar itself. You can climb the 99 steps to the top.

At each corner of the lake is a little arched pavilion. Steps lead down to the water where you can hire boats. The lake is walled in brick and well stocked with fish.

If you are on your way to Islamabad, you do not need to return to Lahore. You can go straight from Sheikhupura to Gujranwala and the Grand Trunk Road to the northwest.

Nankana Sahib, 29 kilometres (18 miles) southwest of Sheikhupura, is an important place of pilgrimage. There are two Sikh temples or *gurduwaras* here: Bal Lila, where Guru Nanak, the founder of the Sikh religion, spent his childhood, and Janamasthsan, where he is believed to have been born. The latter houses sacred relics belonging to the guru, including a holy cloak embroidered with Koranic verses and said to have been presented to Guru Nanak by the caliph of Baghdad.

You can also visit **Chhanga Manga Wildlife Reserve**, 70 kilometres (43 miles) from Lahore on the road to Sahiwal (see page 201), or make a long daytrip to **Harappa**, just off the Multan road near Sahiwal (see pages 172–4).

The **Indian border** is 29 kilometres (18 miles) from Lahore along the Grand Trunk Road at **Wagah**. The border is only open twice a month because of unrest in the Indian Punjab, and you are allowed to cross only between 9 am and 4 pm. Check in Lahore for the latest information. To cross into India you need valid travel documents, health certificates and patience: allow at least two hours to negotiate the numerous officials and forms. In normal conditions you can easily take a bus, minibus or taxi to the border, walk across 500 metres (yards) of no-man's land (porters are available to carry your baggage) and take a bus or taxi from the other side to Amritsar.

There is a good PTDC motel in Wagah where you can stay for Rs70 a room, or Rs30 for a dormitory bed; book through the PTDC office at Faletti's Hotel, Lahore.

In **Amritsar** itself Mrs Bandari's guest house, a large old house with attractive gardens, a pleasant atmosphere and wholesome food, is recommended. It is at 10 the Cantonment, Amritsar. A day is all you need in Amritsar to visit the Sikh Golden Temple and other monuments. If you wish to continue by train to Delhi, Mrs Bandari will arrange train reservations provided you write and ask her far enough in advance. For air-conditioned or first-class train tickets it is essential to book.

Lahore to Islamabad

The **Grand Trunk Road** from Lahore north to Islamabad first runs across the flat irrigated fields of the Punjab plains, which stretch from Delhi to the Jhelum River. The Pakistani belt produces a large proportion of the country's crops—wheat, rice, sugar-cane and cotton—and is irrigated by Punjab's five rivers. The Grand Trunk Road from Lahore to Islamabad crosses the first three of these, the Ravi, Chenab and Jhelum.

Between the Chenab and Jhelum rivers the Grand Trunk Road climbs up onto the **Potwar Plateau**, a strange eroded landscape of flat-topped hills veined with deep gullies. Extraordinary shapes result in the brown mud walls of the ravines: you can imagine Gothic castles with pinnacles, turreted walls and tall brown towers. Here and there scrubby trees add touches of green. This jagged starkness, periodically alleviated by clumps of banyan trees clustered round village ponds, is curiously beautiful. In spring, tiny fields of brilliant yellow mustard nestle on every possible shelf of flat land.

The Grand Trunk Road was built by the Moghul emperors to connect Calcutta with Kabul, passing through Delhi, Lahore, Rawalpindi and Peshawar. The journey from Lahore to Islamabad takes four to five hours by bus or car, and five to six hours by train. There are several places of interest along the way. Most of these are nearer Islamabad than Lahore and make easy daytrips from Islamabad.

Gujranwala, 67 kilometres (42 miles), or 45 minutes, north of Lahore, is a major industrial town and the centre of Pakistan's metalworking and electrical-goods manufacture; it also has flourishing textile and carpet industries. A bypass runs round the town on either side; each bypass is about 15 kilometres (ten miles) long. The one to the east is marginally prettier, as it follows a canal that takes water from the Chenab River above Sialkot and ends near Multan. There is nothing of interest to see in the town except the tomb of Ranjit Singh's father. Ranjit Singh himself was born in Gujranwala in 1780; he is buried at Lahore (see page 183).

Gujranwala derives its name from the Gujar tribe, as do two other towns in this area, Gujrat and Gujar Khan. The Gujars were nomadic pastoralists from the northern subcontinent, but in the 16th century they were brought into the Punjab in large numbers to populate and garrison their new towns and to guard the then-new Shahi (Grand Trunk) Road. Today many of the Gujars in the Punjab are migrant labourers or herders.

Wazirabad, 26 kilometres (16 miles) from Gujranwala, is also bypassed by the Grand Trunk Road. The town was founded in the 17th century by Wazir Khan, Shah Jahan's prime minister and the builder of Wazir Khan's Mosque in Lahore (see pages 189 and 191). Under the Sikhs in the 19th century, Wazirabad was the headquarters of Avitabile, an Italian mercenary who became Ranjit Singh's general, and who built a new enclosed rectangular town.

From Wazirabad a road leads east to the ancient town of **Sialkot** near the Indian border. Some authorities believe that Sialkot was once Sagala, capital of King Menander in about 160 BC; others that it was the capital of the White Huns when they ruled Gandhara. There is an old fort on a hill in the town, where the British took refuge during the Sepoy Mutiny of 1857; those killed in battle are buried at the foot of the hill. Other places of interest include the tomb of Mian Abdul Hakim, a great Muslim scholar, and the shrine and mosque of the popular saint Hazrat Imam Ali-ul-Haq, who converted the local population to Islam. Allama Iqbal, Pakistan's greatest philosopher and poet, was born and raised in Sialkot. His home is open to the public, but it is in poor condition; he is buried in Lahore (see page 184).

Today the town is one of Pakistan's major industrial centres, and is famous for the manufacture of high-quality sports equipment, surgical instruments, saddles and musical instruments. More bagpipes are made in Sialkot than in Scotland.

The Grand Trunk Road crosses the Chenab River about six kilometres (four miles) north of Wazirabad on a toll bridge. The old bridge (closed to traffic) is about 500 metres (yards) upriver, and the old road still leads to it from the Grand Trunk Road on either side of the new bridge. The riverside on the south bank by the old bridge makes a good picnic spot.

Gujrat, eight kilometres (five miles) north of the river and bypassed by the Grand Trunk Road, was founded by the Moghul emperor Akbar on the site of two earlier towns. Akbar garrisoned the fort of Gujrat with Gujars; the town was previously known as Gujrat Akbarabad. After the decline of the Moghuls the town was held by the Ghakkars (see page 209) until their defeat at the hands of the Sikhs.

Gujrat was the scene of the final battle between the Sikhs and the British in the Second Sikh War. The British victory under Lord Gough finally broke the power of the Sikhs in Punjab and led to the annexation of Sikh territories by the British. You can still see the graves of fallen British soldiers in the Shah Jahangir Cemetery.

To the east of Gujrat is the **Shrine of Pir Shah Daula**, a famous 17th-century saint. David Ross, in *The Land of Five Rivers* (1882), describes the Shah Daula 'rats', humans disfigured at birth by 'flattening their heads and pinching their features into a sharpness somewhat resembling that of the rat . . . . Their lives are dedicated, from professedly religious motives, to the saint.' Barren women whose prayers for children are answered still sometimes give their first baby to the shrine.

At **Kharian** the landscape suddenly changes and the road climbs up onto the heavily eroded Potwar Plateau, which stretches all the way to the Margalla Hills, the foothills of the Himalayas. From Kharian a road runs west for Chillianwala, the Rasul Barrage, and an alternative slow route to Islamabad via the Salt Range (see pages 241–53).

The Jhelum River, 12 kilometres (seven miles) beyond Kharian, is spanned by another new toll bridge. The old British road and rail bridge still carries the railway and is almost two kilometres (over a mile) long. From the toll bridge you get a good view of the town of **Jhelum** to the right on the northwest bank of the river. Although there was an ancient town on the opposite side of the river, it was at Jhelum's present site that the British established a military cantonment after their takeover of the area in 1849. It is still an important Pakistani military base, and a salt and timber centre.

It was in the Jhelum area (most probably to the south near Jalapur) that Alexander the Great crossed the river and fought his battle with the Indian ruler Porus. He then marched as far as the Beas River in India, where his weary army refused to go any further. He returned to the Jhelum River and sailed down it to the Indus in boats built near the present city.

Jhelum Church, which you can see from the Grand Trunk Road, was built in Anglo-Gothic style and consecrated in February 1857. The Sepoy Mutiny broke out in Meerut (near Delhi) in May and had spread to the native garrison at Jhelum by early July. The families of the British officers took refuge in the church. The mutineers headed off towards Lahore but were met and defeated by the indefatigable John Nicholson (see page 255), who rushed back from Amritsar with the British Movable Column.

From Jhelum to Islamabad it is 120 kilometres (75 miles) and takes less than two hours by car or bus.

At **Dina**, about 16 kilometres (ten miles) north of Jhelum, the road crosses a high railway bridge, from the top of which you can see Rohtas Fort off to your left and Mangla Dam away to the right. The turnings to both are in the centre of the village.

Mangla Dam lies about 16 kilometres (ten miles) east of Dina; the turning is clearly marked in English. Mangla Dam is reputedly the third largest earth-filled dam in the world. Behind it there is a large lake spanning about 160 square kilometres (62 square miles). The Azad Kashmir town of **Mirpur** is located on its south side. A road crosses the dam to Azad Kashmir. The dam was actually built round a hill topped by a Ghakkar fort that was much altered by the Sikhs in the 18th century. You can drive up to the fort for a good view of the lake.

From the east side of the lake you can drive to the attractive hills near **Pir Gali**. From Mirpur continue round the lake for 26 kilometres (16 miles) where there is a surfaced road leading up into the hills. At Pir Gali you can turn right (southeast) on a rough jeepable road for the **Samani Valley**. The drive takes 90 minutes. From Samani there are some good walks in the surrounding hills (see map on page 228–9). Most maps show the Indian border running through Mangla Lake; the new line of control is further east.

Rohtas Fort

There it stands, sprawling across a low rocky hill a few miles north of Jhelum, its great ramparts growing from the cliff like a Wall of China, looking north across a sandy stream bed to the low hills of the Salt Range and, beyond them, to the snows of the Pir Panjal. The circumference is large enough easily to hold a couple of divisions of troops.

As you approach the fort, the crenellations look like ominous rows of helmeted warriors watching you with disapproval—it is an awe-inspiring sight.

Sir Olaf Caroe, *The Pathans* (1958)

To get to Rohtas Fort turn west in Dina directly opposite the turn east to Mangla Dam. (If you are coming from Islamabad, there is another turning three kilometres, or two miles, before Dina.) An infrequent bus service covers the seven kilometres (four miles) to the fort, but you can often hitch a ride on a lorry. In dry weather you can reach Rohtas in about 20 minutes in an ordinary car, but after the rains you get bogged down in the sand or in the river. The road is paved to the Kahan River, where it divides. Take the left fork onto the sandy river bed and ford the river; provided you keep to the normal crossing point, the sand is quite firm. Alternatively you can leave your car by the river or at the village one kilometre (half a mile) further up, and wade across.

It is about one kilometre (half a mile) from the river up a rough road and past a mausoleum to the east gate of the fort. The road continues through the modern village of Rohtas inside the fort and out through the west gate on the other side, and then on to Tilla Jogian. If you are going by bus, get off at Rohtas village; if you are driving, park at the west gate, where the most interesting ruins are.

The fort was built by Sher Shah Suri, 'the most illustrious Afghan in history', according to Sir Olaf Caroe. Born in India of Pathan parents, he managed to defeat the second Moghul emperor Humayun and take India. However, his reign lasted barely six years (1539–45), and he never extended his sway north of the Margalla Pass (see pages 253 and 255). Yet in this short period he managed to drive the alien Moghuls out of India, to unite the disparate and constantly warring Afghan and Pathan malcontents, and to establish administrative and taxation systems that were later built upon by the Moghul emperor Akbar. He was an outstanding soldier and statesman, and is justly revered by the Pathans even today.

Sher Shah built Rohtas as his northwestern frontier outpost, 16 kilometres (ten miles) beyond his Jhelum borders, to try to keep the local Ghakkar tribe in check and to prevent the return of Humayun. He kept 12,000 men there. The fort also guarded the newly built Shahi Road, which ran straight through Ghakkar territory to the Indus and possibly beyond. Rohtas was named after Rohtas Fort in Bihar (India), which Sher Shah had captured earlier, using the old ruse of dressing his men as women and smuggling them into the fort in palanquins.

Construction work on the new Rohtas began in about 1540 and was finished ten years later, after Sher Shah's death—a stupendous achievement in so short a time.

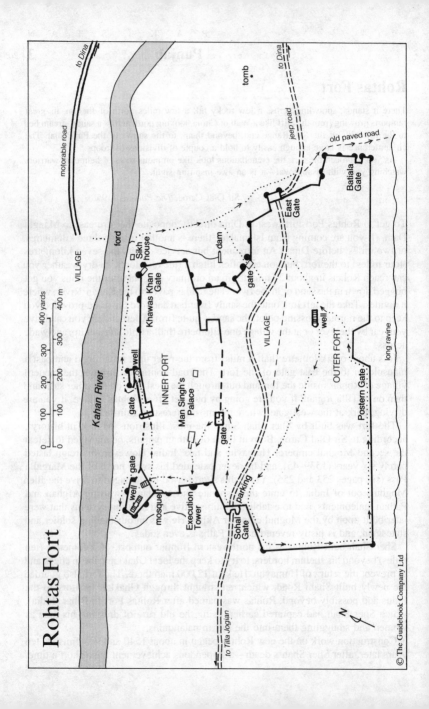

Rohtas Fort

to Dina
motorable road
Kahan River
ford
VILLAGE
VILLAGE
well
well
gate
INNER FORT
gate
well
gate
mosque
Man Singh's Palace
gate
Execution Tower
Sohail Gate
Sikh house
dam
Khawas Khan Gate
parking
OUTER FORT
Postern Gate
long ravine
VILLAGE
well
gate
East Gate
Batiala Gate
old paved road
jeep road
to Dina
tomb

to Tilla Jogian

N

0   100   200   300   400 m
0   100   200   300   400 yards

© The Guidebook Company Ltd

It may seem odd to anyone visiting Rohtas today that the site should once have had any military significance. Yet the Kahan Gorge, which the fort dominates, was the only practicable route from the mountainous country north of the Salt Range to the southern plains. Certainly the Ghakkars used the gorge, and Babur passed through it on his way to the first battle of Panipat. According to the *Akbar Nama*, when Emperor Jahangir, Akbar's son, passed through the fort on his way to Kashmir, he exclaimed that it was scarcely conceivable that Sher Shah could have obtained so strong a position for the building of his fort.

Despite its size and strategic location, Rohtas proved to be something of a white elephant. Ten years after Sher Shah's death in 1545 Humayun returned to Delhi, Sher Shah's two successors having proved worthless. The Afghan governor of Rohtas made no resistance and fled the fort along with his garrison. Thus Rohtas never served the purpose for which it was intended. Rohtas lost its importance as a frontier garrison when Humayun's son Akbar built his great fort at Attock, on the Indus, in the 1850s.

The fort has a perimeter five kilometres (three miles) long, along which are massive walls, bastions and battlements, and ten gates. For about one kilometre (half a mile) along the river the walls are doubled and tiered on the inside; the walkways are wide enough to reassure those who suffer from vertigo. The fort was adapted to the terrain, so that the walls meander and turn with the undulating hills and make use of the river and a number of deep ravines for their defence. The walls are actually more impressive from the outside; the roof of the mausoleum between the river and the east gate affords one of the better views.

It takes about three hours for a thorough exploration of the fort and quite a lot of walking is involved; if your time is limited, concentrate on the northwestern section—Sohal Gate, Man Singh's Palace and the execution tower. If you have young children, be prepared to carry them and hold them on the high walls.

Start from the huge **Sohal Gate**, a fine example of 16th-century fort architecture. It is elaborately decorated on the outside façade and was probably used for triumphal entries. It is flanked by two large U-shaped bastions and is two storeys high with oriel windows and carved stone inscriptions. Inside are spacious apartments where you can stay overnight; book through the deputy commissioner, Jhelum.

From the gate you can walk along the walls in either direction. If you have time, you can go all the way round the top of the southern wall, around the outer fort, to a set of steps nearest to the large **well**, where a wide flight of 135 steps, roofed with pointed arches, leads down to the deep, clear water. A path takes you back from the well to the Sohal Gate about 500 metres (yards) away.

From the Sohal Gate a path leads to the **inner fort** through an L-shaped gate in the curtain wall which separates the inner and outer forts. You can climb to the top of this gate for a good view of the inner fort and the **Palace of Man Singh**, a famous general and governor of Lahore under Akbar. All that remains of this palace are two *baradari* (viewing pavilions) at each end of the hill. The one to the west is the higher of the two and can be climbed by a narrow flight of modern concrete steps without a handrail (not recommended for vertigo sufferers). The top of the tower is the best vantage point from which to view the complete circuit of the fortifications.

The **execution tower**, a huge bastion in the outer wall to the west of Man Singh's Palace, has a stone block and, on the top platform, a hole through which victims were thrown. You can also reach this tower by walking along the wall from the Sohal Gate.

The **mosque** and the **Shisha Gate** are located in the northwestern corner of the fort. The small three-arched mosque features moulded Arabic inscriptions from the Koran and faint traces of paint (possibly original). The Shisha Gate looks unimpressive from the inside but is worth a visit. In the court between the inner and outer gates there is a deep well with steps leading down to the water; arcaded underground chambers around the wellshaft have windows looking onto the well. Vaulted outlets carry off the water. For impressive photographs of the outer walls you can go out the Shisha Gate and down the steps into the ravine.

The next gate, in the centre of the north wall, is surrounded by a well-preserved stretch of wall with the original hooded machicolations (apertures from which boiling oil was poured on attackers). Inside the gate-tower is a vaulted **octagonal room**, with original carvings and moulded calligraphy. From the inner gate a wide, twisting ramp leads down to a **courtyard** with arcaded sides, which may have served as stables or soldiers' quarters. There is another well here.

From this point you can return to Sohal Gate, or if you have the energy, you can go out through this gate, scramble down to the river and walk east through the reeds along the bank to a late 18th-century Sikh house. On the river bank beside the house are the remains of piers which probably anchored a bridge of boats in the wet season. This is where the Shahi Road crossed the river. It is also the best place to wade across the river if you have left your car in the village on the other side.

The track along the east side of the fort is the old Shahi Road. On some sections there are traces of paving and embankment, and in one place you can see the remains of an old bridge. Just before the southeastern corner of the fort is the **Batiala Gate**. From the southeastern corner itself there is a fine view of the south wall running for about a kilometre (half a mile) along the side of a remarkably straight natural ravine.

Tilla Jogian Hill

The highest peak in the Salt Range, at 975 metres (3,200 feet) above sea level, Tilla Jogian is about 14 kilometres (nine miles) to the west of Rohtas Fort. The jeep track starts from Sohal Gate; the ascent is steep, rocky and increasingly difficult. The upper slopes are thickly forested, and the top is covered by the extensive ruins of a Hindu monastery. There is a small hermitage perched at the edge of the cliff and a water storage tank, shaded by pine trees, which was built in Akbar's time. There are also some ruins from the British period, including a vast house where the deputy commissioner from Jhelum held court during the summer months. From the top there is a magnificent view down over the endless fields of the Potwar Plateau.

Tilla Jogian Hindu Monastery has been deserted since Partition in 1947. Its Muslim name is derived from *yogi* (*fakir* or holy man), but the monastery itself dates back to the time of Alexander the Great, when it was called Tilla Ballnath and was dedicated to the sun god. Plutarch (Greek historian c. AD 50–120) called the mountain the Hill of the Elephant: according to legend, King Porus' elephant ran up the hill calling to his king and begging him not to oppose Alexander (see page 250). Later it was renamed Tilla Goraknath, after the Hindu god Goraknath, a transmutation of Shiva.

Tilla Jogian and Rohtas make a good weekend excursion from either Islamabad or Lahore. You can spend the night in the rest house at Rohtas Fort; camping is also possible at both sites.

From Dina the Grand Trunk Road continues northwest across the extraordinary eroded landscape of the Potwar Plateau, and climbs steadily to the top of a line of hills, which it crosses with the railway line. On clear days, and especially after rain, you can see the long line of snow peaks of the Pir Panjal Range on the right, across the Jhelum River in India.

The road follows the railway and descends through **Sohawa**, **Gujar Khan** and **Mandra** to **Riwat**. This area is remarkable for the frequent groups of huge banyan trees, especially in or near the villages along the Grand Trunk Road. These trees, with their thick foliage and hanging roots, were considered holy by the Hindus, and usually grow beside the village pond or tank. Because of the large area of shade they provide, village meetings have traditionally taken place around them.

Manikyala Stupa is about two kilometres (a mile) east of the main road halfway between Mandra and Riwat. You can see it from the main road, but it can easily be mistaken for a clump of banyan trees. A rough track leaves the Grand Trunk Road on a corner a little way south of the radio masts and crosses the railway to the stupa.

Manikyala Stupa is one of the largest in the area. The solid dome supported on a square platform is still intact, but there are no carvings or decorations left other than the simple pilasters around the drum, which were restored in 1891.

You can climb the stupa from a break in the stone facing on the east side and scramble to the grassy top for a good view over the plains below. The deep hole in the top of the stupa was dug by treasure hunters, who removed whatever relics and valuables it once held. (For a description of Buddhist stupas, see pages 24 and 257.)

The **Ghakkar fort of Riwat** is right beside the Grand Trunk Road, on the west side, just past the village of Riwat, about two kilometres (a mile) south of the junction with the Islamabad road. The Ghakkars built the fort in the mid-16th century to defend themselves against the invading armies of the Afghan Sher Shah Suri. But, unlike Sher Shah's vast fort at Rohtas, Riwat is barely 200 metres (yards) square.

The Ghakkars were the most powerful tribe living on the Potwar Plateau. They were probably indigenous to the area and were converted to Islam in the 13th century. They also built forts at Pharwala (see page 231) and Mangla (see page 204).

The Ghakkars were defeated by the first Moghul emperor, Babur, at Pharwala, after which they became loyal allies of the Moghul emperors and in return were allowed a free hand in running their territory. The last independent Ghakkar chief, Mukarrab Khan (1739–65), extended their territories from the Chenab to the Indus. In 1765 the Ghakkars were defeated by the Sikhs at Gujrat, and their territories were taken from them.

What remains of Riwat Fort—the mausoleum, three-domed mosque, two gates and outside walls—is in good condition. Inside the fort it is surprisingly charming and peaceful; it makes a good place for a winter picnic. The fort stands on a long low ridge of black rock which extends in a crescent from Kahuta to the east, around the south side of Rawalpindi, to Kushalgarh on the Indus and beyond. From the top of the mausoleum (you have to climb up some rather precarious stairs), or the main gate, you have an excellent view of this ridge, with the Salt Range behind. To the south you can see Manikyala Stupa and clumps of banyan trees that resemble other stupas.

The undecorated mausoleum is similar in shape to those at Multan (see pages 163 and 166). The outside walls of the fort are lined with chambers that were once the sleeping quarters. A grave in the centre of the fort houses the remains of the Ghakkar chief Sarang Khan. It is marked by a modern inscription in English. Sarang Khan and his daughter were captured by Sher Shah in 1543, and the chief was flayed alive and his skin stuffed with straw; his daughter was married off to one of Sher Shah's generals. Sarang Khan was generally rather unlucky; he lost no fewer than 16 of his sons in action against Sher Shah; only two were left to carry on the line.

The direct road to Islamabad leaves the Grand Trunk Road just past Riwat, and heads north across the Soan River, where it joins the road from the airport shared by Islamabad and Rawalpindi. The Grand Trunk Road continues to Rawalpindi and also crosses the Soan River. Early Stone Age man lived along this stretch more than 100,000 years ago, and hundreds of ancient stone tools can be found near the river. British archaeologists have recently found a 30,000-year-old house near the river between the Grand Trunk Road and the road to Islamabad.

The geology of the Soan Gorge, from Islamabad through the Potwar Plateau to the Indus, is extremely interesting. Here, exposed on the surface, are fossil-bearing rocks between four and 14 million years old. It seems that hominoid primates lived here in profusion, and fossils from this area have doubled palaeontological collections from the rest of the world. Giraffe, gazelle, rhinoceros, crocodile and rodent fossils have also been found here—presumably they were hunted by man's early ancestors.

ISLAMABAD

Pakistan's new capital nestles against the backdrop of the Margalla Hills at the northern end of the Potwar Plateau about 15 kilometres (ten miles) from Rawalpindi. It is a modern and carefully planned city with wide tree-lined streets, large houses, elegant public buildings and well-organized bazaars. There are rarely crowds or traffic jams and few narrow lanes or slums; the walkways are shaded and safe, and separated from the traffic by rows of flame trees, jacaranda and hibiscus. Roses, jasmine and bougainvillea fill the parks, and scenic viewpoints show the city to its best advantage.

The decision to build Islamabad was taken in 1958 under President Ayub Khan. Karachi, the capital since Independence in 1947, and Pakistan's largest city and only port, proved unsatisfactory because of its distance from many parts of the country and because of its debilitating climate. Islamabad, on the other hand, offered a healthy climate, plenty of water and a central position on the Grand Trunk Road, close to the Punjab and North-West Frontier Province. That nearby Rawalpindi was the headquarters of the Pakistan army was another consideration. Finally the site had historical connections because of its proximity to nearby Taxila, for many centuries the region's main city.

A Greek firm of architects, Doxiadis Associates, drew up a master plan, triangular in shape, based on a grid system, with its apex towards the Margalla Hills. The planners envisaged Islamabad eventually absorbing Rawalpindi entirely and stretching well to the west of the Grand Trunk Road.

The city was divided into eight zones: the diplomatic enclave, the commercial district, the educational sector, the industrial area and so on, each with its own shopping area and park. Construction began in 1961, and the first residents moved in two years later. Meanwhile, government offices were temporarily moved up to Rawalpindi.

The 1962 Constitution of Pakistan confirmed Islamabad as the principal seat of the central government, although it was decided that the seat of the central legislature would be Dacca (now Dhaka), in what was then East Pakistan. It was only after the 1971 war, which resulted in East Pakistan becoming the independent country of Bangladesh, that Islamabad came fully into its own as the capital of Pakistan.

When to Go

At 518 metres (1,700 feet) above sea level, Islamabad is at its best from October to March, when the days are crisp and cool, and the nights are cold. Spring is short, but the flowers in March are a riot of colour. The hottest months are May and June, before the monsoon, but even then the climate is usually not oppressive, and you can always escape to the hills, 2,250 metres (7,400 feet) above sea level.

Getting to Islamabad

Islamabad and Rawalpindi share an airport, the Rawalpindi City and Rawalpindi Cantonment railway stations and the Pir Wadhai and General bus stations. It costs Rs70 by taxi from the airport to Islamabad, Rs5 by wagon and Rs3 by bus.

Where to Stay

Expensive: Rs1,000–2,000

Holiday Inn, Aga Khan Road, F-5/1, tel. 826121–35 (s/d Rs1,700/1,900). International class; all facilities.

Islamabad Hotel, Municipal Road, G-6/2, tel. 827311–31 (s/d Rs1,000/1,500). Air-conditioned; all facilities.

Moderate: Rs100–450

Shehrazad, Super Market, tel. 822295–6, 823519 (d. Rs108–205 no AC; Rs325 with AC). Recommended, convenient and good value.

Ambassador, Khyaban-e-Suhrawardy, tel. 824011–5 (s/d Rs300/400).

The three hotels in Shakarparian Park near Rawal Dam are on the main bus line halfway between Islamabad and Rawalpindi; they are quiet and make a good choice for bird-watchers, walkers and horse-riders.

Lake View Motel, tel. 821025, 821057 (s/d Rs350/450).

Dreamland, tel. 826983 (s/d Rs300/550).

Tures Motel, tel. 824503, 813116 (s/d Rs162/215).

Camping ground (Rs10), opposite Aabpara Market, near Rose and Jasmine Garden.

Where to Eat

Great Wall, Blue Area, tel. 815111. Chinese.

Mei Hua, Blue Area, tel. 811242. Chinese.

Kim Mun, Jinnah Market, F-7/3, tel. 822331. Chinese.

Shi Fang, Jinnah Market, F-7/3, tel. 812903. Chinese.

Kao Wah, Aabpara Market, Khyaban-e-Suhrawardy, tel. 829898. Chinese.

Golden Dragon, Round Market, F-7/3, tel. 827333. Chinese.

Orient Express, Round Market, F-7/3. Pakistani and continental.

China Town, Round Market, F-7/3. Chinese.

Usmania, Blue Area, tel. 811345, 812535.

Mariah's, Blue Area, tel. 821578.

Taj Mahal, Jinnah Market, F-7/3, tel. 812932.

White House, Super Market, tel. 828213. Pakistani and continental.

Bunny's, Blue Area. Fast food, beefburgers, chicken-corn soup.

Mr Chips, near Jinnah Market, tel. 821922. Fast food.

Moods, Rama Market, F-7/1, tel. 824747. Fast food.

Kashmirwala's, Daman-e-Koh Viewpoint. Pakistani and fast food.

Useful Addresses

Tourism Division, **Ministry of Tourism**, College Road, Jinnah Market, F-7/2, tel. 820856.

PTDC Head Office, 2 61st Street, F-7/4, tel. 826327.
Telegraph and Telephone Office, behind Holiday Inn, F-5.
General Post Office, Post Office Road, G-6/2, tel. 825957.
PIA, Nazim-ud-din Road, Blue Area, tel. 8225031.
Passport Office, Aabpara Market, near National Bank, tel. 826837.

Sights

Though the straight, tree-lined avenues of Islamabad all look confusingly similar, it is easy to find your way around by using the Margalla Hills, which rise up on the north edge of the city, as a reference point. The good street map available in most bookshops is essential, as most of the streets are numbered rather than named, and no one you ask, even taxi drivers, will know the exact sequence. Some of the main avenues dividing the sectors have several names, such as 6th Avenue, alias Embassy Road, alias Ataturk Avenue; some main roads in different sectors have the same name, like Hills Road F-7 and Hills Road F-6.

The main problem in Islamabad is transport. The city is very spread out, and public transport runs frequently only down three or four of the main streets. You can hire a Morris 1000 taxi for about Rs30 an hour.

The **Daman-e-Koh Viewpoint**, perched halfway up the Margalla Hills, gives the best bird's-eye view south over Islamabad. To get there drive (and pay a Rs2 toll for cars) or walk up from the northern end of 7th Avenue. It is a ten-minute drive or 45-minute walk. There are crowds on Fridays. The viewpoint park is laid out with picnic areas, paths, gardens, viewing points and terraces. From here the straight avenues and neat rows of houses stretch out below you, the President's Palace, Legislative Assembly and Secretariat offices dominating the east end of the city, and the huge Shah Faisal Mosque tucked against the hills to the west. A useful plan painted on a cement block clarifies the city layout. In the distance are Rawal Lake and Rawalpindi, and on a clear day after rain you can see far out over the Potwar Plateau beyond Rawalpindi to the Salt Range on the horizon.

The road behind the viewpoint leads on up to the top of the ridge and then east towards Murree (see pages 234–9).

The **children's adventure playground**, a gift from the Japanese, is at the bottom of the hill below the viewpoint, immediately to the right behind the toll gate. A few hundred metres (yards) away, just beyond the toll barrier, is **Islamabad Zoo**, with a small and inadequately cared for collection of animals, including monkeys, a bear, some birds and deer.

The enormous **Shah Faisal Mosque** is superbly sited at the foot of the Margalla Hills. It represents an eight-faceted desert 'tent' supported on four giant concrete girders and surrounded by four 90-metre (300-foot) -high concrete minarets that look like rockets on launching pads. The central 'tent' is faced in white marble and decorated inside with mosaics and a spectacular chandelier. The mosque was designed by the Turkish architect Vedat Dalokay, and largely financed by donations

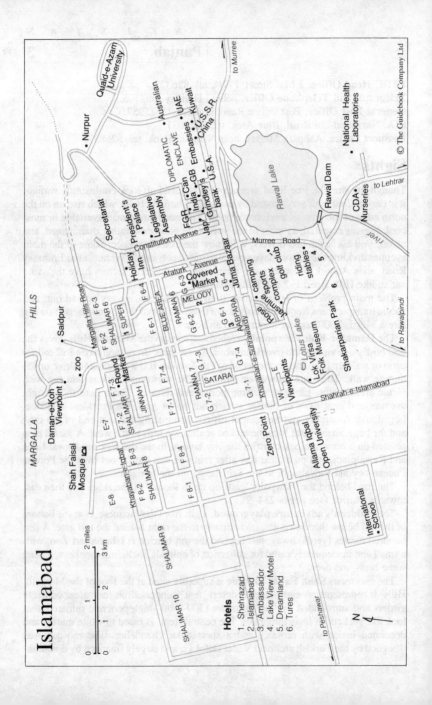

Islamabad

Hotels

1. Shehrazad
2. Islamabad
3. Ambassador
4. Lake View Motel
5. Dreamland
6. Tures

© The Guidebook Company Ltd

Oriental Carpets
by Kent Obee

Pakistan is an excellent place to shop for oriental carpets from neighbouring countries or from Pakistan itself, which is now ranked among the top four producers of hand-knotted carpets in the world.

The carpet industry developed in Pakistan only after Partition, so Pakistani carpets are all 'new' and mostly copies of Persian and Turkoman designs. At their best, however, they are as well made as the Iranian or Afghan originals — only less expensive. They are a sensible choice for the buyer wishing to avoid the uncertainties of older rugs or interested in coordinating the carpet with a particular colour scheme.

Pakistan is also an entrepot for carpets from Afghanistan, Iran and Chinese Turkestan (Xinjiang). Afghan carpets are the most readily available, and doubly so in recent years as a result of the upheaval in that country. Most Afghan carpets are 'tribal' pieces made by either Turkoman or Baluch weavers — though many of the newer carpets are actually made in refugee camps in Pakistan. Smuggled Iranian carpets are available in smaller numbers in the major cities at prices as high or higher than the same carpets would fetch in Europe or America. Tribal carpets from Chinese Turkestan have become increasingly available on the market since the opening of the Karakoram Highway.

Any one of Pakistan's major cities — Karachi, Islamabad, Peshawar, Lahore or Quetta — is a good place to shop for carpets. Lahore is the manufacturing and wholesaling centre of the indigenous carpet industry. Peshawar and Quetta are entry points for goods coming from Afghanistan and Iran, but the better pieces soon make their way to the markets of Islamabad and Karachi, drawn by the more numerous foreign buyers and the resulting higher prices.

Caveat emptor is the golden rule of carpet buying in Pakistan. Although many dealers are well informed and genuinely interested in sharing their enthusiasm for their wares, others are neither particularly knowledgeable nor above duping a gullible tourist with a story that a chemically washed product from a refugee camp is a hundred-year-old Bokhara. Shops in the major tourist hotels can be especially bad in this respect. The collector's knowledge (or that of a friend) of carpets and the current market is the best guarantee of making a worthwhile purchase.

The prospective buyer should be prepared to bargain — and bargain hard. The amount dealers come down varies greatly from shop to shop; it can be as little as five or ten percent, or it might be 50 percent. Many residents of Islamabad, when shopping at the popular Juma (Friday) Market, use as a rule of thumb a reduction of a third.

While there are inherent risks, there are also genuine carpet bargains to be had in Pakistan. Few antiques or museum pieces appear on the market, but the discerning shopper can find carpets of true quality and artistic merit. The pursuit of these can be enjoyable and educational — even addictive.

from Saudi Arabia. The biggest mosque in the world, it holds about 15,000 people inside, and another 85,000 in the courtyard. Underneath the courtyard is a two-storey building housing the **Islamic Research Centre**, library, museum, press centre, lecture hall, cafeteria and the offices of the Shariat (Islamic law) faculty of the Islamic University.

Constitution Avenue and the Diplomatic Enclave are interesting for their range of architectural styles. The **President's Palace** (used for state receptions), the **Parliament Building** and the **Secretariat** are good examples of modern architecture—clean, white and imposing. The embassies in the Diplomatic Enclave are architecturally varied—there are, for instance, pagodas in the garden of the Chinese Embassy. Out beyond the Diplomatic Enclave, and isolated against the Margalla Hills, is the new **Quaid-e-Azam University**.

The **East and West Viewpoints** in **Shakarparian Park**, on a low hill between Islamabad and Rawalpindi, offer the most photogenic view of Islamabad and the Margalla Hills behind. You can get there either from the road to the airport, about one kilometre (half a mile) from Zero Point, or by turning south at the traffic lights at Aabpara Market. An interesting round trip combines a tour of Shakarparian Park with a visit to **Lok Virsa**, the Institute of Folk and Traditional Heritage. Enter from the airport road and drive about 500 metres (yards) down a twisting avenue lined with jasmine. On the right is Lok Virsa, with its open-air exhibition of carved wooden doors in the garden, and a large indoor exhibition of local art, handicrafts and musical instruments from different regions of Pakistan. It also has a research library with microfilm facilities and a recording studio where Pakistan folk traditions are preserved. It is closed on Mondays; telephone 812578 to find out when it is open on other days.

Lotus Lake, a small pool with lotus flowers surrounded by walkways and flowering trees, is just past Lok Virsa, on the right. Opposite this, a side road leads up left to the top of the hill. **East Viewpoint** overlooks Islamabad and has a charming sunken garden laid out as a city plan and bounded by trimmed hedges representing the Margalla Hills. **West Viewpoint** overlooks Rawalpindi. Paved paths wind through the gardens and past fountains and young trees planted by visiting statesmen.

The main drive through the park takes you to a junction. Turn left to pass a huge modern sculpture of a star and crescent, and right a little further on for the **Rose and Jasmine Garden**, where the annual flower and rose shows are held in spring. This road leads past the camping site to Murree Road, near Aabpara Market. The road straight on by the star and crescent passes close to the **Friendship Sports Stadium**, donated by the People's Republic of China, and leaves the park at Rawal Lake, near Rawal Dam.

Rawal Lake is a large artificial reservoir and one of Islamabad–Rawalpindi's sources of water. The area round the lake has been planted with flowering trees and laid out with gardens, picnic spots and secluded paths. The best places to picnic are on the north side of the lake; turn right from the Murree Road on the way towards Murree.

On **Rawal Dam** there is a snack bar, viewpoint and rest house, all extremely crowded on Fridays. There are rowboats for hire, and you can fish in the lake if you have a permit (obtainable from the hut near the Islamabad Club).

The **Islamabad Club**, on the west side of the lake, has various sporting facilities, including an attractive golf course, tennis and squash courts and riding stables. Non-members can hire horses (mostly retired polo ponies) to ride round the lake or into Shakarparian Park. The ride round the lake is superb, especially in spring when the wild tulips are out, the fruit trees are in blossom and the marijuana plants are shoulder high. It takes two to three hours to ride all the way round, through woods, fields and villages; you can hire a groom from the stables to show you the way. It takes about four hours to walk round.

Shopping

Shopping in Islamabad is agreeable and easy; most shops are concentrated in designated shopping areas. The oldest shopping area is the **Aabpara Market**, on Khayaban-e-Suhrawardy, G-6/1, where you can buy household goods, fabrics, hardware, spices and food. **Melody Market**, in the centre of G-6, has souvenir, brass and carpet shops, while **Super Market**, in the centre of F-6, and **Jinnah Market**, in the centre of F-7, offer clothing, jewellery, leather goods, shoes, books, furniture and souvenirs. **Covered Market**, in G-6/3, sells meat, vegetables and groceries, and has good photography and haberdashery shops. In the **Blue Area** are the new PIA offices, most banks, restaurants and some carpet shops.

The **Juma Bazaar** (Friday Market) is the most interesting market for tourists. Every Friday in G-6/4, near Aabpara, wholesale fruit and vegetable sellers set up their stalls, temporary restaurants light their stoves and the residents of Islamabad gather to do their weekly shopping and meet friends. Behind the main market the Afghan refugees lay out rows of carpets, jewellery, antiques and souvenirs. This is a good place to search for gifts.

Handicraft shops

Threadlines Gallery, Super Market. A government-sponsored handicraft shop which has some excellent pieces at most reasonable prices.

Behbud Boutique, Super Market, G-6. Good selection of ready-made shalwar-kameez, table linen, and some traditional embroidery and tribal jewellery; very reasonable prices and profits go to charity.

Afghan Handicrafts and Maharajah Handicrafts, in Super Market.

Ace Leather, in Super Market, for leather goods and semiprecious stones.

Fancy Handicrafts and Kraftman, in Jinnah Market.

Chiltan Handicrafts, Pakistan Handicrafts and Asian Arts and Crafts, in the Blue Area.

Boutiques

Erums and Behbud, in Super Market. Good selection of ready-made shirts, trousers and shalwar-kameez.

Creation, Adam and Eve, and Guys and Dolls, in Jinnah Market. Ready-made clothes, as above.

Bookshops

Vanguard and Book Fair, in Jinnah Market.
Mr Books and Lok Virsa, in Super Market.
London Book Shop, in Kosar Market.
Old Bookshop (secondhand books), in Melody Market.

Carpets

Pak Persian and Qureshi's Carpets, in Melody Market.
Baluch Carpets, Lahore Carpet House, Shiraz Carpets, Nabeel Carpets and others are located in the Blue Area.

Short Outings from Islamabad

Saidpur village is less than one kilometre (half a mile) from Margalla Hills Road opposite Sector F-6, near Daman-e-Koh Viewpoint. The village is a slice of authentic rural Pakistan, with pottery a thriving cottage industry. The potters specialize in garden pots, working on traditional wheels and firing their wares in simple kilns. Before Partition the village was predominantly Hindu and its springs reputedly sacred. There are some fine mango trees in and around the village (the Hindus were the acknowledged experts in mango cultivation). When the site for Islamabad was chosen, the Capital Development Authority bought up the land and resettled most of the inhabitants, but those who insisted on staying ensured the survival of the village.

Nurpur is the most interesting village near Islamabad. It is near the Quaid-e-Azam University, about four kilometres (2.5 miles) from the Diplomatic Enclave; you can catch a minibus from Aabpara Market. At Nurpur is the **Shrine of Syed Abdul Latif Shah**, a 17th-century Sufi saint known as the Bari Imam, the Great Leader. He has an enormous following throughout Pakistan. A Syed (or direct descendant of Muhammad), Abdul Latif Shah travelled widely in the Islamic world gaining knowledge and a reputation as a holy man. He came to settle in what was then the village of Chourpur (Den of Thieves) and earned it its present name of Nurpur (Place of Light).

Many legends are attached to the saint, some very picturesque. When he was born he reputedly told the midwife to go and wash her hands before she touched him! Later he supposedly sat and meditated for 12 years in a rock pool above Nurpur.

Another story tells of a farmer with 70 cows who provided him with milk: when the cows all died in turn, Bari Imam instructed the farmer to milk his bull, who miraculously yielded milk but also died. The farmer was then instructed to throw stones over his shoulder into the stream and call his cows by name, but not to look back. For every stone, one of the farmer's cows emerged from the stream. When it came to the bull's turn, however, the farmer turned round, and the bull was instantly turned to stone. The bull rock is still there behind Nurpur.

The saint's shrine is in the centre of the village above the stream, shaded by a large banyan tree. Walk from the parking area where the buses stop, through the narrow lanes of shops and stalls that provide the pilgrims with refreshments and souvenirs (mainly glass bangles and rings), past the shrines of the saint's disciples, and, finally, to the main shrine.

Foreign visitors are welcome at the shrine as long as they show respect and remove their shoes. Women are not allowed into the inner sanctum but can look in through a window. Threads and locks of hair hang from the banyan tree in the courtyard, placed there by invalids praying for recovery. A small enclosure holds the eternal flame of Bari Imam, and the faithful anoint their foreheads or their wounds with the ashes. Opposite the entrance is an aviary containing hundreds of pigeons.

The saint's annual death festival (urs or *mela*) is a very joyous occasion; for days pilgrims pass through the normally quiet streets of Islamabad on their way to the festival, dancing and singing. The shrine itself becomes a fairground, with foodstalls, sideshows and religious singing and dancing. Foreigners are welcome at the festival, although you may feel more at ease with a Pakistani companion. Women should not go unescorted. Otherwise the best time to go to Nurpur is on a Thursday evening, which is always livelier than other times, as there is usually devotional *qawwali* singing.

Up on the hillside just behind Nurpur is the **Holy Man's Cave**. You can see this easily from Islamabad: look for a cliff face about halfway up the hills with a white-painted shrine along its base. To get there follow the road to the left of Nurpur for three kilometres (two miles), then walk up the hill on a track that starts at the Nurpur Water Headworks. It is hard to get lost; just follow the other pilgrims. Take the righthand path at the fork near the beginning (the lefthand path eventually leads to some cool rock pools—in one of which the Bari Imam is supposed to have sat for 12 years).

It takes about 45 minutes to reach the cave. Halfway up is a banyan tree shading a large rock, on the flat face of which are three small indistinguishable pro-tuberances about 60 centimetres (two feet) long. Apparently, when Bari Imam lived in the cave he was so tormented by a devil that he angrily struck at the demon and turned him to stone. The fairy who lived by the boulder halfway up to the shrine saw this happen and laughed, so the imam came down and turned her to stone too: the two vertical bumps are her petrified wings; the smaller horizontal one below and to the right of the others is her broken neck.

Once you reach the cliff face, follow the path across the bottom of the cliff, take off your shoes and enter the holy area, where the imam meditated for another 12 years. Hanging from the cliff face above is a six-metre (20-foot) -long stalactite from which a drop of water falls every minute or so. This water is considered blessed, and the faithful wait beneath to catch a drop in their hands or on a piece of cloth to drink or suck.

To the right of the cliff the path leads round to the top before dropping sharply down to the entrance of the cave. This is a narrow vertical slit in the cliff about six metres (20 feet) deep. Remove your shoes. The slender and agile can sidle in, one at a time, but it is not possible to turn round inside. For a small fee the guardian of the cave will go in and light an oil lamp at the far end; otherwise you will need a torch or matches. Bari Imam used to sleep here. The faithful write their requests on scraps of paper and tie them to the banyan tree at the mouth of the cave.

The stalactite and the narrow cave may well have been a fertility shrine before the advent of Islam.

The path leads on up the hill, offering beautiful views over Rawal Lake, the Potwar Plateau and Islamabad. On the way you pass another narrow, shallower cave.

Golra Sharif is another important shrine in the Islamabad area. It is the home of a living *pir*, or hereditary religious leader. To reach it take the Peshawar Road from Zero Point and turn right after 11 kilometres (seven miles) at the second roundabout; the shrine is at the end of the road, close to the Margalla Hills. You can also get there by bus from Rawalpindi.

About a million pilgrims visit Golra Sharif every year. The present pir is the grandson of the dynasty's founder, Hazrat Mehr Ali Shah, who lived early this century and was a mystic poet and religious scholar who performed miracles. He was also renowned for having a beautiful, melodious voice. As is usual at Muslim shrines, pilgrims are accommodated free for up to a week in the caravanserais that surround the mausoleums of the former pirs, and free meals are also provided. The tombs themselves are not exceptional, but for those interested in the cultural traditions of Pakistan, a visit to Golra Sharif is well worthwhile.

You can also visit the **snake farm** at the National Health Laboratories on the Lehtrar Road beyond Rawal Dam to see the poisonous snakes being milked for their venom. Children love this visit because they can play with the laboratory's store of rabbits, mice and guinea pigs. To arrange a visit, write to the Director, National Health Laboratories, Lehtrar Road, Islamabad, giving seven days' notice.

Also on Lehtrar Road are the **Capital Development Authority Nursery** and a number of smaller private nurseries where you can buy shrubs, plants, flowers and Christmas trees. The large, cool, shady nursery is an agreeable place to wander round on a hot summer's evening.

Hiking in the Margalla Hills

Among Islamabad's main attractions, particularly for walkers, are the Margalla Hills. The hills are part of the Islamabad National Park, a protected nature reserve covering 31,000 acres; grazing, hunting and shooting are forbidden here. The forest is reclaiming the hills, and the wildlife is slowly returning: rhesus monkeys, barking deer, wild boar and many species of birds are relatively easy to see; leopard, panther and pangolin are more elusive. The peaks behind Islamabad range from 1,217 metres (3,993 feet) to 1,605 metres (5,264 feet), a climb of about 90 minutes to two hours for the average hiker. Most of the paths are rough and stony—strong shoes or boots are recommended. The scrub between the paths is thick and thorny, so shortcuts should be avoided. October to March are the best hiking months. Once over the first ridge it is very easy to get lost, as the hills look bewilderingly similar. The sun can be very hot, even in winter, so take drinking water with you.

The Capital Development Authority has produced a brochure, *Trekking in the Margalla Hills*, which is good as far as it goes, but the map is neither detailed nor accurate enough to be useful. The Asian Study Group (ASG) has published a *Hiking Guide to the Margallas*, which is excellent, with detailed maps and descriptions for ten short family hikes, 20 longer hikes and three hikes lasting two to three days. The ASG organizes regular hikes and bird-watching outings, which the short-term visitor is welcome to join.

In each gully a path leads from Islamabad to the villages on the other side, and there is a paved road to the top of the ridge and along to the east (suitable for ordinary cars), with more paths leading off it. The two maps reproduced here are the ASG overview of trails. They give a general idea of the possibilities and are adequate if you remain within sight of Islamabad. More ambitious hikers should equip themselves with the ASG detailed maps and a compass.

RAWALPINDI

Rawalpindi is a lively, bustling city with crowded streets and colourful bazaars, though it lacks the grand monuments you see in some other Pakistani cities. Nonetheless, the bazaars should appeal to anyone with the desire to see the real Pakistan, and the British cantonment to those interested in colonial history.

Rawalpindi means the Place of Rawal, who may have been a Ghakkar chief (see page 209) some 400 or 500 years ago. Rawalpindi was a small settlement until the Moghuls built the Imperial (Shahi) Road from Delhi to Kabul in the 16th century. It is mentioned by name in the Moghul emperor Jahangir's copious memoirs. Apparently the inhabitants told him that a monstrous crocodile lived in a deep pool nearby. To test the story's veracity, Jahangir ordered one of his men and a sheep into the pool and seems to have been quite disappointed when they emerged unscathed. On other occasions he records that he hunted near the town.

In the early 19th century, Rawalpindi was captured by the Sikhs, who realized its strategic importance and developed it as a trading centre. They also built new houses and to some extent fortified the town. The Sikhs in their turn were ousted by the British after a decisive defeat near Gujrat in 1849. However, a large Sikh community remained in Rawalpindi until Partition in 1947.

The British made their camp, or cantonment, to the south of the old city. As elsewhere in the subcontinent, instead of living cheek by jowl with the locals, they built themselves spacious enclaves, with barracks, arsenals, officer and civilian residences, churches, clubs and other amenities, usually outside the town. Roads were often called lines after the original lines of tents. In the words of James Morris:

Just the look of it on the map suggests the absolute self-sufficiency of the cantonment. It was a world apart. The memsahib and her children need never visit the old city from one furlough to the next, and in the green expanse of the Government Gardens, or on the hopefully sprinkled lawns of the club, a stray native of the country must have felt horribly out of place.

There were down-to-earth reasons why a British garrison, or a British community, should not live in the heart of a tropical town. Plagues and tropical diseases were little understood, women and children were less self-reliant then, the most broad-minded of colonels would hardly wish his soldiers to associate too easily with the bazaar whores. But the detachment of the cantonments had a deeper meaning, for whatever the motives that sent the British out of their islands, a deep instinct kept them perpetually apart from their subjects of other races.

Pax Britannica (1968)

Under the British, Rawalpindi grew rapidly as a military base, and at Independence in 1947 it became the headquarters of the Pakistan Army. In the 1960s the city became the temporary capital of Pakistan while Islamabad was under construction.

Getting to Rawalpindi

Rawalpindi lies on the Grand Trunk Road, 280 kilometres (174 miles) from Lahore and 173 kilometres (108 miles) from Peshawar. It shares an international airport, and railway and bus stations with Islamabad. Murree, Peshawar and Airport roads connect Rawalpindi and Islamabad.

Where to Stay

Expensive: Rs950–3,000

Pearl Continental, the Mall, tel. 66011–21, 62700–10 (s/d Rs1,830/2,150). International class; all facilities.

Shalimar, off the Mall, tel. 62901–21 (s/d Rs960/1,888). All facilities.

Moderate: Rs150–600

Flashman's, PTDC, the Mall, tel. 581480–4 (s/d Rs370/520). All facilities.

Kashmirwala's, the Mall, tel. 583186–9 (s/d Rs540/650).

Gatmell's, Jail Road, near Army House, tel. 65047, 65123 (s/d Rs150/220). Quiet, large rooms, excellent value, storage facilities for expeditions.

Pine, Iftikhar Janjua Road, behind Pearl Continental, tel. 63660, 68017–8 (s/d Rs150/250). Small rooms but quiet; bargain hard.

The big hotels along Murree Road near Liaquat Chowk tend to be noisy and overpriced; the Park, National City, Shangrila, Sandhills, Potohar and Marhaba (there are many more) are all around Rs150–200 for a double.

Cheaper: Rs40–100

Asia, off Murree Road, near Committee Chowk, tel. 70898 (s/d Rs50/80). Quiet, big rooms, helpful management, best value in town.

Rawal, Queens, United and Al Farooq hotels are all in the same square as the Asia. They are slightly more expensive, but still good value (s/d Rs60/90).

Al-Hayat, Murree Road, Liaquat Chowk, tel. 70979 (s/d Rs40/70). Popular with backpackers.

New Kamran, Kashmir Road, Saddar Bazaar, tel. 582040 (s/d Rs60/100).

Inexpensive

Hotels by the railway station are often full of Afghan refugees, and many will not accept foreigners. There are, however:

Railway Retiring Rooms. Rawalpindi City Station. Bring your own bedding.

Youth Hostel, 25 Gulistan Colony, near Ayub Park. Too remote.

YWCA, 64-A Satellite Town. Women only. A bit rundown, but cheap and safe.

Where to Eat

The best Pakistani food is at Kashmirwala's Hotel. The other good restaurants are mostly along the Mall or in Saddar Bazaar.

Shezan, Kashmir Road, opposite GPO, tel. 65743.

Blue Lagoon, the Mall, opposite Pearl Continental, tel. 65377.

Mei Kong, Haider Road, tel. 66377. Best Chinese food.

Chung Wah, Murree Road, Satellite Town, tel. 843803.

Burger Express, Kashmir Road. Fast food.

Seven-Eleven, Bank Road. Fast food.

Cook's 39, Bank Road. Fast food.

The best inexpensive restaurants (about Rs10 per person) are in the Saddar Bazaar area and around Raja Bazaar, the railway and Pir Wadhai bus station.

Useful Addresses

Tourist Information Centre, PTDC, Flashman's Hotel, the Mall, tel. 581480–4.
PIA, the Mall, tel. 67011, 66231.
American Express, Murree Road, tel. 65617.

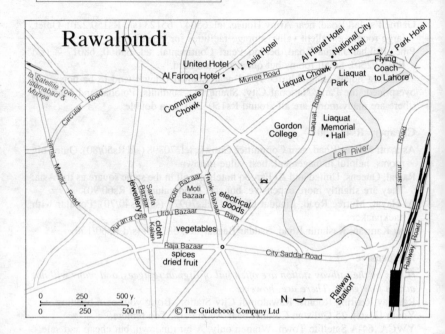

Rawalpindi

(map labels:) to Satellite Town, Islamabad & Murree · Circular Road · Jamia Masjid Road · Committee Chowk · Al Farooq Hotel · United Hotel · Asia Hotel · Murree Road · Al Hayat Hotel · National City Hotel · Park Hotel · Flying Coach to Lahore · Liaquat Chowk · Liaquat Road · Liaquat Park · Gordon College · Liaquat Memorial Hall · Leh River · Sarafa Jewellery · Bohr Bazaar · Trunk Bazaar · Moti Bazaar · electrical goods · Bara · Purana Qila · Sabzi Kalan · Urdu Bazaar · cloth · vegetables · Raja Bazaar · spices dried fruit · City Saddar Road · Railway Road · Railway Station · N

0   250   500 y.
0   250   500 m.

© The Guidebook Company Ltd

General Post Office, Kashmir Road, tel. 65691.
Telegraph and Telephone Office, the Mall, tel. 65854, 65809.
Foreigners' Registration Office, Rashid Minhas Road, Civil Lines, tel. 63866.
Passport Office, 6th Road, Satellite Town, tel. 848051.

Shopping

Saddar Bazaar, between the Mall and the old city, is the place to look for hotels, banks, airlines, travel agents, books, shoes, carpets, leather, furniture, foam rubber, tailors and solar topees. The heart of the bazaar is along Kashmir Road and Massey Gate.

Shamas Din, on Massey Gate, sells boots, shoes, suitcases, saddles and poufs. English Book House and Pak American Bookshop are both on Kashmir Road. Men's tailors are located on Haider Road, ladies' tailors in Kamran Market off Kashmir Road. Look for cashmere shawls along Haider Road. For soft furnishings try the Bombay Cloth Store and Malik Fabrics on Bank Road; for linen try Hyatts. Carpets, brass and antiques can be found on Canning Road behind Flashman's, on the Mall in front and in the lobby of the Pearl Continental Hotel.

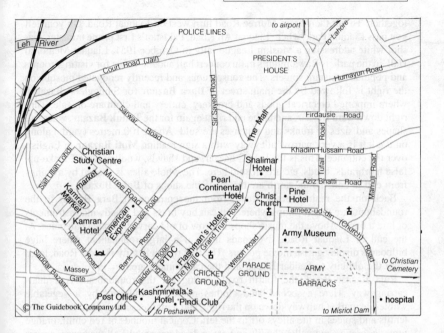

Another good brass shop, Shaukat Ali, 170 D-Block, Satellite Town, tel. 842813, has a large selection of good-quality, ready-polished brass and copper. The shop is in an unmarked private house. Entering Rawalpindi on the Murree Road from Islamabad, turn right at the first traffic lights to Satellite Town. Take the second left. The house is the fifth on the right, about 100 metres (yards) along.

Sights

Rawalpindi has two major roads, Murree Road, the main approach from Islamabad, which runs roughly north to south, and the Grand Trunk Road, which becomes the Mall and runs roughly east to west. The two main bazaar areas are Raja Bazaar in the old city, west of Murree Road, and Saddar Bazaar, which became the cantonment bazaar, between the old city and the Mall.

Bazaars in the Old City

Raja Bazaar is made up of many smaller bazaars, and each is a labyrinth of alleyways. As in all Asian countries, shops selling the same items are grouped together. To get there from Murree Road turn west on Liaquat Road. On your left you pass Liaquat Park, where Liaquat Ali Khan, Pakistan's first prime minister, was shot while addressing a Muslim League rally in October 1951. Liaquat Memorial Hall, in the park, is Rawalpindi's main concert hall and the venue for visiting troupes and popular Pakistani singers. The conspicuous and recently renovated mosque on the right is followed by the main street of **Bara Bazaar** (or Smugglers' Bazaar), where imported electrical goods and crockery, cutlery and cloth are on sale. Turn right down Bara Bazaar, and at the end right again for the **Trunk Bazaar**, where all shapes and sizes of trunks and suitcases are sold. About 100 metres (yards) along on the left is a very narrow alleyway with a sign reading **Moti Bazaar** in English over the entrance. This is the ladies' bazaar, and shawls, woollen goods, make-up, false hairbraids, beads, etc are all sold here. The whole alley is shaded by awnings from end to end. To the north are the medicine shops of **Bohr Bazaar**.

Back on the main Liaquat Road, from the entrance to Bara Bazaar to the roundabout, are **music shops** where you can buy brass and woodwind instruments or hire a band. Above the music shops is a row of old carved wooden balconies. At the end of Liaquat Road, five roads meet at a large roundabout where huge billboards display garish movie posters. The first road left, City–Saddar Road, leads from the old city to Saddar Bazaar and the cantonment area.

Raja Bazaar Road, the fourth road leading off the roundabout, is a dual-carriageway. Here a second-hand clothes market is followed by a vegetable wholesale market halfway down on the right, and a market selling dried fruits, nuts, lentils and spices in the alleys off to the left. Conical mounds of red chilli, orange tumeric, orange and yellow lentils and green dried peas evoke all the bazaar scenes in the *Arabian Nights*.

At the end of Raja Bazaar turn right down a narrow street into **Kalan Bazaar**: shoes and stockings are on display on the left, and bales of cloth, chiffon scarves, hats, hair and beauty oils, and blockprint bedspreads on the right. A narrow but motorable street selling knives, scissors and whips, and overhung with old wooden balconies, branches up the hill to the left. At the top of the hill is the **Purana Qila Bazaar** and a small Hindu temple. Purana Qila means Old Fort, though there is no trace of a fort here now. This is where you can buy wedding dresses, fancily embroidered cloth and heavy gold braid.

Kalan Bazaar runs into **Sarafa Bazaar**, the jewellery market. On your left is a 19th-century red British postbox, Rawalpindi's first. The jewellery bazaar sells gold and silver, and is the best place to hunt for antique tribal silver, some of which is very lovely. (Most of these jewellers also have smarter shops on Murree Road.) Then come the brass shops selling household utensils made of copper, brass, tin, aluminium and stainless steel. Muhammad Shafi and Sons, on the right, is well known for its antique brass and copper ware, and also has a storeroom down an alleyway behind the shop where you can rummage for treasures. Most of the ware is still coated in tin, but the piece of your choice will be expertly polished for you in a few days. Aim at bargaining down to about two-thirds of the asking price, and check that all vessels are waterproof. Any holes can be soldered while you wait. If you continue on down Sarafa Bazaar, you will come out on to Murree Road again.

The Cantonment

The Leh River and the railway line mark the boundary between the cantonment and the old city. The cantonment's main landmark is the intersection of Murree Road with the Mall, where a large Gothic church stands forlornly on one corner. Turning west up the Mall towards Peshawar you pass the old-style Flashman's Hotel on your right. On the left is the cricket ground and Rawalpindi Club behind a row of souvenir shops. The first turning on the right past Flashman's enters the Saddar Bazaar (see page 224).

South along the Mall towards Lahore is the Pearl Continental Hotel, followed by the Shalimar Hotel. Immediately behind the Pearl Continental stands **Christ Church**, formerly the garrison church, built in 1854 and renovated in 1879. Its whitewashed interior with dark wooden beams is typical of many provincial English churches of the same period, but it is prettier than most. In its heyday three services a day were held on weekdays and no fewer than eight on Sundays; now there is one service on Sundays. On the walls are numerous commemorative plaques.

The **Christian cemetery**, off Harley Street, has many graves of British soldiers and their families, a great number of whom died pathetically young from cholera and other diseases; the babies' graves almost outnumber the adults'. One of the graves has a remarkable 'growing stone'; shaped like a wide pipe standing on end and filled with earth, the stone has grown up and around an inscribed cross.

Also in this area are a number of single-storeyed colonial bungalows (the word meaning 'houses in the Bengal or Bangla style') with high ceilings and wide covered verandahs.

The **Army Museum**, also near the Pearl Continental Hotel, houses a rare collection of military weapons, uniforms and paintings covering Pakistan's military history. It is open 9 am–3 pm in winter; 8 am–12 noon and 5.30–7 pm in summer.

Back on the Mall and going southeast towards Lahore, you pass the President's House behind high walls, the jail, the Murree Brewery and Ayub National Park. The park has a lake with boats, a children's amusement park and playground, restaurants, a mini-golf course and zoo, besides many walkways and bridle paths.

Outings from Islamabad–Rawalpindi

Whatever the season there are numerous full- and half-day trips you can make using Islamabad or Rawalpindi as a base. You can explore Pakistani history at a number of archaeological excavations and 16th-century forts; visit the hill stations, dams or lakes; explore the national parks by car or on foot; or go walking, bird-watching or picnicking in the forest. Some trips are accessible by public transport, others require a private car.

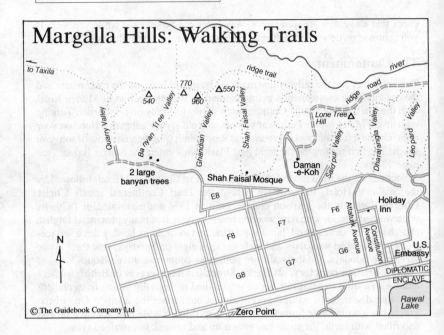

Margalla Hills: Walking Trails

to Taxila

ridge trail

river

ridge road

△770
△550
△540
△960

Quarry Valley

Banyan Tree Valley

Ghandian Valley

Shah Faisal Valley

Lone Tree △
Hill

Said pur Valley

Dharajangla Valley

Leopard Valley

2 large
banyan trees

Shah Faisal Mosque

Daman
-e-Koh

E8

Holiday
Inn

F6

Atatürk Avenue

Constitution Avenue

F7

F8

G6

G7

G8

N

U.S.
Embassy

DIPLOMATIC
ENCLAVE

Rawal
Lake

© The Guidebook Company Ltd

△ Zero Point

Margalla Hills

The easiest outing from Islamabad is to drive or walk to the top of the Margalla Hills, past **Daman-e-Koh Viewpoint** (see page 213) and east along the ridge. You can drive eight kilometres (five miles) along the ridge in an ordinary car, but you need a short, narrow jeep to make the round trip coming back by the Murree Road. On the ridge are cool, shady forests, excellent picnic spots, fine views, and the chance to see a variety of wildlife.

There are two CDA rest houses on the Margalla Hills, bookable at the Directorate of Environment, CDA, Sitara Market, Islamabad. They are at **Pir Sohawa** and **Pharilla**, 16 kilometres (ten miles) and 28 kilometres (17 miles) respectively from Margalla Hills Road. Both are equipped with running water, kitchen and bathroom facilities; bedding is also provided, but it would be better to take your own.

It is eight kilometres (five miles), or about 15 minutes by car, from Margalla Hills Road to the top of the ridge; considerably shorter and about an hour and a half on foot via the paths.

Lone Tree Hill, or Mount Happiness, is the first summit on the right along the ridge road. It is an easy 15-minute walk from the road to the top; it takes one hour

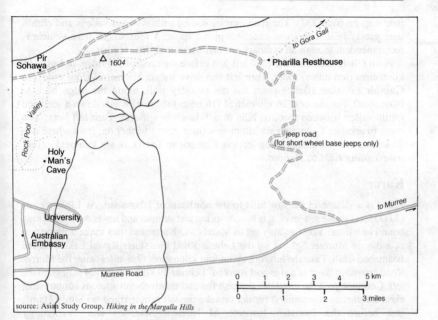

source: Asian Study Group, *Hiking in the Margalla Hills*

to walk from the top down to Islamabad.

The surfaced road ends at Pir Sohawa rest house, at 1,174 metres (3,850 feet), a pleasantly cool place to spend the night, even in summer. It has a well-laid-out garden with paths, steps and benches, and views north over to the next valley and south to Islamabad. From Pir Sohawa it is a hike of 90 minutes to the top of the highest peak in the Margallas.

The jeep track continues to Pharilla rest house, 12 kilometres (seven miles) away; you can walk the distance in two hours or so. About two kilometres (a mile) from Pir Sohawa, a jeep track branches left down to **Sangra** village in the next valley and up the other side to **Makhnial**, where it joins a jeep track to **Khanpur Dam**, an alternative route back to Islamabad through open park-like forest with good views over the valleys. There is a Forestry Department rest house at Makhnial.

From Pharilla rest house it is a six-hour walk to **Ghora Gali** or a one-hour jeep drive for 19 kilometres (12 miles) down a steep track with some tight, gravel-strewn, hairpin bends to Murree Road. When the road forks, keep right.

A scenic full-day round trip over the hills from Ghora Gali, on the road to Murree, to **Khanpur**, beyond Taxila, and thence back to Islamabad, takes about six hours (see map on page 232). The road crosses some fertile wooded valleys and climbs over grassy hills with some excellent picnic spots. A four-wheel drive vehicle is recommended, though an ordinary car can make it in dry weather.

From Ghora Gali take the road left just before the crest of the ridge, to **Lora**, 16 kilometres (ten miles) away. Turn left and drive for six kilometres (four miles) to **Gambir** (another starting-point for the two-day walk along the ridge back to Islamabad). For the next 26 kilometres (16 miles) the road winds down a secluded fertile valley between wooded hills to a T-junction at Serai. Turn left here. You come to another T-junction six kilometres (four miles) further on, from where it is 26 kilometres (16 miles) going left via Khanpur to Taxila, or six kilometres (four miles) going right to Haripur.

Karor

Karor is a village in the low hills to the northeast of Islamabad. At 1,000 metres (3,000 feet) above sea level, it is best in spring and autumn and never becomes snowbound in winter. You can also get to Murree via Karor and thus make a round trip of a day in Murree. Set out on the Lehtrar Road that skirts Rawal Lake past the Islamabad Club. Take the left fork about four kilometres (2.5 miles) after the Murree Road crossing; there is a signpost marked 'Lehtrar 39 kilometres' (24 miles) on the left. Continue past the nurseries through flat and relatively prosperous countryside; eight kilometres (five miles) further on take the left turn marked 'to **Simly Dam**', just before the Pakistan Institute of Nuclear Sciences and Technology (PINSTECH). This is a sensitive area, and you are not allowed to approach the research centre.

A surfaced road takes you across undulating scrubland to **Simly**, 14 kilometres (nine miles) away. The dam is on your left. A paved road continues from Simly to the main Murree Road at Bharakan, about 15 kilometres (nine miles) from Islamabad. A paved road from Simly snakes on up into the hills with good views over the plains behind. About five kilometres (three miles) from Simly you reach the top of a hill from where Murree is clearly visible; there are rockpools below the road one kilometre (half a mile) beyond the summit. A little further on, through a pine forest, are clear views of the snow-capped Pir Panjal Range in India. The pine trees here are tapped for their resin. The large flat-topped stones make excellent picnic tables. There is a Forestry Department rest house in Karor, bookable in Rawalpindi. The paved road continues through the forest to **Lower Topa** and **Murree** (without stops, about two hours from Islamabad to Murree by this route). About ten kilometres (six miles) before Lower Topa a road leads to the right up to the ridge at **Patriata** for excellent views; there is another rest house here.

Pharwala Fort

The footpath to Pharwala Fort starts from the bridge across the Soan river 3.5 kilometres (two miles) beyond PINSTECH. Foreigners may be stopped before passing PINSTECH; Pakistanis may continue by car to the bridge and park there. Pharwala Fort is about five kilometres (three miles) downriver in the Soan Gorge, on the east (left) bank. Allow a full day for this outing and take a picnic. The walk takes about two hours each way, plus an hour to see the fort and eat. The fort is not particularly impressive; the pleasure of the outing lies in the walk. Instead of returning to the Lehtrar road you can make a round trip continuing on the path past the fort for a further five kilometres (three miles) to the Kahuta road. You can arrange for a car to pick you up, or trust to luck that you will find public transport coming from Kahuta towards Islamabad or Rawalpindi.

From the Lehtrar road the beginning of the path is not obvious. Pick your way around the fields and head to the V in the hills, the gorge through which the Soan passes. At the beginning of the gorge you will find the old, roughly paved Moghul track on the east (left) side of the river. All along this track, on almost every suitable flat stone, are carvings of hands or feet, symbols to ward off evil.

Pharwala Fort was the main stronghold of the Ghakkars, the Punjabi tribe who controlled the Potwar Plateau between the 13th century and the advent of the Sikhs (see page 209). In 1519 the first Moghul emperor, Babur, began to raid the subcontinent from Afghanistan. He attacked the Ghakkars at Pharwala, and describes in his memoirs how, with the best of his cavalry, he went from Kallar Kahar, on the north side of the Salt Range, to Pharwala in little more than a day (about 150 kilometres, or 93 miles, over eroded and ravined country) and attacked and captured the fort in time to dine there. When his main force rejoined him, he marched through the gorge and to the northwest (presumably over the site of present-day Islamabad) to the Margalla Pass. The Ghakkar chiefs sued for peace and thereafter became loyal allies of the Moghuls.

Babur's son, Humayun, was ousted from his throne by the Afghan Sher Shah Suri and was forced to flee to Persia. Sher Shah tried to control the Ghakkars by building the huge fort at Rohtas (see pages 205–8). After Sher Shah's death, Humayun prepared to make a comeback from Afghanistan. His treacherous brother Kamran made unsuccessful overtures to Sher Shah's successor and was captured by the Ghakkar chief, Sultan Adam Khan. Humayun was informed and invited to come to Pharwala to decide his brother's fate: Kamran's eyes were gouged out, and he was sent on a pilgrimage to Mecca to atone for his crimes.

The remains of Pharwala Fort consist of sections of curtain wall and three gates. The place of execution was on top of the gate overlooking the river. An elderly gentleman from the village inside the fort invariably greets visitors, guides them round the fort and offers tea.

Below the cliffs on which the fort stands at the southern entrance to the gorge, the Soan River is shelved on huge slabs of rock, where it forms pools. In colonial times, members of the Rawalpindi garrison used to fish and swim here.

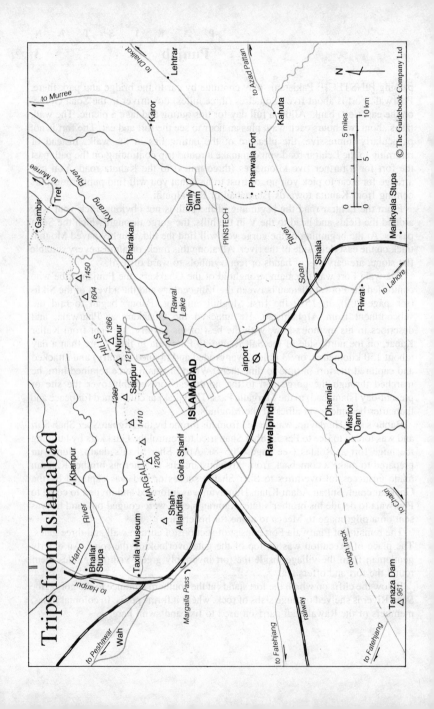

Trips from Islamabad

© The Guidebook Company Ltd

Lehtrar

Lehtrar is a village in the hills 43 kilometres (27 miles) east of Islamabad. There may be a road block at PINSTECH to stop foreigners, but Pakistanis can continue to the extensive pine forest on the ridge at Lehtrar. Again, huge trees growing on the gentle slopes above and below the road are tapped for their resin. There are good picnic spots beside some rock pools along the stream below the road about five kilometres (three miles) past Lehtrar village. There is a Forestry Department rest house in Lehtrar, bookable in Rawalpindi. The paved road continues from Lehtrar down to the Jhelum River, with spectacular views over the valley and into India beyond.

If you approach Lehtrar from the Jhelum River side you can return to Islamabad past PINSTECH without being turned back—unless you are unlucky!

Kahuta

Owing to its proximity to PINSTECH, Kahuta, 32 kilometres (20 miles) east of Islamabad, is also currently out of bounds for foreigners. For Pakistanis it makes a pleasant winter drive of about an hour. From Zero Point take the road for 20 kilometres (12 miles) in the direction of Lahore. Turn left after crossing the Soan River on a long low bridge, cross the railway on a level crossing in Sihala, and follow the paved road through cultivated land and prosperous villages. The low line of hills to the north is cut by the Soan River. You can just see Pharwala Fort, which is about five kilometres (three miles) away, on the hillside to the right of the gorge. The path leading to it is about 11 kilometres (seven miles) from the turning off the Lahore road.

Just before Kahuta, low ridges of jagged rock resembling the back of a brontosaurus form part of the line of rocks that runs east–west from the Jhelum to the Indus and passes to the south of Rawalpindi.

At Kahuta you can see the ruins of several Hindu and Sikh temples. Before Partition this was the scene of serious communal fighting, and in fact it was his visit to Kahuta that convinced Viceroy Mountbatten of the enormity of the Hindu–Muslim problem. Today it is a quiet place, and there is nothing to suggest the horrors of 1947.

Two surfaced roads lead east out of Kahuta to the Jhelum River. One leads off to the left in the centre of town, passes through a cleft in a line of rock, and runs up a pleasant wooded valley to a ridge, before descending to the Jhelum and Azad Pattan Bridge into Azad Kashmir. You can return to Islamabad via Rawalkot, Kohala and Murree, a distance of about 150 kilometres (93 miles). This road is sometimes blocked by snow in winter.

The second road runs straight through Kahuta and eventually reaches a bridge at Karote, further south, across the Jhelum. You can return to Islamabad via either Mangla Dam or Murree.

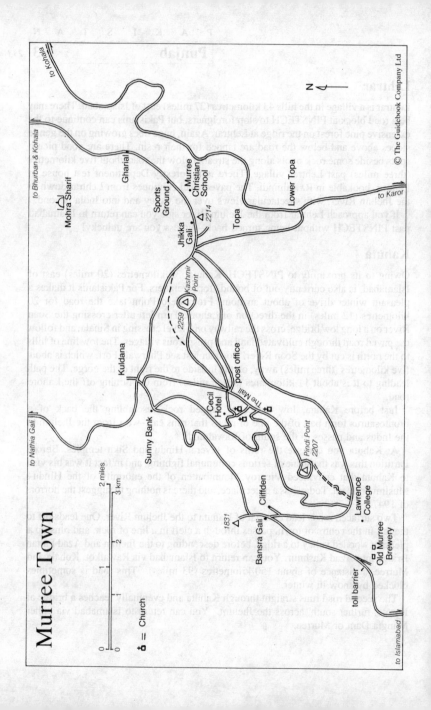

Murree Town

$\dagger$ = Church

© The Guidebook Company Ltd

N

Murree

Murree is a hill resort at 2,240 metres (7,400 feet) above sea level, an hour's drive northeast of Islamabad. This is the first choice for a day's outing from Islamabad. The scenery is superb, the climate cool in summer and crisply cold in winter, the hotels good and the drive easy. As Pakistan's leading hill resort for local tourists, Murree is apt to be very crowded in summer.

The people of the Murree Hills claim descent from Abbas, the uncle of the Prophet Muhammad, who gave his name to the Abbasid Caliphate of Baghdad. Abbasi is a common name in the area.

When the British annexed the Punjab in 1849, they soon decided to establish a hill station at Murree, as it was conveniently near the important military cantonment of Rawalpindi. It was actually founded in 1851 on pastureland on the ridge and developed quickly. The name Murree (or Marhi) means 'high place' in the local dialect. Settlements on the neighbouring ridges at Cliffden, Kuldana, Topa and Gharial were soon added to the original town and military cantonment. The summer headquarters of the colonial government of the Punjab was at Murree until 1876, when it was transferred to Simla.

Murree became increasingly important when the road from Murree to Kohala, and thence along the Jhelum River through Muzaffarabad to Srinagar, was built, as this considerably shortened the traditional route through Hazara. The journey from Murree to Srinagar, a distance of 258 kilometres (160 miles), was divided into 11 stages, each 15–30 kilometres (10–20 miles) long. Dak bungalows, where travellers spent the night and changed horses, were built at regular intervals along the route.

In Murree, as in other famous hill stations, the British attempted to create a little England, with a mall or promenade, parks, churches, schools, clubs and cafes. After Independence, Murree became the summer headquarters of the governor of the Punjab, and when Islamabad became the capital of Pakistan in 1962 the town expanded rapidly. The old wooden buildings and tin-roofed bungalows with names like Primrose Cottage and Woodland Walk have been augmented by stone-built houses belonging to government organizations and embassies, and Murree's popularity as a holiday resort has continued unabated.

The area is lovely all year round. In summer it is cool, and in winter the snow is piled high along the sides of the streets. It often rains, and you will need warm clothes for the evening, even in summer.

Getting to Murree

There is a frequent bus and minibus service between both Rawalpindi and Islamabad, and Murree. If you are driving yourself you can go up by the main road and return via Karor (see page 230). Murree Road leaves Islamabad near the southern end of Constitution Avenue and heads northeast for 15 kilometres (nine miles) across relatively flat agricultural land. You pass a checkpoint at **Bharakan**,

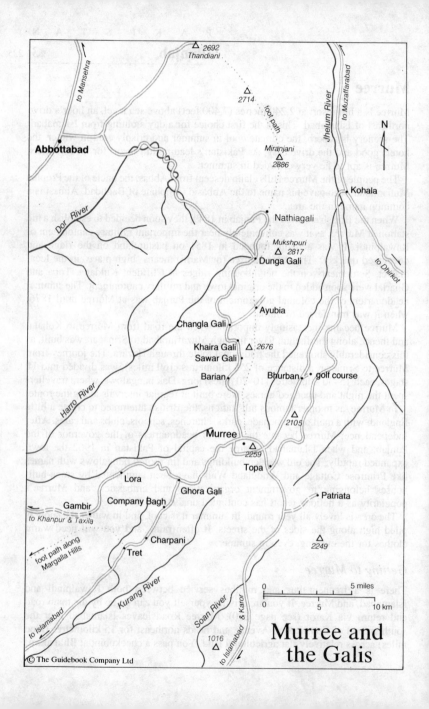

to Mansehra

△ 2692
Thandiani

△ 2714

foot path

Abbottabad

Jhelum River

N

Miranjani
△ 2886

Dor River

Kohala

Nathiagali

to Muzaffarabad

Mukshpuri
△ 2817

Dunga Gali

to Dhirkot

Ayubia

Changla Gali

△ 2676

Khaira Gali
Sawar Gali

Barian

Bhurban • golf course

Harro River

△ 2105

Murree
△ 2259

Topa

Lora

Patriata

Ghora Gali

Company Bagh

Gambir

to Khanpur & Taxila

Charpani

△ 2249

foot path along
Margalla Hills

Tret

Kurang River

to Islamabad

Soan River & Karor

to Islamabad & Karor

0   5 miles

0   5   10 km

Murree
and
the Galis

© The Guidebook Company Ltd

then start climbing, at first gently, then more and more steeply, through shady pine forest. There are a number of villages on the way up with descriptive names like Char Pani (Four Waters), Company Bagh (Company Garden) and Ghora Gali (Horse Station). In the old days you changed horses at Ghora Gali for the final ascent to the ridge. Rawalpindi to Murree was considered a three-day walk, with stops at Bharakan and Tret on the way; in a landau the journey took one day.

Tret and **Ghora Gali** are both starting points for the walk back along the hills to Islamabad. At Ghora Gali a turn left leads down to Haripur or the Taxila Valley (see page 229); turn right to a complex of good old-fashioned rest houses owned by the Forestry Department, where you can picnic in the shady garden or stay overnight. Just beyond the village is a toll barrier (Rs2 for cars), and a little further on are the ruins of the Murree Brewery on the hillside on the right; the Parsee-owned brewery was burned at Partition and has since relocated in Rawalpindi.

Beyond Ghora Gali the road climbs up to **Cliffden**, where it crosses a spur of the main ridge. A road to the right, three kilometres (two miles) beyond the old Murree Brewery, leads up the ridge to **Lawrence College**, originally founded for the sons of British officers, and now one of Pakistan's foremost boys' boarding schools. The convent further up the ridge is one of Pakistan's best girls' boarding schools. The road past the college forks, the left fork coming out at the lower end of the Mall in Murree, the right fork leading to Jhika Gali (see map on page 234).

The main road from Ghora Gali continues to **Sunny Bank**, where there is a roadside bazaar surrounded by three-storey wooden houses. The road to the right leads to the centre of Murree. In summer the Mall is closed to cars; there is a car park at the foot of some steps leading up to the Mall. About two kilometres (a mile) beyond Sunny Bank there is a crossroads: the first road to the right leads back to the north end of the Mall, at the post office; the second road right goes to Bhurban and Kohala; and the road to the left takes you to the Galis (see pages 239 and 241).

Where to Stay

Hotel prices range from Rs20 to Rs800. The season is short, and the hotels are heavily booked in summer, but there are big discounts during the rest of the year. Recommended are;
Cecil, Mount View Road, tel. 2247, 2257 (Rs300–800).
Blue Pines, Cart Road, tel. 2233, 2230 (Rs200–400).
Brightland, Imtiaz Shaheed Road, tel. 2270 (Rs200–400).
Marhaba, Jinnah Road, tel. 2184 (Rs150–300).

There are about 40 other hotels concentrated in the area around the GPO, along Cart Road, Jinnah Road, Imtiaz Shaheed Road and Abid Shaheed Road. The various government and embassy rest houses are all usually booked up in summer, but worth enquiring about if you can find the necessary contacts.

Sights

Murree proper spreads for about five kilometres (three miles) along the top of a ridge running northeast to southwest. At the northeast end of the ridge is **Kashmir Point**, so-called because of the views across the valley of the Jhelum River into Kashmir; at the southwest end is **Pindi Point**, which overlooks Rawalpindi and Islamabad. Between the two stretches the Mall, at the centre of which is the main shopping area, where most people congregate. There are numerous other roads which branch off the Mall, either following the contours of the ridge or descending to the main road.

Promenading up the Mall is Murree's main amusement, particularly in the late afternoon. You can wander through the bazaar below the Mall, where fruit and nuts are sold, and peer into the many stalls and souvenir shops along the way. Cashmere shawls, walking sticks and furs are good buys, and the pistachio nuts are reputed to be the best in Pakistan. In summer you can sit on the terraces of the many tea houses along the Mall and watch the people parade by.

Continuing northeast from the post office at the top end of the Mall, you pass the **Murree Club** down a side road; it was here that in 1955 the Pakistan Constituent Assembly was held. There are some walks down into the woods on your left along forest trails. From the post office to Kashmir Point is the area where many embassies have their summer residences. The road loops around Kashmir Point, the highest spot in Murree (2,260 metres or 7,413 feet above sea level), with the governor's house at the top and views through the trees to the snow-capped mountains in Kashmir.

There are other summer resorts northeast along the Murree ridge on the two roads that connect Murree to Kohala. At **Jhika Gali**, below Kashmir Point, the road forks: left for Gharial and Bhurban, right for Lower Topa. The road to Bhurban passes the Murree Christian School on the right, another of Pakistan's well-known boarding schools; its main building is in the old British garrison church.

Bhurban, eight kilometres (five miles) from Murree, is a much-favoured minor resort on a long ridge that descends northwards to the Jhelum River. The Golf Hotel, one of the best situated in the area, is just beyond a nine-hole golf course (open early April until mid-October). In the high season it is reserved for members only. There are good walks across the golf course, with fine open views back up to Murree and the ridge with the main Galis, and across the Jhelum to Kashmir; on a clear day you can even see Nanga Parbat (see pages 387–8). Below the golf course there is a small flat area with swings and slides for children. From Bhurban you can continue down to Kohala and Muzaffarabad on a good paved road.

Upper and **Lower Topa** on the other, longer road from Murree to Kohala are set in mature pine forests and offer excellent walks through the woods and good places for camping. There is a rest house (bookable through the Forestry Department, Rawalpindi) and an old fire lookout tower at Monkey Hill, beyond Lower Topa. From Lower Topa a new road heads south through Karor to Islamabad, a drive of about two hours (see page 230).

Kohala, 93 kilometres (58 miles) from Islamabad via Murree, is a small village by the bridge across the Jhelum and one of the gateways to Azad Kashmir. From here you can either drive up the Jhelum River to Muzaffarabad, or turn right to join the Makh River at Arja and thence back across the Jhelum at Dhalkot bridge and via Lehtrar to Islamabad.

The Galis

North from Murree towards Abbottabad the road climbs through another string of popular hill stations known as the Galis (_gali_ means hilltop or pass in the local dialect). One of the advantages of the Galis is that they are within a two-hour drive of Islamabad. The road follows the ridge all the way through forests of giant pines. The further you get from Murree, the older and better-preserved the forests are, with much less terracing and cultivation. On really clear days there are magnificent views of the snow-covered Pir Panjal Range, in Indian-held Kashmir, and of Nanga Parbat, far to the northeast. Footpaths cut through the forest all along the ridge, and you can hire horses in every village.

Regular bus and minibus services connect Murree with Abbottabad and stop at the various Galis on the way. If you are driving yourself, follow the road from Sunny Bank, below Murree, to Barian and Nathiagali for about two kilometres (a mile) to the crossroads at **Kuldana**. Turn left again for Nathiagali, 34 kilometres (21 miles) away. The road is surfaced but narrow, with steep drops into the valley below. Most of the road runs at altitudes of 2,000 to 2,500 metres (7,000 to 8,000 feet) and is blocked by snow from December to the beginning of May.

At **Barian**, the first village after the turn-off at Murree, the Punjab ends and the North-West Frontier Province begins. A toll road continues through Sawar Gali to **Khaira Gali**, 11 kilometres (seven miles) from the turn-off at Murree. Turn right just past the signpost for Khaira Gali village, a typical small British cantonment once used for training as well as relaxation. Very few of the houses in Khaira Gali are inhabited now, but the flat parade-ground area near the old British graveyard makes a good picnic spot, with superb views over the Jhelum Valley and the Pir Panjal Range beyond.

At **Changla Gali**, the next village, about 16 kilometres (ten miles) from Murree, the road reaches its highest point, 2,560 metres (8,400 feet) above sea level; there are good picnic spots and fine walks through the pine forest.

A little further on is a prominent sign in English which reads 'Khanispur/Ayubia'. Turn right here for the **Ayubia National Park**, named after General Ayub Khan (head of the military government of Pakistan, 1958–69), where there is a chair-lift to the top of a ridge (closed at lunchtime). The ride is excellent for the views, but the top is rather marred by drink and souvenir stalls.

Dunga Gali, the next village on the main road, is just north of an intensively cultivated stretch of hillside, with terraces rippling down the hill. Behind the village is **Mukshpuri Peak**, 2,817 metres (9,243 feet) above sea level.

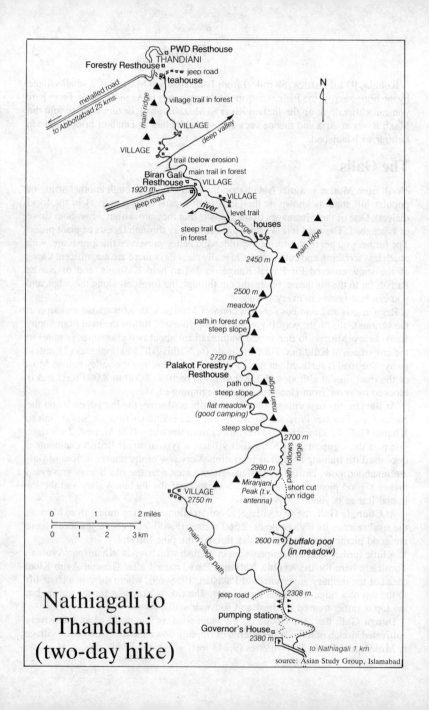

PWD Resthouse
THANDIANI
Forestry Resthouse
jeep road
teahouse
metalled road
to Abbottabad 25 kms.
village trail in forest
main ridge
VILLAGE
deep valley
VILLAGE
trail (below erosion)
main trail in forest
Biran Gali
Resthouse
VILLAGE
1920 m
VILLAGE
jeep road
river
gorge
level trail
houses
steep trail
in forest
2450 m
main ridge
2500 m
meadow
path in forest on
steep slope
2720 m
Palakot Forestry
Resthouse
path on
steep slope
main ridge
flat meadow
(good camping)
steep slope
2700 m
2980 m
path follows
ridge
Miranjani
Peak (t.v.
antenna)
short cut
on ridge
VILLAGE
2750 m
main village
path
2600 m
buffalo pool
(in meadow)
jeep road
2308 m.
pumping station
Governor's House
2380 m
to Nathiagali 1 km

N

0   2 miles

0   1   2   3 km

Nathiagali to
Thandiani
(two-day hike)

source: Asian Study Group, Islamabad

Nathiagali is another little England, with a small timbered church, bungalows, park and colonial governor's house. It is the most popular of the Galis and, for those who like walking, the best place to stay. There are numerous short walks and pony rides through the pine forests, and several recommended longer walks and treks. You can follow the water pipe from Pines Hotel for eight kilometres (five miles) through Dunga Gali to Ayubia, or climb **Miranjani**, at 2,981 metres (9,780 feet), the highest peak in the range. This takes about two and a half hours, starting from behind the governor's house on a path heading north. You can also take a two- to three-day hike from Nathiagali to Thandiani, passing through Palakot and Biran Gali.

Where to Stay

New Green's, tel. 544 (Rs250–500). Recently rebuilt, with fine views.
Pines, tel. 505 (Rs250–500). Small garden, good views.
Valley View, tel. 585 (Rs200–400). Slightly cheaper, good view to the south.
Mukshpuri, tel. 567 (Rs150–500).
New Nathiagali Trekking Club (Rs250).
Dunga Gali Hotel, in Dunga Gali, is another possibility. There are also about six small local hotels and some government rest houses, all very full in summer, and charging Rs20–50 a night.

It takes an hour to drive the 34 kilometres (21 miles) from Nathiagali to Abbottabad. The road drops steeply through terraced valleys with few trees to the Harro River, which passes through a steep-sided gorge. At 30 kilometres (19 miles) from Nathiagali is a turn to the right to Thandiani (see pages 376–7). A few kilometres before this the river runs through a thicket on the left of the road. A walk downstream passes a series of water-powered flour mills and some attractive rock pools.

The round trip from Islamabad to Murree, Nathiagali, Abbottabad and back to Islamabad via the Grand Trunk Road takes five to six hours without stops.

THE SALT RANGE

The Salt Range consists of two lines of low, rugged hills that run east to west between the Soan and the Jhelum rivers, from the Grand Trunk Road near Jhelum City to the Indus near Kalabagh. On the southern side, the hills form a cliff about 700 metres (2,300 feet) high, rising straight up from the plains of the Jhelum. On the northern side, they slope gradually down towards the Soan River and Islamabad. Between the two lines of hills, and protected by them, are a number of relatively prosperous villages containing forts and temples more than 1,000 years old. Many villages are built around a central pond shaded by banyan trees and groves of mango trees, indicating strong Hindu influence in the area before Partition.

The Salt Range is composed of the salt deposits left behind when the sea that extended over the Indus Plain and the Potwar Plateau evaporated 600 million years ago. This is the first natural barrier separating the subcontinent from Asia along the line of collision between the Indian and Asian geological plates. Rocks and fossils found in the Salt Range give a complete record of the earth's history. The layers of rock in the range have been tipped vertically and in some places are even inverted, so that the older, fossil-strewn layers now lie on the surface.

The Salt Range is first mentioned by the historians Arrian and Ptolemy. Alexander the Great passed through Nandana, the traditional pass through the range, on his way to do battle with Porus on the banks of the Jhelum River in 326 BC. In the third century BC the district formed part of the Buddhist empire of Ashoka.

Towards the end of the Buddhist period, in the sixth and seventh centuries AD, there was a kingdom in the Salt Range called Simhapura (or Singhapura), probably centred at Ketas. The Chinese pilgrim Xuan Zang, who visited in the winter of AD 630, described it unfavourably: 'The climate is cold, the people are fierce, and value highly the quality of courage; moreover they are much given to deceit.'

From the middle of the seventh century until the beginning of the tenth, the Salt Range was part of a powerful Kashmiri Hindu kingdom. Most of the forts and temples in the area date from this time. Later, the kingdom was absorbed by the Hindu Shahi Kingdom, which was attacked and destroyed by the first of the Muslim invaders from Afghanistan, Mahmud of Ghazni, in the early 11th century. The local Janjua tribe, the most important in the central parts of the Salt Range, was converted to Islam at this time.

The Janjuas were given a free hand in ruling the area under the Moghul emperors and were not overthrown until the arrival of the Sikhs under Ranjit Singh in the early 19th century. The Salt Range fell under British control after the Second Sikh War in 1849.

The Salt Range is visually extraordinary, with wild eroded gullies and gorges covered in scrub and olive trees. Streaked across the cliff faces is a kaleidoscope of colours. From the top of the cliffs on the southern side, you look out, like an eagle from its eyrie, across the Indus Plain.

Getting to the Salt Range

Buses from Pir Wadhai bus station in Rawalpindi for Khushab, Mianwali and Kalabagh all pass through the Salt Range, and there are services to Chakwal, Choa Saidan Shah and Talagang. The train runs from Rawalpindi to Chakwal and Bhaun; change at Mandra Junction. If you are driving from Islamabad, there are three roads from the Grand Trunk Road to Chakwal, the gateway to the eastern end of the Salt Range, one and a half to two hours away.

The first road leaves the Grand Trunk Road just after the village of Riwat, 28 kilometres (17 miles) from Zero Point in Islamabad; on many maps this road is not marked, and the turning off the Grand Trunk Road is not signposted. After six kilometres (four miles) take the right fork, continue for 60 kilometres (37 miles), then turn right for Chakwal.

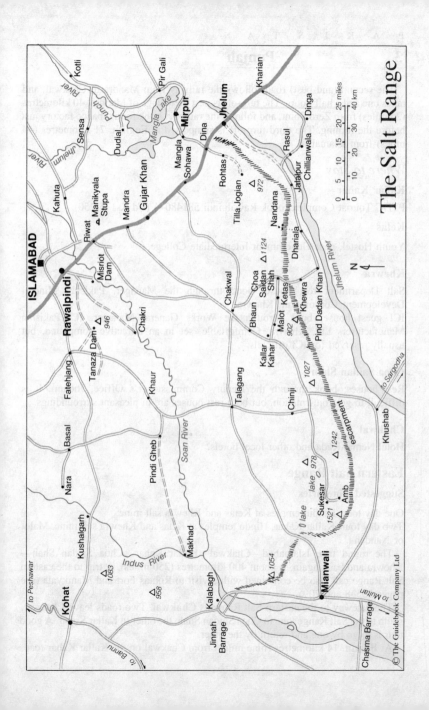

The Salt Range

The second (and best) road follows the railway from Mandra to Chakwal, and takes one and a half hours. The turn-off is past the village of Mandra, 40 kilometres (25 miles) from Zero Point, and follows the railway. Look for a tobacco factory just before the turning. The third turn-off is signposted in English, 71 kilometres (44 miles) from Islamabad.

Where to Stay

Kallar Kahar

PTDC Tourist Complex; book Rawalpindi 581480–4 (s/d Rs175/250).

Ketas

Youth Hostel, near Government Intermediate College.

Khewra

Salt Department rest house; book through the Manager, Pakistan Mineral Development Corporation, Khewra.
ICI guest house; book through the Works General Manager, ICI Pakistan Manufacturers Ltd, Khewra. Comfortable, set in an attractive compound, but usually reserved for ICI officials.

Choa Saidan Shah

Rest houses; book through the Deputy Commissioner's Office, Jhelum. It is difficult to get confirmation, but both rest houses are in pleasant surroundings.

Chakwal

Hotel Nemat Kada and other local hotels.

Eastern Salt Range

Suggested itineraries

One day tour: Hindu temples at Ketas and Khewra salt mine.
Two day tour: Kallar Kahar, Hindu temples at Ketas and Khewra salt mine. Malot or Nandana.

The round trip, Islamabad—Chakwal—Kallar Kahar—Choa Saidan Shah—Khewra and back again, is about 400 kilometres (250 miles). A trip to the eastern Salt Range can also be combined with a visit to Rohtas Fort and Manikyala (see pages 205–8 and 209).

The gateway to the eastern Salt Range is **Chakwal**. Two roads leave Chakwal, south to the Salt Range, one to Choa Saidan Shah, the other to Kallar Kahar. A good tour is to go by one and return by the other.

At **Bhaun**, 14 kilometres (nine miles) from Chakwal on the Kallar Kahar road, the Salt Range begins and the railway line ends. A deserted Hindu temple, used as a store, stands beside the village pond surrounded by banyan trees. The Hindu ashram, with carved wooden doors and graceful arches, is used as a cowshed.

For ten kilometres (six miles) the road twists across jagged hills separated by deep ravines and red cliffs. The country looks impassable, but the road finds a way across the upper ends of the gorges, and rises to the top of the first line of hills. From here you can see back north across the hills to the plains, and the Margalla Hills.

The road descends to **Kallar Kahar** and its salt water lake (*kahar* means lake) and fruit gardens, nestled against the steep hills to the south. The fairly new PTDC Tourist Complex, set along the lakeside, is very bare, and consists of a motel, restaurant and boats for hire.

Kallar Kahar so impressed the first Moghul emperor Babur when he crossed the Salt Range in 1519 that he ordered a garden to be laid out overlooking the lake. The southwest corner of the lake, with its fine trees and orchards, is probably the site of the Moghul garden. On the hillside above the trees is the **Shrine of Sheikh Abdul Qadir Jilani**, a 13th-century Muslim saint from Turkestan. The shrine has peacocks and offers a view down over the lake; the cave below the shrine is the place to which the holy man retired to fast and meditate.

Two roads leave Kallar Kahar, one east to Ketas and Choa Saidan Shah, the other south across the second ridge to Khushab (see page 252). The Choa Saidan Shah road skirts the edge of Kallar Kahar Lake and heads east. There are several places of interest along the way. About six kilometres (four miles) from Kallar Kahar a rough but jeepable track leads south to **Malot** about ten kilometres (six miles) away as the crow flies. Allow at least three hours to find and see the temple.

Turn right just before the Dokh Khushi Waterworks, onto a lorry track (for four-wheel drive vehicles only). The way is quite difficult to find and takes about an hour. From Chhoi village you can see the temple about three kilometres (two miles) away. Take the second track left, which winds steeply up and down. Tracks lead off to several coal mines, which consist of the simplest of galleries running into the hillsides; rickety branches are the only pit-props, and there is no sign of mechanization. Find your way to Malot village, which still retains its old defensive walls and gate. Park here, walk up through the village and climb the hill to the temple.

Malot Hindu Temple stands on a remarkable outcrop on the edge of the cliff—there are deep ravines on either side and a spectacular drop of 700 metres (2,300 feet) straight down to the Punjab plain on the third. Visible from several kilometres (miles) away, the temple is by far the best preserved and most impressively situated of the many Hindu temples in the Salt Range. It is in the Kashmiri Hindu style of the eighth to tenth centuries, and is probably older than others in the area. It is built of fine red sandstone, with three of its four sides identical, the fluted columns suggesting Grecian-via-Gandhara influence. Between these columns are blind trefoil arches with carved reliefs of the temple itself repeating the columns and the

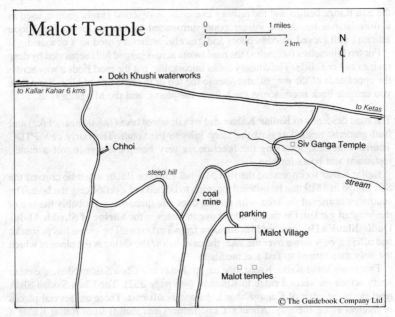

Malot Temple

0   1 miles

0   1   2 km

N

Dokh Khushi waterworks

to Kallar Kahar 6 kms

to Ketas

Chhoi

Siv Ganga Temple

steep hill

stream

coal
mine

parking

Malot Village

Malot temples

© The Guidebook Company Ltd

arches. The original stepped pyramidal roof was replaced with a lookout post by the Sikhs, but you cannot climb up it now.

You can return to the main road by another route, passing on your way another small Kashmiri-style temple of the same period at **Siv Ganga**, at the bottom of the valley east of Malot. It stands in a little oasis of greenery and running water. The temple is surrounded by trees and overhung by a giant banyan tree. It has been plastered over, but the stepped pyramidal roof, typical of the Kashmiri style, is still there, and, like the temple at Malot, it features crude representations of itself in relief on three sides.

Ketas, on the main road between Kallar Kahar and Choa Saidan Shah, was an important Hindu pilgrim centre before Partition. The deserted temples, shrines, fort, bathhouse and rest houses surround a pool sacred to the Hindu god Shiva, and it is to here that thousands of Hindus used to flock every April to bathe. Local tradition has it that when Shiva wept over his wife's death, the tears from one eye formed the pool at Ketas, those from the other a pool near Ajmer in Rajasthan. Ketas is derived from *Kataksha*, or Raining Eyes.

The oldest and highest of the temples probably date from the eighth to tenth centuries, but they have been plastered over and decorated with motifs of a much later period. Ketas has been a holy place for centuries, and it is quite likely that this was the site of the former Buddhist shrine in the Kingdom of Simhapura, described in the journals of the Chinese pilgrims Fa Hsien (AD 403) and Xuan Zang (AD 630). The Hindu temples may lie on top of the older Buddhist shrine.

You can climb up through the fort to the topmost temple and then up some exceedingly narrow stairs to the roof, where a few carvings and wall decorations remain. From here there is a good view of the whole complex.

The Youth Hostel is near the Government Intermediate College.

Choa Saidan Shah, an attractive town six kilometres (four miles) past Ketas, is named after the saint Saidan Shah Shirazi. Apparently, the area was desert until the holy man arrived; when he struck the ground with his staff, sweet water—from the Ganges River, no less—sprang up. The saint's shrine is still standing, and the annual urs is held in April. This is the best place to spend a night in one or another of the two rest houses, which stand in an orchard on the hillside to the west, off the Kallar Kahar Road and overlooking the valley (book through the office of the Jhelum district commissioner). The town is surrounded by trees and orchards and is famous for its roses and perfumes. Like the other towns in the area it was predominately Hindu before Partition.

Choa Saidan Shah is directly accessible from Chakwal if you do not wish to detour via Kallar Kahar and Ketas. Near Choa Saidan Shah on the road from Chakwal is the **Dhok Tahlian Dam** (signposted in English), a good picnic spot. Behind the dam is an attractive lake with a small rest house and two boats (the chowkidar keeps the oars and rowlocks). The fishing here is good.

In the valley to the southwest of Choa Saidan Shah on the road to Khewra is the archaeological site at **Murti**. This yielded a large number of the late-Buddhist and Jain carvings, now in Lahore Museum, and dates from the Simhapura Kingdom period.

Khewra is famous for its salt mine. The town is nine kilometres (six miles) south of Choa Saidan Shah, near the bottom of the Salt Range's southern cliff. The road down is spectacular. The sheer, 700-metre (2,300-foot) cliff runs the full length of the Salt Range and is streaked with vividly coloured rock.

Watli Head, at the top of the escarpment, is the main source of water for the ICI Soda Ash plant at the bottom. The 20-kilometre (12-mile) -long pipeline crosses and recrosses the Watli Gorge on 12 suspension bridges through a variety of rock strata heavily eroded by rains and landslides. A walk down the line in the company of a guide (from Watli Head) is well worth while.

The salt mine is open every day except Friday. If you are interested in going into the mine, write to the manager, Pakistan Mineral Development Corporation, Khewra, giving at least a week's notice. Children under 14 are sometimes (but not always) refused entry. It is a good idea to take a torch.

The salt mine is the largest in area in the world, with 140 kilometres (87 miles) of tunnels, and is the second biggest producer of rock salt. The seams extend the entire length of the Salt Range, of which only a minute proportion are currently mined. It is estimated that if mining is continued at the present rate there is enough salt to last another 350 years in the existing mine alone.

Visitors are taken straight into the heart of the mine in a small electric train. The guided tour includes old and new workings. The rock salt looks like glass and is various shades of red and pink. Inside the mine, a small mosque built of transparent salt bricks with lights concealed in its walls highlights the variety of colours. Salty stalactites hang down from the ceiling.

In the old part of the mine the salt was excavated in enormous sections that created large chambers up to 25 metres (80 feet) high. In the tallest chamber, excavated in Moghul times, the guide lights a flare to show the height. Other chambers have partly filled up with water and carry resounding echos.

The existence of a mountain of salt here was known to the ancient Greek historian Arrian and explains to some extent the historical importance of the area. There is a local tradition that the Janjua tribe began mining here in the 13th century. The Moghuls worked the mines from the 15th century. Under the British the mine, then known as the Mayo Mine, was rapidly developed.

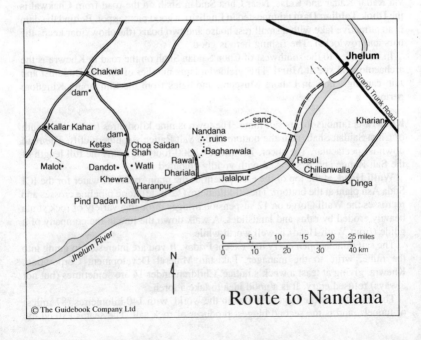

Route to Nandana

© The Guidebook Company Ltd

From Khewra the intrepid walker might like to make a daytrip to **Nandana**, the ancient fort on top of the escarpment to the east that guarded the traditional path to the Salt Range. To get there continue south from Khewra to **Pind Dadan Khan**, on the banks of the Jhelum (another predominantly Hindu town before Partition), where there are several deserted temples. Locally woven bedcovers are a good buy here. Just before the town a road leads east to Jalalpur and Jhelum. At **Dhariala**, 17 kilometres (11 miles) from P D Khan, a new road leads northwards to the cement factory of Gharibwal, at the foot of the Salt Range. At Rawal, just before Gharibwal, the road crosses an old railway line. **Rawal** is famous locally for its spring of sweet water which reputedly promotes fertility. Just after the railway line a jeep track runs northeast (right) along the foot of the Salt Range, stopping short of the village of Baghanwala at the entrance to Nandana Pass.

At **Baghanwala**, the remains of a Moghul gate, called the Shahi Darwaza (King's Gate), stand beside the river bed. Jahangir records in his memoirs that he frequently came here to hunt. Two families in Baghanwala maintain a long-standing feud, which has led to one murder in every generation and is attributed to a dancing girl from the royal court who tried to walk a tightrope slung across the gorge to the west of the fort. When she was in the middle the king cut the rope with his sword, and as she fell the girl laid a curse on all future generations.

An hour's walk from Baghanwala up a steep valley with fresh streams brings you to the foot of the fortress rock, which blocks the pass between huge, almost vertical, cliffs. A partly paved path from a group of water mills leads up to the top of the fortress rock. From the top there is an impressive view, but not much remains of the famous fort.

Nandana Fort was built to guard the original gateway to the Salt Range, the route taken by all the famous invaders of the subcontinent. According to the archaeologist Aurel Stein, Alexander the Great came this way from Taxila before descending to the Jhelum for his battle with Porus. The Hindu Shahi rulers fled here from their capital at Hund (see pages 314–15) after their defeat by Mahmud of Ghazni, and established a new capital at Nandana. It was not long, however, before Mahmud caught up with them and, after defeating the raja in a battle on the plateau to the north, stormed Nandana in 1014. The Hindu Shahis were finally overcome in 1026 and later converted to Islam.

Al-Biruni, the famous traveller, historian and scientist, who came to the subcontinent in the wake of Mahmud of Ghazni early in the 11th century, is said to have measured the circumference of the earth from Nandana—certainly, from the top of the cliff he would have been able to see the earth curving over the Punjabi plain.

In the 13th century, Nandana was held by Jalall-ud-din of Khwarizm. The Empire of Khwarizm, with its centre at Khiva (now in Soviet Central Asia), was shortlived, but at its height comprised most of central Asia and parts of the northwest subcontinent. Unfortunately, Jalall-ud-din fell foul of Ghengis Khan, the great Mongol conqueror, who hounded him as far as the Indus at Kalabagh. Jalaluddin is said to have impressed Ghengis Khan by jumping his horse down a cliff into the Indus after his defeat in battle. Nevertheless, a Mongol force crossed the Indus after him and captured and sacked Nandana before moving on to devastate other parts of the Punjab.

From Nandana you can trek west back to Choa Saidan Shah, passing **Makhiala** and **Kusuk**, two Janjua fortresses which were besieged and captured by the Sikhs under Ranjit Singh early in the 19th century.

Back on the main road at Dhariala you can continue east following the southern cliff of the Salt Range to the Grand Trunk Road. The scenery is dreary and flat beyond Jalalpur, but the route is of historical significance.

At **Jalalpur**, 35 kilometres (22 miles) east of Pind Dadan Khan, the lower outcrops of the Salt Range run down to the Jhelum River in a succession of steeply tilted ridges. Here Alexander crossed the Jhelum in 326 BC. After leaving the Salt Range at Nandana, Alexander moved his army of 50,000 men to the banks of the Jhelum at Haranpur, near Pind Dadan Khan, only to find the Indian ruler Porus waiting for him on the far side with a smaller force but hundreds of elephants, which the Macedonians greatly feared. Alexander, strategically brilliant as ever, moved his army secretly eastwards to where Jalalpur now stands, negotiated the swollen river and, the elephants notwithstanding, defeated Porus near the present-day village of Chillianwala. Porus, however, won Alexander's respect even in defeat and was left with his kingdom intact.

Arrian relates that it was at this battle that Alexander's famous horse Bucephalus was killed. Alexander founded two cities in the area after his victory and named one of them Bucephala in the horse's memory. He personally led the funeral procession, and the horse's remains were laid in a grave in the town. Neither town has been located, but the village of Mong, near Rasul, has some interesting unexcavated mounds under which they may be buried; certainly many coins of the Saka period (75 BC) were found here. In any event, the memory of Bucephalus lingers on, in legend and on ancient coins. In the 19th century, enthusiastic archaeologists were apt to claim that every stupa they discovered was the tomb of Bucephalus.

From Jalalpur the road continues to the **Rasul Barrage**. Fork right and cross the Jhelum on the barrage to Rasul. The flooded area above the barrage is a good place for bird-watching. From Rasul you reach the Grand Trunk Road via Chillianwala and Dinga. (The rough road along the north bank of the Jhelum River crosses sandy nullahs and the wide bed of the Bunhar River. This is just passable in dry weather, but in the wet even four-wheel drive vehicles get bogged down.)

At the village of **Chillianwala**, in 1848, the Sikhs and the British fought a bloody battle which nearly proved disastrous for the British. An entire cavalry regiment took flight. The casualties, including a huge number of camp followers, numbered over 2,000. A large stone cross and an obelisk mark the site of the mass grave of British officers.

Western Salt Range

You pass through the western Salt Range on the way from Islamabad to Mianwali, Kalabagh or Khushab, or you can make a round trip, Islamabad—Fatehjang—Talagang—crest of the escarpment—Kallar Kahar—Islamabad, which is about 400 kilometres (250 miles).

Leave Islamabad on the Grand Trunk Road to Peshawar, and turn left (southwest) after about 15 minutes at the first level crossing to Fatehjang, where you turn left (south) again at the big water tank and head for Khaur. After about ten kilometres (six miles), there is an isolated ridge on your left. You can make a detour on a paved road along the north side of this ridge to **Tanaza Dam** which holds back a small lake where you can fish from hired boats—or you can picnic on the terrace or climb to the top of the 946-metre (3,104-feet) -high ridge.

Khaur, near the Soan River, is the starting point for a detour into the hills along the river, a good area for fossil hunting. The movement of the Indian geological plate into the Asian plate has tipped over the surface of the earth and exposed strata that date back between five and ten million years. There are fossils and stone tools everywhere.

The road forks shortly after Khaur, left to Talagang, or right to **Pindi Gheb** for a full-day excursion to **Makhad** on the banks of the Indus just north of its confluence with the Soan, where the Indus is confined to a deep gorge. The little town of Makhad has steep streets with flights of steps and is the home of Pir Makhad. This was the last point reached by the British Indus flotilla of steamboats which once plied the river.

Talagang, about 40 kilometres (25 miles) south of Khaur across the eroded valley of the Soan River, is the turning point west for Mianwali and Kalabagh. For Khushab, continue south and cross the rolling hilltops of the northern ridge of the Salt Range before descending into the main Salt Range Valley of small terraced fields surrounded by dry stone walls. In March, there is a striking contrast between the green wheat, yellow mustard, red earth and piles of black coal outside the many small coal mines.

Just before the southern ridge of the range the road forks: left (east) to join the road from Kallar Kahar to Khushab, or right (west) for a detour following the Salt Range Valley to the village of **Sukesar**, about 50 kilometres (30 miles) away. Along this valley are saline lakes where the bird-watching is excellent; north of the road is an unusual hilltop resembling an upturned funnel. **Mount Sukesar**, at 1,522 metres (4,992 feet), is the range's highest peak. Unfortunately, there is a Pakistan air force base here, and the road round the mountain and down to Mianwali is closed to foreigners.

Amb, a ruined Hindu town with fortified walls and temples from the eighth to the tenth century, lies about eight kilometres (five miles) southwest of Sukesar. Tucked away in a valley at the furthest southwestern extremity of the Salt Range, Amb can be reached on a rough jeepable track.

The main road from Kallar Kahar to Khushab climbs to the top of the **southern escarpment** of the Salt Range, a cliff about 700 metres (2,000 feet) high and the most dramatic part of the range. Even if you do not wish to go down to Khushab, it is worth driving to the top of the escarpment for the view down the cliff to the cultivated plains below. This cliff runs all along the southern edge of the Salt Range. Three roads zigzag down it: one to Khushab, another further east to Khewra, and the third further west to Mianwali. The Hindu temples at Malot and Amb, and the old fort at Nandana are all perched on its edge, with superb views over the plains. (For Kallar Kahar back to Islamabad, see page 245.)

Talagang to Mianwali is a drive of about two hours, at first rather dreary, then sweeping south and crossing over the narrowest neck of the Salt Range before zigzagging down on an impressive road to the plains. Just before the crossing, to the left, is another of the range's shallow lakes famous for their bird life.

Mianwali

Mianwali can be reached by air from Lahore and Islamabad, or by train or bus from Rawalpindi, Lahore or Multan. This is a district headquarters on the Indus and is important for the irrigation works in the area. There are two big barrages on the Indus nearby, the **Jinnah Barrage** to the north and the **Chasma Barrage** just to the south. Large canals run south from the barrages to feed the Thal Desert, reclaiming considerable portions of it. There are a number of guest houses in Mianwali, bookable at the Deputy Commissioner's office there. Mianwali is a good place to break the nine-hour journey from Islamabad to Multan (see page 170).

Kalabagh

About 50 kilometres (30 miles) north of Mianwali, at the southern end of Attock Gorge on the Indus, is the interesting old town of **Kalabagh**. Here the Indus finally emerges from its 150-kilometre (90-mile) gorge and spreads over the plain. The town is stacked up the steep hillside on the west bank of the river, below eroded cliffs streaked with red, green and grey. If approaching from Mianwali you can cross the river either on Jinnah Barrage (built in 1947), or a few kilometres further upstream on the old road and rail bridge. The best view of Kalabagh is from the eastern end of this bridge.

Seeming almost to hang over the grey and green Indus, Kalabagh's red mud brick houses are plastered like swallows' nests against a series of terraces in the red cliffs . . . . In places the hills are almost solid salt, clear and hard and veined in red. Just downstream, where the Indus begins to widen, there is a sudden abundance of sweet water on the west bank and against the bald redness of the mountains and the barren yellow desert a fountain of green vegetation bursts out of the earth. Growing under and over and through each other, vegetables, fruit trees, roses and oleanders make a rich and brilliant jungle.

Jean Fairley, *The Lion River* (1975)

This green abundance on the west bank south of the town is the estate of the nawab of Kalabagh, who controlled the wild and barren areas of the Salt Range in the vicinity. The nawab's house and guest house and the Highway Inspection bungalow front straight onto the river, shaded by huge banyan and chinar trees, and offer a view of water, mountains, bridge and barrage.

The main street of Kalabagh bazaar is lined with carved wooden doors and overhanging balconies. Narrow alleyways step up the mountain, which is so steep that the houses looking out across the bazaar to the river seem to have been built on top of one another.

Prior to the construction of dams and barrages on the Indus, a British flotilla of steamboats plied the Indus as far as Kalabagh, almost 1,600 kilometres (1,000 miles) from the sea, and up beyond it in the gorges between here and Attock.

A little further up the Indus Gorge from Kalabagh is the place where, in the early 13th century, Jalaluddin of Khwarizm escaped from Ghengis Khan and the Mongols by leaping down the cliffs on his horse and swimming across the river. Ghengis Khan was suitably impressed, although this did not prevent him from sending his horsemen across the river in pursuit and ravaging the northern Punjab (see page 245). The government plans to build the Kalabagh Dam in this gorge.

There are two roads from Kalabagh into the North-West Frontier Province, one north to Kohat, and the other southwest to Lakki. There is also a daily train service from Marhi, on the east bank of the Indus opposite Kalabagh, to Bannu in NWFP.

ISLAMABAD TO PESHAWAR

Along the Grand Trunk Road from Islamabad to Peshawar are some of Pakistan's most important historical sites. Trade routes from east, west, north and south meet here, and all the famous invaders of the subcontinent have passed this way. All stages of Pakistan's history are represented here, from the great civilizations of the three cities of Taxila to the modern Tarbela Dam.

Getting There

Buses ply continuously between Rawalpindi and Peshawar, and you can get off anywhere along the way. The railway line also follows the Grand Trunk Road. If you are driving yourself, head west from Zero Point in Islamabad to join the Grand Trunk Road 14 kilometres (nine miles) away, then turn right on the dual-carriageway towards Peshawar.

Margalla Pass

The Margalla Pass, 28 kilometres (17 miles) from Islamabad, is the first point of interest. The pass's historical importance is out of all proportion to its size, for it is little more than a gentle climb to a cutting through a low line of hills. The dual-

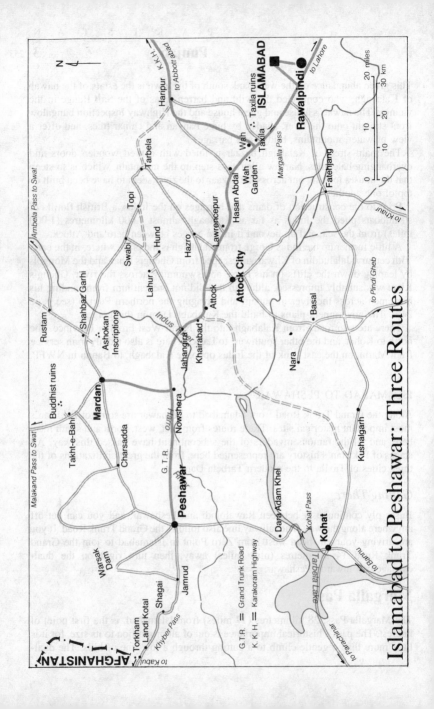

Islamabad to Peshawar: Three Routes

G.T.R. = Grand Trunk Road K.K.H. = Karakoram Highway

carriageway has sliced such a wide path through the hills that you get little impression of a pass at all, and even in the old days it could never have presented a serious obstacle to invaders. Yet Sir Olaf Caroe, distinguished historian of the North-West Frontier, describes it as the real boundary between the subcontinent and central Asia. The Margalla Pass was the ancient route from the west and northwest through the hills.

The old **Shahi (Imperial) Road** lies just to the left of the modern highway. A short section of the cobbled, 16th-century road built by Sher Shah Suri leads up to the original pass, a few hundred metres (yards) to the left of the present cutting.

The first Moghul emperor, Babur, used the Margalla Pass on his invasions of the subcontinent; in his memoirs he called it the Sangjaki Pass, after the nearby village. The Moghuls later used the pass on their way to their beloved Kashmir every spring, when the shorter routes through the Pir Panjal Mountains were blocked by snow. Jahangir wrote in his memoirs that the name Margalla meant 'a place to plunder caravans'.

A tall **granite obelisk** erected in 1868 'by friends, British and Native' to commemorate General John Nicholson stands at the old pass on the left. You can walk up the old Shahi Road to reach it and climb up inside. Nicholson was one of the great folk heroes of Victorian Britain, which saw him as the archetypal Christian soldier, upright and righteous. He was even venerated by the Indians for his strength, bravery and decisiveness; after he died he was known as Nikal Seyn or Nikalsingh and attracted something of a religious following.

Nicholson was an Irishman who came to the subcontinent in 1839, aged 16, as a cadet with the Bengal infantry. As a young political officer he was posted to Rawalpindi in 1846 after the First Sikh War. Henry Lawrence, British resident in the Sikh capital of Lahore at this time, sent out a number of officers, who came to be known as his 'young men' and included Nicholson, Jacobs, Edwardes and Abbott, to 'advise' the Sikhs in the Punjab and the North-West Frontier Province.

When the Second Sikh War broke out in 1848, these officers found themselves isolated in Sikh territory. Most of them not only avoided capture but organized revolts against the Sikhs by exploiting the hostility of the local Muslim tribes. Nicholson duped the Sikh garrison at Attock into surrendering for a short time, and with a small number of Pathan tribesmen harassed the Sikh general Chattar Singh on his way from the north to reinforce the Sikhs in the Punjab. At the Margalla Pass Nicholson tried to capture the old tower guarding the pass, which stood where the obelisk stands today. He did not succeed, but he won the Sikhs' respect for his tenacity and bravery.

Nicholson's subsequent career was no less illustrious, culminating in a magnificent dash to relieve the siege of Delhi during the First War of Independence (or Indian Mutiny) in 1857. (The phrase 'in the Nick of time' comes from this, according to some sources!) He was mortally wounded in the assault on Kashmir Gate, but was the hero of the siege. He was only 34 when he died.

Just beyond the pass on the left is a row of doors in the hillside. These lead to the cave dwellings used by seasonal migrant workers, who are friendly and happy to receive female visitors.

Taxila

The turn-off to the Taxila ruins is unmarked, one kilometre (half a mile) beyond the Margalla Pass on the right and two kilometres (a mile) before the modern town of Taxila. If you are arriving by bus, get off at Taxila town and take a Suzuki or tonga to the Taxila museum. It is three kilometres (two miles) from the turn-off on the Grand Trunk Road to Taxila Museum, the PTDC Information Office, the cafeteria and the guest house. Taxila is also a railway junction on the line from Rawalpindi to Peshawar or to Havelian.

From Taxila you can continue west towards Peshawar, or north to Haripur, Abbottabad and the Karakoram Highway (see page 366). Alternatively, you can hike from Jaulian Monastery across the hills, via Tarmakki and Garm Thon, to Islamabad, which takes about five hours, or north along an irrigation channel to Khanpur, across the Harro River.

Where to Stay

Two Archaeological Department rest houses, one near the museum and the other to the left of the road just before the turning to Jaulian; book through the director general of archaeology, government of Pakistan, Karachi, or the curator of the Taxila Museum.

Youth Hostel near the museum.

Railway Retiring Rooms.

Historical Background

Taxila is one of the subcontinent's archaeological treasures, and was once an important city of the Kingdom of Gandhara. Sir John Marshall began excavating in the area in 1913. His *Guide to Taxila* (1960) is excellent, but rather too technical and detailed for the general tourist. What follows here is a selective description.

The history of Taxila spans about 1,000 years (516 BC to *c*. AD 600). It is simplest, perhaps, to think of the city's development as being influenced, firstly, by the history of the Iranian plateau and, secondly, by a succession of invaders from central Asia. However, though Taxila may rightly be considered a cultural melting pot, the city was only occasionally, and then only for short periods, the capital of the various empires that succeeded one another in the area.

When the Gandharan Kingdom was absorbed by the Achaemenid Empire in 516 BC, Taxila became the capital of this eastern Persian province. The first city of Taxila dates from this period, and is today referred to as Bhir Mound—its original name was Taksashila, which was subsequently altered by Greek historians to Taxila.

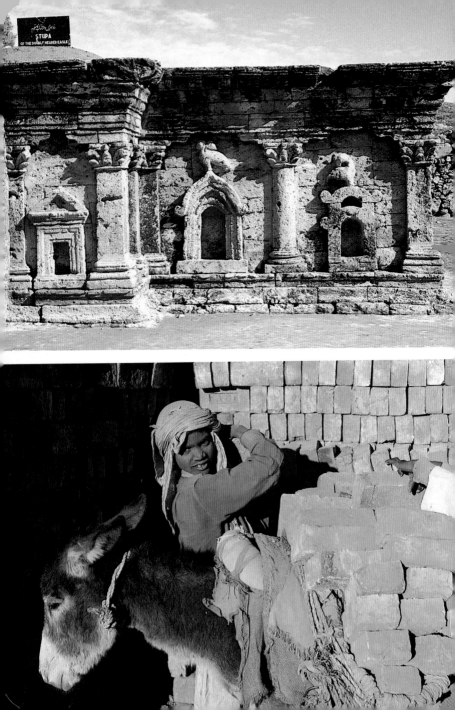

By the late fifth century BC, Taxila had become the site of the best-known university in the subcontinent, which offered courses in mathematics, law, history, medicine, social sciences, the arts, astronomy and military tactics. According to Marshall, the level of knowledge was remarkably high, especially in the fields of mathematics, medicine and astronomy.

It was here in the fourth century that the great Sanskrit scholar Panini compiled his Sanskrit grammar. The Kharoshthi alphabet, derived from the Persian Aramaic alphabet, was also developed here at about this time and subsequently became the national script of Gandhara.

In 326 BC Alexander the Great arrived at Taxila from Pushkalavati and Swat (see page 306). According to Arrian's second-century AD text, *Anabasis*, on his arrival Alexander held philosophical discussions with the resident intellectuals, who were naked ascetics, with the help of three interpreters; he then dined in the great hall. Alexander allied himself with the local ruler against Porus, the more powerful ruler of the Punjab to the southeast and left a garrison at Taxila before setting off across the Salt Range.

Taxila expanded under the Mauryan emperors, who ruled from Pataliputra (now Patna) on the Ganges. The third and most important Mauryan emperor, Ashoka, was his father's viceroy at Taxila. After his succession in 272 BC, Ashoka became a Buddhist and spent the rest of his reign promoting Buddhism and non-violence (see pages 310–11).

Buddha had died some 200 years earlier, in about 483 BC. He was cremated, and his ashes were divided and buried under stupas in eight holy places in the Ganges Plain. Ashoka disinterred them and redistributed them to the principal cities of his empire. Dharmarajika Stupa, at Taxila, was probably built by Ashoka to enclose some of Buddha's ashes. From Taxila Buddhism spread to central Asia and, via Swat, to Tibet and China.

In about 185 BC, the Bactrian Greek rulers of northern Afghanistan and central Asia expanded to the southeast and took possession of Gandhara. They built new Greek cities at Taxila and Pushkalavati, laid out in regular blocks with the streets crossing at right angles. This second city is now called Sirkap; in Punjabi folklore the brothers Sirkap and Sirsukh were evil giants, and the ruins of Taxila's second and third cities have been named—comparatively recently—after them.

The Bactrian Greeks were overwhelmed by other central Asian invaders, the Parthians and the Sakas (related Scythian tribes). The former founded a powerful empire in Persia, while the latter swept into the subcontinent and conquered Gandhara in about 75 BC. The Sakas adopted the existing culture at Taxila and tolerated the various religions practised there—Buddhism, Jainism, Brahmanism, and Zoroastrianism. The Parthians finally overcame the Sakas in AD 20 and absorbed Gandhara into their empire. Gondophares, one of the most famous Parthian kings, is believed to have received St Thomas the Apostle, who brought Christianity to India some time after AD 30.

The Kushans arrived from Afghanistan in about AD 60 and ousted the Parthians.

At first they made their capital at Pushkalavati, moving it to Peshawar in the second century, and built a new city there and at Taxila (Sirsukh).

In Kushan times the majority of the population was Buddhist, and all over the Kingdom of Gandhara thousands of monasteries and stupas were built, mostly in secluded side valleys, or on top of low hills, within easy walking distance of a town where the monks went to beg for their food. (On almost every hilltop around Taxila are the remains of these monasteries and stupas, more than 50 of them within a ten-kilometre, or six-mile, radius.) By this time stupas were being built to symbolize the Buddha, and usually contained some relic in a gold casket. This was the great period of Gandharan Buddhist art; stone and plaster statues of Buddha and scenes from his life decorated every stupa and monastery. Most of the Buddhist sculpture in Taxila museum is Kushan.

Disaster struck Taxila in about 455, when it was attacked by the White Huns who burned the city and monasteries. The city never really recovered. Most of the descriptions of what remained of Taxila can be found in the accounts of three Chinese Buddhist pilgrims, Fa Hsien, Sun Yung and Xuan Zang, who passed through in 403, 520 and 630 respectively, on their tours of famous Buddhist sites. All lamented Taxila's fate.

There were later kingdoms that arose in the area of Kabul and Gandhara after the White Huns mysteriously disappeared from history, possibly being absorbed by the Hindu Rajput or warrior caste. The Kabuli Shahi and the Hindu Shahi kingdoms claimed descent from the Kushans. The Hindu Shahis finally fell in about the year 1000 to the first great Muslim conqueror, Mahmud of Ghazni. One of the most common coins found at Taxila or in the bazaars today is the Hindu Shahi silver coin, with a horseman armed with a lance on one side and Shiva's bull on the other.

You will be offered coins and sculptures as you tour Taxila. Without exception they are fakes.

Taxila Museum

Taxila Museum is open daily, 9 am–4 pm in winter, 8.30 am–12.30 pm and 2.30–5 pm in summer. It houses one of the best collections of Gandharan Buddhist art in Pakistan, an interesting coin collection, a display of artefacts detailing the daily life of the inhabitants of ancient Taxila—utensils, weights, jewellery and toys. The Gandharan stone statues give some idea of what people wore at different times. There is also a useful contour map of the whole Taxila Valley showing the layout of the cities and the other archaeological sites.

Just outside the back door of the museum is a stone wall showing the different methods of building used at different periods at Taxila. Archaeologists have estimated the date of construction by examining the size and shape of the stones used and the different types of jointing. Many of the walls at Taxila are only 50 centimetres (20 inches) high. The upper parts of the walls were generally made of rubble coated with mud and have long since disintegrated. The museum also contains a stone umbrella similar to those that once topped all the Buddhist stupas in Taxila, which helps to give you some idea of what stupas here once looked like.

Touring the Excavations

Those unused to looking at archaeological sites will be disappointed by their first glimpse of Taxila. Initially it seems that there is nothing here but heaps of stones and the odd wall dotted about the valley. It is difficult at first to imagine the cities and Buddhist monasteries in their former glory. Start your tour at the museum.

There are more than 50 archaeological sites in Taxila Valley. They cannot all be visited in one day, and most of them will be of little interest to the general tourist. The first-time visitor should see: Jaulian, a Buddhist monastery (see pages 270–2); Sirkap, Taxila's second city (see pages 264–7); and Dharmarajika, one of the largest Buddhist stupas in Pakistan (see next page).

If you have only time for one site, Jaulian is recommended, but it involves a short walk up a steep hill. If you have three hours, Dharmarajika, Sirkap and Jaulian are recommended in that order.

The more dedicated will want to go to Taxila time and time again. The sites are either poorly labelled or completely unlabelled. Here follows a fairly detailed

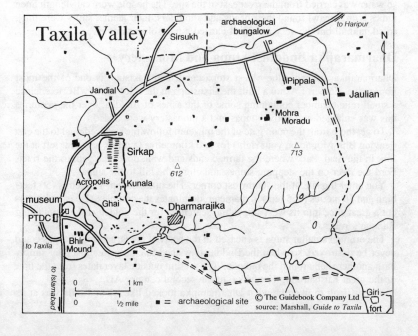

description of all the major sites in chronological order, following Marshall's account.

Bhir Mound

Bhir Mound was Taxila's first city (the sixth to the second century BC). The museum is built on top of its northwest corner. Only a small portion of the centre of the city has been excavated, nothing is labelled and there is very little for the general tourist to see. Bhir Mound lies to the right of the main road as you drive up to the museum, about 200 metres (yards) across the field from the gate to the museum.

According to Marshall, ancient Bhir Mound looked similar to a present-day Pakistani village or the bazaar area of a small town. From the remaining foundations you can trace the layout of the wide main street that twisted round flat-roofed houses made of rough stone and plastered over with mud. The narrow side streets ran between high, windowless walls. The doors of the houses led out onto the street, but all the windows faced inwards to the central courtyard. In each courtyard Marshall found a soakpit, into which the household would have tipped its sewage and slops. The drains in the streets were for rainwater only. At intervals through the city you can see open spaces that were once public squares, each containing a public refuse bin. There were no wells in the city, as the water table was 30 metres (100 feet) down, so water was carried from the river east of the site. The people wore calf-length linen tunics with a shawl round their heads and shoulders; their leather shoes were thick soled, and all but the very humblest carried a parasol in summer.

Dharmarajika Buddhist Stupa and Monastery

Dharmarajika, probably the oldest stupa erected in Pakistan, is one of the most impressive. Emperor Ashoka built the first stupa in the third century BC to enclose a small relic chamber containing some of the ashes of Buddha; over the centuries this was enlarged and votive stupas and a monastery were added.

To get there from the main gate of the museum follow the surfaced road to the east (leaving Bhir Mound on your right) for two kilometres (a mile), and bear left at the fork in the road. Park where the tarmac ends and walk down the path to the river. Ford the river on the stepping stones and climb the hill to the stupa.

You enter the site at the southwest corner. The **main stupa**, 15 metres (50 feet) high and 50 metres (165 feet) in diameter, dominates the complex. Treasure hunters cut a great slice into its west side while searching for the golden casket containing Buddha's relics.

The original smaller stupa is encased in the heart of the larger one. Stupas could never be destroyed, so when the Buddhists wished to enlarge a stupa they simply built another shell around the old one. The present outside layer dates from the time of the great Kushan king Kanishka, in the second century AD.

It is difficult to imagine what Dharmarajika looked like when Taxila was at its

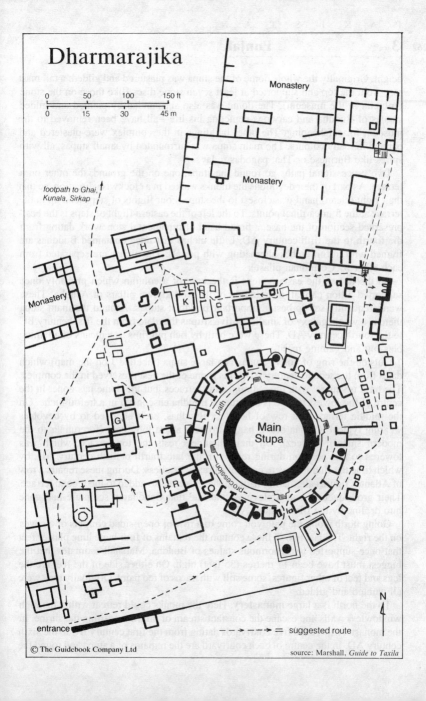

Dharmarajika

0 50 100 150 ft
0 15 30 45 m

Monastery

Monastery

footpath to Ghai,
Kunala, Sirkap

Monastery

H

K

G

R

I

Main
Stupa

path

procession

J

entrance

- - - - ▶ = suggested route

N

© The Guidebook Company Ltd

source: Marshall, *Guide to Taxila*

height. Originally the whole dome of the stupa was plastered and gilded; a tall mast rose from the top and supported at least seven stone discs (like those on the stone umbrella in the museum). The dome was also surrounded by painted and gilded statues of Buddha and carvings depicting his life—all have been removed to the museum for safekeeping. The other buildings in the complex were plastered and painted in many colours. The main stupa was surrounded by small stupas, all with spires like Burmese or Thai pagodas today.

Two processional paths go round the stupa, one on the ground, the other on a terrace. As part of their devotions the monks walked in a clockwise direction, so that their right (clean) hand was closest to the stupa. Four flights of steps lead up to the terrace at the four cardinal points. To the left of the eastern flight of steps is the best-preserved section of the base, a broad band of ornamental stonework dating from the fourth to the fifth century AD. Little niches that once contained Buddhas are framed with trefoil arches alternating with portals. The niches are separated from each other by Corinthian pilasters.

On the left of the eastern steps is the base of a column which probably once supported a lion capital, in imitation of the well-known pillars of Ashoka. These were frequently set up beside important Buddhist stupas. Around the main stupa there is a whole galaxy of smaller **votive stupas** that date from the first century BC to the fourth century AD. These were built by rich pilgrims as a means of attaining blessing and gaining merit.

Outside the ring of votive stupas is a large stupa (labelled J on the map) which dates from the second century AD. This is one of the best preserved in the complex. The base is square, with three diminishing terraces, but the dome has gone. In the centre of the lowest terrace is a statue of Buddha ensconced in a trefoil niche. On the middle terrace is a row of headless Buddhas, each attended to by devotees wearing typical Kushan dress: baggy trousers and a long coat (forerunner to the modern shalwar-kameez). On their shoulders rests the top terrace, which was lowered to this position during repairs in the late fourth or fifth century AD, by which time the Buddhas were probably already headless. During these repairs a row of Atlantes figures alternating with elephants were also added to the second terrace. Their grotesqueness and lifelessness indicate that Gandharan sculpture had gone into decline by the fifth century AD.

Going north along the path you come to a row of open-sided **chapels** or alcoves on the right. The last two of these contain the remains of four huge lime plaster feet that once supported two enormous statues of Buddha. Marshall estimates that the biggest must have been 11 metres (35 feet) high. On either side of the feet are the legs and feet of other figures, some still with traces of red paint. Originally they were all painted and gilded.

To the north is a large **monastery**. Here the monks could retreat within the high windowless walls and escape the constant stream of pilgrims visiting the shrine. In the monastery there are five courtyards dating from the first century BC to the sixth century AD. In the centre of each courtyard are the remains of a stupa and round the edge are the monks' cells, all opening onto the court. The largest court, furthest away to the north, dates from the second to the third century AD; it was two storeys high, and accommodated 104 monks. The bath was in the southwestern corner. The hall of assembly stood in the centre of the monastery. Outside the north wall was a sturdy watchtower.

In the mid-third century AD the Sassanian invaders destroyed all this, and the monastery was rebuilt to a smaller, more easily defended plan. This, in turn, was burned by the White Huns in about AD 455. Six decapitated skeletons, charred and crushed, were found in the small court on the right (east). The monastery was rebuilt roughly and cheaply, and was finally abandoned in about the seventh century.

Retrace your steps to the colossal feet, then take the path to the right (west). It enters a narrow passage between two votive stupas; on the left one sit two headless Buddhas of the fourth to fifth century AD. Their hands rest in their laps in an attitude of meditation.

In the open space ahead is a tank from the first century BC, lined with the original lime plaster. This was the monks' bathing pool. Steps lead down from the north. A votive stupa was built over the top of the steps in the second century AD. West of the tank is a votive stupa (labelled K), on the north face of which a statue of Buddha sits in a niche. The cornice and other details show Greek influence.

To the north of this is a large building (labelled H) that Marshall thinks probably once housed a statue of the reclining, dying Buddha. It was built in the first century BC and strengthened and enlarged after a severe earthquake in about AD 30, when the processional path was added.

Heading south from the building of the dying Buddha, you pass two small water tanks and a washerman's stones, and come to a group of stupas of different ages and styles. In one of these (labelled G) a silver vase containing a silver scroll and small gold casket holding tiny fragments of bone were found. The scroll, written in Kharoshthi, the Gandharan script, and dated about AD 78, claims that these are the relics of the Lord Buddha enshrined by Urasaka to bring health to the Kushan king, to his family, friends, relations and to himself. 'May this right munificent gift lead to Nirvana.'

To the south of these stupas, and nearer the main stupa is another stupa (labelled R), on the back wall of which are some reliefs in stucco plaster dating from the second century AD. The scene on the north side depicts Buddha's horse Kathaka taking leave of his master; the one on the south side portrays the 'Departure of Buddha' (Prince Siddhartha setting off on his search for enlightenment). These are the earliest Gandharan stucco reliefs yet found; earlier statues were made of stone.

To the west of the site is the apsidal—or round-ended—temple (labelled I) built in the first century AD, where the faithful used to gather to pray. It may have had a barrel-vaulted roof, similar in shape to the chaitya halls (caves) excavated in the hillside at Ajanta and Ellora in India, except that here the apse is octagonal. Inside the apse are the foundations of an octagonal stupa. West of the apsidal temple, and next to the exit, is a row of four monks' cells which predate the monastery.

Sirkap City

From Dharmarajika a footpath leads across the hill to Ghai Monastery, then Kunala Stupa, and finally Sirkap, the second city of Taxila, half an hour's walk away. The chowkidar (watchman) at Dharmarajika will provide a guide if necessary. It is easier and more interesting to follow the ridge of the hill all the way from Dharmarajika to Kunala than to walk in the valley and then climb the steep hill at the end. The view from Ghai Monastery down over Kunala to Sirkap is magnificent. If you do not wish to walk, or have no one to bring the car round, you will have to drive round by road (about 15 minutes) back past the museum, to the north gate of Sirkap.

Sirkap, dated from 185 BC to AD 80, is one of the excavations at Taxila recommended for the general tourist. To get there from the museum drive north through a small village famous for its stone cutters who specialize in mortars and replicas of Gandharan sculpture. Cross a narrow bridge and turn right. The car park is outside the main entrance, the city's north gate.

The city wall ran five kilometres (three miles) round the roughly rectangular city, enclosing some rugged hills in the southeast, the isolated hill of the acropolis in the southwest and the large flat area of the city proper. The wall was about six metres (20 feet) thick and six to nine metres (20 to 30 feet) high, with tall square bastions spaced along it.

A large excavated hole beside the city wall, about 50 metres (yards) to the right of the north gate, inside the city, shows the different eras of construction; the neatly made Greek wall, second century BC, at the bottom; the Saka wall, first century BC, in the middle; and the Parthian wall, first century AD, at the top. At the bottom of the hole is the original Greek drain.

The city had no wells. Water was carried from the river, which flows outside the wall on the west side.

The wide main street, 700 metres (nearly half a mile) long, begins a little to the right of the north gate, which prevented invaders from charging straight in. When you look down the main street you can see low walls on either side. These are the exposed foundations of the Parthian city, which was built on top of the older cities of the Bactrian Greeks and the Sakas after the earthquake of AD 30.

Down either side of the main street were rows of small shops with wooden platforms in front, shaded with colourful awnings. Behind the shops were the two-storey private houses, plastered and painted in different colours. You can still trace the layout of the houses, which had doors in the side streets; apparently there were no exterior windows. Each house had up to 20 small rooms on each storey, arranged around a small courtyard. Inside, the rooms were plastered and painted; some had wooden panelling and wooden balconies. The flat mud-covered roof was held up on wooden beams.

The sewage ran down the streets in open drains. In almost every block there was a Jain or Buddhist stupa (you can still see the bottom tiers) with its gilded dome and crowning spire of umbrellas rising above the surrounding walls.

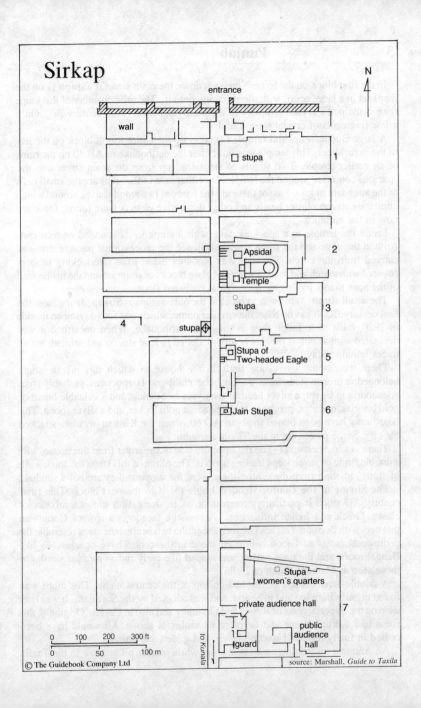

Sirkap

N

entrance

wall

□ stupa   1

□ stupa

□ Apsidal   2

□ Temple

○ stupa

4   □ □ stupa   3

□ Stupa of   5
Two-headed Eagle

□ Jain Stupa   6

□ Stupa   women's quarters

private audience hall   7

□ guard   public
audience
hall

0   100   200   300 ft
0   50   100 m
© The Guidebook Company Ltd

to Kunala

source: Marshall, *Guide to Taxila*

In the first block on the left as you walk down the main street is a **stupa** (1 on the map) set in a large court, with rooms facing onto it. The relic chamber of this stupa once contained a crystal reliquary of the Mauryan period (third century BC). Only a few fragments of crystal were found.

A large Buddhist **apsidal temple** (2) takes up the entire fourth block on the left of the main street. This temple was built after the earthquake of AD 30 on the ruins of an earlier temple. Two flights of steps lead up from the main street into the spacious courtyard around the temple. On either side of the steps are the small cells of the attendant monks. East of these are the bases of two small stupas, around which numerous stucco plaster heads and other decorative objects were found; these are now in the museum.

Inside the temple is a spacious nave with a stupa in its rounded eastern end. Around the nave and the stupa you can still see the processional passage that was entered from the porch. The roof was probably made from interlocking timbers covered with thatch and mud. The line of plain blocks of stone around the inside wall of the apse marks the line of the original timbered floor.

The **small stupa** (3) in the next block is the oldest stupa at Sirkap, dating from the first century BC. It has no base; the circular dome, which was found lying on its side in 1920, must have fallen over in the great earthquake. When unearthed it was decorated with acanthus flowers boldly modelled in lime stucco and painted, but no traces remain today.

There were some interesting finds in the house to which this private stupa belonged: a bronze statuette of the Egyptian child-god Harpocrates, probably from Alexandria in Egypt; a silver head of Dionysus or Silenus; and a valuable hoard of gold bangles, earrings, pendants, rings, beads, a gold locket, and a silver spoon. This hoard may have been buried in about AD 60, when the Kushan invaders attacked the city. Some pieces are in the Taxila museum.

There is another **stupa** (4) on the opposite side of the street from this house, with a double flight of seven steps leading up to it. The plinth of this stupa has thick walls of stone radiating from the centre; these were for support: they are not a sundial.

The **Shrine of the Double-Headed Eagle** (5) is in the next block. This first-century AD stupa is particulary interesting, as its decoration shows a mixture of classic Greek and Indian influences. Across the façade is a row of Corinthian pilasters with decorated niches between them: the two nearest the steps resemble the pedimental fronts of Greek buildings; those in the centre have ogee arches like Bengal roofs; and the ones outside are shaped like early Indian *toranas* similar to those seen at Mathura, south of Delhi.

A double-headed eagle is perched on top of the central niche. This motif was found in early Babylon and in Sparta, and was adopted by the Scythians. It was later used on the imperial arms of Russia and Germany and also in Ceylon. Originally this stupa had a drum, dome and tiered stone umbrella above. All would have been coated in finely moulded stucco plaster, and gilded and painted.

An Aramaic inscription on an octagonal white marble pillar (now in the Taxila museum) was found near this shrine. It relates that the pillar was put up in about 275 BC, when Crown Prince Ashoka was governor at Taxila. As this coincides with Taxila's first city, Bhir Mound, the pillar must have been moved 200 years later.

There is a small **Jain stupa** (6) in the next block. Its rectangular base has five decorative pilasters on each side. The drum, dome and umbrella have all disappeared, but the remains of two Persepolitan columns with crowning lions were found in the courtyard. Parts of these columns are standing on the four corners of the plinth.

The houses of rich citizens and officials and the **royal palace** (7) are further south on the left of the main street. The palace, much of which is hidden in long grass, is very similar in design to the Assyrian palace of Sargon in Mesopotamia. Assyrian influence was very marked throughout Persia, Bactria, and neighbouring countries. The palace is much larger than private houses in Sirkap, but otherwise is no different in design. There is nothing especïally grand or sumptuous about it. According to the Greek biographer Philostratus, who visited Taxila in AD 44, 'The men's chambers and the porticoes and the whole of the vestibule were very chaste in style' (*The Life of Apolonius of Tyana*). Marshall deduced that the rooms, set around little courtyards, were lined with wooden panelling or were plastered and painted.

The foundations indicate that there were only three narrow entrances into the palace: one off the main street leading to the Hall of Private Audience; and two off the southern side street, the first leading to the Court of the Guard and the second to the Hall of Public Audience. The women's quarters to the north had no outside entrance; the women had their private Jain stupa, so they need never leave the palace.

Most of the interesting small treasures found at Sirkap are now in the Taxila Museum. These include some high-quality gold and silver jewellery, household vessels and utensils, tools, stone weights, a few surgical and other instruments, toys, dice, weapons and armour, horse trappings and elephant goads, amulets, seals, pottery moulds, textile stamps and coins. The more expensive items, such as gold combs and hairpins belonging to the wealthy ruling class—the Parthian invaders, indicate western influence, while the cheaper wares of baked clay, iron and stone belonging to the indigenous poorer people are probably of local origin.

Kunala Buddhist Stupa and Monastery

Kunala Stupa is on the hill inside Sirkap City; its high walls are still standing. There are steps up on the left (east) following the old city wall. If you have walked over the hill from Dharmarajika you will walk down this way.

From the tops of the steps there is an excellent bird's-eye view of the entire city, which covered a large area, though only a small section has been excavated. Facing you are the remnants of the city wall, not to be confused with the spoil heaps thrown up by the excavators.

Kunala, the son of Emperor Ashoka, lived in the third century BC. Apparently he had such beautiful eyes that his stepmother fell in love with him. When he ignored her advances she persuaded Ashoka to send him away as viceroy to Taxila. She then sent a dispatch, which she sealed with Ashoka's seal, bringing accusations against Kunala and ordering his eyes to be put out. The ministers of Taxila were loathe to carry out the order, for Kunala was a popular prince, but the prince himself insisted that his father be obeyed and was duly blinded. Needless to say, when Ashoka became wise to this he put his wife to death.

Kunala Stupa supposedly stands on the spot where Kunala was blinded. Built into the side of the main stupa, but now exposed by the excavators, is a smaller votive stupa, which dates from the first century BC. The large surrounding stupa dates from the third or fourth century AD.

Kunala became a well-known place of pilgrimage for the blind, and today Taxila has the best eye hospital in the country.

Kunala Monastery, also of the third or fourth century, is of the usual design with an open courtyard surrounded by monks' cells. In each cell you can see a little arched niche where the monk put his lamp and books. The assembly hall is to the south of the courtyard.

Ghai Buddhist Monastery

To the south of Kunala is another higher hill, still inside the city wall of Sirkap. On top of this is the smaller Ghai Monastery, also third or fourth century. The high walls still stand, and the monastery is unusual because the monks' cells surround a square hall with sloping windows instead of an open court.

Jandial Temple

The Greek temple of Jandial is 700 metres (yards) directly north of the north gate of Sirkap. Built in the mid-second century BC by the Bactrian Greeks, it is a typical Greek temple and the only one in the subcontinent. It was abandoned and probably robbed of its statues of Greek gods when the Sakas invaded in about 75 BC, and was finally ruined by the great earthquake of AD 30.

The temple has a front porch, which is supported on four sandstone Ionic columns and leads into an antechamber. (Sandstone blocks were probably imported to Taxila, the local stone being friable granite.) A heavy wooden and iron door divided the antechamber from the sanctuary. Within, statues of various Greek gods stood on the platform at the back, but no remains were found. Behind the sanctuary is an unusual solid mass of masonry. Normally this space was reserved for another chapel, but at Jandial there was probably a solid tower here: the foundations are deep enough to support a tower 13 metres (43 feet) high. The two flights of steps leading up it from the back probably continued round the outside of the square tower to the roof. The function of this tower is controversial: it might have been used for fire worship, or sun or moon worship. To one side of the tower was a back porch.

Around the outside of the temple is a peristyle or wide verandah. In a typical Greek temple this would be a colonnade with a row of columns supporting the outer edge of the roof. Because there is no stone suitable for columns near Taxila, the roof at Jandial was supported by a wall pierced by 20 large windows. The roof was made of timbers coated with mud.

Sirsukh City

Sirsukh, the last of Taxila's three cities (AD 80–460), was the regional capital of the Kushans. Very little has been excavated, and there is not much to see. Left of the main road, not far east of Jandial, a signpost in English reads 'Sirsukh remains'.

Sirsukh was a rectangular city laid out on flat ground and surrounded by five kilometres (three miles) of wall. Only a small section of the southeast corner of the outer city wall has been excavated. It is about six metres (20 feet) thick and neatly faced in limestone. Semicircular bastions stand at 30-metre (100-foot) intervals along the wall. From inside the city, narrow passages lead through the wall into bastions, which originally were several storeys high and had slits for shooting arrows from on every floor. Along the base of the wall on the outside is a curved stone support to strengthen the wall and make it more difficult to undermine.

The Kushans built a new city at Taxila for three reasons: a terrible plague wiped

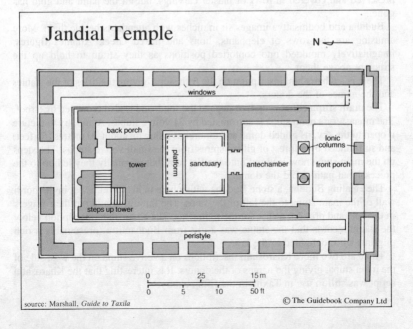

Jandial Temple

windows

back porch

Ionic
columns

platform

tower   sanctuary   antechamber   front porch

steps up tower

peristle

0   25   15 m
0   5   10   50 ft

source: Marshall, _Guide to Taxila_   © The Guidebook Company Ltd out half the population of Sirkap soon after they arrived; they were not accustomed to the Greek city plan and found the hills inside the city walls difficult to defend; and it was accepted tradition, and a matter of prestige, that as conquerors they should establish a new city.

Jaulian Buddhist Stupa and Monastery

The stupa and monastery at Jaulian are the best-preserved buildings at Taxila, and the only ones in Pakistan that give you some idea of what the original decoration round a stupa was like. A roof protects the plaster statues round the stupa, and the site is guarded day and night.

To get there continue east on the main road; a signpost on the right points to Jaulian, 1.3 kilometres (0.8 miles) from the turn-off. A path from the car park crosses the aqueduct and climbs the steep hill to the monastery. From the top of the hill there is a sweeping view over the valley of Taxila.

You enter the complex at the northwest corner into the **lower stupa court**, which has alcoves or chapels round the sides that once contained statues of Buddha. The south side of the court is wired off and roofed over to protect the bases of five votive stupas, which were built as offerings by pilgrims early in the fifth century AD. Try to imagine it without the roof, each domed stupa surmounted by a spire, and all painted and gilded. The remaining bottom levels of the five stupas are well preserved and covered in rows of plaster carvings, but all the paint and gold has gone.

Buddha and bodhisattva images sit in niches with attendants beside them. More amusing are the rows of elephants, lions and naked Greek Atlantes figures, imaginatively moulded into contorted positions as they strain to hold up the structure above them.

There is a Kharoshthi inscription on the fifth stupa, giving the titles of the statues and the names of the donors.

The **main stupa court** is up five steps to the south and is also protected by a roof. The monastery's main stupa is surrounded by 21 votive stupas. Again, try to picture it open to the sky, its gilded dome and umbrellas rising up about 20 metres (65 feet) and surrounded by a forest of gilded spires from the small votive stupas. The steps up the main stupa now lead out onto the flat roof, but originally they led up to the processional path round the dome.

The Healing Buddha, a stone Buddha with a hole in his navel, is set in the north wall of the main stupa to the left of the steps. The faithful would put their fingers in the hole and pray for a cure for their ailments. The Kharoshthi inscription below the statue records that the statue was a gift from Budhamitra (presumably a rich pilgrim) who 'delighted in the law'.

There are two more Kharoshthi inscriptions on a votive stupa on the west side of the main stupa, giving the names of the donors. It is interesting that the Kharoshthi script was still in use in Taxila in the fifth century.

Jaulian: Stupa and Monastery

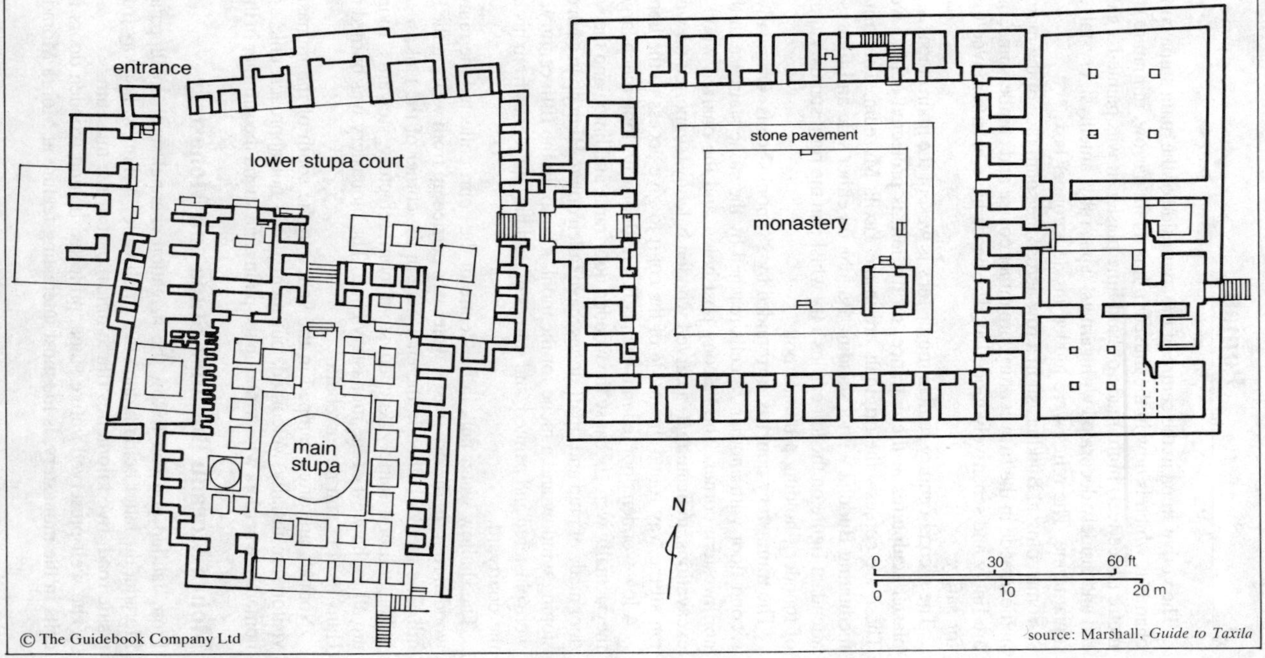

entrance

lower stupa court

main stupa

stone pavement

monastery

N

0   30
0   10

60 ft
20 m

source: Marshall, *Guide to Taxila*

© The Guidebook Company Ltd

The votive stupa in the centre of the south side of the main stupa contained a relic chamber, which is now in the museum. It is a tall, narrow, miniature stupa over one metre (three feet) high; made of hard lime plaster, it was painted a gaudy blue and red and crudely decorated with garnets, lapis, ruby, amethyst, crystal, carnelian and aquamarine. The relics were hidden inside a copper box.

Some colossal Buddhas sit in a row across the south face of the main stupa. Their bodies, made in the fifth century, are rather coarse and cumbersome, but their heads are finely and sensitively modelled. The heads have been removed to the museum for safety.

The second-century Jaulian **monastery** is west of the main stupa. A group of five plaster sculptures at the entrance, on the left, is protected behind wooden doors. These are copies—the originals are in the Taxila Museum. The group shows the meditating Buddha with a standing Buddha on either side and figures behind. The attendant figure on the left carries a fly whisk; on the right stands Vajrapani (the god of thunder), holding a thunderbolt.

The **monastery court** is surrounded by 28 monks' cells. Originally there was a second floor with another 28 cells reached by the stone staircase in the cell in the northwestern corner. The balcony post holes, and the charred wood found in the excavations, indicate that a carved wooden balcony, supported on wooden pillars, ran all the way round the inside of the court to give access to the upper cells.

A low wooden door led into each cell. The doorways look much larger today than they actually were, because the wooden doorframe and lintel, and the wall above the door made of mud and small stones, have fallen down. High up in each cell is a small sloping window and a niche for the monk's lamp. In the fifth century, all the walls were plastered and painted, and statues of Buddha and scenes from his life decorated the courtyard.

The shallow water tank in the centre of the court collected the rainwater off the wooden roof. In the dry season water was carried up from wells at the bottom of the hill. The monks bathed in the enclosure in the corner of the tank.

The hall of assembly, kitchen, store room, refectory, stewards' room and latrine are all to the west of the monastery court. The monastery was burned by the White Huns in 455 and never rebuilt.

Nomads are often camped in the valley to the south of the monastery. Female visitors are usually welcomed, but men should not approach unless invited. The nomads are herders who winter in the plains and spend the summer in the mountains.

Mohra Moradu Buddhist Stupa and Monastery

From Jaulian you can follow the irrigation channel south to Pippala and Mohra Moradu, the latter being hidden in a small valley a short walk away from the end of a side road, five kilometres (three miles) east of the museum.

The well-preserved votive stupa, protected behind wooden doors in one of the cells in the monastery, is the most interesting feature at Mohra Moradu. The stupa is complete in every detail; only the paintwork and gilding have gone. The base is divided into five tiers; the lower tiers are decorated with elephants and Atlantes, the upper ones with Buddhas. The dome and umbrellas are all in place. The stupa was erected in memory of a holy monk who once occupied this cell. There is an exact replica of the stupa in the museum.

The stucco plaster sculptures of Buddha around the base of the main stupa are also worth seeing. These are delicately modelled, dignified and lifelike, and are fairly well preserved. The beautiful heads have been removed to the museum for safety.

Pippala Buddhist Stupa and Monastery

Pippala, halfway between Mohra Moradu and Jaulian, was originally built in the first century AD. A second, larger monastery was built on top of the ruined remains of the first in the fifth century.

Pippala is interesting because some of the rubble-and-mud walls built on top of the 50-centimetre (20-inch) stone base are still standing in the monastery court and between the kitchen and dining room. In one of the cells is a fine plaster stupa, nearly as well preserved as that at Mohra Moradu.

Giri Fort and Monastery

Giri Fort is south of Jaulian, at the end of the jeep track that can be reached from the museum. It was built in the fifth century as a stronghold for the thousands of monks in Taxila Valley. The White Huns had already begun to overrun the northwest of the subcontinent, and the monks may have hoped to avoid the full force of the invasion by retreating outside the main city. About 500 metres (yards) of the fort wall still stand. Part of the monastery is also in good condition.

Wah Moghul Garden

The Grand Trunk Road from the Margalla Pass skirts round the modern town of Taxila and bypasses the industrial town of Wah Cantonment. Between Taxila and Wah there is a turn right to Abbottabad, the fastest of the three routes to Abbottabad and the Karakoram Highway (see page 371).

The **Moghul Garden at Wah** is a pale reflection of the Shalimar Gardens at Lahore or the Moghul Garden in Srinagar. If you are travelling by bus it is not worth a stop, but if you are driving it makes a peaceful picnic spot on the way to Peshawar.

To get there turn left off the Grand Trunk Road about 15 kilometres (ten miles) beyond the Margalla Pass. The turning is just before a new bridge across a small stream and is signposted in English. The garden is about one kilometre (half a mile) from the main road on the right; the track continues to the small village of old Wah.

The garden was laid out by the Moghul emperor Akbar in the late 16th century. He is thought to have stopped and admired the river and surrounding greenery and exclaimed, 'Wah!' ('Beautiful!'); *wah* also means stream in the local dialect. The garden was a favourite resort of Akbar and Jahangir on their journeys up to Kashmir.

The gardens have seen better days, but you can still get an idea of the original layout from the reedy remains of a large pool, the ruins of two pavilions and a bathhouse, with its exposed hot-water plumbing. An avenue of cypress trees lines a dry stream bed where there once may have been fountains, and there are some superb plane trees where parakeets gather. A clear irrigation channel runs along the side.

In old Wah, at the end of the road, there stands a building which resembles a Romanesque church from a distance but which is, in fact, a private 19th-century house. It belongs to the Hayat family, as does the Wah Garden, which the British gave to the family in return for services rendered during the 1857 war. It was Hayat who carried the mortally wounded Nicholson (see page 255) back to camp after the assault on the Kashmir Gate in Delhi.

Hasan Abdal

The little town of Hasan Abdal, on the Grand Trunk Road 48 kilometres (30 miles) from Islamabad, has been considered holy by several religious groups, largely because of its springs. The seventh-century Chinese Buddhist pilgrim Xuan Zang recorded in his journal that the place was sacred to the Buddhists, and that there was a water tank dedicated to the Hindu serpent king Elapatra. There are a number of deserted Hindu temples in the town as well as several Muslim shrines and tombs, various Moghul monuments and the famous Sikh Gurduwara (Temple) of Panja Sahib.

It is not clear who Hasan Abdal himself was, or which of the many tombs in the town is his. In the 15th century, the town was associated with Guru Nanak, founder of the Sikh religion, and with a contemporary Muslim saint, Baba Wali of Kandahar, whose shrine is on top of the hill overlooking the town. In the 17th century the Moghul emperors stopped here annually on their way to Kashmir. In the second half of the 18th century the Sikhs captured Hasan Abdal from the Afghans and later continued west, crossed the Indus and took Peshawar.

The early 19th-century **Gurduwara of Panja Sahib** became a famous Sikh pilgrimage centre, and Sikh pilgrims from India still come here every April for the Baisakhi Festival. The temple, on the right of the Grand Trunk Road in the centre of town, is typical of the rather florid Sikh style, with gilded domes and cupolas, and stands in the middle of a large stone water tank full of fish. The legend attached to the temple is that Guru Nanak asked Baba Wali for a drink of water. The holy Muslim replied by hurling a large rock down at him from his shrine at the top of the hill. Guru Nanak placed his hand on the rock and water sprang up from the place where it had landed. This rock, with its huge 'handprint', has been built into the side of the water tank above the place where the water bubbles up, and opposite steps leading down to the water.

On some days you are allowed into the temple without a permit; on others the custodian will not let you in without permission from the assistant director, Evacuee Trust Properties, Hasan Abdal, tel. Hasan Abdal 57.

Another water tank, with a Moghul tomb next to it, is up a path opposite the Panja Sahib Temple. Hundreds of huge mahseer fish (a kind of carp) swim around in the tank, which may well be the same one described by Jahangir in his memoirs. The emperor amused himself by catching fish, placing pearls in their mouths and throwing them back in. According to Jahangir, the tomb beside the tank belongs to one of the courtiers of his father Akbar.

A paved path leads from the tank and tomb through some gardens to another walled garden with round-domed corner towers. In the centre of the garden stands a simple Muslim tomb.

The climb up the hill to the **Shrine of Baba Wali** takes about two hours up and back. The top of the hill is fairly flat, with trees around the shrine, large table-like rocks and good views.

The turning north to Abbottabad is at the western end of Hasan Abdal, opposite the Cadet College, a well-known private school. West of Hasan Abdal the Grand Trunk Road crosses the Harro River, a tributary of the Indus. The landscape is deeply eroded, partly by nature, partly because clay has been dug for the brick factories.

Lawrencepur, the next town along the Grand Trunk Road, is named for Sir Henry Lawrence, first British resident in Lahore. There is a huge textile mill here which you can visit.

Tarbela Dam

The turning right to Tarbela Dam is 65 kilometres (40 miles) from Islamabad and is clearly marked in English. The dam itself is about 45 kilometres (30 miles) away on the Indus River. You can cross the dam and continue to Peshawar on the other side—a worthwhile detour of about two hours.

About 15 kilometres (ten miles) before the dam, a scenic road leads right (east) along Tarbela Lake to **Srikot** in the Gandghar Hills and, after 29 kilometres (18 miles), comes out on the main Hasan Abdal–Haripur road near Haripur. This makes a good round trip from Islamabad.

For a guided tour of the world's largest earth-filled dam, contact the Public Relations Office of WAPDA (Water and Power Development Authority) at Tarbela, tel. 68941–2, 67050 or 67057.

Eight years after the Indus Waters Treaty of 1960 (see page 110) the World Bank and the Indus Basin Development Fund decided to build a major dam on the Indus at Tarbela, where the Indus emerges from the hills onto the Peshawar Plain. Funds were donated by foreign governments and administered by the World Bank. The contract for building the dam, at an estimated then-record cost of US$623 million, was awarded to a consortium of 13 European companies led by the Italian firm Impreglio.

Statistics and technical data give some indication of its size. It is more than three times larger than the Nile's Aswan Dam. Its length across the top is 2,743 metres (1.7 miles), its width at its base about 600 metres (2,000 feet), and its height 143 metres (470 feet). The 30-kilometre (19-mile) -long lake can hold nearly 14 million cubic metres (18 million cubic yards) of water, and the two giant spillways (the world's largest) take an overflow of 42,000 cubic metres (55,000 cubic yards) a second. When completed it will have an electric generating capacity of 3,478 megawatts; at present it can generate 1,750 megawatts. At full production three tunnels will feed 14 generator units, but only eight generators are currently in operation. There are two further tunnels at either end of the dam to carry water for irrigation.

The best time to visit the dam is mid-July to mid-September, when the main spillway carries the overflow from the melting snow and monsoon rains. When the lake is full, seven enormous sluice gates are opened and a huge volume of water shoots down the 116-metre (380-foot) spillway. At the bottom the water is flipped up in the air to slow it down, and then crashes down into a deep plunge pool. It is the most spectacular fountain in the world, and quite terrifying.

The road runs across the top of the spillway gates to the east end of the dam, then forks. The left branch leads up to a small guest house on top of the hill from where you have an excellent view of the dam, spillways and lake. Below the guest house is a large concrete model of the dam and surrounding hills, and a monument to those who died building the dam.

The road across the top of the dam is often closed. A second road leads down to the bottom of the dam and crosses to the west bank, going past the four main tunnels. Water for irrigation spurts out of the one nearest the bank.

Day trippers from Islamabad have a choice of **three round trips**. They can return via Srikot and Haripur (see above); or along the east bank of the Indus through **Hazro**, 113 kilometres (70 miles) to Islamabad; or along the west bank of the Indus to Attock and the Grand Trunk Road, about 165 kilometres (103 miles) and three hours nonstop to Islamabad.

Those travelling from Islamabad to Peshawar via Tarbela can go along the west bank to Jahangira, near Attock, and continue on the Grand Trunk Road, but it is pleasanter, though longer, to go via **Swabi**, Mardan and Charsadda (see pages 304–13 and map on page 254).

Topi village, eight kilometres (five miles) from the western end of the dam, was the scene of a skirmish between James Abbot and his Pathan allies and the Sikhs. Just past the village there is a right turn (signposted in Urdu) for Swabi, 15 kilometres (nine miles) away, from where you continue west to Mardan. A rough road leads straight on to Attock and comes out on the Swabi–Attock road ten kilometres (six miles) from Swabi.

Attock to Peshawar

The Grand Trunk Road crosses the Indus River at Attock, about halfway between Islamabad and Peshawar. It was a small place of no importance until the 1540s when Sher Shah Suri chose it as the crossing place for his new Shahi Road from Delhi to Kabul.

The most impressive sight at Attock is **Sher Shah Suri's Caravanserai**. It is immediately above the road, just before the new bridge; steps lead up from the road. A 16th-century hotel, the caravanserai consists of four rows of small rooms set around a huge courtyard. From the walls of the caravanserai there is an excellent view of the river, the new bridge and Attock Fort. The small town of Attock, with its Moghul tombs and ruined Hindu temples, is now bypassed by the new road to the new bridge.

Attock Fort was built between 1581 and 1586 by the Moghul emperor Akbar, when he made Attock his base for military campaigns against Kabul. The fort is used by the Pakistan army and is not open to the public. The road up to the front gate is closed to foreigners, but you can get an excellent view of it from the new bridge across the Indus. It stands on a hill at the mouth of Attock Gorge, surrounded by two and a half kilometres (1.5 miles) of high crenellated walls in perfect condition. From the west end of the new bridge you can make a detour left, downstream along the old road, for a fine view back across the river to the fort. The fort slopes down the hill so you can see inside it from across the river. It must have been very exposed to artillery fire from the hill opposite on the west bank.

Akbar established a colony of boatmen whose descendants still live in the little village beside the river below the fort. The boatmen came from further south and were very adept at crossing the river on inflated skin rafts. In the dry season the river was crossed by a bridge of boats anchored on either side to piers which are still there, a little downriver of the fort (see also page 140).

The two-storey road and rail bridge a few kilometres (miles) downriver from the fort was built by the British in 1883. You can reach it from the west bank, but it is now closed to traffic.

The road down the west side of the Indus from Attock to Khushalgarh (see map on page 254) is very rough and suitable for four-wheel-drive vehicles only.

The Indus is the boundary between the Punjab and the North-West Frontier Province. Looking right from the new bridge you can see the confluence of the muddy Kabul River and the clear Indus, the latter having deposited its silt behind Tarbela Dam. The viewpoint on the right, beside a large rock, overlooks the confluence and an island with a rest house midstream.

Jahangira, the next town, is built beside the last bridge across the Kabul River. This is the route to Swabi and to Swat via the Ambela Pass (see pages 327–8 and map on page 254).

Nowshera, 20 kilometres (12 miles) further up the Kabul River on the Grand Trunk Road to Peshawar, is an important military town. Its large cantonment was built by the British to house troops during campaigns on the North-West Frontier. The barracks are on either side of the Grand Trunk Road, and on the left are a variety of tanks and guns used in the 1965 and 1971 wars with India.

The road north to Mardan and Swat crosses a new toll bridge over the Kabul River at the west end of town. It is signposted in Urdu only. From Nowshera to Peshawar stretches 43 kilometres (27 miles) of heavily populated countryside with many factories, and two large Afghan refugee camps. There are still about three million refugees in Pakistan, about a quarter of the original population of Afghanistan. They are placed in some 350 camps, mostly in the North West Frontier Province.

North-West Frontier Province

The North-West Frontier Province, or NWFP, runs for over 1,100 kilometres (680 miles) along the border with Afghanistan. Peshawar is the capital, and the heart of the province is the fertile Vale of Peshawar, which is watered by the Kabul and Swat rivers. This was the centre of the ancient Kingdom of Gandhara and is rich in archaeological remains. The northern half of the province consists of five river valleys (the Kaghan, Indus, Swat, Dir and Chitral), all running north to south. As they are on the northern edge of the monsoon belt, the valleys are fairly green and partly wooded in their southern sections. Northern Chitral and the upper regions of the Indus Valley are mountain deserts and depend on irrigation for cultivation. The area south of Peshawar is also outside the monsoon belt and consists of low rocky mountains and wide gravelly plains. Green oases surround every source of water. Most of the water courses in this area are seasonal; they run from west to east, down to the Indus River, and are dry much of the year.

Today the Khyber Pass is perhaps the province's best-known feature, but it was little used in prehistoric times, and even centuries later was considered too narrow and easily ambushed a route. It was not until the first century AD, when the powerful Kushans invaded Gandhara and pacified the area, that the Khyber, the most direct route from Kabul to Peshawar, became popular as a trade route. (For the full history of Gandhara see page 306.)

In the 11th century, the local population was converted to Islam by Mahmud of Ghazni. The lowlands were subsequently ruled from Delhi by the Moghuls until 1707, by the Durranis of Afghanistan until 1818 and by the Sikhs of Lahore until the British took over in 1849.

The people of the NWFP are mostly Pathans (or Pushtuns or Pukhtuns, as they prefer to be called), as is the majority of the population in northern Baluchistan and eastern Afghanistan. The warlike Pathans form one of the world's largest tribal societies (about 15 million) and are divided into numerous sub-tribes and clans. The Pathans living in the plains paid taxes to the various rulers of the area, but those in the rugged hills that start about 80 kilometres (50 miles) to the west of the Indus River (now known as the Tribal Areas) have never been subdued. The Pathan hill tribes all have a passion for freedom and independence and defend their territory and honour against all invaders. They are fearless guerilla fighters who know the hills and valleys intimately, are crack shots and wear clothes that blend with their surroundings (*kakhi* is a local word meaning 'dusty', and it was as a result of the wars in this region that the British army abandoned its bright red uniforms for the inconspicuous, dust-coloured khaki). No one has ever managed to subdue or unite them: the Moghuls, Afghans, Sikhs, British and Russians have all suffered defeat at their hands.

The British administered the North-West Frontier from the Punjab until 1901, when it became a province governed from Peshawar. The Tribal Areas were left as

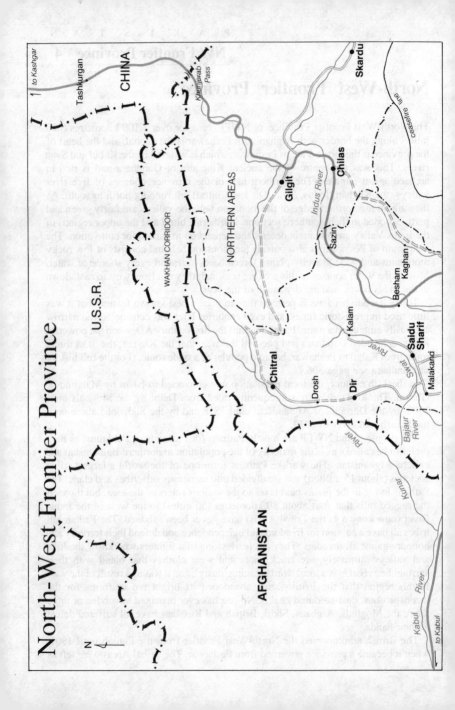

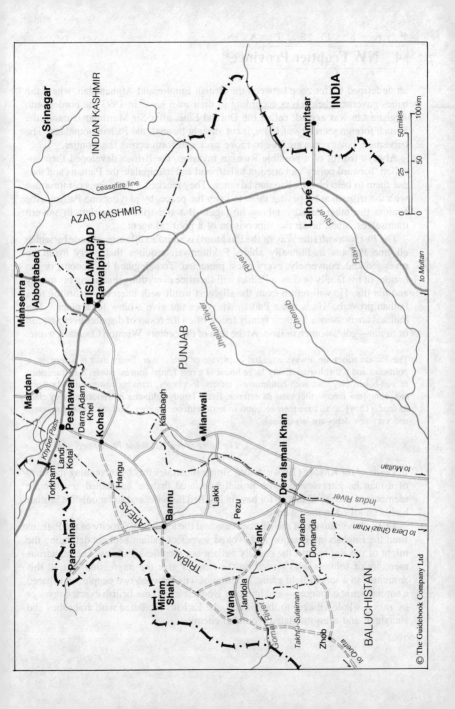

an undefined buffer zone between the British Empire and Afghanistan, where the tribes governed themselves according to their own laws. In 1893 the border with Afghanistan was agreed; called the Durand Line, after Sir Mortimer Durand, the British foreign secretary of India, it cut straight through the Pathan homeland. The tribesmen, however, were free to move back and forth across the frontier.

Always fearful of a possible Russian invasion, the British developed their so-called 'forward policy', an attempt to befriend and manipulate the Pathans and thus use them to help block a Russian advance. They reached a precarious compromise with the tribesmen by paying them to keep the peace, by playing one Pathan tribe against the other and by taking hostages. But the tribes were left to govern themselves, albeit under the supervision of a political agent.

The *Pukhtunwali* (the Way of the Pukhtuns) is an inflexible ethical code by which all true Pathans traditionally abide. Pukhtunwali requires that every insult be revenged and, conversely, every guest protected. To safeguard his honour, or the honour of his family or clan, a Pathan will sacrifice everything, including his money and his life. He will return even the slightest insult with interest. According to a Pathan proverb, 'He is not a Pathan who does not give a blow for a pinch.' The Pathans are notorious for their family feuds, often the result of disputes over *zar, zan* or *zamin*—gold, women or land. At the turn of the century Winston Churchill wrote:

The Pathan tribes are always engaged in private or public war. Every man is a warrior, a politician and a theologian. Every large house is a real feudal fortress made, it is true, only of sun-baked clay, but with battlements, turrets, loopholes, flanking towers, drawbridges, etc., complete. Every village has its defence. Every family cultivates its vendetta; every clan, its feud. [They] . . . all have their accounts to settle with one another. Nothing is ever forgotten, and very few debts are left unpaid.

The Story of the Malakand Field Force (1898)

In *Lords of the Khyber* (1984), André Singer illustrates this by recounting the story of a man he interviewed 'who proudly declared that he had killed seven male members of a Mahsud family for having insulted his wife, and so far only his brother had been killed in the revenge.'

Tales of the dangers of the Khyber Pass and the legendary ferocity of the Pathans fired the English imagination and evoked scenes of gallant soldiers defending the might of the Raj against the equally gallant but merciless Pathans. The numerous memoirs of soldiers who served on the frontier give the impression that all this amounted to a sort of field game, a pitting of wits between two people who shared a similar sense of honour—and humour. Nonetheless, if the British exacted revenge by razing whole villages to the ground, the Pathans retaliated with ambushes and slaughter, and even mutilated wounded enemies.

When you're wounded and left on Afghanistan's plains,
An' the women come out to cut up what remains,
Jest roll to your rifle an' blow out your brains,
An' go to your Gawd like a soldier.

Rudyard Kipling, *Barrack-room Ballads* (1892)

Skirmishes between the British and the Pathans continued unabated for 98 years (1849–1947), and were largely responsible for finally convincing the British of the wisdom of splitting India into separate Hindu and Muslim states. But Partition and the departure of the British did not in fact bring an end to the battles in the NWFP. The Pathans immediately began campaigning for an independent nation of Pukhtunistan and, backed by Afghanistan, frequently clashed with the Pakistani Frontier Force throughout the 1950s and '60s. In 1973, encouraged by Bangladesh's successful bid for independence two years earlier, a band of armed Pathans marched to Rawalpindi to confront Prime Minister Bhutto. The uprising was quickly crushed, but raids, looting, kidnapping and sabotage increased in the NWFP.

In an all-out effort to calm the Pathans, the government has conducted an intensive programme of agricultural development, initiating massive irrigation schemes and settlement projects. The tribespeople are supplied with fertilizers and superior seeds at subsidized prices, and roads and market outlets have been improved.

The Pakistani government adopted the British policy of leaving the Tribal Areas to govern themselves according to their own laws but under the supervision of a political agent, who mediates between the tribal elders and the government. The Tribal Areas are closed to foreigners, and, as a good part of the world's opium is produced here, even Pakistanis need permission to enter. The Khyber Pass is in the Tribal Areas (see page 293 for permits).

About three million Afghan refugees, mostly Pathans, flooded into Pakistan during the Russian occupation of Afghanistan from 1979 to 1988. They were welcomed by the Pakistani government, and housed mainly in 350 enormous refugee camps, mostly in the NWFP.

PESHAWAR

The capital of the NWFP is a frontier town and quite different from any other city in Pakistan. Peshawar has a modern university, first-class hotels, international banks and one of the best museums in Pakistan, and yet the heart of the old bazaar has changed little in the last 100 years. Pathan tribesmen stroll down the street with rifles slung nonchalantly over their shoulders, their hands hidden inside their shawls and their faces partly covered by the loose ends of their turbans. Smuggling, drug-dealing and arms-trading are the day's business, as they have been for centuries. The massive Bala Hisar fort overlooks the maze of narrow streets in the old town and the elegant Moghul mosque. On the other side of the railway is the cantonment, its wide tree-lined streets bordered by gracious administrative buildings and spacious bungalows in large gardens. Clubs, churches, the Mall, schools, Saddar Bazaar and the airport are all part of the British contribution to Peshawar's modernization. Peshawar University, founded in 1950, and surrounded by University Town, is the newest section of town. It lies to the west on the road to the Khyber Pass.

The fortunes of Peshawar have for centuries been linked to the Khyber Pass. The city stands guard at its eastern end, and was founded about 2,000 years ago when the Kushans pacified the area. In the second century AD, Kanishka, the most famous of the Kushan kings, moved his winter capital to Peshawar from Pushkalavati, 30 kilometres (19 miles) further north. The Kushans moved freely through the Khyber Pass between Peshawar and their summer capital at Kapisa (north of Kabul in Afghanistan) and from these two cities ruled their enormous and prosperous empire for the next 400 years.

Kanishka built the empire's most magnificent Buddhist stupa at Shah-ji-ki-Dheri in Peshawar (now the site of a brick factory), and the city became one of the most important Buddhist centres of pilgrimage. When the Kushans were defeated by the White Huns in about AD 455 Buddhism declined; the Khyber Pass subsequently became too dangerous a route, and Peshawar died.

Peshawar regained its former importance with the arrival of the Moghuls in the 16th century. They planted trees and laid out gardens, thereby turning Peshawar into a 'city of flowers' (one of the meanings of its name). None of the Moghuls enjoyed much success with the Pathans, although Babur gained an ascendancy of sorts after 20 years, five major expeditions and a marriage of convenience to a girl of the Pathan Yusufzai tribe. Akbar nearly lost a huge army in the Khyber Pass when it was trapped in its own camp and hounded by an Afridi Pathan war party. Akbar's son Jahangir fared no better.

In 1818 the Sikh Ranjit Singh captured Peshawar, burned a large part of the city and felled its trees for firewood. The Sikhs also destroyed Shalimar Garden and Babur's magnificent fort. In 30 years of Sikh rule the city's population dwindled by almost half.

In 1849 the British took Peshawar from the Sikhs. Many of the British forces were stationed here, and the cantonment area was built as an administrative centre from which to control the North-West Frontier. It was a difficult and dangerous post.

Peshawar is . . . one of the most fanatical cities in India. It has a large and busy and thriving population of war-like people all armed with knives and daggers, and naturally inclined to think little of pointing their arguments with the sword.

Emma Edwardes, *Life and Letters of Sir H B Edwardes* (1886)

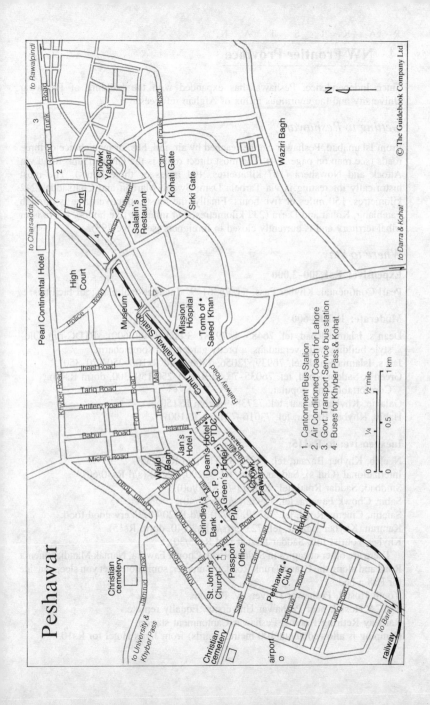

Peshawar

to Rawalpindi

to Charsadda

to Darra & Kohat

to Bara

to University &
Khyber Pass

railway

airport

Grand Trunk Road

3

2

Chowk Yadgar

Fort

Kohati Gate

Sirki Gate

Waziri Bagh

Salatin's Restaurant

Circular Road

City

Qissa Khawani

4

to Darra & Kohat

Pearl Continental Hotel

High Court

Museum

Police Road

Mission Hospital

Tomb of
Saeed Khan

Railway Station

Cantt

Railway Road

Khyber Road

Jheel Road

Tariq Road

Artillery Road

Babur Road

Michni Road

Fort Road

The Mall

Hospital Road

Wajid Bagh

Jan's Hotel

Dean's Hotel

Islamia Road

Islamia Road

The Mall

PTDC

Saddar Road

Bazaar

Chowk Fawara

Grindley's Bank

G. P. O.

Green's Hotel

PIA

Saddar Road

Fakirabad Road

Stadium

Soekarno Road

Christian cemetery

Jamrud Road

Dilazak Road

Khyber Bazaar Road

Bank

St. John's Church

Passport Office

Sunehri Gul Road

Peshawar Club

Christian cemetery

Tang Road

1. Cantonment Bus Station
2. Air Conditioned Coach for Lahore
3. Govt. Transport Service bus station
4. Buses for Khyber Pass & Kohat

0   1/4   1/2   0.5   1 km

0   1/2   1 mile

© The Guidebook Company Ltd

Since Independence, Peshawar has expanded with the building of Peshawar University and the enormous influx of Afghan refugees.

Getting to Peshawar

From Islamabad, Peshawar can be reached by air, rail, bus, or by a choice of three roads (see map on page 254). The most direct route is the Grand Trunk Road via Attock and Nowshera (167 kilometres, 104 miles or three hours). The most historically interesting is via Tarbela Dam, Swabi, Mardan and Charsadda (242 kilometres, 150 miles or five hours. Finally, the most attractive drive is through Fatehjang, Kohat and Darra (232 kilometres, 144 miles or five hours). Darra is in tribal territory and is currently closed to foreigners (see page 297).

Where to Stay

Expensive: Rs1,300–3,000

Pearl Continental, Khyber Pass, tel. 76361–9. International class; all facilities.

Moderate: Rs100–600

Dean's, Islamia Road, tel. 76483–4, 79781–3 (s/d Rs460/600). PTDC-run. Old-style building with verandahs, a pretty garden and some charm.
Jan's, Islamia Road, tel. 76939, 72056, 73009 (s/d Rs100–250/170–350).
Green's, Saddar Road, tel. 76035–7 (s/d Rs100–250/150–300, dorm Rs40). Comfortable and popular.
Galaxie, Khyber Bazaar, tel. 72738–9 (from Rs150).
Habib, Khyber Bazaar, tel. 73016–7 (from Rs100).

Inexpensive: to Rs115

Neelab, Khyber Bazaar, tel. 74255, 62314 (s/d Rs35/55).
International (Gul's), Saddar Road, tel. 72100, 72250 (s/d Rs40/60).
Sindbad, Saddar Road, tel. 75020 (s/d Rs40/60).
Sabir, Chowk Fawara, tel. 75922 (s/d Rs25/40).
Salatin, Cinema Road, tel. 73779, 73770 (s/d Rs20/40). Very good food.
Kamran, Khyber Bazaar, tel. 72345 (s/d Rs20/40, dorm Rs15).
Khyber Tourist Inn, Saddar Bazaar (s/d Rs15/30).
  There are other cheapies in Saddar Road, Chowk Fawara, Namak Mandi, Cinema Road and along the Grand Trunk Road. In summer, some hotels let you sleep outside for Rs8 a bed.
Youth Hostel, Peshawar University. Remote.
YMCA Hostel, near Peshawar University. Equally remote.
Railway Retiring Rooms, Peshawar Cantonment station.
Camping is allowed about 100 metres (yards) from Jan's Hotel for Rs10.

Where to Eat

Salatin's, Cinema Road, tel. 73779, 73770. Best Pakistani food in Peshawar and
famous for its Pathan atmosphere.

Nanking and Hong Kong, both on the Mall. Good Chinese.

Pearl Continental, Dean's, Jan's and Green's, at the respective hotels. All serve
European and Pakistani food.

The street food in Peshawar is famous as some of the best in Pakistan. Try the
stalls along Khyber Bazaar and Qissa Khawani, where you can eat well cheaply. In
and around Saddar Bazaar are more cheap eating places.

Useful Addresses

Tourist Information Centre, PTDC, Dean's Hotel, tel. 79781–3, 76481.
Peshawar Museum, tel. 72252, 74452.
Passport Office, Gunner Road, tel. 78931.
General Post Office and **banks** are in Saddar Bazaar; the **Telephone and
Telegraph Office** is on the Mall.

Sights

Peshawar is divided into three sections: the old walled city, the British cantonment
and University Town.

Bazaar Tour

The most exciting part of Peshawar is the old city, which dates from Buddhist,
Moghul and Sikh times. It is a labyrinth of narrow lanes and colourful bazaars, a
mosaic of traders, travellers, Pathan tribesmen and Afghan refugees. You can
wander for hours in the bazaars, watching the people, drinking sweet green tea
brewed in big copper samovars and absorbing the atmosphere. In typical Asiatic
style, shops selling similar wares are found together; they are almost always open
except during Jumma prayers on Fridays, between 12 noon and 2 pm. The following
tour takes in all the most interesting and picturesque bazaars and some of the
specialist shops and workshops. The tour will take two to three hours even if you
do not stop for the endless cups of tea offered by the shopkeepers.

Start from Jail Bridge across the railway line. You can hire a motorized rickshaw
or horse-drawn tonga here, or walk all the way.

Khyber Bazaar is the main street left from the traffic island, and is full of doctors,
dentists and lawyers. Enormous sets of false teeth gape at you from huge billboards,
evoking nightmares of hours spent in the dentist's chair. This is also the bus terminal
for the Khyber Pass and for Kohat.

Kabuli Gate and the entrance to the walled city is at the end of Khyber Bazaar
by the traffic lights, just before the Kabuli Gate police station. Portions of the old

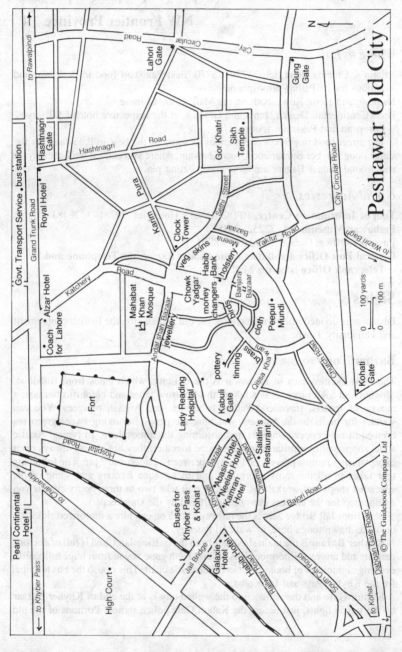

Peshawar Old City

N

to Rawalpindi

Circular Road

City Circular Road

Lahori Gate

Gung Gate

Hashtnagri Gate

Road

Gor Khatri

Sikh Temple

Hashtnagri Road

Pura

Karim

Royal Hotel

Sethi Street

Clock Tower

Meena Bazaar

Yakfut Road

to Wazir Bagh

Grand Trunk Road

Govt. Transport Service bus station

veg skins

Habib Bank

holstery

Alzar Hotel

Coach for Lahore

Katchery Road

Mahabat Khan Mosque

Chowk Yadgar money changers

birds

Banjara Bazaar

Peepul Mundi

Andar shah Bazaar

Jewellery

cloth

0   100 yards

0   100 m

cotton Road

Chutch Road

Fort

pottery

tinning

brass

Dhan Kha wan

Kohati Gate

Lady Reading Hospital

Kabuli Gate

Qissa Kha wani

Salatin's Restaurant

Cinema Road

Bajori Road

Hospital Road

Khyber Bazaar

Abasin Hotel

Neelab Hotel

Kamran Hotel

Pearl Continental Hotel

to Chatsadda

to Khyber Pass

Jail Bridge

Buses for Khyber Pass & Kohat

High Court

Galaxie Hotel

Habib Hotel

South City Road

Railway Road

to Kohat

Dabgari Gate Road

© The Guidebook Company Ltd

city wall still stand on either side. The walls of Lady Reading Hospital, down the street to the left, are old city walls. Peshawar's 16 gates and enclosing wall stood until the mid-1950s; today the names remain, but most of the gates and wall have been removed by the local government.

Qissa Khawani Bazaar, or Bazaar of the Story Tellers, is straight ahead through Kabuli Gate inside the city walls. This was described by Sir Herbert Edwardes as 'the Piccadilly of central Asia'. Tall, narrow buildings line the street, with wooden shutters and intricately carved windowframes and balconies. Here are many of the cheaper hotels and, in the evening, food stalls where you can eat cheaply and well.

The **brass and copper shops** are in the street to the left at the end of Qissa Khawani. These sell a range of new and old wares. Ali Brothers on the left is the best known—all VIP visitors are taken here. 'Poor Honest Ali' has a selection of high-quality brass and copper, as well as Gardner Russian china. Ali will show you testimonials from ambassadors and a photo of himself with Jackie Onassis. Be prepared to bargain hard.

The **Peshawar Pottery** is down a side street on the left, immediately after the brass shops. A wide range of ornamental and utilitarian items, glazed in strong earthy colours, is on display downstairs. Upstairs the potters work from 10 am to 4 pm except Fridays.

Back on the main street are the shops selling the famous **blankets and shawls** woven in pitlooms in Swat and Kaghan. Made of hand-spun wool, they are predominantly red and black with brightly patterned borders. The lane to the right, opposite the one to the pottery, leads to the **cloth bazaar** and the **basket bazaar**, where baskets from D I Khan are sold. Here also is the **Banjara Bazaar**, which specializes in unusual decorative items such as bells, bone and wooden beads and hair braids. Most of the shopkeepers in this area speak only Urdu or Henko (the language of Peshawar). Ask here for the way to **Peepul Mundi**, the main grain wholesale market, where there is a peepul tree believed to be the offspring of the tree under which Buddha preached.

Alternatively you can continue on the main street towards Chowk Yadgar, passing on the way the **bird market** where pet song birds are sold in small cages, as in China. To the left are more cloth shops selling all types of *charders* (multi-purpose sheets) and block-prints.

Chowk Yadgar is the central square of old Peshawar and the best place to leave your rickshaw or car. The monument in the centre commemorates the heroes of the 1965 Indo–Pakistan War and is the traditional town meeting place, where most political rallies and demonstrations take place.

On the left of the square the money changers squat on their hand-knotted carpets with their safes behind them and their pocket calculators at the ready. They will illegally change any currency, but only accept large notes.

From Chowk Yadgar there are two interesting walks, to the west and to the east. Running off the square to the west (left) is the street of the gold and silversmiths, the **Andarshah Bazaar**. This narrow street is lined with shops the size of cupboards selling the usual modern jewellery, plus antique silver, tribal jewellery, old coins, military buttons and buckles. As you sit in the stalls trying on nomad earrings and rummaging through boxes, the shopkeeper sends a small boy to fetch tea from some nearby tea shop. He reappears carrying a brass tray through the crowd with tiny cups of sweet green tea.

The beautifully proportioned **Mahabat Khan Mosque** is at the top of the hill on the right; a narrow gateway between the jewellery shops leads into its large courtyard. Built in the 1670s, the Moghul mosque is orthodox in design, with an ablution pond in the middle of the open courtyard and a single row of rooms round the sides. The prayer hall, on the west, consists of a single hall with no verandah in front but lavishly decorated inside and covered by three low fluted domes. Two tall minarets stand at either end of the prayer hall. According to the late-19th-century *Gazetteer*, the minarets were frequently used in Sikh times 'as a substitute for the gallows'. In June 1895 the mosque was almost destroyed by a fire that raged through the Andarshah Bazaar; it was only saved by the 'unremitting efforts of the faithful'. Mahabat Khan, twice governor of the Peshawar region during the reigns of Shah Jahan and Aurangzeb, financed the building of the mosque.

From Chowk Yadgar, the street to the right (east) leads past fruit and vegetable stalls on the right and an alley full of hardware shops on the left, to the **Cunningham Clocktower**, built in 1900 'in commemoration of the Diamond Jubilee of Her Majesty the Queen Empress'. Sir George Cunningham began his career as politicial agent in North Waziristan and later became governor of the NWFP from 1937 to 1946, and again after Independence from 1947 to 1948. Around the clocktower is the leather and skin market, where many of the shops sell the skins of very young Karakul lambs and have tailors on the premises making astrakhan hats.

The **Meena Bazaar**, the Women's Bazaar, is down the alley to the right from the clocktower. Groups of burqa-clad women shop for beads, trimmings, machine embroidery and trinkets. Here you can buy a burqa (the all-enveloping garment for women in purdah) in a choice of colours. Black coats with matching veils are also on sale for women not required to cover themselves totally.

Retrace your steps to the entrance to the Meena Bazaar. Continue on the main street up the hill. The next alley on the right is the **shoe bazaar**. Some 100 metres (yards) further up the main street, also on the right, is the **block-printing shop**. Cloth is hand-printed using a variety of carved wooden blocks dipped in different coloured dyes. You can have your own cloth printed to your choice of pattern. The cloth bazaar is a little further up the same street, opposite another copper pot bazaar.

Sethi Street continues up the hill to the Moghul caravanserai. Most of the old houses here belong to the Sethi family, one of the oldest merchant families in Peshawar. They once had offices in czarist Russia and Shanghai, which imported silks and china, and exported cloth, indigo and tea. The tall houses with wooden balconies have beautifully carved wooden doors leading into spacious courtyards. Underground are cool cellars, 15 metres (50 feet) deep, where the families can retreat from the heat in summer. Victorian glass chandeliers evoke 19th-century opulence. You can arrange a tour of one of the houses through the PTDC.

The **Gor Khatri** is a large Moghul caravanserai at the top end of Sethi Street. A huge Moghul gateway leads into a large courtyard, over 100 metres (yards) square, that was once surrounded on all four sides by rooms for travellers. The caravanserai was built on a spot that has been a holy place for nearly 2,000 years. In the second century AD it was a Buddhist shrine and monastery known as the Tower of Buddha's Bowl. After Buddhism declined it became a Hindu shrine. In Moghul times, Shah Jahan's daughter built a mosque and the surrounding caravanserai. When the Sikhs arrived in the 19th century they knocked down the Moghul mosque and built a temple to Gorakhnath (Shiva), which is still there on the right at the other end of the courtyard, with a shrine dedicated to the bull Nandi beside it. The Sikhs turned the caravanserai into their governor's residence. It has since been used as government offices and is now used by the police.

Return to Chowk Yadgar, from where you can follow Katchery Road north past a row of **holstery shops**, selling gun holsters and bandoleers, to the Grand Trunk Road.

The **Bala Hisar Fort**, between the Grand Trunk Road and the old city, is a massive structure built by the Sikhs in 1834 on the site of Babur's earlier fort. The fort is used by the army and is not open to the public.

The Cantonment

Peshawar's cantonment is on the other side of the railway line from the old city and follows the layout found all over the Indian subcontinent (see page 222). The streets are straight, wide and shaded by huge trees. The spacious bungalows and government buildings are set back in large gardens. The Saddar Bazaar, between the old city and the cantonment, is full of hotels, restaurants, carpet and antique shops. As usual there are churches, a club, schools, a railway station, and the later additions of a stadium and airport.

Peshawar Museum, formerly the Victoria Memorial Hall, was built in 1905. The long hall, with its side galleries and raised platform at the end, was used for balls. The museum has one of the best collections of Gandharan art in Pakistan, all well arranged and labelled. Sculptures illustrating the life of Buddha are laid out in chronological order. The fasting Buddha here is even more haunting than the one in Lahore Museum. There is also an ethnological section, the Hall of Tribes, with wooden carvings from the Kalash people in Chitral, and a Muslim Gallery. Guided tours are scheduled daily at 10 am and 4 pm, but do not always take place, so telephone 72252 or 74452 for details and opening times.

St John's Church is the oldest church in Peshawar. The foundation stone was laid on 23 March 1851. The Christian cemetery is not beside the church but, as is usual in Pakistan, lies outside the residential area in two different locations on the road to the Khyber Pass. The oldest graves are cemented into the wall closest to the road, and tell of death on the frontier: Lieutenant Colonel Walter Irvine, chief medical officer NWFP 'lost his life in the Nagoman River when leading the Peshawar Vale Hunt, of which he was Master, 26 Jan 1919'; Reverend Isidor Loewenthal, 'Missionary of the American Presbyterian Mission who translated the New Testament into Pushtoo . . . was shot by his Chokeydar, April 27 1864'. There are many sad little graves similar to the one for 'Our Little Mavis, born September 6th 1903, died May 1st 1904. The dearly loved child of Arthur and Maud Tyler'. Donations for the upkeep of the cemetery are welcomed by the bishop at St John's Church.

The **Peshawar Club**, on Sir Syed Road near the Mall (officially Shahrah-e-Pehlavi, but no one calls it that), is for members and their guests only, but you can go in to look around and browse in the library. The swimming pool, surrounded by large shady trees, is open to the public. Before noon, half of it is curtained off by a shamiana, behind which women in purdah swim. Bells ring loudly just before noon to warn the women to leave the pool before the curtain is drawn back.

Edwardes College, another of Pakistan's prestigious boarding schools, was founded in 1855 as the Sir Herbert Edwardes Memorial School. It has splendid Moghul Gothic buildings with ornate cupolas, baubles and pillars.

The **Khalid Bin Walid Bagh**, on the Mall, is a remnant of the old Moghul Shalimar Garden and is full of beautiful chinar trees.

Peshawar, Historic City of the Frontier, by A H Dani, published in 1969 by the Khyber Mail Press, gives a detailed description of the history of Peshawar and a tour of its city walls and ancient monuments.

University Town

University Town is about seven kilometres (four miles) from the centre of Peshawar on the road to the Khyber Pass. The oldest building is **Islamia College**, founded in 1913 to educate the sons of the Pathan chiefs; the college's elegant Moghul Gothic buildings are featured on the Pakistani Rs100 note. In 1950 the University of Peshawar was founded around Islamia College. Various research departments, including the Pakistan Academy for Rural Development and the Pakistan Forest Institute, are in the same area. Surrounding the university is the residential area known as University Town, a sprawling garden town of red brick buildings and watered lawns.

Shopping

Peshawar is famous for its wooden furniture with brass inlay. You can arrange for factory tours. When ordering furniture try to find out if the wood is properly seasoned; otherwise it will crack and the brass inlay will pop out. The best-known factories are: M Hyatt & Brothers, who have a showroom opposite Jan's Hotel and a factory in the Jamrud Industrial Estate; Royal Furniture; Peshawar Woodworks; Khyber Wood Factory; Pak/Danish Industries and Pak/German Industries.

Wax worked on cloth is another handicraft for which Peshawar is well known. You can find it in Saddar Bazaar and in the arcade of the Pearl Continental Hotel. The designs—birds in brilliant colours and dragons—show Chinese influence.

The Afghan Metal Works, behind the Pearl Continental Hotel on Pajjagi (Ashab Baba) Road, are open 8 am–4 pm and welcome visitors. You can watch the moulding, beating, engraving, tinning and polishing of the various copper and brass utensils.

Smoked meat and sausages are available at Brzybrowski's, in the Jamrud Industrial Estate, tel. 50647—they keep well for travelling.

Khyber Pass

When Spring-time flushes the desert grass,
Our Kafilas wind through the Khyber Pass,
Lean are the camels but fat the frails,
Light are the purses but heavy the bales,
When the snowbound trade of the north comes down,
To the market square of Peshawar town.

Rudyard Kipling

The pass is currently closed to most foreigners; UN officials, diplomats and accredited journalists can apply to the provincial home secretary and the minister of tribal affairs for permission to drive through. Pakistanis should apply to the political agent.

From Peshawar to the Afghan border at Torkham it is 56 kilometres (35 miles) or a drive of about one hour. The road is open as far as Jamrud Fort, 18 kilometres (11 miles) from Peshawar, and leaves Peshawar past the university and Islamia College. Afghan refugee camps spread over the fields beyond the university. Beyond these are high, mud-walled compounds of Pathan tribesmen, complete with turrets, gun holes and huge corrugated iron gates.

Jamrud Fort, made of rough stonework and faced with mud plaster, was built by the Sikhs in 1823 on the site of an older fort. The modern stone arch across the road dates from 1964. Those without permits are turned back at the checkpost here.

At its mouth the pass is wide and flat, bounded on either side by low stony hills. The smaller hillocks on the floor of the pass are each capped with a picket manned by the Frontier Force. More pickets are perched on every possible vantage point. In the last century the soldiers used heliographs and semaphore to maintain contact.

The road zigzags up to the first viewpoint, nine kilometres (six miles) from Jamrud. From here you look back down the two roads, one for vehicles, and the other older track for animal caravans and pedestrians. The road sweeps in wide curves down to the rich Peshawar Plain.

From the second viewpoint a little further up, also looking back towards

Peshawar, you get the best view of both the road and the Khyber railway, which threads its way through a string of tunnels on the north wall of the pass.

Shagai Fort is an imposing red fort round the next corner. It was built by the British in the 1920s and is now manned by the Frontier Force; it is not open to the public. Beyond Shagai the road follows a seasonal stream and descends down a small valley past fortified houses for four kilometres (2.5 miles) to the **Ali Masjid** (Mosque). Perched high above the mosque on a commanding spur is the **Ali Masjid Fort**, which guards the narrowest point of the gorge and commands the entire length of the pass. In the cemetery here are the graves of British soldiers killed in the Second Afghan War of 1878. The road through the gorge is one-way, and hugs a narrow ledge beside the river bed, overshadowed by high cliffs; before the road was widened, two laden camels could not pass each other at this point. The return road, and the railway, follow separate ledges higher up on the opposite cliff and offer a less exciting view of the gorge.

Triangular cement tank traps stand in the river bed and are inset into covered holes in the road. The Ali Masjid pumping station is at the western end of the gorge, with subsidiary pumping stations resembling large, vaulted, cement graves at intervals along the road.

The insignia of the regiments that have served in the Khyber are carved and painted on the rockfaces at several places beside the road: those of the Gordon Highlanders, South Wales Borderers, Royal Sussex, Cheshire and Dorset regiments are grouped together.

The pass now opens out into a wide fertile valley dotted with fortified Pathan villages surrounded by high crenellated mud walls with watchtowers at the corners and pierced with narrow gun holes round the top. The villages along the roadside all have their names painted on blue boards in Roman script.

Sphola Stupa, of the second to fifth centuries, stands on the right of the road above the railway at the village of Zarai, 25 kilometres (15 miles) from Jamrud. The stupa has a high hemispherical dome resting on a three-tiered square base. Beautiful Gandharan sculptures were found here when the site was excavated at the beginning of this century, some of which are now in the Peshawar Museum. The side of the stupa facing the road has been restored, but the rest of it is crumbling away.

The **Khyber Rifles' Regimental Headquarters** is up a road to the right shortly after the stupa. Official visitors are often given lunch here and treated to a display of Pathan dancing and bagpipes. The old British mess traditions are still upheld and the mess silver and old photos are proudly displayed.

Landi Kotal, at the end of the railway line, eight kilometres (five miles) from the border, is a smugglers' town. Smuggled electrical goods, cloth and drugs are all sold in the bazaar below the road to the left. The road forks in Landi Kotal: bear right to get back to the Khyber Rifles' Headquarters; bear left to descend to the border. A viewpoint beyond the town looks across more triangular cement tank traps to the border post at **Torkham**, a last oasis of green before the barren brown of the Afghan plain. A continuous stream of donkey and camel caravans plods up and down the pedestrian track to the border; Suzukis and pickups filled with Afghans and tribesmen ply the road. Everywhere you look you see camouflaged pillboxes.

On the hilltop directly south (to the left) of Torkham is a ruined Kafir (Hindu) fort dating from the ninth century. On this ridge the British and the Afghans fought one of the last battles of the Third Afghan War in 1919. The top of the hill is in Afghanistan, with a commanding view down over the Pakistani installations and forts to the east.

The **Khyber Railway** from Peshawar to Landi Kotal is, for rail enthusiasts, a three-star attraction. The British built it in the 1920s at the then-enormous cost of more than £2 million. It has 34 tunnels, which add up to five kilometres (three miles) of darkness, as there are no lights on the train, and crosses 92 bridges and culverts. The two or three coaches are pulled and pushed by two SG 060 oil-fired engines. At one point the track climbs 130 metres (425 feet) in little more than a kilometre (0.7 miles) by means of the Changai Spur, a section of track shaped like a W, with two cliffhanging reversing stations where the train breathes heavily before changing direction.

The Khyber train is currently off limits to foreigners. It leaves Peshawar Cantonment railway station on Fridays only at about 9 am. For station enquiries telephone 74437, for reservations 74436. The 42-kilometre (26-mile) journey to Landi Kotal takes at least three and a half hours, even on a good day. There are frequent stops to clear the line and unload freight. A second-class ticket costs about Rs5, which as train rides go must be the best value in the world. Tribespeople travel free, as part of the contract agreed upon when they allowed the British to build the railway through their territory.

Travelling first class is less exciting as you cannot watch the locals—the doors between first and second class are locked, so you cannot walk through. The only lavatories are in first class; there are no lavatories in the stations.

The train waits two hours at Landi Kotal before returning to Peshawar. It is a short walk of about 750 metres (half a mile) from Landi Kotal Station to the town. It is about one hour from Landi Kotal to Peshawar by road.

Warsak Dam is a favourite picnic spot (closed to foreigners in 1987), 25 kilometres (15 miles) northwest of Peshawar on the Michni Road. The dam was built on the Kabul River between 1955 and 1960 and has created a 42-kilometre (26-mile)-long lake behind it. You can also reach the dam from the Khyber Pass road at Jamrud.

SOUTH OF PESHAWAR

The North-West Frontier Province south of Peshawar is a semi-desert with wide stony plains, mountains rising to about 3,000 metres (8,500 feet) above sea level and irrigated oases. Most of the scenery is similar to Baluchistan to the south; only the valley of the perennial Kurram River is greener. The tribal territories of Kurram (Parachinar) and North and South Waziristan make up about half of the area and can

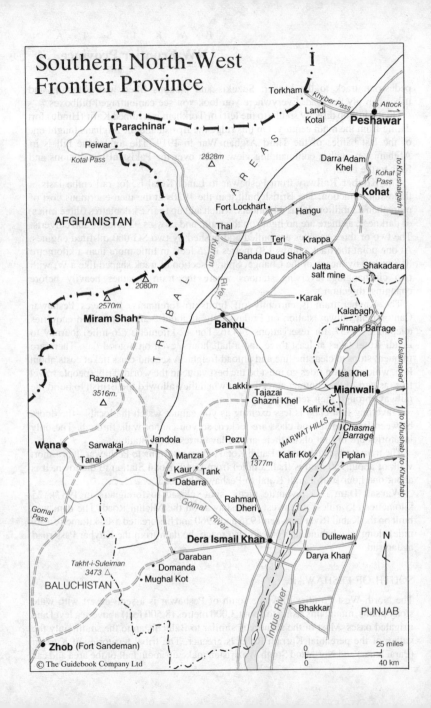

Southern North-West Frontier Province

Torkham
Khyber Pass
Landi Kotal
Peshawar
to Attock

Parachinar
Peiwar
Kotal Pass

Darra Adam Khel

△ 2828m

Kohat
Kohat Pass
to Khushalgarh

AFGHANISTAN

Fort Lockhart
Hangu

Thal

Teri
Krappa

Banda Daud Shah

Jatta salt mine

Shakadara

Karak

△ 2080m

Kalabagh

△ 2570m
Miram Shah

Bannu

Jinnah Barrage

to Islamabad

Razmak
3516m.
△

Lakki
Tajazai
Ghazni Khel

Isa Khel

Mianwali

Kafir Kot

to Khushab
to Khushab

MARWAT HILLS

Chasma Barrage

Wana
Sarwakai
Jandola

Tanai

Pezu

Kafir Kot

Piplan

Manzai
Kaur
Tank
Dabarra

△ 1377m

Rahman Dheri

Gomal Pass

Gomal River

Dera Ismail Khan

Dullewali

Darya Khan

N

Takht-i-Suleiman
3473 △
Daraban
Domanda
Mughal Kot

BALUCHISTAN

Bhakkar

PUNJAB

Zhob (Fort Sandeman)

Indus River

0 ___ 25 miles

0 ___ 40 km

© The Guidebook Company Ltd

TRIBAL AREAS

Kurram River

be visited only with a permit. The other half—Kohat, Bannu and Dera Ismail Khan—is open to foreigners. Most of the NWFP's border with the Punjab is marked by the Indus. Kalabagh is the only Punjabi town on the west bank.

Darra Adam Khel

Darra is the gun 'factory' of the tribal areas, 40 kilometres (25 miles) south of Peshawar on the road to Kohat, or a drive of about 40 minutes. Because of recent drug trading and arms dealing, Darra is now closed to foreigners. There is a checkpost outside Peshawar. (Coming from Kohat it is easier to get through, but if you are turned back, it is a very long way round through Khushalgarh and Attock to get back to Peshawar.)

The Darra arms factory was started in 1897. The British believed it would be better for the Pathans to make their own inferior weapons than to steal British-made guns. In return for allowing the illegal gun factory to operate, the Pathans guaranteed the British safe passage along the main frontier roads.

The main street of Darra is lined with little forges on either side where the guns are made by hand. The tools used are astonishingly primitive, yet the forges turn out accurate reproductions of every conceivable sort of weapon, from pen pistols to anti-aircraft guns, from grenades to rifles. Even the serial number of the original gun is reproduced. Some of the craftsmanship is very fine, but the gun barrels are often made of steel-reinforcing rods from the building trade. The town is quite frightening to visit, as the tribesmen test prospective purchases on the main street.

Kohat

The scenic drive from Darra across the **Kohat Pass** to Kohat is about 25 kilometres (15 miles). At the top of the pass there is a fort and memorial arch to Eric Charles Handyside, who was killed by tribesmen in 1926.

The drive from Islamabad to Kohat via Fatehjang and Khushalgarh takes three to four hours on a good but narrow road. The bridge across the Indus at Khushalgarh is a dual rail and road bridge, a smaller version of the old Attock bridge. From the Indus to Kohat is about 50 kilómetres (30 miles).

Kohat is served by flights from Islamabad on Wednesdays and Fridays.

Where to Stay

Nadria, outside Tehsil Gates, tel. 3162 (Rs20–40; Rs130 with AC).
There are half a dozen cheap hotels around the bus stand and along Hangu Road.

Sights

Kohat is a garrison town. The main road bypasses it, but it is worth going through the centre to see the old British cantonment.

Elphinstone, on his 1809 mission to negotiate an alliance with the Afghan king Shah Shuja against a possible invasion by Napoleon, praised Kohat's gardens, and you can still see why today. One of the most beautiful houses is the residence of the deputy commissioner and formerly the home of Louis Cavagnari, the British resident in Kabul, whose assassination led to the Second Afghan War in 1879. (Cavagnari was half French—his father was a general under Napoleon.) His white house, with its round-topped French windows, is unusually elegant. Kohat Fort is another solid reminder of British days.

It was from Bungalow 26 in Kohat Cantonment that a young English girl, Molly Ellis, was kidnapped by Pathan tribesmen in 1923. She was later released unharmed, but her kidnapping became something of a *cause célèbre* in British circles.

From Kohat you can travel west to Parachinar (about 200 kilometres or 125 miles), or south to Bannu and Dera Ismail Khan (about 400 kilometres or 250 miles).

West of Kohat to Parachinar

Parachinar is a small town at the head of the Kurram Valley, close to the frontier with Afghanistan. The Kurram Valley is in tribal territory, so to go there you need a permit from the minister of tribal affairs in Peshawar. As far as Thal, at the end of the railway line, is an open zone. About halfway between Kohat and Thal, at **Hangu**, you can detour north to the Samana ridge and **Fort Lockhart**, named after Sir William Lockhart, a general serving in the area in the 1890s. The fort was built on the crest of the ridge in 1891. The **Saragarhi Obelisk** nearby commemorates the 21 men killed while defending the Saragarhi post, further along the ridge, during the Tirah campaign of 1897–8 (one of 32 campaigns against the tribespeople). There are spectacular views in all directions, particularly to the north, into the inaccessible Tirah hills.

Thal, on the Kurram River, developed as a trading post on the main caravan route from Afghanistan; Thal Fort commands the river crossing. In 1919, during the Third Afghan War, Thal Fort was besieged by the Afghan army, which had invaded the Kurram Valley.

The Kurram Valley, surrounded by low hills, is treeless and has few villages. Anti-tank defences are reminders that this has always been a major invasion route, though there are few forts. Higher up, the valley broadens and there are impressive views of the snow-clad Safed Koh Mountains.

Parachinar is only about 150 kilometres (95 miles) from Kabul on the main trade route. It is a charming town surrounded by huge chinar trees (a cousin of the maple), from which the town derives its name. The governor's house, a vestige from the time of the British Raj, is set in spacious grounds with views of the Safed Koh. The contrast between the greenness of the town and the barrenness of the surrounding mountains makes the town feel alive and safe. To the east and south, the rolling plain slopes gently to the bed of the Kurram River. Parachinar is at its best in spring and autumn, when the weather is cool, the fields green and the sky clear.

Beyond Parachinar, at the head of the Kurram Valley and near the Peiwar Kotal Pass into Afghanistan, is a small village with the house of Lord Roberts, who commanded the assault on the pass during the Second Afghan War in 1878.

Bannu

Bannu, further south on the Kurram River, can be reached by road from either Kohat or Mianwali and Kalabagh. There is a daily train on the narrow gauge railway from Kalabagh. Bannu has an airport with three flights a week from both Peshawar and Islamabad.

From Kohat to Bannu via Krappa and Banda Daud Shah is 128 kilometres (80 miles) and takes about four hours. At Krappa a new road branches south to Shakadara and Kalabagh, about 65 kilometres (40 miles) away. The main road to Bannu passes through the Salt Range (see page 241). There is a salt mine at Jatta. About 95 kilometres (60 miles) from Kohat the road winds down from the hills to the semi-desert Bannu plain.

Where to Stay

Government Rest House, book through the deputy commissioner, Bannu.
Missionary Hospital, book through the missionary sisters.
There are two small local hotels in the bazaar:
Farid, Tea Bazaar, tel. 4242.
Rashid, Tehsil Street, tel. 3519, 4033.

Sights

Bannu town lies in the centre of a wide valley and is surprisingly green; palms and shady mango trees surround the town. The old city still retains its wall; the gates are closed at night against marauding tribesmen from the hills.

Bannu is known for the missionary hospital and school founded at the turn of the century by the British missionary-doctor T L Pennell; both still bear his name. Some of the outhouses in the hospital grounds are Pennell's original mud and straw huts. Pennell and his assistant, both of whom died of blood poisoning before they were 50, are buried in the graveyard near the hospital; other tombstones tell tales of British soldiers killed in skirmishes with the tribes.

Sir Herbert Edwardes, one of Lawrence's young men, went to Bannu as a political agent in 1846 to 'advise' the Sikhs. Neither the Sikhs nor the Afghan Durranis before them had shown much interest in remote Bannu. The Sikhs' method of collecting revenue was brutal and not very effective—they rode in, destroyed or ate all the crops, rounded up the cattle, and attacked some of the forts with heavy losses. Edwardes, a lone Englishman in the company of a Sikh army, forbade plundering and insisted the troops pay for everything, thereby winning the respect of the tribesmen. Philip Woodruff, in *The Men Who Ruled India* (1954), recounts that a group of tribesmen brought Edwardes a note from the traveller Moorcroft thanking them for their hospitality 25 years before: 'They had saved it as an amulet against any harm from this strange new race and now they produced it, confident it would be honoured. And it was; Edwardes at once gave them a warm invitation to stay in the camp as his guests for as long as they liked.'

On later visits Edwardes convinced the tribesmen to pay their land revenue to the Sikhs and to pull down the fortifications around their villages. The Sikhs then built a single fort, which is still standing today and is used as the headquarters of the local Frontier Force regiment. Edwardes turned his hand to anything and everything; Woodruff recounts how he sat down one night and wrote the Bannuchis a legal code, and the next day translated it into Persian in 18 brisk clauses. Later, in 1848, Edwardes mobilized the tribesmen against the Sikhs in the Second Sikh War. This extraordinary man later became commissioner at Peshawar; Edwardes College in Peshawar is named after him, and Bannu for a time was called Edwardesabad.

From Bannu the road follows the narrow-gauge railway south. A junction left (east) leads to Kalabagh; the road follows the railway all the way. The main road continues south to **Pezu** and Dera Ismail Khan; after Pezu it crosses the westernmost extremity of the Marwat Hills, passing just below their highest peak through barren and eroded country. The hills descend in a profusion of jagged peaks and gorges, but lack the colour of the Salt Range.

Tank

From Pezu a side road to the right (west) follows another branch of the railway to Tank. This is the last town before the tribal areas and the administrative seat of the political agent of South Waziristan. This post has proved dangerous in the past: just before World War I, the then-political agent, Major Dodd, and two other officers were shot by Dodd's orderly on the lawn of his residence.

Sir Henry Durand (father of Mortimer and Algernoon) also met his end in Tank. Sir Henry was feted by the nawab of Tank and given a ceremonial elephant to ride into town. The *howdah* was too high for the town gate and was knocked off, killing Durand in the fall. The gate is now known as the Durand Gate, but Sir Henry is buried in Dera Ismail Khan. Tank, like Bannu, closes its gates at night for fear of marauding tribesmen.

Tank is on one of the early trade routes from Afghanistan through the Gomal Pass. A large, unexcavated (but possibly Indus Civilization) mound is about six kilometres (four miles) out of town on the right side of the road west to Dabarra. The mound is covered in broken pottery, and terracotta figurines are easily found.

Tank to the Tribal Areas and Wana

Dabarra, 11 kilometres (seven miles) west of Tank, is a centre of the falcon trade. Falcons caught by the nomads are sold to Arabian sheikhs for anything up to

Rs200,000 each; the exporter's licence costs another Rs40,000. The birds are caught in the winter when they migrate south from the Russian steppes and can be used only for a few months before they fly north again.

The Powindah nomads (*powindah* actually means 'nomad' in Pushtu) are on the move in March and October (see page 140). They used to migrate from Soviet Turkestan, beyond the Oxus River, to the plains around Delhi and back each year but are now restricted.

There are good views south from Dabarra to Takht-e-Sulaiman Mountain (Soloman's Throne), 3,473 metres (11,290 feet) above sea level, on the border of Baluchistan. The mountain is in tribal territory and a permit is needed for the two-day trek to the top and back.

At **Kaur**, 16 kilometres (ten miles) from Tank, the road forks, left to the Gomal River and Baluchistan, right to Wana. At the fork, on the right, is the lonely grave of a British officer killed in October 1920 by Mahsud tribesmen who attacked a labour camp at Kaur Bridge. Tribal territory begins at the Gomal River, and foreigners without permits are turned back.

The Wana road follows the disused railway to **Manzai**, once the end of the line. A regiment of the Frontier Force is stationed here. The road skirts round the barracks, and a few hundred metres (yards) beyond is a small cemetery with the graves of the British soldiers killed in an ambush at Shahur Tangi in April 1937 (see below).

The impressive fort of **Khirghi Post** guards the valley of the River Zam Tank about five kilometres (three miles) beyond Manzai. Water used to be pumped 100 metres (yards) up to the fort and stored in the reservoir behind. Just beyond Khirghi there is a panoramic view of the river with cultivation on either side and cement tank traps on the river bed dating from World War II.

Jandola marks the beginning of tribal territory; foreigners need permits beyond this point. Kidnapping is a local sport; hostages are exchanged for government concessions and aid. Foreigners command a high ransom and must be heavily escorted if entering tribal territory, so permission is rarely given.

At Jandola the road forks, north to Razmak and Miram Shah in North Waziristan, and west to Wana. There is a famous cadet college at **Razmak** (one of five in Pakistan) run by Major Langland, who is something of a local legend.

The road to Wana follows the Shahur River through a narrow defile called **Shahur Tangi**, where Wazir and Mahsud tribesmen led by the Fakir of Ipi trapped British and Indian troops in April 1937 by laying a dead camel across the road and then shooting out the radiators of the trucks when they were brought to a halt. The road climbs up through barren mountain country past **Sarwakai Fort** and **Tanai Fort** to the plateau of Wana. At Tanai a road branches south to Zhob in Baluchistan.

Wana sits on a well-watered plateau and is surrounded by green fields and poplar and fruit trees. There is a bazaar in the small town, and administrative and military camps beyond; these are approached through a freestanding gateway. Wana is the administrative capital for South Waziristan, and the political agent spends the summer months up here. It is also the headquarters of the South Waziristan Scouts, a locally raised militia with regular army officers on secondment.

Dera Ismail Khan

Dera Ismail Khan, or D I Khan as it is usually called, is on the west bank of the Indus, by a traditional crossing place just upriver of the junction of the Gomal River with the Indus. It has for centuries been an important trading centre, and the Powindah nomads' winter headquarters. It has little industry and moves at a leisurely pace—the bicycle rickshaw is the main form of transport.

D I Khan can be reached by air from Islamabad, Peshawar, Kohat, Bannu, Zhob, Multan and Quetta. Travelling by road from Islamabad via Talagang and Mianwali takes about seven hours.

Where to Stay

Midway, Indus River Bank, tel. 2900, 3100 (s/d from Rs150/250).
Jans, North Circular Road, tel. 3925–6 (s/d from Rs150/250).
New Shobra, near Purani Choungi, Saddar, tel. 2705 (s/d Rs20/40).
Al-Habib, Topan Wala Road, tel. 3106 (s/d Rs20/40).
Dubai Air Line, Circular Road, tel. 3778 (s/d Rs20/40).
Cafee Gul Bahar, Circular Road, tel. 3510 (s/d Rs20/40).
Government rest houses, book through the deputy commissioner.

Sights

The cantonment area is on the banks of the Indus, and its tree-lined promenade follows the waterfront. The river at this point is about ten kilometres (six miles) wide in winter, and twice that in summer. In the dry season several islands emerge midriver where the locals pasture their cattle. Until 1985 a bridge of boats ran from island to island across the river here in winter; in summer a ferry made the crossing. A new bridge now spans the river five kilometres (three miles) south of D I Khan; it is a kilometre (half a mile) long, but its approach embankment adds another 19 kilometres (12 miles). As this makes a very long detour for animal traffic, there are plans to reintroduce the bridge of boats and ferry.

The old ferry boat, the *SS Jhelum*, is still moored at the promenade in the cantonment area. Built in Glasgow in 1917, she is a museum piece and measures about 30 metres (100 feet) in length. She served at Basra in Iraq in World War I and was subsequently moved to Kalabagh; when the Kalabagh Bridge was built in 1931 she moved downstream to D I Khan. The decks of the steamboat are open, with the exception of two small saloons for gentlemen at the bow and an enclosed area for ladies in the stern. You can explore around the boat, and, if you like, take a look at all the different bits of machinery bearing the names and dates of several manufacturers.

Dozens of prehistoric and Indus Civilization sites are scattered along the ancient trade route to the Gomal Pass, which leads to Afghanistan and the west. **Rahman Dheri**, dating from 3200 BC, is one the most impressive of these. It is 22 kilometres (14 miles) out of D I Khan on the Bannu Road; its low mound is visible about one kilometre (half a mile) to the left of the main road. The city is laid out in the typical chessboard pattern of the Indus Civilization, and you can see the ancient brick walls of the houses; pottery shards, lapis and stone tools are scattered everywhere. A similar site is currently being excavated by a British team west of Bannu.

Dera Ismail Khan to Mianwali

Two roads connect D I Khan with Mianwali. The quickest (about two hours) and most scenic route is by the surfaced, single-lane road up the west bank for 90 kilometres (56 miles) to the Chasma Barrage, where you can cross the Indus just south of Mianwali. The road follows the Paharpur Canal through well-irrigated green fields. High bullrushes and reed grasses border the canal, and rows of palm trees stand against the backdrop of the Marwar Hills. On the way you pass the **Southern Kafir Kot Fort**, which stands on low hills and is clearly visible from the road. Like the Northern Kafir Kot Fort, 38 kilometres (24 miles) further up the Indus, it was built at the time of the Hindu Rajput Kingdom (eighth to the tenth century) and was destroyed by Mahmud of Ghazni in the 11th century. Neither fort was rebuilt.

To reach the Southern Kafir Kot Fort take the track a few kilometres (miles) south of the village of Bilot, which leads to some small headworks bridging the canal. Cross here and climb the hill. The best view of the fort is from the south, at the top of the hill. There is a long section of wall with circular towers constructed of well-cut blocks of limestone. At the fort there are three main temple sites, two with groups of temples and shrines on the same plinth. The carving, deep chiselled and reminiscent of Mayan sculpture, is fine and well preserved.

The **Northern Kafir Kot Fort** is about six kilometres (four miles) north of the western end of Chasma Barrage. With binoculars you can see it from the barrage in the distance on the Marwat Hills. Access is on foot, and it would be advisable to take a guide from the WAPDA rest house at Chasma Barrage. You can book the rest house for the night from WAPDA, tel. Mianwali 107.

The fort commands a splendid defensive position, its walls along the top of deep gorges on three sides. It covers a rubble-strewn area of about 25 hectares (62 acres). Inside there are four temples, two badly eroded, the others intricately carved. The best-preserved walls, including a gate, are on the north side of the fort; the walls are about eight metres (26 feet) high. The view from the temple in the southwest corner of the fort is impressive, as it overlooks the Indus with the Punjab Plain beyond.

The fort is just south of the confluence of the Kurram River with the Indus and on one of the main trade routes from the northwest. Other Hindu forts of the same period in the Salt Range are at Amb, Malot and Ketas (see pages 244–6 and 251).

The other route from D I Khan to Mianwali is across the new bridge just south of D I Khan and up the east bank of the Indus. The good two-lane road, shaded by an avenue of mature trees, passes through well-irrigated countryside. It takes about two and a half hours to reach Mianwali by this route.

THE PLAIN OF PESHAWAR

The fertile plain of Peshawar is a large, well-watered area east and north of the city and bordered by the hills of Swat. It was once the centre of Gandhara, one of the great civilizations of the subcontinent.

The Kingdom of Gandhara lasted from the sixth century BC to the 11th century AD, but was at its height from the first to the fifth century AD under the Buddhist Kushan kings. This was a time of great international activity, and Gandhara, at the hub of Asia, traded with China, the Mediterranean and India. Gandhara is chiefly remembered for its Buddhist art: museums all over the world display the fine stone and stucco sculptures that reflect a prosperous, advanced and gentle Buddhist society.

The first capital of Gandhara was Pushkalavati, the Lotus City, now called Charsadda; the Kushans moved their capital to Peshawar, and the Hindu Shahi kings (ninth to the 11th century) to Hund, on the Indus. After Mahmud of Ghazni conquered the area and converted it to Islam in AD 1026, the name Gandhara disappeared.

The visitor in search of Gandharan ruins should not expect to find more than the very slightest trace of the civilization's former magnificence—for a true picture you must visit the museums. And yet it is still something of an experience to stand on the mound where the Lotus City once flourished and to imagine Alexander the Great's army attacking in 327 BC; to read Ashoka's edicts of 260 BC at Shahbaz Garhi; or to visualize the life of a Buddhist monk at Takht-e-Bahi in the third century AD.

The route described here follows some of the original trade routes from central Asia to India. Only a few of the places of historic interest have been excavated, but dotted all over the area are the mounds of former Gandharan towns. Many of the modern villages on the Peshawar Plain are still perched on the top of high mounds; the villagers constantly rebuild their houses on top of old ones, and over the centuries the villages have become appreciably higher than the surrounding plain.

There are many places to see, but the general tourist should concentrate on the **Bala Hisar** (the earliest Lotus City at Charsadda), the Ashokan edicts at **Shahbaz Garhi**, and the monastery of **Takht-e-Bahi**. These three places can be visited in one day from Peshawar, on the way from Peshawar to Islamabad, or from Peshawar to Swat. It makes an interesting round trip to visit Takht-e-Bahi on the way up to Swat via the Malakand Pass, and the Ashokan edicts on the way down from Swat via the Ambela Pass.

Charsadda

The road to Charsadda, 28 kilometres (17 miles) from Peshawar, runs northeast from Peshawar Fort, crossing the productive, well-watered Peshawar Plain where enormous buffalo, known locally as 'black gold', work the land, and tropical sugar-cane and cold-climate sugar-beet grow side by side.

Pushkalavati (the old name for Charsadda), on the banks of the Swat River near its junction with the Kabul River, was the capital of Gandhara from about the sixth century BC to the second century AD. When the capital moved to Peshawar, an important Buddhist shrine at Pushkalavati ensured the city's survival until the seventh century.

Charsadda is surrounded by hundreds of hectares of graves, all decorated with black and white stones in geometric patterns. This graveyard is considered especially holy, like Makli Hill in Sind (see page 70).

The **Bala Hisar** is to the left of the road from Peshawar. About 27 kilometres (17 miles) from Peshawar Fort, just before you enter Charsadda, the road turns sharply right to cross a river over a double bridge. On this corner, just before the bridge, a

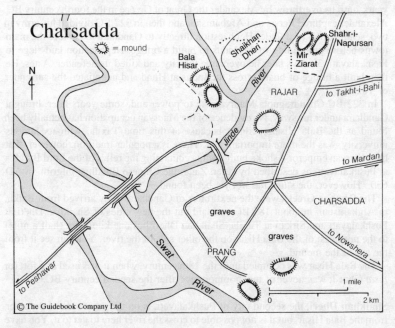

dirt track leads straight on (north) for one kilometre (half a mile). Bear right at the fork. The Bala Hisar, which consists of two high mounds, is on the right of the track.

The Bala Hisar was excavated twice, by Sir John Marshall in 1902 and by Sir Mortimer Wheeler in 1958; the latter cut a trench down through the many layers of mud, stone and pottery to the bottom of one of the mounds. Pottery shards and beautiful round coloured stones are scattered everywhere.

The Bala Hisar was occupied from the sixth century BC. Pushkalavati is first mentioned in the Hindu epic story the *Ramayana*; Bharata, the brother of Ramachandra, conquers Gandharvadesa (Gandhara) and founds two cities, Taksha (Taxila) and Pushkala (Pushkalavati), named after his two sons.

In about 516 BC Gandhara became part of the seventh province of the Achaemenid Empire and paid tribute to Darius the Great of Persia. According to the Greek historian Herodotus, Darius sent the explorer Scylax of Caryanda down the Indus to find the sea—probably from Pushkalavati, where the river becomes navigable. Herodotus describes the Gandharans as bearing bows of reed and short spears, and Wheeler's finds bear this out: the earliest layer of Pushkalavati shows evidence of an Iron Age civilization.

Gandhara probably remained part of the Achaemenid Empire for the next 200 years, until its overthrow by Alexander the Great of Greece in the fourth century BC. Alexander captured Persia and Afghanistan and then in 327 BC divided his army in two, sending half of it under Hephaestion directly to Gandhara to capture the main towns before proceeding to the Indus to build a bridge. Hephaestion laid siege to Pushkalavati; 30 days later he overcame the city and killed its defender, Astes. He then built a bridge of boats across the Indus at Hund and negotiated the surrender of Taxila.

In 322 BC Chandragupta Maurya rose to power and, some years later, brought Gandhara under his sway. No evidence of the Mauryan occupation has actually been found at the Bala Hisar, perhaps because at this time Taxila, with its famous university, was the more important city. There is a popular tradition, however, that the Mauryan emperor Ashoka built a stupa containing the relics of the Lord Buddha at Pushkalavati, as described by Xuan Zang, the Chinese Buddhist pilgrim, in AD 630. However, the stupa has not yet been found.

The Bactrian Greeks were the next rulers of Gandhara. They arrived from Balkh, in Afghanistan, in about 185 BC and laid out the new cities of Shaikhan Dheri at Pushkalavati and Sirkap at Taxila. Shaikhan Dheri lies one kilometre (half a mile) to the northeast of the Bala Hisar on the other side of the river. You can see it from the top of the mound.

The Bala Hisar was occupied until the 18th century, when it was used as a fort (or *hisar*), but it was never of much importance after the second century BC.

Shaikhan Dheri, the second city of Pushkalavati, is on the other side of the river from the Bala Hisar, but it is not possible to cross the river here to get to it. You have to go round by Rajar village (see map on previous page). It is a trip only for the dedicated; for maps and excavation reports see *Ancient Pakistan, Bulletin of the Department of Archaeology*, University of Peshawar, Vol. 2, which is obtainable at the Department of Archaeology in Peshawar or the Asian Study Group Library in Islamabad.

The Bactrians founded Shaikhan Dheri in about 185 BC, at the same time as Sirkap at Taxila. The main streets of both cities were about 750 metres (half a mile) long, with side streets crossing them at neat right-angles. Only a small portion of Shaikhan Dheri was excavated by A H Dani in 1963–4, and no effort has been made to label or preserve the excavations.

The Parthians, the Sakas and the Kushans all occupied Shaikhan Dheri in turn. In the second century AD the Swat River changed course again and the Kushans moved their administrative centre to the new city of Peshawar. But Pushkalavati was not abandoned—it was far too important a Buddhist centre. The Shaikhan Dheri site was flooded, but the town moved one kilometre (half a mile) to the southeast, across the river to what is now the site of the modern village of Rajar. It has not been possible to excavate the high mound on which the village stands; the mounds of Mir Ziarat and Shahr-e-Napursan, a little to the north of Rajar, are covered by modern graves and are also unexcavated.

Prang, south from the crossroads in the centre of Charsadda contains several high mounds—all as yet unexcavated. South of the village the River Swat joins the Kabul River. Prang is probably a corruption of Prayang, also the name of a sacred town in India at the confluence of the Ganges and Jumna rivers, and it seems that Prang, too, is considered sacred: the people of the area bring their dead here for burial.

Takht-e-Bahi

The Buddhist monastery of Takht-e-Bahi is 14 kilometres (nine miles) northwest of Mardan on the road to Swat. A direct road runs from Charsadda to the village of Takht-e-Bahi (see map on page 308). Turn left (north) at the crossroads in Charsadda, and after exactly two kilometres (one and a quarter miles) turn right on the single-lane surfaced road, which leads through rich irrigated farmland. Keep to the main road and after 22 kilometres (14 miles) you come to the main Mardan–Swat road. Turn left here and proceed one kilometre (half a mile) to Takht-e-Bahi.

To get to the ruins cross the level crossing in the centre of the village of Takht-e-Bahi, and after 500 metres (yards) turn right at a sign reading 'Archaeological ruins of Takht-e-Bahi 3 km' (two miles) in English. Cross the railway, turn left at the gate of the sugar mill, and a little further on turn right down a dirt road. You will see the ruins of a large Hindu Shahi fort on top of the hill to the right. Continue on to the end of the track—the ruins of the monastery are straight ahead. It is a steep walk 500 metres (yards) up the hill to the site, and a further 500 metres to the top of the hill.

Takht-e-Bahi is the most impressive and complete Buddhist monastery in

Pakistan. From the top of the hill behind the monastery you can see down across the plains as far as Peshawar on one side, and up to the Malakand Pass and the hills of Swat on the other.

The monastery and stupas at Takht-e-Bahi were founded in the first century AD and abandoned in the sixth or seventh centuries. Surrounding the monastery on the ridge above it to the south, and on the spurs to the east and west, are the ruins of private houses, some three storeys high.

You approach the monastery from the east. On the right, just before you enter the main monastery, is a two-storey block of four monks' cells. In each cell are two niches for the monk's lamp and belongings.

The first court you enter is the **court of stupas**, which is surrounded on three sides by open alcoves or chapels. The excavators estimated that originally these all contained single plaster statues of Buddha, either sitting or standing, dedicated in memory of holy men or donated by rich pilgrims. The largest statues must have stood ten metres (33 feet) high, and all would have been gilded or painted. Around the walls of the chapels, and on the partitions between them, were carved friezes in high relief showing scenes from the life of Buddha; these were carved on slabs of stone and attached to the walls of the shrines with iron nails.

The remains of 38 votive stupas and some more chapels are scattered haphazardly round the centre of the court. These were also built as offerings by pilgrims, and

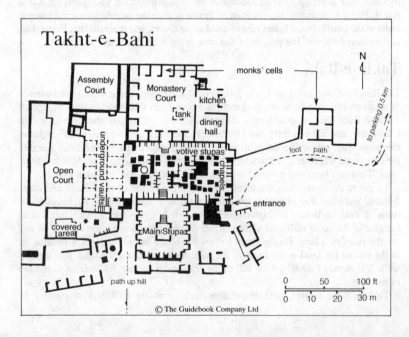

were full of gilded and painted statues and reliefs depicting the life of Buddha. One unusual stupa is octagonal.

The **monastery court** is to the north of the stupa court and up some steps. The monks' cells range round three sides. Originally there was a second storey containing 15 more cells. According to the Buddhist pilgrim Xuan Zang, the walls of the cells were plastered and painted in different colours and the wooden doorposts and lintels were decorated with carvings. In each cell are two niches for the monk's lamp and belongings, and a small window. A water tank in the southwestern corner of the court was probably filled by rainwater draining off the roofs. The kitchen and dining room are to the east of the monastery court. Stairs lead up from the kitchen to the second floor. On the outer wall of the kitchen are two projecting buttresses, which may have been the latrine.

The **court of the main stupa** is to the south of the stupa court and up some steps. The main stupa stands in the centre. The excavators estimate that it was originally about ten metres (33 feet) high, with its umbrellas projecting higher. The square base was surmounted by a hemispherical dome, and all would have been decorated with gilded and painted statues of Buddha and scenes from his life. This court is also surrounded on three sides by roofed alcoves or chapels that once contained statues of Buddha.

The **assembly court** is on the northwestern corner of the complex, surrounded by high walls. This secluded court was the monks' meeting place. The two modern cemented water tanks in the centre of the court were built by the excavators to hold water for workers.

The **chapel** (labelled H on the map) contains two tiers of ornamental trefoil panels divided by pilasters and may have housed a small stupa to commemorate some especially holy or rich person.

The ten **vaulted chambers** underneath the court were used either for meditation or storage. The entrances into the western underground chambers have arched doorways. Two more arched doorways lead west from these rooms out to a large open court; it is not known what this was used for.

In the covered area south of this court are two small elaborately decorated stupas that were in perfect condition when they were excavated in 1910. Today little of the red and gold decoration remains despite the protective shed.

Private houses are scattered up the hill above the monastery and for more than a kilometre (half a mile) along the ridge. Some houses are built around a central court, but most are two storey with one small room set on top of the other. Each is entered by a low door and lit by one small sloping window. The staircases, flat slabs of stone protruding out of the wall, are located outside.

From Takht-e-Bahi you can either continue north up to Swat (see page 316) or turn south to Mardan, 14 kilometres (nine miles) away, and continue east on the ancient trade route.

Some three kilometres (two miles) from Takht-e-Bahi on the road to Mardan a road to the right is marked 'Sahri Bahlol site about 1 km' (half a mile). The modern village of **Sahri Bahlol** is built on top of an ancient mound probably 2,000 years old. More than a hundred years ago the British excavated the site and discovered a walled city and a Buddhist monastery. They removed a great many Gandharan Buddhist sculptures, some of which can be seen in the Peshawar and Lahore museums. Between 1865 and 1870 the British sent army sappers to the best archaeological sites in the Peshawar Plain to collect whatever sculptures they could find. In museums all round the world there are Gandharan sculptures labelled 'from Eusofzai'; Eusofzai (or Yusufzai) is the local Pathan tribe.

Sahri Bahlol village thrives on a flourishing trade in reproductions of Gandharan art. You can spend an interesting hour sitting in private houses drinking tea and looking at the excellent reproductions. Be warned: they are fakes, and the prices are exorbitant.

Mardan

For nearly 200 years Mardan has been a major military base. It is the headquarters of the élite Guides Corps, formed in 1846 to guide regular units in the field, collect intelligence and keep the peace on the North-West Frontier. The Guides were the first British soldiers to wear khaki (see page 279).

The imposing Moghul Gothic memorial arch in the centre of Mardan commemorates the Guides who died at Kabul in 1879 during the Second Afghan War. A plaque reads:

The annals of no army and no regiment can show a brighter record of devoted bravery than has been achieved by this small band of Guides. By their deeds they have conferred undying honour not only to the regiment to which they belong, but on the whole British Army.

For an account of the Guides in action see Charles Miller's *Khyber* (1977) or MM Kaye's romantic novel *The Far Pavilions* (1978). The Guides' cemetery and church in Mardan are also worth a visit.

Shahbaz Garhi and the Ashokan Inscriptions

Shahbaz Garhi is 13 kilometres (eight miles) east of Mardan on the road to Swabi. Down a dirt track to the right, a few hundred metres (yards) before the left turn to Rustam, are the famous Ashokan inscriptions, carved on two rocks on a hill about 300 metres (yards) to the left.

The Ashokan inscriptions date from the third century BC and are the oldest surviving writings of any historical significance in the subcontinent. The Mauryan emperor Ashoka (272–231 BC) ruled over most of the Indian subcontinent from his capital at Pataliputra (now Patna) on the Ganges, in India. He was a Buddhist, but tolerant of all religions. Ashoka ordered a series of edicts to be inscribed on rocks

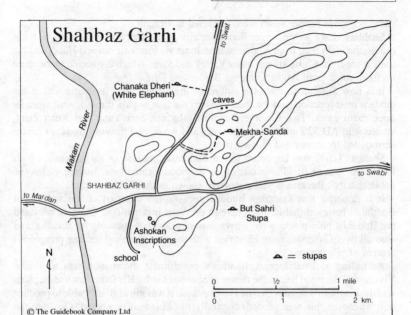

Shahbaz Garhi

to Swat

Chanaka Dheri
(White Elephant)

caves

Makam River

Mekha-Sanda

to Mardan

to Swabi

SHAHBAZ GARHI

But Sahri
Stupa

Ashokan
Inscriptions

school

N

= stupas

0   ½   1 mile
0   1   2 km.

© The Guidebook Company Ltd

and pillars all over his empire; two of these are in Pakistan, at Shahbaz Garhi and at Mansehra (see page 378).

At Shahbaz Garhi 12 edicts are carved on one rock, two on another. Ashoka describes his remorse at the destruction and slaughter that occurred when he overthrew Kalinga in eastern India. He says in future he will conquer only by 'righteousness and dharma', and that, wherever he may be, whether eating or in his lady's apartments, whether on horseback or in the pleasure orchards, he will always be available to hear the petitions of his people.

He tells his subjects that it is their duty to honour their parents, relatives and friends, to give alms to the priests and poor, and not to be extravagant. He forbids the slaughter of animals and suggests that instead of going on hunting trips people should go on pilgrimage. He points out that many religious rites are useless, and that showing self control, respect and generosity are the best ways of gaining merit. And he commands everyone to show religious tolerance to people of other sects.

He orders hospitals to be founded for the treatment of both humans and animals, and medicinal herbs to be planted to ensure a ready supply. He also commands that fruit trees be planted along the roadside and wells dug for the refreshment of travellers.

The Shahbaz Garhi and Mansehra edicts were both inscribed in Kharoshthi, the local Gandharan script; those at Kandahar in Afghanistan were written in Greek and

Aramaic; those further south were inscribed in Brahmi.

Shahbaz Garhi was once an important city at the junction of two major trade routes, the main road from Afghanistan to India via Pushkalavati and Hund, and the trade route from China via the Indus Valley and Swat, which connected to the more northern route from Afghanistan via Bajour and Dir.

It is now difficult to trace the outline of the ancient city. Its centre was at the modern road junction, and the three modern roads now pass through what were its three main gates. Two Chinese Buddhist pilgrims, Sun Yung and Xuan Zang, visited it in AD 520 and 630 respectively and wrote of a thriving Buddhist centre surrounded by stupas and monasteries.

Shahbaz Garhi was important to the Buddhists because of its association with Prince Sudana, or Buddha in one of his previous incarnations. *Sudana* means 'of noble charity'; the area is still popularly known as the Sudana Plain.

It is doubtful that Gautama Buddha ever visited this part of the world, but Buddhists believed that he lived here in previous incarnations. Old folk tales and pre-Buddhist holy places were woven into new legends focusing on Buddha, and sites all over Gandhara were identified with these so that they became prosperous centres of pilgrimage.

According to local legend, Buddha's penultimate incarnation was as Prince Visvantara, the royal heir to the throne at Shahbaz Garhi. His father's white elephant was the kingdom's most prized treasure because it was miraculously able to produce rain whenever this was needed. Naturally the kingdom prospered. One day the prince gave the magic elephant away to a hostile neighbouring kingdom suffering from drought. The people of Shahbaz Garhi were angry at this generous but foolish act and banished Visvantara, his wife and two children. On his way into exile, the prince gave away his horses and chariot and proceeded on foot, carrying the children to Meka-Sanda, where they lived in a cave. One day a Brahmin went to the cave and asked the prince to give him his children, and as a supreme sacrifice the prince handed them over. The Brahmin beat the children until their blood flowed down and reddened the earth, and then, since they were valuable children of royal birth, he put them up for sale in the marketplace in Shahbaz Garhi. There, the children were recognized and rescued by their grandfather, the king. The people, learning of the extreme sacrifices their prince had made in the name of charity, and realizing his holiness, went out to Mekha-Sanda and invited him back.

The sites mentioned in this story still exist. Both Sun Yung and Xuan Zang give clear directions where to find them in their diaries, and they were excavated by the Japanese in the 1960s. Looking for them is a good excuse for a walk on the hill, but there is little to see, except for a few ruins and a magnificent view across the Sudana Plain to Takht-e-Bahi and another line of hills to the north, which is also full of Buddhist ruins.

Mekha-Sanda Stupa and Monastery are on top of a hill. To get there turn north up the Rustam road and after 700 metres (yards), take the second dirt track east (right) round the north side of the hill. It is a 30-minute steep scramble up the hill to the ruins. Two big rocks resembling water buffaloes lie side by side on the hilltop; *mekha* means female water buffalo, *sanda* male—hence the monastery's name.

Two natural caves at the foot of Mekha-Sanda Hill are supposed to be the separate abodes of Visvantara and his wife, who as ascetics could not cohabit. Ask the locals to direct you to the Ghulo-smast, or Thieves' Caves (they were later used as hideouts by bandits). A reddish rock on the hill supposedly marks the place where the children were flogged.

The **Stupa of Chanak-Dheri**, or White Elephant, is on the left of the road to Rustam about two kilometres (a mile) from the turning from the Swabi road and about 500 metres (yards) left (west) across the fields. This was also excavated by the Japanese, but there is little to see.

From Shahbaz Garhi you can continue north on a surfaced road to Swat via the Ambela Pass (see pages 327–8), or east to Swabi. The original east gate of Shahbaz Garhi was at the line of rocks on the road to Swabi about 600 metres (yards) from the Rustam turnoff. **Sahri Stupa**, which commemorates Prince Visvantara giving up his two children, is beside the road on the right, 700 metres (yards) beyond the line of rocks. It has Muslim graves on top and is not excavated.

Swabi, about 50 kilometres (30 miles) from Mardan, was one of Emperor Babur's favourite hunting places. In his diary of 1519 the emperor describes a rhinoceros hunt in the jungle around Swabi:

Feb. 16th. After starting off from the camp for the river, I went to hunt rhinoceros on the Swabi side which place people call also Karg-Khana (Rhino-home). A few were discovered but the jungle was dense and they did not come out of it. When one with a calf came into the open and betook itself to flight, many arrows were shot at it and it rushed into the near jungle; the jungle was fired but that same rhino was not had. Another calf was killed as it lay, scorched by the fire, writhing and palpitating.

Babur Nama (trans. 1826)

At Swabi the road forks left to Tarbela and right to Attock. To Islamabad from Swabi it is 137 kilometres (85 miles), or two hours, via Tarbela, and 119 kilometres (74 miles), or one and a half hours, via Attock. There is a ford before Tarbela which might be difficult for cars during the monsoon.

Hund

Hund was the place where the ancient trade route crossed the River Indus. It was also the capital of Gandhara in the tenth century. However, visiting it is for enthusiasts only. To get there take the road from Swabi towards Attock for ten kilometres (six miles) to the village of Amber. Just past Amber a surfaced road leads left (southeast) to Hund, four kilometres (2.5 miles) away. Park outside the main gate of the village, as its only street is very narrow, and walk straight through to the river.

At Hund the River Indus spreads lazily out across the plain between the mountains and Attock Gorge. In winter, when the water is low, it is shallow enough to ford here; in summer, when it is swollen by melting snow and monsoon rains, the river can still be crossed precariously on inflated cow-skin rafts, or on upturned ceramic pot floats. Udabhandapur, one of Hund's former names, means City of Water Pots.

There are Buddhist, Hindu and Muslim ruins at Hund, the most visible being the 16th-century walls of **Akbar's Fort**, which completely surround the modern village. The fort is square, with a gate in the centre of each wall. The road enters the village through the north gate and exits by the south gate to the river. A cobbled road descends to the Indus, marking the crossing place. The ruined walls have 36 bastions. At the north gate the post holes for the wooden gate posts are still there, but the brick arches that once stood over the gates have fallen down.

The Hindu remains have been badly damaged by floods, but you can still see part of the city wall with two square bastions of diaper masonry on the cliff on the river bank. There are traces of a Hindu gate a little upriver from the Moghul gate on the riverside. To the west of the village is the mound of Samalgarh, which villagers say was the seat of Raja Hodi. There is not much left to see except a bit of diaper wall and some peepul trees, which suggest that this was a sacred area.

Hund flourished from AD 870 to 1001, when it was the capital of Gandhara under the Hindu Shahi kings. Arrian records in *Anabasis* that Alexander and his conquering army of 50,000 men and all their animals crossed the Indus at Hund on a bridge of boats specially built for them by Alexander's commander, Hephaestion, in 326 BC. When he arrived at the river, Alexander made animal sacrifices and held athletic games and a horse show. The omens proved favourable, so the army crossed. More sacrifices of thanksgiving were made on the other side, where King Ambhi of Taxila was waiting to surrender to Alexander. And so Alexander entered India.

When Buddhism arrived in Gandhara in the second century BC, Hund became a Buddhist centre of pilgrimage because it was associated with the place where, in a previous incarnation, Buddha turned himself into a huge fish and fed the people on his own flesh during 12 years of famine. According to Xuan Zang, who visited it in 630, it was 'a city of 20 *li* [four kilometres, or 2.5 miles] in circuit and having the Indus on its south side: its inhabitants were flourishing, and in it were collected valuable rarities from various regions.'

In the seventh century Buddhism slowly died out in Gandhara. In 870 the Turkish Hindu Shahi kings were driven out of Kabul by the Saffarid ruler Yaqub-e-Lais. They set up their new capital at Wahind (as Hund was then known); at this time the Hindu Shahi Kingdom stretched from the Kabul Valley to Kashmir and from Swat to Multan.

The benevolent Hindu Shahi Kingdom was completely destroyed by Mahmud of Ghazni, who had vowed to drive the Hindus out of Gandhara and between 1000 and 1026 led at least 12 campaigns against them. In 1000 he defeated the Hindu Shahi king Jaipala, who a year later committed suicide by climbing on a funeral pyre at Hund. His successor, Anandpala, moved his capital to Nandana in the Salt Range (see page 248). This was to no avail, as he and the other Hindu princes of northern India were roundly defeated by Mahmud in 1008 in a battle near Hazro, on the other side of the Indus from Hund, and by 1026 the Hindus were finally overcome by Mahmud. Thousands of former Hindus embraced Islam, and the area has been predominantly Muslim ever since.

Al-Biruni, the Arab Muslim scholar who lived at Mahmud of Ghazni's court, recorded: 'The Hindu Shahi dynasty is now extinct, and of the whole of the house there is no longer the slightest remnant in existence. We must say that in all their grandeur they never slackened in the ardent desire of doing that which is good and right; and that they were men of noble sentiment and bearing.'

Today Hund is a poor, run-down village. It is, however, beautifully situated on the bank of the Indus. Along the river bank there are millions of pottery shards.

Lahur, a small village three kilometres (two miles) west of the road from Swabi to Attock, was the birthplace of Panini, the great Sanskrit grammarian who taught at Taxila in the fourth century BC. The turning to Lahur is four kilometres (2.5 miles) beyond the turning to Hund.

There is evidence that Lahur was once a large city: five 20-metre (65-foot) -high but as yet unexcavated mounds surround the village. Xuan Zang claims that there was once a stupa in the city that commemorated the conversion of one of Panini's disciples to Buddhism—perhaps one of the five mounds hides this.

It seems likely that the ancient main road did not make the large loop round by Swabi, but cut more directly from Shahbaz Garhi to Lahur, on to Hund, and across the river to Taxila.

The modern main road continues southwest to **Jahangira**, so called because Emperor Jahangir (1605–27) built a bridge of boats across the Kabul River here. This has now been replaced by a modern bridge. At Jahangira you rejoin the Grand Trunk Road. Turn right for Peshawar or left for Attock.

SWAT

Historically Swat is the most interesting valley in Pakistan. It is also one of the most beautiful, as it lies in the monsoon belt and is greener and more fertile than the valleys further north. In lower Swat the valley is wide and the fields on either side of the river are full of wheat and lucerne; the villages here are prosperous and surrounded by fruit orchards. In upper Swat the narrow river tumbles through pine forests hemmed in by snowcapped mountains. Swat offers some of the best walking in Pakistan, as well as excellent fishing and climbing. The excavated archaeological sites here range from prehistoric caves through Aryan graveyards to Buddhist monasteries, of which here were once 1,400 in the valley.

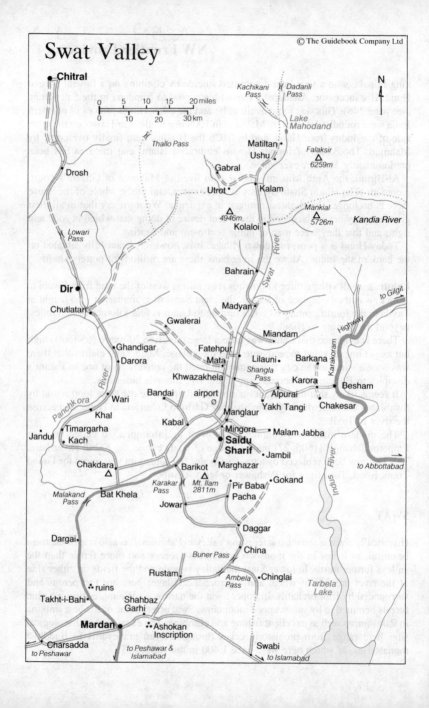

Swat Valley

© The Guidebook Company Ltd

N

● **Chitral**

Kachikani Pass · Dadarili Pass

Lake Mahodand

20 miles

0 5 10 15

0 10 20 30 km

Thallo Pass

Matiltan ●
Ushu ●
Falaksir △ 6259m

● Drosh

Gabral ●
Utrot ●
Kalam ●

Lowari Pass

△ 4946m.
Kolaloi ●
Mankial △ 5726m

Kandia River

Swat River

● **Dir**

Bahrain ●

Chutiatan ●

Madyan ●

to Gilgit

Gwalerai ●

Miandam ●

Karakoram Highway

● Ghandigar
● Darora

Fatehpur ●
Mata ●
Lilauni ●
Barkana ●

Shangla Pass

Khwazakhela ●
Karora ●
Besham ●

Bandai ● airport ⊘
Alpurai ●
Chakesar ●

● Wari

Kabal ●
Yakh Tangi ●

● Khal

Manglaur ●

Jandul ●
● Timargarha
Mingora ●
● Malam Jabba

Indus River

● Kach
● **Saidu Sharif**

Jambil ●

Chakdara ●
△

Barikot ●
Marghazar ●

to Abbottabad

Malakand Pass

Bat Khela ●

Karakar Pass
△ Mt. Ilam 2811m
Pir Baba ●
Pacha ●
Gokand ●

Jowar ●

Dargai ●

Daggar ●

China ●

Buner Pass

Tarbela Lake

Rustam ●
Chinglai ●

Ambela Pass

❖ ruins

Shahbaz Garhi ●

● Takht-i-Bahi

❖ Ashokan Inscription

● **Mardan**

Swabi ●

Charsadda ●
to Peshawar

to Peshawar & Islamabad

to Islamabad

Panchkora River

Getting to Swat

Swat has an airport at Mingora. The daily flight (except Tuesdays) from Islamabad takes 50 minutes and costs Rs210. The thrice-weekly flight from Peshawar takes 45 minutes and costs Rs170. There are daily bus and minibus services from Peshawar; if you are coming from Islamabad, change at Nowshera.

Three roads lead to Swat, all passable in ordinary cars. The shortest is via Mardan across the Malakand Pass, about 250 kilometres (155 miles), or four and a half hours, from Islamabad, or about 120 kilometres (75 miles), or three hours, from Peshawar (see next page). The most attractive route is via Shahbaz Garhi across the Ambela Pass to Buner, and thence across the Karakar Pass, about five and a half hours from Islamabad (see page 327). An interesting and scenic alternative is via Abbottabad and the Karakoram Highway to Besham, then across the Shangla Pass—about seven hours from Islamabad (see page 336).

Swat can easily be visited on the way to the Karakoram Highway and the Northern Areas. There are frequent bus services to the Karakoram Highway at Besham via the Shangla Pass. From Besham there are frequent buses north to Gilgit or south to Manshera. Buses also run to Chitral via Chakdara, Dir and the Lowari Pass.

When to Go

You can visit Swat in all seasons. The valley ranges between about 1,000 and 3,000 metres (3,300 and 10,000 feet) above sea level. In winter you can drive halfway up the valley, and from May to November right to the head of the valley, in an ordinary car.

Suggested Itinerary

October to April

Three days and two nights from Islamabad by car.
Day 1: Drive up via the Malakand Pass, stopping en route to visit:
    —Takht-e-Bahi, Buddhist ruins and monastery (see pages 307–10);
    —Chakdara Museum (see page 322);
    —Churchill Picket (sometimes out of bounds for tourists—see page 319);
    —Shingerdar Stupa (see page 325);
    —Mosque at Udegram and Raja Gira's castle (see pages 326–7).
Check in at hotel in Saidu Sharif or Mingora and in the evening drive to Marghazar, 13 kilometres (eight miles) up the Saidu Valley (see page 331).

Day 2: Drive slowly up the valley as far as you can. Plan to visit:
    —Swat Museum;
    —Butkara Stupa (see pages 329–331).
Stop for shopping in Khwazakhela, Madyan and Bahrain.

If you still have time, explore:
—Birkot Hill (see page 324);
—Gumbat Stupa (see page 325).

Day 3: Drive slowly home over the Shangla Pass if it is not blocked by snow (see page 336); otherwise take the Ambela Pass (see pages 327–8).

May to September
It will be too hot to make any stops on the way up to Swat.
Day 1: Drive straight to Swat over the Ambela Pass. Spend the night in Miandam.
Day 2: Drive up to Kalam, stopping to shop in Madyan and Bahrain. Continue beyond Kalam to the end of the road and walk. Spend the night at Kalam or Ushu.
Day 3: Drive home over the Shangla Pass.

To Swat via the Malakand Pass

From Islamabad go to Mardan either via Attock and Swabi, via Tarbela and Swabi, or via the Grand Trunk Road to Nowshera. (The last is the quickest but least interesting route.)

There is an unmarked bypass round Mardan to the west, but it is interesting to drive through the centre of Mardan to see the Cavagnari Arch (see page 298).

Takht-e-Bahi is 13 kilometres (eight miles) north of Mardan. The Buddhist monastery should be visited only in cool weather. There is a steep climb of 500 metres (yards) up the hill and no shade (see pages 307–10).

The **Malakand Pass** begins at Dargai. The road across the pass is in good condition but is always crowded with a continuous stream of trucks.

From the viewpoint about one kilometre (half a mile) before the top of the pass you can see the Swat Canal in the valley below. It was built by the British to channel water from the Swat River through a tunnel under the Malakand Pass to the plains around Mardan. You can also see the old Buddhist road winding round the side of the hill about 15 metres (50 feet) below the modern road. This originally led to a monastery below the pass, which was destroyed during the blasting of the canal tunnel.

Malakand Fort guards the road at the top of the pass, on the left. Here 1,000 Sikh infantry, under British command, held off 10,000 tribal warriors, led by the fanatical 'Mad Mullah' at the outbreak of the Pathan uprising in 1897, until reinforcements arrived from Mardan to relieve them.

On the other side of the pass the road descends through the market town of **Bat Khela**, with a Hindu Shahi fort perched above it, and continues past the headworks of the Swat Canal to the Swat River. The first bridge across the river is at Chakdara, which carries the road to Dir and Chitral.

Chakdara

Chakdara was an important centre for thousands of years because it was here that the trade route from Afghanistan, via Bajaur, crossed the Swat River.

Alexander the Great came this way in 327 BC with half his 50,000-man army (35,000 of whom had come from Europe). He captured the town of Massaga, now Kat Kala, 13 kilometres (eight miles) from Chakdara, on the road to Dir. The rest of his army undertook the more direct route through Mohmand tribal territory to Pushkalavati (see pages 305–6).

Chakdara Bridge, built in 1896 by the British, is guarded by Chakdara Fort, which was built in the same year on the foundations of Emperor Akbar's 16th-century fort. The fort is still used by the Pakistan army. There is a checkpost at the bridge where you will be asked for your identification papers.

Churchill Picket is on top of Damkot Hill, overlooking Chakdara Fort and bridge, and has a commanding view of the river from the Malakand Pass to Barikot. It also guards the road from Dir as it crosses the Chakdara Plain. Winston Churchill served here in 1897. Sometimes the army prevents tourists from climbing the hill, but if it is not too hot, the 15-minute walk up the path to the top is rewarding.

Winston Churchill writes with youthful exuberance of an incident in this area during the Pathan uprising in 1897, when he was sent to 'chastise the truculent assailants. The chastisement was to take the form of marching up the valley . . . destroying all the crops, breaking the reservoirs of water, blowing up as many castles as time permitted, and shooting anyone who obstructed the process.' Five British officers and 85 Sikhs marched ahead looking for exciting action. Suddenly:

There was a ragged volley from the rocks; shouts, exclamations, and a scream . . . . One man was shot through the breast and pouring with blood; another lay on his back kicking and twisting. The British officer was spinning round just behind me, his face a mass of blood, his right eye cut out. Yes, it was certainly an adventure.

It is a point of honour on the Indian frontier not to leave wounded men behind. Death by inches and hideous mutilation are the invariable measure meted out to all who fall in battle into the hands of the Pathan tribesmen . . . . We all laid hands on the wounded and began to carry and drag them away down the hill.

. . . I looked around to my left. The Adjutant had been shot. Four of his soldiers were carrying him . . . . Out from the edge of the houses rushed half a dozen Pathan swordsmen. The bearers of the poor Adjutant let him fall and fled at their approach. The leading tribesman rushed upon the prostrate figure and slashed it three or four times with his sword. I forgot everything else at this moment except a desire to kill this man. I wore my long cavalry sword well sharpened. After all, I had won the Public Schools fencing medal. I resolved on personal combat à l'arme blanche. The savage saw me coming. I was not more than twenty yards away. He picked up a big stone and hurled it at me with his left hand, and then awaited me, brandishing his sword. There were others waiting not far behind him. I changed my mind about the cold steel. I pulled my revolver, took, as I thought, most careful aim, and fired. No result. I fired again. No result. I fired again . . . . I looked around. I was all alone with the enemy . . . . I ran as fast as I could

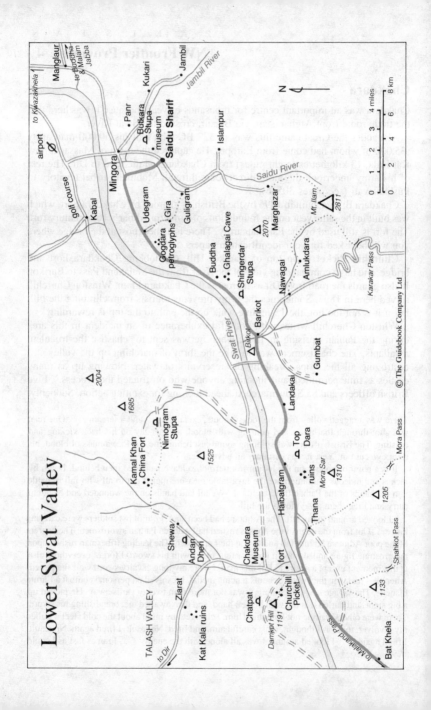

Lower Swat Valley

to Kwazakhela

Manglaur

te Buddha
& Malam
Jabba

airport

to Dir

TALASH VALLEY

Ziarat

Kat Kala ruins

Chatpat

Damkot Hill
1191

Churchill
Picket

Shewa

Andan
Dheri

Chakdara
Museum

fort

Kamal Khan
China Fort

1525

Nimogram Stupa

2004

1685

Kabal

golf course

Mingora

Udegram

Gogdara
petroglyphs

Gira

Guligram

Panr

Butkara
Stupa

museum

Saidu Sharif

Kukari

Jambil

Jambil River

Islampur

Saidu River

Buddha

Ghalagai Cave

Shingerdar
Stupa

Marghazar

Mt. Ilam
2811

2070

Nawagai

Amlukdara

Karakar Pass

Barikot

Bikoi

Swat River

Gumbat

Landakai

Top
Dara

Mora Sar
1310

ruins

1205

Haibatgram

Thana

Mora Pass

Shahkot Pass

1133

to Malakand

Malakand
Pass

Bat Khela

N

0   1   2   3   4 miles

0   2   4   6   8 km

© The Guidebook Company Ltd

.... I got to the first knoll. Hurrah, there were the Sikhs holding the lower one!
... We left one officer and a dozen men dead and wounded to be cut up by the enemy .... We fetched up at the bottom of the spur little better than a mob, ... while the tribesmen, who must have now numbered two or three hundred, gathered in a wide and spreading half-moon around our flanks ....

The Colonel said to me, 'The Buffs are not more than half a mile away. Go and tell them to hurry or we shall all be wiped out.'

... Meanwhile ... I heard an order: 'Volley firing. Ready. Present.' Crash! At least a dozen tribesmen fell. Another volley, and they wavered. A third, and they began to withdraw up the hillside. The bugler began to sound the 'Charge'. Everyone shouted. The crisis was over, and here, Praise be to God, were the leading files of the Buffs.

Then we rejoiced and ate our lunch.

My Early Life (1930)

The top of **Damkot Hill** has been excavated and is covered in ruins of different ages. The newest building is Churchill's Picket itself, a small fort built in 1896. The view from the roof is magnificent. On a clear day you can see the whole of the lower Swat Valley with the snow-clad mountains in the distance.

The Aryans arrived from Afghanistan and settled on the hill in about 1700 BC. They built stone houses, made elegant grey and black pottery on a slow wheel, and used stone and wooden tools for cultivating the land. At first they used only copper and gold for making jewellery, but subsequently they worked iron into knife blades, hoes, sheep shears and needles. Some of these items can be seen in the museum at Saidu Sharif.

There is an Aryan graveyard at the foot of Damkot Hill, on the north side. Excavations have revealed that the Aryans partly cremated their dead, then buried them with various utensils in graves lined and covered with large flat slabs of stone. The Aryans were the forerunners of the Hindus and composed the *Rigveda*, the oldest religious text in the world. In one of the 1,028 hymns still extant, a chief sings of a victory on the banks of the Suvastu—or Swat—River.

In the first century AD, Damkot Hill was occupied by Buddhists, who built a stupa and monastery just below the top of the hill on the south side overlooking the river. The monastery was burnt in the fifth century, probably by the White Huns; it was excavated in 1962–5 by A H Dani; only the foundations remain.

The Hindu Shahis occupied the hill in the eighth century. They built a large fort surrounded by a strong defensive wall that extended down to the river, thus ensuring a safe water supply. The houses, shops, stables and the remains of a smithy are still discernible on the northeastern side of the hilltop. The Hindu Shahi fort was destroyed by fire at the beginning of the 11th century, probably set by Mahmud of Ghazni, who invaded Swat in AD 1001, and the hill was not occupied again until the British came late in the 19th century.

Six boulders with Buddhist carvings on them stand at the foot of the hill to the west. The carved figures are mostly of Padmapani, the Lotus Bearer bodhisattva, here depicted with a slim body and diaphanous robes. The carvings date from the sixth or seventh century, when Buddhism, though on the decline, was still active in Swat.

There is a jeep track from Damkot Hill, along the north bank of the Swat River for 15 kilometres (ten miles) past more unexcavated Buddhist stupas, to another bridge across the river below Bat Khela.

Chakdara Museum is on the road to Dir and Chitral, two kilometres (a mile) from Chakdara Bridge. This small but excellent museum is located on the right at the road junction in the village. The collection of first- to seventh-century Buddhist Gandharan sculpture from nearby sites is well arranged and labelled and is of considerable importance, as many of the sculptures were found undisturbed in the Buddhist monasteries and could therefore be accurately dated. The museum also contains Hindu Shahi and local 19th- and 20th-century artefacts—farming tools, pottery, household utensils and embroidered dresses. The museum is open 8.30 am–12.30 pm and 2.30–5 pm in summer, and 9 am–4 pm from November to March; it is closed on Wednesday.

Enthusiasts visiting in winter can take a short, pleasant walk across the fields to **Chat Pat**, the site of a Buddhist monastery nestled into a fold in the hills beside a small stream. Start 1.6 kilometres (exactly a mile) from the Chakdara Bridge on the road to Dir, where the road fords a small stream. Follow the stream up (left from the road), past a village and into a tiny glen. The monastery is about one kilometre (half a mile) from the road on the left bank of the stream. Here the monks could retreat to meditate and still be within easy reach of alms-giving travellers.

The monastery dates from the late first to fourth century. There is no main stupa, and the monastery on the east side has been buried by a landslide. The Buddhist Gandharan sculptures that decorated the 38 small stupas and chapels show a surprising decline in style from the first to the fourth century. The Kushans brought artists with them from Bactria, in northern Afghanistan, when they first came, but subsequent generations seem to have been less talented. The sculpture is now on display in the Chakdara Museum.

Another winter expedition for enthusiasts is to the remains of **Andan Dheri Stupa**. Its foundations indicate that the stupa once stood 24 metres (80 feet) high. It was, in fact, the most important stupa in the Chakdara Plain. To get there take the road towards Dir for seven kilometres (four miles) from Chakdara Bridge; turn right down a metalled side road. The stupa ruins are just to the left of the side road, 500 metres (yards) from the main road to Dir.

The excavator A H Dani estimates that Andan Dheri dates from the late first to the early seventh century. It consisted of a main stupa, 14 votive stupas, and a monastic area which is now mostly ploughed under. Over 500 pieces of Gandharan sculpture were recovered, some of them in their original positions and therefore datable. Many of these sculptures can be seen in the Chakdara Museum; none remains on the site. Four hoards of coins from the Kushan period, indicating the names and dates of rulers, the style of dress and foreign trade links, were found here.

A famous legend about Buddha, in one of his earlier incarnations, is attached to the site. The Buddhist pilgrim Xuan Zang claims that this is where:

[Buddha] encountered a year of famine and pestilence. In order to save the people's lives, the Buddha, as Indra, changed himself into a great serpent lying dead in the valley. The starving and distressed, in response to a voice from the void, cut from his body pieces of flesh which were at once replaced, and all who ate were satisfied and cured.

The Hindu Shahi fort of **Kamal Khan China** stands on top of the range of hills that divides Dir from Swat. It is in ruins now, but must once have been imposing. To get there continue past Andan Dheri Stupa. At the village of Shewa, three kilometres (two miles) further on, take the footpath east for five kilometres (three miles). A guide from the museum is recommended.

Chakdara to Saidu Sharif

Back on the Malakand to Saidu Sharif road, the first village you come to is Thana, which is actually bypassed by the main road. Stacked steeply up the hillside, this prosperous little town is the starting point for the footpath across the **Mora Pass** to the Mardan Plain. It is a pleasant winter walk to the top of the pass.

From **Haibatgram**, the village on the main road eight kilometres (five miles) from Chakdara Bridge, you can walk up the ridge behind the village where there is an enormous Hindu Shahi fort of the eighth to tenth centuries. For more than two kilometres (a mile) the massive stone walls tumble down the hillside.

Top Dara Buddhist Stupa is nestled into a secluded valley on the side of Haibatgram Ridge, below the Hindu Shahi ruins. Top Dara is well preserved and there is a ruined monastery nearby. It can just be seen from the road if you know where to look.

Landakai, 12 kilometres (seven miles) from Chakdara Bridge, is the gateway to Swat District; all visitors must register at the barrier across the road. A rocky spur juts down from the hilltop to the river, forming a natural defence. Hindu Shahi forts crown each of the low ridges that run down from Landakai spur to the stream on its eastern side.

Nimogram Buddhist Monastery and Stupa are signposted on the left, seven kilometres (four miles) from Landakai. The Nimogram remains are 21 kilometres (13 miles) away on the other side of the river and up a rough road (see map on page 320) that runs through the beautiful and secluded Nimogram Valley.

Nimogram is unique in that it has three main stupas, one for each of the three principles of Buddhism: Buddha the teacher, Dharma (the Buddhist doctrine), and Sangha (the Buddhist order). Surrounding the main stupas are a number of votive stupas, and nearby is an unexcavated monastery site. Some of the superb sculpture found at Nimogram is now in the Swat Museum at Saidu Sharif. None remains on the site.

Birkot Hill is the site of the ancient town of Bazira, which was sacked by Alexander the Great in 327 BC. It is on the left (north) side of the main road, just past the turning to Nimogram, and just before the town of **Barikot**. Alexander took the town with difficulty, then left a garrison there to keep the inhabitants confined in the citadel while he marched further east up the Swat River to capture the town of Ora (near the modern town of Udegram, see page 326).

When the people of Bazira saw [him] departing with the greatest portion of his troops, they made light of the remaining Macedonians as antagonists no longer equal to themselves, and descended to the plain. A sharp encounter ensued in which 500 barbarians were killed and over 70 taken prisoner. The rest fled together [back] into the town.

Arrian, *Anabasis* (second century AD)

Arrian goes on to describe how the defenders of Bazira, on hearing of the fall of Ora, lost heart, and in the dead of night abandoned their town and fled to the Rock of Aornos (now thought to be Mount Ilam, see below).

It is an easy walk to the top of Birkot Hill to see the ruins of the Hindu Shahi fort (nothing remains from Alexander's time). There is one impressive stretch of defensive wall rising to a height of six metres (20 feet), which you can see from the main road beyond Barikot, looking back from the east. This wall originally enclosed a large area on the flattened hilltop, most of which is now cultivated; the small fields are arranged like the pieces of a jigsaw puzzle between the ruins inside the ancient town wall. The fort has not been excavated, but the local inhabitants dig round the ruins searching for coins, arrowheads and other marketable artefacts. The view from the top—the wide fertile plains along the river and sacred Mount Ilam rising up to the southeast of Barikot—is well worth the climb.

Mount Ilam, 2,811 metres (9,222 feet) high, is the largest hill in lower Swat. According to legend it has been sacred since prehistoric times. The locals believed it was the seat of their ancestors and the abode of tribal deities.

At the top are large square blocks of natural stone that may have been used as prehistoric altars. The mountain features prominently in the mythology of many religious groups, including the Buddhists, Lamaists, Hindus and Muslims. According to Xuan Zang, it was here that the Buddha, in a former incarnation, gave up his life to hear half a stanza of doctrine. Xuan Zang called it Mount Hilo, the Tibetans Mount Ilo. The Hindus carved the name of Sri Ram (Rama or Ramachandra, an incarnation of Vishnu and hero of the *Ramayana* epic) on a rock at the highest point. Until Partition in 1974, there was an annual Hindu pilgrimage to the 'throne' of Ramachandra.

Arrian's account of Alexander's battle on the mountain makes exciting reading. It took him seven days to prise the Swatis off the rocky pinnacle. He spent three of those days building a wooden ramp about 500 metres (yards) long across a ravine so that his catapults and arrows could reach the defenders. According to Arrian, Alexander himself 'was present to superintend, commending those that with eagerness advanced the work, and chastising anyone that at the moment was idling'. After the ramp was built, Alexander's soldiers hoisted and pushed each other up the cliff face and 'at the preconcerted signal they turned upon the retreating barbarians and slew many of them in flight; some others retreating in terror flung themselves down the precipices and died. Alexander thus became master of the rock which had baffled Herakles himself.'

At Barikot town the road from the Karakar Pass, Buner and the Ambela Pass joins the road from the Malakand Pass (see map on page 320). This is the most scenic route to Swat.

Gumbat Stupa is about nine kilometres (six miles) south of Barikot. To get there take the road towards the Karakar Pass; about one kilometre (half a mile) from Barikot a dirt road leads off to the right and follows the Kandak tributary for about eight kilometres (five miles) to a village. Ask here for directions. Not only is Gumbat one of the best-preserved Buddhist shrines in Swat, it is also uniquely shaped: its square central cell is surrounded on all sides by a narrow processional passage and is roofed with a 15-metre (50-foot) -high dome. Small windows in the passage and the cell light the inside; it probably once held a colossal standing image of Buddha. Nearby several grassy mounds hide small stupas. On the road between Gumbat and Barikot is a large ruined complex, known locally as Kanjar Kot, the Dancer's (or Prostitute's) Mansion, and also a pair of very dilapidated ruined stupas on large square bases.

The huge but crumbling **Shingerdar Stupa** is on the right of the main road, three kilometres (two miles) past Barikot on the road to Saidu Sharif. Local legend has it that it was built by King Uttarasena to house his share of the relics of the Lord Buddha. There is no record of who King Uttarasena actually was, and since the stupa was built some 700 or 800 years after Buddha's death, the story seems unlikely.

A **large Buddha** dating from the sixth century is carved on the cliff face directly beside the road 1.5 kilometres (a mile) beyond Shingerdar Stupa. The face is very battered; and the pile of stones at the base suggest that the locals, who are all strict Muslims, hurl rocks at the offending image as they pass.

A flight of cement steps to the left leads up to a natural grotto containing more carvings. These are also very battered, but you can just about make out a bearded figure standing on a pedestal supported by lions and flanked by smaller figures. The central figure has a halo round his head and wears a long coat over Cossack trousers tucked into top boots. This central-Asian costume, still worn in Kashgar today, is virtually identical to that depicted on Kushan coins of the first to the third century.

The **Gogdara** rock engravings are about 100 metres (yards) to the right of the road, about six kilometres (four miles) past the carved Buddha, just before the village of Udegram. A sign on the roadside points the way. The rock has recently been seriously defaced by the local villagers, who have chiselled their names all over it, but you can still see some of the charming 3,000-year-old engravings of stick figures driving two-wheeled war chariots, dogs, horses, ibex, leopards, oxen and other (unidentifiable) animals. These engravings are among the earliest petroglyphs found in Pakistan, and may well have been carved by the Aryans, who arrived in Swat driving two-wheeled war chariots.

There are Buddhist carvings from the sixth or seventh century higher up on the same rock, and again on the rock face about 100 metres (yards) further along the path on the right. These depict Padmapani, the Lotus Bearer bodhisattva, who is seated with his right leg tucked up, and flanked by two attendant figures.

Udegram

The village of Udegram is one of the most historically interesting in Swat. The site of the ancient town of Ora, where Alexander the Great fought one of his battles in 327 BC, Udegram was also the capital of the Hindu Shahi rulers in Swat from the eighth to the tenth century. You can see the massive ruins of the castle of Raja Gira, the last Hindu ruler, scattered up the hillside above the town. The earliest mosque in Swat, built in the 11th century in Mahmud of Ghazni's time, was excavated in 1985 just below the Hindu Shahi fort.

For those who enjoy walking and exploring, there is plenty to see on the hillside above Udegram. The best time to go is at dawn or in winter, as it is too hot during the day in summer. The climb right to the top of the hill is recommended and takes about one and a half hours.

The Udegram remains are up a track to the right (south) at the eastern end of the village. The first excavated ruins, 200 metres (yards) from the main road on the left of the track, consist of the foundations of **Ora** and date from the fourth century BC to the fourth century AD. As nothing is labelled, interpretation is difficult, but the Italian excavators deduced that this was the bazaar area and that most of the buildings were shops.

The **Shrine of Pir Khushab** (or **Khushal**) **Baba** is surrounded by a grove of trees about 500 metres (yards) away at the foot of the hill. Local tradition maintains that he was the commander of Mahmud of Ghazni's army and was supposedly killed during the long siege of Raja Gira's fortress. Arrowheads and human bones are scattered all over the hillside below the fortress.

The 11th-century **mosque** is in the centre of the hillside, halfway between the shrine and the main defensive wall of the fort. It is unlabelled, but ask anyone for the *purana masjid*, and you will be shown the way. The south wall of the mosque is protected by the mountain and stands about seven metres (23 feet) high. The west wall, with its arched mehrab in the centre, is also in quite good condition. You can see the bases of the ten pillars that once supported the roof over the prayer hall, and the ablution pool in the centre of the courtyard, surrounded by stone seats.

Raja Gira's castle is a steep but rewarding half-hour climb up the hillside, from where there are fine views down over the Swat Valley. The track up is the old road made by the Italian excavators in the 1950s; it ends at the bottom of a monumental flight of steps, eight metres (26 feet) wide, that lead up to the citadel. From the steps you can see the massive defensive walls built of unmortared stone between the eighth and tenth centuries. Inside the fort corridors separate the rooms. The excavators identified 20 different periods of building and occupation. Nothing is labelled, but you can scramble around the ruins looking for arrowheads, coins and fragments of pottery.

Most of the buildings in the ruined town date from the Hindu Shahi period, but the site was occupied from about 1000 BC up to the 14th century. The enormous town is roughly triangular in shape, with the fort at the northwestern corner.

The defensive walls climb from the citadel for about a kilometre (half a mile) up to the crest of the hill, then follow the top of the sharp ridge separating the Swat and Saidu valleys. There are magnificent views in all directions from the top, up to Mount Ilam, back down the valley to Chakdara, and on up to the snow-covered mountains at the head of the Swat Valley. From the top of the hill the wall runs down the eastern side of the ruined town, along a precipitous rocky spur to a spring at the head of the gully. This was once heavily defended because it was the only source of water for the whole town; water was brought from the well along a series of channels to holding tanks at the foot of the castle's giant stairway. The Italian excavators lined one of these tanks with cement and used the original water system.

To Swat via the Ambela and Karakar Passes

From Islamabad go to Shahbaz Garhi either via Attock and Swabi or via Tarbela and Swabi. From Peshawar go to Shahbaz Garhi via Charsadda and Mardan, or via Nowshera and Mardan (the quickest but least interesting route).

The scenic road from Shahbaz Garhi to Swat is passable in an ordinary car. At Shahbaz Garhi turn north to **Rustam** (see map on page 316); in Rustam turn right (east) and cross the **Ambela Pass** to Buner. The jeep road straight on (north) in Rustam leads to the Malandrai Pass, 25 kilometres (15 miles) away, which also leads to Buner.

From the Ambela Pass you can see down over the Peshawar Plain. This was the scene of the Ambela campaign in 1863, when British troops spent two foggy winter months trying to subdue 15,000 Mujahideen freedom fighters (or 'Hindustani Fanatics', as the British called them), who had been raiding the Peshawar Valley from their hideout in Malka, Buner. You can still see several British forts in the pass.

After the Ambela Pass the road descends into a small valley with a pleasant picnic spot on a small, pine-covered hill on the right of the road. This unexcavated site is now a sacred grave area; it is quiet and secluded and full of birds. From near here a jeep road leads right to Chinglai and south to Swabi. Ask in the village about the condition of the road before attempting it.

The main road climbs up across the **Buner Pass**, 894 metres (2,935 feet), and comes down to **China** (pronounced *Cheena*), from where it is only four kilometres (2.5 miles) to **Daggar**. From Daggar a newly repaired road leads left (west) to **Jowar**, but if you have plenty of time it is interesting to detour north via Pacha and Pir Baba to see the Shrine of Syed Ali, who was reputedly the grandson of the Moghul emperor Babur.

Pir Baba is one of Pakistan's most popular shrines; devotees flock here by the thousands, particularly during the urs. The path to the shrine is lined with beggars on one side and with pretty boys on the other selling khol and perfume. Behind the shrine is a separate mosque for women, and behind this is the *baithak*, where fakirs can meditate.

From Pir Baba to Barikot is 45 kilometres (28 miles), first across the plains of Buner, a fairytale landscape of rugged, steep-sided hills rearing sharply out of the flat plain on the left and views up the rocky slopes of the sacred Mount Ilam on the right. The road then climbs up through mature pine forests to the **Karakar Pass**, 1,336 metres (4,384 feet) above sea level. At the top of the pass there is a Forestry Department rest house (book through the divisional forest officer, Mingora, tel. 2149) and a superb view over the Buner Valley. This makes a good winter weekend base from which to explore Mount Ilam (see pages 324–5).

At the Karakar Pass, Emperor Akbar lost most of his 8,000-man army in his abortive attempt to invade Swat in 1586. From the top of the pass down to Barikot the road runs through the pine forest.

For the route from Barikot to Saidu Sharif see pages 324 and 332.

Saidu Sharif and Mingora

Saidu Sharif and Mingora are twin towns two kilometres (a mile) apart. Saidu Sharif is the administrative capital of Swat Division, and Mingora is the district headquarters and main bazaar area. Both are 990 metres (3,250 feet) above sea level. See page 317 for transport information. The last super-grade **petrol** in Swat is in Mingora; the last ordinary grade is in Bahrain.

The **Tourist Information Centre** is in the Swat Serena Hotel, tel. 2220. You can also change travellers cheques here.

Where to stay

Moderate: Rs300–600

Swat Serena, Saidu Sharif, tel. 4215, 4604. Or book through Serena, Karachi, tel. 537506–9, telex SERENA PK (s/d Rs450/600). International standard, with good food and service in old colonial style.

Pameer, Grand Trunk Road. Mingora, tel. 4926, 4306. In the centre of town.

Cheaper: Rs25–80

Udyana, Grand Trunk Road, Mingora, tel. 4876 (s/d Rs50/80).

Holiday, Makan Bagh, Saidu Sharif Road, tel. 4443 (s/d Rs40/60).

Abaseen, New Madyan Road, Mingora, tel. 2122 (s/d Rs25/40).

There are about 30 other middle-range and cheap hotels in Mingora along the Grand Trunk Road, Madyan Road and around Green Chowk. The real cheapies do not accept foreigners.

Sights

Mingora has been an important trading centre for at least 2,000 years. Its bazaars are worth exploring for semi-precious stones, locally woven and embroidered cloth and tribal jewellery.

At Saidu Sharif there is the Swat Museum, the remains of Butkara Stupa, the Wali of Swat's palace, and the tomb of the Akund of Swat.

The Akund of Swat was a charismatic but bellicose Sufi ascetic who rose to power in the 19th century, united the Swatis and made his capital at Saidu Sharif. He has been immortalized in the west by Edward Lear (1812–88).

Who or why, or which, or what,
Is the Akund of Swat?
Is he tall or short, or dark or fair?
Does he sit on a stool or a sofa or chair, or squat,
The Akund of Swat? . . .

The Akund's death in 1877 was followed by 40 years of tribal feuding until the Akund's grandson, Miangul Wadud, aided by the British, was accepted as *badshah* (king). In 1926 the British acknowledged Swat as a separate state and Miangul Wadud as the *wali* (ruler). In 1949 he abdicated in favour of his son, Miangul Jehanzeb, who continued to develop Swat, building roads, schools and hospitals and revising the laws governing the distribution of land. In 1969 Swat was fully absorbed into Pakistan as Swat District.

The **Saidu Sharif Museum**, on the left halfway from Mingora to Saidu Sharif, has a disappointing collection of Gandharan sculpture from some of the Buddhist sites in Swat; many are reproductions. The ethnographic section features local embroidery, carved wood and tribal embroidery. A few 19th-century coins and weapons are also on display. The museum is open 10 am–4.30 pm, October to March; and 8 am–12 noon and 3–6 pm, April to September.

Butkara Stupa, near the museum, is one of the most important Buddhist shrines in Swat. To get there take the dirt track on the left (north) side of the museum for one kilometre (half a mile); the stupa is 400 metres (yards) from the track across the fields to the left (north).

Butkara Stupa was first built in about the second century BC, possibly by the Mauryan emperor Ashoka to house some of the ashes of the Lord Buddha. In subsequent centuries it was enlarged five times by adding new shells around the

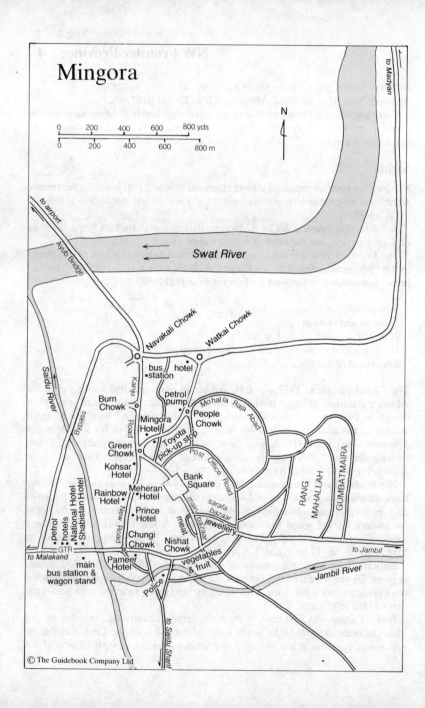

Mingora

0 200 400 600 800 yds

0 200 400 600 800 m

N

to Madyan

to airport

Ayub Bridge

Swat River

to airport

Saidu River

Bypass

Navakali Chowk

Watkai Chowk

Kanju Road

bus station

hotel

petrol pump

Burn Chowk

Mohalla Raja Abad

Mingora Hotel

People Chowk

Toyota pick-up stop

Green Chowk

Post Office Road

Kohsar Hotel

Bank Square

RANG MAHALLAH

GUMBATMAIRA

Rainbow Hotel

Meheran Hotel

sarafa bazaar

New Road

Prince Hotel

main bazaar

meat

Jewellery

to Jambil

petrol hotels

National Hotel

Shabistan Hotel

Chungi Chowk

Nishat Chowk

GTR

to Malakand

main bus station & wagon stand

Pameer Hotel

vegetables & fruit

Jambil River

Police

to Saidu Sharif

© The Guidebook Company Ltd

original stupa, each new stupa completely enclosing the old one inside. In 1955 Italian excavators exposed the successive layers, which showed the evolution of construction techniques. The first stupa was enlarged three times before the birth of Christ.

At the beginning of the third century the peaceful rule of the Kushans brought unprecedented prosperity, and as Buddhism in Swat approached its zenith Butkara became a famous pilgrimage centre. The stupa was enlarged again and richly decorated with stone and plaster carvings depicting the life of Buddha; the whole structure was gilded and painted and topped by stone umbrellas.

Most of the stone carvings have been removed to museums around the world, but two of green schist, dating from the fifth century, have been left in place. There is a headless Buddha low down on the east side, and a Buddha standing on a lotus flower between three rows of acolytes on the north side. Some small fragments of other statues still stand around the base of the stupa.

Votive stupas were built around the main stupa by rich pilgrims hoping to gain merit. There were 215 of these, all decorated with statues, painted, gilded and topped with stone umbrellas. Today only the bases remain. The best-preserved are on the north side of the main stupa. You can still see some of the decoration; green schist columns, lions with full curly manes, eagles, stylized lilies, cupids on lotus flowers, and a few traces of red and blue paint. Scattered all around the site are circular stone umbrellas resembling mill stones that have fallen from the various stupas. According to the excavator Professor Tucci, some pilgrims built columns crowned by statues. The stone and limestone statues of lions crouching on their haunches to the east of the main stupa may well have stood on some of these columns.

Butkara lies between the Jambil and Saidu rivers and was often flooded; it is also on the fault line between the Indian and Asian geological plates and is frequently shaken by earthquakes. While the Buddhists were wealthy the shrine was repaired whenever damaged, but in the seventh century devastating floods covered the area and the monastery was abandoned for a time.

In the eighth century the stupa was roughly repaired. By this time the Hindu Shahi kings had arrived, and most of the remaining Buddhists adhered to Tantrism. Soon after this Butkara was abandoned.

Marghazar is a small village at the top of the Saidu Valley, 1,287 metres (4,222 feet) above sea level and 13 kilometres (eight miles) from Saidu Sharif. The Saidu stream cascades down off Mount Ilam. You can stay in the Marghazar Hotel, the converted summer palace of the first Wali of Swat. The old Hindu pilgrim path up Mount Ilam follows the Saidu stream up behind the palace. It is a superb all-day hike to the top and back, and you can also cross over the shoulder of the mountain and come down to Pir Baba. Even if you do not plan to go all the way to the top, it is worth following the stream a little way up.

At **Islampur**, a village two kilometres (a mile) off the main Saidu–Marghazar road, you can see handloom weaving and buy handwoven shawls and blankets.

Guligram is the starting point for a trek north across the range of steep hills that divides the Saidu Valley from Udegram (see page 326). You can see the defensive walls of the Hindu Shahi town along the top of the hill. The footpath to Udegram crosses the pass to the left (south) of the fortified town.

The **Jambil Valley** can be reached by road from Mingora. This valley is studded with numerous Buddhist ruins and carvings. At **Panr**, Italians have excavated a stupa and monastery dating from the first century, and at Butkara II, Loebanr and Matelai they have unearthed 475 Aryan graves dating from about 1700 BC. From the top of the Jambil Valley a path leads over the hills to Gokand, in Buner.

From Mingora a bridge crosses the River Swat to the airport and to the golf course at Kabal. The road on the other side of the river is motorable down to Chakdara and up to Khwazakhela.

UPPER SWAT

Swat Valley is blocked by snow above Bahrain in winter, but in summer you can drive up beyond Kalam and from there trek north to either the Chitral or Gilgit Valley. Swat becomes more and more beautiful the higher you go. From Khwazakhela the road across the Shangla Pass to the Karakoram Highway and Gilgit is open from May to November only.

From the General Bus Station in Mingora you can catch minibuses to Kalam for about Rs10. The buses from the New Road Bus Station are slightly cheaper but are very slow and dirty, and are not recommended. Buses to the Karakoram Highway cost about Rs15.

Mingora to Madyan

Just north of Mingora a rocky spur juts down to the river. This once formed a natural line of defence for upper Swat, and the main road, built in the 1930s, has been cut along a shelf at the base of this rock. Before the road was built all travellers had either to wade in the river or climb the rock, depending on the season.

At **Manglaur**, the first town north of Mingora, a metalled road leads off to the right (east), three kilometres (two miles) to the Jahanabad Buddha and 30 kilometres (19 miles) to Malam Jabba.

The **Jahanabad Buddha** is a huge seated figure four metres (13 feet) high, carved in the seventh century on the face of a large rock on the other side of the river. The round-faced Buddha sits crosslegged, his hands folded in his lap. To reach the carving cross the river by the next bridge, in Jahanabad village, and walk back.

The metalled side road continues to the ski resort of **Malam Jabba**, with its 50-room hotel, one ski run, and summer pony trekking and mini-golf facilities. The one-hour drive up to Malam Jabba takes you through steep hills, some of which are terraced all the way to the top and covered in fruit and pine trees. You can see the main road across the Shangla Pass to the Karakoram Highway running parallel a few kilometres (miles) to the left (north). It is an easy hike along the ridge from one road to the other.

At **Khwazakhela**, about 30 kilometres (20 miles) from Mingora on the banks of the Swat River, the road across the Shangla Pass to the Karakoram Highway leaves the Swat Valley (see page 336). It is 69 kilometres (43 miles) from here to Besham, on the Indus, and 70 kilometres (43 miles) to Kalam at the top of the Swat Valley. Khwazakhela is the largest commercial centre in this part of the valley. The main street is worth exploring for silver tribal jewellery, locally woven and embroidered fabrics, carved woodwork, semi-precious stones and ancient coins. There is a thriving business in forged ancient coins in Swat, so very few (if any) are as old as they seem. Similarly, most of the antique woodwork is newly carved and blackened.

The bridge across the Swat River at Khwazakhela leads to a metalled road that follows the river down all the way to Chakdara. Jeep tracks lead up most of the side valleys on the other side of the river.

Miandam is a small summer resort ten kilometres (six miles) up a steep side valley, and 56 kilometres (35 miles), or one hour's drive, from Saidu Sharif. The turning is clearly marked, and the good metalled road runs through charming hillside villages, where the roofs of one row of houses form the street for the row above. Tiny terraced fields step up the hillside right to the top. Tools are scarce here, and you often see two or even three men working one spade to dig potatoes, one man holding the handle, and the others pulling on ropes attached just above the head of the spade. Ploughs usually consist of simple wooden pointed beams yoked to two oxen; rakes of simple wooden spikes attached to frames.

From Miandam there are beautiful walks up the Miandam stream past houses with beehives set into the walls and symbols to ward off evil whitewashed around the doors. In the graveyards the wooden graveposts are decorated with floral designs that resemble those used by the Buddhists 1,000 years ago.

Where to Stay in Miandam

At 1,800 metres, Miandam is the best place to spend your first night in Swat in summer. There are four hotels, all moderately priced.

PTDC Motel, tel.10, or book through PTDC, Rawalpindi, tel. 481480–4 (s/d Rs275/350). Well positioned, with a lovely garden and helpful staff. If all the rooms are full, take a spare bed outside and sleep under the trees in the garden.

Miandam Hotel, tel. Miandam 10 (s/d Rs150/300).

Pameer Guest House; book through Pameer Hotel, Mingora, tel. 4926.

Karashma Hotel (s/d Rs50/100).

Camping is allowed.

In the off-season, bargain for lower rates.

Madyan

Madyan is a tourist resort on the Swat River. At 1,321 metres (4,335 feet) above sea level, it is neither as cool nor as beautiful as Miandam, but it has many hotels of all price ranges, and being a large town has many tourist shops and restaurants, as well as a cinema. Antique and modern shawls, traditional embroidery, tribal jewellery, carved wood and antique or reproduction coins are sold in the shops down the main street. The shawls are woven in the side valley east of Madyan, where this cottage industry has been thriving for 2,000 years. Until the beginning of this century natural vegetable dyes were used, but these are now unobtainable, so modern shawls are designed with brilliant red, green, blue and yellow stripes on a black background.

The central mosque at Madyan has carved wooden pillars with elegant scroll capitals typical of Swat. The mud-plastered west wall is covered in floral relief.

A path from the top end of the side valley east of Madyan leads over to the Dubair Valley and down to the Indus River and the Karakoram Highway. This was one of the old trade routes. Do not hike alone here, as the path crosses into Kohistan, where the locals are notorious for their ferocity.

Where to Stay in Madyan

Madyan Hotel, tel. 2, 34 (Rs200–300). Right on the river.
Mountain View, tel. 7 (s/d Rs100/200).
Nisar, tel. 441 (s/d Rs70/140).
Shalimar, tel. 14 (s/d Rs40/60 in season; Rs20/40 off).
Parkway (s/d Rs25/40 in season; Rs15/30 off).
There are other cheaper hotels (s/d Rs15/25).

Bahrain to Kalam

Ten kilometres north of Madyan and about 1,400 metres (4,500 feet) above sea level, Bahrain is another popular tourist resort on the Swat River. The bazaars of Bahrain, like those of Mingora, Khwazakhela and Madyan, are worth exploring for handicrafts. The backstreets, especially the steep street on the northern bank of the side river, are also interesting. Some of the houses have carved wooden doors, pillars and balconies with a remarkable variety of decorative motifs, including floral scrolls and ornamental diaper bands almost identical to those seen on the Buddhist shrines and quite different from the usual Muslim designs. There used to be two old mosques in this street with intricately carved wooden pillars, but recent information indicates that these have been replaced by cement. Ask if there are any other old mosques in the area, as the carving is lovely.

Bahrain has the last petrol pump in Swat. North of Bahrain the metalled road is normally open from April or May to November. The valley it runs through is very narrow and heavily forested. At times the road rises to 100 metres (300 feet) or so above the river, giving fine views on the right across the river to Mankial Mountain; at other times the road follows the bank of the river, which is spanned occasionally by wooden cantilever bridges or by precarious cable cars consisting of wooden platforms suspended from a steel cable strung between two trees on either side of the river, and hauled across by rope. The ride across is smoother and less terrifying than you might expect.

From **Kolaloi** a footpath leads east across the mountains to the Kandia Valley and down to the Indus. This was one of the main trade routes in ancient times, but now should not be followed without a guide.

If you like walking there is a gentle footpath along the far side of the river passing small villages and water mills where grain is ground between revolving mill stones.

At **Kalam**, 29 kilometres (18 miles) from Bahrain, and about 2,000 metres (6,800 feet) above sea level, the valley opens out into a fertile little plain that was probably once the basin of an ancient lake. The administrative office, police station, PTDC motel and information office, and the Falakseer Hotel are up on this plateau. Down by the river, along the main road by the bus stop, are more hotels (some of them cheaper). Kalam is cool in summer and a good base for those who enjoy hiking.

The mosque down by the river at Kalam features excellent wood-carving. Gigantic scrolls form the capitals of the pillars, and some of the beams are ten metres (33 feet) long.

Where to Stay in Kalam

PTDC Motel, tel. 14, or book through PTDC, Rawalpindi, tel. 481480–4 (s/d Rs275/ 350). Nice position with a large garden.

Falakseer, tel. 10 (d Rs325 in season; Rs200 off). Good position.

Khalid, tel. 6 (d Rs300 in season; Rs150 off). Down by the river.

Heaven Breeze, Falak Naz and Kalam (Rs100–150).

Mehran (d Rs45 in season; Rs25 off).

Camping is free in the PTDC Motel garden. It is not recommended elsewhere, as the people in the area (Kohistanis) are sometimes hostile.

Above Kalam

Just beyond Kalam is the junction of the Ushu and Utrot rivers, which together form the Swat. Dirt roads follow each river, both passable in ordinary cars in summer. It is 16 kilometres (ten miles) up the Utrot River to Utrot village, about 2,200 metres (7,300 feet) above sea level, past pine-shaded picnic spots by a rock-strewn stream full of fish. The modern Muslim graves in this area are surrounded by intricately carved wooden railings.

The Gabral Valley enters **Utrot** from the northwest. There are rest houses at both Utrot and Gabral, and the walking and fishing are excellent. A fishing permit is required. For more information enquire at the PTDC motel in Kalam. You should bring your own tackle.

From Utrot it is a two-day hike to Dir.

The **Ushu Valley** runs northeast from Kalam and offers magnificent views of **Mount Falaksir** (6,257 metres, or 20,528 feet), numerous picnic spots, and superlative fishing and hiking. It is eight kilometres (five miles) to **Ushu**, at about 2,300 metres (7,500 feet), where there is the Ushu Hotel ('absolutely safe') and a rest house. You can usually drive a jeep a few kilometres (miles) past the last village, **Matiltan** (also with a rest house), towards **Lake Mahodand**, or the Lake of the Fishes, about ten kilometres (six miles) to the north. It is safe to camp in the grassy pastures by the lake.

From Mahodand Lake you can trek northwest over the **Kachikani Pass**, 4,816 metres (15,800 feet), to Laspur in the Chitral Valley; north over the **Dadarili Pass** to Handrap in the Gilgit Valley; or east to the Kandia Valley and down to the Indus (see maps on pages 338 and 402). For these treks you will need a guide, porters, and all your food for six days, as the area is rugged and uninhabited. You cross glaciers and rough stony ground at high altitude.

There are many more treks of varying degrees of difficulty that are possible in upper Swat. The guides at Kalam can help you choose one and show the way. The PTDC will also advise you. Please note, though, that experienced trekkers claim it is better to trek from Chitral or Gilgit to Swat as the porters in Kalam can be troublesome.

Warning: It is dangerous to swim in the Swat River, to drive at night in upper Swat and to camp other than in recognized camp-sites. Young boys in Swat enjoy throwing stones and are good shots with slings and catapults.

Kwazakhela to Besham

From **Kwazakhela** it is 69 kilometres (43 miles) to Besham, a drive of about two hours on a scenic road through steeply terraced hills and pine forests across the **Shangla Pass**, with views back down to the Swat Valley, and right to the Malam Jabba Valley. It is only 20 kilometres (12 miles) to the top of the pass, a recommended drive even if you do not intend to continue on down to Besham. There is a rest house at Shangla and another at **Yakh Tangi**, five kilometres (three miles) on the other side of Shangla Pass. The road is lovely here, as it twists through the pine forest and is hemmed in by steep hills, the stream rushing far below.

Alpuri, 34 kilometres (21 miles) from Kwazakhela, is an administrative centre with a cluster of buildings roofed in corrugated iron: the assistant commissioner's office, police, school and a few local hotels all nestle together in a hollow. About five kilometres (three miles) past Alpuri is a good place to start walking along the stream back to Yakh Tangi.

At **Dherai** village, 12 kilometres (seven miles) past Alpuri, there is a large deposit of china clay. It is not being exploited—except by the locals, who use the white clay to whitewash their houses.

It is 23 kilometres (14 miles) from Dherai to Besham (see pages 382–3).

CHITRAL

Chitral is a long, isolated valley in the northwestern corner of Pakistan. The Hindu Kush Range, dominated by Tirich Mir, separates it from Afghanistan and the USSR on the west and north, and the lower Hindu Raj Mountains divide it from the rest of Pakistan on the east and south. For five or six months of the year the land route into the valley is blocked by snow. Only two roads enter the valley, one from Dir in the south across the 3,118-metre (10,230-foot) Lowari Pass, and the other, a jeep track from Gilgit in the east across the 3,734-metre (12,250-foot) Shandur Pass. In winter, the one tenuous lifeline with the rest of the country is the small Fokker Friendship aircraft which on clear days flies in through the mountains.

The narrow, 320-kilometre (200-mile) -long valley is home to about a quarter of a million people. North of Chitral town there is very little rainfall, and, as in Gilgit and Baltistan, the villages are small irrigated oases strung along the banks of the rivers. The square stone houses are set amid tiny terraced fields of wheat and maize. Poplars and fruit trees festooned with grapevines border the fields and surround the houses and help prevent them sliding down the mountainsides. It is the contrast between the vivid man-made patches of green, the barren brown slopes, and the towering snow-capped mountains above these, that gives Chitral its startling, unforgettable beauty.

Until 1970 Chitral was an isolated kingdom ruled by a *mehtar*, whose family is still respected in Chitral. Since its incorporation into Pakistan, Chitral has been governed directly by Pakistan through the deputy commissioner in Chitral town.

At some 1,500 metres (5,000 feet) above sea level, Chitral town is snow-bound in winter, but not too hot in summer. Not many tourists find their way into this remote valley, where the moutaineering and trekking are superb.

The valley's other attractions are the uninterrupted view of Tirich Mir (pronounced *Tirishmeer*), at 7,708 metres (25,288 feet) the tallest peak in the Hindu Kush Range, and the Kafir Kalash people, a non-Muslim tribe that lives in three picturesque valleys close to the Afghan border (see page 344).

When to Go

Chitral is best visited from April to October. In April the passes are still blocked by snow, but the weather is clear and there should be no difficulty with flights. In July and August the monsoons, which extend to just south of Chitral town, often result in cancelled flights. Take some warm clothes, as the evenings can be chilly even ir summer.

Getting to Chitral

The easiest way to reach Chitral is by air from Peshawar. There are three daily flights, providing the weather is clear. You need to book several days in advance and

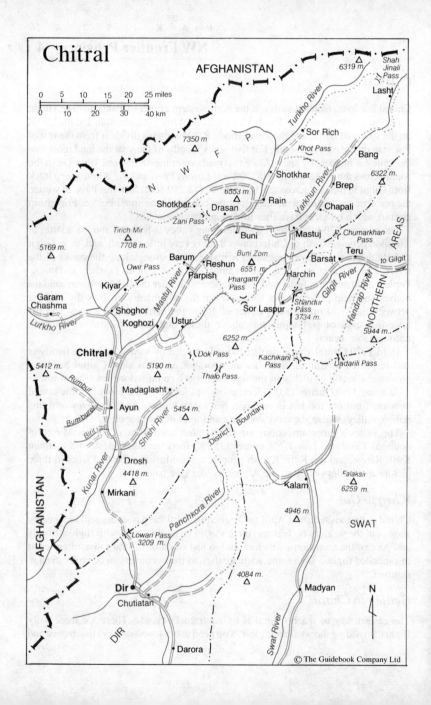

be prepared for cancellation. The flight takes one hour, costs only Rs195, and is spectacular. If possible, sit on the left-hand side of the plane to see the remote tribal areas along the border of Afghanistan, with the sharp, snowcapped Hindu Kush beyond.

The most interesting way to reach Chitral is by road via the Malakand Pass, Dir and the Lowari Pass. During the summer **buses** and **minibuses** leave Peshawar daily for Dir, where usually you must change, but two minibuses daily go right through to Chitral. Buses for Dir leave from the Government Transport Terminal on the Grand Trunk Road near Hashnagri Gate and also from the bus station in Namak Mandi; they cost Rs27. Minibuses for Chitral (the service is known as the Flying Coach) leave from the new bus station on the Grand Trunk Road about three kilometres (two miles) from the main bus station, from Cinema Road, and from the new bus stand in Peshawar city. This arrangement may be temporary. The fare is Rs130 per person, or Rs2,500 for a whole minibus. You can also hire a Datsun pickup for Rs1,500 from Peshawar to Chitral or jeeps in Peshawar or Islamabad for Rs5–6 per mile, plus overnight charges for the driver. Vehicles from Dir into the Chitral Valley do not leave to a set schedule, but there are plenty of them. It costs Rs40 by bus and Rs70 by jeep-taxi from Dir to Chitral.

From Mingora in Swat you can get to Chitral by bus or minibus, but you must change at Chakdara Bridge.

It is a very long day's drive of 10 to 15 hours from Peshawar to Chitral town (add one hour if coming from Islamabad). It is possible, though not very comfortable, to break the journey at Dir town (about five hours from Peshawar by jeep), where you can stay in the rest house, a local hotel, or camp. The Lowari Pass is open only from April or May until November. You do not need a permit, but there are a couple of checks on the way, so take some form of identification with you. It is sometimes possible to get to Chitral in an ordinary car, but for safety's sake a four-wheel drive high-clearance vehicle is recommended for the Lowari Pass.

From Chakdara Bridge across the Swat River in lower Swat it is 226 kilometres (140 miles) to Chitral town. The journey takes 8–12 hours in a private jeep, longer by bus.

Chakdara to Chitral

Dir District begins at Chakdara Bridge. The independent kingdom of Dir was absorbed into Pakistan only in 1962. Since one of the main trade routes from eastern Afghanistan passed through lower Dir, there are several places of historical interest to see along the way.

About 13 kilometres (eight miles) from Chakdara Bridge the main road turns west and enters the Talash Valley. The Buddhists built monasteries and stupas in the side valleys on both sides of the main road; the monks lived off the offerings from passing pilgrims and traders. None of these remains has been excavated, but they date from the second to the ninth century. At the west end of the valley, at the narrowest point, is the Kat Kala Pass. The ancient fort of Kat Kala stands on the left above the village of Ziarat.

Kat Kala (Fort of the Pass) once guarded the entrance to the Chakdara Plains. There has been a fort here for over 2,000 years, but the massive ruins that you see today are the remains of a Hindu Shahi fort dating from the eighth to the tenth century. Its solid walls are strengthened with rectangular bastions and circular towers.

According to Sir Olaf Caroe, Kat Kala may well have been the site of Massaga, once the most important town in the area. In 327 BC Alexander the Great arrived from Afghanistan with half his army and terrified the defenders of Massaga with war engines, movable towers and giant catapults that he had dragged over the mountains with him. His 25,000 men took four days to overrun the town, which was defended by 30,000 infantry, 2,000 cavalry and 30 elephants.

They sent down envoys to the king to sue for pardon. This being granted, the queen came with a great train of noble ladies who poured out libations of wine in golden bowls. The queen herself, having placed her son, a child, at Alexander's knees, obtained not only pardon but permission to retain her former dignity, for she was styled queen, and some have believed that this indulgent treatment was accorded rather to the charms of her person than to pity for her misfortunes. At all events she afterwards gave birth to a son who received the name of Alexander, whoever his father may have been.

Curtius (first century AD)

Soon after the Talash Valley, the main road to Dir turns north again and runs along the east bank of the Panchkora River (River of Five Districts), where fishermen throw circular nets into the water. This area lies within the monsoon belt, so the green hillsides are terraced right to the top; there is no need for irrigation.

Timargarha, 48 kilometres (30 miles) from Chakdara, at the junction of the Jandul and the Panchkora rivers, is the capital of Dir District. The Jandul flows in from Bajaur, a remote tribal area out of bounds for tourists. The ancient trade route from Afghanistan followed the Jandul River, and Timargarha developed as a trading post. According to Aurel Stein, it was here that Alexander the Great probably crossed with his army.

Simple and cheap accommodation is at the New Khyber, on the Grand Trunk Road.

On the right-hand side of the road in the centre of Timargarha is an excavated Aryan grave site dating from 1500 to 600 BC. The graves are lined with large slabs of stone; their contents have been removed to the museum in Swat but are not on display.

Crossing the bridge at Timargarha to the west side of the Panchkora River you reach the excavated site of **Balambat**, just south of the modern fort. This site has been occupied almost continuously since 1500 BC, by Aryans, Buddhists, Hindus and Muslims. Most of the excavated houses date from about 500 BC. The most interesting discoveries here were fire altars—and even today juniper is burnt on fire stands by Swati fortune tellers.

The road hugs the river for the 78 kilometres (48 miles) from Timargarha to the town of **Dir**. Around Dir the valley is narrow and wooded. Dir itself is small and dirty, its one claim to fame being its well-made pocket knives. Most males over the age of 15 parade in the street carrying a rifle or Kalashnikov machine gun. Ordinary-grade petrol is available here, and there is a fairly basic rest house bookable through the PTDC in Peshawar, tel. 72428, 76481 or 76431, and a local hotel.

From Dir there are several trekking paths across the hills to Kalam, in upper Swat. The deputy commissioner, police or Dir scouts in Timargarha will give advice on the condition and safety of the routes.

The **Lowari Pass**, at 3,118 metres (10,230 feet) above sea level, is the most spectacular section of the journey. It is 74 kilometres (46 miles) of pretty rough going from Dir town across the pass to Drosh. The road zigzags up through pine forests to the summit. From the top you see lower Chitral spread below you with row upon row of barren mountains, and in the distance the snow-clad Hindu Kush. The descent is steep and winding, dropping 2,000 metres (7,000 feet) from the top of the pass down to the river.

At **Mirkhani** the road joins the Kunar River. (Confusingly, the main river in the Chitral Valley is known as the Yarkhun in the northern end of the valley, the Mastuj in the central part, and the Kunar in southern Chitral. It then enters Afghanistan and joins the Kabul River at Jalalabad. To add to this confusion the river in the Kaghan Valley is called the Kunhar.) From Mirkhani to Chitral town the road follows the river all the way.

Drosh, the largest town in southern Chitral, is a military headquarters established by the British in the late 19th century. At the officers' mess you can browse through the photo albums and hunting records, and take a look at the map of the Chitral ski slopes. Sadly, the game is all shot out, and no one skis in Chitral now. The rest house in Drosh is bookable through the deputy commissioner in Chitral town, or you can stay at the Drosh View, a small local hotel. Ordinary petrol is available. From Drosh to Chitral town it is 42 kilometres (26 miles).

Just past Drosh a jeep road leads right (east) up the wooded Shishi Valley to **Madaglasht**, from where there are several possible treks (see pages 348–9).

The three valleys of the Kafir Kalash lie to the west of the road, about halfway between Drosh and Chitral town (see page 344).

Chitral Town

Chitral town is surprisingly large, its population having been swelled by Afghan refugees from across the border. The airport is five kilometres (three miles) north of the town. Jeep-taxis meet the planes each day; they are crowded and you need to be quick to get a seat.

The first thing to do in Chitral is to register with the police, who are open 8 am–2

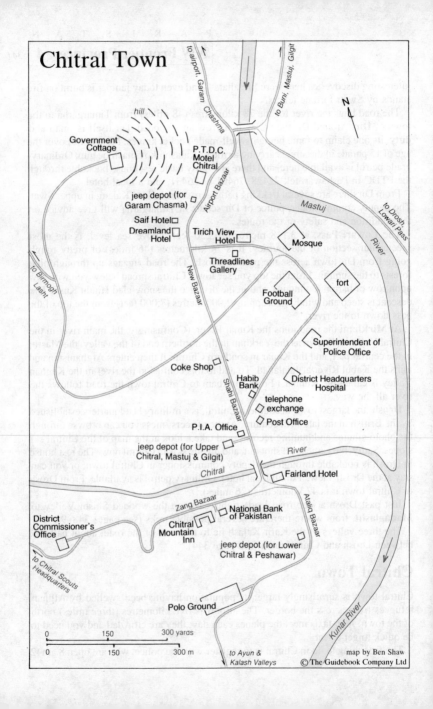

Chitral Town

hill

Government
Cottage

P.T.D.C.
Motel
Chitral

to airport, Garam Chashma

to Buni, Mastuj, Gilgit

N

jeep depot (for
Garam Chasma)

Airport Bazaar

Saif Hotel
Dreamland
Hotel

Tirich View
Hotel

Mosque

Mastuj

to Drosh,
Lowari pass

River

Threadlines
Gallery

New Bazaar

Football
Ground

fort

to Birmogh
Lasht

Superintendent of
Police Office

Coke Shop

Habib
Bank

District Headquarters
Hospital

Shahi Bazaar

telephone
exchange

Post Office

P.I.A. Office

jeep depot (for Upper
Chitral, Mastuj & Gilgit)

River

Chitral

Fairland Hotel

Zang Bazaar

National Bank
of Pakistan

Ataliq Bazaar

District
Commissioner's
Office

Chitral
Mountain
Inn

jeep depot (for Lower
Chitral & Peshawar)

to Chitral Scouts
Headquarters

Polo Ground

Kunar River

0   150   300 yards

0   150   300 m

to Ayun &
Kalash Valleys

map by Ben Shaw
© The Guidebook Company Ltd

pm Saturday to Wednesday, 8 am–12 noon on Thursday, and closed Friday. The hotel staff will show you the way. If you want to visit the three Kafir Kalash valleys of Birir, Bumburet and Rumbur you need a permit from the deputy commissioner, who keeps the same hours as the police; this is usually granted without difficulty, though not without delay. If you wish to see the Kalash women dance you need a second permit from the deputy commissioner. The visitor's permit is free, the dancing permit expensive, at Rs200. By the time you have your permits, and have confirmed your return flight to Peshawar, your first morning in Chitral will be over.

The **Chitral Tourist Information Centre** is at the PTDC hotel. The tourist officer is most helpful in finding transport, suggesting what you should see and helping you plan a trek if you so wish.

Where to Stay

Moderate

Mountain Inn, Ataliq Bazaar, tel. 581, 781, 800 (s/d Rs170–220/250–300). Lovely, peaceful central garden; nice atmosphere. Best in town.

PTDC Tourist Complex, tel. 683, or book through PTDC, Rawalpindi, tel. 581480–4 (s/d Rs250/325). Poor value.

Inexpensive

Dreamland, Shahi Bazaar, tel. 615 (s/d Rs60/120).

Fairland (s/d Rs35–60/70–105).

Tirich Mir View, down by the mosque (d Rs65). Splendid view.

Garden (s/d Rs15/25).

Shabnam (dorm Rs10). Basic.

Afghan-run hotel in Shahi Bazaar (s/d Rs15/25). Good food.

Saif (dorm Rs6).

There are several other cheap hotels in Shahi Bazaar.

Sights

Chitral's bazaars are always thronged and are worth exploring for jewellery, semi-precious stones, local cloth and woollen Chitrali hats with rolled brims. You can find most of the basic food supplies you need for trekking. Above the bazaar the houses are stacked one above the other up the hillside, culminating in the commissioner's residence and governor's rest house, from where there are magnificent views north to Tirich Mir and south over the town.

Chitral Fort stands on a bend of the Kunar (Chitral) River, beside the 100-year-old Shahi mosque surrounded by clusters of enormous chinar trees. The impressive fort is the ancestral home of the mehtars of Chitral (the ex-ruling family), and was considered the most easily defended of all the forts in northern Pakistan. In 1895 Surgeon Major Robertson of the British army and an escort of 400 men were besieged for 48 days here by a combined force from Dir and Chitral. They only just managed to hold out, enduring severe but much publicized hardships. Eventually a force of 250 men struggled through the snows of the Shandur Pass from Gilgit to rescue them (see page 412), and another force marched through the hostile territory of Dir, arriving just too late to help. Thereafter, until Independence, the British maintained a garrison in Chitral.

Part of the fort is now used by the police. On the road leading down to the fort there is an old caravanserai with carved wooden pillars inside the entrance. It stands opposite the open ground and a water-powered flour mill.

The **polo ground**, below the Mountain Inn Hotel, is the scene of fierce polo matches. The major tournaments are held in June and November, when the excitement and tension reach fever pitch. Practice matches are played for weeks beforehand. In August a match against Gilgit is sometimes played in the Shandur Pass. This is the best time to cross from Chitral to Gilgit, as there is plenty of transport up to the pass from both sides. (For a description of polo northern Pakistan style, see page 407).

Occasionally the Afghan game of *buskashi* (pulling the goat) is also played on the polo ground. A horseman carries a goat (or calf) carcass around the field and attempts to drop it in a circle in the centre of the pitch; there are few rules and no effort is spared to make the rider relinquish his goat. Buskashi requires a high degree of horsemanship, stamina and strength.

The ex-ruler's unoccupied **summer palace** is perched on a plateau at 2,700 metres (9,000 feet) above sea level, high above the town. A jeep road goes most of the way, or you can walk, but do not be deceived by what looks like a gentle stroll; it is a hot, strenuous walk over rocks and gravel and can take up to three hours. The climb is worth it, however: at the top the view of Tirich Mir and other snow-clad peaks, including Bunizom in the Hindu Raj to the east, is magnificent. The summer palace is really a small hunting lodge; you can peer in through the windows at the photographs and antlers inside.

You can take a longer walk from Chitral town to **Biron Shal**, another old royal residence 3,000 metres (10,000 feet) high in a narrow wooded valley that is a protected game reserve. The walk starts from behind the deputy commissioner's office. It is too far to get there and back in a day but there is a lovely camping spot in the pine forest especially recommended for naturalists and bird watchers.

Kafir Kalash Valleys

Chitral's prime attraction is the Kalash valleys, home of the 3,000 non-Muslim Kafir Kalash (or Black Infidels) who live in 20 small villages in the valleys of **Birir**, **Bumburet** and **Rumbur**, southwest of Chitral town and close to the Afghan border.

The local Kalash are part of a much larger group who live in neighbouring Afghanistan, in what is now called Nuristan (Country of Light). The whole area was originally called Kafiristan (Land of the Infidels), but in 1896 the Afghani Kafirs were forcibly converted to Islam and the name of their homeland was changed. The Chitrali Kafir Kalash still follow their own religion, a mixture of animism and ancestor- and fire-worship, and have retained some of their original culture. They make offerings to several gods: Sajigor, the highest deity, is in charge of everything; Surisan protects the cattle, Goshedoi milk products, and Praba fruit.

Most of the Kalash are pale skinned, and some of them even have fair hair and blue eyes, all of which give rise to the usual legend that they are descended from the followers of Alexander the Great. Some historians maintain that Alexander did actually go to Chitral, and he was certainly in nearby Dir. The Kafirs were mentioned in classical times, and contemporary chronicles relate that they fought Tamerlane in 1398 and the Moghul emperor Babur in 1507.

The first European to visit Kafiristan may have been the mysterious Scotsman William Watts MacNair, the model for Kipling's Lurgan Sahib in *Kim*. Kipling's famous short story, *The Man Who Would Be King* (1890), is set in Kafiristan, which is depicted as a primitive mountain kingdom where two British renegades found themselves deified by a credulous and savage people. (Kipling, however, never visited the area himself.)

The man who came to know most about the Kafirs was Surgeon Major Robertson, later political agent at Gilgit and the hero of the siege of Chitral. He made two visits in 1889 and 1891, and wrote a thorough and penetrating study of the Kafir people, their beliefs and traditions. His book *The Kafirs of the Hindu Kush* (1900) is still in print and makes excellent reading. Two other good books are Maraini's *Where Four Worlds Meet* (1964) and Loude's *Kalash, Les derniers 'infideles' de l'Hindu-Kush* (1980).

The Chitrali Kafirs are called the Kafir Kalash (*kalash* meaning black) because of their women's black robes. The women also wear magnificent red and white bead necklaces and superb black headdresses which flow down their backs and are covered with cowrie shells and buttons usually crowned with a large red pompom. These headdresses are reminiscent of those worn by women in Ladakh. Unlike the Muslims, the Kalash women do not observe purdah and are open and friendly. You can photograph them, but they always demand payment. If you have a permit, the headmen of the villages of Brun (Bumburet) and Guru (Birir) will arrange for them to dance (but it is more enjoyable to watch the Kalash women dance during their own festivals).

The houses of the Kalash people are built of timber, the cracks between the logs being filled with mud and pebbles. In summer the women sit to cook, spin and weave on the wide second-storey verandah. In winter they cook inside; the smoke escapes through the central hole in the cantilevered wooden ceiling.

The wooden temples are often elaborately carved with zigzag motifs and scrolls, animal heads and flat human faces, especially around the doors, pillars and ceilings. Some of the holy places in the woods can be visited only by men. Only women can enter the menstruation hut, where they retire during menstruation and childbirth.

The Kalash graveyards are quite startling; the dead are left in wooden coffins

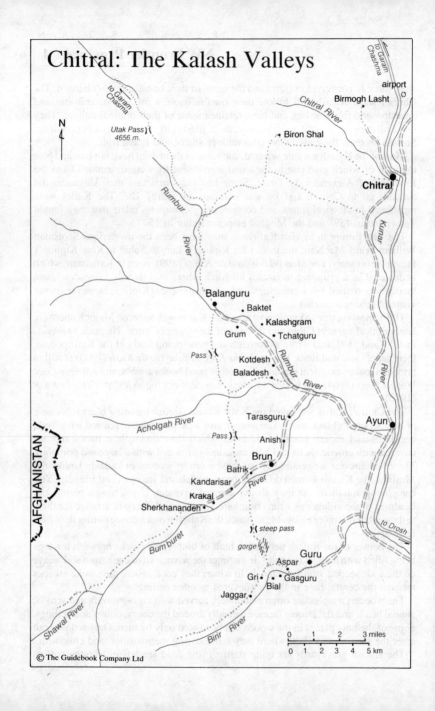

Chitral: The Kalash Valleys

to Garam
Chashma

airport

Birmogh Lasht

Chitral River

to Garam
Chashma

N

Utak Pass
4656 m.

Biron Shal

Chitral

Rumbur River

Kunar River

Balanguru

Baktet

Kalashgram

Grum

Tchatguru

Pass

Kotdesh

Baladesh

Rumbur River

Ayun

Acholgah River

Tarasguru

Pass

Anish

Brun

Batrik

Kandarisar

Krakal

Sherkhanandeh

River

to Drosh

AFGHANISTAN

Bumburet River

steep pass

gorge

Guru

Aspar

Gri

Gasguru

Bial

Jaggar

Shawal River

Birir River

0   1   2   3 miles

0 1 2 3 4 5 km

© The Guidebook Company Ltd

above the ground, and many of the lids have fallen off so that the bones lie exposed to view. Some of the coffins are carved, and the wealthier people make wooden effigies which stand beside the coffins. Few of these can be seen *in situ* today, but there are some in the Peshawar Museum.

The Kalash love music and dancing; you often hear tin flutes being played in the fields. There are different dances for birth, marriage and death, and four annual festivals: the spring festival in mid-May, the harvest festival in mid-August, the autumn festival to mark the walnut and grape harvest, and the December festival to celebrate the winter solstice. There is dancing, singing, drinking and feasting, and sacrificial goats are offered on smoke-blackened wooden altars. The PTDC will advise you of the exact dates, which change yearly.

Getting to the Kafir Kalash Valleys

The easiest way of getting to the valleys, if your time is limited, is to hire a jeep for Rs8 a mile (1.6 kilometres). The PTDC or hotel will arrange this for you. Alternatively you can take a jeep-taxi from Ataliq Bazaar in Chitral town for the much more modest outlay of Rs10 to Bumburet, but you may have to wait a long time before finding one to bring you back to Chitral. Or you can take a jeep-taxi to Ayun, 15 kilometres (nine miles) south of Chitral town, for Rs6, and walk west along the river for about three hours (15 kilometres or nine miles) to either Bumburet or Rumbur. The road into Birir is further south; a private jeep from Ayun to Birir costs Rs120. There is a rest house and a local hotel in Ayun.

Bumburet, the largest and most commercialized of the three Kalash Valleys, is an hour and a half's jeep drive from Chitral town. At Ayun you pay a Rs10 toll before branching off right (west) to follow the Ayun River. There is a police checkpost where the road forks, ten kilometres (six miles) from Ayun; if you do not have a permit you will be turned back. To get to the Kalash valleys, turn left (south) for Bumburet or right (north) for Rumbur. From the checkpost to Brun, the chief village in Bumburet, it is eight kilometres (five miles), to Balanguru, the chief village in Rumbur, seven kilometres (four miles).

Where to Stay

In all three valleys there are rest houses and local hotels; you can also camp. Do not rush your visit, but plan to spend one or two nights in the area.

Rumbur Valley

Kalash Hilton and
Rumbur Hotel, Balanguru (d Rs 25).

Bumburet Valley

Benazir Hotel, Anish (d Rs60). Nice campsite.
Ansaf Hotel, Anish (d Rs60).

Kalash Hilton, Brun (d Rs30).
Frontier Hotel, Brun (d Rs20).
Kalash View Hotel, Brun.
Peace Hotel, Batrik (d Rs30). Popular with backpackers.

Birir Valley

Insaf Hotel, Guru.
Another hotel is being built.

Exploring the Kafir Kalash Valleys

Perhaps the best way to explore the Kalash valleys is on foot. Well-made footpaths follow each of the three rivers, and steep tracks cross the tree-covered ridges between the valleys. The track from Birir to Bumburet leaves the Birir Valley at Gasguru and follows an extremely steep narrow gorge between high cliffs to the top. The gorge divides several times—keep to the left. When you come out of the gorge, it is still an hour to the top; it looks deceptively near, but the trees on top are huge and look closer than they really are. The top of the pass is narrow and pointed, without a flat space large enough to pitch a tent. It takes six hours to cross if you are fit; if you get lost or are unfit, it can take up to 12 hours.

It is better to cross from Bumburet to Birir than vice versa as it is shaded and cooler in the early morning, and the path is more obvious in this direction. Start from the Peace Hotel in Batrik, cross the river and follow the irrigation channel to the gulley; take the central gulley to the top, a climb of about three hours.

From the Bumburet Valley you can trek along the river up to the summer pastures in Shawal, outside the Kalash area, and camp the night with the shepherds.

From Bumburet there is an easy walk back along the jeep track to Rumbur Valley (15 kilometres, or nine miles, from Brun to Balanguru). The trek across the hills takes two days, as there is another valley in between.

From Rumbur Valley you can return by jeep-taxi to Chitral town, or hike there in two days across the top. A guide is recommended. An alternative trek is the more strenuous three-day journey to Garam Chashma, across the 4,656-metre (15,271-foot) Utak Pass.

Garam Chashma

For the non-trekker Garam Chashma (Hot Springs) can also be reached in two hours on a paved road direct from Chitral town, 45 kilometres (28 miles) away. The road follows the south bank of the Lutkho River through a steep-sided gorge and emerges into the green, wooded valley of Garam Chashma, which is guarded by a mud-walled fort. The hot sulphur springs are believed to heal skin diseases, gout, rheumatism and headaches. There is a bathhouse (not very clean), and a good rest house. You need a permit from the deputy commissioner to stay overnight.

You can approach **Tirich Mir** from the south by two jeep roads; both branch off the Garam Chashma road up tributaries of the Lutkho River. One heads northeast across the south side of Tirich Mir from **Shoghor** to **Kiyar**. From Kiyar you can trek across the **Owir Pass** to **Barum** in two days (see page 439). From the top of the Owir Pass there are magnificent views in all directions, especially of Tirich Mir. There are good camping places on either side. The other approach to Tirich Mir is to the northwest, up the Arkari River, which flows down the west side of Tirich Mir.

Upper Chitral

The main jeep track up the Chitral Valley follows the Mastuj River for 107 kilometres (66 miles) to Mastuj and from there jogs south to cross the 3,734-metre (12,250-foot) Shandur Pass into the Gilgit Valley. Again, you need a permit from the deputy commissioner to make this journey.

Public jeeps from Chitral town go to every side valley several times each week. Public jeeps across the Shandur Pass are rarer, but you can hire a jeep from Chitral to Gilgit for Rs5,000.

Koghozi is a small town 19 kilometres (12 miles) from Chitral town. About three kilometres (two miles) beyond Koghozi the **Golan River** flows in from the east. It is a picturesque trek for 14 kilometres (nine miles) along the Golan, through a narrow gorge with vertical sides to **Ustor**. From Ustor there are three possible treks. The shortest is across to Madaghlasht at the end of the jeep road in the Shishi Valley. This takes two or three days. It is 13 kilometres (eight miles) up to the top of the **Dok Pass**, at 4,191 metres (13,700 feet), from where you walk down to Daulatabad, about three kilometres (two miles) up the Shishi River from Madaghlasht.

A second trek takes you back to the main Chitral Valley further up at **Reshun**, 53 kilometres (33 miles) from Chitral town. This involves a 15-kilometre (ten-mile) hike from Ustor up the Golan River to the summer pastures at Dukadaki. A steep dry climb north from Dukadaki leads to the 4,601-metre (15,095-foot) **Shakuh Pass**, from where it is a day's walk down to Reshun.

The third possibility is a strenuous six-day trek to Mastuj across the 5,056-metre (16,588-foot) **Phargam Pass**, from where you follow the Phargam River down to Harchin, on the Laspur River.

Back on the main jeep road up the Chitral Valley you pass many small villages and side valleys with jeep tracks or footpaths leading up them. At **Parpish**, two to three hours and 47 kilometres (29 miles) from Chitral town, a jeep track left (west) leads to Barum, from where you can trek southwest across the **Owir Pass** (4,338 metres or 13,222 feet), with magnificent views north to Tirich Mir, ending up at Kiyar.

Reshun, where the footpath from the Shakuh Pass returns to the main valley, is five kilometres (three miles) beyond Parpish on the main road. At **Kuragh**, seven kilometres (five miles) beyond Reshun, 60 kilometres (37 miles) from Chitral town, the Turikho River flows down from the north to join the Mastuj River.

The **Turikho River** is the most important tributary to the Mastuj. The two rivers flow parallel to each other for about 70 kilometres (45 miles) before joining. There are many possible treks along both rivers, in the area between them, and up the tributaries that flow into the Turikho from the west. The lower Turikho Valley is well irrigated and lush, but the upper part of the valley (known as Rich Valley) is drier and hot in summer. There is a jeepable road most of the way up the Turikho Valley, and a branch road leading west up the Tirich tributary that flows down from Tirich Mir.

Of the many possible treks, the most recommended is from **Uthul**, near Warijum, across the Zani Pass, with its superb views of Tirich Mir, down to Shagram, in the Tirich Valley (there are two Shagrams—the other is on the Turikho River). Then follow the Tirich River up to its source on Tirich Mir (see Trekking Guide, page 439 for a detailed itinerary).

The **Zani Pass**, 3,898 metres (12,789 feet) above sea level, is the best part of the whole trek. If your time is limited, you can spend a rewarding day walking up to the top of the pass, a flat ridge dividing the Tirich Valley from the Turikho Valley, and back to Uthul. The pass offers unrivalled views of the Hindu Kush from Tirich Mir in the west to Saraghrar in the north; in the the other direction lie the Hindu Raj, Bunizom and the mountains round Mastuj. A night camping by the lake just southwest of the pass is made unforgettable by the sight of the changing light on the mountains at dawn.

The two best-known paths connecting the Turikho and Rich valleys with the Yarkhun Valley are little used. One crosses from just north of Shagram (on the Turikho) over the 4,320-metre (14,173-foot) **Khot** (**Cloud**) **Pass** and comes down to the Yarkhun Valley six kilometres (four miles) north of Brep. The other crosses the **Shah Jinali** (**King's Pologround**) **Pass**, at 4,259 metres (13,974 feet). This pass is 20 kilometres (12 miles) from the Afghan border, but the area is sensitive and permission to trek here is difficult to obtain: there is a checkpost at Lasht on the Yarkun River.

Continuing up the main Chitral Valley from the junction of the Turikho and Mastuj rivers, a new road from Buni to Mastuj following the north bank of the Mastuj River has cut out the most terrifying section of the journey.

Mastuj, 107 kilometres (66 miles) from Chitral, is a large town by local standards, with 15 shops and a local hotel. It is set in a wide bowl where the Laspur and Yarkhun rivers join. At Mastuj the river changes its name. Above the town it is called the Yarkhun, below the town the Mastuj.

Mastuj was once the capital of the kingdom of Little Bolor, and an important staging post on the ancient Silk Route (see Gilgit, page 401).

The descendants of the ruling family have opened their fort to tourists. You can stay in tents inside Mastuj Fort (Rs150 excluding meals) where the prince will entertain you. Polo is played every other day on the field below the fort.

At Mastuj the jeep road to Gilgit turns south along the Laspur River to the Shandur

Pass. Another jeep road only passable in winter follows the Yarkhun River north for much of the 60 kilometres (37 miles) up to its source near the Afghan border. The top end of the valley— including the famous **Baroghil Pass** into Afghanistan (one of the paths of the ancient Silk Route), and the Darkot and Thui passes to the Gilgit Valley—is a closed zone, with checkposts at Lasht and Darkot. The Yarkhun Valley is wider, flatter and more cultivated than the Turikho, and you can usually get up as far as Bang without difficulty. Most of the people here are Ismaili (see page 417) and are especially open and friendly.

The shortest route for trekkers to the Gilgit Valley is the path from **Chapali**, 11 kilometres (seven miles) from Mastuj up the Yarkhun River. From Chapali you trek east up the Zagaro River for eight kilometres (five miles), then south across the **Chumarkhan Pass** (4,344 metres, or 14,252 feet) to Barsat on the Gilgit River.

Another alternative is to follow the jeep track along the Laspur River to **Harchin**, then trek up the Harchin tributary to the Harchin Pass, thence down the Ghulbar River to Barsat.

The jeep track across the **Shandur Pass** cuts east from the Laspur River at the village of Sor Laspur. This makes an easy trek because though it is 16 kilometres (ten miles) further from Mastuj to Barsat by this route than via the Chumarkhan Pass, it has the advantage of being 600 metres (2,000 feet) lower. (For more details of the Shandur Pass, see pages 409–12.) It is 40 kilometres (25 miles) from Mastuj to the Shandur Pass.

From Sor Laspur you can also trek across the **Kachikani Pass** (4,766 metres, or 15,636 feet) to Kalam in the Swat Valley (see page 440).

Fishing

The rivers in Chitral are full of trout, their numbers maintained by the trout hatcheries at Chitral and Bumburet. The Lutkho River, which flows from Garam Chashma, is supposed to be the best. The fishing season lasts from April to September; you need a permit from the Fisheries Department in Chitral town, and you would also be well advised to bring your own tackle.

KAGHAN VALLEY

Terraced from river to hilltop and covered in forests of huge Himalayan pine, the Kaghan Valley is one of the most beautiful in Pakistan and is reminiscent of the alpine scenery of Europe. Kaghan is just on the edge of the monsoon belt, so there is no need for irrigation here. The slopes are steep, and villages cling precariously to the sides of the hills, the tops of which are often hidden by clouds. Kaghan is not on the normal tourist route: it is for the lover of nature, hiking, fishing and other outdoor pleasures.

Most confusingly, there is no Kaghan River. The Kunhar River flows through the

Kaghan Valley, down from high in the Indus Kohistan to join the Jhelum at Muzaffarabad. The valley is over 160 kilometres (100 miles) long and climbs from about 900 metres (3,000 feet) at Balakot to 4,173 metres (13,690 feet) at the Babusar Pass. The road through the valley and up over the Babusar Pass to Chilas on the Indus opened in 1898; it was the main route to the Northern Areas and Gilgit before the Karakoram Highway was opened in 1978. Closed for most of the year by heavy snow, the Babusar Pass is only jeepable for the short summer months, and even then landslides frequently block the way.

When to Go

The best times in Kaghan are May, June and early July, before the monsoons, and September and October, before the snows. Naran and Shogran can be reached from April or May until October, but it gets very cold at night in the autumn. August and September is the best time to try to get to the Babusar Pass; the locals repair the road to get the potato harvest out, and you might be lucky and get a ride on a tractor load. Road conditions deteriorate sharply during the monsoon season in late July.

Getting to Kaghan

Several buses a day leave Pir Wadhai bus station in Rawalpindi for Mansehra, a 90-minute journey costing about Rs15. Minibuses leave from the Mall, take three hours and cost about Rs20. Change at Mansehra and head for Balakot one hour away, a journey costing about Rs6 by bus and Rs10 by minibus. From Balakot several buses (Rs16) and minibuses (Rs30) leave daily for Naran, halfway up the valley. In July, August and September, public jeeps travel to the top of the valley on most days, and occasionally cross the pass to Babusar village from where daily jeeps (Rs30) descend to Chilas on the KKH. Alternatively, you can hire a jeep from the PTDC or one of the many private contractors in either Balakot or Naran.

If you are driving you can either approach from Mansehra in Hazara or Muzaffarabad in Azad Kashmir. Both routes take about four hours from Islamabad to Balakot.

Just before Mansehra there is a fork in the road. The left fork is the Karakoram Highway, which takes you to Gilgit; the right fork is a much older road, which leads to the bottom of the Kaghan Valley and to Azad Kashmir. This was the all-weather route taken by the Moghul emperors to their beloved Vale of Kashmir; it was also the route taken by the Pathans in 1947 when they went on a holy war to save Kashmir for Pakistan.

The road goes through the crowded, dusty town of Mansehra (turn right at the T-junction at the other side of the bridge), and then climbs up to a pine-forested ridge, the superb setting for the Batrasi rest house, about 30 minutes' drive from Mansehra and bookable through the PWD Road Maintenance Division, Mansehra, tel. Mansehra 525. This is a quiet, secluded place with good views and gentle walks

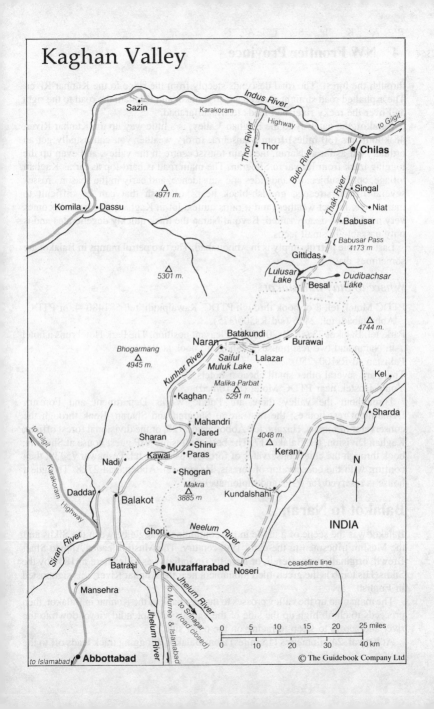

Kaghan Valley

Indus River

Karakoram Highway

to Gilgit

Sazin

Thor River

Thor

Buto River

Chilas

Singal

Niat

Thak River

Komila • Dassu

Babusar

Babusar Pass
4173 m

△ 4971 m.

Gittidas

Lulusar Lake

Dudibachsar Lake

Besal

△ 5301 m.

△ 4744 m.

Batakundi

Naran

Burawai

Bhogarmang
△ 4945 m.

Saiful Muluk Lake

Lalazar

Kunhar River

Kel

Malika Parbat
△ 5291 m.

Kaghan

Sharda

△ 4048 m.

Mahandri

Jared

Keran

to Gilgit

Sharan

Shinu

Nadi

Kawai

Paras

Shogran

Daddar

Makra
△ 3885 m

Kundalshahi

Balakot

Karakoram Highway

N

Siran River

Ghori

Neelum River

INDIA

Batrasi

Muzaffarabad

Noseri

ceasefire line

Mansehra

Jhelum River

to Smagar
(road closed)

to Murree & Islamabad

to Islamabad • Abbottabad

Jhelum River

| 0 | 5 | 10 | 15 | 20 | 25 miles |
| 0 | 10 | 20 | 30 | 40 km |

© The Guidebook Company Ltd

through the forest. The road descends steeply from the ridge to the Kunhar River. The asphalted road straight ahead leads to Balakot and Kaghan; the road to the right and over the rocky river bed leads to Muzaffarabad.

Balakot, the gateway to the Kaghan Valley, is a little way up the Kunhar River, 48 kilometres (30 miles) from Mansehra. In dry weather you can usually get an ordinary car as far as Naran, the main tourist centre in the valley, and even up the logging track from Kawai to Shogran. The main road is hard-top as far as Kaghan village, but is subject to landslides and subsidence, and early in the season crosses several frozen streams, greyish-black heaps of slush that can be difficult to manoeuvre. In wet weather (and it rains quite a lot in Kaghan), the track becomes very muddy and deeply rutted. Beyond Naran the track quickly degenerates and is only passable in small jeeps.

Last reliable **petrol** supply is in Abbottabad. The two petrol pumps in Balakot are sometimes dry.

Where to Stay in Balakot

PTDC Motel, tel. 8 or book through PTDC, Rawalpindi, tel. 581480–4, or PTDC, Abbottabad, tel. 2446 (s/d Rs300/375).

Park, tel. Balakot 23 (s/d Rs200/300). Pleasant position. The Park Hotel runs a hotel in Naran and two rest houses at Shogran; book at Balakot.

Pakistan (d Rs100–250).

There are several other small cheaper hotels.

Youth Hostel, near PTDC Motel (Rs10/bed).

Throughout the valley there are Public Works Department and Forestry Department rest houses; the best are at Shogran and Sharan. Book through the conservator of forests, Hazara, tel. Abbottabad 2728, or the divisional forest officer, Kaghan Division, tel. Balakot 17. The best of all is the VIP guest house at Shogran; book through the chief conservator of forests, Peshawar, tel. Peshawar 75239, then confirm with the conservator of forests, Hazara, tel. Abbottabad 2728. The guest house is reserved for VIPs and diplomats only.

Balakot to Naran

Balakot was the scene of a battle in the continuing struggle between the Sikhs and the Muslim tribesmen in the early 19th century. The Muslim leader Ahmed Shah Brewli, originally from Bereli, or Bareilly (in India), was killed here in 1831 by the Sikhs. His tomb is the green-tiled monument near the Kunhar River; it is signposted in English.

The main road up the valley crosses to the east bank of the Kunhar in Balakot, then proceeds to climb high up the side of the valley, with splendid views down to the river and across to steep terracing on the other side.

At **Kawai**, 24 kilometres (15 miles) from Balakot, a logging track leads off to the right and climbs steeply up to the plateau of Shogran. The track winds up through dense pine forests and can be extremely muddy and rutted in wet weather. Take the right fork where the logging track divides.

At 2,400 metres (7,500 feet) above sea level, **Shogran** stands well above the valley, and is the most beautiful place to spend the weekend. The Forestry Department rest house and guest house (see above) are well furnished and exquisitely situated on the edge of a lush meadow filled with flowers in spring, and offer magnificent views up the valley to Musa-ka-Musalla (Prayer Mat of Moses), Makra and **Malika Parbat**, which at 5,290 metres (17,356 feet) is the highest of all the mountains in the Kaghan Valley. In the clear air the distant wall of mountains looks like a painted stage set you could reach out and touch. The two Park Hotel rest houses are adequate but have no view. Take your own bedding.

It is safe to camp in the meadow. There is plenty of firewood in the forest and water in a nearby stream. The logging track leads up to summer pastures at about 2,700 metres (8,800 feet), where there is another Forestry Department rest house and suitable camping ground. The walk up takes about two hours and is not too steep.

You can trek on over the hill and down into the Neelum Valley, joining the Neelam River at Ghori in the open zone.

The main road up the valley passes through a narrow neck beyond Kawai, then runs alongside the river. From Paras a difficult jeep track leads left over a good bridge and winds its way up to **Sharan** (16 kilometres, or ten miles, or about two hours away), at 2,400 metres (8,000 feet). This spot is almost completely unknown and boasts the least-spoiled hardwood forests in Pakistan. The Forestry Department rest house, nestled in a hollow, is seldom used. Though there are no meadows in the area there are lovely walks through the forest with superb views.

From Sharan you can trek over to Madi and down to Daddar, in the Siran Valley north of Mansehra.

Shinu, the next village up the main Kaghan Valley, has a trout hatchery; visitors are welcome. You can buy a fishing licence here to fish in the well-stocked river. At the small village of **Jarad**, 40 kilometres (25 miles) from Balakot, there is a government-operated shop that sells locally made woollen hats and shawls and carved chests and chairs.

The metalled road ends at **Kaghan**, the small village 60 kilometres (37 miles) from Balakot that lends its name to the whole valley.

Naran

At 2,427 metres (7,963 feet) above sea level and 82 kilometres (51 miles) from Balakot, Naran is the centre of tourism for the Kaghan Valley. Here the mountains stand back a little and protected forests of huge pines clothe the lower slopes. The river takes a leisurely bend forming islands and pools and bubbling over rocks. The place is a fisherman's dream and the starting point for walks and treks into the surrounding hills.

There is no petrol or bank at Naran, and local supplies are limited, so trekkers should arrive with all the provisions they will need. Other visitors might like to bring supplementary foods such as cheese, biscuits, packet soups and tinned or dehydrated food.

Where to Stay

PTDC Motel; book as for Balakot (s/d Rs320/400–1,000).

PTDC tents; book as above (Rs80/tent).

Park, Lalazar, Naran, Shalimar and Zumzum hotels all charge about Rs300 for a double room, more for deluxe. Try bargaining, especially out of season. The telephone rarely works, so booking is difficult except for the Park which you can book in Balakot.

There are many small local hotels offering charpoys for Rs15–20. Camping on the river bank above the village is recommended.

You can eat well in the bazaar on mutton curry, lentils and fresh naan or chapattis for Rs10.

Enjoying Naran

Fishing and walking are the main pastimes for visitors to Naran. The British first stocked the Pakistani rivers in the 1920s with brown trout eggs brought from Scotland; the Pakistan government later augmented the stock by introducing rainbow trout spawn from the Philippines. The trout used to be huge; the biggest ever weighed was over eight kilograms (18 pounds) and came from Lake Saif-ul-Muluk, but uncontrolled blasting in the lakes has depleted the stock.

Fishing permits, which entitle you to land five trout, cost Rs15 a day from the Fisheries Department, PTDC Motel or from a ghillie. Rods can be hired for Rs20, but experienced anglers should bring their own tackle. You can also hire a ghillie, who will show you the best beats and sell you his catch at the end of the day. May, June and October are the best months for fishing. Whether you fish or not, be sure to eat the trout grilled on an open fire.

Lake Saif-ul-Muluk is ten kilometres (six miles) to the east, up a picturesque side valley at an altitude of 3,212 metres (10,537 feet) above sea level. You can either rent a jeep in the bazaar and drive up in one hour (for a set charge of Rs200), or rent a horse for Rs100–200 and ride up, or else walk up the seven-kilometre (four-mile) shortcut in about three hours. The lake is above the tree line and, though marred by a cluster of tacky softdrink stalls, is still exquisite on a clear day when the pointed peak of Malika Parbat is mirrored in its deep-blue waters.

In April, ice islands float like miniature icebergs on the surface, and the surrounding peaks, still covered in snow, stand guard, protecting the sapphire in their midst. In June, flowers fill the alpine meadows around the lake and up the Saif-ul-Muluk stream to the glacier flowing down off Malika Parbat. Early morning and late afternoon are the most beautiful times at the lake. If you have your own bedding there is a basic rest house where you can stay; if you have the equipment, it is a perfect place to camp.

Local legend relates that Prince Saif-ul-Muluk fell in love with a fairy from the mountains. One day he saw her bathing in the stream and crept up and stole her clothes. To preserve her modesty the not-so-reluctant fairy promised to be his wife. The fairy's demon lover appeared in time to see the happy pair together, and in a fit of jealous rage flooded the entire valley. 'Of the fairies in the lake,' recounts the 1907 Kashmir *Gazetteer,* 'some say that they have deserted the place, others aver that still of nights they come to dance their revels on the grass and bathe themselves in the stream, and then woe it is to the mortal who encounters them!'

From the lake you can trek south up the stream to Saif-ul-Muluk Glacier. If you turn west (right) about two kilometres (a mile) before the glacier at **Kach**, a shepherd's summer camp, you can trek up over a 4,237-metre (13,902-foot) pass and come down to settlements on the other side. There are several more ridges to cross before you get back to the main valley at Mahandri, so you would be well advised to hire a local as a guide before attempting it. Mohammad Bashir, son of Mohammad Zaman of Naran, is a highly recommended guide.

Naran to the Babusar Pass

From Naran the valley ascends for another 66 kilometres (41 miles) to the top of **Babusar Pass**. You can usually get as far as Besal by public jeep for about Rs50, or there are plenty of jeeps for private hire—bargain hard, but expect to pay about Rs1,000 from Naran to the top of the pass, or Rs1,200 to Babusar Village, 13 kilometres (eight miles) on the other side of the pass.

Battakundi, 16 kilometres (ten miles) beyond Naran, has an excellent youth hostel, a PWD rest house and three local hotels (Rs10), and was one of the regular stopping places when this was the main route to Gilgit. At an altitude of 2,624 metres (8,607 feet) above sea level, this is the last village in the valley to stay fully open all winter. About two kilometres (a mile) beyond Battakundi, a jeep track leads right up to the village of **Danna Lalazar**, a beautiful spot covered in pine and spruce, with meadows full of flowers in the spring. There is another rest house here. From the Lalazar Plateau (not to be confused with Lulusar Lake) you can walk west across several hills to Lake Saif-ul-Muluk in about five hours.

From Battakundi the main road continues 13 kilometres (eight miles) to **Burawai**, where there is a PWD rest house charging Rs50; a charpoy in the local hotel costs Rs10. From here it is 18 kilometres (11 miles) to **Besal**, a small group of stone houses that blends into the rocky hillside. From June to September you can spend a smoky night in the local restaurant for Rs10. At 3,266 metres (10,715 feet), this village is above the tree line, and most of the inhabitants abandon it in the winter.

A few kilometres (miles) beyond Besal you pass the beautiful **Lake Lulusar**, described thus in April:

. . . about half a mile wide with sheer green mountains rising from the opposite side, their gullies a-glitter with glaciers [snowdrifts]. The water was clear but dark green and one of the loveliest sights of my life was the perfect reflection of the white snow in that depth of greenness. At various points not far from the water's edge were 'icebergs', the tips of glaciers which had slid into the lake and not yet melted.

Dervla Murphy, *Full Tilt* (1965)

At **Gittidas**, 13 kilometres (eight miles) from Besal, the valley finally widens. At 3,634 metres (almost 12,000 feet) this is a summer settlement; in July, August and September whole families come with their animals to the high pastures dotted with tiny lakes. From here it is a steep climb of seven kilometres (four miles) to the top of Babusar Pass, at 4,173 metres (13,690 feet), from where there are superb views down the wooded, fertile Babusar Valley.

The next 13 kilometres (eight miles) down to **Babusar** village are particularly difficult. The track zigzags down a hillside where loose scree often blocks the road; it can be nerve-wracking driving, even in a small jeep. Babusar is a permanent village, at 2,800 metres (9,200 feet), with a rest house and local hotel.

From Babusar village to Chilas it is 37 kilometres (23 miles). If you are hiking, you can spend the night at the local tea shop in **Singal**, a large village in the green, cultivated valley, but as it is downhill all the way you can probably get to Chilas in one day. Every day jeeps ply the road between Babusar village and Chilas; another possibility is to try hitching a ride on one of the tractors or lorries carting wood.

Azad Kashmir and Jammu

Azad (or Free) Kashmir and Jammu, is the area along the Jhelum River assigned to India at Partition in 1947 and later 'liberated' by Pakistan. The least-known part of northern Pakistan, it is one of the loveliest. Lying in the monsoon belt, the valleys here are green and wooded, and there are many well-placed rest houses from which you can take scenic drives and hikes. Being easily accessible by car from Islamabad and Abbottabad, it is ideal for weekend trips. The one problem is that Azad Kashmir is bounded to the east by the 'line of control' (or ceasefire line) with Indian-held Kashmir, and travel for foreigners is banned within 16 kilometres (ten miles) of the border.

Azad Kashmir extends from the plains of the Punjab near Jhelum up through Mangla Lake to the foothills of the Himalayas, and north to the mountains which rise to over 6,000 metres (20,000 feet) above sea level. It is drained by three major rivers, the Jhelum, the Neelum and the Punch; their valleys are steep, forested and very beautiful.

The most interesting part of Azad Kashmir is the area around Muzaffarabad, the capital, at the confluence of the Jhelum and Neelum rivers.

When to Go

The best time to visit northern Azad Kashmir is from late March to early June, and from September through November, avoiding the winter cold, summer heat (although the higher areas are pleasant even in summer) and the monsoons. Southern Azad Kashmir is at its best from September to March.

Getting to Azad Kashmir

Muzaffarabad is an easy four-hour bus ride or drive from Islamabad, or two hours from Abbottabad or Murree. The road via Abbottabad is open all year round, but the road via Murree is sometimes snowbound in winter. Follow the road to the bottom of the Kaghan Valley, ford the Kunhar River (passable in an ordinary car), and continue through Garhi Habibullah up to the col at Lohar Gali, from where there are spectacular views over the Jhelum Valley and Muzaffarabad.

It is a two-hour drive from Murree to Muzaffarabad. There is a checkpost at Kohala Bridge across the Jhelum, from where it is 35 kilometres (22 miles) to Muzaffarabad, following the east bank of the river. The drive from Islamabad to Muzaffarabad is about 130 kilometres (81 miles).

The southern end of Azad Kashmir—the districts of Punch, Kotli and Mirpur— can be reached from Islamabad via Lehtrar, Kahuta or Mangla Dam.

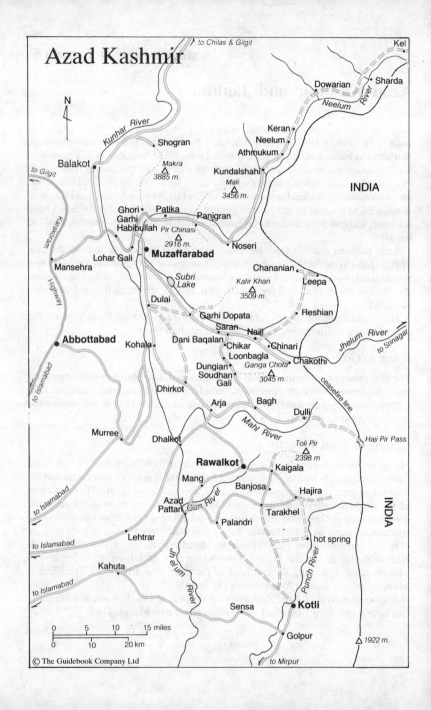

Azad Kashmir

to Chilas & Gilgit

Kel

Dowarian • Sharda

Neelum River

Keran

Neelum

Athmukum

INDIA

Kundalshahi

Mali
△ 3456 m.

Shogran

Makra
△ 3885 m.

N

Kunhar River

Balakot

to Gilgit

Ghori
Garhi
Habibullah

Patika

Panjgran

Pir Chinasi
△ 2916 m.

Noseri

Karakoram

Lohar Gali

Muzaffarabad

Chananian

Leepa

Mansehra

Subri
Lake

Katir Khan
△ 3509 m.

Rawalpindi Highway

Dulai

Garhi Dopata

Reshian

Abbottabad

Saran

Naili

Chinari

Jhelum River

to Srinagar

Kohala

Dani Baqalan

Chikar

Loonbagla

Chakothi

Dungian
Soudhan
Gali

Ganga Chota
△ 3045 m.

to Islamabad

Dhirkot

ceasefire line

Arja

Bagh

Dulli

Murree

Dhalkot

Mahl River

Haji Pir Pass

Rawalkot

Toli Pir
△ 2398 m

Mang

Kaigala

Banjosa

Hajira

INDIA

to Islamabad

Azad
Pattan

Gun River

Tarakhel

Palandri

Lehtrar

hot spring

to Islamabad

Jhelum River

Punch River

Kahuta

Sensa

Kotli

to Islamabad

Golpur

△ 1922 m.

0   5   10   15 miles

0   10   20 km

to Mirpur

© The Guidebook Company Ltd

Muzaffarabad

Muzaffarabad was an important post at the junction of the Neelum and Jhelum rivers on the all-weather route to Srinagar. It is only 180 kilometres (112 miles) to Srinagar along the Jhelum River, but the road is closed 60 kilometres (37 miles) from Muzaffarabad at the ceasefire line with India.

Where to Stay

Government Guest House, tel. Muzaffarabad 3286—ask for the protocol officer.
   Usually reserved for senior government officials.
Assembly Hostel, Chatter Domel, tel. Muzaffarabad 2480.
Tourist Rest House, tel. 3090—ask for the director of tourism.
Forestry Rest House, tel. 2364—ask for the district forestry officer.
   There are various cheap local hotels around the bus station and along Bank Road. There are also many tourist and forestry rest houses along the Neelum, Jhelum and Leepa valleys. Contact the director of tourism (see above) for advice and bookings. Camping is recommended, although there are no recognized camp sites.

Sights

The town is scattered up the side of the mountain in a well-defended position protected by the rivers. Guarding the town and surrounded by the Neelum River on three sides is the **Red Fort**, built in 1552 by the Chukk rulers of the area. The fort was taken several times: first by the Moghuls, then by the Afghan Durranis and finally by the Sikhs. It now stands abandoned. Across the river on top of the hill is the **Black Fort.**

Muzaffarabad bazaar lies on three levels; only one street is paved. It is worth exploring for walnut carving, cashmere shawls, silk embroidery and papier-mâché work.

There are several good walks from Muzaffarabad. Behind the Secretariat, a road climbs up to the east above the town. From here you can walk up to Pir Chinasi, which at 2,915 metres (9,565 feet) offers good views of the Jhelum Valley and the higher mountains to the north above the Neelum Valley. From the col on the Abbottabad road, you can walk along the ridge separating the Jhelum and Kunhar rivers.

Neelum Valley

The Neelum Valley is 200 kilometres (125 miles) long and runs parallel to the Kunhar River (Kaghan Valley). From the top end of the valley trekking paths lead north around Nanga Parbat to the Indus. A fair-weather road goes as far as Khel, 155 kilometres (96 miles) from Muzaffarabad, more than half of which is surfaced.

The drive up the Neelum Valley is highly recommended. There are daily buses from Muzaffarabad and tourist rest houses at Athmuqam, Neelum town, Dowarian, Sharda, Khel and Halmat, all bookable through the director of tourism, Muzaffarabad, tel. 3090.

The road up the Neelum Valley leaves Muzaffarabad past the Red Fort, crosses the Neelum River on a new bridge and heads north through a steep, narrow gorge. After 16 kilometres (ten miles), at **Ghori** (or Kohori), the road crosses the river again. Just before the bridge, a jeepable track leads left and winds its way northwards up a side stream and deep into the mountains. From here it is possible to walk up Makra Mountain, 3,885 metres (12,744 feet), which is visible from Muzaffarabad, and continue on to Shogran in the Kaghan Valley (see page 355). This makes for a pleasant two- to three-day trek.

Continuing up the Neelum Valley, the next village is **Patika**, six kilometres (four miles) further on. You can leave the main road again here, crossing a wooden suspension bridge, and follow a jeepable track north. This offers splendid opportunities for walking to the higher peaks on the Kaghan–Neelum watershed.

Beyond Patika the main road climbs some 250 metres (800 feet) above the river, which rushes through another narrow gorge. At **Panjgran** the valley opens out and rough tracks lead up the mountains to the south, giving access to the Kafir Khan Range. To the north across the river are more tracks to the Kaghan–Neelum watershed.

At **Noseri**, 42 kilometres (26 miles) from Muzaffarabad, the road crosses back to the north side of the river and follows it up past Mali Mountain, 3,455 metres (11,336 feet), to **Kundalshahi**, 74 kilometres (46 miles) from Muzaffarabad, where the Jagran tributary joins the Neelum from the north. There is a trout hatchery and good trout fishing here.

Athmukam, 84 kilometres (52 miles) from Muzaffarabad, lies at 1,371 metres (4,500 feet) above sea level and is the subdivisional headquarters of the region. The tourist rest house is a good place from which to explore the area. You can hire a jeep here to continue up the valley, though buses and jeep-taxis do run to Khel in good weather.

About nine kilometres (six miles) further upstream is the village of **Neelum** with another tourist rest house. The ceasefire line comes close to the river here: you look straight across into India.

Dowarian, 106 kilometres (66 miles) from Muzaffarabad and at 1,615 metres (5,300 feet), is surrounded by pine forest. A track leads west up a tributary to a lake with a Forestry Department rest house. The track continues over the Rattigali Pass to the Kaghan Valley, about 30 kilometres (20 miles) away.

At **Sharda**, 30 kilometres (20 miles) further on and 1,981 metres (6,500 feet) above sea level, the valley opens out and the hillsides are covered in trees. The village is on the other side of the river and can be reached by a suspension bridge. The village is overlooked by Shardi and Nardi peaks, named after two mythical princes. From Sharda the Surgan tributary leads west up to the Nurinar Pass, from where you can cross another pass and get down to Chilas. There is a rest house here.

Khel, 2,097 metres (6,880 feet) above sea level and 155 kilometres (96 miles) from Muzaffarabad, is a picturesque village with a tourist rest house. Here the Neelum is joined by the Shounter tributary flowing down from the Shounter Pass (another possible route north round the west side of Nanga Parbat to Chilas). Khel is at the end of the bus route, but from here you can hire ponies, or continue by jeep for the last 50 kilometres (31 miles) to the border village of Halmat and its rest house.

In both the Neelum and Leepa valleys (see page 364), you see unusual wooden houses, often three-storeyed and with chalet-style pitched roofs that drain off the rain.

Jhelum Valley

This valley lies east of Muzaffarabad; the road follows the Jhelum's south bank and is surfaced all the way to the border at Chakothi. Over 20 buses daily follow this route as far as Chinari, nine kilometres (six miles) before the border, where there is a tourist rest house. There are two spectacular side trips off the Jhelum Valley, one south to the hill resorts (open to foreign tourists), and one north to the Leepa Valley, in the border zone.

Just east of Muzaffarabad the Jhelum Valley is broad; wheat and maize grow on the terraced hillsides. At **Subri**, the river widens into a small lake created by a landslip in 1975. There is a small anglers' hut here and a few *shikaras* (traditional Kashmiri boats) for hire.

The small town of **Garhi Dupatta**, 24 kilometres (15 miles) from Muzaffarabad, is scattered on both sides of the Jhelum and is connected by a wooden suspension bridge. A jeepable track follows the north bank a little way before climbing up into the mountains. From the end of the track you can walk up into the Kafir Kahn Range.

The main road east climbs high above the river through Saran to the village of **Dhani Baqalan**, 33 kilometres (20 miles) from Muzaffarabad. From here a surfaced road to the right (south) crosses over to **Bagh**, in Punch district, from where you can return via Kohala either to Murree or back to Muzaffarabad. The road passes through four charming hill resorts, each with tourist guest houses set in thick coniferous forest.

Chikar, the first resort, at 1,828 metres (6,000 feet), is small and unspoilt and makes a good base for exploring the area. There are four daily buses from Muzaffarabad. Both the PWD and the Tourism Department have rest houses here, bookable from the director of tourism, Muzaffarabad, tel. 3090, and there are several local hotels. There is a lovely walk following the ridge behind the main rest house. From the top of a hill at the end of the ridge, two hours from Chikar, there are fine views of the surrounding mountains and the Jhelum Valley.

Beyond Chikar the surfaced road continues for 13 kilometres (eight miles) to **Loonbagla**, at 2,011 metres (6,600 feet), with another tourist rest house. A third hill resort at **Dungian**, five kilometres (three miles) further on, has a rest house surrounded by a dense forest of silver firs. The fourth resort is at **Soudhan Gali**,

2,134 metres (7,000 feet) above sea level. From here you can walk along the ridge through the forest, then across open pastureland and, after about three hours, up to the top of **Ganga Chota** peak, part of the Pir Panjal Range. The view from the top is spectacular: Murree to the west, the mountains around the Vale of Kashmir to the east, the mountains of the Neelum Valley to the north, and Punch District to the south. The surfaced road descends from Soudhan Gali to Bagh.

Leepa Valley

Back in the Jhelum Valley and continuing east from the turnoff to the hill resorts, you come to **Naili**, 45 kilometres (28 miles) from Muzaffarabad and the turnoff to the Leepa Valley to the north. Unfortunately, Leepa is out of bounds for foreigners, but is open for domestic tourists from May to November. It is reputedly the most beautiful valley in Azad Kashmir. The fair-weather road climbs up over the **Reshian Pass** (2,750 metres, or 9,022 feet) and drops down the other side into the valley. There are three buses daily from Muzaffarabad to Reshian, beyond which the road is jeepable only.

The village of **Leepa**, about 60 kilometres (37 miles) from Naili and 1,921 metres (6,300 feet) above sea level, has lush green rice fields in summer and typical wooden Kashmiri houses with high gabled ends. **Chananian**, at 2,226 metres (7,300 feet), is surrounded by dense pine forest. There are Forestry Department and Tourism Department rest houses here and some local hotels.

Punch District

Punch (pronounced *Poonch*) District, south of Muzaffarabad District, is another thickly forested mountainous area with spectacular views and excellent walks. **Rawalkot**, the district headquarters, can be reached directly by bus from Islamabad on a surfaced road via Lehtrar and the Dhalkot Bridge across the Jhelum. Alternatively, Punch District can be reached from Muzaffarabad, either via Kohala or via the mountain road through Sudhan Gali to Bagh. It is 76 kilometres (47 miles) from Kohala to Rawalkot on a surfaced road.

Where to Stay

Tourism Department rest houses at Rawalkot, Dhirkot, Bunjosa and Thattapani; book through the director of tourism, Muzaffarabad, tel. 3090.

Forestry Department rest houses at Rawalkot, Dhirkot and Arja; book through the district forestry officer, Rawalkot, tel. 818.

Circuit house at Rawalkot.

PWD rest houses at Bunjosa, Palandri and Tarakhel.

Camping is recommended.

Suggested Itinerary

A suggested three-day itinerary, detailed below, is to drive from Islamabad to Dhirkot via Murree and Kohala on the first day. Explore Mahl Valley and drive to Banjosa via Rawalkot on the second day. Finally, return to Islamabad via Tarakhel, Palandri and Kahuta on the third day.

Dhirkot, at 1,676 metres (5,500 feet) above sea level, is one of the most popular resorts in Punch District. There are bus services from Rawalpindi and Muzaffarabad. From Kohala Bridge the road turns south and climbs out of the Jhelum Valley past the tuberculosis sanatorium at Chamenkot to Dhirkot, 24 kilometres (15 miles) and about one hour's drive from Kohala. There is an excellent Forestry Department rest house surrounded by deodar trees, three tourist huts and one long hut; all are heavily booked in summer. There are many scenic walks in the surrounding area.

From Dhirkot the road continues down to **Arja**, on the Mahl River where it forks. The left fork leads up the Mahl Valley to the rest house at Bagh, the four hill resorts (see pages 363–4) and down to the Jhelum Valley; alternatively you can continue east up the Mahl River to **Dulli** and the **Haji Pir Pass**. The right fork leads south to **Rawalkot**.

Banjosa, at 1,981 metres (6,500 feet), is a popular hill resort 20 kilometres (12 miles) from Rawalkot. To get there head east from Rawalkot on the road towards Hajira and after 13 kilometres (eight miles), at **Kaigala** bazaar, turn south for 11 kilometres (seven miles) to Banjosa. From Kaigala there is a jeepable track north to **Toli Pir**, where there are pleasant walks in the forest and good views into the Mahl Valley and the Pir Panjal Range.

Banjosa's beautifully situated and well-appointed rest house makes an excellent base from which to explore the surrounding countryside; there are walks in the neighbouring pine forests, and a climb to the top of the ridge to the east gives marvellous views over the Pir Panjal and into Indian-held Kashmir. There is also a small lake with boats for hire.

From Banjosa the road continues through **Tarakhel**, at 1,982 metres (6,500 feet), where there is a spartan PWD rest house, and descends for 20 kilometres (12 miles) to **Palandri**, and its adequate PWD rest house. From Palandri it is about 95 kilometres (59 miles) to Islamabad via Azad Pattan and Kahuta.

Kotli and Mirpur Districts

The Kotli and Mirpur districts of Azad Kashmir have less to offer the tourist. The countryside is pleasant but unexciting; only in the east, close to the 'line of control', does it become more interesting. Mangla Dam, in Mirpur District, is excellent for boating and fishing, but is best reached from the Grand Trunk Road at Dina (see page 204).

The Karakoram Highway and the Northern Areas

The Karakoram Highway (or KKH), is the greatest wonder of modern Pakistan. It connects Pakistan to China, twisting through three great mountain ranges—the Himalayas, Karakorams and Pamirs—and follows one of the ancient silk routes along the Indus, Gilgit and Hunza rivers up to the Chinese border at the Khunjerab Pass; it then crosses the high central Asian plateau before winding down through the Pamirs to Kashgar, on the edge of the Taklamakan Desert. The Silk Road was actually a series of trade routes linking China with the West: silks, ceramics, lacquerwork, bronze, iron, furs and spices came west; and wool, linen, ivory, gold, silver, precious and semi-precious stones, asbestos and glass went east.

For much of its 1,284 kilometres (798 miles) the Karakoram Highway crosses a high-altitude desert, where there is less than 100 millimetres (four inches) of rain a year. Passing through gorges, the road cuts along shelves on the cliff faces as much as 500 metres (1,600 feet) above the river. The highway is an incredible feat of engineering, and an enduring monument to the 810 Pakistanis and 82 Chinese who died forcing a road through what has reasonable claim to be the world's most difficult and unstable terrain.

The Karakorams and Himalayas began to form some 55 million years ago when the Indian subcontinent drifted northwards and collided with the Asian land mass. India is still trundling northwards at the geologically reckless rate of five centimetres (two inches) a year, pushing the mountains up by seven millimetres (a quarter of an inch) annually. The KKH runs through the middle of the collision belt, where there is an average of one earth tremor every three minutes. *Karakoram* means 'crumbling rock' in Turkish, an apt description for the giant grey slagheaps capped with snow that tower above the narrow valleys between them.

The Indus River separates the Himalayas from the Karakorams, and the KKH hugs the banks of the Indus for 310 kilometres (193 miles) on its journey north. It winds round the foot of Nanga Parbat, the ninth highest mountain in the world and the last in the Himalayan Range. Then it leaves the Indus and cuts through the Karakoram Range, with 12 out of the world's highest 30 mountains. At 4,733 metres (15,528 feet), the Khunjerab Pass is the highest metalled border crossing on a surfaced road in the world.

The highway was a joint Sino–Pakistani project. Completed in 1978, it took 20 years to build, and at the peak of construction employed 15,000 Pakistanis and 30,000 Chinese. The crews spent years in the remote mountains, using pack horses to carry in equipment. The Chinese concentrated on the bridges, the Pakistani army on the road. The first stages required skill in belaying and rock-climbing; often the engineers had to be suspended on ropes hundreds of feet up sheer cliff faces in order to drill holes for explosives. In the rocky stretches progress was measured in metres rather than kilometres; rockslides were a constant threat.

That the road was completed at all was little short of a miracle. The glaciers, brittle rock structures, strong winds, extreme variations in temperature (from 48°C, or 118°F, in summer to –30°C, or –22°F, in winter) and the seismic activity all combined to make the construction (and today the maintenance) of the highway a continual battle. The Pakistani army deploys 1,000 soldiers to keep the road open. They clear the frequent landslides by bulldozing the rockfalls over the cliff and repair the bridges.

When to Go

The Khunjerab Pass is only open for foreigners from 1 May to 30 November. Gilgit and Hunza are at their most beautiful in April, when the fruit trees are in bloom, and in October, when the autumn colours are at their best. In July, it is very hot in Gilgit and along the Indus Valley.

From Islamabad up the Karakoram Highway to Kashgar is a four-day journey (about 30 hours' driving) providing there are no rockfalls. Or you can fly to Gilgit and take two or three days to drive to Kashgar.

Distances

Islamabad—Abbottabad	121 km (75 mi)	2 hours
Abbottabad—Besham	151 km (94 mi)	3.5 hours
Besham—Komila/Dassu	74 km (46 mi)	2 hours
Komila/Dassu—Chilas	129 km (80 mi)	3 hours
Chilas—Gilgit	128 km (79 mi)	3 hours
Gilgit—Aliabad/Karimabad	105 km (65 mi)	2 hours
Aliabad/Karimabad—Passu	56 km (40 mi)	1 hour
Passu—Sost	33 km (21 mi)	40 minutes
Sost—Khunjerab	64 km (40 mi)	2 hours
Khunjerab—Pirali	32 km (20 mi)	40 minutes
Pirali—Tashkurgan	96 km (60 mi)	2 hours
Tashkurgan—Kashgar	295 km (183 mi)	7 hours

Suggested Itineraries

Four days

Day 1	Drive from Islamabad to Chilas.
Day 2	Chilas to Karimabad, with a stop in Gilgit for lunch.
Day 3	Karimabad to Tashkurgan.
Day 4	Tashkurgan to Kashgar.

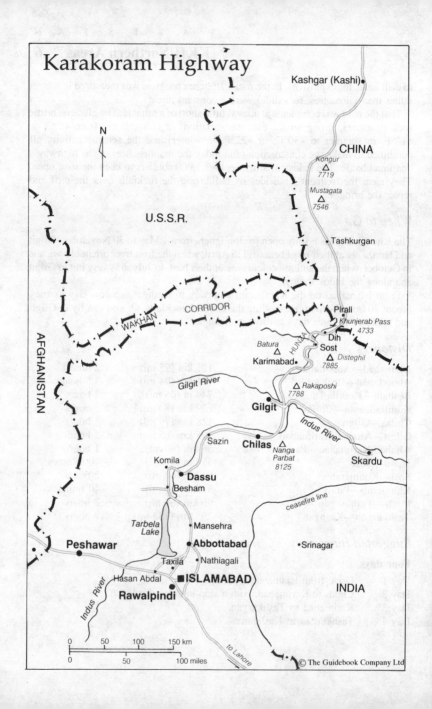

Karakoram Highway

Kashgar (Kashi)

CHINA

Kongur
7719

Mustagata
7546

U.S.S.R.

Tashkurgan

WAKHAN   CORRIDOR

Pirali
Khunjerab Pass
4733

AFGHANISTAN

Batura   Dih
Sost
Karimabad   Disteghil
7885

Gilgit River

Rakaposhi
7788

Gilgit   Indus River

Sazin   Chilas

Komila   Nanga
Parbat   Skardu
8125

Dassu
Besham   ceasefire line

Tarbela
Lake   Mansehra

Peshawar   Srinagar

Taxila   Abbottabad

Hasan Abdal   Nathiagali

ISLAMABAD

Rawalpindi   INDIA

Indus River

0   50   100   150 km
0   50   100 miles

to Lahore

© The Guidebook Company Ltd

Five days

Day 1	Drive from Islamabad to Saidu Sharif in Swat via Bunar.
Day 2	Saidu Sharif to Chilas via the Shangla Pass.
Days 3–5	As above.

Five Days

Day 1	Drive from Islamabad to Besham.
Day 2	Besham to Gilgit.
Day 3	Gilgit to Karimabad, Passu or Sost.
Days 4–5	To Tashkurgan and Kashgar.

Six days

Day 1	Drive from Islamabad to Nathiagali.
Day 2	Nathiagali to Besham.
Day 3	Besham to Gilgit.
Day 4	Gilgit to Karimabad, Passu or Sost.
Days 5–6	To Tashkurgan and Kashgar.

All these itineraries involve long stretches of driving. The most beautiful area lies between Gilgit and Sost. It is recommended that you break your journey for an extra day in Karimabad. Do not be tempted to rush through northern Pakistan in your haste to reach China: it is more beautiful on the Pakistani side of the border, and the tourist facilities are better.

The last reliable supply of super-grade petrol is at Gilgit. Ordinary-grade petrol is usually available at Battal, Batagram, Besham, Pattan, Dassu, Sazin, Chilas, Jaglot, Gilgit, Chalt, Aliabad and Sost, but supplies are erratic.

HAZARA

The first day's journey up the KKH passes through Hazara, a long narrow district between the Indus and Jhelum rivers with its capital at Abbottabad. Most people speed through Hazara on their way north. This is a shame, as the area contains some beautiful and varied scenery, and little-known side valleys that are well worth exploring.

The name Hazara is derived from the Persian word *hazar*, meaning 'thousand'. According to local legend, the descendants of Ghengis Khan, or perhaps Tamerlane, left a colony of a thousand Mongols or Turks in Hazara. (There is another Hazara in central Afghanistan, the Hazarajat.)

Until Partition, the easiest all-weather route to Kashmir was through Hazara, but since 1947 this section of the frontier between Pakistan and India has been disputed, so the border is closed. The ancient trade route ran from Taxila north through Haripur, Havelian, Abbottabad and Mansehra, then east to join the Jhelum River

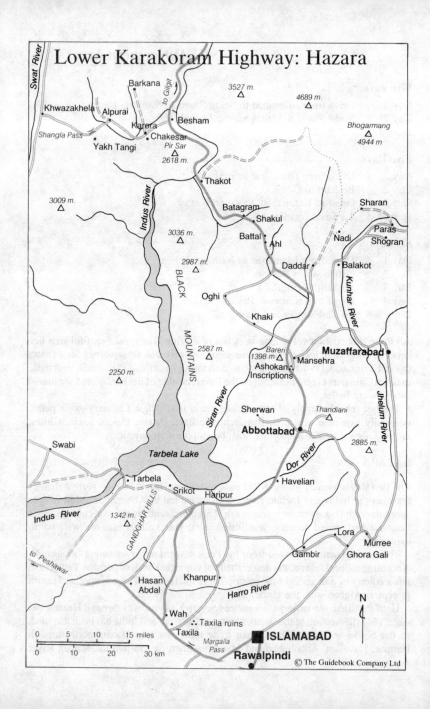

Lower Karakoram Highway: Hazara

Swat River

Barkana

Khwazakhela • Alpurai

Karera

Shangla Pass

Yakh Tangi

Chakesar

Pir Sar

2618 m.

Besham

to Gilgit

3527 m.

4689 m.

Bhogarmang

4944 m

Thakot

3009 m.

Batagram

Shakul

Battal

Ahl

Daddar

Sharan

Paras

Nadi

Shogran

Balakot

Indus River

BLACK

3036 m.

2987 m.

Oghi

Khaki

Kunhar River

MOUNTAINS

2587 m.

2250 m.

Bareri

1398 m

Mansehra

Ashokan

Inscriptions

Muzaffarabad •

Siran River

Sherwan

Thandiani

Abbottabad •

Jhelum River

2885 m.

Swabi

Tarbela Lake

Tarbela

Srikot

Haripur

Havelian

Dor River

GANDOGHAR HILLS

Indus River

1342 m.

Lora

Murree

Gambir

Ghora Gali

to Peshawar

Hasan

Abdal

Khanpur

Harro River

N

Wah

Taxila ruins

Taxila

Margalla

Pass

ISLAMABAD

0   5   10   15 miles

0   10   20   30 km

Rawalpindi

© The Guidebook Company Ltd

and up through the mountains to Srinagar. This was the route the Moghul emperors took.

Following the decline of the Moghul Empire, Hazara came under the loose control of the Afghan Durranis, and then in 1818 passed to the Sikhs under Ranjit Singh. The Sikhs, like the Moghuls, coveted Hazara because they wanted to secure the route to Kashmir, but they had difficulty in quelling the unruly tribesmen. The 1907 Kashmir *Gazetteer* records that in 1835 a traveller passing through the district noted that the fertile Pakhli Plain near Mansehra was still overrun by robber bands; each village had to defend itself as best it could by erecting hedges.

The British took direct control of Hazara when they annexed the Sikh territories in 1849, but they too were given a hard time by the hill tribes of the Black Mountains along the Indus.

The people of lower Hazara are indistinguishable from the people of the northern Punjab. The so-called Swatis of the northern parts of Hazara are the descendants of the previous inhabitants of the Swat Valley, who were driven out of their homeland by the Pathan Yusufzais in the 16th century. The nomadic Gujars still wander up and down the district. In spring and autumn you see them on the march, their camels and donkeys laden with all their belongings, taking their herds of cattle, goats and sheep up to the high summer pastures of the Kaghan Valley and down again to the plains for the winter. Their women wear full gathered skirts over baggy trousers and do not cover their faces.

Islamabad to Abbottabad

There is a choice of four roads from Islamabad to Abbottabad.

The most scenic but longest route is via **Murree** and **Nathiagali**, which takes three to four hours (see page 235). The road is blocked by snow from December to April.

The other three roads all start out on the Grand Trunk Road towards Peshawar, leaving the main road at different points and converging at Haripur, the first market town in the Dor Valley.

The most interesting and second prettiest route is via **Taxila** (see page 256). The road passes the door of Taxila Museum and near six of the more important sites. At the end of the Taxila Valley the road crosses the Harro River at Khanpur Dam, then descends to the bottom of a steep valley. It bears left through eroded countryside and enters Haripur from the east, 41 kilometres (25 miles) from the Grand Trunk Road. Shortly after the railway crossing at the beginning of Haripur township take the right fork. It is two and a half hours to Abbottabad by this route.

The fastest route leaves the Grand Trunk Road 32 kilometres (20 miles) from Islamabad, just before **Wah**, passes through the small, congested township of **Sarai Khola**, and continues past a big heavy engineering complex and other factories. Just beyond the level crossing, nine kilometres (six miles) from the turning off the Grand Trunk Road, is **Bhallar Stupa**, probably dating from the sixth century, and with an unusually high drum, which has been sliced through the middle by treasure hunters. The countryside becomes increasingly eroded, and the road twists and turns through many gullies before it joins the road from Hasan Abdal two kilometres (a mile) before Haripur and 32 kilometres (20 miles) from the Grand Trunk Road. It is two hours to Abbottabad by this route.

The **bus route** to Abbottabad turns right just beyond **Hasan Abdal** on the Grand Trunk Road, 48 kilometres (30 miles) from Islamabad. The road runs through flat country with relatively little erosion, and reaches Haripur 33 kilometres (20 miles) from the turnoff. About 25 kilometres (16 miles) from Hasan Abdal a new road to the left leads up into the Gandghar Hills through Srikot and down to Tarbela Dam.

About a kilometre (half a mile) before Haripur another turning to the left leads down a straight road lined with big trees to the edge of Tarbela Lake. There are fishing boats moored here.

It was somewhere near here that a large force of Sikh soldiers was swept away by a disastrous flood in June 1841 (see also page 386). The *Civil and Military Gazette* reported:

At two in the afternoon, the waters were seen by the soldiers encamped on the banks of the Indus to be coming down upon them, down the various channels, and to be swelling out of these to overspread the plain in a dark, muddy mass which swept everything before it. The camp was completely overwhelmed; 500 soldiers at once perished . . . trees and houses were swept away; every trace of civilisation was effaced.

The entire countryside, to within 30 kilometres (20 miles) of Peshawar, was under water, and many lives were lost.

Haripur is named after Hari Singh, the most trusted and famous of Ranjit Singh's generals. Early in the 18th century the Sikhs rapidly overran the Punjab. Ranjit Singh took Attock Fort in 1813, cutting the Afghan Durrani lines of communication from Kabul to Kashmir, and in 1819 achieved his main goal of wresting Kashmir from the Afghans. The route to Kashmir went through Hazara, where the hill tribes were savage and unruly. Haripur was strategically important because it controlled the route through the hills to the Indus at Tarbela, then a small village on the east side of the river nine kilometres (six miles) upstream from the present dam. Ranjit Singh installed Hari Singh in Haripur to subdue and punish the tribes. He was a successful administrator and ruled in comparative peace until 1834, when he was sent to govern Peshawar.

Haripur became less important when Abbottabad was built in the 1850s. Today it is a busy little town, famous for its orchards and fruit, for it lies in the middle of a lush, fertile valley and is irrigated by the Dor River. This is a good place to buy cheap vegetables and fruit from the wayside stails.

Havelian, 20 kilometres (12 miles) from Haripur, marks the end of the railway and the official beginning of the KKH. It is 795 kilometres (497 miles) from here to the Chinese border. The first stretch of the KKH as far as Mansehra was built in the 1890s and was the earliest surfaced road in the district. The road bypasses the town proper and runs past the enormous walled and turreted enclosure of an ordnance factory to the new bridge across the Dor River. It then begins to climb up through brown and barren hills, crosses the low Salhad Pass, and drops down into Abbottabad.

Abbottabad

Named after James Abbott, Abbottabad is pleasantly cool at 1,220 metres (4,000 feet) above sea level. Abbott (b.1807) was a colleague of Nicholson and Edwardes and one of Sir Henry Lawrence's 'young men' who became 'advisers' to the Sikhs after the First Sikh War in 1846. 'He was,' wrote Lawrence, 'of the stuff of the true knight-errant, gentle as a girl in thought, word, or deed, overflowing with warm affection, and ready at all times to sacrifice himself for his country or his friend.' This may sound rather exaggerated, but it is evident that Abbott was held in considerable affection and respect by the people of Hazara.

In 1927 Sir Olaf Caroe met an old man who actually knew Abbott and told him:

He [Abbott] was a little man, with bristly hair on his face and kind eyes, and we loved him . . . . I was in the *jirga* [council] when he was asking us if we would stand and fight the Sikhs if he stood by us. We swore we would, and there were tears in our eyes, and a tear in Abbott Sahib's eyes too. And we did! He was our father, and we were his children. There are no *Angrez* [English] like Abbott Sahib now.

Sir Olaf Caroe, *The Pathans* (1958)

When the Second Sikh War broke out in 1848, Abbott found himself isolated in Hazara, with the Sikh general Chattar Singh holding lower Hazara and the area round Hasan Abdal. Abbott took refuge in the Gandghar Hills with the Pathan Mishwanis, whom he found to be loyal and willing allies. He led them down to the Margalla Pass to block the Sikh retreat after the battle of Gujrat and helped to enforce the Sikh surrender on the plains of Rawalpindi in March 1849.

After the annexation of the Sikh territories, Abbott became Hazara's first deputy commissioner, which post he held successfully until 1853. He was never promoted, however, but was subsequently transferred to the gun factory at Ishapur near Calcutta. His successor, Herbert Edwardes, later commissioner at Peshawar, made amends by establishing the new cantonment town of Abbottabad.

The town is a useful base for tourists. The **Tourist Information Office** of the PTDC, on Jinnah Road (tel. 2446) next to the church, is particularly helpful. Here you can make arrangements for hiring jeeps to go up the Kaghan Valley and collect reservation slips for previously booked rest houses in the Kaghan Valley, Kohistan and elsewhere.

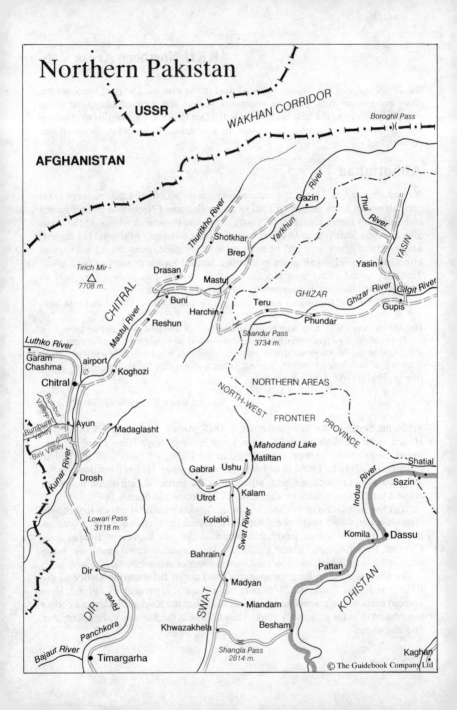

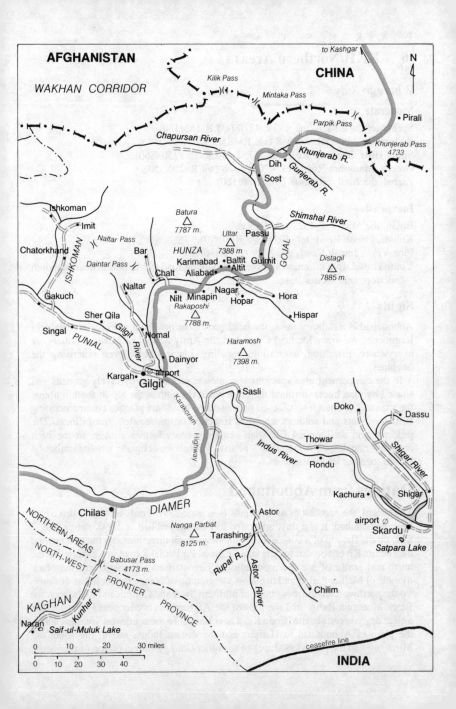

Where to Stay

Moderate

Springfield, the Mall, tel. 4834, 4770 (s/d Rs185/330).
Sarban, the Mall, tel. 4876–8 (s/d Rs185/330).
Simla Hills, Sherwan Road, tel. 5752 (s/d Rs150/250–360).
Greens, Mansehra Road, tel. 4408, 5326 (s/d Rs250/350).
Zarbat, the Mall, tel. 5508 (s/d Rs80/120).

Inexpensive

Bolan, the Mall, tel. 4623 (s/d Rs50/80).
Kohsar, Jinnah Road, tel. 4924 (s/d Rs30/50).
Pine View, Jinnah Road, tel. 2729 (s/d Rs30/50).
Youth Hostel, five kilometres (three miles) along road to Mansehra, near Mandian
    bus stop, near Octroi Post.

Sights

Abbottabad is a military town, the headquarters of the Frontier Force and Baluchi
Regiments, the army Medical Corps and the Army School of Music. Soldiers are
everywhere, marching, exercising, parading, playing polo, even practising the
bagpipes.

    In the cantonment area spacious bungalows, surrounded by lovely gardens and
shaded by pine trees, surround the church and the club at the top of the hill above
the bazaar. The church is still used occasionally. Inside are plaques commemorating
British officers and soldiers who died in action or, more often, from illness. The
peaceful and well-tended Christian cemetery bears further witness to the high
mortality rate despite Abbottabad's relatively salubrious climate: whole families lie
buried together under the trees.

Outings from Abbottabad

Thandiani, the prettiest of all the Galis (see page 239) is only an hour's drive east
from Abbottabad. It is a tiny, unspoiled hill station perched at 2,692 metres (8,832
feet) on the flat top of a conical hill with views in all directions. To the east beyond
the Jhelum River you can see the snow-capped Pir Panjal Range in Kashmir. To the
north and northeast are the mountains of Kohistan and Kaghan, with the black
triangle of Malika Parbat and the snow-covered tip of Nanga Parbat in the distance.
To the northwest are the mountains of northern Swat and Chitral, and to the west the
Black Mountain Range and the hills of the Afghanistan border near Peshawar. On
a clear day you can see the Hindu Kush near Kabul. To the southwest you look across
the plain of Abbottabad to Haripur and the distant Indus, and to the south are
Miranjani and the pine-clad slopes of the other Galis. You feel on top of the world,

and yet it is only 24 kilometres (15 miles) from Abbottabad.

The road to Thandiani is surfaced, in good condition and open most of the year. Take the Nathiagali road out of Abbottabad and turn left after 4.5 kilometres (2.8 miles). At first you drive past strange fractured rocks, then on terraced slopes with houses perched on top of the hillocks. About 15,000 people live on the flanks of Thandiani overlooking the flat Abbottabad plain and the hills beyond. The road twists and turns, climbing steeply. It follows a ravine, with sharp drops into the stream below, crosses a bridge and enters an old pine forest, snaking its way ever upward to the top of the ridge.

At the top are two rest houses, one belonging to the Forestry Department and bookable through the divisional forest officer, Galis Division, Abbottabad, tel. 2433; the other belongs to the Public Works Department and can be booked through the PWD, Abbottabad, tel. 2011. Take all your own bedding and food.

The abandoned church, closed post office and empty bungalows are a ghostly reminder that Thandiani was once a thriving hill station, developed late in the last century for the European residents of Abbottabad and missionaries from the North-West Frontier Province. It fell into disuse after Partition and has only recently been opened up again following the rebuilding of the road. The local restaurants serve Pakistani food and the people are very friendly.

From the top of Thandiani you can take a number of steep walks through the mature pine forests. North from the church it is two kilometres (a mile) to a green glade called Hule ka Dana, a magnificent spot, cool and peaceful, with an even clearer view of Nanga Parbat than from the top. From Thandiani to Nathiagali, it is a two-day walk over Miranjani, with an overnight stay in a Forestry Department rest house midway (see map page 240).

Sherwan, a village on a 1,200-metre (5,000-foot) -high ridge to the west of Abbottabad, makes another pleasant daytrip. Take the road through the cantonment up the hill to Frontier House, once the residence of President Ayub Khan and now a government guest house with a fine view down over the plains. There is a charming Chinese pagoda in the garden. You can park near the guest house and walk along the ridge behind, the brown hills stretching before you.

The road to Sherwan is an unmarked left turn just before the gates to Frontier House. It drops down into a fertile, partly wooded valley before twisting and turning up into the hills. The drive is pretty all the way, and there are good walks and picnic spots at the end.

Mansehra

It is 24 kilometres (15 miles) from Abbottabad to Mansehra through eroded countryside. Just before Mansehra the road divides, left to the Indus and the KKH, right to the Kaghan Valley and Muzaffarabad, on the old route to Kashmir. This was an important junction on the ancient trade routes.

Mansehra developed as a trading centre at this junction. It is ideally situated in the wide, fertile Pakhli Plain and surrounded by hills. It is particularly attractive in spring, when the green fields contrast with the snow-clad mountain.

The KKH bypasses the centre of Mansehra, but most of the buses go through the main bazaar, where you can stay in the Errum Hotel, tel. 2809 (s/d Rs60/90), or in half a dozen cheaper places along Kashmir Road.

Ashokan Inscriptions: the Mauryan emperor Ashoka inscribed another set of his edicts here in the third century BC, outlining his policy of government and instructing his subject on how to lead good and virtuous lives (for a full description, see pages 310–11). The three big boulders on which the edicts are written are right beside the KKH, about four kilometres (2.5 miles) from the road fork. They are signposted in English and protected by roofs, but the Kharoshthi writing is so weatherbeaten as to be barely discernible.

Bareri Hill (1,397 metres, or 4,583 feet), to the left (northwest) of the road, dominates the Pakhli Plain. Named after a Hindu god, the hill is sacred to the Hindus and used to be an important place of pilgrimage. The path to the summit starts from just below the Ashokan edicts.

About five kilometres (three miles) past the Ashokan edicts a road leads off to the left to **Oghi** in the Black Mountains, a slow but scenic detour. The tribesmen of the Black Mountains were particularly hostile to all outsiders and gave continual trouble to the British.

Another sidetrip off the KKH is up the **Siran River** to **Daddar**. This road leaves the KKH to the right about 25 kilometres (15 miles) from the fork at Mansehra. Daddar is an attractive village in a cup-shaped valley with views up to the 4,944-metre (16,219-foot) Bhogarmang Mountain. It is well known for its tuberculosis sanatorium, and has an attractive Forestry Department rest house, bookable through the divisional forest officer, Abbottabad, tel. 2433. The road continues beyond Daddar and climbs sharply through pine forests along the Siran River. From the end of the road a jeep track leads through **Nadi**, and another Forestry Department rest house, then across to Sharan in the Kaghan Valley (see page 355).

The KKH itself follows a picturesque valley, with a shallow boulder-strewn river on the left, then climbs up into mature pine forests. After passing through a small gorge with cliffs of white china clay, the road drops down into a wide fertile bowl with views up to the Black Mountains in the distance. Climbing out of the bowl through another smaller forest, you reach the Nandhiar watershed and the superbly sited PWD three-roomed rest house at **Shakul**, bookable through the PWD, Mansehra, tel. 525. This makes a lovely place to break your journey: it stands on a bluff overlooking the plain and there are good walks through the forest and villages.

Beyond the rest house the road winds gently down through rocky scrub, past poplar trees and rice terraces, to the Indus, 94 kilometres (58 miles) from Mansehra. There is a viewpoint here with a notice board misinforming you that Pir Sar Mountain on the opposite bank of the Indus is the Aornos associated with Alexander the Great and that this was the furthest point north Alexander reached in his travels. Archaeologists now believe this to be false (see page 324), and that Alexander never

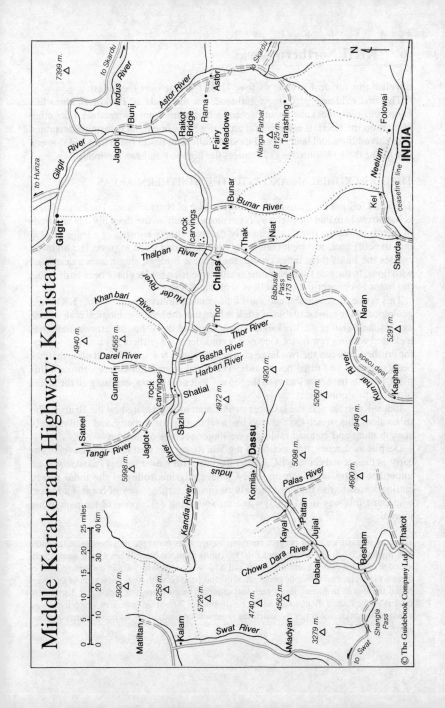

Middle Karakoram Highway: Kohistan

travelled this far. Just beyond view is Thakot Bridge over the Indus.

The first evidence of Chinese influence on the KKH is **Thakot Bridge**, 123 kilometres (76 miles) and about two and a half hours from Abbottabad. Like other bridges on the KKH, it is a graceful arch of white cement, its balustrade decorated with carved lions and lanterns and its side walls with pastel butterflies and flowers. For the next 310 kilometres (193 miles) the highway follows the Indus.

THROUGH KOHISTAN AND INTO THE NORTHERN AREAS

The KKH follows the Indus River round the base of Nanga Parbat. The Indus Valley is so narrow here that the highway is cut along a shelf on the steep hillside hundreds of metres above the river. Occasionally the road simply consists of a ledge blasted into the cliff face, just high enough to allow a loaded truck to pass. The highway crosses the Indus three times on elegant Chinese bridges, single arches decorated with lions. In the past five years nine small suspension bridges have been built across the Indus to connect the side valleys with the KKH.

This is one of the wildest and most inhospitable stretches of the whole KKH, and geologically the most unstable of all. It is here that the Indian geological plate grinds against the Asian plate. Rockslides block the road daily, but the army usually has it cleared within a few hours. Geologists consider this a particularly interesting area, for crushed between the two large continental plates is a small island plate that has been squeezed and tilted northwards. The Karakoram Highway cuts through this plate, from its base near Pattan to the top at Chalt near Hunza, exposing all the layers of the earth's crust.

Indus–Kohistan was the last area of Pakistan to be explored by the British. The tribes along this stretch have always had a reputation for ferocity, and until recently slave-trading and caravan-raiding were major sources of income.

Despite its dangers, this section of the Silk Route was well known to travellers as early as the second century BC. Under the powerful Kushan rulers Pakistan was an important centre of Buddhism; and Chinese pilgrims followed the Indus down, cutting across to the Buddhist monasteries in the fertile valley of Swat. Fa Hsien, who came this way in AD 403, wrote the following description of the path in his journal:

The way was difficult and rugged, [running along] a bank exceedingly precipitous, which rose up there, a hill-like wall of rock, 10,000 cubits from the base. When a man approached the edge of it, his eyes became unsteady; and if he wished to go forward in the same direction there was no place on which he could place his foot; and beneath were the waters of the river called the Indus. In former times men had chiselled paths along the rocks, and distributed ladders on the face of them, to the number altogether of 700, at the bottom of which there was a suspension bridge of ropes by which the river was crossed, its banks being there 80 paces apart.

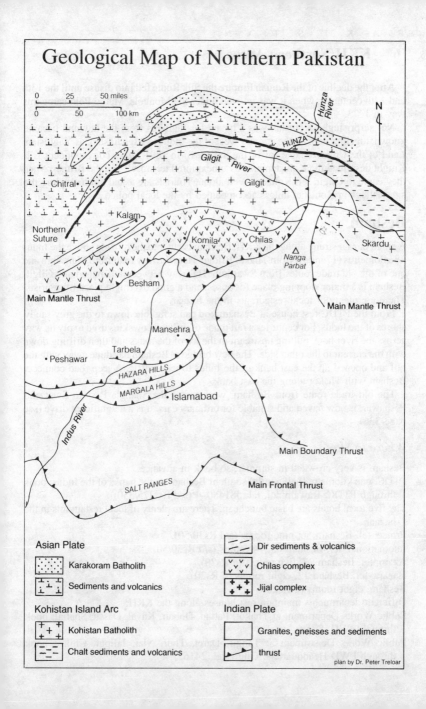

Geological Map of Northern Pakistan

```
0        25        50 miles
0    50        100 km
```

Hunza River

HUNZA

Gilgit River

Gilgit

Chitral

Kalam

Northern Suture

Komila

Chilas

Nanga Parbat

Skardu

Besham

Main Mantle Thrust

Main Mantle Thrust

Mansehra

Tarbela

Peshawar

HAZARA HILLS

MARGALA HILLS

Islamabad

Indus River

Main Boundary Thrust

SALT RANGES

Main Frontal Thrust

Asian Plate

Karakoram Batholith

Sediments and volcanics

Kohistan Island Arc

Kohistan Batholith

Chalt sediments and volcanics

Dir sediments & volcanics

Chilas complex

Jijal complex

Indian Plate

Granites, gneisses and sediments

thrust

plan by Dr. Peter Treloar

After the decline of the Roman Empire the Silk Route fell into disuse until the 13th and 14th centuries, when it was revived under the Mongols. Marco Polo came this way in 1273.

Not surprisingly, Kohistan was a haven for fugitives from the law and became known, together with all the country west of the Indus to Afghanistan, as Yaghistan, Land of the Ungovernable (or of the Savages). In 1891 *Times* correspondent E F Knight described the Kohistan area as 'unexplored territory'; and the British, when they came to Gilgit, left Kohistan well alone. Tourists are asked not to explore the side valleys in Kohistan unless accompanied by the local police.

Besham

A small bazaar strung along the KKH, Besham is cut into the hillside above the Indus 28 kilometres (17 miles) from Thakot Bridge. Here the new road from Mansehra and one of the old trade routes from Swat join. Halfway between Islamabad and Gilgit, Besham is a major stopping place for buses, and a good overnight place for tourists. There are plenty of local restaurants in the bazaar.

From the PTDC rest house at Besham you can scramble down to the grey sandy shores of the Indus. For centuries a raft made of inflated cowskins used to ply its way across the river here, pulling upstream in the lee of the rocks and then drifting down with the current to the other side. The new bridge at Besham has done away with the raft and opened up the east bank of the Indus to jeep traffic. A jeep road connects Besham with Thakot along the east bank.

The old trade route from Besham, west across the Shangla Pass to Swat and Peshawar, is now paved and suitable for ordinary cars. It is a magnificent drive (see page 336).

Where to Stay

Besham is very crowded in summer, so book in advance.

PTDC, one kilometre (half a mile) south of Besham on the banks of the Indus; book through PTDC, Rawalpindi, tel. 581480–4 (s/d Rs 275/350).

The five local hotels are basic but cheap. There are plenty of local restaurants in the bazaar.

Prince, tel. Besham 56, nine rooms (s/d Rs30/50).

International, tel. Besham 65, 14 rooms (s/d Rs30/50).

Azam, tel. Besham 27, five rooms (d Rs20).

Hazara, tel. Besham 12, eight rooms (d Rs20).

Besham, eight rooms (d Rs25).

Different departments maintain rest houses along the KKH:

Public Works Department at Thakot, Pattan, Dobair, Kayal, Dassu, Shatial; book through PWD, Dassu.

Public Works Department at Tangir, Darel, Thor, Niat, Jalipur, Chilas; book through PWD Headquarters, Gilgit, tel. 2416.

Police Department at Dassu; book through the superintendent of police, Dassu.
Forestry Department at Dassu and Shatial.
Government Department at Dassu; book through the deputy commissioner, Dassu.

Besham to Chilas

Beyond Besham the mountains on either side of the Indus rise to 5,000 metres (16,500 feet). They are very rugged, the lower slopes covered in sparse scrub, the higher inaccessible ridges in pine forest. Fertile alpine valleys sandwiched between the mountains have only recently been connected to the KKH and the outside world by rough paths and the occasional jeep track. These side valleys are wider higher up, but are usually very narrow where they join the Indus: it is only from the air that you realize they exist. C E Biddulph described the mouths of these valleys in the 1906 Kashmir *Gazetteer* as being:

. . . so narrow that it is difficult to find a pathway beside the torrent, which issues between overhanging rocks. In addition to this, the enormous rush of water during the summer months from numerous and extensive glaciers and snow fields impedes communication . . . . Several valleys exist into and out of which cattle and horses can only pass during two months of the year, and in which the continual falling of huge masses of rock . . . frequently sweeps away the narrow pathways. The paths are of the rudest kind, and necessity has made the inhabitants intrepid cragsmen . . . . Communication is maintained over the rivers at certain points by hanging bridges of plaited birch twigs—a means of crossing which tries the steadiest nerves.

The people of these isolated valleys are subsistence farmers who cultivate wheat, barley and maize on irrigated terraces stacked up the steep moutainsides. Herds of goats, sheep and mountain cattle find pastures at the top ends of the valleys.

From the KKH you see villages and isolated houses perched on every available spur, the latter almost invisible against the rock and often with no obvious access path. Some of the houses cling to the rocks just above the swirling Indus, with not so much as a field surrounding them. The occasional stone fortress still stands beside its village. Originally the villagers sheltered in the forts whenever attacked and stored their grain there for safekeeping.

The KKH follows the west bank of the Indus and climbs 700 metres (2,000 feet) up the hillside above the river. Framed in the sharp V of the Indus Valley are photogenic views of snowcapped mountains.

Dobair Bazaar, 15 kilometres (nine miles) from Besham, is a typical Kohistani settlement with wooden bazaar stalls flanking the road, where tribesmen with bandoleers of ammunition and rifles slung over their shoulders sip tea. The PWD rest house here is very basic. If the road is blocked and you are stuck here overnight, you would do better to look for a charpoy (rope bed) in the bazaar. The fertile Dobair Valley leads back into the mountains from the KKH. Tourists are advised not to wander alone up here.

Those interested in geology should watch out for the bottom layers of the earth's crust exposed just before **Jujial** (or Jijal) about five kilometres (three miles) past Dobair. The rock formations are extraordinary. A set of tight folds in the cliff on the left of the road is followed 100 metres (yards) later by a small gully, on one side of which are the white quartz rocks of the Indian geological plate, and on the other the green rocks of the bottom layers of the oceanic plate, normally 30 kilometres (20 miles) below the earth's surface.

Round a corner you catch your first sight of the wide bowl of **Pattan**. The village is down below by the river, with a bridge across the Indus and a jeep track leading up the Palas Valley on the other side. A memorial by the road down to Pattan reads:

Some time in the future when others will ply the KKH little will they realize the amount of sweat, courage, dedication, endurance and human sacrifice that has gone into the making of this road. But as you drive along, tarry a little to say a short prayer for those silent brave men of the Pakistan army who gave their lives to realize a dream, now known as the Karakoram Highway.

In December 1974 an earthquake shook the Kohistan region, virtually wiping out Pattan and its environs. Farmers and shepherds were hurled down the mountainsides into the Indus. Several hundred Chinese working on the highway had just returned to their tents and miraculously escaped death in the massive rockslides. In all, the earthquake left 5,000 dead and more than 15,000 injured. The magnitude of the disaster caught the world's attention, and money poured in from all sides. Much of it went towards the longterm development of the region. Today there are few signs of the aftermath of the earthquake; the same frontless shacks selling basic foodstuffs and commodities are to be found here as in other settlements. The PWD rest house in Pattan is right beside the Indus; it has a lovely view of the river and a small garden.

Do not attempt to follow the jeep track up the **Palas Valley** unless accompanied by a local dignitary. The same is true of the **Kayal Valley**, which opens onto the Indus from the west about ten kilometres (six miles) beyond Pattan. The PWD rest house in Kayal stands beside a burbling rock-strewn stream in a shady garden; a jeep track leads for about nine kilometres (six miles) up the valley.

At **Komila/Dassu** the road crosses to the east bank of the Indus. Komila is the bazaar on the west bank of the river; the buses stop here and local hotel/restaurants line the road. Dassu is the administrative headquarters on the east bank, and the deputy commissioner's office, police post and petrol pumps are all located here. A steep track leads up the hill to the DC's house and the comfortable, fully furnished police guest house with a bird's-eye view down to the Indus and Komila huddled along its bank. You can climb up behind the guest house to the top of the ridge which divides the Indus from the Dassu Valley. In the village on the ridge the women wear headdresses fringed with beads and coins, their babies coin-trimmed bonnets with earflaps.

From Dassu the KKH runs due north. The sheer gorge narrows—more workers were killed along this stretch than any other, as the highway here has been blasted

out along a ledge with an overhang above. The olive green river slides along the base of the cliff about 100 metres (300 feet) below the road. Rocks trickle down the cliff face above and scatter on the tarmac. After ten kilometres (six miles) the cliffs slope outwards into a sharp V: the lower slopes are dotted with small shrubs and wild olives, and tiny settlements cling precariously to the mountainsides.

A new bridge crosses the Indus to the Kandia Valley. A jeep road goes into the valley for 35 kilometres (22 miles); from the valley's end it is a 30-kilometre (19-mile) trek across the pass to Kalam, in the Swat Valley. This was the most popular of the routes taken by the Buddhist pilgrims in the first century. Tourists should not come here alone.

The valley narrows down to another tight gorge and turns east. Here the road is gouged into the cliff face 300 metres (1,000 feet) above the Indus.

Just before leaving Kohistan, the hills stand back and the river slows down. A road leads down to a sandy beach where gold panners camp; in winter they pan the streams with flat wooden boards.

Sazin, the first village in the Northern Areas, is a couple of kilometres (a mile or so) away on the right, out of sight of the road. A large, irrigated settlement, it spreads out across the flat shoulder of the mountain. Two unmarked jeep tracks lead up to it. About one kilometre (half a mile) past the second turn you come to a timber dump and army camp near a bridge. Then five kilometres (three miles) later you come to the settlement of **Shatial** and for the first time you see green fields and fruit trees between the road and the river. Here you will find a petrol pump, tea shop, police post, hospital and Forestry Department rest house. A sign by the road reads 'Petroglyphs for the next 70 km' (43 miles), followed soon after by 'Visit Shatial sites'.

The **petroglyphs** are carved on hundreds of rocks along the banks of the Indus and up the side valleys. Invaders, traders, pilgrims and locals—all left a record of their passage. Though people have probably lived in the area since 3000 BC, the earliest petroglyphs are the lifelike leopards and antelopes of the Scythians or Sakas, Iranian nomads (first century BC). The Parthians (first century AD) drew warriors on horseback. In Kushan times Buddhism was brought by missionaries on their way north to China, and in the centuries that followed Chinese pilgrims came to Pakistan to visit the Buddhist shrines. There are thousands of drawings of Buddhas and Buddhist stupas with inscriptions in various languages reflecting the anxiety of the pious pilgrims on their difficult journey along the Indus, and often giving the date, destination and purpose of their journey.

Inscriptions and drawings of different periods are all jumbled together, often with four different languages on the same rock, written centuries apart. The Tibetans describe their dominance of the region in the eighth century, and there are pictures of Hindu warriors waving battle axes at the conquering Moslems. Islam seems to have inspired only the simplest animal drawings, usually of ibex. Today similar drawings are still painted onto the pillars and beams in village houses for good luck.

Some of the drawings are visible from the highway, so you can glance at them without getting out of the car. At Shatial a pathway is laid out through the rocks, and a short walk takes you past the most interesting drawings and many inscriptions, mostly in Sogdian script. If you need to stretch your legs, you can walk along the sandy shore here looking for drawings, or picnic by the water's edge.

A bridge crosses the Indus here, from which jeep tracks lead north up both the **Tangir** and **Darel** valleys. Each valley has a PWD rest house. From Sateel, at the north end of the Tangir Valley, you can hike across to Gupis, in the Gilgit Valley. From the top end of the Darel Valley a path leads over to Gilgit; this was the most popular trade route in former times. There are a number of Buddhist inscriptions on rocks along the Darel Valley, and the carving on the wooden mosques in both Darel and Tangir shows strong Buddhist influence (see also page 334). Tourists should check with the police and deputy commissioner in Chilas before going up these valleys.

From the KKH jeep roads lead to the right up the **Harban**, **Basha** and **Thor** valleys; there is a PWD rest house at Thor. At Basha there is another bridge across the Indus to Khanbari; a new dam is planned a couple of kilometres (a mile or so) further up. Two more new bridges leading across the Indus to the **Huder** and **Thalpan** valleys encourage the development of this traditionally hostile district.

Sandy beaches and wide stony areas flank the river for most of the next 100 kilometres (60 miles) as it curves round the foot of Nanga Parbat. Driving is easier here. In places the road runs straight across acres of gravel and round pebbles that were probably once the floor of a lake. It is somewhere along this stretch that a landslide from the foothills of Nanga Parbat blocked the Indus in 1840, causing the formation of a great lake which stretched nearly to Gilgit. When the dam burst, the resulting floods led to terrible destruction in the Punjab plains (see page 372).

Chilas

Chilas town is three kilometres (two miles) off the KKH to the right, out of sight of the road. The Shangrila Hotel, Chilas Inn, police post and petrol pump are right on the highway. It costs Rs30 by public bus from here to Gilgit.

Where to Stay

Shangrila, on the KKH, tel. Chilas 69, or book Rawalpindi 73006, 72948, or Karachi
    520703, 520261–5 (s/d Rs425/535). Good and modern with 29 rooms.
Chilas Inn, on the KKH (d Rs300).
    Up the hill, in the main bazaar of Chilas town, are six hotels, all charging Rs50 for a double room.

Sights

Chilas, though only a small bazaar town, was an important junction on the ancient trade route. From here the jeep track leads over the Babusar Pass (see pages 357–8) to the Kaghan Valley. At 4,173 metres (13,690 feet), this rough track is passable only in the summer, but until the KKH was opened this was the main route from Pakistan to the Northern Areas. Public jeeps run daily from Chilas to Babusar village, 13 kilometres before the pass.

There are hundreds of rock engravings along the Indus below Chilas. The two most interesting groups are down a jeep track before the Shangrila Hotel and down another jeep track leading to the bridge to Thalpan just after the petrol station. The best carvings face the river. On the north bank, across the Thalpan Bridge, a warrior with a huge knife slaughters a goat and a snow leopard attacks an ibex—both probably date from the first century BC. Later carvings depict Buddhas and stupas of various types. On some rocks whole scenes are portrayed: drinking parties, a ruler with captives, a horse festival (or polo game), a ploughman and a royal couple.

About 300 metres (1,000 feet) up the hill from the petrol station, fifth-century Gupta inscriptions have been carved into a large rock, marking the entrance to the old town. The inscriptions refer to Chilas as Soma Nagar, or Moon City, and name the then-ruling king.

The British left the Chilas area alone until the 1890s, when they built a new, shorter road from Chilas across the Babusar Pass directly to British India. Before this, the only route to Gilgit was long and difficult: from Srinagar across the Burzil Pass and through the Astor Gorge. In 1893 the hostile Chilas tribes rose against the small garrison of Kashmiri soldiers and British officers stationed there to protect the road, and a savage battle ensued. The latter only just managed to quell the uprising.

Opposite Chilas, on the north side of the river, a jeep track leads up the Thalpan Valley; from the valley's end a footpath continues across the hills to Gilgit. Before attempting this hike it is essential to confer with the police and district commissioner in Chilas or Gilgit and to arrange for a guide through them.

Chilas to the Gilgit River

The scenery east of Chilas, where the Indus skirts round **Nanga Parbat**, looks like Tibet. Untouched by the monsoon rains, huge sand dunes roll down to the river. Barren mountain slopes rise to 5,000 metres (16,000 feet) above sea level on the north bank, and to 8,000 metres (26,000 feet) on the south. The Indus and KKH are at an altitude of about 1,200 metres (4,000 feet) and pass through desert. High mud cliffs studded with round boulders, glacial remains and flood debris flank the road. In summer it is cruelly hot; in winter biting winds rush through the gorges. One climber wrote:

I had never seen any valley that compared to it either in kind or in dimensions. It was barren as an Arabian wady; it was floored with the strewn ruins of countless floods, bleached and blasted by the suns of countless summers; it was walled along by rocky cliffs, a maze of precipices and gullies . . . . The naked skeleton of the world stood forth, with every stratum displayed and every mark of the sculpturing chisel undisguised.

W M Conway, *Climbing and
Exploration in the Karakoram-Himalayas* (1892)

You can feel the depressing mass of Nanga Parbat louring above you, too close for comfort, too close to show its beauty. It is in fact a series of successive ridges culminating in an ice crest 8,125 metres (26,660 feet) high, the ninth-highest peak in the world and the westernmost bastion of the Himalayas. No other mountain within 100 kilometres (60 miles) comes anywhere near its size.

Nanga Parbat means Naked Mountain: its southern face is so steep that it is bare of vegetation. This southern wall, with Kashmir at its foot, is one of the greatest precipices in the world—a drop of 5,000 metres (16,000 feet, or three miles). To the east and west the mountain is bounded by the deep narrow gorges of the Astor and Bunar valleys, and it is only towards the north, to the Indus Valley, that the massif slopes rather than plunges.

Nanga Parbat has killed more climbers—45 so far—than any other mountain. The climber Conway was told that the peaks were inhabited by fairies: 'When the sun shines hotly it smokes up there, and that shows when the fairies are cooking their bread.' More alarmingly, it is also believed to be the home of demons, giant frogs and snow snakes 30 metres (100 feet) long. The mountain was successfully climbed in 1953 by a joint Austrian and German expedition, the eighth major expedition to attempt it.

Raikot Bridge carries the KKH to the north bank of the Indus. Just before the bridge there is a Shangrila Hotel (same rates as at Chilas) and a rest house beside a line of hot springs famous for relieving rheumatic and skin diseases. The water channel that runs along beside the road is too hot to put your hand in; at the springs the locals cook by submerging pots in the almost-boiling water.

Fairy Meadows are idyllic alpine pastures surrounded by pine forests on the northern slopes of Nanga Parbat, with breathtaking views of the snow-clad north face above. The meadows are 19 kilometres (12 miles) away up a track that leaves the KKH at Raikot Bridge. Shangrila Hotel is building another lodge up there. For trekkers and climbers it is the perfect camping spot. (See page 443 for trekking details.)

The oppression lifts beyond Raikot Bridge. The river makes another right-angle bend, and once again you follow it due north. About ten kilometres (six miles) on the Gilgit side of the bridge you can finally see the massive bulk of Nanga Parbat behind you, serene and white in the distance. Ahead is a clear view of the triangular points of **Rakaposhi** and **Domani**, part of the Rakaposhi massif. To the east the snow-covered **Haramosh Range** towers above you on the other side of the river.

From here to Gilgit you are seldom out of sight of greenery. Mountain streams fed by the melting snows irrigate patches of flat land along either side of the Indus. Bunji, a large fertile oasis on the east bank, faces **Juglot** on the west side.

The old Gilgit Road which connected Gilgit to Srinagar leads off to the right four kilometres (2.5 miles) past the petrol pumps at Juglot, 74 kilometres (46 miles) from Chilas. The jeep track crosses the Indus on a suspension bridge and turns back south along the other side of the river through **Bunji**, then up the **Astor Valley**. Though

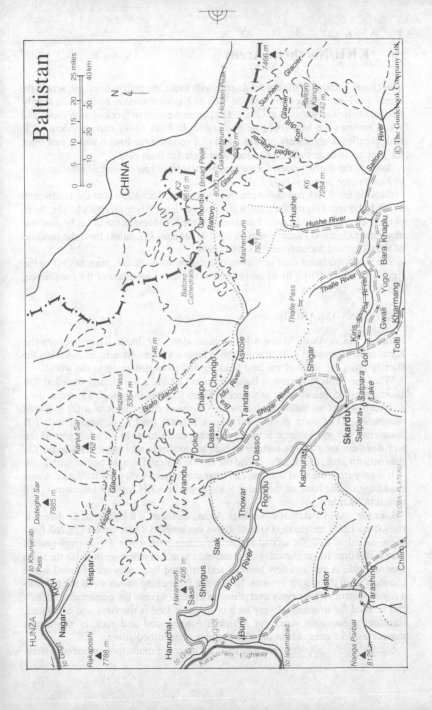

Baltistan

25 miles
40 km
0 5 10 15 20 25 30

N

CHINA

© The Guidebook Company Ltd.

7466 m

Siachen Glacier

Baltoro Glacier

Kanop
7742 m

Konp Glacier

srip

Kaben Glacier

K2
8616 m

8080 m Gasherbrum I (Hidden Peak)
8068 m Broad Peak

Gasherbrum Glacier

Concordia

Baltoro Glacier

Baltoro Cathedrals

Masherbrum
7821 m

K7

K6
7284 m

Hushe

Hushe River

Thalle Pass

Thalle River

Kiris

Shyok River

Satpara Gol

Kharmang

Tolti

Gwali Yugo Bara Khaplu

Saltoro River

7146 m

Hispar Pass
5354 m

Biafo Glacier

Askole

Chakpo Chongo

Bra

Idu River

Kanjut Sar
7762 m

Hispar Glacier

Doko

Dassu

Tandara

Shigar River

Shigar

Skardu

Satpara Lake

Kachura

Disteghil Sar
7885 m

Hispar

to Khunjerab Pass

Haramosh
7406 m

Arandu

Dasso

Thowar

Rondu

DEOSA PLATEAU

HUNZA

KKH

to Gilgit Nagar

Rakaposhi
7788 m

Hispar

Sasli Shingus

Stak

Indus River

Hanuchal

to Gilgit

Bunji

Astor

to Islamabad

Karakoram Highway

Chilim

Tarashing

Nanga Parbat
8125 m

now closed because of the border dispute with India, the path to Srinagar, across the Burzil and Kamri passes and into the Vale of Kashmir, used to be the main supply line for the British garrison at Gilgit. The passes were often blocked with snow, and yet in summer the heat could be intolerable. In 1891 *Times* correspondent E F Knight called it 'the dreary road of slavery'. Even after the British built a new track for pack animals in the 1890s, conditions were far from easy.

Astor is the starting point for various popular treks round Nanga Parbat and east to Skardu (see pages 441–4).

Back on the KKH you come after one kilometre (half a mile) to the confluence of the Indus and Gilgit rivers, the waters of the Gilgit River green and clear, those of the Indus dark muddy grey. From here on the KKH leaves the Indus to continue along the Gilgit and Hunza rivers. It is 43 kilometres (27 miles) from the junction of the Gilgit and Indus rivers to Gilgit town.

The newly surfaced road to Skardu, the capital of Baltistan, branches off to the right, crosses the Gilgit River two kilometres (a mile) upstream of the confluence, and follows the Indus.

BALTISTAN (SKARDU)

Baltistan lies north of Indian-held Kashmir along the Indus River between the Karakoram Mountains and the uninhabited Deosai Plateau. Skardu, its capital, is the starting-point for some of the best trekking and mountaineering in the world.

When the Indus River enters Baltistan from Ladakh, it has already travelled 700 kilometres (435 miles) from its source in Tibet. It comes in through a gorge so deep and narrow that no path can follow it. On the northern bank a solid block of mountains, 60 of them over 7,000 metres (21,000 feet) high, form a wall 100 kilometres (60 miles) thick between Baltistan and China. In no other part of the world is there such a large number of high mountains in such a confined space. On the southern bank, the Himalayas and the Deosai Plateau form the barrier with India.

It is only from the west that you can enter the isolated valleys of Baltistan. A new road hugging the bank of the Indus leads from the KKH for 170 kilometres (110 miles) to Skardu.

Like the rest of Pakistan's Northern Areas, Baltistan is a high-altitude desert. It rises from 1,500 metres (5,000 feet) above sea level to 8,616 metres (28,268 feet) at the summit of K-2, the second-highest mountain in the world. The average rainfall here is less than 100 millimetres (four inches) a year, but wherever possible the steep mountainside is cut into tiny terraces and irrigated by a network of small water channels from the glacier streams. In summer the melting snows swell the Indus to a raging torrent sweeps away everything in its path, so only the gentler side streams can be used for irrigation. Every inch of irrigable land is manured and cultivated: startling green oases stand out against the grey sand and rock of the barren mountains, like emeralds in massive settings of tarnished silver.

Stacked up the hillsides near the fields are mazes of multistorey wood-and-stone cottages honeycombed with narrow unlit alleyways and rough, dark stairwells. Clustered round the houses are apricot, peach, mulberry and apple trees, all festooned with grape vines. Rows of poplar and willow trees line the irrigation channels and terrace walls, holding the soil in place and providing wind breaks. The trees are also vital for firewood and house building.

The quarter million people living in these villages are almost all Shia Muslims, the strictest sect of Islam. They speak Balti, an archaic Tibetan dialect. With its rolling sand dunes and barren mountains, the area round Skardu looks very like Tibet and is, in fact, often called Little Tibet.

The valleys are perhaps steeper and deeper than further east; and they are separated not by rolling plateaux but by lofty spurs. Yet there is the same overall impression of rock and sand, harsh white light and biting dry wind. Natural vegetation is a rare and transitory phenomenon; cultivation is just an artificial patchwork of fields suspended from a contour-clinging irrigation duct, or huddled on the triangular surface of a fan of alluvial soil washed down from the mountains.

John Keay, *When Men and Mountains Meet* (1977)

In comparison to the gentler, greener valleys of Chitral and Hunza, Baltistan appears bleak and forbidding, and is not to everyone's taste. Yet the people, for centuries almost entirely cut off from their neighbours, are charming and hospitable. Until the airstrip was built at Skardu, they were virtually self-sufficient, growing grain and storing rancid butter (a great delicacy) in the ground for the long snow-bound winter. In the summer they ate fruit, reputedly the best in the Northern Areas.

As in so many of Pakistan's northern valleys, there is a vague tradition here that the town of Skardu was founded by Alexander the Great. Although the fort at Skardu is sometimes called Askandria (not unlike Iskander, Alexander's Indian name), neither Alexander nor his followers travelled this far east.

The area's early history is linked to Gilgit's (see pages 401 and 403). Baltistan was known as Great Bolor, Gilgit and upper Chitral as Little Bolor. Baltistan comprised four main kingdoms, of which Skardu was the most important. Of the other three, Khaplu controlled the route along the Shyok Valley; Shigar held the Shigar River and its tributaries; and Rondu guarded the Indus Gorge to the west of Skardu. There were also four lesser principalities: Kiris on the Shyok, and Parkutta, Tolti and Kharmang, which were on the Indus and controlled the path to Leh.

From 1846 Baltistan was ruled by the maharaja of Kashmir, whose cruel Hindu soldiers were hated by the Baltis. The British were only minimally interested in the area, as they considered it of little strategic value. At Independence in 1947, the Balti people, aided by a small number of freedom fighters, including the Gilgit Scouts, rebelled against their Kashmiri rulers and became part of Pakistan. The Kashmiris were for a time isolated within the Askandria Fort.

When to Go

For trekkers and mountaineers, July and August are the best months in Baltistan, but for the ordinary tourist, April, May, September and October are recommended, when the main Indus Valley is not too hot and the trees are covered in spring blossom or autumn gold. There is little shade in Baltistan, and the sun can be very strong, so sunhats and sunblock cream are necessary. At night the temperature falls quickly as the rocks do not hold the heat, so take sleeping bags and extra layers of clothing. The Shia Muslims are very strict, and local women are seldom seen. Visiting women should keep arms, legs and heads covered. Shorts should not be worn, even by men. Take tinned or dried food to supplement the limited local food available.

Getting to Baltistan

The easiest way to get to the Balti chief town of Skardu is by air. The daily flight takes an hour from Islamabad. Boeing jets (Rs300) have replaced the Fokker Friendship (Rs260) on this run—except on Sundays when both fly—so seats are more readily available. As the Boeing flies higher, the view of Nanga Parbat is not as dramatic as from a Fokker, but the cluster of high peaks round K-2, the most magnificent mountain spectacle in the world, can be seen more clearly.

Skardu town is 14 kilometres (nine miles) east of the airport. Jeep-taxis meet the plane and charge about Rs10 for the 30-minute ride to Skardu. The Shangrila Tourist Resort lies in the opposite direction from Skardu and sends a vehicle to collect guests.

The journey to Skardu by road along the narrow gorges of the Indus River is unforgettable. Buses leave daily from Rawalpindi and Gilgit. It takes 17 to 25 hours from Rawalpindi, or five to ten hours from Gilgit.

The Road to Skardu

The junction of the Indus and the Gilgit rivers, 37 kilometres (23 miles) down from Gilgit town, is the turn-off point for the road to Skardu. The Skardu road crosses the Gilgit River on Alam Bridge. Dozens of rock engravings and inscriptions decorate the rocks along the edge of the river between the bridge and the confluence with the Indus (see also page 385).

The single-lane, hard-topped road hugs the north bank of the Indus for 170 kilometres (106 miles) to Skardu. About five kilometres (three miles) from the turn-off there is a superb view looking south, with the confluence of the two rivers in the foreground, and Nanga Parbat in all its shimmering glory beyond.

At **Hanuchal**, 22 kilometres (14 miles) from the turn-off, the Indus reaches the most northerly point in its 3,200-kilometre (2,000-mile) journey to the sea. Blocked on the north by Rakaposhi and Haramosh, it is squeezed between high cliffs and forced to turn south and find a way around the west side of Nanga Parbat to the plains of the Punjab.

A small mountain stream flows down between Rakaposhi and Haramosh at the corner where the Indus turns. The villagers of Hanuchal have built an irrigation channel across the face of the cliff on the north bank. An extraordinary feat of village engineering, it is worth a visit. Park by a sign that reads 'AKRSP CIDA Hanuchal Irig Chnl'; the channel was financed by the Aga Khan Rural Support Programme and Canadian International Development Agency. A steep ten-minute scramble takes you up to the water channel. It is a 20-minute walk along the channel to the source, where you can picnic in the shade of the cliff. Slung across the cliff face on the other side of the stream are the remains of an impassable path which was once the main access to the large village of Dassu (one of several by that name in the Northern Areas), which is out of sight up the stream and now accessible by jeep. From Dassu you can trek north to the base camp of Rakaposhi, or east along glaciers around the north side of Haramosh to Arandu.

An hour's dizzy walking for three kilometres (two miles) along the channel in the other direction takes you to Hanuchal village. It is not recommended for those with vertigo: at one point you must crawl under an overhang with a 150-metre (500-foot) drop straight down to the Indus below.

Sassi, 27 kilometres (17 miles) from the turn-off and 144 kilometres (90 miles) from Skardu, with its petrol pump and a tea shop, is a favourite stopping place for the buses. Beyond Sassi the Indus roars down through a narrow gorge, dropping nearly 600 metres (2,000 feet) in 60 kilometres (37 miles).

Tuar (or Thowar) guards the top end of the gorge and is now the administrative centre for the old kingdom of Rondu. Nearby is **Rondu** village, the one-time capital (and marked on the 1:4,000,000 scale Bartholomew map of the Indian subcontinent). The village consists of a few scattered stone houses perched on a flat shelf of land 150 metres (500 feet) above the Indus and offers a dizzying view down the narrow ravine. A new bridge connects Rondu with the main road. According to the 1906 Kashmir *Gazetteer*, the original bridge of plaited birch twigs that crossed the river here was a terrifying contraption: it was 113 metres (370 feet) long and fell 25 metres (80 feet) in a curve, so that the lowest point was only 15 metres (50 feet) above the rushing water.

Until recently such bridges were commonplace. General Sir Ian Hamilton describes the horror of crossing them:

There were two ropes, the upper one for the hands, the lower one for the feet—far above was the sky, far below ran the Indus. A tight-rope dancer would have been quite all right, I suppose, but these ropes were not tight; they were slack and sometimes my hands went one way and my feet the other. If I live to be a hundred these crossings will come back to me in nightmares.

Listening for Drums (1944)

There are no such terrors on the modern road. The remaining journey to Skardu is relatively easy. The mountains fall back and the wide plain of Skardu opens up before you as the road crosses the Indus near Kachura, 32 kilometres (20 miles) before Skardu.

Kachura Lake is surrounded by orchards that are exquisite in spring, when the fruit trees are in bloom, and in autumn, when the leaves turn gold and red. The Shangrila Tourist Resort on the edge of the lake is comfortable though expensive. The imaginative owner has turned the fusilage of a crashed Dakota into a family suite—a holiday with a difference at about Rs2,000 a night! There are several good walks from the hotel, and you can hire ponies and boats, but being isolated it lacks the human interest and entertainment of Skardu town.

Skardu

This dusty collection of shops and administrative buildings is developing quickly. It is much smaller than Gilgit, and less geared for tourists than Swat, Gilgit or Hunza; most visitors are mountaineers or trekkers. There are only three western-style hotels.

The **Tourist Information Centre** is in the K-2 Motel. There are branches of the Habib Bank and National Bank of Pakistan, but the exchange rate is slightly less favourable than in Islamabad.

Where to Stay

Shangrila Tourist Resort, Kachura Lake, tel. 235; book Rawalpindi 73006, 72948, or Karachi 520261–5 (s/d Rs845/1,145; suite Rs2,000 including meals). Fifty rooms, swimming pool. Expensive.

Karakoram Yurt and Yak Serai, Link Rd; book through Karakoram Tours, Islamabad, tel. 829120, cable: BALTORO (d Rs600).

K-2, PTDC Motel, tel. 104; book Rawalpindi 581480–4 (s/d Rs275/350).

Siachen Hotel, Yadgar Chowk, tel. 286 (Rs50–100).

Kashmir Inn, Naya Bazaar (Rs50–100).

Hunza Inn, Naya Bazaar (Rs50–100).

PWD rest house (also at Shigar, Khaplu and Machlu); book through NAWO headquarters, Gilgit, tel. 2416.

There are other small local cheap hotels. Take your own bedding.

Camping is recommended.

Jeep Hire

The official government rate for hiring jeeps in Skardu is Rs10 per mile plus Rs200 overnight halt charge; if the jeep returns empty the charge is Rs5 per mile. Toyota jeeps cost Rs12 per mile, and tractors Rs15, but the going rate is actually much higher, so bargain hard. Ordinary petrol is available in Skardu only.

Sights

It is fantastic in the precise and literal sense of the word. It is a great oval basin, 7,500 feet [2,300 metres] above sea-level, some twenty miles [32 kilometres] long and eight miles [13 kilometres] wide, enclosed in rocky mountains, purple, red, grey and ochre, that soar up to 17,000 feet [5,200 metres]. The valley is carpeted in fine pale sand through which, green in winter, in summer grey as tarnished silver, the Indus snakes lazily between wind-ribbed dunes and past a single enormous rock standing high and isolated in the river bed . . . . In millions of years the river has progressively cut its way deeply down into the rock, and the cliffs that now wall the valley are ledged and terraced at the different and descending heights of the old beds of the river. Further back the dry and bony mountains rise to their jagged crests intricately folded and overlapping; at the two ends of the basin, where they converge, it seems impossible that even a great river can force a passage through them. The air is so clear that the eye is continually misled; everything looks close, there are no perspectives; only with binoculars does the shrub apparently a few hundred yards [metres] away on the far side of the Indus disclose itself as a large tree at least three miles [five kilometres] off and the children playing with a box at the water's edge become grown men launching a raft.

Jean Fairly, *The Lion River* (1975)

Enthusiasm for the scenery is essential, as there is little else to get excited about in this dusty, one-street town. The **Naya (New) Bazaar** consists of a row of booths down either side of the main street, with a local hotel and bus terminal by the war memorial at the western end, tea shops and general supplies in the middle, and the PTDC K-2 Motel and government offices at the eastern end. The **Purana (Old) Bazaar**, further from the river behind the Naya Bazaar, is more interesting. You can explore the stalls for hand-woven woollen cloth, silver ornaments and wooden spoons. The K-2 shop sells equipment left over from expeditions. Its owner, Ghulam Rasul, an old *sirdar* (leader of porters), is knowledgeable about trekking routes and the hiring of porters. There are several trekking agencies in town, and more opening each year.

The enormous rock which towers over Skardu is crowned by an ancient **fortress** known variously as Karpochu, Askandria or Mindoq Khar. The fortress, possibly built in the 16th century, is a maze of steep wooden stairs, dark passages and low doors. You can take an interesting half-hour walk up the sloping ramp to explore the remains. In 1903, the indefatigable Mrs Fanny Workman (who travelled widely with her husband in this part of the world for the ostensible reason of restoring her to good health!) climbed to the top of the fortress with a sprained ankle and, finding she could not get down again, was forced to spend hours waiting for relief in the blazing sun with no water. In her diaries she merely remarks that by midday the rocks were so hot she could not bear to touch them.

You can also walk from the polo ground round the eastern end of the rock below the fort to the village of Narsok, on the banks of the Indus.

The intrepid rock climber can keep in form by shinning to the top of the rock; this is best attempted from the western end. It involves several traverses along exposed

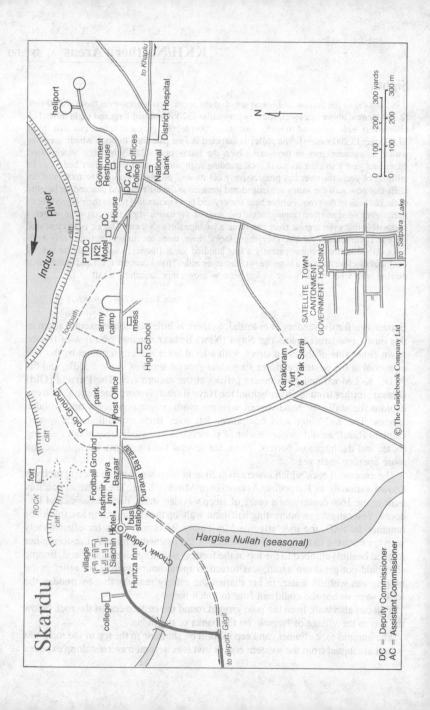

Skardu

Indus River

to Khaplu

heliport

District Hospital

Government Resthouse

offices

DC AC Police

National bank

DC House

PTDC

K2 Motel

to Satpara Lake

cliff

SATELLITE TOWN
CANTONMENT
GOVERNMENT HOUSING

footpath

army camp

mess

High School

Karakoram Yurt & Yak Sarai

cliff

ROCK

fort

cliff

Post Office

park

Polo Ground

village

Football Ground

Kashmir Naya Bazaar

Purana Bazaar

Kashmir Inn

Siachin Hotel

bus station

Chowk Yadgar

Hargisa Nullah (seasonal)

Hunza Inn

college

to airport, Gilgit

N

0   100   200   300 yards

0   100   200   300 m

DC = Deputy Commissioner
AC = Assistant Commissioner

© The Guidebook Company Ltd

ledges and is for the experienced only. On the flattish top are the ruins of another fortress built in the 1830s. A sublime panorama of valleys, gorges, cliffs, terraces and mountains rewards the climber. On the south you look straight down to Skardu. The Shigar Valley, broad and fertile, runs down from the north to join the Indus which flows here in a deep, wide gravelly bed at the foot of the rock.

Outings from Skardu

Satpara Lake, eight kilometres (five miles) south of Skardu, is a 20-minute drive or an easy walk away. The walk along the irrigation channel from the aqueduct in the centre of town is pleasanter and shorter than following the jeep road. You can sometimes find a public jeep-taxi going to Satpara for about Rs10. A small islet in the centre of the lake is reached by the rowboat moored by the PTDC rest house (bookable at the PTDC in the K-2 Motel, or at Rawalpindi). The lake is well stocked with trout. In the nearby village of Satpara most people speak Shina, the main language of the Gilgit Valley; they must at some time have come from Gilgit, and have not intermarried with other Baltis.

The **Satpara Buddha**, a meditating Buddha surrounded by dozens of small bodhisattvas, is carved on the north face of a large rock about halfway between Skardu and Satpara. It is an easy walk from the road of about half an hour across the Satpara stream and up the slope on the other side.

The **Deosai Plateau**, a treeless wilderness at 4,000 metres (13,000 feet), lies south of Satpara and, because of the border dispute with India, is closed to foreigners. Though you are not supposed to cross the plateau to Chilim without a permit, you can take a three-day round trek from Satpara, west to the Burji Pass on the northern edge of the plateau, then north to Skardu by another route. The view of the Karakoram Range from the top of the 4,785-metre (15,700-foot) pass is legendary. Gypsy Davy, who was there in 1924, described dawn on the pass as follows:

[The Karakorams around K-2 came] into the sun's rays several minutes before Nanga Parbat to the west got any light. I thought the Sierras were large, but here, where we could see three or four score miles [100 to 130 kilometres] north, south, east and west, and see only mountains, and most of them above 20,000 feet [6,000 metres], the Sierras seem like sand dunes.

Hugh Swift, *The Trekkers' Guide to
the Himalaya and Karakoram* (1982)

The Shigar Valley

The broad, fertile Shigar Valley is the easiest side valley to reach from Skardu. Its gentle, irrigated slopes with terraces of wheat, maize and barley, and orchards of apricot, mulberry, peach, plum pear, apples and nuts (reputedly the best in the world) are unique in Baltistan. The valley is surrounded by snow-clad peaks and runs down from the north to join the Indus just above Skardu. The road to Shigar bridges the Indus upriver from the confluence and then crosses a level semi-desert before climbing over a ridge for an expansive view of 50 kilometres (30 miles) up to the head of the valley, where the Basha and Braldu rivers join to form the Shigar.

Shigar town, once the capital of the relatively prosperous, independent kingdom of Shigar, sports the most impressive carved wooden houses and mosques in Baltistan. The chief mosque with its pyramidal three-tiered roof was built by Kashmiri carpenters several hundred years ago. Guarding the town is the abandoned four-storey ex-raja's palace. The spartan PWD rest house can be booked in Skardu, or you can stay in the Karakoram Hotel, or camp.

A four- to six-day trek east from Shigar leads up the Bauma stream to the **Thalle** (pronounced *Taalay*) **Pass**, at 4,572 metres (13,935 feet), and down the Thalle Valley to the Shyok River towards Khaplu.

The jeep track continues up the east bank of the Shigar for another 40 kilometres (25 miles) to the junction of the Braldu and Basha rivers, with views across the Shigar Valley, which is about ten kilometres (six miles) wide at this point, to the villages on the west bank. A further 11 kilometres (seven miles) up the Braldu River the road ends at **Dassu**.

The long and famous **Baltoro trek** into Concordia begins at Dassu. Twelve strenuous days of trudging through gorges and scrambling over moraines and glaciers culminate in the fabulous camp at **Concordia**, the innermost sanctum of the Karakorams, at the junction of the Baltoro, Godwin–Austin and several lesser glaciers. 'In the space of about 15 miles [25 kilometres],' writes John Keay, 'the Baltoro [glacier] holds in its icy embrace ten of the world's 30 highest peaks. They line its sides and close its easternmost end like high priests guarding the Holy of Holies.' The peaks include **K-2**, at 8,616 metres (28,268 feet), the second highest mountain in the world after Everest and first climbed successfully in 1954; **Broad Peak**, at 8,060 metres (26,444 feet), and first climbed in 1955; **Hidden Peak** or Gasherbrum 1, at 8,068 metres (26,470 feet), and so enclosed by other peaks that it is virtually invisible, first climbed in 1958; Gasherbrum II, at 8,035 metres (26,362 feet); Gasherbrum III, at 7,952 metres (26,089 feet); Gasherbrum IV, at 7,929 metres (26,014 feet); and on the other side of the Baltoro Glacier, **Masherbrum**, at 7,821 metres (25,660 feet), otherwise known as Day of Judgment and first climbed in 1960. (These are the new 1988 figures as measured by Italian Professor Ardito Desio.) For a detailed description of this trek see page 448.

A permit for the Baltoro trek is required from the Ministry of Tourism in Islamabad, but you are allowed to walk as far as the last village, **Askole** (three days from Dassu), without a permit. From Askole is an open zone (no permit needed) up the Biafo Glacier, across the Hispar Pass and down the Hispar Glacier to Hunza, and it is also open across the Skoro Pass to Skoro, near Shigar.

A bridge at Shigar town leads to the jeep track up the west bank, which follows the Basha River for about 30 kilometres (19 miles) to Doko, ten kilometres (six miles) from Arandu. Strenuous open treks lead from Arandu, west up the Chogo Lungma Glacier, and round the north side of Haramosh, or north to the Hispar Glacier and Hunza.

Khaplu

The largest kingdom in old Baltistan was Khaplu, guarding the trade route to Ladakh along the Shyok River. Khaplu town is 103 kilometres (64 miles) east of Skardu, a dramatic jeep drive of six hours and a recommended two- to four-day trip for non-trekkers. For trekkers, Khaplu is the starting-point for excellent treks to the north, though the area east of Khaplu to the Ladakh border is closed, and nine formally approved treks have been withdrawn because of the border skirmishes with India on the Siachen Glacier.

Public jeep-taxis ply between Skardu and Khaplu and charge Rs20–30 one way. Otherwise you can try to hitch a ride on a tractor-load of equipment belonging to some expedition, or you can rent a jeep from NATCO or one of the tour agents.

The wide sands of the Skardu Basin narrow at the eastern end, and the road turns a corner round the foot of a mountain. It heads south across a stony waste out of sight of the river before descending to **Gol**, about 30 kilometres (19 miles) from Skardu, where there is a bridge across the Indus. The new jeep road on the north bank leads past the small principality of **Kiris** and eventually up the **Hushe Valley**, opposite Khaplu, to Hushe (pronounced *Hushay*) village.

The Khaplu road continues on the south bank round the foot of dark grey mountains, their slopes deeply scored by rockfalls and landslides. Below the road the sand dunes, curved and fluted by the wind, are reminiscent of Tibet.

The Shyok River flows into the Indus about 35 kilometres (22 miles) from Skardu. Near the confluence the road crosses the Indus on the Humayun Bridge and continues east along the Shyok, which at this point looks like the larger river. The Indus Gorge, the trade route to Leh, is closed to foreigners. The tantalizing view from the bridge shows the Indus emerging from the south between high cliffs. Both the Indus and the Shyok rise in Tibet and run parallel for about 500 kilometres (300 miles) before joining. The fertile settlements of **Gwali** (or Ghawari), **Yugo** and **Bara** are separated by long barren stretches where the road follows the river on a new ledge cut in the cliff face. Jagged mountains dominate every view. A new road bridge crosses the Shyok at Yugo.

Khaplu stretches in a wide fan from the base of a semicircular wall of mountain, dropping some 300 metres (1,000 feet) to river level. The scattered houses set amid terraced fields are connected by paths and irrigation channels; the friendly, open villagers welcome visitors. The people of Khaplu belong to the Nurbashi sect of Islam and are more liberal and tolerant than the Shias. The women are unveiled, like the Ismailis in Hunza, and a lone female tourist is accepted as a sister, invited into homes and offered cups of tea, a very different experience from the censorious stares at Skardu.

Dominating the valley from the top end of the alluvial fan, the imposing palace of the ex-raja gazes down on the kingdom. Its whitewashed façade, punctuated by irregularly placed little windows, supports an extravagant four-tier carved wooden balcony up its centre. Built about 150 years ago, it has a faintly Tibetan air, like Baltit Fort in Hunza (see page 419).

To stay in the PWD rest house you need a chit from the tourism officer in Skardu. Bring your own supplies and bedding. There is also a dirty local hotel and restaurant in the bazaar.

At 2,600 metres (8,400 feet), Khaplu is cooler than Skardu, which, combined with the friendly character of the people and the superb walks along irrigation channels, makes Khaplu the nicest place to stay in Baltistan. There are majestic views of Masherbrum, which at 7,821 metres (25,660 feet) is the 24th highest mountain in the world. The British-built rest house close to the river surveys a wide stretch of valley enclosed by slender pointed peaks. It makes the perfect base from which to explore the surrounding villages—labyrinths of old houses, stables, stores and mills that seem to have grown out of the mountainside.

Beyond Khaplu the Shyok loops round a gigantic outcrop of rock nearly 1,000 metres (3,000 feet) high. The new jeep track follows the base of the cliff to **Surmo**, where there is a jeep bridge. Here the river turns south towards Ladakh and the road is closed to foreigners.

The jeep bridge leads across the Shyok and north up the Hushe Valley for 27 kilometres (17 miles) to Hushe village. The valley rises gently with dwarfing views of snow-covered mountain peaks of every shape, the forbidding heart of the Karakoram. Straight ahead is Masherbrum, presiding over the valley.

In Hushe the people still wear the traditional round, peaked Balti cap, white for men and black for women. The people here are friendly and camping is recommended.

Three glaciers flow down to Hushe, the starting point for many treks. In the open zone are the treks up the **Charaksa Glacier** to the base of K-7, and up the **Gondogoro Glacier** and the **Masherbrum Glacier** to Masherbrum base camp. However, you need a permit to cross the Vigne Pass, the Gondogoro Pass or the Masherbrum Pass to the Baltoro Glacier. All the treks that start out up the Saltoro River in the direction of Siachen are now closed.

Fishing

Fishing is excellent in Baltistan, although the trout have a well-earned reputation for shrewdness. The fishing season lasts from April to September, and permits are available from the Fisheries Department in Skardu. Take your own tackle. The best places to fish are Satpara and Kachura lakes, and the Shyok River at Khaplu, where there is a trout hatchery and an appreciative audience.

GILGIT

Gilgit, the capital of Pakistan's Northern Areas, is a thriving frontier town that has expanded rapidly to include about 30,000 inhabitants since the KKH was opened in 1978. It sits in a wide irrigated bowl 1,500 metres (5,000 feet) above sea level at the eastern end of the Gilgit Valley. The snow-covered pinnacle of Domani, 6,134 metres (20,126 feet) and part of the Rakaposhi Range, stands guard at the eastern end of town, while a semicircle of barren peaks around 4,500 metres (13,500 feet) high encloses the valley on the other three sides. There is very little rainfall in the Northern Areas, so all agricultural land must be irrigated by water from the melting snows. Every available square metre of suitable land has been terraced, and tiny fields and fruit gardens are stacked up the lower slopes of the mountains around Gilgit.

The various waves of invaders that passed through lower Pakistan also reached Gilgit. The animism of the early inhabitants gave way to fire worship brought in from Iran; later the Aryan invaders introduced an incipient form of Hinduism. From the first century BC Gilgit, like Kashgar, was an important staging post on the Silk Route from China, and the Chinese had a strong influence on the area. Inscriptions and pictures carved on rocks throughout the region give snatches of history, as does the collection of Buddhist manuscripts discovered near Gilgit in 1931.

From the third to the 11th century Gilgit was part of the Buddhist kingdom of Bolor. Baltistan was called Great Bolor, Gilgit and upper Chitral, Little Bolor. In the early eighth century, three great powers, China, Arabia and Tibet, converged upon the region, and a Chinese force of 10,000 troops temporarily occupied Gilgit and Baltistan before being ousted by the Tibetans. The Arabs, who invaded via the Baroghil Pass, were defeated in upper Chitral. In 725, the kingdoms of Great and Little Bolor merged, with Tibet as the dominant power. About this time Kashmir also became a major power and allied itself with Tibet against the Arabs.

By the 11th century the Gilgit area had become the powerful independent kingdom of Dardistan, equal in strength to Kashmir. Sometime after the 11th century the whole area was converted to Islam, and today the Muslim tribes of the Northern Areas fall fairly equally into three sects: Sunni, Shia and Ismaili. The Sunni sect came via Swat, the Shia via Kashmir and the Ismaili via Afghanistan.

The valleys are so isolated that when the strong central power declined, each valley became a small kingdom with its own customs and language. There were seven kingdoms along the Gilgit and Hunza rivers alone; five different languages were spoken. In the 13th century, Marco Polo called the area 'noisy with kingdoms'. By this time each tiny empire was autonomous and usually at war with its neighbour. Being strategically placed, the kingdoms grew rich from taxing trading caravans that struggled down the rivers.

In 1846 the first maharaja of Kashmir was appointed by the British and the Northern Areas fell under his nominal control. The maharaja's Hindu soldiers could do little to subdue the Muslim tribesmen, despite repeated campaigns in the 1850s

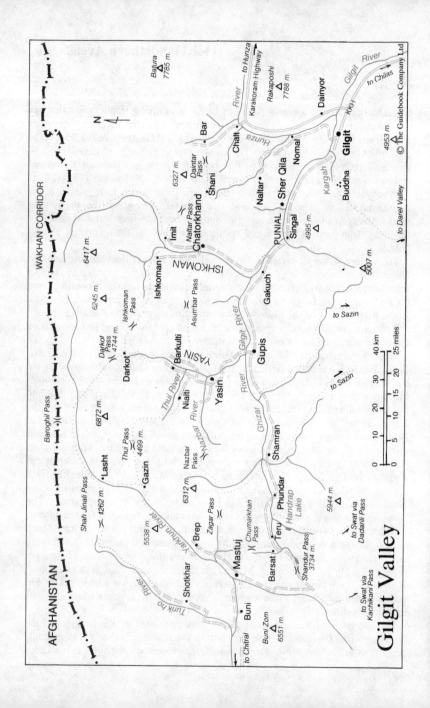

Gilgit Valley

and '60s. The British took an active interest in the region because of its strategic position on the borders of Russia and China. In 1877 they set up an agency in Gilgit to guard against possible Russian attempts to thrust through the mountains to the Vale of Kashmir.

This was the world of Kipling's *Kim* (1901) and of the Great Game, aptly described by John Keay in his excellent book *The Gilgit Game* (1979) as 'a shadowy see-and-run contest between Britain and Russia in the highest mountains'. Ultimately the contest went for nothing; by 1931 the area had been surveyed and it became clear that there was no pass in the region over which the Russians could bring a detachment (let alone an army) to invade India.

Totally cut off by snow for eight months of the year, the first British agency was not a success: it was too small and too remote to make its presence felt, and it ended abruptly in 1881 when it was nearly overrun by the Kohistanis.

The second agency, established in 1889, fared better. By then the route from Srinagar had been improved, a telegraph link had been introduced, and the agency included a full complement of British soldiers. A small ceremonial force called the Gilgit Scouts, who wore the Black Watch tartan, helped to maintain relative peace in the area, as did the British campaigns in Hunza, Chilas and Chitral in the 1890s. Nonetheless, and despite the building of the airport in 1935, it was still the most isolated outpost of the British Empire.

At Partition in 1947, the Northern Areas were designated part of Hindu-ruled Indian Kashmir, but the heavily Muslim population staged a coup against the Kashmiri governor. In 1948 the Indian Air Force bombed Gilgit, a difficult target— they were mocked by the Scouts' pipe band, who played as loudly as they could on the airfield while it was being attacked. Gilgit was undefended at the time, as most of the Gilgit Scouts were fighting the Indians in Baltistan.

Between 1972 and1974 the kingdoms were abolished and the whole area was incorporated into Pakistan. The Northern Areas are now divided into three administrative districts: Diamer, with Chilas as its capital; Baltistan, with Skardu as its chief town; and Gilgit, where the commissioner for the Northern Areas is actually stationed. Hunza is part of Gilgit.

Geographically it is still a sensitive area, as it is bordered by Russia, China and Afghanistan. There have recently been concerted efforts to develop the district by initiating new irrigation and road projects and establishing new schools and medical centres. This applies to the Northern Areas generally. The KKH has made an enormous difference to the standard of living here; the inhabitants can now import goods from, and take their produce to, the rest of Pakistan and to China.

The **PTDC Information Centre** is located at the Chinar Inn. **Banks** in Gilgit only cash US-dollar or sterling travellers cheques, and the rate is not as good as in Islamabad.

When to Go

Gilgit is at its best in April and October. In April the fruit trees are in bloom, and the first green shoots of winter wheat turn each terrace into an emerald carpet. The poplars and willows are a fresh, delicate green, and the jagged grey pinnacles are set like cardboard cutouts against the clear blue sky. In the autumn the trees change colour: brilliant golds, reds and browns stand out vividly against the snowy peaks. Summer is the time for trekkers and climbers. In June, July and August the high mountain pastures are carpeted in flowers, and July to September is the only time of year when the higher passes are open. Winter is bitterly cold. Though Gilgit town gets very little snow, the villages at higher altitude are snow-bound.

Getting to Gilgit

You can fly direct from Islamabad to Gilgit in one hour. The three daily flights are subsidized and at only Rs245 must be the best value in the world; on a clear day the scenery is breathtaking. The PIA pilot of the small Fokker Friendship plane navigates by sight up the Kaghan Valley, over the Babusar Pass, then skirts round the shoulder of Nanga Parbat (8,125 metres or 26,660 feet), with the fancifully named Sleeping Beauty lying on her back across the top. The mountain is so massive that it takes ten minutes to fly past it. The pilot invites the passengers into the cockpit to see the 87 peaks over 7,000 metres (21,000 feet) that stretch, range after range, as far as the eye can see, with the sharp triangle of K-2, the second-highest mountain in the world, clearly visible on the horizon. As the flight can only go in clear weather, it is often cancelled. Remember to confirm your return flight as soon as you arrive in Gilgit.

The drive up the Karakoram Highway from Islamabad to Gilgit is equally spectacular, but takes a minimum of 12 hours by car and 17 hours by bus (see pages 366–90). Two buses and three minibuses daily leave Raja Bazaar, in Rawalpindi, for Gilgit. The bus costs about Rs120. You can hire jeeps or small coaster buses from the tour operators in Islamabad. A jeep costs Rs6 a mile, plus Rs75 overnight charges for the driver. PTDC rates are fixed, others negotiable. If you are not continuing to China, perhaps the ideal solution is to fly up and drive down.

Ordinary- and super-grade **petrol** is available in Gilgit; ordinary-grade can also be purchased in Chalt, Aliabad and Sost. Diesel is widely available in most villages because tractors use it.

Where to Stay

Moderate

Serena Lodge, Jutial, Gilgit, tel. 2330–1 (s/d Rs450/600). Outside town, with a magnificent view of Rakaposhi. Best food in Gilgit.

Chinar Inn, PTDC, Chinar Bagh, tel. 2562 (s/d Rs275/350). Central and popular with tour groups.

Hunza Inn, Chinar Bagh, tel. 2814 (d Rs80–250, dorm Rs30). The best value in town, and popular with independent travellers. Nice atmosphere; good meeting place; good food.

Park, Airport Road, tel. 2679 (d Rs165–200). Central and modern, but slow service.

Gilgit Alpine Motel, on main road near Serena Lodge, tel. 3434 (s/d Rs250/400).

Hunza Tourist Lodge, Babar Road, opposite Jail (s/d Rs200/300). New.

Gilgit View, on riverside near bridge, tel. 3508 (d Rs150). Lovely site.

Riverside Tourist Lodge, Chinar Bagh (d Rs130). Beside river.

JSR, Airport Road, near PIA office, tel. 3971 (d Rs150).

Mount Balore, Airport Road, tel. 2709 (s/d Rs100/150).

Sargin Inn, Shahrah-e-Quaid-e-Azam, tel. 3538 (d Rs100).

Mountain Movers Inn, tel. 2967. Other side of river; helpful management.

Inexpensive

Golden Peak Inn, Bank Road, Rajah Bazaar tel. 3911 (d Rs70, dorm Rs25, tent Rs10). Central, popular with backpackers, camping allowed.

Vershigoom Inn, Airport Road, tel. 2991 (s/d Rs50/80). Central, popular with backpackers.

Tourist Cottage, Jutial, tel. 2376 (d Rs60, dorm Rs25).

Masherbrum Inn, Airport Road, tel. 2711 (d Rs50–80).

Jubilee, Airport Road, tel. 2843 (d Rs80).

Karakoram, opposite airport terminal (s/d Rs30/50).

Along the Gilgit Valley there are **PWD rest houses** at Singal, Gakuch, Chator Khand, Gupis, Yasin, Phandar and Teru. Book through PWD Headquarters, Gilgit, tel. 2416. Take all your own bedding and food.

Sights

Gilgit is the only market town for hundreds of kilometres (miles) in every direction. Traders from central Asia, the Punjab and Sind all converge here, and mountain men from the remotest valleys walk for days to bring their goats to market. Except on Fridays (the Muslim holy day) the bazaars are always bustling and colourful. There is not a woman in sight, but men—Mongols, Tajiks, Kirghiz and Uygurs from central Asia; pale-skinned, often blue-eyed northern Pakistanis; and the darker, swarthier Punjabis, each wearing his own distinctive hat or turban—parade up and down the streets or sit bargaining and gossiping in the open-fronted shops. The single-storey, box-like shops sell an extraordinary range of goods: paraffin lamps and primus stoves, fragile porcelain and lustrous silks from China; powdered milk and iodized salt, tough climbing boots and ice axes (probably once given to high-altitude porters by foreign climbing expeditions), vegetables and fruit, spices and meat, bread and books.

G M Baig's bookshop sells an excellent selection of books and maps relevant to the Northern Areas, as well as antiques and souvenirs, and the two **Chinese emporia**

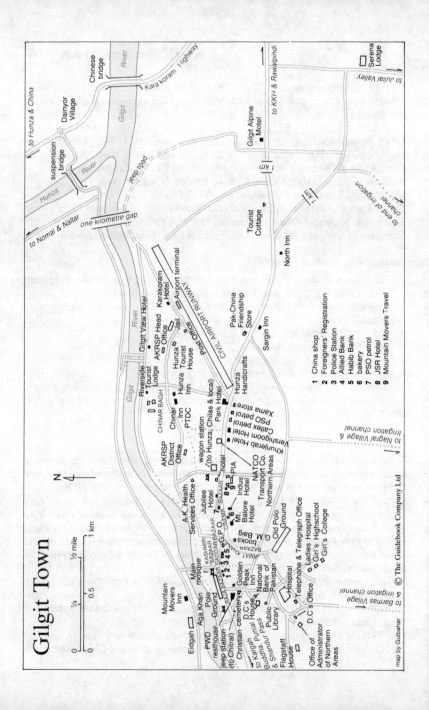

Gilgit Town

map by Gulbahar

© The Guidebook Company Ltd

1 China shop
2 Foreigners' Registration
3 Police Station
4 Allied Bank
5 Habib Bank
6 bakery
7 PSO petrol
8 JSR Hotel
9 Mountain Movers Travel

to Julial Valley

Serena Lodge

to KKH & Rawalpindi

Gilgit Alpine Motel

to end of irrigation channel

1 km

1 km

Tourist Cottage

North Inn

Chinese bridge

River

Kara koram Highway

Dainyor Village

to Hunza & China

suspension bridge

Gilgit River

Hunza River

to Nomal & Naltar

jeep road

one kilometre gap

River

Gilgit

Gilgit View Hotel

Riverside Tourist Lodge

AKRSP Head Office

Karakoram Hotel

Airport terminal

Jail

Post Office

CIVIL AIRPORT RUNWAY

Pak-China Friendship Store

Sargin Inn

Hunza Handicrafts

Hunza Tourist House

Hunza Inn

CHINAR BAGH

Chinar Inn

PTDC

Park Hotel

(to Hunza, Chilas & local)

Xama store

PSO petrol

Caltex petrol

Vershigoom Hotel

Khunjerab Hotel

to Nagral Village & irrigation channel

AKRSP District Office

wagon station

PIA

Prince hotel

A.K. Health Services Office

Jubilee Hotel

NATCO Transport Co. Northern Areas

Indus Hotel

Mt. Balore Hotel

G.M. Baig books

Old Polo Ground

Telephone & Telegraph Office

Ladies Highschool

Girl's College

Golden Peak Inn

National Bank of Pakistan

JAMAT KHANA BAZAAR

CINEMA BAZAAR

G.P.O.

SADDAR BAZAAR

KASHMIRI BAZAAR

RAJA BAZAAR

Hospital

Girl's Highschool

to Barmas Village & irrigation channel

D.C.'s Office

Office of Administrator of Northern Areas

Flagstaff House

Buddha Public Library

to Kargah Punial House

to Shandur Pass (to Chitral)

Christian cemetery

jeep station

PWD resthouse

Aga Khan Polo Ground

Main mosque

Eidgah

Mountain Movers Inn

N

Gilgit

River

0   ¼   ½   1 km
0   ½ mile

near the mosque and the Airport Chowk (Roundabout) stock quality silks, embroidered table linen, irregular pearls and Chinese porcelain from Kashgar at very reasonable prices. **Hunza Handicrafts** at the Park Hotel is an excellent source of trekking equipment and information. **Mountain Movers** is the best local travel agent for tours and trekking.

Up the hill from the bazaar is the old cantonment area, with the military and civil administrative offices, officers' mess, hospital, spacious bungalows, and the Christian cemetery where George Hayward (see pages 410–11) is buried.

In June, August and November, polo tournaments are held in Gilgit. Polo originated in the Northern Areas and is still the most popular sport here. Every important village used to have its team and polo ground, but today only the army, police, Public Works Department, two polo clubs and some of the former kingdoms keep teams. Thousands of supporters flood Gilgit's Aga Khan Polo Stadium. The local game is markedly different from the staider variety that has developed in the rest of the world. There are virtually no rules, the field is unusually long and narrow, the ponies are small and vigorous, and there are five or six players on each side, instead of four. The players even catch the ball in their hands and charge wildly through the goal posts to score. The same ponies are used throughout the match, galloping aggressively up and down with extraordinary energy. The game has essentially replaced the tribal wars, and the spectators get wildly involved, shouting and jeering in a solid mass. Drowning out all else are the clarinets (*surnai*) and drums (*damal* and *dadang*) of the band. Originally the band directed the men in battle, signalling to them with different tunes, and today the coaches blast musical messages at the players, each of whom has his own signature tune. The crowd recognizes all the commands.

Fishing

Fishing in the Northern Areas generally is excellent. The British stocked the rivers with trout—and being underfished they are plentiful and unsuspecting. Fishing permits are obligatory and are obtainable for Rs10 from the Fisheries Department, near the district commissioner's residence in Gilgit. Rods are sometimes available but you would be well advised to bring your own. The best-known beats for trout are at Kargah Nullah, 16 kilometres (ten miles) from Gilgit; Singal, in Punial, 54 kilometres (34 miles) from Gilgit; upstream from Gupis on the Gilgit River; the Yasin River; Phandar Lake, 168 kilometres (104 miles) from Gilgit; Handrap Nullah, 175 kilometres (109 miles) from Gilgit; and Naltar, 45 kilometres (28 miles) from Gilgit.

Trekking

Gilgit is one of the main trekking centres in Pakistan. There are dozens of possible treks of all grades. See the trekking guide on page 431.

Rafting

Rafting is possible on the Gilgit, Hunza and Indus rivers. The sport is new here, and the rivers have not yet been graded, so rafting is for the experienced only and should be arranged through Mountain Movers, beside the PIA office, Gilgit.

Outings from Gilgit

Transport: NATCO (Northern Areas Transport Company) runs public buses and minibuses up the KKH to Hunza. Other companies run wagons and jeeps (called Datsun taxis and jeep-taxis) all over the region, and there are Suzuki vans wherever the road is suitable. The jeep-taxis up the Gilgit Valley leave morning and afternoon from the Punial Road bus stop, beyond the Aga Khan Polo Ground, and tend to be very crowded; NATCO buses, wagons and jeeps leave from NATCO in the main bazaar—check their schedules. The Sargin wagon service runs wagons up the Hunza Valley that leave from near the Nasim Cinema. NATCO, PTDC, Walji/Avis and Mountain Movers all have private jeeps for hire. The rates are fixed at Rs6 a mile, plus an overnight charge for the driver of Rs75 on the paved roads; the rates are higher for remote valleys with unpaved roads.

The **Kargah Buddha**, a rock carving at Kargah Nullah, ten kilometres (six miles) west of Gilgit on the old road to Punial, is the most popular short outing from Gilgit. You can drive to the Buddha, a 20-minute ride, and then walk back along the irrigation channel, an easy two-hour stroll on a flat path through villages and farmland, with a magnificent view down over Gilgit and the valley. The irrigation channel ends near the Serena Lodge, from where you can catch a Suzuki back to Gilgit for Rs2. If you do not have your own transport you can also get most of the way to Kargah by public Suzuki. Ride along the new road towards Punial for about 15 minutes, then walk up the old jeepable track for about one kilometre (half a mile) to a bridge across the Kargah Nullah. From here you can see the Buddha halfway up the cliff face on your left. The statue is about three metres (ten feet) tall and looks down protectively over Gilgit. To reach it walk up the left (Gilgit) side of the stream for ten minutes on a rough path, then follow the irrigation channel round to the base of the cliff. The irrigation channel runs from the Kargah Nullah: you can walk up the nullah and across the hills for two days to the Darel Valley (see page 386) and then on down to the Indus.

The Buddha was carved in the seventh century. A monastery and three stupas about 400 metres (yards) upstream from the Buddha were excavated in 1931, and the Gilgit manuscripts were found there. Written in Sanskrit, the manuscripts contain Buddhist texts and also the names and dates of some of the local rulers and various important pilgrims. More manuscripts were found in 1939 and 1956. They are now housed in museums in London, Delhi, Rome and Karachi.

There is an amusing legend about this Buddha. The villagers asked a passing saint to help them get rid of a man-devouring ogress called Yakhshini who lived at Kargah. The saint succeeded in pinning her to the rock and told the villagers she would be unable to escape again as long as he was alive. He added that if the people buried him at the foot of the rock when he died she would never be free—so the villagers killed the saint at once and buried him at the foot of the rock. The Yakhshini is still there, and the villagers are safe.

Jutial Nullah is behind the Serena Lodge. Like most valleys in the Northern Areas, Jutial has a very narrow mouth, but a six-kilometre (four-mile) walk along the stream, through the steep-sided gorge, takes you to coniferous forests and pastureland. Follow the irrigation channel behind the hotel to the cleft in the cliff face, then take the goat path into the gorge, keeping to the right of the stream.

Naltar, an area of alpine meadows and pine forests 3,000 metres (10,000 feet) above sea level and surrounded by snowcapped mountains, is the loveliest full-day outing from Gilgit. It is about two hours' drive away. The public jeep service is irregular, but you can hire a jeep or trek the 18 kilometres (11 miles) from Nomal up to Naltar.

If you are driving, cross the Gilgit River in Gilgit, turn right and follow the west bank of the Hunza River to Nomal, then branch up a steep, barren side valley, climbing up through a rocky gorge to emerge on the fertile high-altitude pastures. There is a PWD rest house here (see page 405), or you can camp. It is the perfect base for gentle walks through the forest, or up to Naltar Lake, where the fishing is excellent. Naltar is also the starting-point for more energetic treks across the Naltar Pass (4,200 metres or 13,800 feet) to the Ishkoman Valley, or across the Daintar Pass (4,800 metres or 15,700 feet) to Chalt (see page 444 for details). The two ski-lifts at Naltar are reserved for the Pakistan army, which trains here from December to March.

Gilgit to the Shandur Pass

The jeep road to Chitral across the Shandur Pass follows the Gilgit River west. It takes 12 tortuous hours to cover the 210 kilometres (130 miles) to Shandur along a jeep road that is not recommended for the faint-hearted. Though the first half of the road as far as Gupis is currently being improved and widened, it is still only a dirt track cut along the cliff face on the south bank of the river. Passing through the former kingdoms of Punial and Gupis, with Ishkoman and Yasin up side valleys to the north, it connects all the tiny village oases with Gilgit town. (The upper Gilgit Valley is also known as Ghizer.)

In August a polo match between Gilgit and Chitral is sometimes played in the Shandur Pass, and at this time there are plenty of public jeeps up to the pass from both sides. During the rest of the year you can get as far as Teru, at the top end of the Gilgit Valley, by public transport, or to Mastuj from Chitral, but public transport across the pass is difficult to find. You can hire jeeps or ponies in Teru and Mastuj, or you can walk across in two days.

Punial is the first kingdom to the west of Gilgit. It encompasses 12 villages and has a population of 17,000. Its inhabitants call it 'the place where heaven and earth meet'. Its capital is **Sher Qila**, 35 kilometres (22 miles) from Gilgit. Sher Qila means Lion's Fort, so called because it proved so difficult to conquer.

Sher Qila boasts an impressive modern girls' high school built by the Aga Khan, which stands beside the now redundant polo ground; facing the polo ground is an old carved wooden mosque. A 150-year-old watchtower, crowned with a pair of ibex horns, stands guard at the end of the ground, a reminder of past wars. The villagers took refuge in the tower whenever attacked.

The next important village in Punial is **Singal**, 16 kilometres (ten miles) further west, where there is a guest house and a modern Aga Khan medical centre with solar heating.

Punial is full of orchards and small terraced fields and can easily be reached in a daytrip from Gilgit. There is time to walk along the water channels, to look into a local flour mill or blacksmith's forge, to watch the locals ploughing or weaving in outdoor pitlooms, and to photograph rural life.

Gakuch, 72 kilometres (45 miles) from Gilgit, is the turning point for the jeep road north up the lovely **Ishkoman Valley**, another former kingdom. The PWD rest house at Chator Khand, 24 kilometres (15 miles) from Gakuch, is the starting point for the five-day trek east to Naltar across the 4,267-metre (14,000-foot) Naltar Pass. The five-day trek west to Yasin across the 4,432-metre (14,540-foot) Asambar Pass is green and easy all the way. At Chator Khand the road splits, right to Imit, another starting point for a trek to Naltar, and left to the village of Ishkoman, from which you can trek to Yasin across the Ishkoman Pass.

Gupis, the next kingdom west along the Gilgit River, 108 kilometres (67 miles) or six hours from Gilgit, is where you turn north for the **Yasin Valley**, yet another former kingdom. Water is plentiful here, making this perhaps the prettiest of all the Gilgit kingdoms: villages are stacked up the mountainside and surrounded by steeply terraced fields.

From Yasin village, 25 kilometres (15 miles) from Gupis, you can trek east to Ishkoman, or west over three passes to Mastuj. The jeep track from Yasin continues north up the Yasin Valley for 20 kilometres (12 miles) to Barkulti. A road forks left up the Thui Valley for 15 kilometres (nine miles) to **Nialti**, from where it is possible to trek across the **Thui Pass** (4,499 metres, or 14,760 feet, above sea level) to the Yarkhun Valley in Chitral District. This is closed to foreigners, but there is no checkpost.

The main track up the Yasin Valley continues for 24 kilometres (15 miles) to **Darkot**. It was here that in 1870 George Hayward, a Royal Geographical Society explorer, came looking for a way across the Baroghil Pass to the Oxus on his search for the river's source. Hayward never got beyond Darkot: he was murdered by the mir of Yasin. No one knows exactly what happened, but it appears that Hayward was killed in revenge. Apparently he knew that trouble was brewing, for he sat in his tent through the night with a loaded pistol in one hand and a rifle across the table. It was only when he finally nodded off that his 'ever watchful and crafty enemies' rushed forward and overpowered him. He is buried at Gilgit.

> *'Ye have robb'd,' said he, 'ye have slaughter'd and made an end,*
> *Take your ill-got plunder, and bury the dead:*
> *What, will ye more of your guest and sometime friend?'*
> *'Blood for our blood,' they said.*
>
> *He laugh'd: 'If one may settle the score for five,*
> *I am ready; but let the reckoning stand till day:*
> *I have loved the sunlight as dearly as any alive.'*
> *'you shall die at dawn,' said they . . . .*

Henry Newbolt, *'He Fell Among Thieves'*

Darkot is the last village before the Darkot Pass, which leads over to the top end of the Yarkhun Valley in Chitral, in the closed zone close to the Afghan border. From Darkot you can trek either east to Ishkoman or west to Thui. There is a checkpost at Darkot, which you cannot pass without a permit.

Beyond Gupis the road to the Shandur Pass deteriorates, but the 59 kilometres (37 miles) to **Phundar** are usually passable. Phundar, nine hours from Gilgit, is idyllic, and is the recommended overnight stopping place en route for Chitral. The good PWD rest house sits on a ridge looking over the flat, meandering Gilgit River on one side, and down a steep slope into the deep blue of Phundar Lake on the other. If you are not pressed for time, plan one or two nights here. The trout fishing is excellent in Phundar, as it is at Handrap Lake, a little further west up a side valley. There are also gentle walks along the river and irrigation channels or more strenuous climbs up the surrounding hills. From Handrap you can trek south to Swat over the **Dadarili Pass**.

The jeep road beyond Phundar is sometimes closed because of broken bridges, but usually it continues through Teru, 30 kilometres (19 miles) away, with a PWD rest house, to **Barsat**, the last village in Gilgit District. At over 3,500 metres (10,000 feet) above sea level, these villages are deep under snow in winter. The farmers here subsist on one crop of barley or maize a year. From Barsat you can trek direct to Mastuj over the **Chumarkhan Pass**, thence down the Zagaro Gol to the village of **Chapali**, 11 kilometres (seven miles) north of Mastuj. You can also trek from Barsat across the **Ghulbar Pass** to **Harchin**, on the Laspur River, where you rejoin the jeep track to Mastuj and Chitral. Alternatively, you can follow the jeep track all the way by the longer route south over the Shandur Pass.

The **Shandur Pass**, at 3,734 metres (12,250 feet) above sea level, and 12 hours from Gilgit, is blocked by snow from November to May. The top of the pass is flat, open, summer pastureland with two small lakes—an ideal spot to camp. The first European traveller across the pass, Colonel William Lockhart, referred to it as a plateau. On the march to relieve the siege of Chitral in the winter of 1895 (see page 343), the pass presented considerable difficulties:

Here are some 250 men who, working shoulder to shoulder, had brought two mountain guns, with the carriages and supply of ammunition, across some 30 kilometres [20 miles] of deep soft snow, at the beginning of April, the worst time of the year. These men were also carrying their own rifles, greatcoats and 80 rounds of ammunition and wearing heavy sheepskin coats; they had slept for two nights in the snow and struggled from dawn to dark, sinking at every step to their waists . . . .

Lieut W Benyon, quoted in *The Gilgit Game* (1979)

For the route from Chitral through Mastuj to the Shandur Pass, see page 349.

THROUGH HUNZA TO KASHGAR

The Karakoram Highway from Gilgit to the Khunjerab Pass, on the border with China 275 kilometres (171 miles) away, follows the Hunza and Khunjerab rivers through barren gorges, past exquisite terraced oases, and round the bases of Rakaposhi, Distaghil and Ultar mountains, all over 7,700 metres (25,000 feet). It is the most unforgettable six-hour drive. Two glaciers come right down to the road, and round every corner are magnificent views.

Public buses, wagons, Suzuki vans and jeeps leave Gilgit daily (see page 408) for central Hunza (be sure to ask for Karimabad rather than Hunza so that you will be taken up the mountain to Karimabad and not just dropped on the KKH in Aliabad), or you can hire private wagons or jeeps from NATCO, PTDC, Walji/Avis and Mountain Movers for Rs6 a mile, plus Rs75 overnight charge for the driver. Check in Gilgit for up-to-date information.

The Khunjerab Pass is open from 1 May to 31 October for tourist groups, and 1 May to 30 November for individual travellers. The pass is under snow from November to April, but if possible is kept open for the post, trade, and Pakistan and Chinese officials throughout the winter.

You need a valid visa to cross into China, obtainable at the Chinese Embassy in Islamabad. The border post at Sost for customs, immigration and health formalities is open every day for outgoing travellers until 11 am and for incoming travellers until 4 pm. No private vehicles are allowed into China. You can take a private vehicle up to the border for sightseeing, but if you are entering China you must leave your vehicle at Sost and cross on the public bus. Special arrangements can be made for group tours, but these are expensive. From Pirali (Hongqilafu, to Chinese officials), the Chinese run a bus service to Kashgar.

Gilgit to Hunza

There are two ways of getting from Gilgit back on to the KKH. If you are in a private vehicle it is more fun to take the shorter route, for small jeeps only, across the longest suspension bridge in Asia, which crosses the Hunza River near its confluence with the Gilgit River: leave Gilgit on the road to Nomal and branch right towards the river a few kilometres (miles) out of town. The 200-metre (650-foot) -long suspension bridge drops a few inches as you drive onto it and sways and undulates with the jeep's movement. The bridge is attached to the cliff face, and the road disappears into a tunnel at the end, turns a right-angle inside and emerges beside the cliff. This road joins the KKH in Dainyor.

The main road from Gilgit joins the KKH ten kilometres (six miles) east of Gilgit on the south bank of the Gilgit River. The KKH crosses the Gilgit River on the elegant Chinese bridge and climbs up to the village of Dainyor.

The **Dainyor rock inscriptions** are in a private garden in the village. Ask in the street for directions. The inscriptions are dated AD 731 and give the names of the kings who ruled in Gilgit during this period. There is a large Chinese graveyard in Dainyor for those Chinese killed building the KKH.

The KKH follows the east bank of the Hunza River, skirting halfway round Mount Rakaposhi. Hunza is reached through a series of bleak gorges with sheer sides, the river rushing below, the mountains towering above. Between the gorges, wherever there is a patch of flattish land, tiny settlements with terraced fields cling to the feet of the barren mountains. It is a precarious existence. The mountains tremble and settle constantly, and the loose shale on their surfaces slides and shifts, threatening the tiny villages below. There is an average of one earth tremor every three minutes.

On the opposite side of the river you can see the old jeep track, the only southern entrance to Hunza before the KKH was built. Apparently the jeep journey took seven hours on a good day, but the road was often blocked by landslides. Large portions of the old road have already disappeared entirely. The trip was, by all accounts, a terrifying experience and very different from the easy two-hour cruise up the KKH.

The gorges, some of them up to eight kilometres (five miles) long, are so precipitous you wonder how the travellers on the ancient Silk Route managed to negotiate them. In summer the river is in flood and it is impossible to pass on the river bed; in winter the high passes to the north of Hunza are blocked by snow.

The first big settlement on the opposite bank is **Nomal**, 33 kilometres (20 miles) from Gilgit; from here the jeep track leads up to Naltar (see page 409). There is no bridge across the river here, but those wishing to hike to Naltar can take an inflated cowskin ferry across from Rahimabad to Nomal.

A memorial to those who died building the KKH stands on the highway opposite Nomal. To the right about 30 metres (yards) above the highway, you can see the line of the first attempt to build the road before the Chinese came and resurveyed the area.

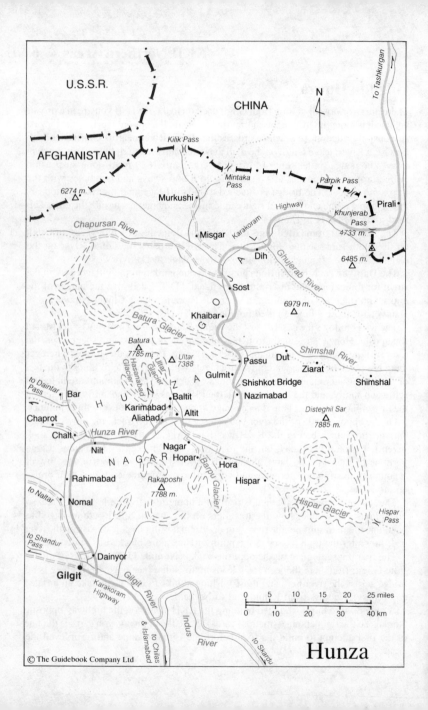

After the first long gorge you come to the large settlement of **Chalt**, also on the opposite side of the river and connected by a bridge with the KKH. From Chalt a jeep track leads north for about 15 kilometres (nine miles) up the Chalt River to the hot springs at **Bar**. There are several easy and picturesque walks along the Chalt River and the irrigation channels on both sides of the valley with flat paths along them. About ten kilometres (six miles) up the Chalt River, the Daintar Valley leads off to the west, along which a path leads over the **Daintar Pass** to Naltar.

Geologically, Chalt is of interest as it lies on the line of collision between two geological plates. The Indian subcontinent is still pushing northwards into the Asian land mass, and a small island plate is being crushed between them (see page 380). The deepest, oldest layers of this island plate are at Patan, on the KKH, the top layer at Chalt. A sign on the cliff reads 'Here continents collided'.

Chalt, with its neighbours **Chaprot** and **Nilt**, nine kilometres (six miles) further on, was, according to *Times* correspondent E F Knight, the scene of 'one of the most brilliant little campaigns in military history'—the British war against Hunza and Nagar in 1891. The war was very well publicized by Knight, and three Victoria Crosses were won in the action. Knight later wrote a stirring account of the battle in his *Where Three Empires Meet* (1893).

Captain Algernon Durand, who had reestablished the Gilgit Agency in 1889 with a large force of Dogra soldiers and British officers, was a sincere if misguided believer in the subjugation of the mountain kingdoms to counter what was perceived as the Russian threat. In late November 1891 he moved a force of 1,000 men to Chalt to prevent the possible invasion of Gilgit from Nagar and Hunza. He built a new bridge and crossed to Nilt, where the tribesmen awaited him, armed with no more than 100 modern weapons. The British eventually managed to blow up the main gate and occupy the fort. Durand, standing in full view of the enemy, was wounded by a home-made bullet of a garnet encased in lead, and was out of action for the remainder of the campaign; he later sent the bullet to his sister as a souvenir.

The tribesmen rushed out of the fort and regrouped behind a network of prepared defences further up the Nilt ravine. It took the British three weeks to root them out. 'One might see many a bigger fight than this,' remarked Knight, 'but never a prettier one.'

An advance party then crossed the Hunza River and occupied the mir's palace in Baltit. The palace was ransacked in the hope of finding 'the treasures of many a pillaged caravan and the results of many a raid'. Little was found except for some beautiful books and a secret chamber containing gunpowder and garnet bullets. The mir of Hunza fled to his relations in Kashgar. That the whole campaign was unnecessary was borne out by the fact that the Hunza people, in 1892 and 1895, voluntarily provided a force of irregulars to serve under British orders in Chitral. And by the time the Pamir Boundary Commission had completed its work in 1893, it was clear that no force from the north or northwest could ever have reached Hunza, let alone Kashmir, over the high passes.

The KKH turns east at Chalt, hugging the Hunza River round the north foot of **Rakaposhi Mountain**. You catch intermittent glimpses of gleaming snowy peaks, glaciers and precipices, kilometres of smooth snow surmounted by triangles and ridges. At 7,788 metres (25,550 feet), Rakaposhi is the 27th highest mountain in the world. It soars magnificently, changing colour according to the time of day. Two of the best views are two kilometres (a mile) past the petrol pump at the turning to Chalt, where you come round a corner to find the great mass of Rakaposhi straight ahead of you, and nine kilometres (six miles) further on, where a sign in English says 'Visitors please Rakaposhi on your right'.

Chalt is the last settlement in the old kingdom of Gilgit. Beyond it Hunza and Nagar begin, Hunza on the north side of the Hunza River, and Nagar on the south. Nagar and Hunza were once part of the same ancient kingdom, but they separated in the 15th century under two warring brothers and have remained traditional enemies ever since. This hostility is exacerbated by the fact that the Hunzakuts are Ismaili Muslims and followers of the Aga Khan, while the Nagar people are Shias and admirers of the late Ayatollah Khomeini of Iran.

The KKH runs through Nagar territory for about 20 kilometres (12 miles) before crossing over to Hunza at **Nazirabad** on another of the elegant Chinese bridges guarded by two rows of ornamental lions. About one kilometre (half a mile) before the bridge a jeep road leads right up to **Minapin**, in Nagar, the starting point for the three-day trek up the Minapin Glacier.

On both sides of the river the cliffs are precipitous. The road climbs high up on the Hunza side with wonderful views of Nagar settlements on the opposite bank and Rakaposhi rising up behind.

When you turn the corner, the Hunza landscape opens up before you in dramatic contrast to the grim desolation of the earlier gorges. Eric Shipton called Hunza 'the ultimate manifestation of mountain grandeur', and at 2,400 metres (8,000 feet) above sea level it is indeed a fairytale land, 'rich, fecund and of an ethereal beauty'. The tiny terraced fields ripple down the mountainside, neatly arranged like fish scales, each supported on a high dry stone wall. The colours change with the seasons: emerald green in the spring, orange and red in the autumn. Everywhere the slender poplar trees cut strong vertical lines in the horizontal terraces and stand out against the glacier-scarred rock.

Above it all stand Rakaposhi, Ultar and Distaghil, guarding the valley on all sides. The scene vanishes again as the road heads up the **Hasanabad Gorge**. If you look left up the stream at the Hasanabad Bridge you see the terminal moraine of Hasanabad Glacier, which ends a kilometre (half a mile) above the road. The new road up to Karimabad leaves the KKH 2.2 kilometres (one and a quarter miles) past Hasanabad Bridge, marked only by a sign to the Mountain View Hotel. **Aliabad** straddles the KKH one kilometre (half a mile) further on. The alternative way up to Karimabad is the steep jeep track that leaves the KKH in Ganesh, at the memorial to those killed building the highway, six kilometres (four miles) past Aliabad.

Hunza

Hunza's 30,000 inhabitants have been ruled by the same family since the 11th century. Because of their isolation and impregnability they long believed themselves the equals of the great powers. A legend relates that the Hunzakuts, as the people of Hunza are known, are descended from five wandering soldiers from Alexander the Great's army. Although many of the people are fair-skinned and have blue or green eyes, the legend is unlikely. In central Hunza the people speak Burushashki, an aboriginal language; in upper Hunza (Gojal) they speak Wakhi, a language related to that spoken in Chinese Turkestan.

Hunzakuts lived off the fruits of caravan-raiding, slave-trading and attacking their neighbours. The kingdom retained its isolated independence until the British took over in 1891, and did not become part of Pakistan until 1974. Even now the mir of Hunza retains much of his traditional importance. The society is co-operative rather than competitive; each family grows enough wheat, maize, apricots and walnuts for its own use. The people used to be self-sufficient, making their own clothes, shoes, wooden and stone bowls and growing all their own food, but now that the KKH has made it so easy to import goods from the rest of Pakistan and China this has changed.

The people are cheerful and friendly. Almost all are Ismailis (followers of the Aga Khan), the most progressive sect of Islam. The women wear bright clothes, long shirts over baggy trousers, and little embroidered pillbox hats over which they drape light shawls. They do not cover their faces, but you should not embarrass them by trying to photograph them.

The modern green-roofed *jamat khanas* (community centres) that dominate every village are the Ismaili places of worship. They fly the green and red flag of the Aga Khan and are not open to the public. Notices in every village announce the development work of the Aga Khan, who takes a deep interest in the area.

Hunza was probably the model for James Hilton's Shangri-La in *Lost Horizon*. The myth concerning Hunzakut longevity may well be the result of a *National Geographic* article that claimed that in Hunza people lived longer than anywhere else, being free from social stress and living on a low-fat diet. Fruit, especially the apricot, was and is the staple food. Nothing is wasted—even the apricot stone is used for fuel, and the kernel is ground into flour, pounded for its oil or eaten as a nut.

Though you see many old people in good health in Hunza, few, if any, live to the fabled 120. Life is as hard in Hunza as it is elsewhere in the Northern Areas, particularly in the early spring, when food supplies run low. The infant mortality rate is high; only the strong survive. Many women aged 50 look older than they are.

Where to Stay

Moderate Rs100-300

Serena Lodge, Karimabad (opening 1991); book through Serena, Karachi, tel.

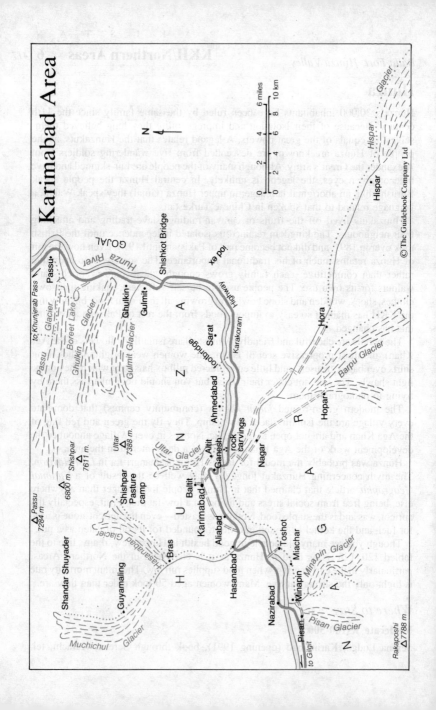

Karimabad Area

© The Guidebook Company Ltd

537506–9, telex SERENA PK.

Mountain View, Karimabad, tel. 17 (s/d Rs200/250). New, large, with good view.

Hilltop, Karimabad, tel. 10 (s/d Rs125/200). Convenient; good food.

Tourist Park, Karimabad, tel. 45 (s/d Rs150/200).

Rakaposhi View, Karimabad, tel. 12 (d Rs100–175). Overpriced.

Silver Jubilee, Karimabad, tel. 62 (d Rs100–200, dorm Rs30). Magnificent view.

Hunza Lodge, Karimabad, tel. 61 (d/t Rs100/120).

Garden (d/t Rs120/150, dorm Rs50, tent bed Rs25).

Domani View, Aliabad (s/d Rs175/250).

New PTDC hotel (opening 1990) in Aliabad.

Inexpensive

Hunza Inn, Karimabad (d Rs50, dorm Rs15). Popular with backpackers.

Rainbow, Karimabad, tel. 49 (d Rs60). Basic.

Village, Karimabad, tel. 26 (d Rs50–100).

Karim, Karimabad (d from Rs50).

Karimabad, Karimabad (d Rs40, dorm Rs20). Fantastic view.

New Hunza Tourist, Karimabad (s/d/t Rs40/70/75).

Friends, Karimabad (charpoy for Rs10).

Diran, Karimabad (camping for Rs10).

PTDC camping ground with facilities in Aliabad (tents Rs60, camping fee Rs10).

The Prince, Jubilee and Delux in Aliabad along the KKH are cheap.

Sights

It is well worth spending a night or two in Karimabad, the capital of Hunza. Walkers should be happy here for days. From Karimabad you look across the valley to Rakaposhi, with the whole valley laid out below you enclosed by a complete ring of snow-covered mountains. Princess Bubuli's peak culminates in a 600-metre (2,000-foot) needle of sheer granite, too steep to hold the snow. According to local legend, King Kiser of Tibet conquered Hunza and married a Hunza princess named Bubul. He dreamt that he saw Tibet invaded and decided to return there, telling his wife that he would come back to Hunza 'when donkeys grow horns, when millstones grow beards, when the river flows uphill'. Lest the princess get into trouble in his absence he seated her on the granite spike with a 90-kilogram (200-pound) bag of millet seed and a cockerel and said: 'Give him one grain a year and when the grain is done, I shall return.'

Below Ultar Glacier the whitewashed **Baltit Fort** stands guard over the entire valley. This was the old palace of the mirs of Hunza and was inhabited until 1960, when the mir's new granite house was built just above the hotels. The fort is about 400 years old. The local people say that a princess of Baltistan married a reigning mir and brought with her some Balti masons, carpenters and craftsmen to build Baltit as part of her dowry.

Baltit stands on a cliff edge; behind the fort is the deep ravine of the Ultar stream, and above, Ultar Glacier forces its way down a cleft in the sheer mountain face.

To visit Baltit you must first collect the keys from the gate man at the mir's new house; any small boy will show you the way. From Karimabad to Baltit it is about one kilometre (half a mile), a steepish but interesting walk through the old village, where men sit gossiping together under the trees outside the shops. (The women seem to do all the daily work, fetching water and wood, taking the animals to pasture and weeding the fields.) Alternatively you can take a jeep almost all the way, walking only up the steep ramp below the fort. Forming a bridge across the path is part of the house of the former *wazir* (prime minister) of Hunza; there is intricate wood-carving across the front.

Baltit is a curious, rambling old place with 53 rooms scattered on three storeys; it is sturdily built of stones reinforced with timber beams and plastered over with sun-dried mud. You approach the main door up a zigzag ramp, and enter the ground floor into a dark hall with guard rooms off it. On the same floor are guest rooms, prisons, storerooms, the kitchens and the dowager queen's apartments. A rough wooden staircase with banisters of poplar poles leads up through a square hole to the floor above.

You emerge into a central courtyard, off which are the main reception rooms where the mir held court. There is a throne room, summer and winter living rooms, bedrooms, bathrooms, stores, guards' quarters and arms depots. There is even a royal balcony, from which the mir could survey his kingdom; behind this is a room containing photographs of the mirs and important visitors. In the museum room are coats of mail, weapons and the drums that sounded the alarm when enemies attacked, warning the villagers to run into the fort for shelter. It was a feudalistic society; though the mir taxed his subjects, he also provided for them in times of famine or need, distributing grain from the stores in the fort.

Another wooden ladder leads to the roof for a view straight across the valley to Rakaposhi beyond. Nestled below the walls are the villages of Baltit and Karimabad. The polo ground in Karimabad is now used as the school playground. The mir's new palace is a kilometre away to the south; his family graveyard lies beyond. To the east you look up the Hunza River across the fields of Altit, guarded by Altit Fort. To the north you peer straight over the edge at a sheer drop into the Ultar ravine, which leads up to Ultar Glacier.

For a spectacular view of Baltit Fort, walk along the irrigation channel that comes from Ultar Glacier. You can also climb the steep path to the hill on the other side of the ravine behind Baltit, and from there walk down to Altit village.

Altit Fort is even more impressive than Baltit and is probably 100 years older. Perched on a rocky cliff that falls 300 metres (1,000 feet) sheer into the Hunza River, it is a two-kilometre (one-mile) jeep-ride away. The road passes through an arch in the aqueduct feeding Karimabad just above the mir's new palace and winds, in a series of hairpin bends, over a frail suspension bridge and across a polo ground to Altit village. The road is so rough it is more pleasant to walk; this does not, in fact,

Baltit Fort

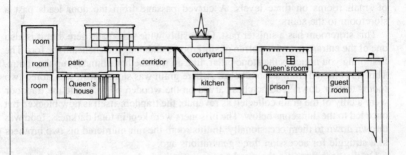

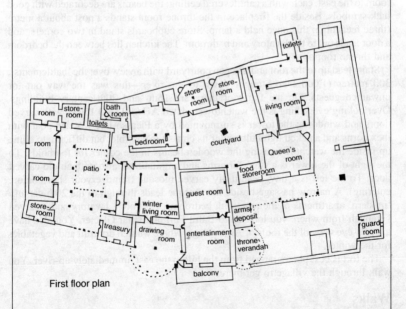

First floor plan

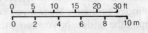

	0	5	10	15	20	30 ft
	0	2	4	6	8	10 m

take much longer.

A guide with a key to the fort meets you in the village and leads you on foot through an orchard and up a steep rock to the door. Like Baltit, the fort has a maze of small rooms on three levels. A curved passage from the door leads past a storeroom to the stairs.

This storeroom has a sinister past. Ostensibly wine was made here, but it is also one of the entrances to the warren of storerooms and dungeons beneath the fort. The first thing you notice is the stone pillar, like an Elizabethan chimney, up the centre. This was entered from a room below, where grain was stored; fruit was stored two rooms further down. The notches carved on the wooden pillar beside the trapdoor were a tally of the grain collected as revenue; the trapdoor itself is now blocked but once led to the dungeons below. The prisoners were kept in total darkness; food was thrown down to them occasionally. In this room the mir murdered his two brothers in a struggle for accession three generations ago.

On the next floor are the royal apartments, the bedroom to the west, the throne room to the east, each with a cantilevered ceiling; the beams are decorated with good luck symbols. Beside the fireplace in the throne room stands a post about a metre (three feet) high; this once held a lamp. Store cupboards stand in two corners, and a door leads out to the lavatory and bathroom. The kitchen lies between the bedroom and throne room.

Stairs lead up to the roof and an open courtyard with a view over the 'battlements', 300 metres (1,000 feet) straight down to the river—this was the way out for unwanted guests. On the flat roof there are 16th- and 20th-century buildings. Overlooking everything is the watchtower, dated AH 909 (AD 1503), with carved doors and windows; the tower is surmounted by a Picasso-like wooden goat with ibex horns and a naked lightbulb under its chin. It is possible, but difficult, to climb up inside the watchtower using the wooden beams in the corner for footholds. To the right of the tower is a store for arms and ammunition, also with an old carved door. To the left is a tiny, beautifully carved mosque (remove your shoes before entering). A narrow passage beside the mosque leads through to the 20th-century 'modern' apartments of the raja, with bedrooms, bathroom, lavatory and a carved verandah from where you look up to Baltit Fort and Ultar Glacier. You also have a bird's-eye view of the roofs of Altit village, where women dry fruit and vegetables for the winter.

The fort is best photographed from the hill to the east, immediately up-river. You walk through the village to get there.

Walks

There are wonderful all-day walks along the clifftop from Altit to Sarhath, halfway to Shishkot Bridge, where the KKH crosses the Hunza River. At Sarhath there is also a footbridge across the Hunza; you can arrange at your hotel to have a vehicle pick you up at the bridge, or you can hitchhike back.

A flat, easy walk takes you from below Baltit Fort along the irrigation channel for a couple of kilometres (a mile or so), from where you can look back across the wide bowl of cultivated terraces to Baltit in the background.

The walk along the irrigation channel to the base of the **Ultar Glacier** behind Baltit is easy and spectacular, but the hike up to the glacier is more difficult. It is a three-hour climb to the summer pastures, where you can stay with the shepherds and watch them make butter and cheese. Follow the lowest irrigation channel from Baltit Fort, then take the path up the left side of the gorge. Ultar Peak is still unclimbed.

Hasanabad Glacier is easier to get to. Start from the bridge on the KKH across the Hasanabad Nullah, three kilometres (one and a half miles) downriver from Aliabad, and follow the stream up, scrambling over the high mound of the terminal moraine. There is a two-day trek along the edge of the glacier to the summer pastures on the slopes of Batura Glacier (see page 447).

The less energetic can visit the **Pakistan Mineral Development Corporation** project in Aliabad, which is developing Hunza's mineral wealth. You can buy precious and semi-precious stones here. Some two kilometres (a mile) further on, a path to the ruby mines leads off to the left.

Ganesh

Six kilometres (four miles) beyond Aliabad, the KKH makes a sweeping S-bend down past Ganesh village to the bridge across the Hunza River. Ganesh, on fertile flat land above the river, is guarded by an old watchtower and fort. The old carved mosque is also worth a visit. In the pool in front of the tower all the local children learn to swim. Until this century boys had to swim across the Hunza to prove that they could escape or attack across the river when necessary. Until the British came in 1891, the men of Hunza used to keep a sword, gun, shield and a loaf of bread (which was replaced every eight days) beside their doors; when the drums beat the alarm from Altit Fort, heralding the approach of raiders, each man would grab these things and run for the fort. (Presumably his family went too.)

Like Gilgit, Hunza was an important staging post on the Silk Route and was heavily travelled for thousands of years by traders going back and forth between China, India and the West over the Kilik, Mintaka, Parpik and Khunjerab passes. The most convincing proof of this lies in the inscriptions on the **Ganesh rocks**, a sort of Silk Route guest book. The rocks are immediately beside the KKH, between the road and the river, a few hundred metres past the bridge across the Hunza River.

The inscriptions are in Kharoshthi, Brahmi, Gupta, Sogdian and Tibetan. Among them is a portrait of the first-century Kushan king of Gandhara, Gondophares. Another inscription reads 'Chandra sri Vikramaditya conquers'; the date of the inscription corresponds to AD 419. Chandra sri Vikramaditya was Chandra Gupta II, the greatest of the Gupta emperors, who ruled over most of India in the early fifth century AD.

Most of the drawings are of hunting scenes with horses and riders shooting at ibex, ibex surrounded by horsemen, and men dancing round ibex. The ibex was extremely important to the people of Hunza, Afghanistan, northern Pakistan and northern India, as it was believed to be the pet animal of the mountain fairies and symbolized fertility and prosperity. In the more remote parts of Hunza the people still perform ritual ibex dances: a holy man dons an ibex headdress and drinks ibex blood (or nowadays the blood of an ordinary goat), then falls into a trance and proceeds to tell fortunes and answer questions about the future.

Nagar

Public jeeps leave Aliabad daily for the kingdom of Nagar, or you can hire a private jeep at one of the Aliabad or Karimabad hotels for about Rs500 to take you to the end of the road at Hopar and back. The jeep will wait for an hour while you view the glacier.

The jeep road into Nagar leaves the KKH just beyond the rock of Ganesh. The first six kilometres (four miles) are dry and barren, then the road divides. The track straight on along the north bank of the river leads 10 kilometres (six miles) to Hora and the beginning of the trek up the Hispar Glacier: the right fork crosses the Hispar River on a suspension bridge and climbs up to the fertile villages of Nagar, where you can walk along irrigation channels and through the fields and villages. The Mir (ex-ruler) of Nagar lives on top of the hill between the jeep road and the Hispar River. His private compound includes an old carved mosque, audience pavilion and polo ground. Almost all the people here are Shia Muslims, and the women are in stricter seclusion and less friendly than the Ismaili Muslims of Hunza.

The jeep road ends at Hopar (about 15 kilometres and 1 1/2 hours from the KKH) a magnificent bowl, terraced and fertile, with views up to Miar Peak, Golden Peak and Malubiting (all part of the Rakaposhi Range) and down onto the Bualtar Glacier (also known as the Balkie or Hopar Glacier) which is racing forward at about 20 centimetres (8 inches) a day. You can trek across this glacier and on up the Barpu Glacier to summer pastures. The Hopar Hilton overlooking the Bualtar Glacier offers basic accommodation in tents and serves adequate food.

The KKH is at its most spectacular between Ganesh and Gulmit. The road runs high on the eastern side of the river, twisting and turning round the barren foot of the Hispar Range which has six peaks of more than 7,000 metres (23,000 feet). On the opposite bank, villages cling to the side of Ultar II Mountain, 7,388 metres (24,240 feet) above sea level. Below the villages, grey scree slithers down to the river; above, jagged teeth along the ridge hide the highest snow-covered peaks from view.

The rocks in Hunza are full of rubies and garnets. About 200 metres (yards) past the turning to Nagar on the KKH, you will notice shallow caves dug in the cliff face—these are mines. You can actually see the garnets in the rocks and collect them along the base of the cliff. Soon after this you enter a gorge streaked with lines of white marble like trickled icing.

At **Shishkot Bridge** the KKH crosses back to the west bank; from here to Tashkurgan in China the people speak Wakhi, a Turkic language.

Gulmit

Gulmit (2,500 metres or 8,200 feet above sea level), eight kilometres (five miles) past the bridge, is a fertile plateau with irrigated fields on either side of the road. Halfway between Gilgit and the Khunjerab Pass, it is a good place to spend a night or two.

The small museum belonging to the ex-ruler, Raja Bahadur Khan, is full of interesting ethnic artefacts—wooden bowls, spoons, and farm implements, woollen coats and embroidered hats and shawls. The raja shows you round with charm and enthusiasm.

There are many walks along irrigation channels in the area, and the people are very friendly. One recommended walk is across Ghulkin Glacier to **Boreet Lake**, then across Passu Glacier and down to Passu village. For a longer walk continue from Passu Glacier across the Husseini Ridge to **Yunzbin**, at the bottom of Batura Glacier (see map on page 446).

Where to Stay

Silk Route Lodge, on KKH, tel. 18 (s/d Rs225/300). Camping allowed.

Horseshoe Motel, on KKH, tel. 6 (s/d Rs200/250).

Tourist Cottage, on KKH, tel. 19 (d Rs60, dorm Rs25).

Village Inn, tel. 12 (s/d Rs125–200). Traditional room upstairs. Up in Gulmit village 500 metres (yards) from the KKH.

Marco Polo Inn, tel. 7 (d Rs125–250) Traditional rooms. In Gulmit village.

The **Ghulkin Glacier**, covered in gravel and rocks, comes right down to the road about one kilometre (half a mile) past Gulmit. The road crosses the snout of the glacier at the very edge of the river, then climbs up onto the lateral moraine, a great grey slag heap. The glacier, Boreet Lake and a small hotel are up a track to the left.

About five kilometres (three miles) further on you round a corner to find **Passu Glacier** straight ahead. It is white and shining and deeply crevassed, and looks exactly what you expect a glacier to look like; most other glaciers in the area are covered in rocks and gravel. The glacier flows down to the east, so the morning sun glints off the ice. Above the glacier to the left the jagged line of the Passu and Batura peaks, seven of them over 7,500 metres (25,000 feet), shine clean and white and hostile. Some of these peaks are still unclimbed and are referred to by number, not name, on the map. Behind, on the opposite side of the river, a semicircle of saw-toothed summits hems in the valley. Their rugged beauty catches the evening light at sunset, and grey alluvial fans slide down their flanks to the river.

Passu

Passu, 14 kilometres (nine miles) beyond Gulmit, is a village of farmers and mountain guides. This is the setting-off point for climbing expeditions up the Batura, Passu, Kuk and Lupgar groups of peaks, and trekking trips up the Shimshal Valley and Batura Glacier.

For non-trekkers there are two easy walks from Passu. It takes about 20 minutes to scramble up through the rocks to the Passu Glacier, or an hour to follow the irrigation channel up to the Batura Glacier. Or you can wander through the small village of Passu, watch the villagers at work in the fields, and see yaks and dzos (yak-cow hybrids).

Batura Glacier comes down from the left a couple of kilometres (a mile or so) north of Passu. There are several scenic treks up the side of the glacier to the summer pastures with magnificent views of the mountain (see page 447).

Where to Stay

Passu Inn, on KKH, tel. 1 (d Rs70, traditional family room sleeping six Rs200). Popular with hikers; good meeting place. Inn-keeper has detailed maps of the region and can arrange for guides for treks in the area.
Shishper (d Rs70).
Batura Inn (d Rs40–50).
Boreet, up by the lake and popular.

Shimshal

The road to Shimshal leaves the KKH six kilometres (four miles) past Passu. Shimshal is an isolated, unspoiled valley, three to four days' walk away through a narrow barren gorge. You need a guide to lead you in; once there you can take several different treks up to the surrounding glaciers (see page 448). The villagers of Shimshal are currently building an access road from the KKH.

Sost

The KKH passes through four more villages before reaching the immigration and customs post at Sost, 34 kilometres (21 miles) from Passu.

Where to Stay

Shangrila Hotel, due to open in 1990. (Book Rawalpindi 73006, 72948, or Karachi 520703, 520810, 520261–5; rates will be under Rs1,000.)
Tourist Lodge, tel. 9 (s/d Rs150/200, dorm Rs25). Popular with tours.
Khunjerab, tel. 12 (d Rs150, dorm Rs15–20).
Hunza Dreamland (d Rs150, dorm Rs15–20).

Mountain Refuge (d Rs100).
New Mountain Refuge (t Rs100, dorm Rs25).
Sarklin (d Rs100).
Carawan (d Rs100).
National (d Rs40).
Pak-China (d/t Rs40/60).
Al Zaman (dorm Rs20).
Shahin (dorm Rs15).

The border post at Sost is open until 11 am for outgoing traffic to China. It is four to five hours' drive from here to Tashkurgan, and you must allow time for passing the Chinese customs and immigration at Pirali. The time difference between China and Pakistan is three hours, so it will be at least 7 or 8 pm, Chinese time, before you arrive in Tashkurgan. The post is open for incoming traffic until 4 pm Pakistani time.

NATCO runs daily buses from Sost to Pirali. Sometimes if there are not enough passengers the bus does not run, so be prepared for a day's delay. The charge is Rs150 for the 120-kilometre (75-mile) journey. The mail wagon crosses on Wednesday and can accommodate eight passengers. Private vehicles are not allowed into China, though they may proceed to the top of the pass for sightseeing.

The jeep road west up the long, wide **Chapursan Valley** leaves the KKH just past Sost. This valley leads to the Irshad–Unwin Pass (4,880 metres or 16,000 feet) to Afghanistan and is closed to foreigners. The Chapursan Valley also leads to the Chillinji Pass (5,291 metres or 17,359 feet) and on to Ishkoman, which used to be the main route for Hunza people to Gilgit when the Nagar people, their traditional enemies, controlled the route down the Hunza River.

About eight kilometres (five miles) further along the KKH, another jeep road leads left for ten kilometres (six miles) to **Misgar**, from where paths cross the Kilik and Mintaka passes to China (also closed to foreigners). Until the KKH was built across the Khunjerab Pass, the Mintaka Pass was the most popular route from Hunza to Tashkurgan; the KKH was built across the Khunjerab because the Mintaka Pass lies too close to the Afghan and Russian borders.

For the next 20 kilometres (12 miles) the valley is narrow and barren. You leave the Hunza River and follow the Khunjerab. The cliff face is shattered into huge cubes and slabs of rock like giant building blocks that peel off and tumble into the road. Alluvial fans flow down every gully, frequently blocking the way.

The **Khunjerab National Park** begins 30 kilometres (19 miles) from Sost. The hills stand back from the road, the valley opens out and the Khunjerab dwindles back to a tiny mountain stream with the odd tuft of grass and willow and birch tree along its banks. The checkpost at **Dih** consists of six lonely stone houses.

Driving the last stretch to the top of the pass is easier. There is less mountain above you now, the slopes are gentler and the road follows the banks of the stream for 35 kilometres (22 miles) before winding up round 12 wide, well-engineered hairpin bends to the top.

Khunjerab Pass

The Khunjerab Pass at 4,733 metres (15,528 feet) is the highest border crossing on a paved road in the world. A red sign announces 'China drive right', a rival green sign 'Pakistan drive left'. A monument tells you that the pass is 16,000 feet (4,877 metres) above sea level and was opened in 1982. The Khunjerab Pass is the continental watershed, water on the Pakistani side flowing down to the Indian Ocean and that on the Chinese side being swallowed up by the Taklamakan Desert in the Tarim Basin. The name Taklamakan means literally, 'If you go in you don't come out.'

The scenery is remarkably different on either side of the pass. On the Pakistani side you wind up through barren deserted gorges with no sign of human life for the last 40 kilometres (25 miles) before the border. The Chinese side is a wide, open, grassy, high-altitude plateau, with herds of yaks, sheep and goats tended by Tajik herders who live in yurts. Children and dogs play around the camps. The Tajiks are smiling and friendly, and even the women are happy to be photographed. The small two-humped Bactrian camels sport hairy 'jodphurs' down to the knees, and look quite different from their big, short-haired, one-humped cousins on the Pakistani side.

The first Chinese checkpost is five kilometres (three miles) beyond the top, a single house manned by two young soldiers. The road runs straight across rolling grassy steppe for another 30 kilometres (19 miles) to the immigration and customs post at Pirali.

Pirali, at 4,100 metres (13,451 feet), is a collection of half a dozen barracks, the customs and immigration houses and a meeting hall. Away across the flat plains is the distant line of the Pamirs. A sign tells you it is 1,860 kilometres (1,156 miles) to Urumchi, the capital of Xinjiang.

Covering the 96 kilometres (60 miles) from Pirali to Tashkurgan takes about one and a half hours. There is a bus; or sometimes you can hire a jeep and driver from the border guards for FEC1.50 (US$0.50) per kilometre (0.6 miles), or hitch a ride on a lorry. The road runs due north and parallel to the border with the USSR, only 15 or 20 kilometres (about ten miles) away. You are never alone. Men ride horses, donkeys or Bactrian camels across the grasslands, chasing the herds of yaks, sheep and goats. The villages of square stone houses have schools, hospitals, and even the odd cinema and basketball court, and are surrounded by unirrigated fields of barley.

Tashkurgan, at 3,180 metres (10,433 feet), has one wide paved street about one kilometre (half a mile) long lined by three rows of poplars on each side. The population of 4,000 are mostly Tajiks, Ismaili Muslims whose language is written in the Arabic script. The government hotel is primitive with no running water and smelly outhouses. A second 200-bed hotel is proposed for 1990.

You can explore the whole town in two hours—the crumbling, mud-walled fort on the northeast corner, the 'old' town with its small wooden mosque, the flour mills on the mill stream to the north beyond the fort, and the old graveyard in the fields to the north, where some of the graves are decorated with the horns of Marco Polo sheep and ibex, while others consist of great mud mausoleums. The plains to the east of the town are swampy and covered with the stone houses of Tajik herders who settle there for the winter but roam around after their herds in summer.

Tajik men wear heavy black overcoats tied at the waist, trousers tucked into tall boots and hats trimmed with sheepskin (wool-side out). The women wear skirts over thick stockings or trousers, jackets and pillbox hats covered with headsquares. Some still wear their hair in four long plaits decorated with rows of buttons.

The one government shop, and half a dozen **bazaar** stalls are interesting for their range of goods, from silks to psychedelic socks, blocks of tea to wooden pitchforks, horse bridles to bottled beer. In the local restaurant you can watch the cook make noodles, swinging and folding the wheatflour dough: 14 folds make 16,384 noodles. The steamed dumplings in soup are delicious.

Stirring martial music, long harangues, news and commentary are piped through loudspeakers to the whole town morning and evening.

From Tashkurgan to Kashgar it is a magnificent seven- to 20-hour drive of 295 kilometres (183 miles) north across the high-altitude plateau close to the Russian border. The road climbs up across another pass at 4,100 metres (13,451 feet), then curves round **Mustagh Mountain** and **Kongar Mountain**, both at over 7,600 metres (25,000 feet), with the beautiful **Lake Kalakuli** nestled between them. The Pamirs close in for a dramatic 70 kilometres (43 miles) through **Tiger's Mouth Gorge**, where the sheer cliff consists of folded and contorted rock—thin layers of slate and mud, whisked into whorls and folds, like two-coloured cake batter in a mixer bowl. The final 80 kilometres (50 miles) to Kashgar is across flat, irrigated farmland, the fields outlined by straight rows of tall poplar trees.

Kashgar

Kashgar (Kashi, in Chinese) lies at 1,289 metres (4,229 feet) above sea level and is hot from May to October. Once known as the Pearl of the Silk Route, this oasis between the mountains and the desert was a resting place where travellers used to prepare themselves for the next leg of their journey. It is a city of 200,000 people; the old mud town is perched on its high mound of debris and spills down to join the new city with its wide paved streets and utilitarian, Russian-style buildings. There is almost no motorized traffic. Everyone rides bicycles or donkey carts. (For a map of Kashgar, see page 468.)

Where to Stay

Xin Binguan (Kashgar Guest House), tel. 2367–8. Furthest out of town (half an hour by donkey cart) and usually used for conferences.

Lao Binguan (Seman Hotel), tel. 2129, 2060. This was the Russian Consulate. The most comfortable, with the best food.

Qinibagh Hotel, tel. 2291, 2103. This was the British Consulate. The cheapest, with smelly outhouses and no running water, but adequately clean and conveniently located.

All three hotels have cheap dormitory accommodation for individual travellers.

Sights

The town is at its best on Sunday, market day, when hundreds of country Tajiks ride into town on their donkey carts laden with vegetables, fodder and firewood for sale. The bazaars are crammed from early morning until late afternoon with traders selling everything from cloth and pearls to painted cots and aluminium water butts. The blacksmiths shoe horses, the milliners make a delightful range of caps and hats, and the skin merchants sell everything from tabby-cat furs to snow leopard skins.

Apart from the Sunday market and the old town, the other sights worth seeing in Kashgar are the main **Eidgah Mosque** (one of 130 mosques in town), the 18th-century **Tomb of Abakh Hoja** and the enormous **Uygur graveyard**.

It is possible, but difficult, to find a bicycle to rent (see map). A bicycle makes your stay in Kashgar very much more enjoyable.

Leaving Kashgar can be a problem. It is three days by bus round the edge of the Taklamakan Desert to Urumchi, or three hours by air. The flights are heavily booked and you may have to wait more than a week for a ticket.

Trekking Guide

North Pakistan contains the most concentrated block of high mountains anywhere in the world, and the longest glaciers outside the polar regions. The views of unspoiled villages set against a backdrop of glaciers and snow-covered peaks are unrivalled. The Hindu Kush, Karakorams and Himalayas of Pakistan are less crowded than the mountains in India and Nepal and, being outside the monsoon belt, are ideal for trekking from June to September. Shorter, lower-altitude treks can be made throughout the year, even in January, the coldest month.

Trekkers have two choices. You can either go on a fully organized trek arranged by one of the large international tourist agencies or a reliable local agency, which means that everything from tents and food to guides and entertainment is laid on; or you can arrange your own private trek and hire a *sirdar* (foreman), cook and porters either through an agency in Pakistan or directly from a village near the start of your chosen trek.

Experienced and confident trekkers with some knowledge of Urdu may prefer to trek with just one or two porters to guide, carry and cook. If you use a Pakistani travel agent to find porters for you they will charge more per day (the travel agents take a commission), but you will be saved a certain amount of hassle and uncertainty. Only the very experienced should trek alone as many of the tracks are little used and pass through isolated territory.

With only 100 millimetres (four inches) of rainfall a year, northern Pakistan is virtually a desert. The villages are all man-made oases dependent on irrigation. There are long stretches of barren mountainside between villages, so you need to carry all your own food and supplies. Living off the land in the Nepalese style is generally not feasible here, but you can stock up on the most necessary foodstuffs in Gilgit, Chitral and Skardu.

Maps

Good trekking maps are not available in Pakistan, so you must buy them before you go. The best set are the US Army U502 Series (scale 1:250,000), seven of which have recently been issued in colour and can be ordered from the Library of Congress, Geography and Map division, or any good map shop. The relevant maps are sheets:

NJ 43–13—Edition 1-AMS Mastuj (Northern Chitral)
NJ 43–14—Edition 2-AMS Baltit (Hunza)
NJ 43–15—Edition 1-AMS Shimshal (Shimshal and Hispar)
NI 43–1—Edition 1-AMS Churrai (Upper Swat)
NI 43–2—Edition 2-AMS Gilgit (Gilgit and Nanga Parbat)
NI 43–3—Edition 2-AMS Mundik (Skardu)
NI 43–4—Edition 2-AMS Siachen (Concordia and K-2)
NI 43–6—Edition 1-AMS Srinagar (Kaghan Valley and Azad Kashmir)

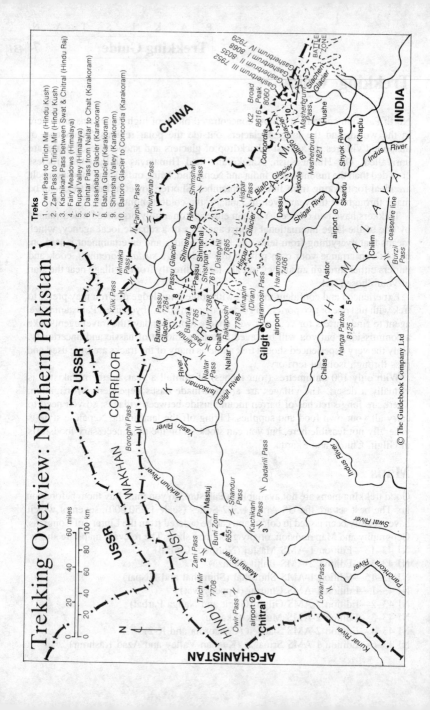

Trekking Overview: Northern Pakistan

Treks

1. Owir Pass to Trich Mir (Hindu Kush)
2. Zani Pass to Trich Mir (Hindu Kush)
3. Kachikani Pass between Swat & Chitral (Hindu Raj)
4. Fairy Meadows (Himalaya)
5. Rupal Valley (Himalaya)
6. Daintar Pass from Naltar to Chalt (Karakoram)
7. Hasanabad Glacier (Karakoram)
8. Batura Glacier (Karakoram)
9. Shimshal Valley (Karakoram)
10. Baltoro Glacier to Concordia (Karakoram)

© The Guidebook Company Ltd

Warning: The ceasefire line between India and Pakistan is not marked—if you are trekking in Kashmir or Baltistan be sure you know where it is. Each map gives a reliability diagram—good, fair and poor—so be sure to note the accuracy rating of the map for the area in which you are trekking.

Another good set of maps is published in Japan in the mountaineering book *Mountain Maps of the World: Karakoram, Hindu-Kush, Pamir and Tien Shan* (1978). The text is in Japanese, but the maps are labelled in Roman script. The maps cover most of the Pakistani mountain region at a scale of 1:200,000. This book is hard to find and very expensive, but a good map shop may have colour photocopies.

All maps can be ordered from:

Travel Bookshop, Rindermarkt 20, 8001 Zurich, Switzerland.
Artou, 8 rue de Rive, 1204 Geneva, Switzerland.
Bauer SA, 1 route de Crissier, 1020 Renens, Switzerland.
Stanford International Map Centre, 12–14 Long Acre, London WC2E 9LP, England.
McCarta Ltd, 122 Kings Cross Road, London WC1X 9DS, England.
Cordee Books, 3a De Montfort Street, Leicester LE1 7HD, England.
Geo Center GmbH, Honigwiesenstrasse 25, Postfach 80 08 30, 7000 Stuttgart 80, German Federal Republic.
Geo Buch, Rosental 6, 8000 Munchen 2, German Federal Republic.
Libreria Alpina, Via C Coronedi-Berti 4, 40137 Bologna, Zona 3705, Italy.
For travel agencies in Pakistan, see page 459.

Permits

Trekking in Pakistan is defined as walking below 6,000 metres (19,700 feet) and is divided into two zones, open and restricted. No permit or approved guide is needed in the open zone, which covers most of Pakistan. The restricted zone is along the borders with India, China, Afghanistan and Iran; most of Baluchistan and Chitral; and certain very popular treks in Baltistan where the number of trekkers at any one time needs to be regulated. Around most of the country you may not approach within 30 kilometres (19 miles) of the border, though there are exceptions to this—in Azad Kashmir the restricted zone is within 16 kilometres (ten miles) of the border. The Ministry for Tourism has approved eight treks in restricted zones, for which a permit is necessary.

Permits are issued by the Tourism Division, College Road, F-7/2, Islamabad, within 24 hours of application (in duplicate), which must be made through an approved travel agent. An approved guide must accompany all treks in restricted zones. Guides and porters must be insured for the sum specified by the government. All trekkers must register at the checkposts along the way.

It is possible, but difficult, to get permission to take treks along restricted routes other than the eight mentioned above. This takes time. Applications must be accompanied by a route map and passport particulars of all trekkers. If permission is given, an approved tourist guide will be assigned to accompany the trek. Those trekking in restricted zones must be briefed in Islamabad before departure; this can cause some delay.

For detailed information on all the trekking rules and regulations—open and restricted zones, rates and conditions for hiring porters, guides and liaison officers—and mountaineering rules and regulations (these are different from the trekking ones), apply to the Tourism Division in Islamabad. Specify that you require the rates for hiring porters and jeeps, as these are a special appendix and not in the booklets. The rates differ in the different valleys.

The trekker must never forget that certain areas of Pakistan are still hostile to outsiders and are dangerous for Pakistanis and foreigners alike. For your own protection let the police know where you are and follow their advice about which areas are unsafe. It does not cost much to hire a villager (usually non-English speaking) to walk with you. Having someone along who speaks the local language and can explain who you are to others is highly recommended.

Trekkers in Pakistan must be flexible, ready to change their itineraries and plans at a moment's notice. If your flight is cancelled, take a bus. If your chosen trek is closed, take another one. Always be friendly with the deputy commissioner and the police: they are all-powerful, and it is essential to have them on your side. They are easily irritated and it is not worth arguing with them. Though at times you may be extremely frustrated, it pays to appear relaxed and cheerful. If you can establish a good rapport with your guide and porters they will be much more willing to help you. On the whole, Pakistanis find Westerners tense, selfish and obstinately inflexible. Take the time to greet everyone, to shake hands all round and to ask polite questions about health and family. This is the Pakistani way.

Hiring Guides and Porters

The rules and regulations for hiring porters are clearly defined by the government. The official daily wage differs in each valley but ranges between Rs90 and Rs110 a day for low-altitude porters, plus a specified daily food ration or Rs30 a day food allowance. You must expect to bargain, as you are unlikely to find anyone who will work for the basic wage. It is essential that porters should sign a contract specifying exactly what is expected of them before setting out. The porters in Diamer (Nanga Parbat area) have a particularly bad reputation for going on strike. A normal day's march is only ten to 13 kilometres (six to eight miles). There are recognized stopping places and it requires tact and determination to get the porters to walk further, and you will usually have to pay more to persuade them. It is perfectly possible to walk two stages in one day, but the porters will charge double wages. Agree on the wages to be paid on rest days (usually about half) and forced rest due to bad weather (normally full wages), and on the porter's wage if walking back unladen (usually half or less). Porters are entitled to one day off in seven. Low-altitude porters work below 5,000 metres (16,400 feet) and are expected to carry 25 kilos (55 pounds). It is normal to pay 50 percent of the first week's wages in advance; thereafter payment is at the end of each week.

What to Take

—Comfortable trekking boots with spare insoles.
—Trainers or running shoes as a comfortable change.
—Liner socks and thick outer socks, at least two pairs of each.
—Baggy trekking trousers. Shorts are never worn in Pakistan, as they offend the Muslim sense of propriety. Local _shalwar_, the baggy trousers worn by all Pakistanis, are comfortable and recommended; you can buy them in Karachi or Rawalpindi, or have them made by a local tailor in a few hours.
—Long, loose fitting, wash-and-wear shirts, both lightweight and warm, with button-down pockets. Women should wear men's shirts with long tails.
—Several T-shirts and underpants.
—One set of thermal underwear.
—Down-filled or thermal jacket.
—Light plastic rain cape with hood or Goretex jacket with hood.
—Gloves or mittens.
—Warm ski hat and broad-brimmed sunhat.
—Umbrella.
—Women will need bras and tampons and may find it very useful to have a lightweight length of cloth, two metres (yards) by one metre (like a sarong). This can be wrapped around you when washing and offers some cover when there is no other privacy. It can also be used as a shawl to cover your head so as not to offend the strict Shia Muslims in some villages.
—Sleeping bag warm to −10°C (14°F) with detachable cotton liner.
—Tent.
—Foam pad to sleep on.
—Stove, kerosene or gas. Stoves bought locally are not very efficient, so it is better to bring your own from overseas. You can buy kerosene locally, but gas is difficult to find. (Dad Ali Shah in Gilgit sometimes has gas for sale.)
—Fuel container. Again, local containers are not so good.
—Two cooking pots and a pressure cooker are recommended.
—Nylon stuff bags with drawstring tops for carrying supplies.
—Clear plastic bags to protect spare clothes from damp.
—Backpack.
—Washing things, soap, towel, lavatory paper.
—Washing-up sponge, scouring pad, drying-up cloth.
—Pliers, Swiss army knife, torch (a head-torch is recommended).

—Matches in waterproof bag.
—Sewing kit, scissors, safety pins.
—Enamel cup, fork, spoon, tin opener.
—Water bottle.
—Moleskin, plasters.
—Lip balm, sunscreen lotion, total sun block, skin moisturizer.
—Flea powder, insect repellent, soothing bite cream, calomine lotion.
—Sunglasses and/or glacier glasses.
—Thin nylon cord for hanging washing and tying bundles.
—Ice axe.
—Maps, note books, pens.
—Money pouch that hangs round your neck on a string.
—Fishing rod (the rivers are full of unsuspecting trout).
—Fishing licence, obtainable in Chitral, Gilgit and Skardu.
—Old shoes, jacket and sunglasses as presents for your porter.
—Whistle.

Health

You need to start out healthy and fit. You would be wise to have up-to-date immunization against typhoid, tetanus, diptheria and polio. (For malaria prophylactics and gamma globulin see page 32.)

The most likely health problem while trekking is an upset stomach. Diarrhoea, dysentery, and a variety of parasites are all caught from contaminated water and food. Always boil water for at least ten minutes or treat it with water-purifying tablets, and never eat anything which is not cooked.

Altitude sickness is the other hazard: read up on this before you go so you know how to recognize and treat it. It is caused by a lack of oxygen above 2,500 metres (8,000 feet). The usual signs are a combination of any of the following: headache, nausea or vomiting, irregular breathing, dry cough, loss of appetite, lassitude and fatigue, loss of coordination, loss of judgement, oedema (resulting in swollen face and hands and reduced urine production—you should produce at least one pint of urine a day—and in severe cases, pneumonia and a waterlogged brain). These symptoms should be taken seriously: altitude sickness can be fatal. The cure is to go to a lower altitude and rest. The best preventative is to gain altitude slowly: the height at which you sleep should not increase by more than 300 to 400 metres (1,000 to 1,300 feet) per day, though it is all right to climb higher and return.

Be prepared for enormous temperature changes. On glacier treks the temperature can vary from –10°C (14°F) at night to 40°C (104°F) in the afternoon. You can get severely sunburned at high altitude. You should drink six pints of fluid a day and take salt tablets.

Some doctors recommend a high carbohydrate diet.

Suggested Medical Kit

—Water-purifying tablets (Micropur).
—Malaria prophylactic tablets.
—Gastrointestinal tablets (Imodium).
—Antibiotics (Septrin and penicillin).
—Aspirin and/or some other painkiller (take enough to offer to the locals when needed).
—Antiseptic ointment to soothe infected bites and blisters.
—Adhesive tape and gauze.
—Adhesive plasters or Bandaids.
—Crepe bandage for binding sprains.
—Anti-allergic treatment for those with known allergies.
—Antibiotic eye ointment (for treating the locals).
—First aid instruction booklet.
    Remember to consult your doctor before you set off.

Food

Pakistan produces a reasonable range of tinned meats and packet soups, though they are not as tasty as those available in the west. Pakistani chocolate and cheeses are not recommended, though the biscuits are good. If possible, bring a few treats with you from overseas. You should buy all your Pakistani tinned and dehydrated supplies in Islamabad or Rawalpindi. In Gilgit you can buy rice, wheatflour, several types of lentils, milk powder, nuts, dried fruit, sugar, cooking oil, biscuits, jams and cornflakes. Skardu and Chitral bazaars are smaller than Gilgit, but you can still stock up on most basic foodstuffs there.

Choosing a Trek

There are hundreds of possible treks in Pakistan, from easy two- or three-day walkabouts through the villages, to tough treks of a month or more along glaciers and over snow-covered passes. Various treks and walks have been suggested throughout the guidebook. The dotted lines on the maps indicate a few of the more popular treks, but there are many more. What follows here is a more detailed description of ten treks in the Hindu Kush, Karakorams and Himalayas working from west to east. To give an idea of what the treks are like:

    C-grade treks are long, strenuous walks requiring fitness and common sense.
    B-grade treks also involve the use of rope, crampons and ice axes.
    A-grade treks require technical mountaineering skills.

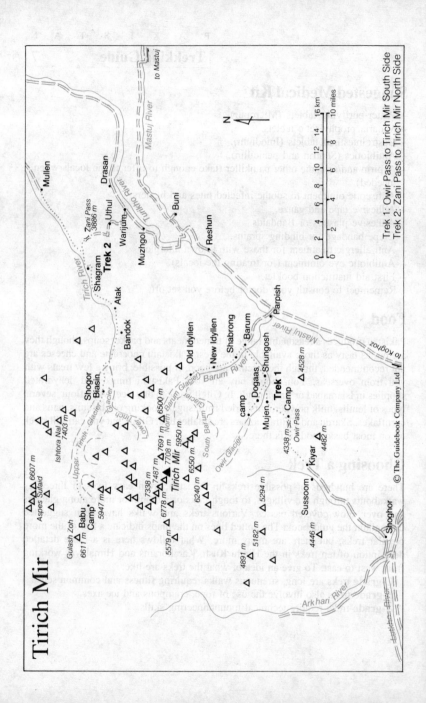

Tirich Mir

to Mastuj

Mastuj River

Mullen

Drasan

Uthul

Buni

Zani Pass
3886 m

Warijun

Trek 2

Muzhgol

Shagram

Reshun

Turikho River

Tirich River

Atak

Parpish

Bandok

Masuj River

to Koghozi

Shogor
Biasin

Old Idyllen

New Idyllen

Shabrong

Barum

Ishtora Nal
7403 m

Upper Tirich Glacier

Glacier

Lower Tirich Glacier

Barum River

Shungosh

Dogaas

Aspes Sulaid 6607 m

Babu
Camp

5947 m

North Barum Glacier

6500 m

South Barum Glacier

camp

Mujen

Trek 1
Camp

Gulash Zoh
6611 m

5579 m
6778 m
7487 m
7691 m
7708 m
Tirich Mir
7338 m

6550 m

6240 m

5950 m

Owir Glacier

Owir Pass

4338 m

4528 m

4482 m

4891 m

5294 m

Sussoom

Kiyar

4446 m

Shoghor

5182 m

Ark hari River

© The Guidebook Company Ltd

N

0   2   4   6   8   10   12   14   16 km
0   2   4   6   8   10 miles

Trek 1: Owir Pass to Tirich Mir South Side
Trek 2: Zani Pass to Tirich Mir North Side

Chitral–Zani Pass and Eastern Tirich Mir

Restricted zone—permit necessary from Ministry of Tourism and from deputy commissioner, Chitral, but there is no checkpost.
Mid-May to October, grade C, 3–10 days.
Maximum height: 4,703 metres (15,430 feet).

Day 1: Jeep from Chitral to Uthul, the village below the Zani Pass on the west side of the Turikho River, four to five hours. Camp at about 3,000 metres (10,000 feet).

Day 2: Either jeep or walk through Uthul, along the village jeep road and climb up to Zani Pass, 3,886 metres (12,750 feet), three hours on foot, from where there is a superb view of Tirich Mir, Saraghrar, Bunizom and the mountains around Mastuj (see page 349). The jeep road ends at the lake southwest of the pass where you can camp if the weather is good; otherwise you can descend steeply down the other side to the Tirich River and camp in the green pastures of Shagram.

Day 3: Trek west along the Tirich River to Atak and lunch by the shepherd's hut. Continue along the river to Bandok, a pasture surrounded by birch trees. Camp in the wood at about 3,400 metres (11,150 feet).

Day 4: Continue west along the river to Tirich Glacier, from where there is a difficult trek along the glacier to Shogor Basin, opposite where Lower Tirich Glacier joins Tirich Glacier. There is a magnificent view of Tirich Mir up Lower Tirich Glacier. Camp at about 4,100 metres (13,500 feet).

Day 5: Continue along Tirich Glacier to Babu camp, the advanced base camp at about 4,700 metres (15,400 feet). From here you can see Ghul-Lasht Zom, Aspes Sufaid, Noshaq and Ishtora Nal, but not Tirich Mir.

Return by the same route to Shagram and then, instead of crossing Zani Pass, continue down the Tirich River through several villages for another three hours to the end of the jeep track. For a shorter trek, turn back sooner.

Chitral–Owir Pass and Southern Tirich Mir

Restricted zone—permit necessary from Ministry of Tourism and from deputy commissioner, Chitral, but there is no checkpost.
June to September, grade C, 3–11 days.
Maximum height: 4,338 metres (14,232 feet).

Day 1: Chitral town to Barum (five hours). Jeep up main Chitral Valley to Parpish, then turn left (west) up a narrow track with steep hairpin bends to Barum, where the jeep track ends. Camp at Barum at about 2,500 metres (8,200 feet).

Day 2: Barum to New Idyllen (four to five hours); side-trip north following Barum stream up to glacier. One-hour walk to Shabronz, a green and fertile village, then 30 minutes along a dramatic water channel on a narrow path with a steep drop. The last three hours involve a scramble across scree to New Idyllen or Shokor Shol.

Superb views southeast to Hindu Raj and west to Tirich Mir the Lesser. Camp at about 3,300 metres (10,800 feet).

Day 3: New Idyllen to Old Idyllen (three hours). Follow Barum stream up to North Barum Glacier and explore the glacier. Camp at Old Idyllen at about 3,600 metres (11,800 feet). It is dusty but offers some shade, a good water supply and superb views.

Day 4: Explore the ridge between North and South Barum glaciers to a height of about 4,300 metres (14,100 feet) for excellent views of Tirich Mir and subsidiary peaks. Camp at Old Idyllen.

Day 5: Old Idyllen to Shabronz (five hours). Camp in shaded, pleasant village at about 2,700 metres (8,900 feet).

Day 6: Shabronz to Dogaas, at base of Owir Glacier (five to six hours). Follow the Owir stream up to northwest. It is an easy contour walk along waterways up the wide valley. Camp at base of Owir Glacier, at about 3,300 metres (10,800 feet), by a clear stream in a grassy meadow; superb views.

Day 7: Optional side-trip up Owir Glacier, a hard five-hour trudge over rough scree and rubble for a not very distinguished view from the top. Return to Dogaas for night.

Day 8: Dogaas to below Owir Pass. Go down from glacier towards west. Passing last village in the valley at about 3,200 metres (10,500 feet), climb up for about two hours to about 200 metres (650 feet) below the Owir Pass. Camp on grassy col, a superb site, the best of the trip with magnificent views and an excellent water supply (but no shade) at about 4,000 metres (13,100 feet).

Day 9: Walk up to Owir Pass and spend the day exploring the ridge. Walk along towards Tirich Mir for staggering views in all directions. Return to camp 8 for night.

Day 10: Owir Pass to Kiyar (three hours). Cross Owir Pass and descend steeply across shale to Kiyar. Camp above village with another superb view of Tirich Mir.

Day 11: Kiyar to Chitral. Jeepable road all the way; or you can walk down along the stream to Shoghor in four to five hours.

If your time is limited, you can trek from Barum directly to the top of Owir Pass, camp overnight as for day 8 above and continue to Kiyar the next day.

Chitral to Swat—the Kachikani Pass

Open zone.
June to September—early September best time—grade C, 7 days.
Maximum height: 4,766 metres (15,635 feet).

Chitrali porters are reported to be more amenable than Swati ones, so the trek from Chitral to Swat and not vice-versa is recommended. The disadvantage of this is that the first two days are very strenuous. Swat is in the monsoon belt, so pine-covered hillsides and green pastures make for a pleasant end to the trek. Upper Chitral is dry and barren. It is 22 kilometres (14 miles) from Mastuj to Sor Laspur, the end of the jeep track on the Chitrali side. It is about 16 kilometres (ten miles) from Kalam to Matiltan, the end of the line for public transport in Swat.

Day 1: Jeep from Chitral town via Mastuj to Sor Laspur. Public jeep-taxis are readily available as far as Mastuj. Camp at Sor Laspur beside stream at about 3,000 metres (9,800 feet).

Day 2: Sor Laspur to Bashar (seven hours). Follow the Laspur River up through rough stony terrain with no greenery to where the Kachikani stream joins it from the south. Camp by muddy glacier stream.

Day 3: Bashar to base of Kachikani Pass (five hours). Follow the Kachikani stream south up through barren gravelly terrain, cross the bottom of Kachikani Glacier and turn east for the steep climb across the moraine to below Kachikani Pass. Camp.

Day 4: Cross Kachikani Pass at 4,766 metres or 15,635 feet (five hours). Steep climb up across gravel and patches of snow to the pass. The south side of the pass is completely snow-covered but not so steep; several glaciers flow down from various directions. Descend below a dramatic icefall to grassy meadow with birch trees and flowers. Camp at 3,840 metres (12,600 feet) by clear stream full of trout.

Day 5: Follow stream down through birch wood for four to five hours, or 14 kilometres (nine miles). It is an easy walk. Camp at the junction of two clear streams.

Day 6: Continue downstream for three to four hours, an easy 12-kilometre (seven-mile) walk to Lake Mahodand, Lake of Fishes. Beautiful camp at about 2,900 metres (9,500 feet) in meadow beside lake surrounded by birch trees.

Day 7: Follow stream down to Matiltan, an easy walk of ten kilometres (six miles). Camp at 2,400 metres (8,000 feet).

Day 8: Jeep down to Saidu Sharif.

Nanga Parbat–South Side–Rupal Valley

Open zone.
This can be an easy six-day hike up the Rupal Valley to about 4,000 metres (13,000 feet), or it can turn into a strenuous grade-B trek across the Mazeno Pass at 5,377 metres (17,640 feet).
June to September; the Mazeno Pass is best crossed in August.

Day 1: Jeep from Gilgit to Chorit and on to Tarshing if the road is open. Lush green meadows surround these villages. Camp at Tarshing at about 2,900 metres (9,500 feet).

Day 2: Tarshing to Bazhin (four hours). Trek across Tarshing Glacier to Rupal village and on through upper Rupal along a narrow green valley to Bazhin camp; this is located in a narrow field between the lateral moraine and the mountain, with running water, a small wood and spectacular views up the east face of Nanga Parbat. Camp at about 3,650 metres (12,000 feet).

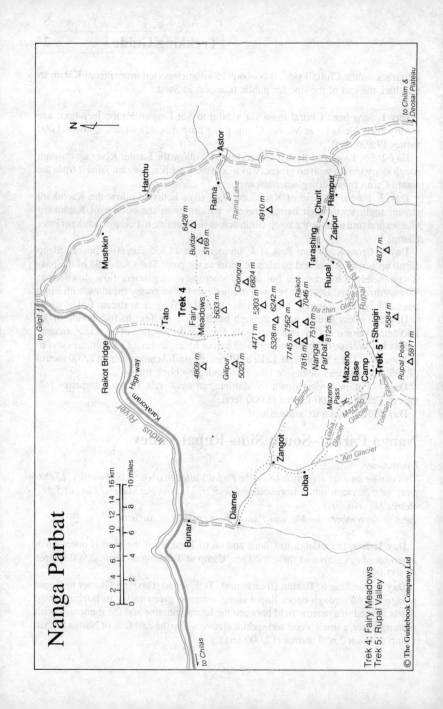

Nanga Parbat

N

to Chilim &
Deosai Plateau

Astor

Harchu

Rama

Rama Lake

Mushkin

Buldar △ 6428 m

△ 5169 m

Chongra
6824 m
△

△ 5633 m

Trek 4

Fairy
Meadows

Tato

4910 m △

Churit

Rampur

Tarashing

Zaipur

Rupal

4877 m △

Rupal River

Raikot
△ 7046 m

Bazhin Glacier

Rupal Glacier

△ 4471 m
△ 5203 m 6242 m △
5328 △ 7562 m △
7745 △ 7510 m △
7816 m △ Nanga 8125 m
Parbat ▲

Shaigiri

Trek 5 △ 5584 m

Mazeno
Base
Camp

Rupal Peak
△ 5971 m

Gilipur
△ 5029 m

△ 4809 m

Karakoram
Highway

Raikot Bridge

Indus River

to Gilgit

Diamir

Zangot

Loiba
Glacier

Mazeno
Pass

Mazeno Glacier

Airi Glacier

Toshain Glacier

Diamir Glacier

Bunar

Diamer

Loiba

0 2 4 6 8 10 12 14 16 km

0   2   4   6   8   10 miles

to Chilas

© The Guidebook Company Ltd

Trek 4: Fairy Meadows
Trek 5: Rupal Valley

Day 3: Bazhin to Shaigiri (four hours). Cross Bazhin Glacier to Tupp meadow, surrounded by summer settlements, and continue on an easy flat walk along Rupal stream past Herrligkoffer base camp and Latboi base camp to Shaigiri, from the where you can see the whole south face of Nanga Parbat and other peaks. Camp by the white rock at about 3,650 metres (12,000 feet).

Optional return from here back down Rupal Valley or spend two days climbing Rupal Peak (5,971 metres or 19,586 feet) for magnificent views north across the valley to Nanga Parbat's south face.

Otherwise,

Day 4: Shaigiri to Mazeno base camp (three hours). In the afternoon, explore the glistening white Toshain Glacier with views south to Toshain Peak, at 6,325 metres (20,750 feet), and to Rupal Peak. Camp at about 4,170 metres (13,600 feet).

Day 5: Mazeno base camp to Mazeno high camp (five hours). From here there are views of high peaks in all directions. Camp at about 4,600 metres (15,100 feet).

Day 6: Mazeno high camp across pass to Loiba (nine hours). Mazeno Pass is 5,377 metres (17,640 feet) above sea level and requires rope and crampons. Beyond the pass walk down Loiba Glacier, which is white for a short way then covered in rocks and gravel. Camp at Loiba at about 4,200 metres (13,800 feet).

Day 7: Upper Loiba to Loiba Meadows (two to three hours). A lovely easy descent to birch woods and lush green meadows, with shepherds' settlements and herds of dzos, sheep and goats. Camp at about 4,000 metres (13,100 feet).

Day 8: Loiba to Zangot (four hours). Zangot is a small village surrounded by fruit trees at the base of Diamer Glacier with magnificent views of Diamer Peak. Camp at about 2,700 metres (8,850 feet).

Day 9: Zangot to Diameri (four hours). Follow the Diamer stream down to the confluence with the Bunar River. Diameri is located at the junction. Camp at about 1,750 metres (5,700 feet).

Day 10: Diameri to Chilas. There is a jeep road to Diameri, so you can drive all the way; otherwise walk for about four hours down to the KKH and hitchhike from there.

Nanga Parbat–North Side–Fairy Meadows

Open zone.
June to September, grade C, minimum four days.
Maximum height: optional, between 4,000 and 5,200 metres (13,100 and 17,000 feet). (From Fairy Meadows there are many optional treks.)

Day 1: From either Gilgit or Chilas jeep to Raikot Bridge, on the KKH. Trek up to Tato village (five or six hours). In 1988 a jeep track was under construction, so you can jeep part of the way. Camp at Tato, at about 2,600 metres (8,500 feet).

Day 2: Tato to Fairy Meadows (three to four hours). Fairy Meadows is an area of wide summer pastures with shepherds' huts surrounded by pine forest. The Shangrila Hotel chain is building a lodge here. Camp on the meadows where there is shade and clear water—the perfect campsite—at about 3,200 metres (10,500 feet).

Days 3 and 4: Easy daytrips exploring and trekking from Fairy Meadows. There are magnificent views of the north face of Nanga Parbat.

Day 5: Fairy Meadows to base camp of Nanga Parbat (five to six hours). Visit German memorial to those expedition members killed in 1937. Camp at about 4,000 metres (13,100 feet).

Day 6: Explore around base camp and climb up to foot of Gilipur Peak. Camp at 4,200 metres (13,800 feet).

Day 7: Optional climb west to Gilipur Pass, at 4,900 metres (16,075 feet), and from there to top of Gilipur Peak, at 5,029 metres (16,500 feet). Return to about 4,000 metres (13,100 feet) to camp.

Day 8: Optional climb east up to Bulder Cleft at 5,200 metres (17,060 feet) and return to base camp.

Days 9, 10 and 11: Trek down to KKH.

Gilgit–Naltar to Chalt Across Daintar Pass

Open zone.
July to September, grade C, 5–7 days.
Maximum height: 4,800 metres (15,750 feet).

Day 1: Jeep from Gilgit via Nomal to Naltar; beautiful alpine pastures surrounded by mature pine forest. Camp or stay in PWD rest house or local hotel. If you have time, continue with day 2's trek.

Day 2: Naltar to Naltar Lake, also called Kuti Lake (three to four hours). Walk upstream through forest, past Gujar herders' summer settlements to Naltar Lake. Camp by the first lake (the other lakes are at a higher level 15 minutes away).

Day 3: Naltar Lake to Lower Shani (four hours). Follow stream north, leave the forest and cross a wide swampy pasture to Gupa, a Gujar settlement in sparse pine wood. (If you do not have a guide, ask the Gujars to point out the pass to you as it is not obvious.) Follow east bank of stream to the Naltar Glacier and continue for a few kilometres (miles) on the eastern lateral moraine (the glacier on your left) across snow fields and stones on a clear path to green pastures beside the glacier below the pass. Camp by small stream.

Day 4: Lower Shani to upper Shani (one hour). Spend the day getting acclimatized by walking up to the head of the valley and the foot of the Naltar Pass (to Ishkoman), and return to upper Shani, 500 or so vertical metres (yards) above lower Shani. Camp beside snow field at the highest possible flattish ground on the ridge leading to the pass.

Day 5: Cross the Daintar Pass (six to eight hours). Follow the very steep ridge up sliding shale for two to three hours to the top, then scramble to the right along the pointed crest to the cairn (you would be well advised to rope up for this). Find your way through the snow corniche and down the extremely steep shale slope to a large snow field on the other side. There is a flower-filled pasture where you can camp, below the snowline, but most people continue down to the first shepherds' huts at Toleybari. Camp in birch woods beside stream.

Day 6: Toleybari to Tarbetar Das (four to six hours). Walk for two hours down a narrow gorge (the path on the left bank is steep, but easier) to Tali, a large summer village with fields of wheat and a polo ground. This is the end of the jeep road, but even if the road is open you are most unlikely to find a jeep here. Walk down jeep road to Tarbetar Das, first through cultivated fields, then through a barren gorge. Camp at Tarbetar Das.

Day 7: Public jeeps leave early each morning for Gilgit, about three hours away (or half that in a private jeep).

Hunza–Up the Hasanabad Glacier to Summer Pastures

Open zone.
May to October, grade C, four to six days.
Maximum altitude: optional.
Start from the KKH in Hunza.

Day 1: Hasanabad to Bras (three hours). Start trekking at the Hasanabad Bridge, three kilometres (two miles) below Aliabad on the KKH. Walk upstream, scramble up over high terminal moraine to where the Hasanabad and Muchichil glaciers meet. Camp at the summer village of Bras.

Day 2: Bras to Shishpar (four hours). Follow edge of Hasanabad Glacier up to the summer pastures of Shishpar. Camp by shepherds' huts.

Day 3: Spend the day with the shepherds and explore the summer pastures from where there are views of Ultar and Passu peaks and Hasanabad Glacier. Camp as for Day 2.

Day 4: Return to KKH; alternatively return to Bras and trek up Muchichil (also known as Muchuar) Glacier to Guyamaling (five hours). Camp.

Day 5: Guyamaling to Shandar Shaynder (four hours). Continue up side of glacier to the summer pastures of Shandar Shaynder, where there are shepherds' huts and a watermill. Camp with the shepherds.

Day 6: Return to the KKH.

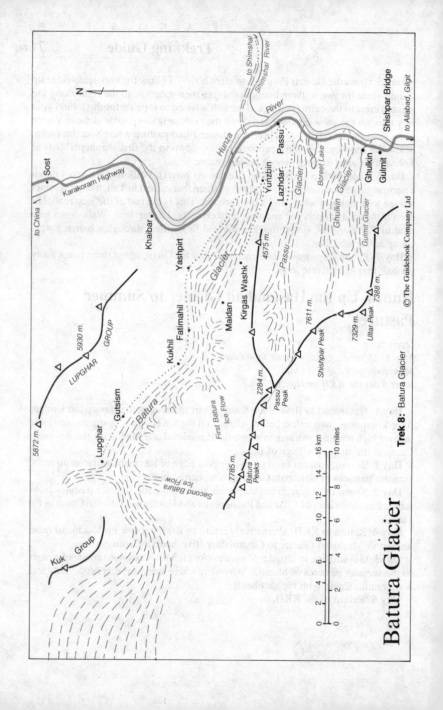

Batura Glacier

Trek 8: Batura Glacier

© The Guidebook Company Ltd

Hunza–Passu Up the Batura Glacier

Open zone.
May to October, grade C, 6–8 days.
Maximum height: 4,000 metres (13,100 feet).

Day 1: Passu to Yunzbin (three hours). From Passu village follow irrigation channel to base of Batura Glacier, covered in black gravel and rocks. Follow south side of glacier on shepherds' trail across scree with views of the forepeaks of Batura and the Passu Massif. Dusty with some juniper, buckthorn, wild roses and purple vetch, and some pastureland for sheep and goats. Camp at Yunzbin, at 2,930 metres (9,600 feet).

Day 2: Yunzbin to Yashpirt (six hours). Turn north across glacier, a grey sea of gravel and rocks, then continue west following the glacier lateral moraine up to Yashpirt, a summer village where women and children come with herds of sheep, goats, cows and yaks. Pastures with juniper trees, berberis, spirea and wild roses surround the village. Views across Batura Glacier to the first Batura icefall. A clear stream flows by the camp site at about 3,200 metres (10,500 feet).

Day 3: Yashpirt to Kukhil (three hours). Follow lateral moraine past occasional birch and willow trees. Stop for lunch at Fatimahil, a summer village with magnificent views across Batura Glacier to the Batura group of peaks (about nine peaks between 7,500–7,785 metres, or 24,600–25,540 feet). Continue along the edge of the glacier to Kukhil, another summer settlement beside a stream. You can sleep in empty huts (beware of the bugs) or camp at about 3,400 metres (11,150 feet).

Day 4: Kukhil to Gutshism or Lupdor (two to four hours). Continue up side moraine past juniper and mountain ash across sparse summer pastures. Gutshism is the last summer settlement, Lupdor the last pasture. Camp on the last grass. Lupdor is at 3,700 metres (12,140 feet).

Day 5: Optional exploration around the area, walk from Kukhil up to Shelmin (three to five hours) and camp by the stream. Alternatively, you can walk on the glacier or climb one of the peaks.

Day 6: Optional, continue from Shelmin up to Wortham (three to five hours) up a slippery slope on to grassland where you camp by a clear spring.

Days 7 and 8: Return by same route. Alternatively, cross Batura Glacier below Yashpirt and descend on the south side, which is shadier and greener with good views down onto the glacier.

From Yunzbin you can climb up to the Yunz Pass on the ridge between the Batura and Passu glaciers for superb views of both glaciers and surrounding peaks. Then descend to Passu Glacier and return to Passu that way.

There are also treks up both Gulmit and Ghulkin glaciers.

Hunza–Passu Up the Shimshal Valley

Open zone.
April to November, grade C, 7 days minimum.
Maximum altitude: optional.

Day 1: Passu to Jurjur or Shugarden (two to three hours). Take a jeep up the KKH from Passu to the bridge across the Hunza River, turn east across the river and follow new jeep track to the end, about nine kilometres (six miles). Trek into Shimshal Gorge along difficult, rocky path following Shimshal River. Camp.

Day 2: Jurjur to Dutt (three to five hours). Continue upriver through Shimshal Gorge. Still rocky but not quite so difficult. Cross river at Dutt, where there is a hut where you can cook. Camp at Dutt.

Day 3: Dutt to Ziarat (five hours). The path is difficult and steep, cut across the cliff face. For part of the way you must cross back to the west bank of the Shimshal. No drinking water available all day. Ziarat is a shrine with a large pilgrim shelter that can sleep 50.

Day 4: Ziarat to Shimshal (six hours). Walk along river for three hours to the Molunguti Glacier which takes one hour to cross. Then follow an easy road for about 1 1/2 hours to the first village of Shimshal where the valley widens to a fertile bowl. Camp near Shimshal.

Days 5, 6 and 7: Explore the Shimshal Valley. The valley is beautiful east of Shimshal village, wide and green with shepherds' huts and herds of sheep, goats and yaks. Up by the Chinese border there are even herds of wild asses. Nine glaciers flow down from the south to the Shimshal River: four between the KKH and Shimshal village, and five between Shimshal village and the Chinese border. Paths lead up all of them to summer pastures.

Leave the Shimshal Valley by the same route you came or via Gunjerab River.

Skardu–Baltoro Glacier to Concordia and K-2

Restricted zone—permit necessary to go beyond Askole, obtainable from Ministry of Tourism.
June to September, grade C, 18–24 days.
Maximum height: 4,985 metres (16,355 feet).

About 35 mountaineering expeditions and numerous trekking groups follow this trail every summer. Several groups share every campsite.

Start from Dassu, at 2,438 metres or 8,000 feet (four to five hours north of Skardu by jeep).

Day 1: Dassu to Chakpo (six hours). Follow river, then climb up a fairly gentle slope to cross the shoulder of Talam Mountain at about 2,900 metres (9,500 feet).

Descend gradually to river for lunch. It can be very hot at noon: have your umbrella handy. In the afternoon pass villages of Biano, Tseder and Ho surrounded by green fields and fruit trees. Camp at 2,680 metres (8,800 feet) in field at Chakpo village.

Day 2: Chakpo to Chongo (seven hours). The most difficult day of the trek, through Braldu Gorge. Loose gravel slopes above path make it dangerous when it rains—climb up hill above river to avoid landslides. Descend to river for lunch, then follow river up to Chongo with views ahead (to the east) of Bakhordas Mountain, at 5,809 metres (19,058 feet). Camp at about 3,000 metres (9,800 feet).

Day 3: Chongo to Askole (four to five hours). An easy day mostly through cultivated land. Stop during the first hour at hot springs for bath. Continue through villages of Tongol and Surungo. Arrive at Askole, the last village for lunch. Camp at 3,050 metres (10,000 feet).

Day 4: Askole to Dumordo (six hours). Reach Biafo Glacier after three hours. (The open trek up Biafo Glacier across Hispar Pass and down to Nagar on the KKH takes 12 days.) It takes one hour to cross the glacier and then a further hour to Korophon. This is the usual camp site, at 3,100 metres (10,200 feet), but it is worth continuing for one more hour to the Dumordo River and camping there.

Day 5: Dumordo to Paiyu (seven hours). Wade across river in early morning when it is still low. If the river is too swollen, trek one hour up-river to Jula Bridge, a private pulley bridge with a toll of Rs10 per person and Rs5 per bag. If delayed by river crossing spend night at Bardumal, the traditional campsite, which is rocky with unclean water. Otherwise, continue for a further five hours, an undulating walk with the first views of dramatic mountains ahead, to the green pastures and trees at Paiyu with fresh spring water. Camp at 3,480 metres (11,420 feet). (This camp is often crowded.)

Day 6: Paiyu to Khobutsi (six hours). After one hour walking past some trees and greenery, you come to the Baltoro Glacier. Walk across the glacier for two hours then along the southern edge, across sand and rock to Liligo, the traditional campsite on a stony waste below muddy cliffs, but with fine views of jagged rock spires. It is better to continue for another hour and a half to Khobutsi, on a sandy beach beside a small stream. Camp at about 3,800 metres (12,470 feet).

Day 7: Khobutsi to Urdukas (five hours). Cross the Khobutsi River in early morning and climb across two glaciers to the pleasant camp on grassy slopes at Urdukas, with splendid views across Baltoro Glacier to the granite needles of Trango Towers flanked by Biaho and Biale. Camp at 4,130 metres (13,550 feet).

Day 8: Urdukas to Goro (six to eight hours). (It is easy to reach Concordia from Urdukas in two days, but porters may bargain for three days' pay.) The walking is all on Baltoro Glacier. On the south, Yarmandu Glacier flows down from Masherbrum Mountain and joins the Baltoro. Lunch at Biano camp. In the afternoon continue walking along glacier, with magnificent views of Masherbrum and Mitre Peak on the right and Mushtagh Towers on the left, to Goro camp. Camp on the glacier at 4,500 metres (14,760 feet).

Day 9: Goro to Concordia (six hours). Follow Baltoro Glacier to Concordia, the junction of the large Abruzzi and Goodwin Austin glaciers and the smaller Biarchidi, Vigne, West Gasherbrum, Broad and Khalkhal glaciers. Camp at 4,720 metres (15,485 feet). There is usually a tent city here, where up to five groups camp at any one time. Surrounding Concordia are K-2, Broad Peak, Gasherbrum, Sia Kangri, Baltoro Kangri, Masherbrum and Chogolisa. Within a radius of 15 kilometres (nine miles) are 41 peaks over 6,500 metres (21,300 feet), many of them unnamed.

Day 10: Concordia to base camp of K-2. Tours usually spend four nights at Concordia to give those who wish time to explore the area and either trek north up Goodwin Austin Glacier to the base camp of K-2 at 4,985 metres (16,335 feet), or south up Abruzzi Glacier.

It is possible to trek back to Dassu in five or six days if you are fit.

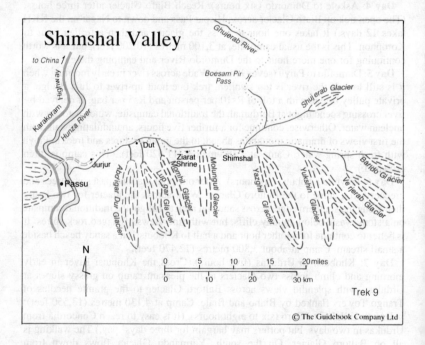

Shimshal Valley

to China

Karakoram Highway

Hunza River

Ghujerab River

Boesam Pir Pass

Shujerab Glacier

Dut

Jurjur

Passu

Ziarat Shrine

Abdigar Dur Glacier

Lupgar Gia Glacier

Momhil Glacier

Malunguti Glacier

Shimshal

Yazghil Glacier

Yukshin Glacier

Baridd Glacier

Virjerab Glacier

N

| 0 | 5 | 10 | 15 | 20 miles |
| 0 | 10 | 20 | 30 km |

Trek 9

© The Guidebook Company Ltd

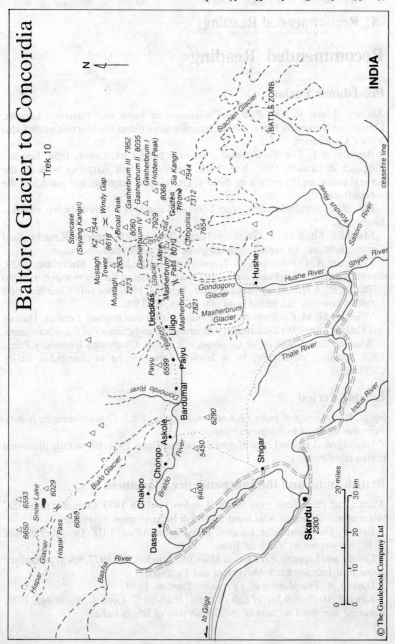

Recommended Reading

Pre-Islamic Period

Allchin, B and R, *The Rise of Civilization in India and Pakistan*: London, Cambridge University Press, 1982. Comprehensive recent introduction to the Indus Valley Civilization.

Basham, A L, *The Wonder that was India*: New York, Grove, 1954; London, Sidgwick & Jackson, 1967; New York, Taplinger, 1968. Excellent book for the general public on the prehistory, history, art, religion, language and politics of the subcontinent.

Fox, R L, *Alexander the Great*: London, Lane, 1973. Scholarly but readable biography.

Marshall, Sir J H, *A Guide to Taxila*: Delhi, 1936; reprint Karachi, Sani Communications. Extremely detailed guide with good plans and maps.

Stein, Sir A, *On Alexander's Track to the Indus*: London, Macmillan, 1929; reprint Karachi, Indus Publications, 1975. An account of Stein's research in Swat.

Thapar, R, *A History of India*: London, Penguin, 1966; two vols. Clear historical narrative covering the period from 600 BC to AD 1500.

Wheeler, Sir M, *Civilisations of the Indus Valley and Beyond*: London, Thames and Hudson, 1966. Well-illustrated prehistory and early history of the subcontinent.

Wheeler, Sir M, *The Indus Civilisation*: London, Cambridge University Press, 1968. Detailed description by a leading archaeologist of the Indus Valley Civilization.

Islamic Period

Spear, P, *A History of India 11*: London, Penguin, 1965. Concise readable history from the Moghuls to the present day.

Gascoigne, A B, *The Great Moghuls*: London, Cape, 1971. Beautifully illustrated coffee-table book.

British India and the Independence Movement

Allen, C, ed. *Plain Tales from the Raj*: London, Deutsch, 1975. Compiled from BBC interviews with people who lived in British India — most enjoyable.

Barr, P, *The Memsahibs*: London, 1976. Delhi, Allied, 1978. Describes the life of British women in Victorian India.

Collins and Lapierre, *Freedom at Midnight*: London, Pan 1977. Racy, journalistic account of Independence Movement and Partition.

Durand, A, *The Making of a Frontier*: London, 1899.

Kincaid, D, *British Social Life in India, 1608–1937*: London, Routledge, 1938. Amusing anecdotal account of the British way of life in India.

Knight, E F, *Where Three Empires Meet*: London, Longmans, 1893; reprinted Karachi, Indus, 1973. Travels in Ladakh and Kashmir, and the British invasion of Gilgit and Hunza in 1891.

Lelyveld, D, *Aligarh's First Generation*: Princeton, Princeton University Press, 1977. The Muslim response to the British in India.

Miller, C, Khyber, *British India's Northwest Frontier*: London, MacDonald and Jane's, 1977. History of the Khyber region.

Morris, J, *Pax Britannica, Heaven's Command and Farewell the Trumpets, trilogy*: London, Faber & Faber, 1978. Beautifully written history of the British Empire.

Singer, A, *Lords of the Khyber*: London, Faber & Faber, 1984. Yet another history of the Pathan–British encounter in the NWFP.

Tandon, P, *Punjabi Century, 1857–1947*: Berkeley, University of California Press, 1968. A fascinating biography of a family living during the last century of British rule.

Wolpert, S, *Jinnah of Pakistan*: London, Oxford University Press, 1984. Classic study of the lawyer who founded Pakistan.

Woodruff, P, *The Men who Ruled India*: London, Cape, 1954. The British involvement in India and the men who worked there.

Younghusband, G J and F E, *The Relief of Chitral*: English Book HouseReprint 1980. A contemporary account of the relief of Chitral in 1895 by two brothers.

Pakistan Since Independence

Burki, S J, *Pakistan under Bhutto, 1971–1977*: New York, St Martin's, 1980. Excellent analysis of the Bhutto years.

Feldman, H, *From Crisis to Crisis — Pakistan 1962–1969*: London, Oxford University Press, 1972. Describes the Ayub Khan years.

Feldman, H, *The End and the Beginning — Pakistan 1969–1971*: London, Oxford University Press, 1975. Covers the breakup of Pakistan and the birth of Bangladesh in 1971.

Lessing, D, *The Wind Blows Away Our Words*: London, Picador, 1987. An articulate and impassioned account of the Afghan Refugees in Pakistan and their fight against the Russians.

Geography

Miller, K, *Continents in Collision*: London, Philip, 1982. Royal Geographical Society scientific expedition to the Karakorams.

Anthropology and Sociology

Caroe, O, *The Pathans*: London, Macmillan, 1958; reprinted Karachi, 1975. Scholarly but readable history.

8 Recommended Reading

Loude, J Y, Kalash, *Les dernier 'infideles' de l'Hindu Kush*, Berger-Levault 1980. A study of the Kaf ir Kalash of Chitral. With superb photos.

Maraini, F, *Where Four Worlds Meet*: Hamilton, 1964. Journey through northern Pakistan, interesting discussion of the Kafir Kalash.

Muslim Literature

Jamal, Mahmood, *The Penguin Book of Modern Urdu Poetry*: 1986. Good selection of modern Urdu poetry.

Enevolodsen, J, trans., *Selections from Rahman Baba*: Herning, Denmark, Kristensen, 1977. Loose translations from the best-loved Pushtu poet.

Kiernan, V, trans., *Poems by Faiz*: London, Allen & Unwin, 1971. Translations of Pakistan's most prominent post-independence poet.

Lorimer, D L R, *Folk Tales of Hunza*: reprint, Lahore, Allied

MacKenzie, trans., *Poems from the Divan of Khushal Khan Khattak*: London, Allen & Unwin, 1965. Translation of the Pushtu poet.

Malik, H, ed., *Iqbal: Poet-Philosopher of Pakistan*: New York, Columbia University Press, 1971. Collection of essays on the intellectual who helped found Pakistan.

Russell, R, and Khurshidul Islam, *Ghalib: Life and Letters*: London, Allen & Unwin, 1969. Fascinating letters by Urdu's best-known poet.

Sorley, H T, *Shah Abdul Latif of Bhit*: Oxford University Press, 1940. Classic introduction to the leading poet of Sind.

Art and Architecture

Mumtaz, K K, *Architecture in Pakistan*: Singapore, Concept Media, 1985. Excellent, well-illustrated and readable history of architecture from the Indus Civilization to the present.

Fiction in English

Fraser, G M, *Flashman*: London, Pan. Hilarious, irreverent, sexy account of the 1857 Indian Mutiny. Historically accurate, a terrific read.

Fraser, G M, *Flashman in the Great Game*: London, Pan 1976. Flashman carouses through the First Afghan War and survives, another terrific read.

Kaye, M M, *Far Pavilions*: New York, St Martin's, 1978. First half mushy romance, second half well-researched account of the Guides fighting in the Second Afghan War.

Kipling, R, *Kim*: London, Macmillan, 1899. Classic novel of the Great Game.

Lambrick, H T, *The Terrorist*: London, Benn, 1972. Sindhi rebellion, explains the power of the Pirs, excellent read.

Masters, J, *The Ravi Lancers*: New York, Doubleday, 1976.

Moggach, D, *Hot Water Man*: London, Cape, 1982; Penguin, 1983. Interesting and funny about expatriates and locals in Karachi.

Scott, Paul, *The Raj Quartet*: London, Heinemann, 1952; Panther, 1973. Life in India before Partition.

Scott, P, *Staying On*: London, Heinemann, 1977; Longman, 1985. The life of a British couple who stayed on after Partition. Set in India, but could just as easily be Pakistan.

Sinclair, G, *Khyber Caravans*. Light, amusing, also describes the Quetta earthquake.

Singh, Kushwant, *Last Train to Pakistan*: New York, Grove, 1961. Describes the horrors of Hindu/Muslim slaughter at Partition.

Sidhwa, Bapsi, *The Crow Eaters*: London, Cape, 1980. Parsee family in Lahore, very amusing, good insight.

Sidhwa, Bapsi, *The Bride*: London, Cape, 1983. Starts with the horrors of Partition, ends less convincingly in Kohistan, a good read.

Travel and Adventure

Amin, Willetts and Hancock, *Journey through Pakistan*: London, Bodley Head, 1982. Coffee-table book with beautiful photographs, light text, none too accurate.

Bechtold, F; H E G Tyndale, trans., *Nanga Parbat Adventure*: London, Murray, 1935

Braham, T, *Himalayan Odyssey*: London, Allen & Unwin, 1974. Trekking and climbing in Pakistan, 30 years' experience.

Buhl, H, *Nanga Parbat Pilgrimage*: London, Hodder & Stoughton, 1981. Autobiography of the climber who finally conquered Nanga Parbat.

Burnes, Alexander, *A Voyage on the Indus*: Bombay, 1828; reprint Karachi, OUP, 1972. British 19th-century explorer on the Indus.

Churchill, Winston, *My Early Life*: London, Butterworth, 1930; Fontana, 1959. Exuberant tales of life as a young officer in the North-West Frontier.

Conway, W M, *Climbing and Exploration in the Karakoram-Himalayas*: London, 1892.

Fairley, J, *The Lion River*: London, Allen Lane, 1975. Good account of the Indus River from source to mouth.

Hamilton, I, *Listening for Drums*: London, Faber & Faber, 1944.

Herrligkoffer, K M, *Nanga Parbat—the Killer Mountain*: New York, Knopf, 1954. Describe the tragedies of Nanga Parbat and the first successful ascent.

Houston and Bates, *K-2—the Savage Mountain*: New York, McGraw Hill, 1954. American attempt on K-2.

Keay, J, *When Men and Mountains Meet*: London, Murray, 1977. Readable stories of the exploration of the Karakorams and Himalayas between 1820 and 1875.

Keay, J, *The Gilgit Game*: London, Murray, 1979. Continuation of above between 1865 and 1895.

Masson, C, *Narrative of Various Journeys in Baluchistan, Afghanistan, and the Punjab 1826—1838*: London, 1842; reprint Karachi, OUP, 1974. Fascinating early journey through what is now Pakistan.

Matheson, S, *The Tigers of Baluchistan*: London, Barker, 1976. Western woman encounters Baluchistan.

Moorcroft, W, *Travels in the Himalayan Provinces*: London, 1841.

Moorhouse, G, *To the Frontier*: New York, Holt, Rinehart and Winston, 1985. A journey round Pakistan with a description of people and places.

Murphy, D, *Where the Indus is Young*: London, Murray, 1977. Diary of an eccentric Irishwoman who spent a winter walking in Baltistan with her six-year-old daughter.

Naipaul, V S, *Among the Believers*: London, Deutsch, 1981. Travels in Iran, Pakistan and Indonesia, comparing the Islamic peoples.

Newby, E, *A Short Walk in the Hindu Kush*: London, Pan 1981. Side-splitting account of a hike through Afghanistan along the Pakistan border.

Pennell, T L, *Among the Wild Tribes of the Afghan Frontier*: London, 1909; reprint Karachi, OUP, 1975. Story of the life of a British missionary doctor in Bannu, NWFP.

Polo, Marco, *Travels*: 1485 in Latin; *Travels Retold*, Penguin, 1958.

Reeves, R, *Passage to Peshawar*: New York, Simon and Schuster, 1984. Excellent analysis of present-day Pakistan.

Rowell, G, *In the Throne Room of the Mountain Gods*: San Francisco, Sierra Club, 1977. New edition 1988, with colour photos. Describes 1975 expedition by Americans to K-2. Superb description of Concordia and candid view of what mountain climbing is really like.

Schaller, G B, *Stones of Silence*: New York, Viking, 1980. Description of wildlife in Chitral and elsewhere in south Asia.

Stephens, I, *Horned Moon*: London, Chatto and Windus, 1953. An early post-independence journey through Pakistan, Kashmir and Afghanistan.

Swift, H, *The Trekker's Guide to the Himalaya and Karakoram*: San Francisco, Sierra Club, 1982. Excellent trekking guide, mainly for Nepal and India, but with 50 pages on Pakistan.

Tilman, H M, *Two Mountains and a River*: Cambridge University Press, 1948. An attempt by Shipton and Tilman to climb Rakaposhi and Mustagh.

Theroux, P, *Great Railway Bazaar*: London, Hamilton, 1975; Penguin, 1977. A train ride from Europe to Asia including a brief passage through Pakistan.

Appendices

Some of Pakistan's Best-known Mountains

Most mountains have several peaks, some of which are numbered, not named. In Pakistan there are five peaks over 8,000 metres, 29 over 7,500 metres and 101 over 7,000 metres.

Mountain	Height m (ft)	Range	World Rank
K-2	8616 (28,268)	Karakoram	2
Nanga Parbat	8125 (26,656)	Himalaya	9
Gasherbrum I (Hidden)	8068 (26,470)	Karakoram	11
Broad Peak	8060 (26,444)	Karakoram	12
Gasherbrum II	8035 (26,362)	Karakoram	14
Gasherbrum III	7952 (26,089)	Karakoram	15
Gasherbrum IV	7929 (26,014)	Karakoram	17
Disteghil Sar	7885 (25,869)	Karakoram	20
Kunyang Kish	7852 (25,761)	Karakoram	22
Masherbrum NE	7821 (25,660)	Karakoram	24
Rakaposhi	7788 (25,550)	Karakoram	27
Batura I	7785 (25,541)	Karakoram	28
Kanjut Sar	7760 (25,460)	Karakoram	29
Saltoro Kangri I	7742 (25,400)	Karakoram	33
Trivor	7720 (25,330)	Karakoram	36
Tirich Mir	7708 (25,289)	Hindu Kush	41
Chogolisa I	7654 (25,111)	Karakoram	46
Shishpar (Batura)	7611 (24,970)	Karakoram	49
Skyang Kangri	7544 (24,750)	Karakoram	58
Pumari Kish W	7492 (24,580)	Karakoram	67
Noshaq	7492 (24,580)	Hindu Kush	68
Tirich Mir NW	7487 (24,563)	Hindu Kush	69
K-12	7468 (24,500)	Karakoram	73
Teram Kangri	7463 (24,485)	Karakoram	74
Malubiting W	7452 (24,448)	Karakoram	76
Sia Kangri	7422 (24,350)	Karakoram	79
Skil Brum	7420 (24,344)	Karakoram	80
Teram Kangri II	7406 (24,298)	Karakoram	82
Haramosh	7406 (24,298)	Karakoram	84
Istoro Nal	7403 (24,288)	Hindu Kush	85
Mount Ghent	7400 (24,278)	Karakoram	86
Yukshin Gardan	7400 (24,278)	Karakoram	87

Ultar I	7388 (24,239)	Karakoram	88
Teram Kangri III	7381 (24,216)	Karakoram	90
Sherpi Kangri	7380 (24,212)	Karakoram	91
Karun Koh	7350 (24,114)	Karakoram	100
Momil Sar	7342 (24,088)	Karakoram	103
Saraghrar Peak I	7338 (24,075)	Hindu Kush	104
Bajohagur–Duanasir	7329 (24,045)	Karakoram	106
Gasherbrum V	7321 (24,019)	Karakoram	107
Baltoro Kangri I	7321 (24,019)	Karakoram	113
Urdok Peak I	7300 (23,950)	Karakoram	114

Selected Travel Agencies for Touring and Trekking in Pakistan

Travel Walji's Ltd, PO Box 1088, Islamabad, tel. 823963, 828324–6; cable WALJI'S; telex 5769 WALJI PK.

Sitara Travel, Bank Road, PO Box 63, Rawalpindi, tel. 64750–1, 66272; cable CEETARA; telex 5751 STARA PK.

Karakoram Tours, 1 Baltoro, Street 19, F-7/2, Islamabad, tel. 829120; cable BALTORO; telex 54480 MIRZA PK.

Nazir Sabir Expeditions, PO Box 1442, Islamabad, tel. 853672; cable CLIMBING; telex 5811 NAIBA PK.

Baltoro Adventure Tours, 112 Rahim Plaza, Murree Road, PO Box 1769, Rawalpindi, tel. 63014; cable HIMALAYA; telex 5576 TTISM PK; or Skardu, PO Box 621, tel. 280; cable BAT.

Mountain Movers, Airport Road, Gilgit, tel. 2967.

Adventure Tours Pakistan, Ashraf Aman, PO Box 1780, Islamabad; tel. 852505; telex 5948/5909 PLORP.

Pakistan Tours Ltd, Flashman's Hotel, The Mall, Rawalpindi, tel. 64810–11, 65449; telex 5260 FH PK.

Selected Foreign Embassies and Consulates

Islamabad

Afghanistan, 176 F-7/3, tel. 822566, 820707.
Australia, Diplomatic Enclave, tel. 822111.
Austria, 13 Street 1, F-6/3, tel. 820137.
Canada, Diplomatic Enclave, tel. 821101–4.
China, Diplomatic Enclave, tel. 826667.
Denmark, 121 Street 90, G-6/3, tel. 824210, 824211.
France, 11 Street 54, F-7/4, tel. 823981–3.
Germany (Democratic), 218 Street 3, F-6/3, tel. 824475, 824472, 823845.
Germany (Federal), Diplomatic Enclave, tel. 822151, 822155.
Great Britain, Diplomatic Enclave, tel. 822131–5.
India, Diplomatic Enclave, G-6/4, tel. 826718.
Iran, 3 & 5 Street 17, F-6/2, tel. 822694–5, 823612.
Italy, 448 Margalla Hills Road, F-6/3, tel. 825791.
Japan, Diplomatic Enclave, tel. 820181–4, 821008–9.
Nepal, 506 Street 84, G-6/4, tel. 823754.
Netherlands, PIA Building, Blue Area, tel. 822631, 822887, 825279, 811814.
Norway, 15 Street 84, G-6/4, tel. 824830, 822046.
Poland, 13 Street 88, G-6/3, tel. 821133.
Portugal, 8 Street 90, G-6/3, tel. 823395.

Saudi Arabia, 1 Street 4, F-6/3, tel. 820156–9.
Spain, 180 Ataturk (6th) Avenue, G-6/3, tel, 821070–1.
Sri Lanka, 2 Street 48, F-7/4, tel. 820754.
Sweden, 6 Agha Khan Road, Markaz, F-6, tel. 822557–9.
Switzerland, 25 Street 19, F-6/2, tel. 821151–2.
Thailand, 23 Street 25, F-6/2, tel. 824967.
United Soviet Socialist Republic, Diplomatic Enclave, tel. 824604.
United States of America, Diplomatic Enclave, tel. 826161–70.
Yugoslavia, 14 Street 87, G-6/3, tel. 821081, 820234.
UNICEF, 58 & 62 Khayaban-e-Iqbal, F-7/2, tel. 825135, 825142.
UNDP, FAO, WHO, UN Bldg, G-5, tel. 822070–9.
UN High Commission for Refugees, 18 & 25 Street 8, F-7/3, tel. 826003.
UN Information Centre, 26 Street 88, G-6/3, tel. 823465.
ILO, 58 Khayaban-e-Iqbal F-8/2, tel. 854963, 852313.
World Bank, 35–37 Street 1, F-6/3, tel. 820280.

Karachi

Afghanistan, 43J Block 6, PECHS, tel. 437346, 436146.
Austria, 43 N-1, Block 6, Razi Road, PECHS, tel. 430111–12.
Belgium, 108–4 Charles Fox 1–5, Clifton, tel. 531011–12.
China, 207 Dr Daud Pota Road, tel. 514784, 514934, 512334.
France, 12A Md Ali Bogra Road, Bath Island, tel. 532047–8.
Germany (Democratic), 41Q Block 6, PECHS, tel. 430568.
Germany (Federal), 90 Clifton, tel. 531031–2.
Great Britain, York Palace, Runnymede Lane, Clifton, tel. 532041, 532046.
India, 3 Fatima Jinnah Road, tel. 512542–3, 522275.
Iran, 81 Shahrah-e-Iran, Clifton, tel. 530638–9.
Italy, 85 Clifton, tel. 531006–7.
Japan, 233 Sommerset Street, EI Lines, tel. 551331–2, 516439.
Netherlands, 4A Choudhary Khaliquzzaman Road, tel. 525879.
Norway (Hon), 5 & 6 Chartered Bank Chambers, II Chundrigar Road, tel. 231888.
Poland, 10B Lalazar, Maulvi Tamiz-ud-din Khan Road, tel. 552147, 552177.
Saudi Arabia, 27 Khayaban-e-Hafiz, Phase V, DHS, tel. 532518, 531055.
Sri Lanka, 6D St 8–5, Scheme 1, KDA, tel. 430890, 439990.
Switzerland, 98 Clifton, tel. 532038, 532039.
Thailand, 1 G-18, Sasi Homes, Kahkashan, Clifton, tel. 530696, 530706.
USSR, 26–8 Flench Sreet, Bleak House Road, tel. 512852–3.
USA, 8 Abdullah Haroon Road, tel. 515081–8.
Yugoslavia, 43 H-7, Block 6, PECHS, tel. 432225.

Lahore

Austria (Hon), 12C Gulberg II, tel. 871537, 880571.
France (Hon), 43 Shahrah-e-Quaid-e-Azam, tel. 321566, 321329.
Germany (Federal) (Hon), 60 Main Gulberg, tel. 870976.
Iran, 82 E-1, Gulberg III, tel. 870274, 870257.
Italy (Hon), WAPDA House, tel. 323104, 323039.
Norway (Hon), 295/3 Sarwar Road, tel. 310618.
Saudi Arabia, 5/6–5 Gulberg, tel. 322118, 870250, 872289.
USA, 50 Zafar Ali Road, tel. 870221–5.

Peshawar

Afghanistan, 17 CB-1, Gulmhar Lane, University Town, tel. 40503.
France (Hon), 10 Fort Road, tel. 73177.
Germany (Federal) (Hon), Jamrud Road, tel. 50584.
Iran, 3 Sir Syed Road, tel. 74643, 75543.
USA, 11 Hospital Road, tel. 79801–3.
USIS, 1C Chinar Road, University Town, tel. 41463, 40422.
USAID, 26C Chinar Road, University Town, tel. 40420, 40422.

Quetta

Afghanistan, 4 Lytton Road, tel. 74160.
Iran, 2/33 Share Hali, tel. 75054, 75320, 74373.

Historical Dates

3000–1500 BC	Indus Civilization.
1700 BC	Aryans invade from central Asia.
516 BC	Northern Pakistan becomes the easternmost province of the Achaemenid Empire of Persia. Gandhara is a semi-independent kingdom.
327–325 BC	Alexander the Great invades Pakistan.
272–236 BC	Ashoka, the greatest of the Mauryan emperors, promotes Buddhism.
c.185 BC	Bactrian Greeks from Afghanistan conquer northwest Pakistan.
c.75 BC	Arrival of Scythians (Sakas) from central Asia.
AD 20	Parthians conquer northern Pakistan.
60	Kushans from central Asia overthrow Parthians.
3rd century	Kushans decline and are dominated by Sassanian Empire of Persia.
4th century	Kidar (Little) Kushans come to power.
c.455	White Huns invade Gandhara and are converted to Hinduism.
565	Sassanians and Turks overthrow Huns.
Late 6th to 7th century	Turki Shahis control area west of Indus, including Gandhara.
711	Muhammad bin Qasim conquers Sind and southern Punjab.
870	Hindu Shahis from central Asia arrive.
1001–26	Mahmud of Ghazni invades. Mass conversions to Islam.
1034–1337	Sind ruled by Sumrahs, a Sindhi tribe.
1150	Ghaznavid Kingdom destroyed by Ghorids.
13th century	The consolidation of the Muslim sultanate of north India.
1221	The Mongol Ghengis Khan invades the Punjab.
1337	Sammah Rajputs overthrow the Sumrahs in Sind.
1398–9	Tamerlane invades from central Asia.
15th century	Decline of the Delhi Sultanate. Founding of the Sikh religion.

Early 16th century	Babur, the first of the Moghuls, raids the Punjab.
1524	Sind is overthrown by Shah Beg Arghun from Kandahar. Amir Chakar Rind unites Baluchi tribes and also defeats Sammahs.
1526	Babur defeats the Lodis, the last of the Delhi sultans, and establishes Moghul Empire.
1530–56	Emperor Humayun, Babur's son, forced into exile in Persia by Sher Shah Suri.
1545	Death of Sher Shah Suri. Tarkhans obtain power in Sind.
1556–1605	Akbar, son of Humayun, is emperor.
1605–27	Jahangir is emperor.
1627–58	Shah Jahan is emperor.
1658–1707	Aurangzeb is emperor. Sikhs organize themselves as warrior sect.
1736	Founding of Kalhora dynasty in Sind.
1739	Nadir Shah of Persia invades the subcontinent.
1747–73	Ahmad Shah Durrani founds Kingdom of Afghanistan and acquires the Indus territories, Punjab and Kashmir.
1760s–1830s	Sikhs become dominant force in the Punjab.
1789	Talpur Baluchis overthrow Kalhora dynasty in Sind.
1799–1839	Ranjit Singh rules the Punjab from Lahore.
1843	The British annex Sind. First British–Afghan War.
1845–6	First British–Sikh War.
1848–9	The British defeat the Sikhs in the Second Sikh War and annex the Punjab and NWFP.
1857	First War of Independence (Indian or Sepoy Mutiny).
1858	British government takes over direct rule of India.
1887	All districts of Baluchistan are in British hands.
1889	British agency established in Gilgit.
1891	British conquest of Hunza and Nagar.
1906	All India Muslim League founded.
1930	Muhammad Iqbal proposes the creation of a separate Muslim state.

1947	Independence and the Partition of the subcontinent.
1948	Death of Muhammad Ali Jinnah. Fighting between India and Pakistan over Kashmir.
1949	UN sponsors ceasefire in Kashmir.
1958	Military government of General Ayub Khan.
1965	17-day Indo–Pakistan War. UN ceasefire declared.
1969	General Yahya Khan takes over leadership of Pakistan.
1971	War between West Pakistan and India leading to secession of East Pakistan and establishment of Bangladesh.
1970–7	West Pakistan governed by Zulfikar Ali Bhutto of the Pakistan People's Party.
1977	General Zia-ul-Haq takes over government of Pakistan.
1985	Non-party elections held. Zia remains in power.
1986	End of Martial Law.
1988	Zia killed in plane crash. General elections held; Pakistan People's Party returned to power with Benazir Bhutto as Prime Minister.

The Muslim Calendar

The Muslims use a lunar calendar. The year is divided into 12 months alternately 29 and 30 days long. The year has either 354 or 355 days (11 years out of every 30 have 355 days, an extra day being added at the end of the year). The Muslim months shift in relation to the seasons, falling back 10 or 11 days each western year. Every 30 years a cycle is complete. The 12 months are: Moharram, Safar, Rabi-ul-Awwal, Rabi-ul-Sani, Jumada-ul-Awwal, Jumada-ul-Sani, Rajab, Shaban, Ramazan, Shawwal, Ziquad and Zilhaj.

Ramazan is the fasting month, when Muslims do not eat or drink from sunrise to sunset. The approximate dates of Ramazan for the next few years are:

28 March–27 April (1990)
17 March–16 April (1991)
4 March–3 April (1992)
22 February–21 March (1993)

The most important Muslim dates are:

First day of Moharram: New Year's Day.
Ninth and tenth of Moharram: Shias commemorate the massacre of Hussain (the Prophet's grandson) at Kerbala, Iraq, by processing and flogging themselves in mourning.
Twelfth of Rabi-ul-Awwal: Milad-ul-Nabi, or birthday of the Prophet Muhammad.
First of Ramazan: beginning of the month of fasting.
Twenty-first of Ramazan: Shab-e-Qadr, or Night of Prayer.
First of Shawwal: Eid-ul-Fitr, a three-day festival to celebrate the end of Ramazan, marked by the new moon.
Tenth of Zilhaj: Eid-ul-Ajha, two-day festival commemorating the sacrifice of Ismail (Muslims believe it was Ismail, not Isaac, that Abraham offered to sacrifice). Pakistanis sacrifice animals on this occasion, and this is the time Muslims make their pilgrimage to Mecca.
The Muslim calendar begins on 16 July AD 622, the date of the Hijra, when the Prophet Muhammad migrated from Mecca to Medina. AH stands for Anno Hijrae.

AH	AD	AH	AD	AH	AD	AH	AD	AH	AD
1	622	300	912	700	1300	1100	1688	1410	1989
10	631	400	1009	800	1397	1200	1785	1411	1990
100	718	500	1106	900	1494	1300	1882	1412	1991
200	815	600	1203	1000	1591	1400	1979	1413	1992

Urdu Glossary

Urdu is the national language of Pakistan, but is the mother tongue of only a small proportion of the population. Urdu is a mixture of Persian, Arabic and various local languages. It is similar to Hindi, but is written in Arabic script.

All nouns are either masculine or feminine and the adjective agrees with the noun. Most masculine nouns end with -a, most feminine nouns end with -i, while all plural nouns end in -e.

Verb endings differ if it is a man or a woman speaking. In the present tense, a man ends his verbs with -a, a woman ends hers with -i, eg *meyn jata hun* (m), or *meyn jati hun* (f), which means 'I go'.

1	*ek*	11	*gyara*
1.5	*dehr*	12	*bara*
2	*doh*	13	*tera*
2.5	*dhai*	14	*chawdra*
3	*teen*	15	*pundra*
4	*char*	20	*beess*
5	*paanch*	25	*pacheess*
6	*che*	30	*teess*
7	*saat*	40	*chaleess*
8	*aath*	50	*pachaass*
9	*naw*	100	*ek saw*
10	*dus*	2,000	*doh hazaar*

(Beware of similar-sounding 25 and 50.)

greeting (Peace be with you)	*Salaam alay kum.*
reply (With you also be peace)	*Waalay kum as salaam.*
How are you?	*Aapka* (or *Tumhara*) *kya hal heyh?* (nb 'aap' is formal, 'tum' informal)
I am well.	*Teekh heyh* or *Teekh takh.*
What is your name?	*Aapka* (or *Tumhara*) *naam kya heyh?*
Do you speak English?	*Kya aap ungrezi boltay heyn?*
I am English/American/French.	*Meyn ungrez/amrikan/fransisi hun.*
thank you	*shukria*
good bye	*khoodha haafis*
yes	*jihaan, haanji* or *haan*
no	*naheen (na'en)*
okay/good	*achaa*
When?	*Kub?*
three o'clock	*teen bujay*

three hours	*teen gentay*
morning	*subah*
evening	*shaam*
Which way to Lahore?	*Lahore kiss turaf heyh?*
go	*jaana*
near	*nazdeek*
far	*dur*
food	*khana*
eat food	*khana khana*
drink	*peena*
meat	*ghosht*
beef	*gai ka ghosht*
goat meat	*bukri ka ghosht*
chicken	*murghi*
fish	*muchli*
egg	*unda*
vegetable	*subzi*
potato	*aalu*
spinach	*palak*
lentils	*daal*
rice	*chavel*
bread	*roti, naan, chapati*
yoghurt	*dahi*
water	*pani*
tea	*chai*
salt	*namak*
sugar	*cheeni*
home/house	*gher/mekaan*
bed	*pulang, charpai*
blanket	*kambal*
pillow	*takya*
sheet	*charder*
fan	*punkha*
candle	*moom butti*
hot	*guram*
cold	*thanda* (m) *thandi* (f)
small	*chota/choti*
big	*burha/burhi*
clean	*saaf*
expensive	*mengha*
How much is this/that?	*Yeyh/Voh kitnay ka heyh?*
What is this/that?	*Yeyh/Voh kya heyh?*

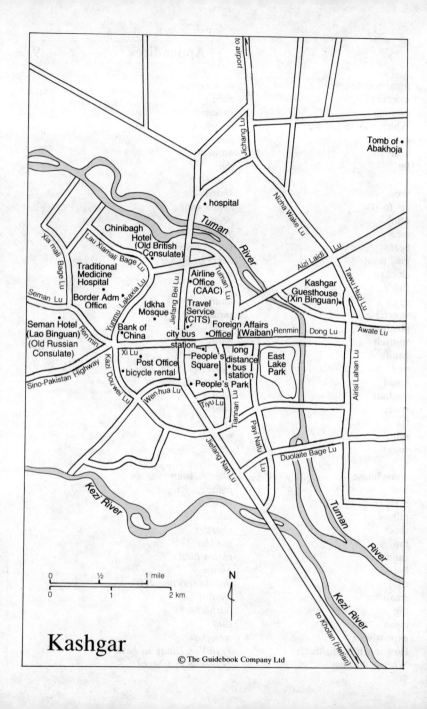

to airport

Tomb of • Abakhoja

Jichang Lu

Nizha Wake Lu

• hospital

Tuman River

Chinibagh Hotel (Old British Consulate)

Xia mali Bage Lu

Lau Xiamali Bage Lu

Aizi Laidi

Tawu Huzi Lu

Airline Office (CAAC)

Tuman Lu

Kashgar Guesthouse (Xin Binguan) •

Traditional Medicine Hospital

Seman Lu

• Border Adm Office

Yunmu Lakaxia Lu

Jiefang Bei Lu

Travel Service (CITS)

Idkha Mosque

Awate Lu

Seman Hotel (Lao Binguan) (Old Russian Consulate)

Renmin

Bank of • China

Foreign Affairs • Office (Waiban)

Renmin Dong Lu

Airisi Lahan Lu

Kazi Dou wei Lu

Xi Lu

city bus station

People's Square

long distance • bus station

East Lake Park

Sino-Pakistan Highway

Post Office

• bicycle rental

Wen hua Lu

• People's Park

Tiyu Lu

Tiannan Lu

Payi Natu Lu

Jiefang Nan Lu

Duolaite Bage Lu

Kezi River

Tuman River

Kezi River

to Khotan (Hetian)

0   ½   1 mile

0   1   2 km

N

Kashgar

© The Guidebook Company Ltd

Index